Distinctions of Class

Born in Gillingham, Kent, in 1937, Lady Burgh was
educated at Chatham Grammar School. She trained as
a nurse at a London teaching hospital but left in the
middle of her training to marry the future Lord Burgh.
Now divorced, she has four children and spends part of
the year in Sutherland, in the northern Highlands, and
some months in the West Country. *Distinctions of Class* is
her first novel.

Anita Burgh

DISTINCTIONS
OF
CLASS

Pan Books
London, Sydney and Auckland

First published 1987 by Chatto & Windus Ltd
This edition published 1988 by Pan Books Ltd,
Cavaye Place, London SW10 9PG
in association with Chatto & Windus
9 8 7 6 5 4 3 2 1
© Anita Burgh 1987
ISBN 0 330 30199 3
Printed and bound in Great Britain by
Richard Clay Ltd, Bungay, Suffolk

The rich man in his castle,
    The poor man at his gate,
God made them, high or lowly,
    And ordered their estate.

Mrs C. F. Alexander

Prologue

Jane Reed sat alone at the back of the plane. Jane always sat alone as the engines revved to a screaming intensity and the fuselage began to shudder with the strain. She needed to be isolated with her fear; the confidence, the banter of the others only fuelled her terror. She was better by herself.

The great machine began to roll. This was the point when she always intended to change her mind, to stand up and insist on getting off, but never did. The force, as the plane began its headlong catapulting down the runway, pressed her back into her seat. She closed her eyes so as not to see the terrifying speed she could feel, the knuckles of her hands showing white as she clenched them tightly together.

We're just like suicidal lemmings, sitting here, she thought as the plane hurtled towards its point of no return.

Jane had tried everything – hypnosis, Valium, gin, even pot – but there was no drug, no treatment known to man, that could calm this otherwise confident woman into acceptance of air travel.

The large, chintz-covered armchair in which she sat accentuated her smallness. She was dressed casually for travel in a well-cut tracksuit made of the finest silk and not intended for the running track. The grey of the fabric matched exactly the grey of the large eyes hidden now by the firmly shut eyelids. The handmade shoes, the Hermès scarf draped about her shoulders, the cascade of gold chains around her neck, proclaimed her wealth before one even noticed the large diamond rings sparkling on the manicured hands.

Had she not been so famous it would have been impossible to be certain of her age. Her skin was clear and still had the bloom of a much younger woman. The few fine lines around her eyes seemed only to emphasize their size and beauty, as if they had been applied by an expert beautician. Her mouth was full and generous. The high cheekbones and the firm chin were as nature had made them, unhelped by surgeons' skills. The small, light body gave an impression of fragility that disguised the toughness of which Jane was capable. People always wanted to help and protect her, and Jane had learned to use this fact to her advantage. But she was famous, and wherever her name appeared, there in brackets beside it, for all the world to see, was her age. Not that Jane minded, for with her looks, being in her forties seemed irrelevant.

'You can open your eyes, undo your seatbelt, have a fag. We're safely up!' Jane heard the patient humour in Fran's voice. Gingerly she opened her eyes and grinned at the woman who stood opposite her.

'Silly, aren't I?'

'Damn silly when you think how often you fly.'

'Safer than crossing the road?'

'Exactly. Safest form of travel there is.'

'But I always feel as if I'm stepping into my own coffin when I get into this thing.'

'I know.'

'You know?'

'I should do.' Fran laughed. 'We have this inane conversation every time we take off.'

'Do we?'

'Yes, dear Jane, word for word!' Fran flopped down in the opposite chair. 'Drink?'

Jane nodded agreement and Fran pressed the bell to summon the stewardess. With her unvaried smile the stewardess placed the already poured drinks before them.

Jane watched the girl undulate back up the plane. Her tartan uniform looked ridiculous. It just didn't suit the decor. Jane knew it was her own fault. The chintz seat covers, slubbed silk walls and matching curtains had been intended to make the interior look like a drawing room, to delude Jane into thinking she was not airborne. It had failed. Chintzy aeroplanes did not look right. That epicene young designer, stamping his Gucci shoes with rage at her suggestions, had been right all along. She would have to have it changed.

'Cashmere! Green cashmere, that's the answer.'

'What for?' Fran looked up from the papers she was working on.

'This plane. Just look at it, like a flying bordello. It's dreadful. I want it changed immediately we get back. The stewardess's uniform as well. Something Scottish, but not bloody tartan, and get rid of all this chintz.'

'I agree about the chintz – shame about the tartan.'

'But it always looks so out of place outside Scotland, like refugees from *Brigadoon*!'

'Light or dark?'

'Light.'

'I'll get on to Campbells of Beauly.' Fran made a note in the huge notepad that she always carried.

'You know, Fran, I can't think why we don't manufacture it ourselves. We've the tweeds, wool, silk – why not cashmere? We must find out if it needs special looms or whatever.' She looked at the now offending chintz. 'Do you think you can upholster in it?'

'Shouldn't think so. Wouldn't stand up to my huge arse for long, if you did.' Fran snorted.

Jane frowned. 'Don't put yourself down, Fran.'

'It's true, I do have a huge arse.'

'There's no need to keep harping on it,' Jane said sharply. She hated the way that Fran disparaged herself. Fran's shape was certainly unique – square face, which seemed to melt, chinless, into an equally square neck above her solid trunk, which ended in a pair of stocky legs. After all these years, Jane was only aware of Fran's shape when Fran chose to mention it. But Fran, within seconds of greeting a stranger, would make some remark about her size. She claimed she did it to get in first, but Jane felt it was done out of embarrassment for her unfashionable bulk. While it upset Jane to imagine what pain and insecurity must lurk in Fran, it also had the uncomfortable effect of reminding Jane of the agonies and insecurities she herself had suffered in the past and which she liked to imagine she had buried.

'Irritates you, does it?'

'A bit.' Jane smiled apologetically, already regretting snapping at her friend.

'It's all right for skin-and-bone fashion plates like you.'

'Skin and bone! Me? You must be joking. My boobs are far too big.'

'So you can say your boobs are too big but I'm not allowed to comment on the memorable size of my arse?'

'Touché!' Jane offered Fran a cigarette from her heavy, gold cigarette case, decorated in sapphires with initials which had once been hers.

'You looked lovely the other night at Max Shielberg's party.' Jane smiled.

'Bah! I looked like a Bedouin's tent, more like!'

'I haven't always looked like this. It took years of practice. And the money helps.'

'All the money in the world wouldn't make me look any different.'

'I love you as you are.'

'I don't know if that's a compliment or not.' But Fran smiled broadly at her.

'God, I feel tired,' sighed Jane, stretching her hands over her head.

'You don't look it — as usual.' Fran looked at her friend. 'I quite expected you to pop in last night for a natter.'

'I would have, Fran, but it was so late. I didn't want to wake you.'

'Official receptions don't usually go on that late.' There was a teasing note in Fran's voice.

'It didn't, it ended at ten, I went on . . .'

'Anywhere interesting?'

'Anyone, you mean.' Jane laughed at her friend. 'No . . . not the way you're thinking! But a very interesting man. He's a Brazilian diplomat — wanted to talk about the trust and the possibility of setting one up in Brazil, so there!'

'Affairs have to start somewhere.'

'Fran, you're impossible! Worse than a mother! A couple of drinks and you think I'm having an affair.'

'I wish you would, Jane,' Fran said, suddenly serious. 'You don't have nearly enough fun for a woman who's still as attractive as you are.'

'My dear friend, the idea of starting an affair, at my age, is too daunting. Getting to know a stranger, all that agonizing waiting for the phone to ring — "Will he, won't he?" — Quite honestly, I couldn't be bothered.'

'Then don't have an affair with a stranger — have one with an old friend.'

Jane looked up sharply. 'And what exactly do you mean by that?'

'What I say . . .'

'One can't go back. It never works, Fran.'

'You know what? I think you're scared to try. I never thought I would think of you as a coward.'

'Well, you learn something new every day, don't you?' Jane said lightly.

Jane saw that Fran was settling herself for a long talk, but Jane kicked her shoes off and curled up in the large armchair.

'You going to sleep?' The disappointment in Fran's voice was blatant.

'Just a little snooze. Wake me up for dinner.' She lay back, her eyes closed. There were times when she thought that Fran could bore into her mind. It was almost if she knew about the letter.

Her hand rested protectively on her handbag. Now and again she would pat it, as if it were a pet dog, and a gentle smile hovered about her mouth. Inside lay a letter, creased from constant reading; a letter that years ago she would have had no problem in answering. But now? She was thankful to have these moments, above the Atlantic, to think. Jane Reed had a decision to make: one that could change her extraordinary life, once again.

One

1951–55

I

It had been a noisy childhood. The traffic rumbled a pavement's width from their front door; trains shunted monotonously in the sidings two streets away; the piercing shouts of children playing in the street continued from morning to night; the neighbours bickered endlessly beyond the paper-thin walls. At regular intervals the mournful wail of the factory hooter, summoning the various shifts to work, punctuated this tapestry of noise.

Jane lay in her narrow bed. The bed had to be narrow because the room was so small that the bedside table, low bookcase, and child's desk and chair filled it to capacity. A dingy, black-and-brown peg-rag rug lay on the linoleum floor which had once been patterned in blue and pink but was now faded from continual polishing to a dull beige. The unused gas bracket loomed above her bed, capped off but full of gas, a constant source of nightmares for Jane. The walls were distempered, the brushmarks clearly visible on the surface. As the paint flaked constantly, it was renewed every year so that, with each application, the colour darkened. Now the original pale pink colour had become a lurid salmon pink. The green curtains at the small sash window did not complement the pink walls, nor did the blue, flowered material hanging across the alcove which served as a wardrobe.

As the factory hooter pealed out its first summons, Jane stirred and lay waiting for the next significant noise of her morning. Through the flimsy wall she heard the shrill ringing of her neighbour's alarm clock. He swore as he attempted to stop the bell and sent the clock crashing to the floor. The bed springs twanged as he heaved himself up. She could imagine him flicking his greasy, black hair out of his eyes as he fumbled for his heavy boots. Two loud steps and the sash window was raised. She closed her eyes as if, by not seeing, she could blot out the sound she dreaded and which she heard every waking morning, except Sunday. On Sundays, when he lay in, she was spared the hawking and gobbing noises as he cleared the phlegm from his lungs, the globules of sputum rattling onto the corrugated iron roof of the shed beneath his window. Later, his mother would come with a bucket of disinfected water and sluice the slime away, so that always about Jane's room hung the institutional smell of disinfectant. The very sight of him filled her with disgust. She knew the neighbours thought her stuck-up but she could never bring herself to speak to him.

Beneath her, in the kitchen, she heard her father stirring the sugar in the teacups. Apart from scrubbing the yard once a week, it was the only thing she had ever seen him do about the house. She was surprised that after last night's row, he should even bother. A door slammed, and then the heavy footsteps on the stairs. Her door opened – how nice, she thought, if, just once, he would knock. He placed the cup on the green painted teachest that served as a bedside table. He grunted. He always grunted in the mornings, rarely spoke. She did not look at him. Silently he turned and shuffled along the landing to her mother's room.

She sipped the sweet, orange-coloured tea and wished that she need not remember last night, but the memory kept slinking into her consciousness. There had been no warning, but that was not unusual. In this house, rows and violence flared up with depressing regularity, from nowhere and frequently about nothing.

They had been sitting around the table eating their tea – fishcakes for Friday.

'I've spoken to the foreman, Jane. You can start work next month,' her father announced.

'Pardon?'

'You heard.'

'I heard, but I didn't understand.'

'Oh, didn't you? Then let me explain,' her father said in a sarcastic tone. 'You're over fourteen. It's time you quit school and got a job and started paying your way, like everyone has to.'

'Charlie! Don't talk such rubbish!' her mother interjected.

'I'm not talking rubbish. Fourteen is school-leaving age, so why hasn't she left?'

'Fourteen is for those who didn't pass the scholarship, and well you know it. I want Jane to stay on into the sixth form. Then she'll get a proper job and all the expense will have been worthwhile.'

'Sixth form!' he snorted. 'Now who's talking rubbish, woman?' He glared at his wife.

'But, Dad, they're putting up the school-leaving age to fifteen.'

'Exactly! So now's the time for you to leave, before they do.'

'But I haven't finished, I'd leave with no qualifications. It would all have been a waste.'

'I always said it would be a waste. But, that aside, truth is, young woman, I've had enough of supporting you. I'm fed up to the back teeth, working my fingers to the bone, seeing you lolling about on your fat arse doing nothing. I'm not paying out a penny more.'

'You bastard!' her mother shouted. 'You "work your fingers to the bone", that'll be the day! No, you're up to something, you rotten sod! You're doing this to spite me, aren't you?'

'Don't talk so bloody silly. I said why I'm doing it.'

'No, there's more to this.' Her mother stared hard at her husband. 'There's something else. You never wanted her to go to the Grammar, never. And now she's there, you want to ruin everything. Have you no pride in her?'

'Pride? In that?' her father sneered at her. 'Stuck-up little cow, that's all she's become with her fancy education. And thinking she's superior to me all the time.'

'Dad, that's not fair . . .'

'Jealous!' her mother interrupted triumphantly. 'You pathetic creature, you're jealous of your own daughter. Jealous, 'cause she's getting the chance you never had.'

Jane looked sharply at her father. She had heard the story so many times – how her father had won a scholarship to the grammar school, and how his own father had refused to let him go. Could that really be the reason for his actions? She looked at the once handsome face now marred by bitterness and her anger began to fade. She felt sorry for him. Tentatively she put out her hand to him.

'Dad, I'm so sorry. I didn't think . . .'

'Don't talk bloody stupid, girl! I don't know what rubbish your mother is going on about. Jealous? Why should I be jealous of you? I work hard for my money and I've decided I don't want to spend any more on you. It's as simple as that, you see . . .' He smiled at her but the smile was full of malice.

'Boozing!' Her mother had not finished with him yet. 'So you can have more money to go down the bloody boozer, that's your reason, you selfish bugger!'

'I spent my money how I bloody well want and if you don't shut your face, Maeve, you won't see a penny more of it either.'

Both parents purposefully lit cigarettes, inhaled deeply, and, in unison, pushed the plates in front of them to one side, as if clearing a space for combat. Like boxers flexing their muscles they faced each other across the table. The snarling and sniping continued, each cutting the other a little deeper with every remark. There was no longer any place for Jane in this argument, her parents had taken it entirely to themselves and, ignoring her, concentrated with practised ease on the task of destroying each other.

It was a familiar enough scene and Jane knew there was no point in her staying. She collected the plates, washed them up, put them neatly away and slipped up to the haven of her room.

It was Friday, too, she thought sadly. All her life Friday had been different. When she was a child, it had meant bath night. The water-filled copper was lit, two huge saucepans bubbled on the gas stove. The tin bath was taken from its rusty hook in the yard and placed in front of the banked-up fire, and she would sit in the water and enjoy the warmth and the pretty colour of the firelight glistening on her skin. Her mother would shampoo her hair and rinse it with jugs full of water that cascaded over her face as if she were sitting in her own private waterfall. She would be lifted out and wrapped in a heated towel and then allowed to spend the rest of the evening in her pyjamas, ready warmed on the hearth, listening to the wireless. As she grew older and her body began to develop, she was not allowed to bath in front of the fire any more but had to endure the chill of the kitchen. However, alone in the kitchen, she could cut her nails on Fridays, something her mother had never allowed, declaring it an invitation for the devil to enter her body.

And, once a month, Friday meant a trip across town to see her aunt. Her uncle owned a shop and they lived on a hill, in a house which had bay windows and a door with stained glass in it, and a little garden in front. It was her mother's dream to live in such a road with a front garden separating them from the traffic.

The main reason for the visit was that her aunt owned a television set. They certainly did not go there for the conversation. As soon as they arrived, they would sit down in front of the magical machine and, when the screen went blank, they left. If she was very lucky, her aunt would invite her to stay the night. Then she had the luxury of a bath in a real bathroom with shiny tiles on the wall and endless hot water from the giant geyser that wheezed and sighed above the bath.

She lay on her bed and longed to sleep but the row progressed with increased ferocity. She wondered where they got the energy from. The sound of crashing glass made her sit bolt upright. She leaped from her bed and rushed downstairs. In the living room both parents stood in frozen attitudes, looking at a smashed glass bowl, its pieces lying in the hearth and on the fireside rug.

'Mum! Dad! For God's sake stop this!'

Slowly her mother turned to face her. Jane was shocked by the ravaged, tear-stained face, the eyes blazing with anger, the mouth contorted by her inner bitterness.

'Look at that! Look at that! The one lovely thing I possessed. The only thing . . .' and the woman started to cry with a harsh wailing noise which sounded more animal than human.

'Dad, how could you? Mum loved that bowl!'

'That's right, blame me. I didn't break the bloody thing. The silly cow did it herself!' he shouted back.

Jane stepped forward and gingerly began to pick up the sharp fragments of glass.

'Maybe we can mend it,' she said hopefully.

'Don't be so stupid. It's gone.' Suddenly her mother pushed her. Jane looked at her with surprise. Her mother pushed her again, harder, her fingers prodding painfully into Jane's flesh. 'See what you've done? See my glass bowl?'

'But, Mum, I wasn't even here, I didn't touch it.'

'It's your fault! It's because of you it's all broken. If it wasn't for you, we wouldn't have been arguing in the first place. Oh, Christ! Why were you ever born . . . ?'

Jane stood shocked and speechless. The sentence seemed to hang suspended in the air between them. Her parents both looked as surprised as she. Her first instinct was to cry but a sudden swell of anger doused all feelings of self pity.

'I never asked to be born, certainly not into this hellhole!' she screamed. She turned from them and rushed blindly out of the door and up the stairs to her room. There, with the door safely shut, she allowed the tears of anger and pain to flow.

2

Now it was morning. There had been other mornings after other rows when life had simply gone on as usual, but this time Jane could not see how anything could be the same again.

It was fairly common, after a row with her husband, for Jane's mother to say to her child, 'If it wasn't for you, I'd be off . . .' But she had never gone. Jane had always assumed that she had stayed because of love for her. Consequently, Jane could not remember a time when she had not felt guilt for her mother's unhappiness, seeing herself as the trap which had prevented the woman from finding a better, happier life. But now . . . 'Why were you ever born?' How could you love someone if you wished she had never been born, and, from wishing that, how big a step was it to wishing her dead?

Jane knew that her father did not like her — she could hardly have escaped the fact since he frequently told her so. But she was certain it had not always been that way. She could just remember a time, during the war, when she had sat on his lap, enjoying the smell of his tobacco, her head on his chest, her cheek against the rough serge of his uniform, his voice rumbling deeply against her ear as he read her the story of Jane Squirrel from the only book that he had bought her and signed 'with love'. She still had the book but she did not know, or understand, what had changed his attitude to her. It all seemed so long ago. Of course, there had been the incident of the bird. Maybe that was it.

A neighbour had given her a kitten, and she was overjoyed when her mother said she could keep it. She lavished love on the little animal, delighting in its purring contentment. Two weeks after the cat had come into her life, he strayed into a garden at the bottom of the alley. The old woman who lived there had hurled a brick at the cat, shattering the tiny creature's spine. Jane had found him, blood spewing from his mouth, writhing in agony. She scooped him into her arms and tried to love him better as he died. Her grief had been such that her mother had said she could never again have a pet. So she was surprised when on her birthday her father had appeared with a budgerigar in a cage. Her father was angered by her lack of enthusiasm. She had tried to explain that she was frightened to have another pet in case it, too, died. Nor did she want to own a poor creature locked up in a cage. Perhaps her explanations had been clumsy, for he had hit her hard, declaring her an ungrateful bitch, and stormed off to the pub. He looked after the bird himself and, secretly, she would watch him stroking its green and yellow feathers, looking at it with tenderness. She felt herself wishing that she was the little bird and that he would look at her and touch her like that. But she could not remember how soon after the book the bird had come, or even if it was her attitude to the bird that had made him dislike her.

She slipped out of bed. In the kitchen her father sat with a cup of tea, studiously reading his *Daily Mirror*. He ignored her. She washed her face and hands, wishing as always that there were somewhere more private. She poured herself some tea and, sitting down, noted with distaste the chamber pot, placed by the back door to be emptied – she turned her back on it.

'Dad, can we talk?' she asked nervously.

'There's nothing to talk about.'

'But school, it means so much to me.'

'I expect it does, but there's one important lesson to learn in life and that is that you can't always have what you want. The sooner you learn that the better.'

'But –'

'The subject is closed. I'm going to my allotment.' He struggled into his jacket and made for the door. 'Empty the piss pot for me,' he said as he clattered out into the yard in his heavy boots. She heard the scrape of his bicycle as he dragged it out of the shed. He had asked her to do that to humiliate her. He knew how she loathed the chamber pot, how for years she had refused one of her own, preferring to brave the cold and the dark, and to pick her way, torch in hand, to the outside lavatory. With an expression of distaste she picked up the pot and carefully carried it down the yard, fearful that she might be seen with her shameful burden. The yeasty smell of the urine hit her nostrils as she hurriedly threw it down the lavatory and pulled the chain. Back in the kitchen, she boiled the kettle to scald the chamber pot, and afterwards scrubbed her hands vigorously with the 'Lifebuoy' soap.

She went into the small living room and cleared the grate, carefully picking up the remaining pieces of broken glass, putting them to one side in the vain hope that something could be done with them. She looked around the tiny room, at the moquette-covered settee, her father's worn, imitation-leather armchair, the dining table with its ugly, bulbous legs which seemed to attract the dust spewed out daily from the factory. She straightened the picture of camels striding across the Sahara Desert, and wondered why it always depressed her. She looked at herself in the mirror – 'bevelled-edged' her mother would declare with pride – and she hated this tiny house, and this ugly room with the dado starting to peel from the walls. She hated this life where neighbours gobbed out of windows, and chamber pots had to be emptied, and knew with a heart-sinking certainty that if she could not stay at school there would be no escape for her, ever.

Her life had changed dramatically the day she had passed the exam that had given her a place at the local grammar school. She had rushed home with the news, bursting with pride and excitement, slipping around the back way to avoid the local women gossiping on their doorsteps. And the news tumbled out of her in breathless excitement.

'My God, think of the cost of the uniform!' was her mother's reaction.

'Right!' her father agreed for once. 'We can't afford it. And anyhow, it's a ridiculous waste of money. What's the point of educating a girl? She'll only land up at the kitchen sink.'

For Jane, his reaction was the best thing that could have happened. Had her father been happy for her to go to the school, then her mother would inevitably have objected, so deep was her distrust of him. But, by declaring that he would never sign the necessary papers, her father inadvertently secured Jane's future.

Going to the new school, she became alienated from her friends in the street who went to the secondary modern school where they learned to hate all grammar-school kids, including herself. She would cycle miles out of her way to avoid passing them, for she was likely to be met with a hail of abuse and occasionally with stones. The gulf which had opened up between herself and her friends saddened and puzzled her. She was still the same person, a uniform couldn't change that. They had all had the same chance – it wasn't her fault that she had passed while they had failed. Now she had no one to play with, for the resentments continued long after school was out.

But at school there were wonderful compensations. She discovered that some people thought reading was a thing to be encouraged, not, as her mother saw it, a waste of time, and unhealthy too. She had not been allowed to join the library because her mother thought that the books were dirty and full of germs, so she had to make do with the few books in the house. By the age of ten she had read all the works of Dickens from the matching set which her father had won in a raffle, and the *Complete Home Doctor*. She saved all her pocket money for books, which worried her mother who confided to Aunt Vi that she thought Jane was odd in the head.

For the first time she learned that there was music which, when you listened to it, washed through your brain and could make you sad when you were happy, and happy when you were sad: music which made her feel that anything in her young life was possible.

She discovered paintings, in prints on the walls, and in the large books in the library, which could lift her soul as the music had done. She learned poems which explained emotions she knew but had been unable to express.

At first she was shy of the other girls in her class. Not only did they speak with a different accent from hers, but there was an ease of manner about them and a confidence in their own ability which she lacked, and which puzzled her. She wondered where it came from. Having until now moved only within her own class, she had not given the existence of any other a thought. Now, faced with it, she felt uncomfortable and retreated behind a shield of shyness.

There she might have remained had not one of the girls, Sylvia, invited her home for tea one day. Not only did she find a friend but her whole view of her life was subtly changed.

She had watched, amazed at first, then envious, at the easy, affectionate relationship between Sylvia and her parents. She was speechless with surprise when they had asked her how her school work was going, what her plans for the future were. She listened to this family chatting to each other and realised for the first time that at home she was lonely. Until now she had accepted the hours spent alone, the silence of parents who, in any case, barely spoke to each other. How could she have known she was lonely when she had nothing with which to compare her state? Now she recognized it and wished her relationship with her parents could be different. But, think as she might, she could see no way of changing things.

Instead she spent as much time with her new friend as possible. Jane observed intently how her friends behaved, their manners, their rituals, the way they spoke. Should the mother tell her daughter to sit up, to take her elbows off the table, to pass the cream and help herself last, it was

Jane who absorbed the instructions. The niceties of which way to hold a soup spoon, the difference between breaking and cutting a roll, were of no importance in Jane's house. At home there were only two rules. The first, and probably the most important, was to do nothing that would make the neighbours talk. The second was never to let any man 'mess about with you'. What this meant Jane was not quite sure, but instinctively she felt that the two were somehow connected.

Now, with her father's ultimatum, all her dreams were at risk. And they had been such modest dreams, too. She would have liked to go to university but had rejected that idea as being too costly. What she wanted most was a home of her own, a home like Sylvia's, and a husband. The only way she could hope to achieve her dream was by continuing her education. If she went to work in the factory, she knew that she would end up like her mother, married to someone like her father. Then she could forget her fine hopes of a husband who wore a suit each day, of china that matched, of bookcases full of books, of records of Bach and Beethoven.

It was not true what her father had said: she did not look down on them, did not feel superior, even though daily she knew more than they did. The ever widening gap between her and them was not of her making. Wasn't it natural that having been shown a more pleasant way of life she should want it for herself? There was so much that she would have loved to share with them, but of what use was poetry and art to them? The more she learned, the more they became strangers to her.

3

Jane had been right. This morning everything had changed. She had changed. She saw that she must fight for herself and her dreams.

The memory of her mother's remark returned. But she must not allow herself to show resentment: she could not afford to alienate her mother. Her best weapon was her mother's hatred of her father. He would not change; his mind once made up remained constant.

She felt, with the sadness, a strange lightness, as if the knowledge that her mother wished she had never been born relieved her of the guilt which had dogged her whole life.

But there was an emptiness within her at the recognition that her mother did not love her.

Hearing her mother stir she put the kettle on, and quickly finished the last of the clearing-up – at least that would please her. Her mother entered the room, and glowered at her, on her guard for any onslaught from Jane.

'I've put the kettle on, Mum, do you want anything to eat?'

'Just tea,' her mother replied, visibly relaxing. 'Where's your father?'

'Gone to the allotment.'

'Good, maybe he'll fall down a bloody big hole and not get out again! Miserable sod!' She sipped her tea. 'You'll never know what I've had to put up with from that bastard, Jane. How much I hate him for all the happiness he's deprived me of.'

'I know, Mum.' Jane tried to interject sympathy she was not feeling into her voice.

'God, I wish I could leave him!'

'Why don't you?'

'Don't be bloody daft! How would we manage?'

'I could get a job in the factory – after all he's arranged one for me – and then I could help you with money,' she replied with a mixture of guilt and satisfaction at her own deviousness.

'Not on your nelly!' her mother exclaimed excitedly. 'And have that bastard win? You'll finish at that school if it's the last thing I do.'

'But how? I suppose I could see if there are any grants going, but that wouldn't mean much — you have to be a war orphan to get any real help.'

'The bugger couldn't even get himself killed either, which would have been a help.'

'Mother!'

'Well, if I think like that he's only himself to blame for making me,' she said defensively and continued noisily sipping the tea, deep in thought. 'I don't know how yet, but I'll work something out. The bastard needn't think he's won this one.'

Jane felt she could begin to relax a little, certain her mother would resolve the problem and now convinced in her mind that whatever she did it was not for love of Jane but for hatred of her husband.

'Shall we go to the pictures tonight? There's a new Bette Davis at the Plaza.'

'Why not? We'll get the shopping in, go and have tea at Lever's and then go to the pictures. Sod him, let him get his own bloody tea for a change.'

'Remember what happened last time we saw a Bette Davis film there?'

'No, what?'

'That man fainted two rows in front of us, remember? Right in the middle of that scene when Bette Davis wouldn't give her dying husband his pills. Really messed it up, all the noise and fuss!'

'Lor', yes, I remember. And you were all disappointed he hadn't got a knife stuck in him, and that we would be witness to a murder.' Her mother laughed at the memory and how she had scolded Jane for her overactive imagination.

A death in the cinema would have had a certain element of glamour about it, which was more than could be said for Jane's only experiences of real death — death near to her, death in her street, death in the family. Terrifying experiences — for it was customary, and expected, that neighbours should pay their last respects to the deceased. This custom included children as well as everyone else in the street. She would be dragged, protesting, into the darkened, curtained front room and by the flickering lights of candles forced to stare at the waxen corpse in the coffin, hear the crying of the bereaved relatives. She would never for the rest of her life be able to look at violets with pleasure, not since the day she had been held over the corpse of her grandfather in his coffin, and been forced, screaming, to kiss his ice-cold, rigid face goodbye. The

perfume of the sweet violets pinned to his lace-frilled pillowcase per-
meated the room and flooded her brain for ever with remembrance of
death.

So they went to the cinema and they sat in the one-and-nines and ate a
box of chocolates. An uneasy truce was established.

And her mother did solve the problem by getting a job herself in the
factory, the very one destined for Jane. But Jane, despite telling herself
that she didn't care any more, found the old guilt returning, and as she
saw her mother's tiredness, her guilt increased.

Her father rarely spoke to either of them now. In some ways this was a
good thing for it made the rows less frequent. He spent more time in the
local pub, just as her mother had predicted, and he kept to his word not
to spend another penny on Jane. Their life settled back into its former
rigid routine – if it was stew it must be Wednesday.

Because her mother worked, one of the great banes of Jane's life, the
ritual Monday washday, was no more. In the past, Monday had been her
least favourite day of the week, the day when the large copper which
dominated the kitchen came into its own. The fire was lit beneath it and
the clothes piled in. To the smell of her mother's dreadful cooking was
added the dank, sickly-sweet smell of the boiling clothes. Sometimes,
when the wind was particularly strong, her mother would decide to
wash the blankets. When she was small, Jane was lifted into the tin bath
to tramp up and down on the washing. Her mother seemed to think it
was fun for her, but she loathed it, hated the slimy feel of the soda-filled
water, and she was frightened to see her little pink feet turning white, the
flesh becoming swollen, bloated and crinkled. She was terrified that her
feet would never return to normal. Mondays meant that her mother
would be in a foul mood from morning to night. Even when it rained the
washing ritual had to be observed, as though her mother regarded the
washing as a religious rite that if not performed invited catastrophe to
the tribe. On wet days the living room would be festooned with wet
washing, the steam rising off it in white tendrils, the dampness permeat-
ing the whole house. But now her mother hired a washing machine,
which was delivered each Saturday morning. The washing was done in a
quarter of the time, and her mother was less bad-tempered and moody
about washing day.

The visits to her aunt's house continued. And, even better, since her
uncle had bought a caravan they now enjoyed odd weekends at the
seaside. He paid extra rental for his site because it was on the edge of the

field packed with caravans, as close to the sea as possible. Jane loved to lie in her bunk at night, listening to the gentle hiss of the Calor Gas lamps and the endless sound of the sea pounding onto the shingle beach. She would listen to the scrabbling, hissing, sliding noise of the shingle as it struggled with the might of the sea, imagining the tiny shards of shell being thrown carelessly from one wave to another, rather as she saw herself sometimes when she had become embroiled helplessly in one of her parents' rows.

Always in shapeless black or maroon dresses worn in an unsuccessful attempt to camouflage her enormous bulk, Aunt Vi was the kindest and funniest person Jane had ever known. With such layers of fat, her face should have been a featureless blob, but instead it was lit by dark-brown eyes which glinted constantly with merriment. The warmth and strength of her character transcended her appearance. Jane was fascinated by her aunt's mouth. The lips were large and soft and when her aunt ate a chocolate they closed around the sweet with a pleasure so sensual that it was possible to envy the chocolate its caress. There was no television in the caravan to dampen conversation, so Jane was to learn for the first time what a quick wit her aunt possessed, the particular joy she took in the ridiculous. Anything to do with bodily functions would reduce her aunt to tears of laughter. No matter which orifice was involved, Aunt Vi would find something funny to say about it. There were many times when Jane wished that she were her mother, but then she would feel pangs of guilt at her own disloyalty.

Her aunt had discovered a new interest, and when not at the seaside, she would collect Jane and her mother and together they would join a coach party to visit one of the large houses newly opened to the public. Neither of the two older women seemed the least bit interested in the treasures on show, but reserved their scrutiny for worn curtains, threadbare carpets, or dust on the Chippendale. The success of the trip for them depended, it seemed to Jane, on the value of the tea and the cleanliness of the lavatories. But Jane loved these outings, trying, as she walked around with the parties, to imagine the rooms a hundred years ago, lit by candles, with women in long dresses working at their needlepoint.

The weekends, and the trips they took, were to prove the happiest times of her childhood and Jane would always remain grateful to Aunt Vi. In her sister-in-law's company even her mother became relaxed, a different person, catching some of the lightness and joy in life which Aunt Vi possessed in abundance. Jane would watch her mother laughing and catch a glimpse of the carefree person she must once have been. On these weekends the bitterness would leave her face, and her lips, usually set in a thin, intransigent line, would relax and even smile. But by Sunday evening and the return home, her good humour was wiped away, her eyes were hooded again with suspicion, her mouth reset in its mean line.

As her childhood slipped away, Jane felt more and more like two people: the one at school who could laugh and joke and was full of ideas, and the girl at home, the moody one, as her mother called her.

Her mother despaired of Jane's looks. Mrs Reed's ideal was a cousin of Jane's with blonde hair, a pert pretty nose and the vacuous expression of a china doll. Since both Jane's parents had brown eyes, her mother regarded the grey of Jane's with suspicion, as if she thought her daughter a changeling. As a small child Jane's dark, straight hair had been twisted with rags each night. The resulting bobbing ringlets were at total variance with her strong-featured face. Her mother had finally tired of her attempts to coax curls where curls were not intended and eventually Jane's hair was cut unbecomingly short with a fringe. So it remained until at fourteen Jane decided to grow both hair and fringe and made no attempt to wave it.

It came therefore as something of a surprise to her, at sixteen, to find that boys did not agree with her mother's assessment of her looks.

She became part of a large group of teenagers who eddied from tennis club to youth-club dance, who cycled to the coast, rambled the downs, drank copious cups of coffee, put the world to rights, and flirted mildly with each other. A couple of times, attracted by a boy's looks and a strange feeling in her stomach that had nothing to do with food, she had gone out alone with him. She would set out on the date full of excitement and anticipation, only to return perplexed and irritated by his clumsy kisses and fumbling at her body. Sweaty palms and awkward attempts at lovemaking quenched that strange feeling within her, and certainly did not lift her to the heights of passion that the poets spoke of.

Her school days drew to an end. She rejected her mother's offer of help to send her to university. She knew that she could no longer deal with her guilt about her mother's having to work to support her: there was guilt enough without adding to it. Nearly eighteen, she did not know what she was to do. The only firm resolve she had was not to work in an office. It was one of her teachers who suggested that she might like to become a nurse. She had never thought about it, but there were certain advantages

– she would be paid while she trained, she would meet interesting people, she would be in London, she would get away from home. So, with no sense of vocation, just a need to find an escape, she began to plan on a nursing career.

4

Knowing nothing of London hospitals, she applied to the only one she had heard of – St Thomas's. When the application form arrived, demanding that one of her referees be a minister of the church, she tore it up. Her churchgoing had been restricted to her baptism and a short spell at the local Methodist chapel, which she had attended, not from any religious zeal, but because they had the best Sunday-school outings. She worried that perhaps the blessing of the church would be required by all the hospitals.

'Here, look at this.' Her mother handed her the daily paper. 'If it's good enough for her, it'll do you!'

Jane scanned the report which said it was rumoured that a foreign princess was to enter a London teaching hospital to train as a nurse.

'It will probably be like the other one and want a vicar's reference.'

'Go on, try it, you don't know. Fancy, you could be hobnobbing with royalty!' Her mother seemed amused at this idea.

'It's only a rumour, Mum. Still, it's the name of another hospital, and if she's going there, it must be a good one.'

'I don't understand why it has to be a London hospital. A nasty place, London – you could get into all sorts of trouble there. What's wrong with the local hospital? I could keep an eye on you then.'

'I want the best, Mum.' It wasn't strictly true. It was logical to try for the best training, but the main reason was her longing to get away from home, and she could hardly tell her mother that. She was encouraged, when the form arrived, to see that this hospital was not interested in what the church thought of her. She applied and two months later, with money earned as a part-time waitress, Jane bought a ticket and took the train to London for her interview.

Since she had only drifted into the idea of nursing, she was not in the least bit nervous as she entered the ornate Victorian building, smelling for the first time that combination of boiled cabbage, disinfectant and polish peculiar to hospitals.

The waiting room into which she was shown was already crowded with girls. There was no vacant seat, so she leaned against the wall. There was an oppressive atmosphere and Jane noticed that none of the girls could sit still. They twisted in their seats, picked imaginary flecks from their clothes, patted their hair and tortured their handkerchiefs. There was a constant clicking of handbag clasps as mirrors were produced and anxious faces were scrutinized. The tension was catching and Jane soon found herself straightening her skirt and fiddling with her hair.

The door opened and a girl appeared, her face gaunt with strain. The others leaped up.

'What was it like?' several asked.

'It was dreadful.' The girl slumped on a chair offered her solicitously by one of the others. 'She's terrifying! Absolutely terrifying!'

'What did she ask you?' one demanded.

'I can't remember! I'm sorry, I can't remember a thing.' She put her hands to her face.

A name was called, and cries of 'good luck' followed the next girl as she disappeared through a door with 'Matron' stencilled on it.

A buzz of conversation started but, instead of lessening, the tension increased as the more knowledgeable among them trotted out statistics concerning numbers of candidates and the shortage of places. Jane began to regret wasting train-fare money on what was obviously a fool's errand.

By the time it was her turn she had been completely infected by the nervousness of the others, and felt her palms clammy with perspiration, her stomach churning with fear.

She noticed nothing of the room she entered for she found herself in the presence of a person whose aura of absolute authority made the back of her throat dry so suddenly that she feared speech would be an impossibility. All she noticed was how white the collar and cuffs were against the navy-blue uniform of the thin woman, whose upright posture made Jane involuntarily straighten her shoulders.

'Be seated,' a firm and surprisingly deep voice told her. Jane sat and found herself being surveyed from the other side of the desk by a pair of blue eyes with no hint of warmth in them. They scrutinized her, as if seeing through the stuff of her clothes and checking whether her underwear were clean. Embarrassed by the stare, Jane studiously examined her hands.

'Why nursing?' the voice rapped out at her.

'I . . .' Jane coughed. 'I can't afford to go to university, miss.'

'What employment is your father in?'

'He's a storeman in a factory. My mother works in the same factory, on the assembly line. They make nuts and bolts and things . . .' Her voice lamely tailed off, as the woman scribbled on the pad in front of her. She finished writing and again stared at Jane with her unblinking eyes. Jane felt that more was expected of her. 'You see, miss, I don't want my mother to work any more, it's too much for her. It's time I started supporting myself, really.' She studied her hands again, unable to think of what else to say.

'There is slightly more to nursing than the pay packet at the end of the month.'

'Oh, I know, miss.'

'Do you feel you have a vocation?'

It was a question Jane should have had the sense to anticipate, but she had not. In fact she had not really given any thought to what questions she might be asked. Now she began to regret her lack of preparation.

'What? Like a nun . . . ?' Jane giggled nervously, desperately playing for time as she tried to think what the right answer might be. The woman's eyes did not waver. 'I'm sorry, miss. It's a serious question, isn't it?'

'All my questions are serious, Miss Reed.'

'Well, if I'm honest, no. I applied because I didn't know what else I could do, and I don't want to work in an office.'

'Hardly a reason to attempt a career in nursing.'

'No, miss. But I have thought about it, and I think nursing will be interesting work and it will exercise my mind. And I like meeting people. I think it will be a satisfying career . . . miss.' She watched wretchedly as the matron made further notes. Undoubtedly it had been a stupid answer to give but it was the only one possible. She knew that she could not have lied: those ice-cold eyes that seemed to bore into her made lying impossible.

'Tell me, Miss Reed, what would be your reaction when dressing the wound of a postoperative colostomy? A colostomy, Miss Reed, is a surgically made opening into the surface of the abdomen through which evil-smelling, liquid faeces are evacuated,' the matron explained. It must have been the woman's matter-of-fact tone that made contemplation of such a horrifying prospect possible.

'I think, miss, the most important thing would be not to allow the patient to see any feelings of disgust that one might have at the sight and the smell. He would certainly be in a very sensitive state of mind.'

'I see.' More notes were made. 'What qualities do you think a nurse should have?'

Pleased with her answer to the previous question, Jane relaxed for a second. 'Good feet?' Flustered, she coughed. 'I mean, she should be strong,' she added quickly. 'And level-headed. She must like people and have a sense of humour,' Jane finished in a rush, feeling now that everything was pointless and wishing she could get out of this room.

'Do you think you have these qualities?'

'Yes,' Jane answered promptly.

'Kindly stand up. Come round here, Miss Reed. Would you lift your skirts?'

Jane did as she was asked, feeling very puzzled and foolish as the woman carefully studied her legs.

'It's a bit like auditioning for the chorus line, isn't it, miss?' she joked weakly, more to cover her embarrassment than to make anybody laugh.

'Your legs are very important. They have to be strong, you will be spending long hours on them. By the way, you call me "Matron" not "miss", I'm not a schoolteacher.'

'Sorry, Matron.'

'Thank you, Miss Reed. There is a tour of the hospital at the end of these interviews. I shall inform you within the week of my decision.' The woman returned her attention to her notepad, and Jane miserably picked up her handbag from the floor, turned, opened a door, and walked into a cupboard. For a wild, hysterical moment she thought to close the door and hide, hoping that Matron had not seen her.

'The door is to your left, Miss Reed,' the humourless voice announced.

Back in the waiting room the others clustered about her, plying her with questions.

'Don't ask me anything! It was dreadful. I said I had no vocation and I walked into a bloody cupboard!'

She did not need the others to tell her she had made a complete mess of it all. She put on her coat and left the hospital, not even waiting for the hospital tour.

A week later the letter from the hospital arrived. She could not believe the contents. She had been accepted. In some mysterious way her answers had been the right ones. She had yet to learn that the last thing a nurse needed was a burning sense of vocation, that such types soon fell by the wayside. Neither did she realize that her weak little jokes had shown a sense of humour despite her nerves, nor that strong legs and a strong back would be her greatest allies. And in her answers, most importantly, she had put the patient first. She had also yet to learn that Matron was no fool and could read a character with one glance of her cold, blue eyes.

Jane was ecstatic. Suddenly nursing was the only thing in the whole world that she wanted to do.

Six months later, she and her mother stood on the platform of the station, waiting for the London train to pull in.

'You'll write?'

'Of course I'll write. Bet you don't answer!'

'Don't get into any mischief!'

'No, Mum.'

'You know, don't let any dirty bugger mess about with you.'

'No, Mum.'

'And keep your underwear clean.'

'Yes, Mum, "in case of accidents", I know, Mum.' She grinned.

They stood now in an awkward silence. Not knowing what to say to each other, both wanted the train to come.

At last the train drew in and Jane made for an empty compartment.

'No, Jane, the middle. Always travel in the middle of the train.'

'Why? What's wrong with the front?'

'In case of an accident, of course! You're less likely to get killed travelling in the middle.'

'Mum, your world is full of possible accidents.'

'It makes sense to take precautions. You can never tell when that bastard up there might drop something on you.' Jane laughed at her mother's irreverent remark and resignedly allowed herself to be loaded into the middle of the train. 'And,' her mother continued, 'always travel in a coach with other women.'

'I know, I know, so I won't be raped! Oh, Mum, stop worrying, do, I'm only going to London.'

Her mother looked unconvinced that her warnings would be heeded. She climbed back onto the platform and stood looking up at Jane who, leaning out of the window, was taken aback by how small and vulnerable her mother looked standing on the platform, and how lonely she suddenly seemed.

'Don't worry, Mum, I'll be all right.'

'Worry? Me? I'm not going to worry about a big lump like you.' But she did not laugh, instead her voice sounded strained, as if it was difficult for her to speak. She looked dejected.

'Mum, don't be sad, please.'

'I'm not sad. Glad to wash my hands off you, more like,' and her mother smiled, but the smile crumpled and seemed to slide off her face like melting wax.

'Mum . . . !' A great cloud of steam gushed out from the engine and raced down the platform towards them, enveloping her mother. 'Mum . . .' but the train began to pull away, making speech impossible. She hung from the window and blew a kiss, but doubted if her mother saw it through the steam.

The rows of terraced houses of her home town slipped by as the train gathered speed. Streets in which she had played all her life, streets where she knew the people, streets where she felt safe.

She was surprised to feel sad. Hadn't she waited impatiently for the day when she could get away from her home and her parents? Yet, back there on the platform, she was certain that if her mother had said, 'Don't go,' she would have leaped off the train. In those moments she had been closer to her mother, and felt more affection from her, than she had ever experienced before. Nothing had been said: it was only a feeling. Should she trust such a feeling? She was puzzled by the emotion, for she thought she had constructed solid barriers, that she no longer cared. Yet here she was, full of joy that her mother did care, that under the layers of bitterness and nagging there remained some affection for her.

And now? London! The prospect excited her. At eighteen, she had not yet learned to be afraid of the unknown. Her future filled her only with anticipation.

5

It was warm for September as she struggled with her heavy suitcase up the long road towards the Nurses' Home. She was hot – her suit was too thick for this weather, the skirt too tight for easy walking, even without a case. Her stiletto-heeled shoes, which she had bought to celebrate her new liberty, were still unfamiliar, and she wobbled about the pavement as she fought to keep her balance. Her outfit and the pretty little skullcap, decorated with blue flowers, had looked so right in the mirror at home. But now the sight of the other girls, in simple skirts and blouses, flatties, and without hats, made her feel overdressed.

'Gosh, just like first day back at boarding school after the hols, isn't it?' a cheerful girl gushed at her.

'I wouldn't know,' Jane said abruptly, as she battled her way through the throng and up the steps of the building.

The hallway was bedlam. The high, piercing shrieks of overexcited girls mingled with the deep-voiced banter of red-faced fathers who struggled valiantly with the ever-increasing piles of luggage. Tearful mothers could be heard giving last-minute instructions to inattentive daughters. A phone rang continuously in a small porter's lodge, but no one answered it. A short woman in blue overalls checked each girl in and issued her with a room number. The lift doors clanged at regular intervals and its mechanism creaked and groaned as it carried load after load of girls, with their parents, to the rooms above.

Jane found her room. Hanging out of the window she could see a landscape of roofs and chimneys, and could hear the muted rumble of the traffic seven floors below. Twice the size of her room at home and with basin, cupboard, desk and bookcase, the room was perfect.

Looking at herself in the full-length mirror, Jane was irritated at how wrong she looked. The suit and lace blouse, which had cost weeks of work as a part-time waitress, at home had seemed the most beautiful garments she had ever possessed. Suddenly, she hated them, and felt stiff and gauche. She opened her case – to her mother and to her, London meant dressing up and so she had not packed any clothes which could be regarded as casual. She found a navy-blue jumper, hastily discarded her blouse and jacket, draped a scarf about her shoulders, and threw the hat to the back of the cupboard shelf. That would have to do.

The noise of fifty young women, chattering excitedly, made it easy to find the right lecture room. Jane went to the back and sat at a desk, silently watching and listening. Many of the others bounded about the room, noisily introducing themselves or emitting sudden shrieks as they recognized one another from some long-forgotten interschool hockey match, or realized that they had friends in common. She watched them, admiringly, as effortlessly they made friends. Everything about them – their voices, their clothes, the noisy confidence – made her feel isolated.

'Grim lot, aren't they?' The voice made Jane jump. Swinging round she found a dark-haired, plump girl was sitting beside her. 'Right stuck-up crowd, if you ask me.' She smiled and two large dimples appeared on either side of her mouth.

'They do seem very confident.' Jane smiled back, relieved at last to have someone to talk to.

'Bleeding dreadful! "Oh golly!" "I say!", "Samantha, darling, how's Nigel?"' Expertly the girl imitated the accents all around them, making Jane laugh. 'I'm Sandra Evans, not from Wales, from Battersea.' She held out her hand, and Jane grasped it.

'Jane Reed, from Kent.'

'I gather Kent's quite posh.'

'Not the part I come from,' she said hurriedly. 'Do you think they're all like this? I mean, they all seem to know each other.'

'No, I shouldn't think so, there must be some other normal people about. All the big hospitals take a quota of grammar-school girls each year. We can't be the only two.'

'Really? I didn't know that.'

'Oh yes, it's true. But this princess business has probably made matters worse. I expect some of this lot hope they'll meet and marry her brother and become royal. Otherwise they would probably have chosen St Thomas's.'

'Is she coming?'

'No! A laugh, isn't it? Now they're stuck here instead of swanning about Tommie's in frilly caps!' The girl laughed loudly.

'I thought all London hospitals were the same.'

'Not likely!' She warmed to her theme, delighted to find such a willing audience. 'Only five of the London hospitals are acceptable to this lot. St Thomas's is the tops. They wouldn't be seen dead in a place like the Westminster –'

A noisy scraping of chairs heralded the arrival of a tall, stout woman in the uniform of a sister. The woman waited for the chattering to cease. So imposing was her manner that silence was immediate. Her gimlet eyes scanned the room as if inspecting each girl in turn.

'I'm Home Sister,' a deep voice rumbled at them.

'More like Home Brother with a voice like that,' Sandra whispered, making Jane choke as she fought to suppress a giggle, her face turning red with the effort.

'Silence!' Sister raised herself to her full height, her ample breasts heaving as she shouted, making the pleats of her apron bib open and shut from the strain forced upon them.

'Crikey, she's got tits like an accordion!' Sandra whispered again and Jane choked loudly.

'What is the problem, Nurse?' Sister's voice boomed across the lecture room. Jane continued to fight the laughter that was rippling up within her, her face growing puce with the effort. 'Your name, Nurse?' Everyone in the room turned to stare at Jane. 'Nurse, I asked for your name, kindly have the courtesy to answer!'

'I think she wants to know your name, Jane.' A straight-faced Sandra nudged her.

'Me? But I'm not a nurse,' Jane whispered.

'You are now, matey!' The dimples flashed at her.

Confused, Jane stood up. 'Did you mean me, Sister?'

'Of course I meant you. No one else is disrupting this talk. Your name?'

'Jane Reed,' she spluttered.

'I'm not interested in your Christian name, Reed. What's wrong with you? I do hope you haven't arrived here carrying nasty germs. That would never do!'

'No, no, Sister. I seem to have a tickle in my throat.'

'Someone give her a drink of water.' A glass of water appeared from the front row. 'Now, perhaps Nurse Reed will give me permission to continue? Blushing with confusion, Jane sat down. 'I must emphasize,' the deep voice boomed on, 'that we will not have illness in the Nurses' Home. Your duty to your patients is to remain healthy. You will remain healthy by having an adequate amount of sleep, eating sensibly, taking your vitamins. Clean living, nurses, clean in body and mind!'

'Spoken in the true Flo Nightingale spirit!' Sandra sighed exaggeratedly.

'Sandra, shut up, you'll get me going again!' Jane pleaded.

Her reward was another glare from Home Sister, who continued pointedly. 'As I was saying, I am your home sister. I am responsible for your wellbeing. I stand for no nonsense. Understood?' A murmur of assent rippled around the room. 'Your rooms will be inspected daily. I will not tolerate untidiness. You are to be neat in your appearance – hair is to be worn off the face, none on your collar. No ponytails . . .' Several hands, nervously, patted offending ponytails. 'You will wear no make-up or perfume when on duty. Understood?'

'Why?' Jane whispered to Sandra who shrugged her shoulders.

'You have a question, Nurse Reed?'

'I was just wondering why no make-up or perfume, Sister.'

'We do not permit perfume because the last thing an ill patient wants to smell is cloying scent – it could make them nauseous. And no make-up, Nurse, because you are not a shopgirl or secretary, and in any case it could prove a distraction to your male patients. To continue. You are Set 128 – remember that number, you will use it frequently. You are not to fraternize with nurses in sets above or below you – it is bad for discipline. Likewise you will refer to each other by surname only, no Christian names are allowed. Do you understand?' The girls began to shuffle uncomfortably in their seats. The sister held aloft a large book. 'This is *the Book*. When you leave the Home you will sign out, and when you return you will sign in again. Failure to do so means instant report to Matron.' Others apart from Jane and Sandra began to whisper. 'While in preliminary training school, PTS for short, you will sign in by ten at night. T-E-N.' The whispering was louder. 'What is worrying you, Nurse?' she asked at random of a girl in the front row.

'It seems frightfully early, Sister.'

'You have hard work to do, my girl. It's quite late enough.'

'But when we are out of PTS, Sister, what then?'

'Midnight, Nurse. And before you ask, in your first year you are permitted three late passes until 2 a.m. You apply to me for them, and I warn you now, I shall require to know where you are going and with whom before I issue them.'

For another half-hour the sister droned on with an endless succession of rules that Jane knew she would never remember.

'Christ, it's like a bleeding nunnery!' sighed Sandra.

'And I thought I had found freedom,' Jane said with a rueful smile.

In batches of six they trooped down to the basement to be issued with their uniform. A harassed supervisor gave every girl a neat pile of clothes, each item of which had to be signed for. Then the girls had to parade in uniform dress and apron in front of Home Sister.

'You two bend over,' she ordered Jane and Sandra. The two girls bowed to her. 'Stupid girls! Turn around and bend over.' Proffering their rear ends to the sister was too much for them and they both began to giggle uncontrollably. 'And what do you find so funny, Nurses?'

'Why are we bending over, Sister?' Sandra gasped between her laughter.

'This is no laughing matter, Nurse. Control yourself, at once. I am checking that when you bend there is no sight of your suspenders.'

'No, Sister.' Sandra struggled to reply. 'But . . .'

Jane stuffed a handkerchief into her mouth.

'But what, Nurse Evans?'

'But, Sister, the dresses are so long, surely no one could glimpse anything.'

'I like to check for my own satisfaction, Nurse. It would not be fair to our poor, sick, male patients, now would it?'

'No, Sister,' they chorused in muffled voices, both now with handkerchiefs clutched to their mouths.

Once outside the room they collapsed in helpless laughter against the wall.

'Do you really think the wards are full of sex-crazed men?' asked Jane.

'I do hope so. Yummy!' shrieked Sandra. 'Imagine rows and rows of frustrated men waiting for a flash of our stockingtops!' Two other girls in the room looked with undisguised dismay at her.

'I can't imagine any man wanting us looking like this,' Jane pointed out as she looked at her reflection in the mirror. The long, thick dress reached to below midcalf. The undarted bodice flattened her breasts, and the stiff, starched apron embraced her like a large chastity belt.

Sandra flung the short red cape about her shoulders.

'Well, this is bloody daft. Look where it comes to. Right bum-freezer and no mistake.'

'Do you have to be so vulgar?' one of the other girls snapped.

'That's not vulgarity, that's fact. Mark my words, your bum will freeze just as fast as mine, come winter!' Sandra replied, laughing.

'God, the types they let in these days,' the girl drawled to her friend, exaggeratedly rolling her eyes.

'You can say that again, Miss Bumless. I wonder what she sits on if she hasn't got a bum?' Sandra aped the drawling voice. 'Come on, Jane, let's get out of here. Stuck-up cows!' Still giggling they rushed from the room and spent the rest of the afternoon in Sandra's room attempting to make their caps up, failing miserably at every attempt, and laughing uncontrollably at every failure.

The next day lectures started in earnest. It was easy to slip into the routine; it was just like being back at school, with homework to do and tests to revise for. The only difference was the uniform and having to get used to being called Nurse. Without a patient in sight, Nurse Reed felt a fraud.

Gradually Set 128 split into four distinct groups. There was what Sandra christened the Bible Belt, serious-faced girls who bustled about like eager novices trying to interest the others in Bible and prayer meetings.

'Put me on one more prayer list,' glowered Sandra at a small mouse-like creature, 'and I'll shove your head down the lav and pull the chain!'

'She means well,' pleaded Jane as the frightened girl scuttled away.

'I'll pray when I want, not when some smug, self-satisfied do-gooder tells me to! They won't last. All vocation and no guts.'

'San—Evans!'

'You're sometimes too bleeding reasonable for your own good, Reed,' Sandra said with mock severity.

Then there were the quiet studious ones, always with anxious expressions. Every spare moment was devoted to study, testing each other, even practising bandaging on each other. They had been labelled the keenies.

'Sisters in the making,' groaned Sandra. 'They'll be hell on the wards.'

'At least they're certain to pass out of PTS,' said Jane, conscious that she spent far too much time gossiping and slipping out to the Cat's Whisker coffee bar with her own gang.

The third group was Sandra's particular *bête noire* – the ones who had originally earned her scorn – the Deb Brigade.

'Joined to snare doctor husbands, that lot, depriving some poor girl of a chance to be here,' was Sandra's studied opinion of them. They kept very much to themselves, never inviting any of the others to their frequent sherry parties; they received the most phone calls, were always away at weekends and were the first to make contact with the medical school next door. 'See,' Sandra said smugly.

Sandra made no secret of her loathing and the group studiously ignored her, inspiring Sandra to greater heights of verbal abuse. But they fascinated Jane who admired not only their clothes, their hair and their social life, but especially the way they did not seem to give a damn about anybody, including the dreaded home sister. They even managed to look attractive in the dreadful uniform.

'They've had them doctored,' announced Sandra as they debated this phenomenon.

'What do you mean?' Jane demanded.

'Mummy's little dressmaker put the odd tuck in here and there, shortened it, that sort of thing.'

'You're kidding!' Jane exclaimed, too nervous of Home Sister even to wear her cap at anything but the regulation angle.

'No, I'm not. Campbell-Grant's dress is definitely shorter than it was last week. You look.'

This fact only increased Jane's awe at such daring.

The Deb Brigade seemed to have fun, too, and Jane would have liked to be friends but the few overtures she plucked up courage to make were ignored.

'You're wasting your time, Jane. They only want to know their own sort.'

'But I had all sorts of friends at school. My best friend's dad was an army officer,' she said with pride.

'What was she doing in a grammar, then?'

'I don't know. I never asked.'

'Probably skint – father came up through the ranks, I shouldn't wonder. They wouldn't have wanted to know your friend either.'

'You're so cynical!'

'No, I'm not. I'm a realist. Stick with your own kind, it's safer.'

'You sound just like my father. In any case, you don't help to make friends, always sniping at them. They probably think I feel the same way.'

'You're free to choose, Reed. You don't have to kick around with the rest of us if you don't want to. Go and join the others, it's no skin off my nose!'

'Oh, Evans, you can be such a bitch at times.'

'Well, shut up about the others then.' Sandra grinned at her, knowing from the start that Jane would never desert the tight-knit group made up of the grammar-school intake, who went everywhere together and with whom Jane was relaxed and felt at home.

6

At the end of the first month, with her small savings and first pay packet, Jane went shopping. She knew exactly what she was going to buy. Within an hour she was the proud possessor of a red, circular felt skirt, a tight-fitting jumper, two frilled petticoats which made the skirt stand out in a most satisfying way, and the longed-for flat leather pumps. At last, she would look like the others. With what was left, she went home for the weekend.

'Good God, girl! How much did that lot cost?' her mother greeted her. Jane twirled around, the petticoats flashing beneath the skirt.

'It's what all the girls are wearing, Mum.'

'More suitable for a square dance than walking around the street in. What with all those frills, you look like the rear end of an ostrich!'

'You've never seen an ostrich in your life.'

'I've got imagination, haven't I?' Irritably her mother put the kettle on. 'What happened to that nice suit and smart shoes you spent all that money on? Thought that was what everyone was wearing.'

'I still wear it, it's just that casual clothes are all the rage now.'

'I should hope you bloody well do still wear it. I hope you're not going to fritter all your money away like this.' Aggressively she spooned the tea into the pot.

'I felt like treating myself, Mum. I was excited getting my first wage packet,' Jane answered, annoyed that she should feel guilty.

'It's all right for some, I suppose.' Her mother sniffed, pouring the boiling water onto the tea. 'Seen any stiffs yet?' she suddenly asked.

'Lord, no. I haven't even seen a live patient, let alone a dead one.' Jane was relieved that the inquisition on her clothes appeared to be over.

'What do you do all day then, buy clothes?'

'No, Mum.' Jane sighed. 'We go to school, have lessons in anatomy and things and we do practicals on dummies or each other.'

'I thought you learned all that as you went along. Sounds boring. I thought you'd have all sorts of interesting cases to tell me about.'

'Sorry, Mum,' Jane said apologetically.

Her mother sipped her tea, gazing blankly out of the window at the wall outside, where the galvanized tin bath hung. 'Bath's sprung a leak. Christ knows when I shall be able to afford another.'

Jane looked down at her skirt, her pleasure in it finally destroyed. 'I'm sorry, Mum. I didn't think.'

'Didn't think what?'

'I should have given you some of my money, instead of buying all this.'

'Did I ask for anything?' her mother snapped. 'No, I never ask for nothing. If you want to spend your money on rubbish like that, that's your affair.'

'No, Mum,' said Jane mechanically.

'In any case, it's too late now, isn't it? All gone, I presume.' She smiled a tight-lipped smile that had no humour in it. She stood up. 'I promised Mrs Green I'd pop in this evening. Didn't know you were coming home.'

'I thought I might go up to the Palais.'

'Yes, you do that, nice for you.'

Jane sat alone, angry with herself that she hadn't thought to buy her mother something — flowers, chocolates. It probably wouldn't have made much difference, though: her mother would still have disapproved. That fleeting moment of intimacy on the station platform four weeks ago was past. Perhaps, in her overexcited state, she had imagined it in the first place.

She went to the local dance but none of her friends were there. Like her they had moved on; already girls junior to her in school had taken their places. As she noticed their shy, sly glances she felt as though she were trespassing on their territory. It was extraordinary how quickly she felt she did not belong in her home town.

The next morning, she lied and said she had to be back in the hospital by lunchtime. There seemed little point in staying longer or, for that matter, returning for some time.

Weekends at the Nurses' Home dragged. Most of the girls, making the most of the free weekends in PTS, went home. Jane caught up on work that never seemed to get done when Sandra was about, and used the time to wander around the museums and art galleries, exploring London as she did so. It would have been more fun with someone else. When Sandra invited her home for the weekend, she accepted gratefully.

Sandra's home in Battersea was in a road just like her own. The only differences were that it had one more room and half the garden was taken up with an extension containing a brand-new bathroom. Even with the extra room it was a squeeze. Sandra was the eldest of six, and the only one to have left home.

The house was in chaos when they let themselves in. Piles of damp clothes adorned every surface, papers and magazines lay where they had been dropped and there were toys everywhere. Sandra scrabbled among the dirty crockery to find two cups, kicked a fat sleeping cat off a chair and dumped the washing from another chair onto the floor.

'Shirley, get down here!' Sandra shouted up the stairs. 'We've an hour till Mum gets back. Lazy bitch,' she said, settling back to her cup of tea. 'Now I've left she's supposed to supervise the others and make sure they straighten up for Mum.'

'What's everyone called?'

'There's Shirley, she's seventeen, Sharon's fifteen, Sherry's twelve, Sheena's eight and Sean's six.'

'So many Ss!'

'That's one of Mum's little economies, saves on the Cash's name tapes, see? S. Evans does us all.'

'Do you like being part of a large family?'

'Varies from bliss to sheer hell.' Sandra laughed. 'We never have enough money for anything. And how I hate sharing! You'll never know the paradise it is, having my own room at the hospital. On the other hand, you're never lonely. And if you've a problem, there's always someone to listen . . . that sort of thing. I guess I wouldn't have it any other way.'

'Sounds lovely to me. I mean, never being alone. But, are you Roman Catholics?'

'No. Everyone asks that, I suppose it's the only way they can under-stand such a large family. I don't think my parents planned it that way — it just happened. As Mum says, my dad was born oversexed and he always seems to know when she's got her knickers off!'

'Your mother said that to you?' Jane sat bolt upright in amazement. 'She talks about sex with you? Jokes about it?'

'Nothing odd in that, is there?'

'It's the most extraordinary thing I've ever heard.'

'Why? Doesn't your mother talk about it?'

'My mother doesn't even think about it, let alone talk about it. And she certainly doesn't do it.' Jane laughed at the very idea.

'Come off it, all husbands and wives do it.'

'I'm pretty certain mine don't. They don't even sleep together.'

'I'd hate twin beds.'

'I mean they have separate rooms,' Jane explained.

'Crikey, how grand! Have they always had separate rooms?'

'No. I can just remember when Dad came back from the war, they slept together then. I should remember: I had to get out of my mother's bed – how I hated him for kicking me out. But I don't think it was for long, 'cause he moved into the other back bedroom and I went back to sleeping with Mum.'

'How sad!'

'Oh, I don't think so. I think my mother was relieved. All she ever said to me about sex was that it was disgusting, and something a woman would have to put up with in marriage. It was the price we paid.'

'Poor woman, think of all the fun she's been missing! My mum doesn't think like that. She enjoys it. You should hear them at it some nights.'

Jane was out of her depth and could only smile, wide-eyed with amusement.

'Have you ever thought, perhaps that's why your father doesn't like you?' Sandra went on, undeterred. 'He blames you for taking his wife away from him – back from the war and you in his bed, that sort of thing. Poor man, he must be dreadfully lonely and frustrated. More tea, Reed?'

Jane was stunned. Silently she held her cup out for Sandra to fill. How could she have been so insensitive and blind? If Sandra was right, so much made sense. With her mother's emphatic views that sex was disgusting, it had never struck Jane that it could be anything else. She had a natural curiosity about the subject, but had presumed that her mother's attitude was perfectly normal. But if Mrs Evans enjoyed it, why didn't her mother? Was her mother different? Or was her father a bad lover? Since she had never given the subject much thought, the very idea of her parents making love seemed too ludicrous to contemplate.

'You've gone quiet, Reed.'

'You've given me a lot to think about, that's why. Shouldn't we start clearing up for your mum?' As Jane spoke, Shirley, a mirror image of Sandra, appeared, yawning exaggeratedly.

'About bloody time. Tired, are we?' Sandra sneered.

'Shut up! Two minutes in the house and you start,' her sister retorted. While the two sisters argued about who was the lazier, Jane began to do the washing-up. An hour later, once the sisters had formed a truce, all was tidy, the vegetables were peeled, and the kettle was on again as Mrs

Evans, a short, fat woman, as wide as she was tall, bustled in. She gave Jane an expansive welcome and busied herself preparing the supper.

'Sit down, Mum. We'll do that. You look tired out.'

'Tired, me? Nonsense. But a cup of tea would be nice.'

She sat, sipping her tea with relish and, although she never seemed to stop talking, within ten minutes she knew what Jane thought about the hospital, her mother, her father, the government, even stiletto heels.

'And how's your week been, Sandra?' She turned to her daughter.

'Fine. Reed and I came top in the tests again. That put the noses of the snooty lot out of joint, I can tell you.'

'Still not made friends with them, then?'

'No. And I don't want to either. They're so stuck-up, Mum. I reckon if I fell down in a dead faint at their feet they'd step over me.'

'Sounds to me as if you're getting a nasty chip on your shoulder. You're as good as anyone, both of you, and don't ever forget it.'

'But, Mum, it's difficult not to let them get you down.'

'Nonsense! That's life, my girl. Don't think it's just St Cuthbert's. You'll find people everywhere who think they're a cut above you and want to put you down. You just have to learn to live with it and prove them wrong. And being rude to them isn't the way, Sandra.'

'Well, I'm not having anything to do with them, and that's that,' announced Sandra.

'It's difficult, Mrs Evans,' said Jane. 'I know what Sandra means, but I do wish we could all be friends. It all seems so silly.'

'Traitor!'

'Let her finish, Sandra, don't be so bossy.'

'Well, it's easier for Sandra, she seems to see everything so clearly in black and white, whereas . . . oh, I don't know, I don't think it's as simple as that.'

'Piffle! In any case, I didn't come home to spend the weekend talking about that lot.'

'All right, we'll drop it. God, my feet ache! Any more tea in that pot?' Mrs Evans asked, kicking off her shoes and vigorously rubbing her toes. 'Do you know, we had six post-ops today, a Saturday, I ask you.'

'Sandra told me you were a nurse, Mrs Evans,' Jane said with interest.

'A private nursing home isn't the same, is it, Mum?' Sandra butted in. 'Full of moaning women having hysterectomies!'

'Don't you listen to her, Jane. I like it there. I can't seem to stop. I've left once or twice, but I always go back.' The little woman spoke in quick staccato sentences, each word coming out in a rush, as if she were making the most of the short time she had to sit down and talk to them.

'But how on earth do you manage? I mean, all the family and everything,' Jane asked.

'It all gets done sooner or later, and what doesn't get done wasn't worth doing in the first place.'

Jane looked with admiration at this woman who must do the work of six and yet seemed so happy and contented. And she was so easy to talk to. Even when she disagreed she didn't hector them. It was difficult not to compare her with her own mother, whose endless moaning and nagging was still a sharp, guilty memory.

Sandra's father arrived. Tall and thin, a complete contrast to his wife — like the Sprats, Jane thought. She was immediately on her guard, wishing he had not returned to spoil the pleasant evening. And then he smiled at Jane, welcoming her to his house with gentle charm. There would be no shouting in this house from him, that was obvious. Instead he joined in their chatter as he mended his son's toy. By the end of the evening, Jane felt as if she had known this warm and welcoming family all her life. As she lay in bed, it was difficult not to envy Sandra her family.

The following day, as they were about to leave, Mrs Evans took Jane to one side.

'You're always welcome here, Jane. If ever you want someone to talk to, you come to me. It's hard when you first leave home, it's good to have a second mum to turn to.'

'Thank you, Mrs Evans, you're very kind.'

Jane was thoughtful after the visit. She felt Sandra was wrong to be so intransigent about the other girls. By being so bigoted, wasn't Sandra risking being as selective as the others? Maybe it just needed time. Certainly she would never be able to confess to Sandra how she envied the others and secretly longed to be like them. She was preoccupied, too, by her new insight into her parents' behaviour. It explained so much — the bitterness, the nagging and the rows, their general air of unhappiness. The resentment that had built up within began to soften into sadness and even sympathy for them.

7

No amount of time in the training school could have prepared Jane for the shock of the wards. The ordered routine of the practical nursing in the demonstration room, performed on life-size dummies, fell apart when real flesh-and-blood patients were the object of her care. The dummies in the school felt no pain, they did not curse her, nor did they smell.

She had presumed that her patients would be grateful; instead the majority were cantankerous and never ceased complaining. There were times when she felt that they seemed to be blaming her personally for whatever was wrong with them.

Jane seemed to live in a sea of urine. As soon as one bedpan round was complete and she had scrubbed and scoured the sluice room, it was time for the next. When she was not issuing bedpans, she was testing or measuring their contents. Her whole life seemed to be filled with specimens. She felt as if the patients did not exist, only their urine. To think how she used to object to her father's chamber pot. If he could see her now, he would have the last laugh.

The sister's voice could be heard from the start of duty to the end. The mere sound of it sparked terror in the student nurses' hearts. Sister seemed incapable of being satisfied with anything. What difference could it possibly make to the patients whether the bed wheels were all at the same angle, or whether the sheets were turned down exactly 15 inches? Or that the bath plugs were set in a particular position and the bath soap in another? It could not have been of any interest to them — they probably did not even notice such minutiae — but to the nurses it was a constant source of worry and irritation.

Everything was so drab: the buildings, and the endless corridors painted in dull, institutional green. The long wards painted the same green stretched noisily into the distance, with ugly bedsteads standing like iron sentries at measured distances. Everywhere Jane thought she could smell the sickly-sweet stench of death and decay, of the cancers eating away at so many of the wretched souls in those ugly beds in the noisy wards; and everywhere there was the never-ending, depressing green. It seemed incredible that people could recover in such surroundings.

She always felt tired. No matter how many early nights she had, she could never completely shake off the exhaustion. It was not just physical fatigue, though that was real enough, it was mental tiredness too. Fatigue induced by fear, fear that she might do something wrong, fear of being shouted at, fear of instant dismissal.

She was relieved that she did not have any sense of vocation for, if she had, the reality would have come as a heartbreaking shock. Jane felt she was totally unnecessary to anyone's recovery.

'What the hell are we here for, Evans?' she asked her friend as they lay on her bed, lazily smoking and resting their aching feet.

'It'll get better. Once we sign on, they'll let us do more interesting things, like dressings and injections.'

'Dressings! Injections! Don't make me laugh! I'm not even allowed to give a blanket bath!'

'I've heard Sister Field is a bit eccentric.'

'I hate it. I can't take it – the boredom, the yelling, the smells, the bloody patients. I hate it!' she shouted loudly.

'Love, don't give up. Wait until you've been somewhere interesting – then decide. I mean, to give up after one ward seems a bit silly, doesn't it? You might feel completely different about the next one. The men on my ward are lovely, and so appreciative that it makes it all worthwhile.'

'Great for you! You should try my moaning women.'

'They say that Gynae is one of the worst.'

'It's true, I can tell you! Half of them are moaning because they're not pregnant, and the other half are in because they were and they tried to get rid of it. It's crazy. So on top of their moans, the "want-to-be-pregnant brigade" hate the guts of the "get-rid-of-it-by-any-means brigade". And me? I loathe them all!'

'Oh dear, you are fed up.' Sandra smiled at her friend.

'And when you come off duty, what is there? The food's atrocious. Why do you think they give us all those vitamin pills?' Jane angrily lit another cigarette. 'Look at our raw, rough hands. And this bloody uniform – look at us, we look like drabs! It's sexless, it's uncomfortable, and I can never pleat this bloody cap right.' Petulantly she threw the cap she had given up folding across the room. Sandra retrieved it and started neatly folding it for her. 'And no one's died yet!' she said, almost as an afterthought.

'How remiss of them!' Sandra grinned at Jane's pink face, noticing with amusement that the colour did not make it any less attractive, the grey eyes glinting in rage at the whole system.

'Shut up! I'm not joking. I want a death to see if I can cope with it. If I can't, I might just as well give up now and save everyone a lot of trouble and money.'

'Make sure you don't use someone dying as an excuse to get out. It's never pleasant, my mum says. She says it doesn't matter how many you've laid out, it's always upsetting.'

'Your mum's a proper nurse. I'll never be one, I know that now.'

'Don't talk so bloody daft. A minute ago you were complaining that you didn't have enough contact with the patients. So how do you know that you aren't going to make it? Wait until you're on a decent ward, or Theatres.'

'God, I dread Theatres! I'd drop everything, I know I would. As it is, everything breaks if I go anywhere near it – I broke the sterilizer today. I just looked at it and it exploded. Sister was furious and we had to borrow one from the ward next door,' Jane said in a woebegone voice.

'You can't break a sterilizer by looking at it.'

'You tell Sister Field that. She says I did, the miserable old cow!'

'Is she as bad as they say?'

'Bad! She's evil! She's a bad-tempered, sexually frustrated old shrew. Do you know she made Tyler-Smith stand on a stool in the middle of the ward today? She'd dropped a dressing tray, and the old bitch made her stand on this flaming stool, just like an orphan out of *Jane Eyre*. And, what's more, she made her stay there while the Prof did his round with that gawping gaggle he calls students.'

'That woman Field can't be normal. There must be something wrong with her head, if you ask me.'

'I hate it all. And those bitches with their superior airs, I hate them too. Have you noticed how they all have double-barrelled names – that's another thing that gets on my nerves.'

Sandra laughed at her outburst.

'What's so funny?'

'I thought it was you wanted to be friends with them. Sounds as if you've changed your mind – dramatically.'

'I hate being made to feel inferior. Why should I? I'm as good as them.

Honest, I didn't know such snobbery existed!' She flopped back onto her pillow, lapsing at last into a sullen silence.

Sandra wandered over to the window and peered out at the soot-laden, yellow fog swirling thickly against the panes.

'Great! There's a right peasouper building up out there.' Jane glanced without interest at the window.

'What's good about that?'

'The bronchitics will be pouring in, snuffing it left, right and centre. That will please my dad.'

'Why on earth should a rush of bronchitics please your father?'

'Didn't you know? He makes coffins!'

Jane shrieked with laughter, her anger with everything evaporating. 'You're making it up to make me laugh. You told me your dad was a carpenter.'

'He is. What do you think coffins are made of, clot? This is his busy season, a good load of stiffs now sets him up nicely for the summer and then he can do what he really likes doing, making furniture. He'd like to do that all the time, but the coffins pay well.' She watched Jane rolling on the bed with uncontrollable laughter. 'He's very good!' she said defensively.

'Oh, Sandra, I'm sure he is. It's just the idea of someone listening to the weather forecast and hearing it all in terms of how many corpses he could count on – it's so funny!'

'Well, at least you're laughing.' Sandra sat down again on the bed. 'You know what you want? Get you out of this doom – a man.'

'Fat chance we have of meeting anyone.'

'There's loads of lovely blokes about. You're so busy moaning that you don't notice them. And with your looks you shouldn't have a problem.'

'Where are all these men?' asked Jane sitting up with interest.

'For a start, there's the doctors, the medical students, the –'

'Doctors! They're so grand they don't even know we exist. Same with the medics: they only talk to the seniors. Where are we supposed to meet anyone? This place is like a nunnery.'

'There's the Cat's Whisker.'

'I'm sick to death of cappuccino. In any case the students there are as skint as we are.'

'There are some yummy porters. Have you seen the one in Casualty?'

'A hospital porter isn't my idea of romance.'

'And who are you, Nurse Reed, to be so high and mighty? Don't tell me you're turning into a snob!' Sandra laughed.

'You know what I mean. I can't imagine anything remotely romantic happening in this place.'

'I suppose the love of your life will come charging in on a coal-black stallion.'

'That would be nice!' Jane smiled.

Sandra took her hand, her expression suddenly serious. 'Don't give up, Jane. It'll get better, honest it will. If you went, I'd miss you dreadfully.'

'It's probably out of my hands, Sandra. I expect the hospital will politely ask me to get lost after this three months' probation, which would solve everything.'

Jane survived her three months on the ward full of moaning women. It was with mixed feelings that she approached Matron's office to be told whether the hospital was willing to train her. Part of her was certain that she was wasting her time and everyone else's; part of her was afraid — what else could she do? It was the perennial question to which there seemed to be no answer. A very small part of her felt she would be sad to go, that perhaps things would get better.

She entered Matron's room. Nothing seemed to have changed since she had last been here at her interview. It was as if the woman hadn't moved from her position behind the desk.

'Nurse Reed, sit, please.' As before, there was no welcoming smile to help Jane read the woman's mind. Jane sat silently as Matron read her ward report.

'I think we should have a talk, Nurse Reed, don't you?'

'Yes, Matron,' a very subdued Jane replied.

'Nurse Reed, your appearance is a disgrace. Just look at your shoes! They are filthy and appear to be falling apart.' Jane looked guiltily at her shoes and attempted to twine them around the legs of her chair to hide them. 'Your stockings are laddered, and inking in the ladders with black ink fools no one, especially not me. Your apron has a black mark on it. Ink? And your cap is a mess! What have you to say, Nurse Reed?'

'I'm sorry about my shoes, Matron. It's the water in the sluices — they're always wet, and they were cheap to start with. I snagged my stockings as I was changing to come to see you and I didn't have another pair, and I hoped you wouldn't notice. And I have a dreadful time with the cap, I can never get it right, I do try . . . but each time I screw it up into an unholy mess!' she finished breathlessly.

'Save up for better shoes. Always have a spare pair of stockings. Ask a friend to help you with your cap.'

'Yes, Matron,' Jane replied dejectedly.

'Apart from that, Nurse Reed, your ward report is excellent. Sister Field is pleased both with your work and your willingness and keenness to learn, also your cheerfulness in what, after all, is not one of the easiest wards in this hospital.'

Jane could feel her mouth opening in disbelief. 'I am pleased to inform you that the hospital will be willing to enter into a contract with you, should you wish to join us, for the rest of your training.'

'Oh yes, please, Matron. Thank you.'

Matron dismissed her and as she stood to go, she smiled at Jane. 'You will find, Nurse Reed, that nail varnish remover is quite good for getting ink stains off flesh.'

'Thank you, Matron.'

'And by the way, Nurse Reed, the door is to your left!' To her astonishment, Jane saw that Matron was grinning broadly.

Two

1956 – 57

I

Jane had been nursing for a year. In that time she had come to terms with the pettinesses of their small, enclosed world. She had learned to ignore the snobbery. On the ward she performed, without arguing, tasks which previously she had thought pointless. She did not get so tired. She was more tolerant of her patients, realizing that often their bad temper and depression were caused by fear. Finally she had to face death for the first time, with every pore of her body crawling with terror. But as she held the wasted, pain-racked body of the frightened old man, comforted him and helped to ease his fear, she conquered some of her own. As the last breath left the emaciated figure, she placed his hands on his chest and bent and kissed him on the forehead. It seemed the right thing to do. Then she ran into the sluice room and, among the bedpans and urine bottles, sobbed her grief for the old man she hardly knew. She knew now that Sandra's mother had been right, that death would never become a routine occupational hazard.

Now, as a second-year nurse, she had a different-coloured belt, two additional late passes, five shillings extra a week and far more confidence.

She was on her second tour of night duty. Last night on Male Surgical had been terrible. The ward was available for casualties, which meant that some beds had to be kept free for the victims that the city would damage and spew up each night.

It was a rare night that the beds were not all filled and this was no exception. A multiple pile-up in the Edgware Road, two knifings from Soho, and an Irishman who had decided to climb some scaffolding only to fall four storeys and live, despite two broken legs, a broken back and concussion so severe that it was doubtful if they would ever know what had possessed him to climb it in the first place. Two regular patients, of whom Jane had grown fond, chose that night, amid the noise and chaos, to give up the struggle and die, quietly and unnoticed.

It was the sort of night that really summed up Jane's fragmented feelings about being a nurse, when she felt there was no better job. It was also the sort of night when she felt she could not cope, was totally inadequate to the task in hand and too young to bear the responsibility of all that pain and anguish.

She went off duty exhausted. Fully dressed she lay on her bed, meaning to wash and change, but instead she fell rapidly into a deep sleep, happy in the knowledge that she had four nights off and could sleep as long as she liked.

An insistent banging on her door punctured this sleep. She stirred restlessly. The banging persisted.

'Reed! Reed? I know you're in there.'

'Go away,' she mumbled, putting her pillow over her head. The knocking continued. 'Go away, Evans!' she shouted, irritable now.

Instead the door was thrown open and Sandra burst into the room.

'I knew you were in here,' Sandra exclaimed triumphantly. 'You're on nights off, aren't you?' Blearily Jane nodded. 'Good. Then get up! Come on.'

'Go away, please. I want to sleep.'

Sandra sat herself down firmly on Jane's bed. 'You are bad-tempered! Come on, cheer up! We're going to a lovely party, so get up.'

'You might be going, but I'm sleeping for days.'

'God, you're wet! You've had hours already. Come on, wake up!'

'My feet are killing me,' Jane moaned.

'Then you need something to take your mind off them. A party!'

Sandra leaped up and, opening Jane's wardrobe, began to riffle through her clothes.

'Now, what will you wear?' She held up dresses, considering each for a second and then, rejecting them, threw them in a heap on the floor and burrowed back into the wardrobe. Jane watched the systematic destruction of her orderly room. 'Come on, misery, don't just sit there mooning. Take an interest, do. What are you going to wear? Not that it matters. You always look stunning, whatever you wear.'

'Is there any point in my repeating that I am not going to this bloody party?' Jane asked, sitting up wearily.

'None whatsoever. It'll do you good to get out and meet some new people. In any case I can't go on my own, now can I?'

'Ask someone else.'

'I don't want to go with anyone else, I want to go with you.'

Jane looked at the large brown eyes, and knew that she would go. It had been a foregone conclusion the minute that Sandra had come into the room. She could never resist her friend, and her objections had merely been a form of ritual.

'Whose party is it?'

'There, I knew you'd come. I don't know who's giving it, but it's sure to be super. You know those two Cambridge students working on Casualty as porters? Well, it's a friend of theirs. They're super, not the least bit stuck-up.' She picked out a blue dress. 'You've half an hour to have a bath, OK? You don't mind if I borrow this, do you?'

'Yes, I do mind. If I'm going, I want to wear that dress!' But it was too late, Sandra was already scurrying along the corridor to her own room, triumphantly holding Jane's dress aloft.

Half an hour later, she entered the hall of the Nurses' Home. As usual, at this time of the evening, it was crowded with off-duty nurses. Some were waiting for their dates to appear, others had no dates and nothing better to do than to watch what was going on and who was going out with whom.

Jane had been too well tutored by her mother's disappointment in her looks to regard herself as beautiful. Sandra's compliments she interpreted as acts of friendship. The admiring glances she received from the other girls' dates were, she thought, the stares of curiosity. She stood looking around the hall, in her red felt skirt and black jumper, her long dark hair tied back with a red ribbon, totally oblivious of how lovely she looked.

Across the room she saw Sandra in animated conversation with a young man Jane remembered seeing around the hospital, but he looked different in his sports jacket.

'He can't go like that!' Jane heard Sandra say angrily.

'Why not?' the young man asked.

'Don't be bloody daft, he looks as if he's dying!'

'No, he's not, he's just had a bad day.'

Jane noticed another man slumped on the settee. His face was grey, his eyes were glassy, and he was sweating profusely.

'What's the problem? Is he ill?' Jane interrupted, concerned.

'Bad day, my foot! He's drunk,' hissed Sandra. 'Just look at him.' Suddenly she noticed Jane. 'John, this is Jane. She's supposed to be this slob's partner,' Sandra said angrily.

'Jane, hullo. I'm dreadfully sorry, but I don't think David will be coming to the party, do you?' he said apologetically, turning to look at his friend with a perplexed expression. 'I really don't know what we can do.'

'We get him out of here and to his bed, that's what we do!' Sandra snapped, her dark eyes blazing with fury. Together they began to manhandle David from the settee. Suddenly he came to life and swiftly swung round, hung over the back of the settee and, with heaving shoulders, vomited.

'Oh, Christ!' said John.

'Bloody hell!' exclaimed Sandra, looking nervously around the room. They were lucky, the room was so crowded and the noise level so high that miraculously no one had noticed. 'Quick,' ordered Sandra, 'push that flaming settee back against the wall. Get him out of here, quick!' Surreptitiously they edged the settee back against the wall.

'How do I get him out?'

'God, you're impossible! Frogmarch him. Carry him. I don't care, but just get him out of here, fast. We can't risk the portress seeing us with you. We'll meet you outside.'

John supported his swaying friend and sheepishly led him past the portress's lodge. The woman leaped up and eyed them suspiciously as they stumbled past.

'The heat . . .' they heard John mumble in explanation.

Sandra and Jane waited a minute until the portress was busy with a crowd about her window and then slipped past. Mrs Grant, the portress, was one of the banes of their lives. She sat her life away in her pigeonhole of an office, behind a little window which opened and shut with a crack, like the jaws of a predatory animal. Each morning a queue of girls hoping for mail would form outside the window. At the appointed time, not a minute early or late, the window would snap open and Mrs Grant would reluctantly hand out mail. The Nurses' Home was her world, and very little escaped her sharp eyes. But tonight they were in luck, and they managed to get outside without her seeing.

They found David leaning at an angle against the railings and, on the corner, they saw John looking for a taxi.

'This evening is going to be a disaster. I'm not coming,' Jane declared. 'Oh, hell!' Her hand shot up to her mouth. 'The bloody Book – we forgot to sign out.'

'Stop flapping, Reed. I've arranged all that. Sykes is signing us out and in. And, yes, you are coming. Look, we'll dump David back at his digs. You can hardly let me go on my own, after this!'

'Well, how about neither of us going?'

'Damn that! We're all dressed up now. Come on, Jane, it still might be fun.'

Against her better judgement, Jane climbed into the taxi. The driver was none too keen to take them.

'I don't take drunks! Who'll clear it up if he's sick?'

'My good man . . .' started David, only to collapse back into the seat, winded by a vicious jab from Sandra's elbow.

'He's not drunk, driver. He has this dreadful collapsing illness, and we must get him to his bed quickly,' Sandra lied, giving the driver one of her largest smiles. 'It's not infectious, and we are nurses,' she reassured him. Sandra's smile did the trick and the taxi sped off towards David's lodgings. As he disembarked unsteadily from the taxi, David bowed low to both of them.

'I come from haunts of coot and hern . . .' he began cryptically, then buckled at the knees. The girls waited, sitting stiff-backed with indignation, while John deposited his friend in bed.

'Look, girls, I'm so sorry about this,' John said, climbing back into the taxi. 'He's always doing it. He can't drink, you see, it always makes him throw up.'

'Why does he do it then?' Sandra asked in a frigid voice.

'Habit, I suppose.' John gave them a weak grin. 'I promise you the rest of the evening won't be like this, honestly. It was much worse last time, he was sick in the Ritz.'

'"Coot" is right!' said Jane. The two girls looked at each other and started to laugh.

'You are coming then?' They nodded. 'Fabulous!'

A little later, the taxi pulled up in front of a small house in Fulham. As John paid it off, Jane stood on the pavement and looked through the open windows at the silhouetted shapes of a large crowd. Even from the street the noise was deafening; the very walls of the house seemed to bulge in time to the rock and roll that was bellowing out. She shouldn't have come, she thought. She never knew what to say to people at parties and this looked larger than any party she had ever been to. If they were all Cambridge types, they were likely to be arrogant, very intelligent, and she would have nothing in common with anyone.

'Evans, I don't want to go!'

'Lor', don't start that! We're here now. What's the matter with you? You've hardly said a word all the way.'

'I don't know. I've got this horrid floaty sort of feeling in my stomach and it makes me nervous, as if it's warning me.'

'Hell, you are a clot! That's excitement.' Jane did not look convinced. 'Stop behaving like an old woman! It'll be fine, I promise you. This is our chance to broaden our horizons. If we play our cards right we might even get an invitation to Cambridge.' She grabbed Jane confidently by the arm and eagerly followed John up the steps to the front door.

Inside, the crush was unbelievable. John had to push a path for them through the crowd. There did not appear to be anywhere to hang coats and reluctantly they threw theirs onto a large pile on the floor.

'Where's the booze?' John asked of a young man making his way with difficulty in the opposite direction, holding aloft two glasses of wine which slopped in all directions.

'Kitchen. Back.' He indicated with a jerk of his head.

The surfaces in the kitchen were covered with bottles of every shape and size. The floor was awash with spilled wine. A beer barrel stood on a table in the centre of the room; beneath it lay a young man apparently asleep, but with his mouth open so that the drips from the tap trickled down his gullet.

'I do hope he doesn't drown!' Jane tried to joke. The other two peered at him. As John gently prodded him with his foot, one eye opened and winked at them.

'I thought he'd be all right. And if not, what a way to go!' laughed John loudly. Jane did not laugh. She had seen too many drunken brawls in her street. She could understand that her father and his cronies needed to drink – for them it was an escape – but what on earth could this fortunate young man possibly need to escape from?

She followed the others back through the crush to the front room where the crowd was even denser. She need not have worried about making conversation with strangers: the crashing music made talking impossible. To her pleased surprise, one young man after another asked her to dance, and all she had to do was to smile as they valiantly tried to talk to her. The crowd seemed good-natured enough, but she could not put out of her mind that at any moment it might erupt in violence.

By three o'clock, and after a visit from the police requesting that they turn the volume down, things began to quieten. Softer music was put on. People began to sprawl on the floor. Jane searched for Sandra but could not find her among so many bodies. In a sudden lull, tiredness began to creep up on her. Sinking to a large cushion on the floor, she leaned her back against the wall and gratefully closed her eyes.

'Hullo.'

Jane looked up, shading her eyes to try to make out the tall figure standing over her.

'I'm sorry. You'll have to forgive me, I can't dance another step.' She laughed apologetically.

'I wasn't going to ask you to dance, I wanted to talk to you. May I?' He indicated the big cushion and she moved over to make room for him. He sank down beside her, elegantly jackknifing his tall frame.

'Alistair Redland,' he introduced himself.

'Jane Reed.'

They solemnly shook hands and smiled at each other. She thought he looked handsome, almost Nordic with his blonde hair, but it could be a trick of the light, she thought. She smiled again, shyly.

'Are you enjoying the party?' he asked.

'Not much,' she replied.

'I'm sorry.' He laughed. 'What's wrong with it?'

'It's too crowded, and with so many drunks around, it's bound to end in a fight.'

'Really? Are you sure?' Again he laughed.

'Yes. It always does, doesn't it – drink, I mean?' She turned to him and for the first time he saw the real fear in her beautiful grey eyes.

'Jane, I don't think you need worry. They're just having a good time, you know, letting their hair down. I've never seen a real fight break out, not with this lot.' He sounded incredulous. 'I'm sorry you don't like my party, though.'

'I didn't realize it was your party.'

'Obviously, otherwise you wouldn't have told me you didn't like it.'

'Yes, I would,' she replied. 'There wouldn't be much point in lying, would there?'

'Well, no, I suppose not. It's just . . . well, usually people aren't quite so honest. Do you like my house?'

'It seems very nice. Do you share it with anyone?'

'No.'

'It's a bit big just for one person, isn't it?'

'I don't think so, it only has two bedrooms.'

'Only!' She laughed.

'Why are you laughing?'

'Just that my friend Sandra's family of eight live in a three-bedroomed house.'

'Oh, I see.' He looked thoughtful. 'Cigarette?' As she took the cigarette, she noticed what beautiful, strong hands he had. So many men were spoiled by ugly hands, but she liked his. 'Are you a student?'

'A student nurse at St Cuthbert's.'

'Do you like it?'

'Not much. I'm not a very good nurse, you see. I can't remember things. I mean, the other day I assisted a doctor with a blood transfusion and I'd forgotten to put the blood on the trolley; he wasn't amused. And I drop everything and break things.'

He smiled. 'It sounds dreadful. Couldn't you do something else?'

'Not really. I'd hate to work in an office and I couldn't work in a bank – I can't add up!'

He laughed. It was a good, open, honest laugh – nothing polite about it, she thought.

'And you?' she asked.

'I'm at Cambridge doing estate management. Not nearly as lively as nursing.'

'You don't sound as if you're at Cambridge.'

'What does that mean?'

'You talk normally, not as if you're strangling to death half the time.'

'Jane, you are funny!'

'Well, you know what I mean.' She grinned at him. 'Our hospital is full of them, and really sometimes it's difficult to understand what they're saying. But you, you have a beautiful voice, I could listen to you for hours.'

'I'm relieved to hear it. Let's hope you will.'

Jane found herself blushing.

'You blush, too! I don't believe it!'

They were too engrossed in each other to notice John and Sandra approaching.

'We thought of going on to a club. Coming, Alistair?'

'No, thanks, John, not tonight.'

'Coming, Jane?' Sandra asked her. Jane discovered to her surprise that suddenly she did not want to leave at all. Reluctantly she began to get to her feet.

Alistair's hand restrained her. With delight she heard him say softly, 'Stay here with me, Jay, please.'

'I think I'll stay here, Sandra.'

It was the easiest decision of her whole life.

2

The light shining down on their cushion was the only one in the room. Jane felt as if they were sitting on an isolated island, the sleeping bodies around them like large rocks in a dark sea. Alistair fetched a bottle of wine prudently hidden before the party.

Talking to him was easy. He seemed genuinely interested in her, and what she thought and felt about things.

As dawn began to filter into the room, her feeling of isolation began to fade. In the daylight, the romantic rocks became again the crumpled shapes of sleeping guests, the darkened sea the bare floorboards littered with glasses, bottles and cigarette ends. Alistair shuddered at the sight.

'Let's walk down to the river,' he suggested. They left the sleepers, the upturned bottles and the smoke-laden air. As they walked along the deserted street, he suddenly took her hand in his. It was a warm handclasp, and it felt right and comfortable. She looked at him shyly and he smiled, and in the full light of day she could see that he was handsome. It had not been a trick of the light, after all. A good foot taller than she, he was slim but muscular. His hair was the Nordic blonde she had thought it to be. It was straight with a hank that continually fell across his forehead. He had a habit of running his hands through it, flicking it back into place. His eyes, unusually in someone so blonde, were brown and flecked with gold. When he smiled fine lines appeared around them, as if he smiled a great deal. He walked with a long-legged stride so that Jane found herself almost running to keep up.

'Sorry.' He grinned at her, slowing down. 'I always forget that not everyone walks as fast as I do.'

They reached the wall of the Embankment and leaned against it, watching the greenish-brown water of the Thames sluggishly slip by. Two swans swam majestically towards them, inclining their heads elegantly in their direction, as if bidding them 'good day'. They laughed with pleasure and both solemnly called, 'Good morning!' to the passing birds. She squealed with horror as a large sleek rat slipped from the deck of a houseboat but they watched with fascination as it walked the mooring rope with the grace of a tightrope walker, manoeuvring intelligently around the cowls put there to baulk its progress. They applauded with delight as the rat safely reached the shore, but they regretted the noise they had made when it turned bright eyes on them and, startled, slunk away.

Although they stood apart as they leaned against the parapet, Jane was as aware of his body as if he were touching her. She wished he would. He talked about Turner. She tried to listen but found herself planning to move her hand, unnoticed, so that it would brush against his. She moved slightly to the left, but as she did, he turned around, widening the gap between them, and he talked of Wordsworth. Instead of listening, she watched his mouth. It was a generous mouth with full, fleshy lips. A mouth she would like to kiss. But then perhaps he didn't want to kiss her, otherwise surely he would have done so by now. He began to talk of Browning . . .

'Oh, to hell with the lot of them!' He stepped forward and, awkwardly, took her into his arms and was kissing her. She was so surprised her wish had been granted that she stood rigidly, her mouth passive against his. 'I'm sorry, I shouldn't have done that. I apologize, I don't know what got into me. You looked so pretty.'

'Don't apologize! I wanted you to kiss me. I didn't think you would and it took me by surprise.' She laughed with delight, unaware how ingenuous she sounded.

'Really? I mean, we've only just met.'

'I know. Silly, isn't it?'

'Shall we try again?'

'Yes, please.'

Gently his mouth brushed against hers. His arms tightened about her. The pressure of his lips upon hers strengthened. Involuntarily her lips parted and his tongue caressed the inside of her mouth. She felt as if he were drawing her into his own body. Nerves within her, dormant until now, kindled into life, sending rapid messages all over her. A dull ache consumed her, an aching she had never felt before. To Jane's disappointment, the kiss ended.

They broke apart. Cupping her face in his hands, he looked at her for a long, silent moment. His expression made Jane feel weak; there was a look of longing in his eyes which was new to her, but which excited her.

'Now,' he said, 'I'm starving! Let's get something to eat.' Jane began to laugh.

'What's funny?' he asked.

'It's not exactly what I wanted to hear.'

'Oh? What should I have said?'

'Something romantic, like "Come with me to Sidi Barani".'

'Where's Sidi Barani?'

'I don't know, but it sounds romantic.'

'My sincere apologies,' he teased her. 'As an alternative, might I suggest we go to this fantastic, intimate, exclusive transport café round the corner?'

'That's better.' She laughed.

The café was full. They sat at the only free table oblivious of the slopped tea, the fat congealing on the plates, the ribald comments of the lorry drivers, and grinned at each other.

'It's not the Ritz,' he said apologetically.

'It doesn't have to be,' she answered happily. 'In fact I prefer it here, especially if your friend David has been there recently.' She told him about David's disgrace the night before.

'Good Lord, I'm sorry. He's famous for that but no one told me about last night. No wonder you were so edgy about the drinking.'

A harassed waitress quickly cleared the rickety table, took their order and within minutes their breakfast arrived. They ate the huge fried breakfast with relish and with no thought of diet or digestion. They lingered over their tea, smoking cigarettes, talking, and in the crowded café managed to find again an isolation.

Finally they wandered back to the house. One or two of the bodies remained asleep, others were sitting like rag dolls, propped against the walls, staring with glazed eyes into space.

'Don't think they're going to be much help,' said Alistair good-naturedly.

'I'll help you clear up,' Jane volunteered.

'Would you? That would be marvellous. I'll buy you lunch if you do.'

'That won't be necessary. I want to help,' she said stiffly.

'Jane, don't be so prickly! I said that because I would like to buy you lunch, not as a payment.'

'Sorry. Am I prickly?'

'Yes.'

'I don't want to be, not with you. I'm afraid lunch is out, though. I have to get back to the hospital. If there's been a row about David, poor

Sandra will be having to cope with the thunder on her own. It wouldn't be fair, would it?'

'Dinner, then?'

'That would be lovely, thank you.'

'That's better,' he said and kissed her on the forehead. They found some cardboard boxes and began to collect the empty bottles and glasses, opening all the windows to clear the fug which had settled in all the rooms. By the time they returned to the kitchen with their boxes of rubbish, there was barely room to move. The young man had gone from under the beer barrel and in his place there was a large puddle of beer. The sickly, sour smell of it hung in the air.

'You hang on here,' Alistair ordered. 'I'll pop round the corner and get some tea towels and things.' He banged noisily out of the house. Jane found a bucket under the sink and an old rag; the water was hot and she started to mop up the offending puddle of beer.

'Who are you?' a voice demanded.

Startled, Jane looked up to see standing over her a girl of her own age. There the similarity ended, for every inch of this young woman was groomed to perfection. Perched jauntily on her curled blonde hair was a neat little white hat. Not a wrinkle marred the pencil-slim skirt of her suit. No dust spoiled the pristine whiteness of her gloves. The gloss of her high-heeled shoes was so bright that Jane was fascinated to see her own face reflected in them as she knelt on the floor, peering up at this elegant creature. The girl stood, one hand on hip, her feet elegantly positioned like the feet of a ballet dancer or model.

'I said, who are you?' she repeated imperiously.

Flustered, Jane got to her feet, conscious of her lack of make-up and her untidy hair. In her confusion she knocked the bucket and some of the water spilled on her skirt, which now flapped damply against the backs of her legs.

'I'm a friend of Alistair's,' she explained.

'I don't know you,' was the brusque reply.

'No, but I am all the same.' She felt anger welling up in her.

'Where is he?'

'Out.'

'I realize that. Where?' the other girl snapped.

'I said, out.'

'You needn't make a state secret of it!'

'You can leave a message with me, if you like.'

'I'd rather deliver my message personally. That way, I'll know he's received it,' she said unpleasantly. 'Don't let me stop your work.' She indicated the bucket.

Jane felt her antagonism increasing. She had no intention whatsoever of getting back on her hands and knees in front of this creature. Pointedly she pushed the bucket to one side with her foot. Leaning against the sink, arms folded, she glared belligerently across the small room at this girl who epitomized everything she secretly longed to be, smoothly, expensively sleek and confident.

'Could you move these?' The girl indicated the only chair in the room, on which there was a tray of glasses. Used to being ordered, Jane automatically did as she was asked and dusted the seat with the only towel in the room. Suddenly realizing what she was doing, she swiped the towel viciously across the chair, angry with herself for reacting like a servant. Again she took up her position by the sink. The girl looked suspiciously at the chair and gingerly sat on it. Snapping open her handbag she took out a cigarette but did not offer one to Jane.

'Is there any coffee?'

'No.' Jane did not know if there was or not, but she had no intention of looking and took a perverse pleasure in not being helpful, relishing the small sense of power it gave her. The feeling did not last long, for as she glanced surreptitiously at the other girl, she saw that she was very pretty and, but for the arrogant expression on her face, could have been lovely, despite the heavy make-up. She longed to know who she was but was not going to risk being rebuffed again by asking. She feared that perhaps she was a girlfriend and found the thought made her feel strangely cold inside.

She began to fret that Alistair had not returned. This girl's arrival made his absence seem interminable. At last, with relief, she heard the front door slam and Alistair appeared in the doorway weighed down with parcels.

'Sorry I was so long. I thought I'd better get some supplies in and I've got a fridge coming, too. At least we'll be able to keep the gin cool!' Stepping into the kitchen he saw the girl. 'Hullo, Clar, I didn't think it would take too long before you came snooping around.'

'If you must know, I didn't want to come. Mother sent me. Your telephone isn't working.'

'It is.'

'Not this morning it isn't,' she said tersely. Alistair went out into the hall.

'Some fool knocked the receiver off the hook,' he explained. 'You two met?'

'Hardly,' the girl drawled.

'This is Jane Reed, isn't she the most beautiful creature you ever saw?' Alistair said proudly. The girl looked hard at Jane but said nothing. Jane stood, feeling astonishment, as for the first time in her life she heard a man describe her as beautiful. 'Jane, this is my sister, Clar.'

'Clarissa Cotham, actually. How do you do?' Jane found herself offered a very limp hand. She took it, relieved that she was his sister but puzzled that she had a different name.

'I see you had a party last night. So kind of you to invite me, Alistair!' she said sarcastically.

'I didn't for one moment think you'd like to come. You're always at pains to tell me you don't like my friends.'

'Is it so surprising? They're always so vulgar!' She looked straight at Jane.

'Clarissa, shut up, do. You're not impressing either of us. You're too childish for words. Why are you here?'

'Mother wants you to come to dinner tonight,' she said shortly. She did not seem capable of normal speech, Jane thought: everything was either said with a sneer or a snap.

'I can't come, I'm taking Jane out to dinner.'

'Well, you can tell her, Alistair, not me. She's got Fortescue coming round and wants everyone there. That's an order.' She stood up, brushed imaginary dirt from her suit, and picked up her handbag.

'You off? I thought perhaps you'd come to help.' It was Alistair's turn to be sarcastic.

'Me!' She snorted rather than laughed. 'I should get your little friend here to help you. She looks the capable sort,' and she swept from the room.

'Heavens!' exclaimed Jane.

'Dreadful, isn't she? She likes to think she's being sophisticated. In fact she's just bloody rude. I can't stand her myself.'

'Really?' She was curious. 'I always thought it would be marvellous to have a brother or sister. Someone to confide in.'

'Confide in? Confide in Clarissa! You're joking! If you're an only child, I envy you.'

'It can be very lonely being an only child.'

'It's a loneliness I could do with.' He laughed.

'No, really. I was always very lonely.'

'Poor Jay.' He crossed the room to her. 'I won't let you be lonely any more.' He kissed her with great gentleness. 'I'd much rather kiss you but I had better telephone Mother.'

Jane began to wash up the piles of glasses. She could not hear what he was saying on the phone, but from the tone of his voice it sounded as if he was arguing. He returned to the kitchen looking angry.

'Bloody family! I buy this house to get away from them for a bit and still they bother me. Jane, I'm sorry, I so wanted to take you out tonight but I have to go to this family dinner.'

'It's all right, I don't mind. I've got another three nights off duty after this.'

'Look, tell you what, it shouldn't go on too late. If I give you a key you could come here and I'll get back as soon as possible and we can go out for a drink. What do you think?'

'That would be lovely.'

'Great!' He had switched moods and the arrival of the new refrigerator completed his change in temper. He took a boyish pleasure in supervising the delivery and installation of the machine. Then they put the shopping away. It was an enormous fridge and the pack of butter, the pound of bacon and the six eggs looked lost in it.

'Why so big?'

'To get lots of bottles in, of course.'

'Alistair, we're off now, thanks for a super party.' A young man appeared in the doorway. Jane jumped with surprise at the sound of his voice. She had forgotten that there were still others in the house. She was so wrapped up in being with Alistair that it was as if life only existed in the room they were in.

'Right, Simon, I'll see you,' said Alistair. 'I wonder how many others are left, I'd quite forgotten they were here.'

Jane felt quietly satisfied that he felt the same. 'Perhaps you'll still be finding guests in three weeks' time.' She laughed.

'Let's check.'

They wandered around the house but everyone else had gone. In the dark of last night she had not realized what a pretty house it was. There were two large bedrooms and a third that had been turned into a bathroom. Last night she had not noticed that the sitting room had large double doors opening into an equally large room beyond it. There was a basement that opened into a small, well-stocked garden.

'I want to turn the whole of this basement into a kitchen-dining-room,' he explained. 'You see, it'll open straight into the garden,' and he opened a glass door to show her. 'I don't want a formal dining room, it'll be more fun to eat down here.'

'What will you do with the dining room upstairs?'

'Those doors fold back into the wall. It'll make a terrific, roomy drawing-room.'

'And the kitchen that's there already?'

'That's going to be my study.'

'A study! I thought you didn't like work very much?'

'I don't, but a chap's got to have a room to make his phone calls and read his letters, hasn't he?'

'If you say so,' but she didn't sound too sure. 'It's going to be very expensive to furnish, isn't it?'

'Not if I scour the junk shops. Furnish it bit by bit.' He looked at the stains on the floor. 'It was certainly a good idea to have the party before I started furnishing it, wasn't it?' Remembering the chaos of the morning, she laughingly agreed.

He tried to dissuade her from returning to the hospital, suggesting that she join him on a shopping expedition to find things for the house. She wanted more than anything to go with him, but, as she explained, there was Sandra to think of. Not only that, she was beginning to feel very tired and knew she should get some sleep.

'No, I'd better get back.'

'You promise you'll be here tonight?'

'I promise.'

He drove her back to the hospital in the dark green MG he obviously doted on and which he had christened Flo. She noticed with smug satisfaction the envious stares of the nurses who happened to be around as they screeched to a halt in front of the Nurses' Home. He slipped her a key and kissed her cheek. Guiltily creeping past the portress's lodge she was only too aware that her creased skirt could only mean that she had been up all night. Luckily she managed to get to her bedroom without meeting anyone in authority and, with relief, got out of her clothes and into a long, relaxing bath.

3

The warm water relaxed her tired body, but it did nothing to calm her mind. She could almost feel her thoughts, tumbling about in chaotic confusion, banging one against the other.

It had happened, she was sure it had, just as she had always known that one day it would. It had not been exactly as she had dreamed it would be – when she had met him no voice within her shouted, 'He's here!' The heavens had not tumbled. Instead she had thought he was 'nice'. Hardly the stuff of poetry. A bit disappointing, she thought, and giggled to herself. But something had happened by the river, no doubt of that. That longing to be kissed, the way he had looked at her, and that weird aching feeling she had experienced. And now something new – she was missing him. She had only just met him, he had not yet become part of her life, so what was there to miss? She examined this thought and spun every facet of it in her mind. Did it matter why? She missed him; that was enough. She smiled and lay back contentedly in the water. And what was it he had called her? J or maybe Jay? She hugged herself with pleasure; no one had ever given her a pet name before.

She stepped out of the bath and looked critically at her reflection in the mirror. She had been planning to cut her hair, having grown tired of putting it up in a bun. Now she wondered what to do with it. She shook her head, the black hair falling about her face. She had read that men preferred long hair; maybe she should wait before cutting it, maybe she would ask his opinion. She looked at her white body, wishing she was not so pale. He would be brown all over, she was certain of that, but the English summers were never long enough to turn her into the tawny creature she would have liked to be. She touched herself. She had good skin. She had learned that from handling patients, so many of whom had rough skins while hers was very smooth, she thought with satisfaction.

It was not that she never looked at her body – she often did – but now she was looking at it and trying to see it with his eyes. Could it please him, would he like it? She wished her breasts were smaller. At least her waist was small, but then the trouble with a small waist was that, irritatingly, it seemed to make her hips look inches bigger than they really were. She wondered what it would feel like, having a man touch her naked body. She closed her eyes and ran her hands down her body, she caressed her breasts, teased at her nipples – pretending her hands were his. It was as if these hands had a life of their own as they slipped, sensuously, across her flat belly and between her legs. An unfamiliar sensation, an intense feeling of excitement, jolted her body. Her eyes opened, and she looked at her reflection with surprise, shocked by the excited sparkle in her eyes. She shook herself, laughed at the girl in the mirror and swung the towel about her. What would her mother say if she could read her daughter's thoughts?

In her room she found Sandra lying on her bed. 'There you are!' Sandra exclaimed. 'I've lost count of the number of times I've trekked along here to see if you were back. Where on earth have you been all night?'

'If you must know, it seemed safer to stay there than to climb back in. And for your information, we sat and talked and then went for a walk, had breakfast, and we spent this morning clearing up the mess. So there!'

'Did he kiss you?'

'Mind your own business!'

'Ha! He did. Seeing him again?'

'Yes, tonight.'

'Fast work. Look.' Sandra pointed to Jane's basin, in which was a large bouquet of flowers.

'Who the hell . . . ?'

'David. I got one too. He wants to take us out tonight.'

'That was sweet. Was anything said about the mess in the hall?'

'Not a dicky bird. Seems no one has discovered the puke yet. Mind you, the standard of cleaning in this dump, it'll probably still be there in fifty years. You coming out with us, then?'

'No, I told you, I'm seeing Alistair.'

'Perhaps we could get someone else and go out in a sixsome.'

'Thanks, I'd rather not.' Jane felt herself blushing.

'So! What have we here? Serious, is it?'

'Very. But then I always knew it should happen like this.'

'What?'

'Falling in love.'

'You've only just met him!'

'I know. Daft, isn't it?'

'Romantic but, yes, daft too. Don't you go doing anything silly, Jane,' Sandra said, suddenly serious, and lapsing back into the Christian names which they had learned never to use. 'You wouldn't, would you?'

'Yes, Sandra, I would. It's him, I just know it is. There doesn't seem much point in waiting.'

Sandra sat up on the bed looking at her friend anxiously. 'You mean sleep with him? Don't be bloody daft, Jane – you can't sleep with him, not on a first date! What the hell would he think of you? For heaven's sake, look at the hours we've spent debating whether we should allow a bloke to kiss on a first date. Now this!' Agitatedly she lit a cigarette. 'You've gone stark staring bonkers, that's what's happened.'

'It must seem odd, but you weren't there, you didn't see the way he looked at me.'

'You can't have thought this through, Jane. What if he sleeps with you and then ditches you? It happens. And what if you get pregnant? You can say goodbye to your career then.'

'I'll have to risk it. If I'm wrong about how he feels it doesn't alter how I feel. He could ditch me without my having slept with him, and then I would never know what it would be like to sleep with the man I love. So, you see, I can't wait, can I? I can't take that risk, can I?'

'I've never heard such balderdash in my life. He won't be the only man you fall in love with.'

'Yes, he is. I'll never feel like this again.'

'Christ, you risk losing everything. If he loves you he won't mind waiting, will he?'

'But if he loves me too, then why wait?'

'I suppose there's logic in there somewhere. But how can you be so sure?'

'You don't understand. I never wanted to sleep with anyone ever before, never, never! Now I do. So this has to be different. I didn't really know myself until just now, lying in the bath, and thinking I just wanted to be with him, and to make love to him.'

'Dangerous places, baths!' Sandra grinned at her. 'But aren't you scared?'

'Terrified. But all bubbly as well. I think I'll get a little bit drunk, I'm sure that will make it easier.'

'You are a rotten moo; I always wanted to be the first. There you've been guarding your virginity, going on about the right man coming along, and there have I been trying to get rid of the bloody thing and no one wants mine.'

'And you've been lecturing me! Sandra, you're a fool. You make it sound like some dreadful impediment.'

'It is an impediment to being a complete woman, and I want to be a woman. Every man I meet, though, is either too gentlemanly, too scared or too drunk.' She pulled a wry face. Jane laughed despite herself.

'What about John? He seemed really taken with you, and he's very nice. Anything likely to happen with him?'

'He's no good. Too fond of his booze. I suppose I might be lucky and catch him one afternoon before he gets his nose in a glass.'

'I don't mean to sleep with, fool! I meant how did you get on with him?'

'Fine,' Sandra said airily. 'Judging by the way he necks, I should think he'd be pretty good in bed. But he's not likely to be the love of my life. He's fun but he'd run a mile at anything serious. Anyhow, if you're going out on this heavy date, you're going to need some sleep. I'm going. But you promise, if you do it you will tell me all?'

'Maybe.' Jane laughed as Sandra left her alone. With her thoughts in such confusion, she had not expected to sleep, so she was surprised when her alarm bell woke her to find that it was eight in the evening.

Excitedly, she dressed. Hurriedly she packed a small overnight bag. For a second she thought of her mother's horror if she knew what her daughter was doing, and just as quickly she put the thought to the back of her mind. She ran downstairs, too impatient to wait for the lift. As she signed herself out in the Book, she wondered, if she did sleep with Alistair, would she look different when she returned? Would it show on her face? Would people guess?

'Good evening, Nurse Reed. Nights off?'

Jane swung round to find the enormous bulk of Home Sister blocking her way. She felt a wave of guilt, terrified that the woman could read her thoughts and would stop her.

'Yes, Sister.'

'Going home?'

'Yes, Sister,' she lied.

'I hope you have a nice time.' Jane looked astonished at the sister's words; the woman had never spoken to her pleasantly before. It made Jane feel worse about lying and, feeling herself begin to blush, she bent down and fumbled with her case on the floor, relieved to see the sister's sturdy legs move away, as she mumbled, 'Thank you.'

She was too deep in thought to notice the bus journey across London. Arriving in Fulham, she hurried along the road to the little house. She let herself in and felt her way along the unfamiliar hall, stumbling over rolls of carpet as she searched the walls for a light switch.

A new carpet had been laid in the sitting room, from wall to wall. New curtains hung at the windows, the pelmets ornate and fringed. There was a chintz-covered sofa, its covers worn and faded. Beside it stood an intricately carved Indian coffee table, on which glowed an old bottle, converted into a lamp. A single abstract painting hung on the wall. Jane turned her head from side to side, studying it, in the hope of understanding it. She gave up the effort. Packing cases littered the floor and other paintings were stacked against the walls, waiting to be hung.

In the kitchen the greasy old gas cooker had been replaced by a gleaming new machine, covered with clocks and shining dials. In the corner the new fridge gurgled. She opened the door. It was now full of bottles of wine and some gin.

On the kitchen table stood a collection of shorter, sturdier bottles with unfamiliar, exotic names. A bright-green one looked fun but she settled for a familiar brandy. Her mother always had a small bottle in the medicine chest ready for the first twinge of toothache, when a brandy-soaked ball of cotton wool would be placed on her gum. Jane poured a glass, took a sip of the dark, golden drink, and immediately began to choke as the burning liquid touched the back of her throat. She found a bottle of lemonade, added that to her brandy and sipped the mixture nervously. She was pleased with the taste.

Clutching her glass she returned to the sitting room. One tea chest was full of books which she began to unpack and arrange on the empty alcove shelves. The majority were dull, about estate management, but at the bottom she found a pile of tattered and well-read children's books. Like her, Alistair had saved his books from his childhood.

Alistair found her in the kitchen, mixing herself another drink. She smiled with delight as he entered the room.

'I hope you don't mind my helping myself to a drink?'

'Of course not. I'll join you. Here, let me, what are you drinking?'

'Brandy and lemonade.'

'What?' he exclaimed, laughing. 'It sounds disgusting!'

'It's quite nice really. It was disgusting without the lemonade.'

'Don't ever tell my father what you've been doing with his best Napoleon brandy. He'd have apoplexy!' He continued to laugh but, seeing a shadow of confusion flicker across her face, he added hurriedly,

'Jay, drink whatever concoctions you want. But would you rather go out for a drink?'

'I'd rather stay here.'

'Fine. Then I have a treat for us.' He opened the fridge door and, like a magician, produced a bottle of champagne. 'Do you like champers?'

'I don't know. I never had it before.'

'Never had champagne? What an extraordinarily deprived life you've had!' He started to laugh but stopped himself. 'That was rather a stupid remark to make, wasn't it? Sorry.'

'I don't mind. It's true. After all, there isn't much call for champagne at the Railway Arms,' she replied easily. Alistair opened the bottle carefully, and she was disappointed that the cork did not pop. 'It always pops in the films,' she complained.

'That's because they're not opening it properly, it shouldn't really. There, try that.'

Gingerly she took a sip, and smiled broadly. 'Oh yes, I like that. Very much!' and with greater confidence she took another larger sip.

'Brandy and champagne. I thought you didn't like to drink?'

'I don't mind drinking, it's when people get drunk that I get frightened. In any case, I'm boosting my confidence.'

'Really? Might I ask why?'

'I want to be relaxed. I want you to —' She stopped abruptly. 'Oh, I don't know. I'm feeling shy, I suppose.' She looked earnestly at her glass.

'Shy? Of me?'

'No. Yes.' She shook her head in confusion, wishing convention were different and that she could be honest and tell him she was building up her confidence to go to bed with him.

'You funny creature!' He put his arm about her shoulder and kissed her, but this time gently. Just as in the morning, Jane felt great waves of excitement flood through her body and she clung to him with an intensity that puzzled but pleased him. 'Let's go and sit somewhere more comfortable,' he said softly and, taking her by the hand, led her into the drawing room.

She hoped he was going to kiss her again, but instead he returned to the kitchen for the champagne. 'Whose case is that in the hall?' he asked, coming back with the bottle.

'Mine,' she replied, blushing furiously.

'Oh, I see. Are you planning to stay the night?' he asked with an attempt at nonchalance, as he refilled the glasses.

'If you don't mind.' Her blush intensified.

'I've only got one bed. But I don't mind sleeping on the sofa.'

'Oh no! I wouldn't dream of putting you out. In any case you're far too tall. There'd be nowhere for your feet. I'll sleep on the settee,' she said quickly, regretting as she did so the turn the conversation was taking, the fact that he was misunderstanding her intentions.

'We'll toss for it.' He grinned at her.

They sat side by side on his new sofa which, he proudly told her, had cost him a pound in the King's Road.

'It's lovely,' she said, disappointed that still he was not kissing her but appeared to prefer to talk. 'Can I have more champagne?' she asked, proffering her glass.

'What about the rest of the room? Bet you were surprised how much got done while you were away,' he said, refilling her glass.

'It's amazing. The men must have worked like greased lightning.'

'They did. Plus a little bribe from me to stay on and finish this room. I wanted somewhere halfway furnished for us. So what's your verdict?'

'I'm sorry, but I don't like those curtains. They're too fussy.'

'Pretty ghastly, aren't they? That's Mother. "Leave the curtains to me," she said. I didn't realize she'd produce those things.'

'The carpet's nice, though.' She hiccoughed discreetly.

'We had a row about that. She said wall-to-wall carpeting was vulgar.'

'What's vulgar about it?'

'Search me. She says it should be bare boards and rugs. But I won, I thought it would be easier to keep clean.'

'Bare boards! Fancy having bare boards if you can afford lovely carpets like this. It's just like being in a cinema.' With surprise she discovered that her glass was empty.

'Do you like my picture?' He poured more champagne.

'No, I think it's horrible. Really ... horrible!' She searched for another word but her brain seemed to be slowing down.

'What's wrong with it?'

'I don't like the colours and the shapes are silly, really ... silly.' Where had all the words gone? she wondered. 'I can't get excited about a green egg on a wobbly frying pan.' She shook her head slowly from side to side.

'It's a Picasso,' he said, watching her closely.

'Is it? He must have been feeling ill when he painted it then. Sorry, Mr Picasso, I think your picture – stinks,' she said with exaggerated care.

'That painting is a good test of how genuine people are. You have no idea, the number of people who suddenly change their minds when they know who the artist is.'

She turned sharply and looked angrily at him. 'I think that's horrible. Testing! Can't you trust yourself to judge people?'

'You're being prickly again, Jane.'

'I'm not surprised. Who the hell do you think you are, going around setting traps for people? What do you think I am, a liar?'

'No, Jane.' He laughed. 'That's one thing I'm certain you're not. Oh, come on. I didn't expect you to get het up about it. I only meant it's a sort of game. It's fun. Don't be cross with me.' He took hold of her and kissed her gently, and her anger melted away. In fact she could not remember what had made her angry in the first place.

'Do you always say exactly what you think?'

'Yes. Don't you?'

'No, not always.'

'Why not?'

'Well, sometimes it's more diplomatic not to.'

'You mean you lie?'

'No, Jane.' He laughed. 'I mean sometimes I try to be tactful.'

'I don't think I'd be any good at that.' She giggled, peering at him through her fingers.

'I agree. I don't somehow think you would either,' he said, kissing the nape of her neck.

'Would you like more champagne?' He took her glass.

'I'd rather you kissed me properly!'

'My pleasure.' Jane felt as if she were floating, conscious only of the closeness of their bodies, and the almost intolerable need for him that was building within her.

'I'm sorry,' he said, suddenly breaking away from her. 'I'm rushing things. But you looked so lovely and . . . Oh, Christ, it's hard to sit here and not touch you, and try to talk about bloody curtains and paintings.'

'It was lovely, Alistair. I don't mind you rushing it at all. I thought it was super. More, please . . .' She pursed her lips at him. 'Please . . .'

'Sweetheart, look, I think I'd better take you home.'

'No!' she shouted, sitting up so suddenly that she spilled her drink. 'No! That's what I am afraid of, that you'll take me home and not want to see me again.'

'Jane, darling, don't be silly, of course I'd want to see you again. It's just . . . sweetie, you're getting so drunk . . . it wouldn't be right, don't you see? I'm only human and I'm afraid if you stay here, well, if you stay, I don't know what will happen.'

'Oh, lovely!' she said brightly, busily mopping up the champagne.

'Jane, you are going to get into awful trouble if you persist like this.' He smiled fondly at her.

'No, I won't. I wouldn't behave like this with anyone else.' She leaned towards him, her face a mere inch from his. 'I feel safe with you, you see. I trust you.' She said earnestly.

Alistair put his head into his hands. She watched anxiously, not quite sure what the problem was: she kept forgetting what they were talking about, which made understanding difficult. He looked up at her, an expression of mild exasperation on his face.

'OK,' he said, as if he had made a decision. 'Let's both get drunk!'

'Oh yes, what a good idea! I'd like to get drunk, that's what I wanted to do all along . . .' She laughed at this idea as Alistair went to fetch another bottle of champagne.

They settled on the sofa, he in reach of the bottle, she with her head on his lap. 'Don't you think that tid – Oh Lor', I can't say it, even.' Alistair laughed helplessly. 'It's even too funny to say!'

'Try again,' advised Jane seriously.

'Don't you think the funniest word you ever heard is . . .' He paused dramatically and then, taking another deep breath, declared triumphantly, 'tiddlywinks!'

They slipped from the sofa on to the floor, laughing until they ached.

'What about – winkle?'

'Hippopotamus!' They both shrieked at their own cleverness, and word followed word.

Suddenly Jane could not think of any more words and her head slumped forward.

'Come on, Jay, my love,' he said as he lifted her gently from the floor. 'Time for bed.'

'Yes, please,' she said dreamily. He carried her unsteadily to the staircase.

'Up the wooden stairs to bed we go. With a tiny candle for . . .' she crooned to herself.

In the bedroom he placed her on the bed. She sat, still humming the little tune, studying her stockinged feet intently.

'You can borrow a pair of my pyjamas, that is, if I could find them.' He started to rummage through the cases that were scattered about the room.

'Doesn't matter. Doesn't matter a damn!' she said airily, flopping back on the bed fully dressed. She felt him cover her with the eiderdown.

'Alistair.' She groped with her hand for his. 'Alistair, don't go. Stay with me.'

She heard his shoes fall to the floor and she felt the bedsprings give as he slid in beside her. Beneath the warm eiderdown she settled contentedly into the crook of his arm. There was something she wanted to say to him, but she just could not remember what it was, as sleep overcame her.

4

She woke up, lifted her head and felt dreadful. It was as if, in the night, someone had placed in her head two large glass marbles with broken edges which were relentlessly rolling about inside her skull, rubbing one against the other to create a pain that seemed to break her head in two. She had a moment of total panic, when she thought she was dying, before she remembered the night before, and the cause of her bad head.

'Oh dear,' she sighed. 'What a fiasco!' She looked around the unfamiliar room. Cases were strewn about the bare floorboards, their contents spewing out as if they had burst. A sheet was pinned to the window in place of a curtain. The only furniture in the room was the double bed in which she lay, alone. What had happened? She shook her head, wincing with pain as the recalcitrant marble rolled around within her skull. If only she could remember! Despite the pain in her head she slowly sat up, flicked back the eiderdown and, with nervous fingers, ran her hands over the bedding. It was dry. She lifted her skirt, her pants were in place. With relief she sank back on the pillows. It would have been dreadful if the most important moment of her life so far had passed by without her knowing. But even as she thought this, she knew she was also disappointed. Trouble with you, Jane Reed, she said to herself severely, you don't bloody well know what you do want. But what if it had happened? He could have put her pants back on, he could have used a Durex. But surely she would be sore? Surely she would feel different? Surely she would know?

Slowly she swung her legs over the side of the bed. Standing made the pounding in her head worse. Never again, she vowed vehemently, as, finding a hairbrush, she feebly dragged it through her hair. She longed for a toothbrush.

She found Alistair in the kitchen, concentrating so hard on cooking the breakfast that he was not aware of her standing in the doorway, shyly watching him.

'Hullo. How long have you been there?' He smiled at her.

'Not long. How long have you been up?'

'Ages. I can't lie in bed, never have been able to. You spoiled my surprise, I wanted to bring you breakfast in bed.'

'I don't like breakfast in bed, it always reminds me of illness. And I get crumbs everywhere!'

'Just as well you woke up, then.'

'Alistair?'

'Yes?'

She still stood in the doorway, wondering if she looked as awkward as she felt, as he went on with his cooking.

'Yes?' he repeated, looking up at her.

'Alistair? I . . .' She did not know how to ask him the question uppermost in her mind. It was such a silly-sounding question to ask.

'The answer's no, Jane. We didn't. We slept as innocently as babes.'

'Oh! I see. I thought not.' Wondering, at the same time, why he had not. One unwelcome conclusion was that perhaps he had not wanted to. God, she was in such a muddle! Did everyone get as confused as she did?

'What are you thinking?' he asked.

'I was thinking what an indecisive fool I am.' She smiled apologetically.

'That's not exactly the word I would use to describe you,' he said gently. Then, briskly breaking an egg into the pan, he changed the subject. 'Come on, sit down and have your breakfast.'

'I couldn't eat a thing, really. I feel dreadful.'

Alistair laughed at her woebegone face. 'Then you must make yourself eat. It'll make you feel a new woman, I promise. Best thing for a hangover is food. I should know, I'm the expert on the subject.'

'But you look fine.'

'It takes more than we had last night to affect me. You mixed the drink, that's why you're feeling so dreadful. Lesson number one, one spirit drink only, then stick to the wine. I know, from experience.' He laughed loudly, making her wince. 'Oh, my poor love, I'm sorry.' He crossed the kitchen and softly kissed her.

'Alistair. I am sorry about last night.'

'There's nothing to be sorry about.'

'No, really, I was stupid. I didn't think it through. I just crashed in presuming all sorts of things I hadn't the right to presume.'

'Like what?'

'Well . . . that you'd even want me,' she said in a small voice.

'Of course I wanted you. Too much.'

'Then why didn't you take advantage of me?'

'"Take advantage of me"!' He shouted with laughter. 'What a wonderfully archaic expression! Where on earth did you get that from? No, Jane, you really don't understand about sex. You would have to enjoy it, too, for it to work. And last night, well, last night you weren't in any state to enjoy anything.'

'I think you're right. I don't understand much about sex.'

'Then I'll teach you.' He smiled at her, but it was not like an ordinary smile: there was an intimacy to it which made a strange shiver snake down Jane's spine. 'Now eat! And then we'll go shopping,' he said, mock-sternly. The little moment of intimacy passed and Jane wondered if she had imagined it.

Their breakfast finished, they went out on what was to be the first of many shopping safaris for the house. Together they delved into the junk shops, shouting with delight as they found a lamp that took their fancy, or a chair that would be fine with a new cover. To her delight Jane found that they seemed to have the same taste, and agreed on everything.

Alistair stopped at an Italian restaurant, suggesting lunch. Reluctantly she followed him in.

'But I hate Heinz spaghetti!' she confided in a whisper. She was flustered when Alistair laughed out loud. 'Please!' she pleaded.

'I'm sorry.' He took her hand and leaned across the table, lowering his voice. 'Darling Jane, that's not Italian food. Let me order for you. I promise you, you'll love it.'

For Jane, who until now had eaten simply to stay alive and had never enjoyed eating for its own sake, the meal was a revelation. She gorged herself on the delicious food and wine.

'I'll take you to Italy one day,' he announced. 'The food is even better there. We'll sit in the sun and peel fresh figs, drink Frascati and make love all day.'

'That sounds like paradise. I've never been abroad.'

'You're the most wonderful girl to know. You've not done anything! May I be your Svengali?'

'I thought Svengali was a baddy.'

'I'll be a good one.' He laughed happily over his glass. He laughed so much and so often that she wondered if he was ever sad or depressed. It was difficult to imagine it. She could only think that she would always be happy when she was with him.

'Where's your home?' she asked.

'In the West Country. And yours?'

She told him and he pulled a face. 'Yes, it's pretty horrible, I agree. The funny thing is, I didn't realize it was until I left, and when I went back I was shocked at how drab and dirty it looked. I've only been away a year and already I feel I don't belong any more.'

'I couldn't imagine belonging anywhere else but my home. I was born there and I expect to die there too.'

'Has your family lived there long, then?'

'Ages.'

'That must be nice. But when you had dinner with your family last night, you didn't go home. It would have been too far.'

'They have a house in London, too.'

'How grand!'

'Is it? I suppose it is, if you think about it. It's always been there, so I never do.'

'What does your father do?'

'He farms.'

'I think I'd like him. Farmers are such jolly people, aren't they?'

Alistair snorted with laughter. 'I don't know which farmers you've met. Most of them moan like hell. I say he's a farmer, but he doesn't exactly dig the land.' He smiled to himself. 'You would like him, though, I'm certain of that. He's the most honest person I know. I'd like to be like him.'

'You love him a lot, don't you?'

'Yes, if I think about it, I do.'

'That's what I envy so much in people like you and Sandra – you never ever have to think about it.' Before Alistair could ask her what she meant, she continued, 'And your mother?'

'Ah! That's more difficult. She means well, but she will interfere in my life. She doesn't seem to realize that I've grown up. Last night's summons was typical: it wasn't really essential for me to be there. She seems to think that I don't have other things to do.'

'It must be difficult to accept that your children have grown up, especially if you love them.'

'If? Don't all parents love their children?'

'No,' she replied simply. 'Are your parents divorced?'

'No. What made you ask that?'

'Just that you and your sister have different names.'

'Oh, that. We're one of those odd families where everyone has a different name.' He smiled. 'Come on, if we're going to be back at the house when that furniture arrives, we'd better get going. Shall we come here for dinner tonight?'

'Dinner! You're joking. After that enormous meal, I couldn't eat another thing. And the expense, Alistair!'

'I think I can afford the odd dinner out, but, if you don't want to, we can get some stuff in and cook at home.' He spoke seriously but somehow Jane felt he was laughing.

They paid the bill and walked quickly down the King's Road, stopping to buy food for supper. They arrived back at the house just as the lorry with their treasures drew up outside.

The afternoon passed in a flurry of cleaning and polishing and deciding where to put the furniture they had bought. By the evening they were exhausted. Alistair mixed them two gins and tonics, and Jane found another drink to add to her repertoire. She settled at the kitchen table with her drink and watched with admiration as Alistair expertly prepared a meal. The evening was chilly. Alistair found some kindling and coal and lit a fire. They sat on the floor in front of it to eat their dinner, sipping claret, and Jane had her first lesson in wine.

She lay back on the large cushion, the firelight playing upon her. The wine, food and the warmth of the fire made her feel totally relaxed. Alistair stroked her hair, and she stretched languorously, feeling as she imagined a contented cat would feel. He kissed the nape of her neck. His tongue traced the outline of her ear. Tentatively his hand slipped open the buttons of her blouse, and as she made no objection, it slid with more confidence to fondle her breast. Her body began to stir beneath his gentle caressing; she moved closer to him and lay, eyes closed, enjoying and relishing these new sensations. Suddenly he removed his hand and she felt a moment's disappointment. Then feverishly he removed her blouse, cursing softly as he struggled to release her brassiere, and then to her joy he was sucking her breast and she was holding his head to her. This was what she had waited for, this was what she had lived for – this man's hands and mouth to be on her. Suddenly it was not enough, she wanted his hands where the ache and longing was intolerable. Her body curved towards him as if to tell him what it wanted, just as if she no longer had control over it.

He knelt above her, quickly removing his own clothes. She watched him, excitement sparkling in her eyes, and wondered if perhaps she should have done that for him. And what about her own skirt and stockings? Was she supposed to take them off, or would that be too forward? Oh, dear, what would he think of her? He began to remove her skirt. Gingerly she moved towards him, a great longing to feel him propelling her hand. She loved the velvet feel of his hardness.

'Good girl,' he said in a strange voice as if he had difficulty in speaking. She smiled at him, happy that she was pleasing him, but there was a strange faraway look in his eyes, as if he did not see her, which frightened her. The sound of his breathing grew faster. 'Oh, Jane!' he cried. She liked the feel of his weight on her but she could not help feeling disappointed that he had stopped kissing and caressing her. There was some resistance as he guided himself into her. He began to thrust harder. She had expected it to hurt more than it did; only a small cry escaped her lips. His pounding of her body intensified, his breath coming in great gulps. She felt buffeted by the great strength of this man, suffocated by him. She had lost complete control and for a second sheer terror filled her.

'Alistair!' She screamed arching her back with all her strength to get him off her.

'Jane!' he bellowed and, instead of stopping, his penetration of her increased in its ferocity. She felt it was going on for ever. 'Jane!' Again he shouted her name, his body looming above her as he lifted his weight momentarily from her. A great groan escaped from him and he collapsed on her, sweat pouring from him, forming in little pools on her own flesh.

She thought he had fainted, he lay so still, but slowly he began to move, gently kissing her, licking the sweat from her, and back to her body came the flickers of enjoyment, the shivery feeling down her spine.

He rolled away from her and smiled tenderly at her.

'You were marvellous,' he said.

'Was I?' She sounded surprised.

'Absolutely marvellous!' He laid his head against hers. 'You know, it's never been that good for me before! So together, so total.' He relaxed contentedly, stretching in the firelight. He cupped her face in his hands. 'Jane, darling, you should have told me you were a virgin, I would have been more gentle. Did I hurt you?'

'No, not much,' she said, covering her legs with her skirt to hide the streaks of blood. 'I thought you realized, you see. It's odd, though, I –' she began and then stopped.

'What, my darling?'

'Oh, nothing.' She smiled back and curled up in the firelight with him. She realized that he had slipped into a light sleep, and she lay thinking. How could it have been as he said, when, at the moment which should have been the most precious, she had not really felt anything but afraid?

And yet it had all started so beautifully – and ended that way too. Perhaps she was doing something wrong. She laughed quietly to herself: she always had preferred starters and puds.

That night, in bed, he took her twice more. Each time, as he climaxed, she did not feel afraid any more but she cried out his name, for it seemed to be expected of her. Really, after all the build-up, the debating with Sandra, the fearful anticipation, it was all rather disappointing.

5

Alistair's long vacation passed by in a haze of parties, dinners, exhibitions and an endless stream of his friends calling.

Jane's time was spent in scheming for changes in the duty rosters, to fit in with Alistair's plans. On the wards she watched the clock constantly; she became expert at split-second changing in and out of uniform, and rushing for buses – buses to take her to Alistair and early morning buses bringing her back to the Nurses' Home to face the heart-thumping terror of sneaking back in, unseen. She should have been tired but, miraculously, she was not. It was as if her love for him acted as a stimulant and gave her boundless energy.

But, finally, it was a tearful Jane who stood on the platform at Liverpool Street Station and watched the Fenman pull out, carrying Alistair and their carefree summer back to university.

Now she was tired again. Off duty all she wanted to do was sleep, as if only then could she escape the dreadful loneliness of life without him. But she dared not sleep in case the phone rang for her and she missed his call. She would not go to the Cat's Whisker coffee bar with the other nurses. Instead she lay daydreaming on her bed until ten o'clock and the certainty that no more calls would be accepted by the portress, when she would sink into the longed-for escape of sleep.

Each day it was an agitated Jane who joined the long queue of nurses waiting hopefully for mail. She wrote each day but Alistair replied only spasmodically. She hated the portress with a vehemence that surprised her when no letter had arrived, as if it were the woman's fault he had not written.

Near Christmas he returned and they spent two precious days in his house in Fulham. He had told no one he was there and so the phone never rang and no one called. They ate, drank, made love and talked. They hardly seemed to sleep. Apart from the budgerigar, Jane had only ever received practical presents; she gave Alistair a bright-red jumper. He gave her a leather-bound, gold-tooled edition of the metaphysical poets. Holding the beautiful book in her hands, she regretted the jumper and wished she had thought harder about a gift for him or at least had knitted it herself, but he seemed overjoyed with the sweater.

Then it was Paddington station on which Jane found herself, saying another tearful goodbye as he took the train to the West Country for Christmas with his family. She began to feel she was always saying goodbye on dirty, crowded station platforms.

She had to work through Christmas, having swapped her day off to have the earlier two days with Alistair. She had dreaded Christmas, fearing that she would be swamped with miserable longing for him. Instead the next few days passed at hectic speed as she was swept along on the tide of the hospital's festivities. When he phoned, she could tell him with conviction that she was fine and happy.

But then she was back to the waiting – the waiting for letters, phone calls, and for time to pass. Sometimes she was ashamed at the careless way she longed for the days to fly, knowing that on the wards there were patients whose lives were numbered by the very days that she non-chalantly wished away.

At the end of January she had a week's holiday and went for the first time to Cambridge.

It was a mystery to her how any studying was done. Alistair's life seemed to consist of sprawling in chairs, drinking coffee and talking all morning. At lunchtime they went to the local, the Pickerel, for beer, food, darts and more talking. They would return to his room in Magdalene College, overlooking Benson Court. He would sport his oak, shutting the second door to his rooms, which by tradition meant that under no circumstances was he to be disturbed and that, as far as the authorities were concerned, he was working. It was a useful university tradition for lovers. They would emerge for tea. Tea in Cambridge was a sacred ritual and there appeared to be an unwritten roster of whose turn it was to provide it, as each day they went to different rooms and each day the same crowd was there. This way, Jane sampled every cake that Fitzbillies bakery produced, and consumed so many crumpets she felt she never wanted to eat another.

In the evening he would leave her at the Pickerel, in the care of the landlady, Muriel, while he slipped across the street to dine in Hall. Muriel was used to looking after young ladies waiting for their lovers to return

and she would make certain Jane had enough to eat and that no one
bothered her. She had a soft spot for nurses and always piled Jane's plate
with too much food.

'Got to keep your strength up, girl,' she would say and wink at a
blushing Jane, her fat, jolly face creasing into a hundred laughter lines.

When the students returned, the drinking would start in earnest, the
talk became louder and the little pub began to disappear in a haze of
cigarette smoke. Sometimes the talk became too abstruse for Jane and
she felt out of her depth, but often she thought that they were deliberately using long words and complicated arguments to show off to her.
Frequently she had serious doubts whether they really knew what they
were talking about. She would listen amused as they heatedly postulated
the problems of the real world, and what they would personally do to
solve those problems. She, however, was well aware that none of them
had ever experienced the reality of that world. Cambridge was an unreal
place, a delightful never-never land, she decided.

Alistair took a great risk by having Jane live in his rooms with him.
Had he been found out, he would have been sent down immediately.
Each night at ten they would play a charade of her leaving, loudly saying
goodnight outside the porter's lodge; then she would either slip in
quickly by a side gate before it was locked for the night, or much later
Alistair would haul her up over the wall at the back of his court, while
she suppressed her giggles as best she could, and laddered innumerable
stockings. In the morning they would rise early, hiding away all evidence
of Jane's belongings, and she would crouch in the wardrobe while his
bedder cleaned the rooms. Shut up in the darkness, she was convinced
that a sneeze was imminent or that the heavy thudding of her heart
must be audible to the amiable, chatty bedder who did her chores so
slowly.

Saturday was party night. They went to four parties, each larger and
louder than the previous one, and finally ended up in the cellars of the
Union building, where the noisiest gathering of them all was taking
place, with a trad band making conversation impossible. As the evening
progressed, Jane watched, alarmed, as everyone became increasingly
drunk.

'God, Jane, what's got into you? You're being such a wet blanket,'
Alistair shouted at her above the noise of the party.

'They're all drinking so much. It's no fun,' she shouted back.

'As far as I remember, madam, you quite like the stuff yourself. It
seems it's all right if you get drunk when you want, but it's not all right

for other people.' He glared at her, rocking back and forth on his feet. 'Oh, come on, Jane, have a drink. Cheer up, for Christ's sake!'

'No, thanks. You enjoy yourself. I'm fine here,' she replied through clenched teeth.

'Oh, hell, sod you then! Sulk on your bloody own,' he yelled angrily, and made his way through the swaying mob to the other side of the room.

How could he ruin everything? Jane asked herself desperately. She had to leave tomorrow: she had wanted this evening to be perfect and romantic. Instead, it threatened to turn into a drunken mêlée.

The sound of glass shattering silenced even the trumpet in the band. A great cheer went up from a crowd gathered around the door. Instinctively she knew that the crashing glass had something to do with Alistair. Elbowing her way through the throng, she reached the door around which a curious group still stood. The cold East Anglian wind whipped in through the gaping hole where the plate glass had been. Dangerous shards of glass glinted viciously in the muted light.

'What happened?' she asked anxiously, but everyone was talking at once and no one paid attention. 'Please, tell me, what's happened?' She tugged the sleeve of a man standing beside her.

'That mad bugger Redland just walked through the door.'

'He did what?'

'Someone bet him he couldn't and he did,' another voice told her, full of admiration.

Jane's hand flew to her mouth to suppress a horrified groan. She looked at the cruel, razor-sharp glass still hanging precariously in the door. 'Let me out!' she screamed.

Someone opened the door and the last of the glass crashed to the floor, shattering into small splinters, and the crowd leaped backwards, laughing, as they avoided the splinters flying everywhere. Jane pushed her way through them and emerged, coatless, into the bitter, dark night. Of Alistair there was no sign.

She hung over the wall of the Round Church shouting his name. Silence. There was only the noise of the party, muted now. In Bridge Street, the white snow accentuating their indecent redness, drops of blood littered the pavement. Sobbing, she followed the trail of blood, racing, skidding on the snow. On the apex of Magdalene Bridge, he must have stopped: there was blood on the parapet as well as on the pavement. She hung over the bridge, her eyes desperately searching the swirling, black water, vainly calling his name. Peering up the road she was relieved to see the neat spots of blood, like an obscene visiting card, trailing up to the gate of Benson Court.

She raced up the street, around the back, and began laboriously to climb the wall. Without Alistair there to bunk her over she had to search for foot and finger holds, shivering now with the extreme cold. It took ten minutes before, with torn skirt and ruined blouse, she was racing across the forbidden grass, uncaring of college regulations, and pell-mell up the stairs to his rooms.

In the middle of the floor, flat on his back, lay Alistair, a happy smile on his face, and blood caking his skin as it coagulated.

Quickly she fetched a bowl of water, tore a handkerchief into strips and began gently to clean his face, finding with relief that the cuts were superficial. A deeper one in his hand still oozed blood. She would have liked to get him to hospital – she was certain his hand needed stitches – but, however hard she shook him, she could not wake Alistair, and she could not risk adding to his troubles by raising the porter. She bound the hand tightly, and put a cushion under his head which she turned to one side in case he was sick. Then she covered him with the eiderdown. Taking off her ruined clothes, she sank onto the bed, leaving the light on in the sitting room and the door open so that she could keep an eye on him where he lay on the floor.

She meant to stay awake but at some point fell into a restless sleep.

'Ah, there you are. Move over.' Her fuddled brain heard Alistair's voice. Roughly he pushed her across the bed, up against the cold wall.

'You all right, darling?' she whispered.

'I will be in a minute when I've fucked you.'

She did not have time to react to the way he spoke before he was upon her, his knee prising her legs apart, and forcing himself into her. She lay rigid with fear. This very immobility seemed to infuriate him and goad him into thrusting at her more violently.

Mercifully it was soon over. He slumped from her and within moments was snoring in his sleep. But Jane could not sleep. She lay wide-eyed, looking at the darkness, afraid to move for fear of disturbing him, with tears rolling down her cheeks unheeded. Wishing it were all a terrible dream that she could wake from, she wept for the Alistair she loved and who seemed lost to her. What had happened, she wondered, to make him change like this? Not until the weak wintry dawn filtered into the room did she, in turn, sleep.

'Morning, Jay, my sweet.' She awoke to Alistair kissing her. She shrank from him. 'Here, what's the matter . . . ?' He lifted himself from the bed. He moaned. 'Christ, my head, what the hell happened to my head? Oh, darling, what the hell was I up to? Kiss me better, there's a love.'

Suspiciously she looked at him, at the multitude of scratches and the large bruise that was already black on the side of his face. The kind expression was back in his eyes. 'I think I was a bad boy last night!' He grinned his little-boy grin at her. She gently kissed the cuts and bruises, softly massaged his temple. 'Ah, that's lovely, that's better, much better,' he sighed. He turned to her and began to make love to her as she was used to him making love to her. Only the soreness of her body told her that the previous night had not been merely the nightmare she had hoped it was.

Alistair stood naked in front of the mirror, inspecting his cuts and bruises.

'Christ, what did I do?'

'You walked through a plate-glass door. A bet or something.'

'I did what? Christ, there'll be hell to pay. I could get sent down for this. Oh, Lord! Why didn't you stop me?'

'I wasn't there, you told me to "sod off". I followed the trail of your blood back here.'

'Darling, I'm sorry. Your last night, too. I am an oaf! Will you ever forgive me?'

'It could have been worse.' Relief made her lenient. She managed to smile at him, knowing that despite last night she loved him, and always would.

'It's the whisky. I don't know what it is but I go berserk on the bloody stuff if I don't watch out. I can't remember a thing!'

'Don't drink it, then,' she said as reasonably as she could.

'I don't, normally, but John had a big bottle and, oh, I don't know, it just seemed like a good idea at the time!' He grinned sheepishly at her. 'You're a brick, Jane, not nagging me or anything when I was obviously a bloody pain. But promise me, the next time you see me with a Scotch in my hands, take the glass away.'

'I will, darling, I promise I will,' she said with feeling.

He crossed the room, opened the door and closed the outer one. 'Right, Sunday, no bedder. And no interruptions. I want you all to myself . . .' He leaped back into the bed with her and cradled her in his arms. She determined to put the incident to the back of her mind. It had not been the real Alistair who had come to her last night.

6

When she thought about it, Jane was well satisfied with the way her life had turned out.

She had an interesting and rewarding job. Sandra had been right: the more senior Jane became and the more responsibility she was given, the more involved she became in her work.

Her friendship with Sandra was stronger than ever. There was a patience and tolerance in their relationship that enabled them to weather the odd bouts of irritation they felt for each other. There was an openness that allowed them to air causes for such irritation. She loved her friend.

There was Sandra's family who welcomed her on her frequent visits, making her feel that their home was truly hers too, if she wanted it. And she did. In return, she gave them her time, helping with household chores, baby-sitting, anything that could, in any small way, thank them for the warmth they showered on her. There were days when she felt she belonged with them, that these people were her real family.

Having, at last, adjusted to Alistair's absence in Cambridge, she filled her days with new interests. She joined a library and read voraciously. She took advantage of the free tickets given by theatre managements to the nurses, and she went to plays, saw her first ballet, heard her first opera. With her free tickets she sat in rapt wonder listening to a full-sized symphony orchestra playing music she had until now only heard on records. She prowled through art galleries and museums. Without realizing it, Jane was educating herself.

At the centre of her life was Alistair. She had pined for love, planned for it, waited patiently for it. She was not to be disappointed in the reality and all the suppressed love within her overflowed. She adored him. She never questioned what he might think of her way of loving him. Had she been more experienced with men, she might have wondered if, at first, he might be perplexed and possibly afraid of her intensity. But, as the months went by and she asked nothing of him, only to be allowed to love him, she would have seen, had she been looking for it, that he began to relax in his attitude to her.

Alistair's friends saw a change in him. No one was sure if it was Jane's love that changed him, or the fact that he had been gated for the rest of the term after the incident of the glass door. But now he was working harder, drinking little, and writing to her often. Before Jane had come into his life he had rattled from one affair to another. Now suddenly he stopped, as if he no longer needed these inconsequential adventures.

The only cloud, for Jane, was that after months of love, she still did not enjoy the climax of their lovemaking. She lied to Sandra, pretended that everything was fantastic, that she was totally fulfilled. This was not strictly untrue – she did feel fulfilled in a sense, her love for him fulfilled her. Physically she did not mind; it did not bother her. The cloud, and it was really quite a small one, was her nagging worry that this was not how it should be. If making love had consisted only of foreplay, she could honestly have said she enjoyed it. She was certain that Alistair did not know how she felt: relishing his lovemaking up to that point, she found it easy to fake the rest.

She did not think of the future and what she would do when this love affair was over. She was convinced that she would never cease to love him as long as she lived. Sometimes, alone in the dark, she feared that he would tire of her. But, with the emptiness of her past, she could not contemplate an empty future – it would have destroyed her. So she lived for the present and never thought of the time beyond her next meeting with Alistair.

She rarely went home now. Her friends from her school days had dispersed. The gulf between her and her parents seemed even greater. They were totally engrossed in their loathing for each other and her visits seemed only to be unwelcome intrusions on their hatred. She tried to tell her mother of her love for Alistair, but her mother, having no faith in the existence of love, lectured her on the dangers of lust. And so, since she could not talk about him when she was home, she went there less and less often. For when she was not with him, she liked to talk of Alistair, to say his name, to hear it said. On her days off, when she could not see him, she would go to Sandra's home where she was free to speak of him with pride. She wrote to her parents, but they never replied. She did not really expect any reply.

Nearly a year after their first meeting, Jane had two weeks' holiday. She arranged this holiday to coincide with Alistair's coming down from Cambridge for good. They planned to spend it in the Fulham house. Two weeks of nights together and long leisurely breakfasts instead of having to get up at dawn to get back to the hospital. She wrote to her mother explaining that friends had invited her to join them for the holiday, and consoled herself that it was only half a lie.

With two heavy suitcases she indulged in a taxi to take her to the house. She found Alistair already there, in the kitchen, preparing their evening meal. As they chatted and argued good-naturedly about what they should do during these two weeks of holiday, the phone rang.

'Jane, answer that, please, my hands are greasy.'

'Flaxman 2433,' she said into the receiver.

'Oh! Did you say 2433?' a surprised-sounding female voice asked.

'Yes, 2433.'

'May I speak to Lord Redland, please?'

'Who?' Jane asked incredulously.

'Alistair Redland.' The voice sounded exasperated.

'Sorry. Yes.' She placed the receiver carefully on the table. 'It's for you, Alistair,' she said, her voice sounding unnaturally formal.

'Who is it?'

'I forgot to ask.'

'Clot!' Alistair playfully patted her behind as he went to pick up the phone.

'Hullo?' He signalled to Jane to get him a cigarette. 'Yes, Mother,' she heard him say. There was a pause, 'Jane, Jane Reed.' Another pause. 'A nurse, Mother, at St Cuthbert's.' He pulled a wry face at Jane. 'R-E-E-D!' He was grinning widely as he listened. 'Jane, my mother wants to know if you are related to the Fenton-Reeds of Plympton?'

'Of course I'm not.' The exasperation she felt at hearing herself explain to his mother was clear in her tone.

'No, Mother, she's not related to them.' He rolled his eyes with impatience, and smiled at Jane as she returned to setting the table.

'Yes, Mother. No, Mother. Three bags full, Mother,' he said, returning to his cooking. Jane continued to lay the table. They had bought candles and she noticed as she lit them that her hand was shaking. She felt sick and ice cold inside. How could he not have told her, she thought angrily.

'Right, darling. Table ready? Great, sit down, the food's going to be marvellous.' He was too busy collecting the dishes and putting them on the table to notice that she sat silent, a sad expression on her face. 'Now, the wine. This is a very special one, to celebrate our holiday.' He lifted his glass to her. 'You look lovely, Jane, even more beautiful in the candle-light.' She did not look up but stared steadfastly at her plate. 'Jane, what's the matter?'

'Nothing.'

'Why so moody then?'

'It's nothing.'

'I hate people who sulk.'

'I'm not sulking.'

'It's a bloody good imitation then. If you're not sulking, then why have you gone so silent?'

'Because everything is different now.' She could feel tears began to prick her eyes, felt the skin of her face go stiff as she fought not to cry. She could hear the strain in her voice.

'Different? What's different?' he demanded irritably.

'You could have told me you were a bloody lord!' she blurted out.

'Oh, for heaven's sake, is that all?' He laughed.

'I don't think it's funny! You should have told me. It's ruined everything!'

'What the hell do you mean? Don't be so melodramatic. Look, I'm sorry you're upset. I didn't think. Maybe I should have told you, but when? How? I don't make a habit of going around saying, "Oh, by the way, I'm a lord." That would be daft.' He roared with laughter at the very idea.

'Don't laugh! It's changed everything.'

'Jane, don't be so bloody silly.'

'I am not being bloody silly!' she shouted. 'It has changed everything. You've been keeping it secret, laughing at me behind my back.'

He laid down his knife and fork and took her hand. 'Jane, listen to me.' She turned her head away from him. 'Jane.' He turned her face to him, but she would not look up at him. 'OK, don't look at me, then, but at least listen to me. I can't help being a lord. I was a lord when I met you. Nothing is different about me.'

'You could have told me at the beginning.'

'What? And have you react like this then?'

'No, I wouldn't have.'

'You would have, everybody does. It happens all the time. People react to a title, they're either all over one or they back away. It can take ages to cement a friendship if you're lumbered with one. I should know.' She said nothing. 'Christ! I know exactly what you're thinking. You think I'm playing with you, using the poor working-class girl. That I'll drop you when I've tired of you. Hell, it sounds like a Victorian melodrama.'

'It could happen. I think it's a reasonable assumption.'

'Reasonable! What the hell is reasonable about it? Just because I've got a stupid title doesn't mean I'm automatically a bastard, for God's sake!' He was shouting with anger at her. She studied her hands intently as she always did when nervous. 'You're a snob!' he yelled. 'A sodding snob!'

'Me?' She reacted angrily. 'Me, a snob? You're being ridiculous!'

'Yes, you are! You're rejecting me because of who I am. You're an inverted snob. Don't you realize I don't give a damn about you and your background? It's not *who* you are, it's *what* you are that matters. I like you for being Jane, my straightforward Jane. That's what attracted me to you in the first place. I was fed up with silly women playing games with me, and lying. You were the complete opposite. When I saw you, my guts turned over and I wanted to hold you and make love to you and make you mine and look after you. I can do that just as well as a lord, as I could as a plain bloody mister!' There was anger in his face but mixed now with an expression of sadness.

Jane began to cry. 'Do you really feel like that about me?' she mumbled through her tears.

'Yes, of course, I wouldn't have said it otherwise.'

'It's just it was such a shock when your mother asked to speak to you. It meant I didn't know who you were, and I thought we knew everything about each other. I mean, what else don't I know?'

'There's nothing else to know. You know all the important things. This title business, it's nothing.'

'I'm always so afraid of losing you.' She dried her eyes. 'I've never met a lord before,' she said, almost shyly.

Slowly he grinned at her. 'Don't make a habit of it, will you? They tend to be a randy lot!'

She did not laugh. 'I feel such a fool, Alistair, not knowing, and everyone else knowing.'

'Not everyone does, I don't advertise it. My friends at Cambridge are used to it and couldn't give a damn. I don't mix in the circles where it matters.' He smiled at her. 'Perhaps I should have said something. I'm sorry. But we get on so well and, oh, I don't know, perhaps it did become a bit of a game, after a while, wondering how long it would be before you found out my dreadful secret.'

'But you never suggested I meet any of your family. And you've obviously never mentioned me to them. Is not wanting me to know your secret the only reason?' she asked, pretending a calm she did not feel.

'I don't like the implication behind that question. Are you implying I'm ashamed of you?' His voice rose angrily. 'I've not taken you home simply because everything has been so perfect I didn't want interfering families involved. That's all. And, while we're on the subject, you've never once suggested you take me to meet your parents.'

'That's different.'

'Balls! It's no different at all. Are you ashamed of me, then?'

'Don't be silly. I didn't want them interfering either.'

'There you are, then.'

But it wasn't as simple as that. She had not suggested it because she knew that her parents would not understand, and her father in particular would have objected to Alistair simply because he was not one of them. Now, it would be impossible ever to take him home, for within her father lurked a dark and bitter hatred for the upper classes, and a deep resentment of those with titles. She knew she was not being totally honest with Alistair. And if she could deceive him in this matter, was it not probable that he was doing the same, lying to protect her feelings?

'You OK now?' he asked anxiously.

'Still feeling very stupid. I think my pride is hurt the most!' She managed to laugh.

'Thank God you're laughing. Now if all that is settled, can we get on with our dinner before it's ruined?' he asked practically.

Their dinner finished, the awkward incident past, they were lying on their cushion listening to their favourite piece of music, Sibelius's Fifth Symphony, when the phone rang again. Alistair was gone a long time. Jane dreamily lay back on the large paisley-covered cushion. The cushion was a joke, really, it did not match anything in the room, but they felt sentimental about it, since they could honestly claim it was where they had first met. So it stayed, in nonharmonizing splendour, and they would often lie on it together listening to music, as they had tonight. She watched the sun as it slid behind the rooftops opposite. She thought of Alistair being a lord, and decided that she might quite like the idea once she got used to it. It was definitely romantic. And different. How she would love some of those snobs at the hospital to know – they would strangle her with jealousy. She smiled to herself.

'The great debate whether or not you meet my family seems to have been decided for us. That was my mother again. She wants us to go home for the weekend. She wants to meet you.'

'Alistair, I couldn't!' Jane said, her voice shaking at the very idea.

'Jane, they aren't monsters. It's time you met them, really. She asked me if our relationship was serious. I said it was and so it's only natural that they should want to meet you.'

'But our holiday?'

'It's only for the weekend. They have no one staying this weekend, and it's the only one for months. I didn't think you would want to go if the house was full of people.'

'It's all too much!' she said, with rising panic in her voice.

'Darling, I'd like us to go,' Alistair said, his voice very serious.

'Will you be angry with me if I say no?'

'Extremely.'

'Then I suppose we have to go. But I think your parents are going to be very disappointed in me.'

'Don't talk daft. They'll love you. Have you got a long frock?'

'Good God, no, why?'

'We always dress for dinner. We'll have to buy you one tomorrow.'

'Alistair, I can't afford a dress! I've got £14 in the whole world.'

'I'll buy it for you.'

'I couldn't possibly let you. Hell, what would my mother say?'

'What would she say?'

'She told me never to accept clothing from a man. He would take it as his right to remove it!'

'Wise woman, your mother.' He grinned at her. 'Bit late, though. Come here, I want to make love to you. And stop worrying!'

But she could not. And long after he was asleep, she lay in the darkness, fearful of the ordeal before her, afraid of what his family might think of her, and afraid that, by meeting them, her relationship with Alistair would in some way be changed. If they let the outside world into their little personal paradise, Jane feared that it would be tarnished.

Alistair seemed so confident about the weekend, but Jane had an animal instinct which told her that trouble lay ahead.

7

The next morning, despite her protestations that she 'couldn't possibly', 'the expense' and 'what would people think?' He insisted on buying her not one but two dresses.

They hurried back to the car, adding the dress boxes to their other luggage. As they left London behind, the excitement she had felt at buying the new clothes slipped away as rapidly as the miles that separated them from the dear, familiar house in Fulham.

Apprehension began to seep through her, pierced with shafts of fear. Like building bricks, these emotions piled one on another, until she was filled with trepidation. For once she was glad that the car was too noisy for conversation. She did not want Alistair to know how fearful she was becoming. They were his family, and he loved them, she could not expect him to understand her terror at the idea of meeting them.

Why hadn't she had the courage to refuse? That was what she should have done: she should have explained to him reasonably that it was silly for her to go, that it would only cause trouble, that she and his family would have nothing in common. What if they were all like Clarissa? Far better to have left things as they were, persuaded him to live his life in separate boxes. Then why had she not? Curiosity? Perhaps, a bit. Not wishing to hurt him? No, that was a stupid idea. By going, she was much more likely to cause him hurt. Pride, she finally decided, that was why she was here – because of her stupid pride. Look where her insistence that she was as good as anybody, and to hell with the rest, had got her. That worked at the hospital, but now, she would be alone in totally alien surroundings. What havoc could his family wreak on their relationship? Once Alistair had seen her in the environment of his home, among those he loved, would he not see how pointless it was? Silly pride, too, knowing that when she got back to the Nurses' Home she would let it be known where she had been just so that she could see the expression on the faces of the Deb Brigade. Oh, God, what a fool she was!

They left the green meadowlands where fat cows grazed. They began to climb and soon the countryside had changed into a bleak and barren moor, the scrubland stretching as far as the eye could see. Large outcrops of rock loomed menacingly against the skyline. The desolation of the landscape matched the hopelessness and fear that she felt within her.

The car stopped in front of a pair of large, intricately wrought iron gates. To the summons of the car's horn, an old woman came out to heave the huge gates open. As the car slid through, she bobbed; Alistair waved and drove on. Jane turned round to see the woman swinging the gates shut.

'She's closing the gates again.'

'Of course. Don't worry, it's not a prison. You can get out any time.' He seemed amused by the astonished expression on her face.

'But she's old. Those gates are so heavy.'

'I wouldn't let Mrs Trevinick hear you say that, she wouldn't be at all pleased with you. She's done that job for forty years, to my knowledge. In any case, the gates are well oiled,' he added defensively.

'But why not keep them open? Seems silly to keep opening and shutting such huge things.'

'Good God, those gates have been kept shut for centuries; you can't change tradition like that. Then what would the old girl do?' He manoeuvred the car over a cattle grid. 'In any case it keeps snoopers out.'

She began to think she had dreamed the wild, fearful moorland, for suddenly here was a parkland of idyllic lushness. Large trees swayed in the gentle breeze, each obviously planted according to an overall design, to carry the eye forward across the land. They drove past a herd of deer, so tame they merely stopped cropping the grass for a second and with benign curiosity watched them pass by. The drive wound seemingly endlessly through this landscape which was like something in an eighteenth-century painting. Passing through a copse of beech, Alistair stopped the car and pointed to the valley below.

'There you are, darling, Respryn!'

'Bloody hell!' she exclaimed breathlessly.

Set against a wooded hill, which curved around and held it protectively in its folds, stood a house. It was of such age and beauty that it seemed to have grown there from the rock itself, as if it were an inspiration of nature and not of man. A hundred windows glinted in the sunshine. A battalion of chimneys, ornately decorated and twisted like sticks of rock, made it look more like a village than a house. Creepers grew abundantly on the grey stone walls, softening them so that no sharp

angles disturbed the eye. In front of the house, the garden was surrounded by a low grey wall of the same stone. Clipped box hedges,
planted in intricate geometric patterns between the smooth lawns, were
guarded by several dozen tall, neatly trimmed ornamental conifers
which marched like soldiers across the bright-green grass.

'Alistair, it's unbelievable. It can't be real, it's too beautiful!'

'It's a bit nice, isn't it?' He grinned proudly.

'Don't be so blasé!' She hit him playfully. 'It's fantastic! Almost too
good to be true, like the lid of a biscuit tin or a jigsaw. Heavens! And you
live there?' He nodded. 'Crikey, you never think of people living in
places like that. It's the sort of place you pay your half-a-crown to visit,
not to live in.'

'Gracious! We haven't come to that yet!' He smiled as he slid the car
into gear and they carried on down the drive past a turreted gatehouse.

'We used to play in that as children, used it as a glorified playhouse.'

'But it's as big as a house!'

'Yes, but small when you compare it with the real house, isn't it?'

As they drove nearer, the size of the house became truly apparent.
They passed under another gatehouse into the stable yard, where a large,
gilt stable clock chimed the hour as they came to a halt. Several horses'
heads appeared inquisitively over the stable doors. Taking her hand,
Alistair led her towards an oak side door over which was cut a large
stone crest.

'Anyone home?' he yelled as they entered a surprisingly small, oak-
panelled hall. His call echoed through the corridor, then there was
silence again, interrupted only by the ticking of a grandfather clock.
From the wall a stuffed badger in a glass cage gazed glumly down at
them. A tall, rather sombre man, dressed in immaculate, thinly striped
trousers, moved silently and smoothly towards them.

'Anyone here, Banks?' asked Alistair.

'Her ladyship and Lady Clarissa are out to tea and his lordship is in the
library,' the measured tones informed them.

'Splendid! Which room has my mother put Miss Reed in?'

Hearing her name mentioned, Jane stepped forward and, extending
her hand, said brightly, 'How do you do?' The man looked at her hand,
at her, then glanced at Alistair. Finally, and almost suspiciously, it
seemed, he took her hand and inclined his head.

'The Rose Room, Lord Redland.'

'Fine. See to the cases in the car, will you, Banks? Thank you. Come
on, Jane, let's find father.'

Alistair led her along a perplexing number of red-carpeted corridors so rapidly that she could only glimpse the pictures on the walls as they sped by.

'Alistair.' She pulled at his jacket and he slowed down, turning questioningly to her. 'Who was that?' she whispered.

'Back there? That was the butler, Banks. Been with us as long as I can remember.'

'Oh, gosh! Should I have shaken his hand?'

'Darling, do whatever you want.'

'I don't think you're supposed to shake hands. With butlers, I mean. Sorry!'

'Jane, you are a clown. It doesn't matter a fig. If you want to shake the butler's hand, then shake it. No need to apologize. It probably made a pleasant change for him; he spends his life being taken for granted.'

They set off again at the same speed, and crossed the main hall, their heels clattering on the mosaic tiles. She had only seconds to take in the glowing tapestries on the walls, the faded standards hanging from the ceiling. Briefly she glimpsed a large oak staircase sweeping up to the floors above, and then they were racing along yet more long, red-carpeted corridors. At last they stopped, and Alistair opened a linenfold panelled door.

She looked in wonder at the beautiful room. The long walls were covered in bookcases, the light from the tall casement windows glinting on the gold of the bindings, enhancing the rich colours of the leather covers. The sun shimmered through a stained-glass window, scattering the jewel-like colours onto the pale oak floor in rainbow-coloured puddles of light. On large tables about the room, maps were strewn in a random jumble. An enormous terrestrial globe, its surface sepia with age, stood to one side of a stone fireplace which reached the ceiling and was decorated with an intricately carved coat of arms. A fire burned in the grate but the room was so vast that it could never possibly heat it. Comfortable leather chairs were placed at random about the room and the air was heavy with the scent of books and leather.

'Hullo!' a voice called from the far end of the room and only then did Jane notice a tall, slender man with silver-grey hair standing on the top of a pair of library steps. He climbed down and Jane felt a nervous constriction in her throat. He had a natural elegance about him that triumphed over his bizarre choice of clothes. His well-worn trousers, neatly pressed, were of a grey and yellow check. His jacket with large leather elbow pads was equally worn and was of a different check and colour. His bright yellow shirt clashed alarmingly with the red polka-dotted scarf about his neck. Only a man of supreme confidence could have got away with such a collection of colours and patterns, Jane thought.

'Alistair, how lovely to see you,' he said, and the two men embraced warmly.

'Pa, I'd like you to meet a friend of mine, Jane Reed. Darling, this is my father, Lord Upnor.'

'Miss Reed, how kind of you to visit us.' Jane looked at him shyly. The blue eyes were surrounded by lines which could only have been caused by laughter, so gentle was his expression. The fine bones of his face showed beneath the tanned skin which set off the bright silver of his hair. She felt a warm, strong hand clasp hers. 'Did you have a good drive down?'

'Thank you,' she whispered, frowning with puzzlement that he too had a different name.

'I do hope you are not too tired, Miss Reed?'

'No, thank you, I'm fine.'

'Jane, why are you whispering?' Alistair laughingly asked.

'Was I?' She giggled nervously. 'Well, it's a bit overpowering, isn't it? A bit like being in church.' Still she whispered. The two men looked at her quizzically.

'Of course, the stained-glass window! Yes, I suppose it is a bit,' Lord Upnor said kindly. 'We have to blame my Victorian ancestor for that, the purists complain he ruined this room.'

'Oh, I like it. It's pretty.'

'I tend to agree with you, my dear, especially when the sun shines through it as now. A drink! Would you care for a drink, Miss Reed?'

'No, thank you.' She was regaining control of her voice, she realized with relief.

'Too early?' he enquired.

'Yes, Father, much too early, I'm afraid.' Alistair laughed.

'Pity,' the older man replied.

Jane stood awkwardly clutching her handbag in front of her so tightly that her knuckles gleamed whitely against the red chapped skin of her hands.

'Are you interested in books, Miss Reed?'

'Oh yes, I love them. Are these all yours?'

Lord Upnor laughed. 'Well, yes. Mind you, I tend to think I'm only looking after them, that they belong to the house, really. Would you like to see some of our treasures?'

'Yes, please.' She stepped forward eagerly, tripped over a rug and knocked against a table, sending a pile of books tumbling to the floor with a crash. 'Oh, bugger!' she exclaimed in her confusion, blushing red as she dropped her handbag in her haste to kneel down and pick up the books. 'Oh, dear, I'm sorry, these lovely books! I shouldn't have sworn like that either, I . . .'

'My dear Miss Reed, I don't think there is any risk that I will faint from shock.' Lord Upnor laughed with delight and both men helped her replace the books. 'Now, what shall we show her, Alistair?'

'What about the Book of Hours?'

'Splendid choice!' The older man crossed the room and, taking a large bunch of keys, opened a tall bookcase. He selected a small book and laid it reverently upon the table. 'Come, Miss Reed,' he beckoned her. He opened the book and the brilliant golds, vermilions and blues of the illustrations seemed to jump from the page, surely as bright as the day they were painted.

'How beautiful!' she exclaimed, her hands instinctively moving towards it. Then quickly she put them behind her back.

'Please. Please, you may hold it if you wish.' Lord Upnor handed her the book. Gently she turned the pages, her eyes devouring the pictures, hardly believing that she could be holding anything so old and precious.

'It's so beautiful, it makes me want to cry.' She looked up and the tears glinting in her eyes emphasized their excited sparkle.

'Ah, Alistair, we have another enthusiast here,' Lord Upnor said, pleasure at her care and interest evident in his voice. 'Then perhaps you would like to see my collection of botanical books?'

One beautiful book after another was produced to her exclamations of delight. She was fascinated by his large collection of ancient maps; they laughed over the strange spellings of the place names, admired the unbelievable accuracy. He had begun to catalogue the maps, he told her, they were his most prized possessions. The time flew by as the three of them sat, heads close together, studying the treasures. A loud gong sounded far away in the house.

'Good God! Is that the time?' Lord Upnor exclaimed. 'I'll get us all shot!'

Alistair showed her to her room and told her she had an hour in which to dress for dinner. He closed the door and left her alone.

8

Jane looked around her bedroom with awe. It was dominated by an intricately carved four-poster bed, whose rose-coloured curtains matched exactly the bowl of roses on the oak dressing table in front of the window. The window itself looked out on a flower garden from which, as the evening drew in, the sweet smell of roses and lavender mingled with the headier scent of night-scented stock. The floor was highly polished and scattered across it were rugs whose colours glowed even in the dim light.

An open door led into the bathroom. The large bath, its massive bulk encased in shining mahogany, sat splendidly on a raised dais. The taps were of gleaming brass; a huge rod of equally shiny brass slipped into the plug hole with ease. Turning on the taps, she jumped at the ominous gurgling they emitted before the water came gushing out. She undressed hurriedly, throwing her clothes about the room in her haste. She chose some jasmine bath oil by Floris from a collection beside the bath, then lowered herself into the huge tub. The bath was too long for her to lie down comfortably so she sat up, barely able to see over its rim, to examine the room. It was more like a sitting room than a bathroom, with its patterned wallpaper, paintings, armchairs – not a ceramic tile to be seen. There was even a fire laid in the pretty fireplace. But there was no lavatory. What was one supposed to do?

It was a bath for lingering in, but Alistair had said she had only an hour. Reluctantly she hauled herself out and, taking a soft, thick towel from the pile provided, she found she could wrap it twice around herself and still it trailed on the floor. Hearing noises from her bedroom, she peered cautiously around the door to see, to her consternation, a young maid tidying her clothes away.

'Please! Oh, gracious! I'll do that,' she said in some confusion.

'Good evening, miss. Did you find everything you needed? I came earlier to run your bath, but you were still downstairs,' the girl said in the soft tones of the West Country.

'Thank you, it's all lovely.'

'I wasn't sure which evening dress you would be wanting, miss, so I pressed them both to be on the safe side.'

'Gracious, you shouldn't have bothered. Perhaps you can help me decide which one to wear tonight?'

The girl crossed to the wardrobe and with only a second's hesitation said, 'The green one, miss. There's a big dinner tomorrow and I think the black would be a little more formal, don't you?' Gently she smoothed the folds of the dress. 'It is lovely, such good quality,' she said longingly.

'It's gorgeous. I . . .' Standing now beside the maid, Jane saw her other clothes neatly pressed and hanging in the wardrobe. This girl had unpacked her case! It was a horrible idea, this stranger touching her things, like being burgled, she thought angrily. 'But you . . .' She stopped as the girl turned and smiled at her pleasantly, waiting to hear what she had to say. It was not her fault: she was no doubt only doing what she had been ordered to do. 'It's the bath plug, I can't move it to let my bathwater out,' she said instead.

'They be horrible old-fashioned things, miss. You have to learn the knack of them. I'll see to it.' She bustled off into the bathroom and within seconds Jane heard the water sloshing about. Following her, she found the maid busily scouring the bath.

'You mustn't do that, please. I can clean my own bath!' Jane said, appalled.

'Gracious, miss! That would never do. It's my job, you'll be getting me the sack.' The girl laughed good-naturedly, and continued with her cleaning. It was so wrong, thought Jane, a girl of her own age cleaning up after her, as if she were some sort of invalid.

'I'd prefer it if you didn't do it again. I promise I won't tell anyone. It's just, well, I don't like you doing it.'

'Very well, miss.' The girl looked puzzled and Jane was afraid that she had hurt her feelings.

'You see, I don't like being waited on like this.'

'Yes, miss. Whatever you say, miss,' the maid said stiffly. They had been getting on so well, thought Jane sadly, and now she had offended her and she would go. Jane did not want to be left alone, not yet. All the time she was talking to this girl she did not have to think of the ordeal ahead. She must think of something to delay her going, she thought, as she saw the girl moving towards the door.

'Can you tell me where the toilet is?'

The maid crossed to the corner of the room and, with a flourish, opened what Jane had taken to be a cupboard.

'There you are, miss,' she said, giggling.

Looking round the door Jane saw, in a room no bigger than the cupboard she had thought it was, a magnificent, polished mahogany lavatory, enthroned on a small dais. Jane laughed out loud. 'I've never seen a toilet like that, ever,' she snorted.

'It is grand, isn't it? Fit for a queen. We've never had a queen use it, not in my time, but we have had several duchesses!'

'Heavens! Are they all like this?'

'Only in the best rooms along this floor. Mind you, I wouldn't use it, I'd get all claustrophobic in there,' and the two young women collapsed in giggles together. The girl glanced at her watch. 'Gracious, the time, miss! You'll be late. Would you be wanting any help?'

'What with?'

'Dressing, miss.'

'No, thanks, I think I can manage that after all these years.' She grinned broadly and the maid laughed with her. 'What's your name?'

'May, miss.'

'Mine's Jane.'

The young girl stopped laughing and looked uncomfortably at her feet, and began to shuffle them. A heavy silence fell between them. Jane, realizing her mistake, did not know what to say. 'Will that be all, miss . . . Miss Jane?'

'Yes. Thank you. And thanks for pressing my dress.'

'It was a pleasure, miss.' Quietly the girl let herself out of the room and Jane sat despondently at the dressing table. Absent-mindedly she toyed with the silver dressing-table set, not seeing the fine engraved crest on the handles, oblivious to everything but her own confusion. She was never going to get things right. First the butler and now the maid. If she could not behave properly with her own kind, how the hell was she going to manage with the others? That was the problem, she was no different from the butler or May, so why should she be expected to behave differently?

With little enthusiasm she made up her face, brushed her hair so that it fell loose about her face, and only cheered up a little when she caught sight of her reflection in the cheval glass. She had not been sure of the dress in the shop, but Alistair had insisted they buy it. Now she was glad that they had for, as she twisted from side to side, she was pleased with the way the fine, dark-green jersey wool seemed to mould to her body, accentuating its curves. It was a feminine sort of dress, one she would never have dared to choose for herself. She stood on tiptoe – like most short women, she had a dream of growing at least another six inches in the night. It was odd, though, how the clinging lines of this dress made her seem taller, she was sure. If only she were blonde, she sighed. Conditioned by years of her mother's admiration for the blonde, baby-faced cousin, Jane was still unaware of how striking she looked with her dark hair, pale skin and haunting grey eyes.

From far away she heard another gong sound. She presumed that she should respond to it, but since no one had told her where to go she thought it safer to stay where she was. She sat on her bed and investigated the contents of her bedside table. There was fruit, a tin of biscuits, a jar of boiled sweets and a bottle of French mineral water, a pretty pin cushion, needle and thread, hankies – the list was endless. She could survive a siege in here, and she managed to smile to herself. Idly she inspected the books. They had obviously been chosen with her in mind, for she was amused to see a couple of hospital romances and a book on Burke and Hare. She got up and wandered about the room, looking at the paintings – a pastel of a child, a rather sombre oil of a Madonna and child. She studied the carving on the chimneypiece, smelled the roses, hung out of the window and worried about what she should do if Alistair did not appear.

There was a loud knock on the door.

'Come in,' she said nervously. To her relief it was Alistair. 'Oh, you look so handsome!' She smiled at him in his dinner jacket. She had never seen him dressed like that before.

'And you look wonderful. I was right about that frock. Come on, you're late, everyone is waiting for you.'

'I'm sorry, I didn't know where to go. I was frightened of getting lost.'

'My fault, I forgot to explain. That second gong is to tell everyone my mother is down and drinks are being served. We'd better hurry or you won't have time for even a tiny one.' Taking her hand he raced down the staircase with her, and it was with a thudding heart that Jane was led to a door behind which she could hear a babble of voices. As they entered the room the chatter stopped and to Jane's horror she saw that there was a crowd, when she had expected only Alistair's parents. Her heart sank as she saw his sister across the room.

'Miss Reed, at last!' A dark-blonde, tall and upright woman approached her with outstretched hand. Alistair introduced his mother.

The woman's elegance was emphasized by her thinness. She had a pale complexion but her fair skin had the dryness to which so many English women fall prey, so that her make-up seemed to sit uncomfortably on top of her skin. But this was the only flaw that Jane could see. Although now faded, she had once been beautiful. 'We thought you were lost.'

'I'm sorry, I didn't know what the gong meant, or where to go.'

'Silly Alistair. However, you're here now. I do hope you find your room comfortable?'

'Yes, thank you. It's lovely, thank you. My room is lovely.' Too late she realized how repetitive her mumblings were, and how gauche she must sound.

'Let me introduce you to everyone. I gather you have met my husband.' Lady Upnor put her hand under Jane's elbow and expertly propelled her across the room to join the others. 'May I introduce my sister-in-law, Lady Honor Calem?'

Jane looked up shyly to see a face of the most extraordinary loveliness smiling at her. No matter how long this woman lived, people would never say of her, 'She must have been beautiful, once.' It was not just the creamy, clear skin, virtually unlined and covering fine bones, nor the large generous mouth smiling in welcome at Jane, nor even the mane of golden red hair which she shook unselfconsciously as she took Jane's hand. Her true beauty lay in the kindness, joy and vitality that shone in her large, expressive eyes. There was a warm vibrance to the woman, an inner charm, which would keep her beautiful.

'My daughter, Clarissa,' Lady Upnor continued.

'We've met,' Clarissa's clipped voice announced. 'I met her charring for Alistair.'

'Really? Did you help Alistair? How kind of you,' Clarissa's mother said smoothly. 'Perhaps you have met Clarissa's friends, too? No?' Jane found herself shaking hands with a young girl, Amanda Duckworth, whose prettiness was marred by a sulky expression. James Standard was a pleasant, rather red-faced young man, who looked as if he might be fat one day. 'And lastly, my friend, Roderick Plane.' Lady Upnor introduced her to a small rotund man in his late forties, who took Jane's hand in a damp, limp grasp. His mouth was large and slack, and he had the ruddy complexion and broken veins of a heavy drinker. His cheeks were like two large pouches, which gave the odd impression that his face was slipping off his skull. As he greeted her, Jane noticed that he was not looking at her but at a point over her left shoulder, as though she did not exist for him.

'There, now you know everyone.' Alistair's mother smiled at her but, with a chill feeling, Jane saw that it was with her lips only. There was no warmth in her eyes.

Jane was given a drink, and with her gin and tonic in her hand she moved over to a large window seat which set her outside the circle of the others as the conversations resumed. She admired the self-assured way the talk was batted back and forth across the room. There never seemed to be an awkward silence. She was struck by how loudly they talked and laughed and with what confidence they stated their opinions, as if the idea that they might be wrong had never crossed their minds.

'You look out of things over there, Miss Reed.' Alistair's mother smiled graciously at her.

'I'm fine, thank you, Lady Upnor.'

'Tell me, Miss Reed, do you like monkey-puzzle trees?'

'Yes, I do.'

'Rupert, you monster!' Lady Upnor shrieked, playfully tapping her husband's hand. 'You got to her first. Admit it! You are not to be trusted for one moment. It's true, Miss Reed, isn't it? He persuaded you to say that?'

'No. I really do like monkey-puzzle trees,' Jane insisted, angry with herself as she began to blush.

'Well, I agree with you, Lady Upnor,' Roderick Plane lisped. 'Ugly trees, should all be cut down.' Everyone began to argue, without explaining to Jane what the problem was.

'We will ask Miss Reed's opinion,' Lady Upnor said eventually. 'Miss Reed, tell me, don't you think my husband is being unreasonable? He knows I hate the trees and they are totally out of keeping with the period of the house. Since it pains me to look at them, don't you think he should cut them down?'

Everyone turned and looked at Jane expectantly. She wanted to say something bright – like 'It would probably pain the trees more to be cut down' – but, as she saw all the faces turned in her direction, she found her mouth was dry and the words would not form.

'I don't know,' she said lamely and hated herself for her lack of courage. Oddly, she felt as if she had failed a test, and sat miserably looking at her hands as the argument continued unabated. She looked up as she felt someone sit beside her. It was Alistair's aunt.

'At last we meet Alistair's mysterious lady! We knew something was up – he's never home these days – and Blanche was convinced it was a young woman. We have all been agog to meet you,' she said with a low, gentle laugh.

'Meet me? Gracious, how embarrassing!'

'Not at all. A beautiful young woman like you should have oodles of attention.'

'Beautiful, me?' she said ingenuously.

'Certainly. Hasn't Alistair told you? With your lovely hair and those grey eyes – it's a ravishing combination. Are you Scottish, perhaps?'

'No, I'm English. Yes, Alistair says I'm beautiful but that doesn't count, does it? When you're fond of someone you see them differently.'

'Ah ha. So he loves you, you mean! Oh, what fun!' She laughed again with that soft, throaty chuckle.

'I didn't say he loved me,' Jane countered hurriedly.

'Of course you didn't. Silly boy, if he hasn't told you, but I assure you he does. "Fond of" for Alistair, that is being in love.' Although Jane liked what the woman was saying, it embarrassed her and she quickly changed the subject.

'If we're talking about beauty, Lady Calem, I think you are beautiful, in fact I think you're the most beautiful person I've ever seen.'

'Sweet of you to say so,' Lady Honor said, with the ease of one used to a lifetime of such compliments. 'I adore it when a woman says something nice to me. Their comments are so much more reliable, and such a rare commodity.' She leaned across and whispered in her husky voice, 'By the way, Jane, you call me Lady Honor. Calem was only a mister.'

'Crikey! I'm sorry. It's so confusing. Everybody seems to have a different name. I mean, Alistair's is different from his parents' and his sister's – where I come from that would only mean one thing –' Aware of what she was about to say, she stopped abruptly and put her hand in front of her mouth.

'And what would that be?' Lady Honor's eyes twinkled in such a merry way that Jane heard herself saying:

'Why, that they were illegitimate.'

'Oh, of course!' Lady Honor laughed loudly. 'What a wonderful idea! How I should love to tell Blanche, but I don't think I had better.' She smiled broadly at Jane. 'The name bit is really quite simple. Our family name is Cotham, you see, but our titles are different. Rupert's is Upnor, and Alistair takes the lesser title of Viscount Redland. And Clarissa and I, being daughters of earls, use our Christian names, which shows the title is our own. Do you see?'

'Yes,' answered Jane so doubtfully that Lady Honor pealed with laughter again.

'Poor sweet! You'll catch on. It's really quite unimportant but I thought it might make you more comfortable if you got it right.'

'Might I hear the joke?' Roderick Plane had sidled up. Jane's heart jumped. It was odd that she should feel completely at ease with Lady Honor and free to say whatever came into her head; but with this man . . . never.

'No, you can't, Roddie. It was far too naughty for your delicate ears,' the older woman teased him.

'I gather you're at St Cuthbert's?' he asked Jane. 'Do you know Sir Peter Willoughby or Sir Alexander Disney?'

'Hardly,' Jane answered with a smile. 'They're like gods, and they don't talk to mere mortals under the rank of staff nurse.'

'I see,' Roderick said without interest and drifted off.

'That's you finished for Roderick,' Lady Honor said cheerfully. 'He only speaks to people with titles, who are important, or who he thinks might become important, or might know people who are important.'

'How daft! Think of all the interesting people he never meets, then. What does he do?'

'Shrouded in mystery, my dear. He never says, but it's bound to be something shady. I have never understood what Blanche sees in him.'

'Tell me, Lady Honor, what was all that argument about the monkey-puzzles?'

'My dear, it is so boring. They have been arguing about those damn trees ever since the day they got married. My sister-in-law thinks they are out of place and my brother loves them and refuses to cut them down. Every new person she meets gets the same quizzing. I have a theory that she then only bothers with those who agree with her.' She laughed as she said it, but the information made Jane's heart sink even further.

'But the whole garden is Victorian, isn't it, so they aren't out of place. I mean, you would have to dig the whole garden up for it to be truly in keeping with the house.'

'Did I hear you discussing my garden?' Lady Upnor called to Jane across the room.

'Well, yes.'

'And what were you saying?'

'I was just asking Lady Honor . . .' She could feel herself blushing again. 'I was just saying that since the whole garden is a Victorian one, it would seem a shame to exclude the monkey-puzzles since they are so much part of a Victorian garden,' she answered with a courage she was far from feeling.

'I see. And are you an expert on the subject of Victorian gardens?' Lady Upnor asked.

'No. It's just that I've visited a lot and, well, you get used to what's in them, and I rather like them . . .' she trailed off.

'So you frequently stay in houses like this, then? I suppose you would have to, to be such an expert.'

'Oh no, I didn't mean that. I never stayed anywhere like this before. I meant houses where the public can visit, I've been to a lot of those.'

'God preserve us from such a fate!' Lady Upnor said feelingly. Jane felt Lady Honor gently squeeze her hand. She wished she could disappear and sat waiting miserably for Lady Upnor to quiz her further. She was rescued, however, by the butler, who came to announce that dinner was served. Jane stood up.

'Are you going somewhere, Miss Reed?' Lady Upnor asked imperiously. Jane, blushing bright red, hurriedly sat down again, aware of Clarissa and her friend in the corner smirking at her. Alistair crossed the room to her side.

'How are you getting on?'

'Terrified!'

'You silly goose, you're doing fine.'

'Alistair, I think you have found a dear girl here,' she heard Lady Honor saying to him.

'She's an absolute cracker, isn't she?' Alistair said proudly and, as his mother stood up, he took Jane's arm to lead her in to dinner.

9

She was getting used to large rooms now, for everything in this house seemed to be on a monumental scale, but even so she was amazed at the size of the dining table that stretched for yards down the centre of the cavernous room. She sat with Alistair and his father on either side of her, but, because of the size of the table, they were some distance from her. There was no chance of intimate conversation here, which perhaps explained why they all talked so loudly.

The battalions of cutlery and lines of cut glass promised a feast. Candlelight glowed from enormous silver candelabra, placed at measured intervals. The whole table was a blaze of light as the candles reflected on the highly polished glasses and silver. Each piece of the individual place settings – cutlery, cigarette box, ashtray, pepper pot and salt cellar – was heavily engraved with a crest. The cutlery at the hospital was engraved and she knew for certain that this was to stop the staff stealing it. Were they frightened their staff or even their guests would walk off with the silver here? Perhaps it was to remind them that it was theirs or even who they were.

The butler and the footmen began to serve the food. The butler's glance was everywhere, checking and rechecking that all was well, that no one lacked or needed anything. Plates were smoothly removed and replaced. Wine glasses were unobtrusively refilled. The men worked quickly and quietly, seeing all but appearing not to listen. It gave them the air of assiduous robots.

The stage had been set for a banquet and Jane was astonished and disappointed at how unappetizing the food was. It was lukewarm and bland, the vegetables as overcooked as her mother's. Everything was covered with a sticky white sauce which tasted of nothing. Lord Upnor ate with noisy relish. Jane toyed gingerly with her food: even if it had not been so repulsive, she was far too nervous to eat.

The wines, however, were wonderful and as they seeped into her bloodstream she could feel a little confidence returning. Alistair's father, and his aunt who sat opposite, were both attentive and coaxed her to talk. She started to enjoy herself.

'It's a ludicrous waste of money, James!' they heard Roderick Plane exclaim from the other end of the table.

'What's a waste of money, Roddie?' Lord Upnor asked with interest.

'Money spent on education, Lord Upnor. James and I cannot agree on the subject.'

'We would be in a fine old pickle if people weren't educated, Roddie. I mean doctors and bankers and vets especially, useful chappies like that,' Lord Upnor reasoned.

'Lord Upnor, I did not make myself clear. I do apologize to you,' Roderick Plane continued obsequiously. 'I'm not against education, provided you pay for it yourself. I'm against educating the masses. That's where the money is wasted. Our money, yours and mine!'

'And what do you mean by "masses", Mr Plane?' Alistair asked with what, to Jane's surprise, sounded like amusement.

'I mean the working classes. Mind you, I think the phrase "working class" is a misnomer – none of the bastards know what work is. I apologize for my language, Lady Upnor, but it is something I feel strongly about.' Lady Upnor inclined her head graciously to him.

Jane had read about people saying they heard warning bells in their heads. Now she knew what it felt like. As her anger rose, the noises in her head were almost deafening.

'Daddy would agree with you,' Amanda added helpfully. 'He has dreadful trouble with the beastly unions. He says we might as well be living in Russia.'

'Salt of the earth, more like scum of the earth!' her incredulous ears heard Roderick Plane blubber. Her anger was concrete, like a hard lump inside her. It rose into her throat until she felt she would choke. She noted the footmen standing impassively by and felt anger for them as well as for herself. Her face began to redden but from fury this time. She glanced across the table. Clarissa smiled coldly at her and, with a blinding certainty, Jane was convinced that Clarissa had in some way engineered this whole conversation.

'But surely, if what you say is true, and I don't for one minute think it is, by not educating them you would make them even more idle, take all ambition away from them?' Alistair argued reasonably. How could he be so calm and polite to this dreadful man? Jane fumed inwardly.

'My dear young man, you miss the point entirely. When they were not educated we never had any trouble with them, they knew their place and were content to live there and their children after them. Now, with education, you fill their empty heads with unnecessary information when all they are going to do is empty dustbins – a complete waste, you see.'

'But Roddie, not everybody becomes a dustman,' Lord Upnor interrupted.

'No, and the ones who don't get heads full of dangerous learning so that they begin to question the order of things. That is the path we are travelling, and we face disaster if we don't stop.'

'Daddy says it's cruel, really, educating them,' Amanda chipped in. 'He says that we send them to lovely schools, like the new ones the government is putting up, costing thousands, with plate-glass windows and afrormosia floors, and then at night they have to go back to their dreadful slums. Daddy thinks it can only lead to discontent.'

'How right your father is,' remarked Roderick unctuously.

'Balderdash!' The word exploded from Jane.

There was a moment's silence round the table.

'Are you an expert on education as well as gardens, Miss Reed?' asked Lady Upnor in a pleasant tone of voice which completely disguised the sarcasm of her question.

'No, Lady Upnor, but I know about state education and the need for it and the desire that people have for it –'

'I have not noticed a burning desire in my maid to improve her education. However, servants are certainly a lot more difficult these days than their fathers and mothers were and I think that education must take the blame for that. I think there is a lot of truth in what Roderick says.'

Lady Upnor had interrupted her, but anger gave Jane courage.

'If your argument were valid, Lady Upnor, then we would all have stayed in the trees.'

'Pity some didn't,' drawled Clarissa.

'And you keep talking about "them" as if "they" were some sort of different species to yourself. We are not, we are human just as you are and we have the right to the same opportunities in life.'

'Good gracious, Miss Reed, are you a Communist? How dreadful!' Lady Upnor smiled her cold smile at Jane.

'No, I'm not a Communist. But I do believe that everyone should be given a chance. If they don't take it, that is their mistake. But to say that such a large proportion of the population shouldn't even be given a chance is both malicious and stupid.'

'Do you have to be quite so rude?' demanded Clarissa.

'I think calling the working classes "scum" is pretty offensive!' replied Jane with an equal snap to her voice.

'Such a silly expression, "working class". After all what does it mean, someone who works. Well, if someone works he's got to be educated, Roddie. Far better not to educate old drones like ourselves,' Lord Upnor broke in, in an attempt to take the tension out of the situation.

'Jane really is the only person at this table who can speak with any authority on the subject. After all, she is the only one of us who does any work, isn't she?' Lady Honor asked, smiling sweetly at Roderick. 'That is unless you work, Roddie? Tell me, do you work?' She smiled mischievously at him.

'If people are going to become offensive than I think it is better that we ladies withdraw,' Lady Upnor said, getting to her feet.

'I don't think Jane was being offensive, Mother. She was defending her point of view,' Alistair said hurriedly.

'Don't you, darling?' Again she smiled that cold smile. How could something as pleasant as a smile become so fearsome? thought Jane. It was unfortunate that this had happened, but there had been no alternative. She would never have forgiven herself if she had not spoken up – even if, as she thought, it had been an elaborate trap set by Clarissa and her cronies. If she was never invited again it did not really matter, she did not want to know people who could talk and think like that, Jane consoled herself. She would be sad if she never saw Lady Honor and Alistair's father, but she could not change her opinions just to suit her ladyship.

As the women moved from the room, Jane continued to sit in her seat. Alistair leaned over to her. 'Darling, you go with the ladies,' he whispered.

'I want to wait for you.'

'No, darling, you can't. I'll be along later.'

Miserably she followed the other women, trailing behind them as they slowly mounted the wide oak staircase to the drawing room.

She sat and watched the others as they fluttered about Lady Upnor, who was pouring coffee. She was struck yet again by their unselfconscious elegance. They were all so tall and slender that every movement they made looked graceful. They sat entwining their legs one around the other, as only very tall women can. Their heads were poised on long slender necks and, as they talked and turned from side to side, she was reminded of a group of ballet dancers in repose. She felt awkward beside them. The smallness and rounded curves that delighted Alistair precluded her, she realized, from ever being as truly elegant as they were.

Lady Upnor was assiduous in caring for Jane, pointing out the best chocolates in the silver basket she offered her. She seemed a different woman from the one in the dining room. Jane smiled gratefully, confused by the woman's sudden swing of mood. Everyone by now had coffee and Lady Upnor took the chair closest to Jane.

'Tell me, Miss Reed, where did you manage to meet my son?'

'He gave a housewarming party. Some friends of his who were working at my hospital invited me. It was a lovely party.'

'Which friends?'

'John and David, I don't know their surnames.'

'Oh, those friends. Dreadful, vulgar young men!'

'I like them,' Jane said loyally.

'What's Alistair's house like?' asked Lady Honor. 'I must pay him a visit.'

'It's a horrible, poky little thing. Why on earth he insisted on buying it, I shall never understand – with all the room we have in the London house. He wouldn't listen to me, but then he never does.'

'It's natural, Blanche, that he should want a home of his own, surely?' Lady Honor argued.

'One realizes why now,' Lady Upnor said, looking pointedly at Jane, who looked quickly down at her hands. Compared with the elegant white hands of the other women, hers appeared even more red and chapped than usual. Despite copious use of hand cream, they never seemed to improve. She felt Clarissa staring at her hands, too, and quickly placed them at her side, wishing she could sit on them and hide them away. 'My dear Honor, you should see inside. It is simply ghastly. I offered him whatever he wanted to furnish it, but no, he had to buy piles of the most awful, evil-smelling junk. Quite ridiculous of him.'

'But his furniture is lovely. Really, Lady Honor, it's super and it doesn't smell!' Jane leaped to the defence of the Fulham house. Lady Honor smiled understandingly; Lady Upnor stared coldly at Jane.

'I gather you have known my son for a year?'

'Nearly, not quite.'

'I see,' said his mother. 'But your nursing, I presume you are not qualified yet?'

'No, I have another year, after August, to finish.'

'A year? I see. And of course you want to qualify?'

'Some days I do, other days I could quite happily walk out.'

'You mustn't do that!' Lady Upnor said hurriedly. 'It would be such a waste, if you did.'

'Yes, I suppose so.'

'Ghastly profession,' interjected Clarissa. 'Digging around in other people's orifices. Ruination to the hands!'

'Cla-ris-sa!' her mother enunciated. 'Don't be so vulgar!'

'It's true, Mummy. That's all it is, really, quite disgusting. What on earth made you choose it?' she asked Jane unpleasantly.

'It chose me. I needed to earn some money.'

'Couldn't you have worked in a shop or something?' Clarissa waved her hand vaguely.

'It's probably more interesting than working in a shop. And at least I'm using my brains.'

'Really?' Clarissa arched her brows. 'I wouldn't have thought it took much brainpower to give someone a bedpan.' Amanda giggled in the background.

'Clarissa, you go too far sometimes. In fact, the exams are terribly hard, I hear,' Lady Honor said, turning to Jane. 'Isn't that so, Jane?'

'Well, my hospital won't accept you without A levels.'

'Ha! Well, that cuts you out, Clarissa!' her aunt declared triumphantly.

'I suppose you could always marry a doctor. That's why people take up nursing, isn't it?' Clarissa said, ignoring her aunt's taunt.

'Not me, I don't like the medical students and have nothing to do with them, if I can help it.' Jane preferred to think she had not heard Clarissa say, 'More's the pity.'

'And what does your father do?' Lady Upnor continued.

'He works as a storeman in a factory.'

'I see. How interesting,' Lady Upnor said in an icy tone. Jane wished she would not keep saying 'I see' like that. What did she see? It was obvious that she was drawing conclusions from Jane's answers, but what conclusions?

'Fancy a game of backgammon, anyone?' She was relieved to hear Clarissa change the subject and presumed that she was at last bored with baiting her. 'How about you, Jane?'

'I'm sorry, I don't know how to play.'

'You can't play backgammon? But everybody plays backgammon,' her tormentor continued.

'Not everyone. I don't.' It was Jane's turn to snap.

'Do you ride?'

'No.'

'Play tennis?'

'Badly.'

'Heavens, what are we going to do with you all weekend?'

'Don't worry about me. I'm quite capable of looking after myself,' Jane replied.

'Evidently.' Clarissa smirked. Jane could feel tears of frustration pricking her eyes. How she longed to be back in Fulham, not here with this bitch baiting her at every turn. If only they were on their own, she could tell her exactly what she thought of her, but that was probably what she wanted. With relief she heard the men's voices and looked eagerly for Alistair, who came immediately and sat on the arm of her chair, stroking her hair.

'Alistair, you look most uncomfortable there. Sit on a chair properly,' his mother ordered him.

'I'm fine, Mother.'

'No, you're not. You will break the chair,' she said with irritation in her voice. Reluctantly, he got up and moved away.

'Drinks?' Lord Upnor asked and there was a bustle while drinks were arranged. 'Miss Reed?' He smiled at her.

'Might I have a gin and tonic, please?'

'A *gin and tonic*!' Roderick Plane bellowed. 'Good God, I never heard anyone order a gin and tonic after dinner in my life.' He roared with laughter, opening his mouth wide, exposing his bad teeth and spraying those nearest him with spittle.

'It's the only drink I like,' a bright-red Jane explained.

'If Miss Reed wants a gin and tonic I can't think why she shouldn't have one. In fact I think it's a very good idea, it's damned hot tonight. Make that two, Banks,' ordered Lord Upnor.

'Three, Banks,' Alistair added loyally.

'Ice, Miss Reed?' the butler asked imperturbably.

Until midnight, when people began to drift away, Jane sat silently, nursing her drink. She had decided it was safer if she kept her mouth shut. So she listened as they talked. The talk was fairly general, mainly about the estate and the farm, until Lord Upnor excused himself and retired. Then the tone changed completely. Roderick was obviously the master of ceremonies and was soon talking cruelly about their friends, and tearing their characters to pieces. She thought he was despicable but everybody else was shrieking with laughter.

All the adults had gone to bed and only the young remained. It was with them that she felt most uncomfortable. Their self-confidence and loud assurance made her feel inadequate and at the same time angry that she should feel like this. They seemed such a closely knit group, with their own jokes and private vocabulary. Alistair was a part of it. She was an outsider and realized that, no matter how long she knew them, she would always remain one.

When someone suggested a game of billiards, she used the game as an excuse to go to bed. Lying alone in the dark, listening to the unfamiliar noises of the old house, she longed for Alistair to be with her and, as if in answer to her wish, the door opened and Alistair crept in.

'Christ! What a route march I've had to get here,' he said, chuckling. 'My bloody mother's put us as far apart as possible. My room's in the other wing.'

He climbed in beside her. It was wonderful to feel his familiar arms about her.

'Where's your mother's room?'

'Along the corridor, miles away. Don't worry, she can't hear through these thick walls. Come here,' he said as he took her in his arms and began to make love to her. But Jane found it impossible to relax: she lay in his arms as unfeeling as a piece of wood.

'What's the matter?' he asked concerned.

'I don't know, I think it's because I feel it's wrong in your mother's house.'

'It's my father's, too, and he wouldn't mind for one minute!' he replied jokingly. 'Well, if it's going to be like this, remind me not to come here often!' he said, snuggling against her.

10

Jane awoke, disappointed to find that Alistair had gone. He must have crept stealthily away at first light as he had come to her in the darkness. She rolled onto his side of the bed, burying her face in the indentation he had made in the pillow, breathing deeply, searching for his smell which might still linger on the linen. If only it were just the two of them here, how happy she could be! The memory of last night made her shiver. How awkward, how gauche she must have seemed! The unnerving feeling of not belonging and the knowledge that she never would swept over her again. She was angry that she had been so tongue-tied, unable even to argue her case well. But then, how could she with that ice-cold hag smiling at her with her dead fish eyes?

Last night after dinner she had been interrogated. The questions had not been posed out of interest, but rather to analyse and place her; not to investigate her as a person but to find out where she fitted in the structure of their lives. Of course, she had not fitted into any approved slot.

It had all been so coldly performed that Jane began to appreciate that her suitability in human terms counted for nothing. She had proved herself socially inferior and that was the issue which counted. Her rejection was not personal. Those little sparks of irritation which she had seen in Lady Upnor were not directed at her personally but were caused by the older woman's discomfort at the position in which she found herself – of having to contemplate a social inferior as a guest. Had Jane met her simply as a patient, no doubt Lady Upnor would have been charm personified.

Jane began to feel afraid, afraid that Alistair would be prevailed upon to see her as his mother did, that she might deliberately make Jane look stupid so that he would himself become aware of her unsuitability. She felt as if by coming here she had stepped into the Victorian era petrified in its strict social codes. The injustice of it, the unfairness, the stupidity that distinctions of class should still be regarded as important, made her sad and then, with mounting emotion, angry.

How dare that woman stand in judgement? Why should she not be Alistair's friend if he so chose? Her underprivileged background did not alter her character. It was ludicrous that one's rightness and standing should depend on an accident of birth. It was as ridiculous as her father's preconceived ideas about class. Social behaviour could be learned. She had known which knife and fork to use, how to eat her soup; she had learned a lot over the years and she was quite capable of learning a hell of a lot more. Why should she be made to feel ashamed of her background? At least she was achieving something in her life, unlike Clarissa who, having had everything from birth, appeared to do nothing, thought less, and yet expected respect. When Jane was with Alistair she did not feel inadequate, so what was wrong with her, allowing that woman to make her feel like this?

A soft knock at the door brought her back to the day ahead. It was May with a tray of tea. A single red rose in a tiny crystal glass was reflected in the silver teapot.

'Good morning, miss,' May said as she pulled the curtains and bright sunshine flooded into the room. 'It's a lovely day, miss – it's going to be a really hot one." She settled Jane with the tray. 'Lord Redland says to tell you he's gone riding and will be back about ten. He gave me the rose for you.' She began to giggle. 'Real romantic, isn't it?'

'It's a lovely rose,' Jane replied, unaware of her dignity in not commenting further.

'Yes, miss, sorry, miss,' the maid replied, far more aware than Jane of the limitations that bound her. 'Shall I run your bath?'

'If you must.' Jane smiled at the girl. 'But remember you mustn't expect to clean it out!'

'Yes, miss. You win!' Laughing, May went to run the bath. Jane sat in the large canopied bed, sipping her tea and gazing dreamily at her red rose. At least the rose showed that Alistair had not been affected by last night's bickering or her inability to make love to him. She was relieved that he had not expected her to go riding. Like a true city girl, she was terrified of horses.

"May," she called, and the maid appeared in the doorway. 'May, tell me, what am I supposed to do? I've never stayed anywhere like this in my life and I'm completely at sea.'

'It's the mealtimes you really have to watch out for. Her ladyship's a real stickler for punctuality and she gets ever so cross if people are late. It doesn't matter who it is, I've seen her tell a cabinet minister off before now,' she said admiringly. 'Breakfast doesn't matter – most of the ladies have theirs in bed – but Lord Redland said as you didn't like to eat in bed.'

'Oh no, I hate it, all the crumbs!'

'Wish all the ladies felt like you.' The maid warmed to her subject. 'A right mess some of them make! Crumbs, spill their tea, marmalade on the sheets. And sometimes it's lunchtime before we can get into their rooms to straighten them!'

Jane tutted in sympathy at the maids' plight. 'And after breakfast?' she asked.

'I expect Lord Redland has plans for the morning. Lunch is at one. Dinner at eight. Tea is served at four, but you don't have to have that if you don't want.'

'What do people do all day?'

'Eat, it seems to me!' She giggled. 'Oh, they walk in the gardens, some ride, write letters, that sort of thing.' From the tone of her voice it was easy to see that May thought the regime very boring. 'There's a swimming pool, up past the rose garden. If the weather is nice, they might have a swim. But really, I think that's all they do. Most of the ladies have a rest in the afternoon, but God knows why!' She laughed.

'Would you come for a walk with me, if Lord Redland has other plans?' Jane asked. The girl looked at her, puzzled. 'I mean, you could show me where the rose garden is.'

'Good God, miss! That would mean instant dismissal.'

'If you went for a walk?' Jane asked incredulously.

'I can go for a walk. But not in the rose garden or anywhere I would be seen. Gracious, no.'

'Seen by whom?'

'Her ladyship, of course, miss. She won't even have the gardeners about when she's in the garden. Many a time they have to jump into a bush if she suddenly appears.'

'But that's Victorian! I never heard of such a thing! And you don't mind?'

'It's always been like that.'

Jane couldn't think what to add. The girl lived in a different world from hers. It was none of her business, after all.

'I was thinking, miss, that big dinner tonight. Would you like me to do your hair?'

'My hair?' Jane questioningly fingered the ends of her hair. 'What could you do with it?'

'I thought it would look lovely done up in a big chignon. You've such lovely long hair, so shiny too.'

'Do you really think so? Anything that gives me confidence, May, anything!' She grinned. 'Yes, let's.'

'Oh, miss, thank you. You'll look lovely, I promise. I want to be a lady's maid, you see, but I hardly ever get a chance to practise – most of the ladies who come here to stay, they bring their own. But your bath, miss, the water will be getting cold.'

Her bath finished, Jane cleaned it. Back in the bedroom she had to laugh at May. Not only was the bed made, but everything had been neatly folded and put away. Dressed, she followed May's directions to the breakfast room.

She was relieved to find the room empty. She ignored the rows of heated silver chafing dishes, containing everything from fried eggs to kippers and kedgeree, and helped herself to coffee. On another side table was a pile of newspapers. She would have liked to read one but they were aligned in such pristine order that she did not like to touch them, remembering how angry her father became if anyone read his *Daily Mirror* before him.

The door opened and Banks sidled into the room. She had noticed last night that the butler did not appear to walk but rather glided across the floor as if on casters.

'Good morning, Miss Reed.'

'Good morning, Mr Banks.' The butler gave her one of his rare smiles. He noticed her empty plate.

'Have you everything you need, miss? Perhaps I could fetch you something else that you would prefer to eat?' he asked with concern.

'Oh no, thank you, Mr Banks. It all looks lovely, I'm just not hungry. The coffee is delicious,' she added hurriedly, hoping to prevent him feeling hurt by her refusal. She stood up, uncertain of which of the two doors facing her was the correct one. Noticing her dilemma, the butler smoothly opened one of the doors for her.

'Might I suggest, Miss Reed, that the Long Gallery is particularly beautiful at this time of day?'

'A long gallery, I'd like to see that. If you could point me in the right direction.' She giggled.

'Allow me,' and the butler escorted her silently through the long corridors. Eventually they stopped before double doors which Banks opened with a dramatic flourish.

'There, Miss Reed, the Long Gallery!'

Jane gasped. She had thought the library grand, but it had not prepared her for this. At the foot of a small flight of steps stretched a long room which appeared narrow only because of its extraordinary length. Long windows let in a flood of light which reflected dazzlingly on the white plaster ceiling and the large pair of matching marble fireplaces. The oak-plank floor gleamed, reflecting more pools of light. The room was so shining and bright that it was like stepping into a long prism of glass.

'What a lovely room!' Involuntarily she clapped her hands with pleasure.

'It is 116 feet long, miss. In winter there are curtains at all the windows but in summer we take them down and then, I think, the room looks its best.'

'Oh yes, Mr Banks, I can see that. It's as though it were made of crystal, not wood and plaster.'

'Exactly.' The butler warmed to her appreciation of this room, which he obviously held dear. 'Note the ceiling, miss.' She craned her neck to look up. The plasterwork was so ornate and heavy it seemed to be defying gravity with its weight and intricacy. 'Italian plasterers came especially to do the work. They lived here for years, I gather. If you walk down the window side, Miss Reed, and up the other side you will see that each panel is a scene from the Bible.' Sure enough, there were Adam and Eve and the serpent.

'It is used for dancing, Mr Banks?'

'Very occasionally. Originally it was designed as a place for the ladies of the house to walk and take exercise when it was raining.' Far away in the depths of the house a telephone rang. Reluctantly excusing himself, Banks went to answer the phone, leaving her alone.

She soon discovered that the room was a museum, with some cases containing letters, none of which she could decipher. One case held embroidered gloves and stockings, a note in copperplate writing explaining that they had belonged to Queen Victoria and Elizabeth I. What strange people queens were, she thought. In many of the houses she had visited on coach trips were bits of clothing left by these two monarchs. Did they lose them, forget them, or give them? she wondered. She could not resist turning the key on a large clockwork china doll. Slowly the doll's small hands rose and moved across the miniature keyboard of a tiny piano and the room was filled with tinkling music.

It was possible, moving down the room, to see the interests that had amused the earls down the centuries. One had obviously had a passion for clocks. Another for Africa. Here was India's case, with jewel-encrusted knives, an ivory Taj Mahal. There were mementoes of war. And endless cases of silver spades and forks used for planting trees, laying foundation stones. Upper-crust bric-à-brac, she decided.

Finally she came to the end of the room and sat in a window embrasure on a beautiful tapestried cushion and surveyed the whole gallery. It was easy to imagine it full of graceful women in their sweeping dresses promenading about, laughing and gossiping, perhaps playing with a ball, a small dog joining in, fat babies rolling and sliding on the polished floor. It would not have been a museum then but full of noise and activity. This room must remember those days with longing.

That was true of the whole house, really, she thought. It had been built to house scores and now only a handful lived here. The walls must long for the fun to start again. Until then it seemed as if it were waiting.

Beneath her in the garden a man was hoeing a flowerbed, years of practice making his body move in a perfect flowing action. Gardeners had stood in that same place doing that same rhythmic hoeing through the ages. Across the park she saw Alistair and his father approaching on fine black horses. How many women had sat here waiting for their menfolk to ride across that parkland? It seemed that wherever she looked, the people and the scenery made a timeless tableau. The house would always be here, the situations would always be the same, only the people and their clothes had altered down the centuries.

She ran back down the long room, skidding on the highly polished floor, raced down the stairs and, after trying two doors, finally found the one that led into the stable yard as Alistair and his father clattered under the clock tower.

'Darling!' Alistair called, slipping from his horse. As he came towards her, leading the animal, she backed away nervously. 'Darling, I want to kiss you!' Alistair laughed at her.

'Does it bite?' she enquired anxiously.

'Of course he doesn't. See.' He kissed the horse on its muzzle. 'Major here wouldn't hurt a fly!'

'Trouble is,' she said with an apologetic laugh, 'I'm not a fly!'

'Good morning, Miss Reed.' Lord Upnor approached. 'How pretty you look!' He beamed at her.

'Isn't she a lovely sight to come back to, Pa?' Alistair asked proudly.

'She certainly is. I must say, it's a real pleasure to see a young woman without her face covered in goo.'

'Where's everyone else?' Jane asked quickly to cover her delighted amusement.

'In bed, probably,' Alistair explained.

'But last night Clarissa said something about riding . . .'

'That's as far as Clarissa's riding goes, talking about it, eh, Pa?' Alistair said dismissively. 'They've all got hangovers, I expect. They stayed up long after us.' He started towards the stable. 'Don't go away, Jane. Just let me get Major settled, then I want to show you something.'

'Not bothering with coffee, Alistair?'

'No, thanks, Pa. I want to show Trinick to Jane.'

'A good idea. See you both at luncheon, then.' The older man left his horse to a groom but Jane waited while Alistair rubbed down and watered Major.

They drove across the park for nearly a mile and then passed through gateposts from the top of which benign stone bears looked down on them. They followed a short shrub-lined drive and came to the front of a granite-built house, its walls covered completely in climbing plants. Virginia creeper swarmed over most of the façade, entwined with climbing roses and clematis. The walls of the house were a riot of colour. It appeared small, but this was only in contrast to the vast size of the main house.

Taking her hand Alistair led her through the open front door into a flagged hall, where an elegant, curving staircase swept up to the floor above, and light filtered through a large creeper-covered window on the half landing.

Admiring each room in turn, she followed him through the pretty house. Upstairs they stood in the largest of the five bedrooms, where a large bow window seemed to fill the whole of one wall. Jane exclaimed, 'Oh! This is my favourite.'

'What do you think of it?'

'Alistair, it's gorgeous. Whose is it?'

'It's mine. I shall live here now I've finished at Cambridge. I've got to get it decorated, of course, and find some furniture. It won't take long, and Pa says I can take whatever I want from the attics at Respryn.'

He rattled on about his plans for the house, but Jane felt a coldness growing within her as she thought of him so far away from London, and from her. As she had never looked to the future, she had never paused to think what his plans might be. She had been stupid; of course his time at Cambridge had to come to an end, she had known that. So why could she not have had the sense to think ahead and to wonder what his plans might be? She could have asked and then she would have been fore-warned, instead of finding out like this. How on earth was she to exist without him? How was she to get through all those days which now stretched bleakly before her? 'But your house in Fulham?' she eventually managed to ask.

'I'll keep that on, can't bury myself away down here all the time.' So she would see him sometimes; she wasn't to be cut entirely out of his life. 'Come here!' He dragged her down on to the bare floor.

'Alistair, someone might come!' she protested.

'No, they won't, and what if they do?' he asked, feverishly unbuttoning her blouse, searching for the softness of her breasts. She tried to resist but at his touch the familiar warmth flooded through her and she knew that it was too late.

'I've dreamed of making love to you here,' he whispered, his voice taking on the huskiness it always did when he wanted to make love. The sun, filtering through the greenery at the window, bathed their bodies. Oblivious to the bare boards and the dust, Jane responded to his caresses with a passion fired by fear of the future and anguish that this might be the last time, and further fuelled by anger at his mother's disapproval. She lay in the morning sunshine, Alistair's hands and mouth upon her. That woman could say what she wanted – it was Jane's breast in his mouth now, it was Jane's body he was about to enter. His mother had no control over his passion for her. For this moment, that was Jane's precious possession. Therein lay her power.

'I just knew that it would be perfect here in this room,' he said with satisfaction as he lit two cigarettes and handed her one. He propped himself against the wall, unselfconscious in his nakedness, his blonde hair hanging damp and dark on his forehead. When Jane went to pick up her clothes, he put out his hand to restrain her. 'Leave them, please. I want to look at you naked, here in this room.'

She settled down beside him, resting her head on his chest, listening to the beat of his heart as his pulse began to slow down. 'Well, what do you think of it?' he asked.

'Of what?'

'This house, Trinick, of course.'

'I told you, I think it's lovely. You're very lucky.'

'Do you think you'd like to live here?'

'I should think anyone would love to live here.'

'I'm not interested in "anyone". I want to know if you would like to live here?' Gently he lifted her chin so that he was gazing at her. 'You silly thing, Jay, I'm asking you to marry me.' He laughed as her mouth dropped open in astonishment. 'Don't look so surprised. What do you say? Yes or no?'

'Alistair, it's such a shock. I never thought about marriage, never allowed myself to. Heavens!' was all she could think to say.

'So, are you saying yes?'

'I don't know. It's all so sudden. I mean, your parents, what will they say?'

'I don't give a damn what my parents say, I'm not marrying my parents.' Agitatedly he lit another cigarette. 'I didn't realize it was to be such a difficult decision for you. I thought you'd say yes right away,' he said, a hint of petulance in his voice.

'Oh, my darling, I want to say yes, I really do.'

'Good, so that's settled.' He stubbed out his unfinished cigarette. He looked longingly at her full breasts, gently stroking them. He began to pull her towards him again.

'No, Alistair, we have to talk.'

'No?' he said, disappointed. Resting his elbow on the floor, he looked at her. 'What's there to talk about? It's settled and now I want to make love to you again, to celebrate,' he said with a triumphant laugh.

She moved away from him. 'It's not as simple as all that,' she insisted. Her concern removed any embarrassment she might feel at the ludicrousness of sitting naked, in midmorning, talking earnestly on the floor of an unfurnished room.

'It is.'

'No, darling, it isn't. For a start, you've never told me that you love me. I can't marry you if you don't love me.'

'That goes without saying.'

'It doesn't.'

'I'd hardly ask you to marry me if I didn't.'

'OK, then, say it.'

'All right! I love you!' He grinned sheepishly. 'Now can I make love to you?'

'No, I want to talk. I don't think you've thought this through.'

Alistair sighed and, seeming to resign himself to her refusal, propped himself back against the wall again.

'What haven't I thought through?'

'Your parents, for a start. What are they going to say?'

'I should think they'll be pleased. They both think it's time I got married.'

'Married, yes, but not to someone like me.'

'Why, what's wrong with you? Have you a past that I don't know about? Are you a reformed prostitute or do you have a criminal record?' He laughed at his own joke.

'Alistair, please, I'm being serious. Look, until this weekend I'd no idea how you lived outside Cambridge and Fulham. I'd no idea it was so frighteningly grand. They're expecting you to find someone more suitable than me, someone who won't be terrified by all this.'

'Good Lord, girl, if that's all that's bothering you? My father's as fit as a fiddle, I shan't inherit for years. Meanwhile, we live here, I learn to run the estate and you'll be learning a different life style. Simple, nothing to it,' he concluded, satisfied with the logic of his argument.

'But I could never be like your mother.'

'Maybe I don't want a wife like my mother.'

'Or Clarissa or Amanda. They know instinctively how to do things, they know what's what, they've been trained for it.'

'Heaven save me from someone like Clarissa!' He took her hand. 'Look, Jane, they like you, my father told me so this morning.'

'Yes, I think your father likes me, but that doesn't mean that he would want me as your wife. Of course your mother is going to say she does, or at least pretend she does. To do otherwise is to risk your running straight into my arms – any woman knows that. No, she doesn't like me, I sense it.'

'Rubbish!'

'It's true, she'll be disappointed in me.'

'Well, that's her problem. It's me you're marrying, and I can't see any problems that can't be surmounted. OK, so it's all very strange at the moment but you're intelligent. You'll soon learn and adjust, I know you will.'

'But at dinner last night. That argument about education – you could see then the chasm between me and them. Even then I let myself down by arguing so feebly. There was so much more I wanted to say but the little I did say did not amuse your mother.'

'Jane, you were splendid last night, I was proud of you. My mother will have respected you for standing up for what you believe. She likes a good argument and she'd regard that as a successful dinner. Had you sat and said nothing, then she would have been disappointed in you.'

'Oh, Alistair, you don't see, do you? You're so nice, you just don't realize.'

'Realize what?'

'It doesn't matter what I'm like, it matters who I am. That my dad works in a factory, that I'm working-class. They don't want that for you.'

'My parents aren't like that,' he protested. 'I've always been allowed to have what friends I want. For years my best friend here was the farm manager's son. No, they're not snobs, darling.'

'Friends are one thing, a wife is something entirely different.'

'Rubbish, you don't know them.'

'But last night, Alistair, I felt so out of everything. It's difficult to describe but I felt all the time that I was a spectator. You all seem to have a way, a code, even a language of your own and I haven't been given the dictionary.'

'Jane, my darling, sometimes I think you're bloody paranoid. I love you – there, I said it again. I like you, which is probably even more important than love in the long term. I need you, yes, I need you in my life. I want you to be the mother of my son. I don't give a damn about anyone else, I really don't.'

Jane felt a lump form in her throat at his words. 'Alistair, I love you. I would so like to marry you. I just don't see it happening, though.'

'Then you will? Thank God,' he said. 'You worry too much. We'll work it out. In a couple of years no one will know you weren't born to this life. Now can I make love to you?'

'What did you do last night after I went to bed?' she asked, coiling away from his outstretched arm.

'Hell, what's that got to do with this? You know what I did, I sat talking to Clarissa and Co for a while and then I sneaked along to you, and a right disaster that was.'

'Did you talk about me with Clarissa?'

'No,' he said, but his eyes did not meet hers.

'You're lying, Alistair. What was said?'

'Nothing, really . . . Oh hell, you know Clarissa.'

'I can imagine, then.'

'So, she's snooty about you. I don't see what that's got to do with you and me.'

'You rowed about me,' Jane said, nodding sagely. 'It could have a lot to do with us. Perhaps you feel sorry for me, perhaps that's what's made you suddenly propose.'

'Christ! How insulting can you be? How the hell could you think like that about me, after all this time?'

'It seems odd to me.'

'Glory be, you are a paranoid. Listen, Jay, I love you. I want to marry you. I don't give a damn what my bloody sister says or does. I've been thinking about this for some time. I just wanted it to be here, in this house. Romantic, that's me.' She could never resist his boyish smile.

'Oh, Alistair . . . I'm sorry.'

'I should bloody well think so. Now, can we make love again?'

'Please!' She clung to him.

Later, as they lay relaxed in each other's arms, she said, 'Alistair, there are a couple of things.'

'Yes?' he mumbled drowsily.

'If we get married, it's for ever for me. I couldn't bear it if you were unfaithful to me. I could never share you.'

'Married to you, my darling, is it likely that I would even want to look at another woman?' he replied, stretching contentedly. She leaned over and kissed him.

'The other thing is, can we keep it a secret for now? Let your mother get used to me first?'

'Sod! No!' He sat up, suddenly wide awake. 'I want to tell the whole world.'

'It would be best, Alistair.'

'No. We've decided. I'm sure you're wrong about my mother. She's a bit stiff and formal, that's all. Oh, crikey, don't let's go over all that again. Please!' He looked at his watch. 'Hell! The time! We'll be late for bloody luncheon, then she most definitely won't approve.' He laughed. 'Come on!'

Hastily they dressed, desperately dusting each other down. 'I guess it's pretty obvious what we've been up to,' he said happily. 'Let's race back. We might just be in time for a shower.'

12

Luck was with them and they were able to slip up to their rooms without being seen. Jane quickly washed and changed out of her dusty clothes and she and Alistair arrived simultaneously in the morning room at five minutes to one. Holding her hand, he led her in.

'Alistair, you are almost late,' his mother admonished him.

'Almost, but not quite!' He grinned goodnaturedly back.

Lunch was a simpler affair than dinner had been but, for all that, it was still formally served and lengthy. Jane tried hard to concentrate on the conversation as it eddied around her but it was difficult; she could not seem to focus her mind. She wanted to curl away in a quiet corner and blanket herself around with happy thoughts. If she and Alistair loved each other, everything could be resolved, their love would make sure of that . . .

'I'm sorry, Lady Upnor, I didn't hear what you said,' she apologized nervously.

'I asked if you had passed a pleasant morning?'

'Lovely, thank you,' Jane replied. Alistair grinned from ear to ear.

'Alistair, why are you grinning like a Cheshire cat?' his mother asked him pleasantly.

'I'll tell you later, Mother,' Alistair said, still grinning widely.

'I'll look forward to that. Meanwhile I'd be obliged if you would take that asinine expression off your face. It's preventing me from enjoying my luncheon,' she teased.

Jane looked around at the happy faces, laughing at Alistair and his mother. Maybe he was right and she was being paranoid? Did she worry and think too much, as he said? It could be that her problems were of her own making. After all, her uncle loved an argument, she'd heard him change his opinions just to get an argument going. Arguing was not necessarily quarrelling, she must try and remember that. At last lunch was over. Alistair spoke quietly to his mother.

'Come on, Jane,' he called across to her. 'Let's go for a walk.' He led her out. 'We're to meet my parents at four, they're both busy until then.'

For the next two hours Alistair took her around the grounds of the house, showing her his favourite childhood haunts. They walked quickly through the formal gardens, which would have held no interest for a little boy, to a summer house in a copse, built like a woodman's cottage and looking as if it were made of gingerbread. They crossed a patch of wild ground where weeds, some flowering, grew in profusion among the bushes and under the trees. It was in dramatic but still beautiful contrast to the formal gardens.

'This is called the wilderness,' Alistair explained. 'When I was a child this place used to terrify me. I was convinced it was the wilderness in the Bible, you know, forty days and all that. I always expected to bump into the devil himself here!' He laughed at the memory. Beyond the wilderness, they came to a long brick wall. Alistair opened a small green gate and led her into the huge kitchen garden. The high walls seemed to trap the smells of the herbs and ripening fruit in a heady and concentrated essence. She touched the walls, which were warm from years of sun. The buzzing of the bees filled the air. This was another place of timelessness. These gardens must have looked, smelled and sounded like this for centuries. The idea made it a comforting place to be. Alistair picked a peach for her.

'It's no fun any more,' he said sadly. 'When we used to pinch them from under the gardeners' noses, that was fun. Now I'm allowed to pick what I want the fun's gone out of it and I swear they don't taste nearly as good.'

She would have liked to linger, but he insisted they press on, he wanted her to see his favourite place on the whole estate. They walked through a pretty wood which in spring, he told her, was a carpet of bluebells. They passed an ancient swing, suspended from the branch of an old beech, the rope now frayed and rotting from the weather. She could hear water cascading and around the next bend in the path was a small waterfall tumbling over rocks and down into the dark-green, limpid pool. Trees inclined themselves over the sides, their branches trailing in the water like slender fingers.

'Alistair, it's a magic place.' She found herself whispering.

'Pretty, isn't it?' he said with a satisfied expression. 'If things are going wrong, half an hour here watching and listening to the water and I'm fine again.' They sat on a flat rock. 'We used to play ghosts here in these woods. We had a pantry boy called Henry, he'd cover himself with a sheet, pop a torch in his mouth and jump out at us from behind the trees. It was the most exquisite terror. I wonder what happened to Henry – he went off to the war. I must ask Pa.'

'Are the public ever allowed in here?'

'The gardens are open a couple of days a year – some pet charity of my mother's.'

'It seems such a shame more people can't see and enjoy it.'

'Heavens, mother would never allow that. "People will make it look untidy!" I can just hear her.' He imitated his mother's voice.

'But the house, it seems wrong that it can't be seen and appreciated.'

'Good God, Mother would have a fit! She has the proletariat in the garden twice a year on painful sufferance. I mean, she goes out for the whole day when it happens. Can you imagine what she would think of people crashing about in her house?'

'I think things should be shared.'

'This is subversive talk, Miss Reed, I don't think it would go down too well with my mother.' He laughed and kissed her teasingly.

They sat a while in silence, listening to the sound of the waterfall. She wished that the water would work its magic on her, but as the time drew closer and closer to four o'clock and their appointment with Alistair's parents, she could feel the now familiar constriction of her throat, the quickening of her heartbeat.

'Come on, sweetheart, time to go.' Alistair helped her to her feet.

She was so nervous that she did not take in the attractive proportions of the room they entered, nor did she notice Alistair's father standing by the fireplace. She was conscious only of the older woman sitting rigidly upright at her desk and she noted the studied way with which she slowly and deliberately capped her pen, straightened the letter she had been writing, and patted her immaculate hairstyle. Only then did she turn to face them.

'Well, and what is the big secret, Alistair?' she asked. Alistair was beaming from ear to ear.

'I've asked Jane to marry me and I still can't believe it but she accepted. Isn't it marvellous? Of course we wanted you two to be the first to know.'

The silence that followed seemed to Jane to last for ever, though in reality it lasted only a fraction of a second. But within that time, as if watching a film in slow motion, Jane saw with horrified fascination that Lady Upnor's back became even more rigid, she noticed the almost imperceptible lift of the older woman's head, noticed how she closed her eyes as if in silent prayer or pain.

'This is splendid news!' It was Alistair's father who spoke. 'My dears, I am so pleased for you both.' He took their hands and smiled at Jane. 'Alistair, I think you've made a very wise choice. And now I may call you Jane,' he said, and bent forward to kiss her cheek.

'This is a surprise,' Lady Upnor said eventually. 'You might have given us some warning, Alistair. That was very naughty! Champagne, Rupert, we should have champagne.' Lord Upnor picked up the house phone.

'There you are, darling, it's all right,' Alistair said to Jane. 'She seemed to have some nutty idea that you wouldn't approve, Mother.'

'Really?' said Lady Upnor in a glacial voice. 'What on earth gave you that idea?' She looked calmly at Jane but there was no warmth in her eyes and Jane knew for certain that she had been right.

The champagne arrived and Lord Upnor proposed a toast. 'Welcome to our family, Jane. We wish you both the best luck in the world and every happiness.' The toast was drunk but from the corner of her eye Jane saw that Lady Upnor said nothing and, although she raised her glass to her lips, did not drink.

'But what about your nursing? I thought you said only last night that you hoped to qualify?'

'I did, Lady Upnor, but that was before Alistair proposed to me. I think I'd rather be his wife than finish my training.' She tried to laugh but without success.

'And how do you think you will adjust to living in the country? I gather you are a city girl from what you were saying. Do you think you will settle? Alistair will have to spend a lot of time here away from the bright lights of the city. There's not much to do in the country. How will you like that?'

'I think I can adapt, Lady Upnor. I have never been one for the bright lights. I just want to be with Alistair, and so long as I'm with him I'd be happy down a mine shaft.'

Lord Upnor beamed at her response. 'When is the wedding to be?' he asked.

'As soon as possible.' Alistair was grinning again, he seemed unable to stop.

'I presume you will want a quiet wedding?' his mother asked.

'Why?' Alistair asked.

'Yes, I think that would be best,' answered Jane, and for once the two women looked at each other with mutual understanding.

'Well,' the older woman continued relentlessly, 'I hope that you know each other well enough. Marriage is a big step, Alistair, and one not to be taken lightly.'

'Yes, Mother, I know. But Jane and I have spent a lot of time together this past year, I think we know each other pretty well,' Alistair said seriously, the grin momentarily disappearing.

'You're a fine one to talk, Blanche. We decided to get married a week after we met.'

'That was different,' his wife said curtly, and, as if aware that her guard was slipping, quickly added, 'We were older.'

'Jane seems a sensible girl to me, very grown-up for her years.' He turned to Jane. 'You must arrange for us to meet your parents, my dear.'

'Thank you,' she answered, feeling only dread at the prospect.

'Have you spoken to her parents, Alistair?' his mother asked.

'Not yet, but I will, of course. I've never even met them, I think she's ashamed of me,' he said laughing.

'Don't be so ridiculous, Alistair,' said his mother, not joining in the joke. 'In that case I hope you won't mind my suggesting that we shouldn't say anything about this to anyone until you have spoken to them. It would hardly be fair, would it?'

'I suppose not,' Alistair replied, disappointment in his voice.

'That was a surprise!' said Lady Upnor, and with a complete change of subject, as if washing her hands of the matter, added, 'I suggest we all get changed for dinner early tonight. I want everyone down on the dot of seven, in case people arrive early. It is so difficult for people who live in the country and who have to travel long distances to arrive punctually.' It was obvious that they had been dismissed and the subject was closed.

Later, sitting alone in her room, Jane felt it had been a very unsatisfactory interview. She was certain she would have felt better had the woman voiced her objections outright, said honestly what she was thinking. Then at least they could have put their case. Instead, the woman had said nothing, expressed no pleasure, no displeasure. Jane was aware that she had witnessed someone exerting a great deal of self-control and she admired Lady Upnor for that. Had Alistair noticed that his mother had refrained from calling her by name, had not kissed them, had not drunk her champagne? She felt that Lord Upnor's reaction was one of genuine pleasure. If he could accept her . . . ? But that was a riddle to which there seemed to be no answer.

She had been proved right, but there was no satisfaction in being right on this occasion. Alistair loved her, that was the important point. She must try not to be so sensitive. She must watch and learn and, given time, maybe even his mother would begin to learn to like her.

13

As promised, May presented herself in plenty of time to do Jane's hair.

'Oh, miss, isn't it exciting,' she babbled.

'What, May?'

'Why, you and Lord Redland getting engaged. I think it's all so romantic.' The young girl giggled.

'But how do you know?' Jane asked astonished.

'You can't keep anything from us below stairs, miss! We thought something was in the wind. Lord Redland's never brought a young lady here before, and then the champagne.'

'But you can't jump to conclusions every time the family have champagne, May.'

'Yes, we can. His lordship hates the stuff, so it's only drunk on very important occasions – you see? Everyone wants to know what you're like, and I'm the only one that knows,' she said with pride.

Jane laughed at the girl's obvious excitement but made her promise, no matter how much people pestered her, to keep it a secret. Reluctantly, May promised, and started to do Jane's hair.

'I thought, miss, if we pulled it back like this, off your face, it would look ever so sophisticated. See?'

'Won't it look too severe?' Jane asked, studying her image in the dressing-table mirror.

'Oh no, miss, it'll look lovely. It'll show off your face something proper. And then I'll twist the rest into a super chignon.' Silence descended as May, frowning and with great concentration, brushed, combed, teased and coaxed Jane's hair into place, entwining it with small white rosebuds she had picked. 'There!' she eventually proclaimed, holding up a hand mirror so that Jane could see the back.

'May, it looks fabulous! The best hairdresser in London couldn't have done better.'

May beamed proudly at Jane's praise. 'Now the dress.' Gingerly she lowered the dress over Jane's head, taking care not to disturb her hair. 'Oh, miss, you look a treat!' May clasped her hands together with pleasure at her handiwork.

Excitedly, Jane twirled in front of the looking glass. The heavy folds of the black crepe dress, with scooped neckline and tight, wrist-length sleeves, made her look taller, an elegant stranger. 'Come in,' she called happily to the knock at the door.

'Wow! Jane, you look stunning,' Alistair exclaimed.

'Thanks to May. What do you think of my hair like this?'

'Fantastic. It makes your eyes look even larger – if that's possible. Haven't you any jewellery? Is it a bit plain?'

'Oh, Lord Redland, Miss Jane is perfect like that. It's more dramatic with no jewellery. Don't you think, M'Lord?'

Alistair studied Jane. 'Yes, May, you're right.'

'In any case, darling, I could never compete with the other women's jewels, could I?'

'Suppose not. But, I tell you, they're going to have one hell of a problem competing with your beauty,' he said proudly, while May beamed at them as if she had created this handsome pair single-handed.

As on the previous evening they all met for drinks, but the house party had grown to include two elderly couples whose name Jane did not catch. Four more friends of Clarissa's had arrived, including two girls who shook her hand casually and then swooped upon Alistair, making a great fuss of him. Tonight Jane could afford to be amused by their obvious flirtation with Alistair. She hugged the secret to her. He was not the available and highly prized bachelor they thought. Alistair winked at her across the room, and from his grin she felt certain that he was thinking exactly the same.

James Standard came over with a drink for her.

'Gin and tonic, isn't it?' he asked.

'Yes.' She laughed. 'Is anyone ever likely to forget?'

'You look really super, Jane,' he announced shyly.

'Thank you, James,' she replied, for once not blushing.

'I was wondering if you would like to have dinner with me one night back in London?'

'That would be lovely. I'm sure Alistair would enjoy that very much.'

'Ah, yes, well,' the young man muttered abashed, 'we must arrange something.'

Lady Upnor's fears were confirmed by the early arrival of some guests full of flustered apologies and obviously aware of her ladyship's views on punctuality. The room began to fill up. From the hearty greetings it seemed that they all knew one another. It still puzzled Jane why these people were so loud and why they had to shout. At school, she had always been taught that it was bad manners to make too much noise in company, and yet this group brayed and bellowed at each other with no such inhibitions.

'How do you do?' A strident voice made her jump. 'I'm Linda Talbot.' A tall, angular woman stood before Jane. Her wild grey hair looked as stiff as wire wool, and sharp intelligent eyes shone like a bird's in her lined face. She proffered her hand.

'Jane Reed,' she said, shaking the hand, surprised by the force of the grasp and the roughness of the skin.

'You dinner or house guest?'

'House. I'm a friend of Alistair's.'

'Splendid!' the loud voice proclaimed. 'He always had a good eye for the ladies. Bertie!' she bellowed. An equally tall and angular man responded to her call and approached, glass firmly clutched in hand. He had large spectacles that kept slipping down his nose and which he pushed back with the regularity of a metronome. 'Bertie, come and meet Jane Reed here, friend of Alistair's from London.'

'How do you do?' He stood back and peered at her through his spectacles. 'And what a fine filly you are, plenty of heart room and good quarters!' he said appreciatively.

Jane had never been compared to a horse before but from his smile presumed he was being complimentary.

'Bertie, you'll embarrass the poor girl, stop it. Do you hunt?' Linda Talbot asked Jane.

'No.'

'Pity.'

'Actually, I'm afraid of horses,' Jane confided.

'Afraid of horses, good Lord, did you hear that, Bertie, she's afraid of horses?' They both shook their heads in disbelief. Alistair joined their little group.

'Hello, Linda, Bertie, see you've met my Jane?' He kissed Linda on her weather-beaten cheek.

'Glad to see you've taken my advice, boy. Choose your women as you'd choose your horse!' Bertie guffawed.

'She doesn't hunt, though,' Linda said, astonishment still lingering in her voice.

'No, but she'll learn,' said Alistair, taking Jane's hand protectively.

Banks announced that dinner was served. Jane was fascinated at how smoothly the men paired off with women to take them in to dinner.

'How do they do that?' Jane asked Alistair, as the crocodile formed. 'How do they know who they are with?'

'Organization. Each man is told as he arrives who his dinner partner is to be. You see, never man and wife together.'

She noted and stored the information away. Tonight there must have been over thirty people dining. The table was longer than the night before, with even more silver on its immaculate damask. More flowers stood in frozen arrangements. More candles blazed, reflecting the women's jewels, making the diamonds flash in answer to the candles' glow. At least the spaces between the guests were not so wide tonight and normal conversation should be possible.

'Who is everyone?' she whispered. Alistair identified various people around the table.

'That pretty woman on the right of my father, she's the Duchess of Wessex: she's a good sport. On the other side is the Lord Lieutenant's wife – she's rather dull.'

'Where's your aunt?'

'Down there, see?' He indicated Lady Honor further down the table, already in animated conversation with a young man. 'He's an actor. Mother always sits Honor beside the artistic types, she's good with them. Have you met Admiral Sir Percy Wing?' Jane found herself being introduced to the guest on her right who looked like an illustration of an admiral, large, with a brown face and piercing blue eyes.

As the meal started and the babble of talk increased, she felt she should say something to the man beside her.

'My dad was in the navy,' she told the admiral.

'Really, my dear? How interesting. What was he?'

'A stoker.'

'Ah now, there's a fine breed of men. Without them the war at sea would certainly have been lost.' He warmed to his theme. 'In action I always felt for them, down below in the dark and heat, not knowing what was going on topside, just hearing the fearful noise. In many ways it was easier for us seeing the hell of it all. Splendid fellows!' he repeated with enthusiasm.

'Who are splendid fellows?' the Duchess asked from across the table.

'Stokers. This young lady's father was one.'

'Really? How awful for him,' the Duchess said with sympathy. 'One of my gardeners was a stoker, it was dreadful, he told me. Do you know that sometimes the only way they could keep those poor souls down in the stoke hole was for an officer to pull a gun on them? Dreadful.' She clucked.

'I didn't know your father was in the navy,' Lord Upnor joined in. 'Where did he see action?' The Duchess and the admiral as well as Alistair's father leaned forward with interest. Jane told them what she knew, apologizing that it was so little because her father rarely spoke of his war to anyone.

'Poor fellow,' the Duchess said sympathetically. 'He probably had a bad time. It would be better for him if he could talk, get it out of his system,' she advised Jane kindly.

'The Russian convoys were some of the worst,' and the admiral began to tell them of his war.

At least tonight she was enjoying the company, but still the meal seemed endless. The food was a little better, the white sauce was less in evidence, and the dishes were more imaginative. However, with so many guests to be served, the food tonight was not lukewarm but stone cold, since everyone had to wait until the last person had been served before starting. The meal ended, and with sinking heart Jane rose with the other ladies to retire to the drawing room.

As was becoming her habit she found a window seat and gazed out on the park below. To her surprise the Duchess chose to come and sit beside her. Jane decided that duchessses were easy people to talk to as she chattered away, answering the woman's questions about everything under the sun.

'May I ask you a question?' Jane asked.

'I doubt if I'll know the answer, I'm terribly thick.' The Duchess twinkled back at her.

'Why do the men stay behind in the dining room after we have left?'

The Duchess laughed. 'Irritating, isn't it? It started, I suppose, when man used to pee in pots kept in the sideboard.' She laughed even louder at Jane's shocked expression. 'Then, after they'd stopped their filthy habit, liking the custom, they continued it. Then, it was alleged, they discussed politics and important affairs deemed far too boring and difficult for our shell-like ears.' She snorted. 'It also gave us gals a chance to go to the loo and powder our noses so that the men could continue to think that we never sank to such basic functions. Now, of course, it just gives them a chance to drink more than we do, gossip, and tell dreadful stories.' Jane roared with delight. 'You've given me an idea. It is an antiquated notion. At my next dinner party, I shall have the men leave the room, and we gals will down the port! Yes, I shall. What fun! What's more –' but the Duchess was interrupted by Lady Upnor.

'Constance, my dear, I do want you to meet Mrs Griggs, whose husband has just bought the old Frangers place. I think she might be a good committee woman for you.'

'Excuse me, my dear,' the Duchess said, 'I'll be back for more interesting social discussions with you. Duty calls.' She sighed and, to Jane's astonished amusement, winked at her. She had somehow imagined that a duchess would never wink. It seemed here, in this company, that all the rules of her childhood were being turned upside down. As the Duchess moved away, Lady Honor came to join her on the window seat.

'Jane, my dear, I've been let into the secret, I'm thrilled to bits.' She took Jane's hand.

'Thank you, Lady Honor,' Jane said with relief. 'Who told you?'

'My brother. He's very chuffed. I think it's all too divine. Clever Alistair, I'm so thrilled for him. You're so right for him – sensitive yet practical – you'll be a great help to him. He never fitted into the 'young man about town' image like Clarissa and her friends. He had more sense! I love him dearly, you know.'

Jane felt tears of gratitude prick her eyes. Lady Honor squeezed her hand again.

'Don't you worry, my dear. It will all be fine.' She smiled her beautiful smile and for a sweet moment Jane could not even begin to think what it was that threatened her. They watched the throng of women.

'Isn't the Duchess lovely?' Jane asked.

'Duchesses always are. Dukes being so important and so rich and so thin on the ground, they get the pick of the bunch.'

'Then why aren't you a duchess?' asked Jane.

'Sweet little Jane! That's a long story, I'll tell you one day.'

A number of women drifted over and Lady Honor introduced them to Jane. Jane found that they seemed to fall into two categories: those who asked her if she hunted and moved away when she said no, and those who asked her if she played bridge and also moved off at the same answer. She confided her findings to Alistair's aunt.

'That's rural life in England for you. Why do you think I spend most of the year abroad?'

'Do you?'

'Yes, mainly in Italy, I have a villa there.'

'So you're *that* aunt. Alistair told me about your house.'

'Yes, he loves it there. It's gorgeous and I find the company more amusing. And it's easier to be naughty abroad!' She laughed.

The men began to filter back into the room. Jane watched anxiously for Alistair, but he was one of the last. He was in deep conversation with his father, the older man's arm about his shoulder. Seeing her, they came straight over.

'My dear Jane, such a sparkle in your eyes, it's a wonder that people have not guessed your secret.' Lord Upnor smiled at her.

'Yes, Rupert,' said Lady Honor, 'I think all this secrecy is very stupid. It would have been such fun to announce it tonight.'

'It would have been fun, Honor, but Blanche is right: we should not say anything until Jane's parents know. It would not be fair.'

'Well, telephone them, Alistair, and ask them,' Lady Honor suggested practically.

'They're not on the telephone,' Jane explained.

'Of course not, how silly of me,' said Lady Honor. 'How about sending them a telegram?' she added brightly.

'Heaven forbid! They would think I was dead or something. It would give them a terrible shock,' Jane protested with a laugh.

'It is possible for people to survive without that infernal machine and telegrams, Honor, although we realize you couldn't,' Lord Upnor teased his sister affectionately. They moved away, leaving Alistair and Jane alone at last.

'Enjoying yourself?' he asked.

'Yes, I am. The Duchess is a poppet and people aren't nearly as scary as I thought.'

'See, no need to worry. God, Jane, you look so beautiful tonight, I wish we could slip away,' he said with longing.

'Alistair, help with drinks, there's a dear.' It was his mother. For the rest of the evening, every time Alistair managed to sit with Jane, his mother would come to drag him away.

Some of the younger guests clattered noisily off to a party. Alistair declined and Jane was surprised that Clarissa, pleading tiredness, did not go either.

The evening was a long one and it was not until well past one that the other members of the house party had gone to bed and Alistair's parents returned from seeing off their last guests.

'Let's have a last snort. Just the family,' Lord Upnor suggested, pouring the drinks himself for he had dismissed the servants. 'That was a very successful evening, Blanche, very successful.'

'I'm glad that you think so. I was mortified.'

'Mortified, what on earth happened?' her husband asked, concerned. Lady Upnor swung round to Jane, her face blazing with anger.

'Was it absolutely necessary to tell everyone that your father was a stoker?' She spat the last word out with vehemence.

'I was asked,' Jane replied, her voice already beginning to tremble. Alistair crossed the room and stood protectively at her side.

'You could have just said he was in the navy. It was not necessary to be quite so specific.'

'The admiral asked me what he was.'

'Blanche,' — Lord Upnor put a restraining hand on his wife's arm — 'I think you are going too far.'

Lady Upnor wrenched her arm away from his hold. 'You might not mind, Rupert, with your wishy-washy liberal ideas. I mind very much — that the whole county should know just how working-class my future daughter-in-law is.'

'Future daughter-in-law!' Clarissa exclaimed, looking with dismay from Jane to Alistair. 'You bloody fool, Alistair, you can't marry her. Sleep with her if you must, but for Christ's sake don't be such a bloody fool as to marry her. God, what are people going to say? Marrying that! How could you?'

Jane stood rooted to the spot with shock. Alistair, his father and aunt all began to defend her loudly at the same time.

'Clarissa, you will apologize,' Jane heard Lord Upnor say.

'I won't, Father! Never! I've nothing to be ashamed of. He's the one who should be doing the apologizing. I knew she was a scheming little tart the first time I met her,' she screeched. 'Hell, the only thing acceptable about her is her name, for Christ's sake.'

'You little bitch!' Lady Honor said with quiet vehemence.

'My name?' Jane asked, perplexed.

'If you have to marry a peasant, the least you could have done was choose a foreign one — at least her accent wouldn't give her away then,' Clarissa said spitefully.

'My name, what about my name?' Jane persisted, but no one seemed to hear her.

'I will not have my future wife spoken to like this,' Alistair stormed.

Lady Upnor sank on to the settee; her cast-iron self-control had completely disappeared and her hands shook as she turned angrily on her husband.

'This is all your fault, Rupert. You and your woolly ideas. You've filled that boy's head with your liberal rubbish. This would never have happened had he gone to Eton, as I wanted. Now you've ruined his life,' she concluded dramatically.

'Blanche, stop talking such utter rot.'

'Imagine, the future mistress of Respryn – it doesn't bear thinking about. How on earth do you think she'll manage?'

'I can learn,' Jane said weakly. She, too, was shaking.

'Learn? Don't be so stupid, girl. One is born to this position, you can't learn how to behave.' The babble around Jane was dreadful as everyone began arguing at once.

'Please, shut up!' She put her hands over her ears, trying to shut out the fearful sound.

'Don't you speak to me like that, young woman! This is my house. I shall say what I like in it!'

'My house, Blanche, and I object to Jane being treated in this way.'

'Rupert, I despise you,' Lady Upnor hissed at her husband.

'Oh, please, will everyone stop arguing about me?' Jane broke in desperately. 'Please, I can't stand it!' Alistair put his arm round her and Honor gently took her hand. 'I don't understand this hatred. We love each other, how can you spoil it all? And what the hell has my name got to do with all this?' She felt obsessed with the conundrum of her name.

'I meant at least your name is acceptable, even if nothing else is. You could have been called something unutterably awful like Sherry or Dawn,' Clarissa finally explained.

Jane began to laugh, a dangerous shrill laugh. 'You can't be a real person, Clarissa. You judge people by their names, their names! You're mad!' She was angry now, angry at such stupidity, angry at their rejection. Her eyes glinted with fury as she shook off Alistair's and Honor's touch. 'Who the hell do you think you are? How dare you? Why do you keep talking about me as if I'm some terrible virus? I'm a human being with pride, too! I'm not going to apologise to you, Lady Upnor, for being me – why should I? And how can you expect me to deny my father? I'm proud of what he did in the war. I'm proud of me.' She gulped desperately for breath. 'I'm sorry if I'm the cause of a family row. I don't want to cause any trouble, but I would like to point out, Lady Upnor, that I was invited here as a guest, even if you have decided not to treat me as one.' Flushed with her anger she turned to Alistair. 'I want to go to bed now, I can't cope with scenes like this . . .' She turned on her heel and, with head held very high, went to the door. Her hand on the doorknob, she paused, turned and faced them. 'And, Lady Upnor, if the truth is known, I'm not too sure if I want to be a member of this family!' She slammed the door shut behind her, but the noise of their argument mounted in a crescendo which she could still hear despite the thickness of the wood.

Alone in her room she allowed herself to cry. She lay on her bed, her body racked with long sobs, the tears pouring down her face and dampening the pillow. This should have been the happiest day of her life, but her worst fears had been realized.

She must have cried herself to sleep with exhaustion for she awoke, with a start, as her door burst open and Alistair stormed in.

'Pack,' he commanded. 'We're leaving.'

'But, Alistair —'

'No buts. Come on, I'll give you a hand.'

Within minutes she had collected her few possessions together and, still in her evening dress, her pretty hairstyle dishevelled and falling about her ears, she miserably followed Alistair down the stairs. His father stood in the hall.

'My dear Jane, I am so sorry. I cannot apologize to you enough.' He took her arm and looked with concern at her tear-stained face.

'Lord Upnor, I'm sorry too. I never wanted to be the cause of trouble between Alistair and his family.'

'My dear sweet girl, you must not blame yourself for one moment. What Alistair is doing is the right thing. You are to be his wife: his duty and loyalty must lie with you.' He kissed her gently on the cheek. 'Drive carefully, Alistair,' he said.

The car roared across the park, its headlights picked out the faces of the startled deer. In his anger Alistair crashed the gears and the little car protested. She huddled low in her seat, shivering more from misery than cold, as Alistair headed the car towards London.

She would always remember the wretchedness that she felt on that journey, the myriad emotions that engulfed her. Fury at being so insulted. Humiliation and shame at what she had endured. Pain at the rejection; and surprise at the realization that, after all that had happened, she felt a fierce pride in her father and her background. Puzzlement that she should be treated as if she had some dreadful disease just because she was working-class. And a gut-freezing fear that his mother might win and that she would lose Alistair.

Near Winchester, Alistair turned to her and said, 'I love you.' Those were the only words he spoke on the entire journey, hunched as he was over the steering wheel, driving far too fast, his mouth set in an angry line. For once Jane did not mind the speed, felt no fear. She was too far down her pit of misery even to notice.

14

They let themselves into the house as dawn tinged the London sky. Without consulting each other, they headed wordlessly for the bedroom. Miserably Jane sat on the side of the bed, her whole body slumped in dejection.

'Jane,' he said, and put his arms about her. She leaned against him. He sat stroking her hair, gently caressing her until, like a child, she slept in his arms. She would never know that he sat for hours holding her, watching her, guarding her. She would have feared nothing if she could have seen the expression of tenderness on his face as he sat the creeping dawn away and resolved what to do. Eventually he laid her gently on the bed and covered her; in her exhaustion she did not even stir. He bathed and changed and then went downstairs, for he had a lot to do.

The sound of church bells woke her. She lay for a while listening to the familiar sound. She loved Sundays in London: they would often walk for miles through the deserted streets . . . Then she remembered.

'Oh no!' she wailed to herself. 'Why couldn't I have stayed asleep?'

She heard noises from the kitchen and crept down. Alistair was making breakfast for them as he so often did. She stood watching him, memorizing the way he moved, the shape of his head, the way his hair fell forward as he bent intently to his cooking. She stored away the picture in her mind so that in the future she would easily be able to recall him.

'Good morning, Jay.' He smiled at her. 'You look a right old mess, you know.'

She looked down at her lovely black dress, now all crumpled, and became aware, for the first time, of her tangled hair and the fact that her face must be swollen from crying.

'I wanted to see you,' she said simply, holding her arms out to him. He came over, took her in his arms and kissed her swollen face tenderly.

'It will be all right, darling, I promise.' Gently he led her to the stairs. 'Now, you go up and get washed and I'll finish our breakfast.'

In the bathroom she was shocked at what she saw in the mirror. What a wreck she looked! She sponged her face and the ice-cold water began to reduce the puffiness about her eyes as it washed away the salty streaks which had made her skin feel stiff as parchment.

'That's better,' he said later when she returned to the kitchen. 'Here.' He set a plate of bacon and eggs before her.

'Alistair, I can't eat.'

'Yes, you can, you need it. I insist. You've had an exhausting night; you'll feel better for something to eat.'

She forced the food into her mouth but it seemed to taste of nothing, as if she were chewing cardboard. She managed only half her food but drank, almost with desperation, large mugs of sweetened tea. He had said that everything would be all right but her fear remained, as they ate in silence.

'Jane.' He spoke eventually. 'I must apologize for last night. I really had no idea that my mother and sister thought like that. I can't explain to you how ashamed I feel. You were right all along.' He looked despondent, his dark eyes reflecting his concern for her.

'It's all right, really. I'll get over it. At least I expected it. I won't say "I told you so"!' She tried to laugh but it failed.

She looked at her hands, studying them carefully. She knew what she had to say, but feared to say it. She sat silently shaping and reshaping the words in her head. Finally she looked at him. 'Alistair, I don't want to come between you and your family . . . I realize you love them too and, it . . . well, darling, it just wouldn't work if you were torn in two . . . Maybe your mother's right . . . perhaps it would be better if we split up now . . . ?' Her whole speech came in quick breathless bursts, the words competing with sobs, which finally won.

Quickly, Alistair came round the table, knelt beside her, took the hands she was so ashamed of and kissed them. 'Oh, sweet Jane, you've got it all the wrong way about. I'm not going to have my family damage us, or come between us. It's made me more determined than ever to marry you and the sooner the better now. Come on, Jane, no more tears. You never warned me that life with you would be so damp,' he teased her as gently he dried her eyes.

'Alistair, I thought I was going to lose you,' and she shuddered at the thought.

'What rubbish! You'll find I'm much more difficult to get rid of than that.' He grinned. 'At least you can be proud of the way you stood up for yourself last night.' He got to his feet, chucking her under the chin, trying to coax her to laugh. 'Now, I've been very busy this morning. I've had a long talk with my father on the phone—he's in complete agreement with my plans, and he sends his love to you. I've phoned my lawyer and he's arranging a special licence for us to get married. This week, I hope. We have to go to your parents and get their consent since you're under twenty-one. My lawyer is bringing round a consent form today. Once we're married, then I think we should go away for a few weeks to let the dust settle a bit. There is one problem, though.' He leaned forward and looked at her intently. 'I have to return to Respryn, Jane. It's what I've spent all these years training for and I can't let my father down.'

'What about your mother?'

'My mother will pretend that all this hasn't happened; I know her. In fact, we need see very little of her: she tends to spend most of the week in London. We can have our own set of friends. So life there will be possible for you, if not altogether ideal. You do understand the position I'm in?'

'Yes, darling,' she said uncertainly.

'So, we settle at Trinick. We make love morning, noon and night. We'll have hundreds of children and live happily ever after. Agreed?'

'Agreed.' She smiled for the first time that morning.

The front-door bell rang. 'That'll be the lawyer.' Alistair jumped up to answer but returned with Lady Honor, who immediately took Jane into her arms.

'My poor, sweet, little thing! What a ghastly night, what a drama! Are you all right? I thought you were absolutely marvellous, Jane. What an exit! I do hope you didn't mean your threat – some of us are quite nice, you know.'

'That was temper, Lady Honor. I didn't mean it. I want to marry Alistair more than anything else in the world.'

'Thank God for that! And cut the Lady nonsense – call me Honor. You're family, or almost. Now, I'm off to Italy today and New York on Thursday but I simply had to see you two before I left. When are you getting married?'

'This week,' Alistair answered.

'Good, I'm glad to hear it. Very sensible. I should make it as soon as possible. I'd like you to have my villa for your honeymoon, if you have nothing else planned.'

'Thank you, Honor, fantastic. I can't think of anywhere I'd rather take Jane, it'll be perfect.' The front-door bell rang again. 'That must be the lawyer this time. Cheer Jane up, will you, Honor?' Alistair rushed off to attend to the lawyer.

'I've a presie for you, Jane. Look.' Honor held out a red velvet box to the young girl. Gingerly Jane opened it. Nestling inside was a beautiful four-stranded pearl choker with a diamond clasp.

'Oh, Honor, it's lovely! I don't know what to say,' Jane exclaimed, stunned.

'It was my mother's. I know that she would have liked Alistair's wife to have it.'

'Honor, it's the most beautiful thing I have ever seen. I'll treasure it. Thank you.' Honor patted her hand. 'I can't help how I was born, Honor,' Jane suddenly burst out. 'I can't understand how one's background can be so important, how if it happens to be the wrong one you're treated as if you're an untouchable.'

'I know, my dear.'

'You don't think it matters, my being me, do you?'

'Loving each other and being good to each other, that's all that matters.'

'But, Honor, I just know Lady Upnor won't give up. She will still try to break us up. I sensed it right from the start. At least, I knew there would be trouble. I tried to warn Alistair, but he was so convinced that everything was going to be all right. I really feel sorrier for him – after all, it's his family.'

'Alistair's strong enough – don't you worry about him. He won't give in, it's Blanche who'll end up the loser. No, you must never let anyone come between you and the man you love. I did, you know. Years and years ago, I fell in love with someone my mother didn't approve of and she forced me to give him up. I've often wondered how my life would have been if they had let me marry Bob. Maybe I wouldn't have had so many husbands. And, you know, Jane, the silly thing is, he's a cabinet minister now and frightfully respectable. Stupid, isn't it?' She laughed, but Jane noticed a look of sadness cross her lovely face.

'But you're not against me, nor is Alistair's father. It's Lady Upnor. Why?'

'She's showing her middle-class origins, darling. They're the worst snobs of all.'

'What do you mean? You mean she wasn't born an aristocrat?'

'Good God, no! There was an awful shemozzle when Rupert fell for her. Her father was a manufacturer of something or other, filthy rich of course, but anyone in trade was beyond the pale to my mother. Blanche still has an enormous chip on her shoulder.'

'But she plays the part so well.'

'Of course. Expensive education, right clothes and the right training work miracles, but when the chips are down all her nasty, sordid middle-class pretensions come out.'

'But you'd think that she'd be even more understanding, then.'

'Heavens, no! She buried her origins: no one remembers any more. Now you'll stir them all up again. I can just hear the old ducks in the county trotting out, "Of course it's history repeating itself. The Redland boys always marry beneath 'em . . ." What a hoot it will all be!'

'But, Honor, I don't think any of it matters.'

'Of course it doesn't, darling, that's the great joke. You know it and I know it, only fools don't know it.' She lit a cigarette. 'What are your plans now?'

'We have to go and get my parents' consent. I'm under twenty-one.' Jane pulled a face.

'Problems?'

'Probably. My father's slightly left of Lenin. He'd abolish hanging and bring in the guillotine for aristocrats if he had his way.'

'Well, make sure he chops Blanche first!' Honor chuckled with joy at the prospect.

'What's the joke?' Alistair had appeared in the doorway.

'We're having a profound sociological discussion,' Honor announced airily.

'So early?' Alistair laughed.

'Anyway, darlings, I must fly – literally. I'll tell my staff to expect you any day next week.'

'You're an angel, Honor. I wish you could come to the wedding,' said Alistair. 'Any chance?'

'No, darling, impossible. In any case, with my track record, I find weddings deeply depressing affairs. I feel I put a curse on them if I attend, like the wicked fairy. Now, be happy, the pair of you. Don't let anyone interfere.' And she was gone.

'I like your aunt so much. She seems to understand,' Jane said as they heard the car drive away.

'She's probably enjoying all this secretly. She loathes my mother and I know it's mutual. Come on, sweet,' Alistair said cheerfully, pulling her to her feet. 'Now it's your lot's turn.'

There was little traffic on the road and they drove quickly out of London and through Kent. She guided him through the warren of narrow streets in her home town.

Alistair sighed. 'My God, this is depressing. You told me your childhood was bleak but I wasn't prepared for it to be as gloomy as this.'

'But all towns have rows of streets like this – you must have seen similar ones.'

'Yes, but I never really noticed them before. I never knew anyone who had to live in them. It makes one see them in a different light.'

She debated with herself whether or not to knock. Usually the sound of an unexpected knock on the door would throw her mother into a fit of anxiety. Certain knocks were expected and came at regular intervals – the rent collector, the club man, an insurance agent – but in these streets an unexpected visitor usually meant trouble. On the other hand, if she just walked in with Alistair her mother was likely to be angry since she hated to be taken unawares. At least a knock would give her warning and time to hide the papers under a cushion, or to stuff the washing in a cupboard.

Her father answered the door, in shirtsleeves and slippers.

'Oh, it's you,' he said without enthusiasm, turning his back to return to the living room, where he sat back in his armchair and resumed reading the newspaper. They followed him.

'Dad, this is Alistair Redland.'

Alistair stepped forward, his hand outstretched. 'Good morning, sir.' Her father looked at the proffered hand and the young man suspiciously. He shook hands and grunted something.

'Where's Mum?'

'Out the back, yakking as usual.'

She left Alistair standing in the middle of the tiny room, looking lost and embarrassed, and quickly went to find her mother, who was in the garden gossiping across the rickety fence with their next-door neighbour.

'Hullo, Mum, Mrs Green.' The two women looked up in surprise at her sudden appearance. 'Excuse me, Mrs Green, but, Mum, I've brought a friend home to meet you.'

Mother and daughter walked up the narrow garden path.

'Who is it?'

'Alistair. The one I told you about.'

'You could have warned us. You can't stay to dinner, the joint's not big enough.'

'That's all right, we didn't plan to, it's only a flying visit.'

'You look terrible. What have you been up to?'

'Nothing. Too many late nights probably,' she lied and her mother sniffed, knowing she lied.

They found Alistair very relieved to see them. He had stood there in silence and her father had not said a word to him. At least her mother was polite and offered him coffee.

'I think Alistair would prefer beer, Mum.'

'No, Jane, coffee will do fine,' Alistair interrupted.

'I really think you would prefer a beer, Alistair,' Jane said pointedly, imagining his puzzlement if faced with her mother's idea of coffee, which was boiled milk, a teaspoon of Camp coffee and far too much sugar.

'Well, if you have beer that would be very nice,' Alistair complied.

'Charlie, get the gentleman a beer,' her mother ordered.

'That's my dinner beer,' Jane's father complained.

'Get the beer, Charlie,' her mother said with barely controlled anger.

'I'll get you some more, Dad,' Jane promised. Still muttering under his breath, her father reappeared with his jug of beer. They settled themselves around the dining table while her father sorted out the glasses. She had never thought about the smallness of the room, but now, after her visit to Respryn, the contrast was ridiculous. This one room would have fitted into the drawing room at Respryn a dozen times. It was not that they were untidy; it was that the room was so small that one person made it look crowded. With the four of them it was chaotic. Her father took out his tobacco tin and laboriously began to roll a cigarette.

'And to what do we owe the honour of this visit?' he enquired, unpleasantly.

'I wanted you to meet Alistair, Dad.'

'You this Cambridge chap she's been knocking about with?' her father asked.

'Yes.'

Her father concentrated further on the rolling of his tobacco. An awful silence hung in the air.

'Actually, sir,' Alistair began, 'I've come to ask your consent to marry Jane.'

Both parents looked at her simultaneously.

'Your nursing, Jane. You won't be allowed to finish. Oh, what a pity!' her mother exclaimed.

'I realize that, Mum.'

'But after all the sacrifices I made! You should have a qualification, Jane. You never know what's going to happen, and with nursing you can always get a job anywhere.'

'She will be well provided for, Mrs Reed, I can promise you that.'

'Quite honestly, young man, I'd rather you waited until Jane has finished her course and is qualified. It all seems such a waste of time otherwise.'

'We don't want to wait, Mum. Having decided, well, we want to get married now. I've never been really happy nursing, I'll be glad to see the back of it.'

'First I've heard of it,' her father interjected. 'If my memory serves me right, you made enough fuss to start nursing, against my wishes. Now suddenly we're to believe that you don't like it.'

'We won't go into that now, Charlie.' His wife stopped him. 'Where would you live? Finding a house isn't too easy these days, you know.'

'Alistair is going to help his father and we'll have a lovely house of our own. It's so pretty, Mum, right in the country, with two bathrooms, imagine that, Mum. And it's got a huge garden and no traffic.'

'You could come and stay any time, Mrs Reed, any time you wanted. All you'd have to do is phone and we would come and get you.' Alistair smiled. Jane could see that her mother was beginning to succumb to his charm.

'It all sounds lovely.' Her mother sighed wistfully.

'And this job with your father, what does that entail?' her father enquired.

'At first I'll be watching and learning.'

'Oh yes, what?'

'Farming.'

'And what sort of wage can you expect?' her father persisted.

'Well, I won't actually get paid.'

'Not paid? Then you're a bloody fool. If you're worthy of hire then you're worthy of pay commensurate with the work you do.'

'It wouldn't actually be necessary, sir.'

'Money not necessary? What a strange world you must live in, young man, where there's no need for money. How will you eat, may I ask?'

'Oh, I'm sorry, sir. I misunderstood. I already have enough money to support us from my investments.' Alistair smiled broadly.

'Investments?' Jane's father's eyes glinted dangerously. 'You mean you make money sitting on your arse while the poor bloody workers tear their guts out for bloody peanuts?'

'Charlie . . .!' Her mother tried to stop him.

'I don't think that's quite fair, sir. If no one invested then there would be no work for anybody.'

'If the parasites didn't invest, then the government would be forced to step in and then maybe the profits would go to the right people, the workers who created the profits in the first place, and the fucking drones in the City would get nothing!' Her father sat back with a satisfied expression on his face.

'But it doesn't work that way, sir,' Alistair said almost desperately.

'I know it bloody doesn't, more's the pity. But it will one day, oh yes, one day it will!'

Alistair nervously tightened the knot of his tie. Jane sat helpless, knowing too well that when her father got into his stride, there was no stopping him. He would continue to pursue, needle and goad Alistair.

'But you said something about farming. That's a proper job, Charlie. Farmers work really hard,' her mother interrupted helpfully.

'Real farmers do,' her father sneered. 'He isn't going to work that hard if he isn't going to get paid for it, is he? Stands to reason.'

'It's like an apprenticeship, really. A way of learning to manage the estate –'

'Estate?' Her father pounced eagerly on the word.

'Yes, sir. So that when I inherit –'

'Inherit?' Her father's eyes shone with anger as he spat the word out venomously. 'Estate? Inherit? Inherit what?' he said as if the words left an unpleasant taste in his mouth.

'Well, everything, sir. The land. The house. The title.'

'Title?' Her father's voice was too controlled now. It frightened Jane.

'Oh, of course, sir, I'm sorry, you probably don't know,' Alistair continued blithely. Jane desperately pulled a face at him across the table but his eyes were intent upon her father's face. 'Silly of me, sir. I'm Viscount Redland and my father is the Earl of Upnor.' Jane noticed her mother surreptitiously straightening her skirt.

'Jesus Christ!' The oath exploded from her father's angry and distorted face.

'Oh, that's nice,' her mother simpered.

'The answer's no,' her father announced loudly.

'Dad!'

'No, and that's that.'

'But I'll be twenty-one next year and then you can't stop me.'

'Right, do what you bloody well like next year but until then the answer's No, understand, N-O.'

'Might I ask why, sir?' Alistair asked.

'You can, young man, and I'll tell you. I've no truck with the likes of you and never have had and never will have, and I won't rest until your sort's dead and gone for good.'

Alistair reeled back in his chair at the vehemence in her father's voice and the hatred which showed in his eyes.

'But, Dad, Alistair can't help who he is – it's an accident of birth.'

'He can't help it, Jane, I agree. But I can stop you joining them and stop you I will. Christ, I'd be a laughing stock on the shop floor.'

'Typical of you, that is, Charlie. As usual, it's not Jane you're thinking of but your stinking bloody pride and what your bloody workmates will say. When have you ever thought of her, I ask?'

'I am thinking of her, you stupid cow – it won't work, it never does. She'd be miserable. Stick with your own class, that's what I say. His lot won't ever accept her: she'd always be an outcast.'

'On the contrary, sir, my father likes Jane very much and is very fond of her already.'

'Your father, you say, what about your mother? I notice you don't mention your mother,' her father said sharply.

'It goes without saying, sir.'

'Nothing goes without saying, sir.' Her father sarcastically emphasized the 'sir'. He stood up. 'Well, if that's all you came for, I'm off to the pub.'

'Charlie, you can't leave like this. If Jane's made up her mind and he seems a nice young man –'

'You women are all the same. A good-looking boy, smarmy manners, a title, and you're wetting your knickers with excitement. Women, you're all pathetic!' He slammed out without saying goodbye.

'Whew!' Alistair whistled.

'I did warn you,' Jane said miserably.

'My husband is an animal, um . . . Viscount . . . an animal!' Jane's mother twisted her hands in anguish. 'He's done nothing for Jane, it's been all me. He's never taken an interest, then suddenly he decides to play the father.'

'Can Mum sign?' Jane perked up at the thought. Alistair dug out the form and studied it.

'It doesn't make it clear, it says "parent or guardian".'

'Then it doesn't matter which parent signs it. You sign it then, Mum.'

'Jane, I daren't. It's hell living with him as it is.'

'Please, Mum,' Jane pleaded.

'No, I'd better not.'

The three of them sat looking at the form on the table. Jane was the first to speak.

'Mum, I think you'd better sign. I'm pregnant!' Her mother stared at her, a look of disgusted horror twisting her face.

'Jane, how could you? You dirty little bitch, you slut, letting a man do that to you!' She shuddered. 'My God, the shame, the whole street's been waiting for something like this to happen, they'll laugh their heads off over this.'

'Jane?' Alistair looked at her quizzically.

'It's true, Mum, you'd better sign it. So the street laughs, but it'll be better than having a bastard grandchild, won't it?' She pushed the form across to her mother.

'That's me finished with you, Jane, I don't ever want to see you again. How could you, after all I taught you? And after all I've done for you – the sacrifices, all those hours in that bloody factory; and this is how you repay me! You can count your lucky stars that this young man here has some sense of decency and wants to do the right thing by you. It's more than you deserve, my girl. You give me no bloody choice then, do you, you mucky little cow!' Jane watched her mother signing the paper, writing her name with an angry flourish. The set of her mouth was even more bitter than before. Jane felt a flicker of anger at her mother's predictable reaction.

'Thanks, Mum, you won't regret it.' Jane hurriedly snatched up the form and stuffed it quickly into her handbag. 'Come on, Alistair, let's go.' Alistair said a hurried goodbye and her mother replied automatically. Alistair drove the car down the street, round the corner, and stopped.

'Jane, what the hell was all that? You're not pregnant, are you?'

'No. But I knew it was the only way to get one of them to sign.'

'But that was cruel.' He sounded shocked, but there was a small glimmer of amusement in his eyes.

'I know, I didn't want to lie to her but it seemed the only way. I'm afraid that if we don't get married right away, we never will. And I'm her child – I can be as bitchy as they are.'

He put his arms about her. 'Of course we'll get married. Do you think that we should go back and explain to your mother, though?'

'No, Alistair.' Jane laughed a hard little laugh. 'You heard her, she's not worried about me, only what the street will say. And I can assure you that the fact that I'm not pregnant is irrelevant to the street. They will presume that I am, anyway.' She thought a while. 'I'll tell her when we're safely married.'

They drove out into the country and stopped for lunch at an old coaching inn. As he was eating his roast beef, Alistair began to laugh.

'What's the joke? I thought that was a bloody awful scene back there,' Jane complained.

'Jay, it's the funniest thing that ever happened,' he spluttered over his food. 'Imagine, neither of us is socially acceptable to the other side. God, it's so incredibly funny!' She began to laugh with him. He pushed his plate away, unable to eat more for laughing. 'I just wish that my mother could have heard all that.'

15

On the Monday they applied for and were granted their special licence to be married on the following Thursday.

Alistair was immersed in a whirlwind of preparations, making arrangements with lawyers and the bank, as well as travel plans.

With only £14 to her name, Jane had to face the problem of what she was to wear at her wedding. She would have liked to buy a new suit but that was out of the question. It was then she remembered Mrs Baum's suit. A year ago a grateful patient had given her a grey silk outfit by Hartnell, hardly worn. Jane was used to receiving chocolates, nylons, the odd scarf, but nothing like this. Mrs Baum had insisted she accept it, saying the silk matched her eyes, but Jane had never worn it, thinking it too dressy for her. She did not even know why she had bothered to pack it for this holiday. While Alistair was out, she tried it on. Twirling in front of the mirror, with full skirt billowing round her, she admired the pinched-in waistline, the tight-fitting bodice. It really was perfect; she wished she'd been nice to the patient now. She studied her reflection thoughtfully – perhaps a little too long. She'd ask Mrs Evans to help her alter it.

Jane took the bus to Battersea, the suit in a box beside her. She was excited at the prospect of telling her second family the news.

'My, Jane! What excitement, taken me really by surprise,' said Mrs Evans over tea. 'I do hope you're not rushing things.'

'I love him so much I could burst.'

'And how are you so certain it's love?'

'Oh, I know it is. I mean, I wouldn't mind peeling potatoes for him or washing his socks!'

Mrs Evans laughed. 'That sounds like true love. Mind you, I don't think you'll be doing much washing or peeling of spuds, from what you say.'

'It's like a fairy story, isn't it?'

'It's that all right. With the mother as the wicked fairy.'

'She's dreadful, Mrs Evans, really terrifying. Ten thousand times worse than Matron.'

'From what you say, she may be called 'Lady', but it doesn't sound as if she behaves like one to me. I've never heard of such rudeness!'

'It was so unexpected. I knew she didn't approve, but she'd hidden it well until that last night, and then . . . wow.'

'Mind you, Jane, what that woman says is right in some ways. You're taking on a lot and even more will be expected of you. Marriage is hard enough without the problems and added responsibilities you'll be facing.'

'I'll learn, Mrs Evans, I know I can.'

'Let's hope you're right, Jane. It's a shame you'll have to resign. Have you seen Matron?'

'No, I'm too frightened to. I'll write.'

'Matrons have that effect.' Mrs Evans laughed. 'Now, what about this skirt that needs shortening?'

Jane slipped on the skirt and stood on the kitchen table while Mrs Evans began to pin up the hem. 'You were wrong to lie to your mother, though. I'd never have expected it of you, Jane,' she said through a mouthful of pins.

'I know.' Jane blushed. 'But, you see, if I don't marry him now, I know his mother will work on him and stop it. I couldn't risk that.'

'If he really loves you, nobody can change his mind, not now or in six months. And, Jane, I want you to write to your mother straight away and tell her what you've done – it's wicked, Jane, the poor woman will be sick with worry.'

'Yes, Mrs Evans, I will, you're right. You will come to the wedding, won't you? Thursday at noon.'

'Come? You try and keep us away – we'll all be there, I promise. Do stand still, Jane, or this will take hours.'

'I want Sandra as my witness. I hope she can get off duty. If she can't make it, will you stand in for her?'

'Don't you worry, my love, Sandra will be there, if she has to abscond to do it.' She stood back. 'Is that the right length? Right, you put the kettle on, Jane. This'll take me just a minute to hem up.'

It really had been the most satisfactory day, Jane thought, as she returned to Fulham. As she let herself into the house she heard raised voices coming from the sitting room. She peeped around the door in time to hear Roderick Plane saying, 'But the poor woman is prostrate with grief.'

'She brought it on herself,' Alistair answered stiffly.

'Hullo,' Jane said shyly.

'Dear Miss Reed.' Roderick bore down on her and took her hand. 'Such exciting news!' From his reaction Jane could only presume that overnight she had become a person of importance to him. 'Miss Reed, I am here from Lady Upnor. She is in such distress. She wants to see you.'

Jane looked across at Alistair. 'It's up to you, darling, you must do what you want,' he said.

'Will you come?' she asked hopefully.

'No, I'm afraid I can't. I've arranged to meet my father at his club in half an hour – it's important. After that I want to take you out for a very special dinner. Do you realize, we haven't celebrated yet? You go if you want – Roderick will take you – but if you don't want to, I'll quite understand.'

'I'll go,' she quickly decided. It was the last thing she wanted to do but she knew she must. She had to grasp at any chance to patch things up: perhaps that was what Lady Upnor was hoping, too.

'That's a good girl,' Roderick lisped and bustled her out of the house to his waiting car. He talked incessantly as they travelled through the rush-hour traffic but she barely listened to what he had to say. The car halted in front of an imposing double-fronted house which dominated the square in which it stood.

When Banks opened the door to them, Jane greeted him as if he were a long-lost friend. He bowed solemnly and led them across the black and white marble hall and up the wide imposing staircase; the brass handrail glinted in the evening sun pouring into the stairwell from a glass dome above. Generations of Upnors gazed down stiffly at them from the gilded frames which marched up the walls of the staircase. The house was intimidating in its opulent elegance. The butler opened shiny mahogany double doors and led them through the large drawing room and into a smaller sitting room, where the curtains were half drawn and a single lamp glowed in the corner.

'Miss Reed and Mr Plane, Your Ladyship,' the butler announced in a loud voice. In the dim light Jane could just make out Lady Upnor lying on a chaise longue, a book unopened on her lap. She raised her arm feebly and Jane was not sure if this was to dismiss Banks or to welcome her.

'Miss Reed.' Lady Upnor indicated a seat beside her. 'I thought we should talk.'

'Yes, Lady Upnor, I agree.'

'Please sit down. No, Roderick, I want you to stay,' she said as the little man sidled towards the door. Jane saw him lick his lips as though in anticipation at the interview ahead.

'Miss Reed, the other night was so unnecessary.'

'Oh yes, Lady Upnor, I do agree,' Jane said warmly and smiled with relief.

'Had you not been so tactless, none of this unpleasantness need have happened.' Jane felt her face stiffen, her smile disappear. 'However,' Lady Upnor continued, 'one thing is certain: you do appear to care for my son and so you won't marry him, will you?'

'I don't understand,' Jane said shakily.

'Miss Reed, you're an intelligent young woman, you must comprehend how unsuitable you are for the position my son will eventually hold. It is imperative that he marries someone of his own class. You could only harm him, and, if you really care for him, you will not want to be an encumbrance to him.'

'I don't see that I would be an encumbrance, as you put it. I want to marry him because I love him. I think our love for each other is all that matters.'

'I am fully aware of what you think, Miss Reed, but I must disagree with you. This love that you speak of . . .' Lady Upnor shuddered as she used the word 'love'; she spoke it reluctantly, almost as if she were uttering an obscenity. She coughed discreetly. 'Love is not enough. For one thing, it never lasts, and when it is no more, what are you left with? Two completely unsuitable people, with nothing in common, inflicting unhappiness upon each other.'

'I think that love can last.'

'That is because you are young and naive, Miss Reed. You will become a burden to my son, a very embarrassing burden.'

'I thought I'd come here to be friends with you.'

'I assure you, Miss Reed, I choose my friends with far greater care than my son does.'

'My God, Lady Upnor, you're so bloody rude!'

'How dare you speak to me like that?' The older woman sat bolt upright, her book clattering to the floor. 'Such impertinence!'

'Then watch what you say to me!' Jane retorted quickly, with anger.

'Ladies, ladies,' Roderick intervened. 'Please, this will get us nowhere.' He turned to Jane. 'What Lady Upnor says is true, my dear. You have no idea what will be required of you in the future.'

'I can learn.'

'My dear girl, we are talking about breeding, you can't learn that,' Roderick continued in a patient voice as though speaking to a small child.

'I gather Lady Upnor has learned,' Jane said sharply.

'Well, really!' Lady Upnor exclaimed.

'Behaviour is ingrained,' Roderick persisted. 'It cannot be acquired. Small things, I agree, like not calling Banks mister, those can be learned, but not the important attributes like grace and style.'

'I call Banks mister, because he is a mister and he's older than I am and it would be rude to call an older man by his surname.'

'But Banks is a social inferior and is used to being called Banks. It embarrasses him to be called anything else.'

'Have you ever asked him? And, in any case, this whole argument is because I am socially inferior, too. In that case, how can I be superior to Mr Banks?'

There was no answer to Jane's logic and Roderick slumped back into his chair, giving the floor once again to Lady Upnor.

'Is there anything you have not told us about that perhaps we could help you with?' Lady Upnor continued, forcing herself to speak calmly.

'I don't understand,' said Jane.

'Miss Reed, what do you want from me?'

'I've told you, I want to marry Alistair and I wish we could all be friends.'

'Might I, Lady Upnor?' Roderick insinuated himself again. Lady Upnor waved her hand at him in a gesture of exasperation. 'Miss Reed, what Lady Upnor is trying to say, I think, though of course being a lady she is finding it very difficult, is, well, are you pregnant and do you want help with an abortion? These things can be easily arranged. No one need know.'

'Pardon?' Jane exclaimed in horror.

'Oh, my God,' Lady Upnor sighed. 'She says "pardon"!'

'Are you pregnant?' Roderick repeated.

'I heard you the first time! No, I bloody well am not and if I was, what business would it be of yours?' she shouted.

'Well then,' the unctuous little man continued, 'how much do you want? Lady Upnor is quite prepared to be generous, say £2000? That's a good sum of money, my dear Miss Reed.'

'I don't believe this is happening!' Jane exclaimed, jumping to her feet. She was shaking with rage. She wanted to smash the face of this horrible man, see his blubbery lips split wide open. 'You can stop calling me "dear", I'm not your dear,' she yelled angrily at him. 'I'm getting out of here. You tricked me into coming . . . I don't want to hear any more from either of you!' She stumbled across the room and, as she left, her unbelieving ears heard Lady Upnor wail, 'But Roderick, he can't marry her – she says "pardon"!'

She sped down the sweeping staircase. Banks, standing in the hall, watched her descend with genuine concern on his face as he saw the expression on hers.

'Mr Banks?' He looked at her enquiringly. 'Mr Banks, do you mind me calling you mister?'

'It's unusual, Miss Reed.' He thought for a moment. 'But I must confess I find it rather charming.' He smiled.

'Thank you, Mr Banks,' she said with a sense of triumph.

He opened the door for her, she stood on the steps and, taking a long, deep breath, put two fingers in her mouth and summoned a taxi with an ear-splitting whistle. As she got in the cab, she turned to see the discreet Banks standing on the steps, a broad grin on his face.

In the taxi she began to calm down a little. She felt as if she had been in a bad play and someone had forgotten to give her her lines. The whole situation was turning into a farce. She began to laugh.

'What's the joke, miss, can anyone join in?' the taxi driver asked her.

'People, that's the joke.'

'People! That says it all, miss. They are the biggest comedy around. Learn that and you'll be all right, I can tell you.'

She was relieved, as she paid the taxi off, to see that the lights were on and that Alistair had returned. She found him in the sitting room, mixing himself a drink.

'How did it go?' he asked. She started to laugh.

'You can't marry me, I say "pardon".' She laughed and could not stop laughing, and the laughter began to hurt. She leaned against the wall weakly but still the laughter came, rising to a crescendo. Alistair stepped across the room and slapped her face sharply. Immediately she stopped, surprise registering on her face.

'I'm sorry, darling, but you were hysterical. I think you need a stiff drink,' he suggested.

She sat with her drink while Alistair coaxed out of her a confused account of what had happened at his mother's.

'Shit!' he exclaimed. 'The old bitch, and I thought I knew her. In front of the greasy toad Roderick, too.'

'But why can't I say "pardon"?' It was the only thing she could think of, it was becoming a fixation.

'You're supposed to say "What?" or "I beg your pardon". It's one of those words that are supposed to label people, like saying "toilet" instead of "loo" or "serviette" instead of "napkin".'

'You mean, on top of everything else, I've got to start relearning my own language?' she asked in disbelief.

'No, my love. You can say what you damn well like. I love you when you say "pardon".' He smiled broadly at her and playfully smacked her rear end. 'You see, there's another one, you'd say "bottom" and I'd say "arse"!' He laughed.

'No, I wouldn't, I'd say "bum".' She laughed too as she took a swipe at his.

But she remained perplexed. Everything about this family puzzled her. They spoke too loudly, almost shouting at each other. They roared with laughter, displaying filled teeth and tonsils. They made noises when they ate, they burped – why, she had even heard Lord Upnor fart, and instead of ignoring it, everyone had joked about it. And now there was a vocabulary which was different from everything she had learned. A code by which people graded each other. And what was oddest of all was that if she had said 'What?', her mother would have hit her. Of one thing she was certain: she was not going to bother; people would have to take her as she came or not at all. She was not going to change for anyone.

That night Alistair took her to the Connaught. Family treats, all his life, had been held here, he explained. She gazed around the opulent, plush room which, although full, seemed to have more waiters than clients. All round her were faces she recognized, faces from the cinema, the newsreels. Alistair was amused at the simple pleasure she took in spotting the famous. She, in turn, was amused by the attentive service as her napkin was unfurled, her wine glass refilled, her peach peeled, her cigarette lit.

'Makes me feel just like a baby,' she said, as she sipped her liqueur contentedly.

On the way back to the house, Alistair stopped the car on the Embankment. They leaned on the parapet where they had stood the night they had first met.

'Jane, I want to give you this.' She looked down: in his hand he held a beautiful, antique sapphire and diamond ring.

'Will you marry me, Jane?'

'Yes, please, Alistair, oh yes.'

He slipped the ring on her finger. 'It had to be here,' he said, 'where we first kissed.' And he kissed her again. It amazed Jane that after a year, the minute Alistair touched her, her body reacted, needing to be caressed and closer to him.

Remembering the scene at his mother's, Jane began to laugh.

'What's so funny?' he asked, bewildered. 'This is a serious moment.'

She told him about her defiant whistling for the taxi and Banks's amused smile. He started to laugh too, clutching her shoulder.

'At last I know the real reason why I'm marrying you,' he said.

'Why?'

'Think how useful you'll be when I'm old and riddled with gout and it's pissing with rain in Bond Street.'

16

Jane walked jauntily towards the house in Fulham. She swung her carrier bags almost triumphantly. In one was a perfect wisp of a hat; in another, dove-grey, peep-toed shoes. And lastly there was a dreamy white nightdress. She would have liked to buy the gloves she had seen in Harrods – Italian, with the new gauntlet effect – but her money had run out. She would have to make do with an old pair. However, in her present mood, the lack of new gloves was a minor disappointment. Everything was working out perfectly. Her passport was ready at Petty France in her future name. They could collect it after the wedding in time to catch the flight to Italy. Everyone seemed bent on helping them. Everyone, that is, except Lady Upnor. Jane shook her head, hair flying loose, in a gesture of defiance. She had decided not to worry about her. There was nothing she could do about Lady Upnor's attitude. Nothing and no one, she was determined, would mar the day after tomorrow. She was in love, she was loved, that was all that mattered.

She continued along the leafy road, the early evening sunshine dappling the pavement. She was smiling, she could not seem to stop smiling. People passing her, seeing her smile, continued on their way, made happier by the young woman's evident joy.

As she put the key in the door, the telephone began to ring.

'Miss Jane Reed?' A man she had noticed standing by the gate had followed her up the path.

'Yes?' she replied, smiling, struggling to turn the key and get to the phone.

'Francis Greenstone,' he announced, digging in the pockets of the rather grubby raincoat he wore, despite the heat, and produced a card. Juggling with the bags and the key, Jane popped the card between her teeth.

'Excuse me. Minute. Phone,' she muttered. And, despite the card, she still managed to smile. She slipped into the narrow hall and picked up the receiver. 'Hullo?' The door slammed shut. She swung around, her smile disappearing immediately. The man had not only followed her into the hall, but had shut the door and was leaning against it, his arms folded, watching her. Jane felt afraid. 'What the hell?' She started. 'No, not you,' she explained into the phone. She looked at the man and then at the telephone, unsure which to attend to. 'Yes, hullo?' She finally decided.

'Miss Reed?' a voice asked. 'This is the *Daily Bugle*. Is it true that you are to marry Lord Alistair Redland on Thursday?'

'Yes.'

'And is it true that Earl Upnor's objecting?' She slammed the phone down, her stomach lurching, making her feel suddenly sick.

'Press?' the man asked. She nodded, white-faced, her mind racing. 'I'd take the phone off the hook, if I were you,' he said, almost kindly. As he spoke, the phone rang again. She jumped and looked at it, wide-eyed with alarm. 'Shall I answer it?' he asked helpfully, and picked up the receiver without waiting for her reply. 'Hullo,' he barked into the instrument. 'It's for you,' he said, handing her the phone.

'Who the hell was that?' she heard Alistair demand.

Remembering the card, now crumpled in her hand, she glanced at it. 'Oh, darling, he's a reporter, please come quickly, I don't know what to do or say.' Her voice expressed the mixture of relief and alarm she was feeling. Relief that he was not a burglar, and alarm that he was from the press, an unknown quantity, but one that made her feel vulnerable.

'Don't say anything,' Alistair ordered and, before she could say more, the phone went dead. She replaced the receiver on the cradle and immediately it rang again. Without a word Francis Greenstone swooped on it.

'Too late, mate, *Echo* here, piss off!' He disconnected the call. 'As I suggested, Miss Reed, you'd better leave it off the hook. Do you know what, I could do with a cup of tea, and you look as if you need one, too.'

Wordlessly she led him down the stairs into the basement kitchen and put the kettle on. As she did so, she noticed the man peering into her carrier bags.

'Do you mind, that's mine.' She grabbed the bags and stuffed them under the table.

'For the wedding outfit? Any chance of a preview photograph?'

'No! Certainly not!' She glared angrily at him, and then added, 'Do you take sugar?' The mundane question struck her as ludicrous in the circumstances.

'Three, please,' he answered. As she spooned the sugar into his tea he

noticed her ring. 'Nice ring you've got there. Part of the Upnor collection
– or wouldn't his lordship cough up?'

'There's no point in you staying, I'm not going to say anything to you.'

'I can't go, I'd get the sack. I'm only doing my job. Shall we wait for
your fiancé? It's all the same to me. You make a good cup of tea, by the
way.' He smiled amiably at her. As they sat in silence, drinking their tea,
he seemed totally oblivious to Jane's anger and discomfort. After what
seemed an age she heard Alistair's key in the lock. She rushed to meet
him on the stairs.

'Alistair, thank goodness you're here! Get him to go, darling, please,
he gives me the creeps.'

'Good evening, Lord Redland. I've just been trying to have a chat with
the young lady here.'

'Get out,' Alistair ordered. 'We don't want anything to do with damn
reporters.'

'What you want and what you get are two different things, M'Lord. I
suggest you cooperate with me. It'll be better in the long run.' The
pleasant tone of his voice made his words sound even more ominous.
Jane shuddered.

'I don't want to give any interviews,' Alistair said.

'I think you will, M'Lord. You see, at this moment one of our
reporters is with Miss Reed's parents and if you don't cooperate with
me, then we'll just use that interview instead.' He smiled. 'Got a match?'

'Oh, Alistair, Mum and Dad can't cope with this.'

'What we want, Lord Redland, is complete exclusivity and in return
we'll keep the other papers away from the old couple, and that's a
promise. All we want is an interview with you two and a nice photo with
the parents, OK?'

Despondently, Alistair shrugged his shoulders. He picked up his car
keys.

'We'll take my car, Lord Redland, more satisfactory in the long run.'
Again he smiled, but each time he did so, it made Jane even more
alarmed. It was an automatic, unfeeling smile. A professional smile, she
realized.

Outside, the man whistled and a car drew up, driven by a young
woman with bright blonde hair. 'Lottie Carter,' he said, introducing
them. The young woman barely acknowledged Alistair and Jane as they
climbed into the back seat and grimly held hands. Francis Greenstone
swung around in his seat and leaned over towards them.

'Now, just a few questions, like where you met, that sort of thing.'

Alistair coldly told him that they had met through mutual friends, and added no details.

'And has Miss Reed met your parents?'

'Of course.'

'Sticky, was it?'

'I don't know what the hell you mean.'

'I mean, Lord Redland, the difference in your backgrounds. She's not exactly what your parents expected, I'm sure.'

'Mr Greenstone, I don't like your attitude. Of course my parents have no objections. Why should they? They have met Jane, like her and are very happy that we're getting married. I don't know where you got these peculiar ideas.'

The reporter did not look convinced. 'Bit sudden, though, isn't it? Any particular reason?' he asked, looking pointedly at Jane's stomach. Alistair shifted his arm and put it protectively around Jane's shoulder.

'I don't like the implication of your question.'

'I'm sorry about that, Lord Redland, but I'm only doing my job.' There was a detachment about him and Jane knew he was telling the truth. It was just a job to him, it didn't matter one way or the other what they did or said; he would write a story, print it and move on to the next one. The feeling it gave her, of not being of any real interest to him, was a chilling one.

Halfway to her home, they stopped at a mock-Tudor road house for a snack. The two journalists were obviously on expenses and determined to make the most of it. Jane ordered orange squash, she wanted to keep a clear head. Alistair ordered beer, but Francis and Lottie ordered double whiskies and steak sandwiches. 'Best steak sandwiches in the Home Counties,' Greenstone announced, but the last thing Jane or Alistair wanted was food. Jane stood up to go to the lavatory. 'Where are you going?' asked Francis Greenstone. Jane swept past him without answering.

Lottie joined her in the ladies'. The young girl stood at the mirror playing with her hair. Jane locked the cubicle door, glad to be alone for a moment. She supposed it was funny, really, that the only place she could find peace was in a lavatory. Funny or sad? One or the other. When she came out the girl was still looking in the mirror. Jane washed her hands.

'You've been sent to spy on me, haven't you?' she said accusingly.

The girl laughed. 'Well, I'm supposed to keep an eye on you, if that's what you mean.'

Jane angrily piled her make-up into her bag and swept out to battle her way through the crowded bar back to Alistair.

'Alistair, we've been kidnapped!' she announced dramatically, her eyes flashing with indignation. 'That girl's been spying on me.'

'Yes, darling, I'm afraid so. They're protecting their story.'

'But what possible interest could we be to anyone?'

'Plenty, Miss Reed,' the reporter interrupted. 'You're a big story. It's not every day of the week a working-class girl like you marries a lord, now is it?'

'But how the bloody hell did you find out where we were?' Alistair asked.

'Impending marriages are always pinned up on the notice board in the Register Office – they're inspected every day. It was clever of you to put your father's address and not your own, though. It took the others a time to find out where you were.'

'You didn't answer my question,' Alistair persisted.

'I was luckier, I had a tip-off. Not only where you lived but also that there were – how shall we put it – a few difficulties?'

'But who told you? Nobody knows.'

'Sorry, Lord Redland, I can't give secrets away like that – just an impeccable source, close to the family, as we say,' he said, tapping the side of his nose with a grubby finger.

Alistair and Jane looked at each other. 'Roderick Plane!' they said in unison. The reporter grinned but said nothing.

'The bastard!' exclaimed Alistair angrily. 'The slimy little bastard.'

'It's a very lucrative business, informing on friends in high places,' Greenstone told them.

'That's the end of that little creep's weekend house-partying,' Alistair said bitterly.

'I didn't say it was him, Lord Redland.'

'You didn't have to. He's the only person who knew anything, outside our families.'

Francis Greenstone abruptly stood up. 'Now, if you two lovebirds are ready, I think we'd better be on our way.'

They drove in silence and an hour later pulled up at Jane's house. The lights were on in the front room, a sure sign of momentous events. The front door was wide open and from inside the noise of a monumental row could be clearly heard. They rushed in, in time to see one young man hitting another and splitting his lip open, then grabbing his camera and removing the film.

'Hullo, Jimmy, what seems to be the problem?' asked Francis Greenstone.

'Local press, Francis, he won't leave.'

'Oh no? I think you'd better, sonny,' and so saying he manhandled the astonished young reporter out of the door, throwing his camera after him and slamming the front door firmly shut. They found Jane's mother in the front room.

'Thank God you're here! It's been like a zoo and with your father on nights, I've been at my wits' end,' Jane's mother complained.

'Mrs Reed, I'm so sorry, I'd no idea,' Alistair apologized.

'That's all right, dear, it's not your fault, it's these wolves. Disgusting behaviour! That poor local reporter – that was Maggie Baker's eldest, Jane – he was only trying to do his job.' She glared at the London reporters. Jane thought that if she heard just one more person claiming that they were only doing their job, she would scream.

'And what do you think of your future son-in-law, Mrs Reed?' asked Francis Greenstone, ignoring her thunderous looks with nonchalant detachment.

'He's a very nice young man.'

'And what about him being a lord?'

'He can't help that, can he?' she snapped back.

'Splendid.' The reporter laughed. 'What a quote! And what about your daughter becoming a lady?'

'She's one already, thank you very much, young man.' Her mother sniffed audibly. Alistair and Jane looked at each other astonished at the assured way her mother was handling the reporter.

'Mrs Reed, have you got a nice photograph of Jane we could use?'

'Sorry, no. I gave it to that nice young reporter from the local paper.'

'You did what?' Francis Greenstone groaned. 'How the hell did you let that happen, Jimmy?'

'Sorry, Francis, I was in the loo when he arrived, she must have slipped it to him then.'

'That's our bloody photo exclusivity gone for a burton.'

'It was my photograph, I can give it to anyone I want. I didn't "slip it", as you put it, young man. He asked for it and I gave it to him. I really don't know who you people think you are,' Jane's mother said angrily.

'Of course, Mrs Reed. Never mind, what's done is done. At least he didn't get a photo of you three together. How about our taking one now? Would you mind?'

Lottie stopped filing her nails long enough to pose them and to take the photos of three very stiff and unsmiling people.

'Are you going to the wedding, Mrs Reed?'

'I doubt it, if people like you are going to be there.'

For the first time in the whole evening Jane and Alistair laughed. Try as he might, the experienced reporter could get nowhere with Jane's mother. Resigned that no more information was forthcoming, Francis bundled them back into the car, leaving the young reporter, Jimmy, guarding Mrs Reed from the attentions of the other papers.

The car sped back to London. It was a silent journey. Francis appeared to be asleep, but both Jane and Alistair were afraid to talk to each other in case he was not. So they sat lost in their own thoughts, tightly holding each other's hands.

Finally, the car ground to a halt in front of the loading bay of a tall building. They were ushered out of the car and through a door, and only when the door was firmly shut were the lights put on. Francis led them to a lift, and they travelled several floors up to emerge in the newsroom of the newspaper. The place was a hive of chaotic activity, reporters frantically typing, shouting across the vast room at each other. Several telephones were ringing; some were answered, others ignored. No one took any notice of them. Francis opened his desk and took out a bottle of whisky which he offered them and this time they did not refuse. For the first time in the whole evening Francis left them alone, but no doubt one of the many staff in the room had been instructed to keep an eye on them. The frantic activity began to decline, desks were opened and bottles appeared. Finally Francis returned.

'Our compliments,' he said and handed them a sheet of still-wet photographs. They were terrible: in all of them they looked stiff, rigid and far from happy.

'Can we go now?'

'Not just yet, Lord Redland, if you don't mind. We'll run you home, of course. I must say you've been very helpful. If I might suggest, I'll pop round first thing in the morning, keep the rest off you, though it's a bit late for them now.' He laughed.

A sudden gigantic shuddering reverberated through the building.

'What on earth's that?' Jane asked alarmed.

'It's the presses, Miss Reed. The paper's been put to bed, we can all go home.'

'You mean it's safe for you to let us go. I presume that all the presses of your rivals will be rolling too by now?' said Alistair.

'Well, give or take a few minutes, yes. Nothing will stop them now except the Queen dying or World War Three starting.' He laughed again.

Wearily Jane stood up. It had been the most extraordinary evening in her life. No one had been unpleasant to them, but what had happened was far from pleasant. For a whole evening they had lost control of their own lives and wishes.

By now Lottie had gone home and it was Francis who drove them, at breakneck speed, back to Alistair's house. 'See you in the morning,' he called cheerily as he drove away.

'We want to have a lie-in,' Alistair shouted to the departing car. As they turned on the pavement they were blinded by the popping flashbulbs of a dozen cameras.

'Lord Redland, could you comment on the rumour that your father has disinherited you?' shouted a voice from the darkness.

'Oh, go to hell, the lot of you!' Alistair stormed into the house, slamming the door with a resounding crash.

17

The phone rang at six in the morning. No sooner had Alistair angrily replaced the receiver than it rang again.

'Don't these bastards ever sleep?' Alistair muttered bitterly.

'Francis Greenstone suggested I took it off the hook, yesterday. It'll never stop. I'll make us some tea.' She slipped a shirt of Alistair's over her naked body and quietly padded down to the kitchen. It was going to be a lovely day. She wound up the venetian blind to let the sun in and opened the window. The figure of a man popped up from nowhere, framed by the window.

'Miss Reed? Do you have any comment to make . . . ?' A camera shutter clicked.

'Leave us alone!' she screamed, slamming the window shut and racing out of the room and back up the stairs. 'Alistair! Alistair! Come quick, they're everywhere! They're even outside the kitchen window.'

'Bloody bastards! It's unbelievable,' he muttered as he pulled on his slacks and a pullover. 'You'd think there were enough people who actually wanted publicity.' She heard him run down the stairs, and then the sound of raised voices, Alistair shouting, the door slamming. Jane huddled under the sheet, beginning to fear that at any moment a camera would poke out at her from somewhere else. Nowhere seemed safe. Alistair returned with their tea.

'Can't we complain to their editors?' Jane asked.

'It's the bloody editors who sent them in the first place. Thank God, we'll be away from all this tomorrow.' He peered out through the curtains. 'The street looks full of them. They're like locusts.' He looked at her sitting white-faced and dishevelled, the sheet still clutched about her. 'My poor darling Jane, I'm sorry about all this. I expect you always planned a lovely white wedding in a rustic church with bridesmaids – the full works – and look at the carnival this is likely to turn out to be.'

'I'm O K, darling. They startled me, that's all. I mean, you don't expect it, and me in your shirt too.' She managed a wan grin.

'I feel so useless. I don't know what to do to protect you. I should have guessed this was going to happen.' Alistair banged one hand into the palm of the other with frustration. 'The press have sniffed around me all my life, but nothing like this.'

They spent the rest of the day in a half-light with all the curtains drawn because as soon as a crack appeared they saw the sinister, black snout of a camera. Francis Greenstone arrived at nine, as he had promised, and, to her surprise, Jane was glad to see him, hoping that he might provide some measure of defence against the men outside.

'Can't you get rid of them?' she implored him.

'Too many, I'm afraid, they wouldn't listen to me. Any chance of some tea?' Jane poured him a cup.

'I'll try reasoning with them,' Alistair said, going to the front door. Francis Greenstone gave a short laugh over the rim of his cup. The clicking of cameras heralded Alistair's appearance on the doorstep. It was as if a swarm of crickets had descended on the street. She could hear their raised voices as they fired questions at Alistair. 'Where's the bride?' she heard several shout, but she could not catch what he said in reply.

Alistair reappeared. 'Jane, I think if we agree to let them take our photograph, they might just go away.'

'But I look such a mess.'

'You look lovely.' Jane hurriedly dragged a comb through her hair and went to the front door, holding Alistair's hand tightly. The reporters had agreed to photographs only but, as soon as she appeared, they began shouting questions at her. They asked about Alistair's parents; they asked her when the baby was due. Alarmed, she ran back into the house. They had had their photographs, but they did not go away.

She tried to concentrate on doing her ironing and packing their cases. She had even become resigned to Francis, who sat reading the huge pile of newspapers he had brought with him. His only requirement was countless cups of tea.

'Seen your press?' he asked, handing her a copy of the *Echo*. The headlines in bold print announced: 'HE CAN'T HELP BEING A LORD' SAYS EX-STOKER'S WIFE – 'HE'S REALLY VERY NICE!'

Below was the terrible photograph of the three of them. 'Turn to centre page for full story –' but she could not bear to see any more. She thrust the paper back to Francis. She did not know why but she felt overwhelmed with shame at what she had seen.

'It's ghastly, I don't want to see any more.'

'Pity. I thought it came off rather well.'

A loud banging on the door began. Alistair bellowed up the stairs to them to go away, but the banging and bell-ringing continued. It even disturbed Francis, who, with a sigh, heaved himself up from the table and, muttering, 'I'll see to the buggers,' disappeared up the stairs. He reappeared with John and David, who were grinning from ear to ear.

'Crikey, what a song and dance! We had to rugby tackle our way in,' John declared.

'Your phone's broken,' David informed them.

'We took it off the hook. But am I glad to see you two! Beer?' Alistair asked them.

'Anything we can do?' they asked, gratefully gulping at the tankards of beer.

'Keep us sane!' suggested Alistair.

'I'm about to write a couple of letters that you could post for me,' Jane replied. 'I'd begun to think I wouldn't be able to post them. I didn't know who to trust,' she said, looking pointedly at Francis. 'I've written to Sandra – I'm frightened she won't get it in time. You couldn't pop into the hospital and leave her a message? Tell her it's noon at Chelsea Register Office?'

'I'll go,' John volunteered. 'I don't think David had better show his face in there.' They all laughed at the memory. It was wonderful to be laughing again; Jane had feared she would never again see the funny side of anything.

She left the men heatedly debating with Francis Greenstone the right of the individual to privacy. Upstairs she struggled with her letters.

Jane wrote to Matron first, handing in her notice. The letter to her parents to explain her lie about being pregnant was more difficult. She made several attempts before she got it right. Alistair, bringing her a glass of wine, read them both.

'They're fine, darling. I'm sure everyone will forgive us eventually. Look, I'm sorry I hadn't told you, but I'm having dinner with my father tonight.'

'Alistair, do you have to? I don't think I can cope with that pack of jackals on my own.'

'Jay, I promised my father: it's a mini-stag-night he's laid on for me. Francis reckons that if I leave here, most of that lot will follow. Perhaps it's best if I'm not here tonight.' Jane's grey eyes widened in panic, and Alistair took her hand. 'Sweetheart, imagine the pictures in the papers, the snide remarks, if we leave for the wedding together. I've asked John and David to stay with you. No one will get in if those two oxes are here, will they? And they'll take you to the Register Office in the morning.'

'Well,' she said uncertainly, 'it is supposed to be bad luck to sleep under the same roof the night before you marry. But where will you sleep?'

'I can stay the night at my parents'.'

'Is your mother there?' she asked anxiously.

'If she is then I'll sleep at my club. I promise.' He laughed tenderly. 'She won't get me to change my mind, you know.'

'I worry . . .' She smiled lamely.

'Don't stand me up, will you?' he said, kissing her gently before he left.

She made the boys some supper and left them playing cards with Francis while she went to bed early. But it felt wrong to be in bed there without Alistair.

She woke far too early to a glorious, perfect June day. She spent as long as possible getting ready, taking immense care over each fingernail, each strand of hair. At last, finding nothing else she could do to her appearance, she nervously entered the sitting room.

'Jane, my love, you'll slay them,' David said appreciatively. 'Scared?'

'Absolutely terrified.'

The two boys shielded her with their massive rugby players' shoulders and cleared a path through the mob of newsmen to a waiting taxi. Outside the Register Office a crowd had gathered. Jane braced herself for their stares but relaxed visibly as they shouted good-luck wishes. Francis Greenstone bounded up to her with a bouquet of gardenias. 'Compliments of the *Echo*,' he said, kissing her on the cheek, and for the first time gave her a genuine smile. A bouquet was the one thing they had forgotten to arrange. She thanked him, and the reporters were finally rewarded with a photograph of a happy bride-to-be.

She was to remember little of the actual ceremony. She was vaguely conscious that the room was full, but she saw only Alistair. He told her later that she had stumbled over the words. At the time she had not even noticed, but she did remember the look of love in Alistair's eyes as he bent to kiss her.

'Good morning, Lady Redland,' he whispered in her ear.

Only then did she see their guests and was amazed that there were so many of them. Sandra was there with several other nurses from the hospital, tears streaming down their faces. She saw some friends of Alistair's and, right at the back, Mr and Mrs Evans with their children looking as if they had been polished for the occasion. Sitting in monumental isolation, smiling like a Cheshire cat, was her aunt, in a voluminous magenta dress and hat with the most dramatic feather Jane had ever seen.

'Auntie Vi!' Jane rushed into her aunt's expansive embrace. 'You wonderful person, you came!'

'What did you think? When I saw the paper yesterday I was straight over to your mother's, but she wouldn't budge. You're not pregnant, are you?'

'No. I lied.'

'I said you had. I said, "Our Jane isn't that stupid." Even if you were, they should have been here – silly behaviour, I think. Your mother thinks you're going to get hoity-toity with us.'

'Auntie Vi! I never would.'

'Course you won't. Your mother's a doomy old cow sometimes. Your husband looks very nice, Jane.'

'Heavens, yes, my husband!' Jane said with wonder. She introduced her aunt and the Evans family to Alistair. The atmosphere of the Register Office was rapidly becoming like that of a party.

'Excuse me, Lord Redland, but I do have another wedding in ten minutes,' the registrar said apologetically.

With difficulty Alistair shepherded the noisy group out to a line of waiting taxis, inviting everyone to join them for lunch at the Connaught. Alistair and Jane stayed to pose happily for photographs. Finally the press let them leave, and to cries of 'Good luck' they stepped into the Upnor Rolls-Royce.

'Who arranged all this – the taxis and the Rolls?'

'Pa did. He's organized the lunch too. He's at the Connaught now. He felt that if your parents weren't coming it was better if he stayed away from the Register Office as well. The press would only twist it.'

'You can't win with them, can you?'

'Never, Lady Redland.'

'Oh, please, don't call me that. It makes me feel silly.' She tried to smile at him. That might be her name now, but she knew it was going to take her a long time to get used to it.

By the time they arrived at the hotel, everyone was into their second glass of champagne. Sandra was first to throw her arms about her friend.

'Sandra, thank God you're here! I was so afraid that you wouldn't get time off,' Jane exclaimed, hugging her.

'I'd have gone sick, I wouldn't have missed this for anything. You should have been at the hospital, though, Jane. What a laugh! Home Sister crashing around in her curlers like a demented hen, flapping the newspaper and yelling, "She can't do this, she's Senior Nights next week!" God, it was so funny!'

'Don't even talk about it – I couldn't face them, I wrote to Matron instead.'

Mrs Evans and her aunt hit it off immediately and, looking like two brightly coloured galleons come to rest, were soon deeply engrossed in conversation. As the champagne flowed, so the colour of the two women changed from pink to bright red. Aunt Vi eventually matched the magenta of her dress. Alistair's Cambridge friends began to flirt with the nurses. The Evans children, sampling champagne for the first time in their lives, were rapidly becoming overexcited. Lord Upnor beamed with pleasure on the whole proceedings. It was a wonderful, happy lunch. Much to his amusement, she thanked Lord Upnor at least a dozen times for his kindness. She was so afraid he wouldn't realize how much she appreciated the lunch, and especially how much she appreciated his being there.

The cool, oyster-grey interior of the Rolls-Royce epitomized the change in Jane's life. She leaned back against the soft leather upholstery and smiled a broad, satisfied smile. The bathroomless terraced house, the ugliness, the lack of privacy – that life had gone for ever and she could contemplate the fact with no regret. A new life now beckoned. She faced it eagerly, determined to succeed, determined to show them all that she could.

'What are you thinking?'

'That you're my husband and no one can separate us now, ever!' She kissed him gleefully. 'And bathrooms for the rest of my life!' She flung her arms excitedly into the air.

'Now I know why you married me,' he teased.

'That's right. For a bathroom and because I love you.'

He took her in his arms and they saw none of the suburbs of London as the car glided on towards the airport.

By nine that night they were driving up to Honor's villa. Her staff stood on the steps waiting for them, headed by her major-domo, Guido. He ushered them into the villa like a fussy nanny.

Whiteness. Everything was white, she had stepped into a marble, silken, luxurious, shimmering cube of white. Everywhere she looked, walls, floors, furniture, flowers, the billowing lawn curtains and the

ornaments were white. Only the paintings on the wall were coloured –
magnificent, blazing abstracts – and in their bedroom there were subtle
pink tuberoses whose scent filled the air.

For fear of hurting the feelings of Guido and his staff, they had to eat
the dinner prepared for them. They sat at a marble table on the wide,
white marble terrace. Below them, far away, the lights of a little town
reflected in the sea. The warm air clothed her like a light wool coat. The
black sky seemed to hold a million new stars which shone brighter than
she had ever seen stars shine before.

They bathed together in the sunken bath, water pouring from gold
dolphins. They sat in the water, the air heavy with expensive perfume,
and toasted each other in the chilled champagne they found at the side of
the bath.

'Alistair, darling, it's unbelievable, like a Hollywood film set.'

'Great fun, isn't it? My mother thinks it's vulgar.'

'I think it's lovely. Lovely, extravagantly lovely!'

'Opulent decadence.' He laughed.

They climbed into the giant bed, their bodies slipping between the fine
lawn sheets. The setting and the night air, sensuous with the heady smell
of unfamiliar flowers, contributed to their passion. As Alistair slept in
her arms she looked at him and knew that she would never love anyone
as much. She had found him, and now she would use her life to love him.

It was an idyllic month. They had plans to go touring and sightseeing,
but these came to nothing. Instead, they whiled the days away in their
white villa making love, drinking Frascati, eating fresh figs, just as
Alistair had promised they would. They grew brown and he more golden
as the sun drenched his hair. They began to put on weight with the
delectable food which arrived in astonishing variety each day. They
purred like cats as the staff spoiled them, pandering to their every wish,
treating them with that special understanding that Latins give to lovers.

She did not want to leave. For a month she had been able to forget the
problems at home, to be herself, to be alone with him. But a letter from
England settled their plans. Alistair had been mildly vexed that, because
of his mother, he would not be able to go to Scotland to shoot as he
always did in August.

'Fantastic!' he exclaimed over his letter. 'Listen, darling, it's from
Mother: "I presume you will be arriving at Drumloch as usual in
August? Shall you be bringing your wife? Will she be a gun? Let me
know . . ." Isn't that great, Jane? She's obviously coming around.' His
eyes were shining. 'I think we should leave here at the end of this week.

We'll get back to Trinick and start getting some order there. We can stay with Father.' Jane pulled a face. 'It'll be all right, darling, Mother will be in Scotland. She always goes up first to open the house. It will just be the three of us.' She listened to him happily making his plans.

'I wish we could stay here for ever,' she sighed.

'I know, Jay, but you'll love Scotland, too.'

Three

1957—69

I

Without Blanche Upnor's presence, Jane was happy at Respryn. Rupert, as he had now insisted she call him, gave them free run of the attics in the big house to choose whatever they wanted for Trinick House. It was like sorting through a large antique shop but with no bill to pay.

They spent several days in London choosing wallpapers and fabrics. The elegant designers' showrooms they haunted were as far removed as possible from the Co-op wallpaper department to which Jane was used. Jane wallowed happily in a sea of prints, chintzes, silks and fabrics of which she had never heard. Attentive, epicene young men plied her with emphatic ideas of what she should choose, of what was the rage this season. She blithely ignored their advice, confident, with the picture in her mind's eye, of how their house was to look. Having ordered carpets and curtains, they returned to Respryn, the car loaded with wallpaper and paint.

Nothing moved fast enough for Jane. If only the house could be finished overnight – instead she had to wait patiently for the workmen to finish one room at a time. But, as soon as one was finished, she was moving furniture, polishing, hanging paintings, unpacking the cases of porcelain and china they had chosen from the seemingly endless treasures of the attics of Respryn.

Jane's excitement knew no bounds, nor her burgeoning pride in her home. She would willingly have done without the trip to Scotland, so desperate was she to move in, but Alistair was adamant.

'When we return from Scotland will be time enough,' he insisted. 'Time for the smell of fresh paint to have disappeared. In any case, the curtains won't be ready until we get back.'

She found an old rocking horse called, incongruously for such a fine dapple-grey, Fred. He had been Alistair's. She rescued him from the dark attic, washed and polished him, patiently combed his mane and tail and placed him in the hallway.

'That's a strange place to put Fred.'

'I think he looks nice there,' she replied.

Alistair stood back and studied the horse. 'You know, you're right. I have to hand it to you, Jane, you really are putting this place together well.'

'You needn't sound so bloody surprised.'

'You needn't snap.'

'Well, you needn't be so patronizing! Just because I'm working-class doesn't mean I have no taste or that I'm colour-blind,' she said crossly.

'Jane, please, don't be so prickly.'

'What do you expect, for Christ's sake?'

'You know, darling, I shall call you Hedgehog if you continue to be so sensitive.' He smiled at her but she did not smile back.

'Of course I'm sensitive. You can blame your family for that!' She glowered in return.

'I'm sorry, darling. I didn't mean to sound patronizing. I'm so proud of what you're doing.' Gently he coaxed her back into a good humour; she was so happy that she could not remain angry for long.

In this fortnight, not only did she begin to build her home, but she began to consolidate her friendship with Alistair's father, whose acceptance of her, she confidently felt, was total and genuine.

Too soon the fortnight was over, and as the day of departure for Scotland drew near, her spirits began to sink.

Life with Alistair was turning into a long series of firsts. With him she had experienced her first champagne, foreign food, fine wines, gin and tonic. Her first trip abroad, with her first flight; and now Scotland, as they set out with Rupert on her first journey on the overnight sleeper. She loved the train, the comfort of their tiny sleeping compartment, the noise of the train thundering through the night, its whistle echoing across the sleeping countryside. At each stop she peered out, trying to make out where they were, as the train took on mail. She loved the hiss as the great steam engine was fed water and great clouds of steam billowed out across the station. As they progressed north, so the accents on each station changed, until finally she heard the lilt of the Scottish accent. When she awoke properly, it was to the beauty of the northern Highlands. She was to learn that the Highlands had their own special colours – with the improbable purple of the heather, the violent yellow of the broom and the scarlet of the rowan – as if God had mixed an especially bright palette for Scotland. At Inverness they left the train and she breathed air as crystal clear as gin.

The Rolls, with Tucker, the chauffeur, was waiting for them. Once off the main road, they seemed to travel for hours along single-track roads no better than cart tracks. They travelled up glens so narrow she had to peer to see the sky. Waterfalls cascaded down the mountainsides like liquid silver and yet the rivers frothed like brown beer.

'Why are the rivers so brown?'

'The peat,' they answered.

'What's peat?' she asked. They explained, astonished that she had never heard of it. Suddenly on the skyline they saw a magnificent stag silhouetted against the blue sky. Tucker stopped the car so that they could get a better look.

'Pa, look at that! If only I had a rifle on that beauty.'

'He must be a royal,' his father answered. 'Fine beast.'

'Alistair, you couldn't kill anything as beautiful as that, surely?' Jane asked, horrified.

'I damn well could, my girl,' he replied firmly.

After two hours of bumpy, curving roads, they arrived. The house had always been referred to as a 'lodge'. Jane had been expecting a small gatehouse. No one had explained a Scottish lodge to her and she was astonished when Drumloch Lodge appeared in all its grandeur. Turrets proliferated, windows were positioned in the most unexpected places and she saw a front door through which an elephant could have passed.

'What do you think?' Alistair enquired, smiling.

'It's very grand,' she answered unsurely.

'I always think it looks as if it was built by Ludwig of Bavaria on a bad day,' Rupert laughed.

She knew without going into the house that she did not like it. It was too big. It did not look as though it belonged here in the way that Respryn looked as if it had grown from the soil. It was so large and the place so inaccessible that she wondered how many men had toiled and for what pitiful wages, and how many had died, to build this giant, crenellated house in this remote place. Some Lord Upnor in the last century had ordered a castle, had chosen a design, said 'put it here' and then basked in the stone and mortar which were proof of his own importance.

Large deerhounds lolloped out to greet them exuberantly. Banks was at the door, and Jane smiled with delight. 'Mr Banks, how lovely to see you!'

'Lady Redland.' The butler bowed. She hated her new name, felt embarrassed by it, as if she had no real right to it.

The hall was like a banqueting hall. It seemed that every square inch of the walls was covered with the heads of dead animals; their staring glass eyes seemed to follow her everywhere. Animal skins were scattered over the floor, some with heads on, some without, so that crossing the floor was like an obstacle course.

Banks showed them to their room. He led them up a dark, creaking staircase and along a narrow corridor on both sides of which large portraits of dour-looking men in kilts glowered down on them. Like so many rooms in this strange house it was circular, and a large oak four-poster with tartan curtains dominated the room. The window was small and set in walls several feet thick; very little light filtered into the room and Jane searched for a light switch.

'There's no electricity here – oil lamps only,' Alistair informed her. 'We've a small generator for the fridges and the kitchen, but that's all. Fun, isn't it?'

'Yes,' she said, unconvinced. She would never like this house: she already loathed this dark cold bedroom and she hated the dead animals everywhere.

'I'm going for a walk. Coming?' he asked.

'No, thanks, I think I'll unpack.'

'Leave it to the maid, come on.'

'No, thanks, I'd rather sort things out myself.'

He shrugged and left her. As soon as he had gone she regretted her decision, the room seemed to press in on her. No sounds penetrated the thick walls and there was a chill in the room that an extra sweater did not eliminate. She started to unpack but the silence was unnerving. Leaving the cases for the maid, after all, she grabbed her coat and ran out of the room, down the long staircase, hoping to be able to catch up with Alistair.

She found her way out into the grounds – there was no garden that she could find. On either side, the dense forest seemed to come almost to the walls of the house itself, as if trying to engulf it. Only at the front of the building did a vista of meadows lead down to a steel-grey, glinting loch with the mountains rising majestically beyond. That view was breathtakingly beautiful and now out of the house with its oppressive atmosphere Jane felt distinctly happier. She sat on a wall admiring the view.

The sound of running water attracted her attention. She eased herself from the wall and made her way into the trees. She paused to enjoy the sweet, unfamiliar scent of the decaying leaves, and for the first time the comforting, warm smell of the soil. She bent down and inhaled deeply: it was a new idea to her that from death and decay should emerge something so consoling.

The sound of the water was louder. She walked further and found herself standing on a ridge above a river, the water flowing fast, as brown and frothy as stout, between the jagged rocks it had once carved and shaped but which seemed now to guard it. A short way up the river a waterfall tumbled urgently. She carefully clambered over the rocks to reach the bottom of the fall, amazed that here the frenetic water formed a dark, almost still pool. She sat mesmerized by the water.

From the corner of her eye she was aware of something moving. She looked up. There was nothing there. About to turn away, she stood rigid with astonishment as a large fish, the sun glinting on its scales, shot out of the peaty water of the pool like a silver blade and propelled itself into the air with such power that it cleared the fall. Another one appeared, missed the fall and crashed back into the river only to emerge again, seeming to balance on its tail fin and once again unleash its great force in another jump. The pool seemed to boil with swirling fish, all jumping, some clearing the fall, others falling back into the pool time and time again, only to try once more. She found herself cheering them, willing them to succeed. One poor fish misjudged his leap and landed at her feet on the rock, half stunned. Gingerly she felt it, frightened that it would be slimy to her touch: instead, she enjoyed its cool smoothness. As she gently picked it up to replace it in the water, the fish jerked into life, and Jane was staggered at its strength as it broke her hold and knifed across the pool like a javelin.

For over two hours she sat, fascinated by the courage of these great, shining fish, before she reluctantly made her way back to the house to be on time for lunch. Several cars now stood in the forecourt, a crowd of young people spilling out of the latest arrival. Her sister-in-law was among them. Clarissa looked straight at Jane and pointedly turned her back. Jane steeled herself to walk past the group, her head held high, conscious of their stares as she let herself in the door.

Banks was in the hall, accompanied by some maids bearing huge silver trays of glasses and ice buckets. She asked Banks where she should go, and he ushered her into a large sitting room. The furniture was surprisingly shabby compared with Respryn. Large chintz-covered sofas, their seats sagging, their covers worn, were scattered about the room. It was a comfortable, lived-in room and was light compared with the rest of the house, with four large casement windows looking down across the meadows to the loch.

'There you are. Where have you been?' Alistair asked.

'I found a waterfall and a pond. Darling, it was magical – these great big fish, so brave, some of them, they jumped it, they actually jumped the waterfall.' Her eyes sparkled with excitement, the words tumbling out. 'What were they, Alistair? They were beautiful.'

Clarissa and her friends, who had followed Jane into the room, burst into laughter.

'Salmon, you ignoramus!' she heard Clarissa sneer. She swung round to her adversary. So, there was to be no respite from her sniping and bitching.

'I've never seen a salmon, so how the hell was I to know? We haven't all had your advantages, Clarissa,' she said with spirit.

'That is painfully obvious to us all,' Clarissa drawled.

'Clarissa, behave yourself or leave the room,' her father admonished her. Behind his back Clarissa pulled a face at him. 'They are beautiful, Jane, you're quite right.' Rupert spoke reassuringly. 'I must speak to Mac tomorrow, Alistair, there's obviously a grilse run on. We should get some good fishing in the next few days.'

Immediately Jane regretted mentioning the fish. By talking about them she seemed to have ensured that someone would go out and kill them.

In her excitement she had not noticed Lady Upnor sitting in a large wing chair. She greeted her and apologized for the lapse, but her mother-in-law ignored her and said to Alistair, 'Could you make sure that your wife keeps to our timetable while she is here?'

Alistair looked thunderous, but said nothing. Jane felt the usual wave of fear which this woman engendered in her. Like so many of her generation and class, Lady Upnor was an imperious being who would brook no dissension. Since her own mother-in-law had died, her word had been law at Respryn and no one could recollect her ever being contradicted, except by her husband. So she sailed on a sea of rudeness and bigotry, oblivious to the harm and hurt she caused: everyone accepted her behaviour as her right and perfectly normal in the scheme of things.

Jane survived lunch, but only because she was sitting at Rupert's right hand. She had already learned enough to know that she was placed there because of Alistair's title. What a strange woman Lady Upnor was, rude to the point of ignoring Jane herself yet strictly observing the codes of etiquette as far as Jane's position in society was concerned. As the only other married and titled woman present, Jane was given the seat of honour beside Rupert. It showed a depth of hypocrisy that only widened the gap between Jane and her mother-in-law.

More guests arrived in the afternoon and in the bustle of greetings, Jane was able to slip away. She decided that the oppressive room was more welcoming than Lady Upnor.

Alistair, in high spirits, joined her to change for dinner. She watched with fascination as he donned the paraphernalia of Highland dress. It made him look different, more masculine somehow: even the way he moved had altered, with a proud strut as the kilt pleats swung behind him.

'You look fantastic, Alistair.'

'I like wearing the kilt. I'm told I've the ideal arse for it. Don't you agree?'

She laughed at him preening in front of the mirror.

'What happens tonight, Alistair? Why the party clothes?' she asked.

'Pa's first night here is always a party. Lots of local friends come over. But you can slip off to bed when you want – the ladies usually do. We men tend to drink the night away and play billiards. It's great fun!'

The hall certainly looked different. Giant candles lit the room and a huge log fire burned in the grate; the long table was ablaze with more candles. Fortunately the walls were in shadow, so that Jane was spared the dead animal heads glaring accusingly at her.

Lord Upnor's friends began to arrive, the men all kilted and the women in soft, coloured, long cashmere skirts and jumpers. They all knew each other and the noise of their reunion was deafening. A piper appeared and piped them in to dinner, where the food was the best Jane had tasted in an Upnor house: a succulent saddle of venison with perfectly roasted potatoes and bright red rowan jelly. As a married couple, Jane and Alistair were separated at the dinner table and he was seated several places away. Jane found herself between a deaf old general, who tried to hear what she said but with whom conversation was impossible, and one of Clarissa's smooth male friends from London.

'Pity you missed the May ball,' he said without preamble.

'What May ball?' she asked.

'First week in June. It was good fun. Alistair was in cracking form. He's topping fun when he's drunk, isn't he?' The man chortled.

'I was working,' she said, her face stiff with the inner shock she was feeling.

'Yes, Alistair said you were. Ghastly job, nursing, I mean. What?'

As if from a long way away she heard the young man prattling on, but for Jane conversation was impossible. She sat isolated at the noisy, glittering table. It seemed to her that everything had gone dark. She could only sit and try to sieve through the turmoil of her thoughts. What she minded most was not that Alistair had gone to the ball, but that he had not told her about it. There had to be an explanation, she reasoned. She would not think about it now. She must not let her thoughts spoil this evening. With great control she turned once again to the young man to ask him what he did.

After dinner they returned to the hall where the large refectory table had been manhandled to one side. The piper reappeared. People took up positions on the floor, talking idly while the man tuned his pipes, making an agonizing wailing noise as he did so. Everyone seemed to know exactly which reel he was going to play, for as soon as he started, the dancers hurled themselves into the patterns of the dance. In the afternoon Jane had noticed a gallery above the hall and, finding the staircase, she climbed up to get a better view. Beneath her the dancers moved from one reel to another, each of them knowing the steps perfectly. No one put a foot wrong. Jane was reminded of the ever changing patterns of a child's kaleidoscope as she watched the swirling tartans of the kilts, and the plaids worn by the women across their shoulders. There was much whooping and shouting from the men as they twirled the women around in intricate formations. While the dances were beautiful to look at, there was a barely controlled violence to them.

By one o'clock she felt tired enough to drop, and searched out Alistair.

'Can we go to bed now, darling?'

'Don't be daft, the night's young. You go if you want. I'm not.' With a loud whoop he put his arm round a pretty girl and led her off in another dance.

Jane slipped away and found their room with difficulty. Two oil lamps glowed, casting long, dark shadows on the walls. She slipped into the giant bed and peered into the shadows. She began to hear noises, a faint tapping and a strange sighing. She was shivering and put on a jumper and a pair of Alistair's socks. She longed for Alistair. She was hurt that he had not come when she asked – after all, they had only been married for seven weeks – but realized this was unreasonable. He was having such fun she should feel happy for him. But she did not. She knew she could not have fun without him beside her; yet he seemed capable of it without her. On the other hand it was not his fault that she could not dance the reel. She would learn: yes, she would ask a maid or someone to teach her, then she would not have to stand and watch. It must look odd, though, she thought, newly wed and he downstairs while she was alone in bed. She lay wide-eyed in the flickering light, trying not to think of Alistair dancing with other women, and of him at May balls without her. She shivered again. She knew she would never get to sleep in this ghostly room . . .

Despite her fears she slept, only to be woken by a heart-stopping shock as Alistair crashed drunkenly through the door.

'You missed a good party,' he slurred as he struggled out of his finery.

'God, you startled me, Alistair! This room is creepy.'

'Christ, Jane, don't be so bloody wet!' he snarled.

His tone of voice was so contemptuous that she felt as if she had been struck. The whisky fumes on his breath made her turn her head away in disgust. Violently he made love to her and she cried out because he hurt her, but he either did not hear or did not care. Finished with her, he slumped to his side of the bed and quickly fell into a deep sleep. For Jane sleep was a long time coming.

2

'Come on, darling, up you get! It's the Glorious Twelfth. It's the big shoot today.'

She opened her eyes. There was her Alistair, the man she loved, not the violent stranger of the night before. He kissed her tenderly as he did each morning.

'What's that?' he asked, pointing at a large bruise on her breast.

'It's a bruise. You made it last night.'

'Darling, I'm so sorry. Was I a brute?'

'Yes.' Her voice was cold.

'I was drunk.'

'I know.'

'It won't happen again, I promise.'

'I'm your wife, you know, not a whore,' she spat at him.

He looked so downcast that, despite herself, she felt a rush of love for her husband. Surely he meant it this time. Abruptly she changed the subject. 'Darling, I was scared stiff last night. Before you came up, I heard these terrible noises.' She attempted to imitate them, and he laughed.

'Poor darling, I should have warned you. It was the wind howling in the turret and the hot-water pipes tapping – and then I crash in like a monster . . .' He held her in his arms, kissing her hair, the bruise on her breast. 'This won't do, though. Come on, we'll be late. I want you to see the shoot.'

'What are you shooting?'

'Grouse, of course.'

'What's grouse?'

'Jane, you're so funny. You don't mean to say you don't know what grouse are? They're birds, delicious things.'

'I never heard of them.'

'You know, sometimes it amazes me how ignorant you are.'

'I'm sorry,' she said stiffly. 'I don't think you get grouse in Kent and, if you don't mind, I'd rather not go.'

'I do mind. I want you to come, it's great fun. You can stay in my butt with me, and I'll even let you have a go.'

'But I know I'd hate seeing animals shot, and I certainly have no desire to "have a go".'

'For heaven's sake, Jane, they're only birds, don't be so soft. Why on earth do you think we came here?' He tugged at the blanket. 'Come on.'

Reluctantly she did as he bid. She knew this constant carping was bringing out the worst in both of them. They ate a quick breakfast and then joined the rest of the party in the hall. The others were dressed in hairy tweeds and thick boots and sported the most extraordinary collection of headgear. The whole party looked shapeless and sexless.

'Jane coming? Good girl,' said Lord Upnor.

'Yes, Pa, I want her to see the shoot.'

'Well, she can't go dressed like that,' his mother snorted. Jane was conscious of everyone looking at her in her slacks and Wellington boots, trench coat tightly belted, and with a scarf on her head.

'I haven't got anything else to wear,' she retorted, glaring pointedly at Alistair, who rarely noticed what she was wearing.

'She'll get soaked,' Lady Upnor snapped.

'I've got another riding mac she can borrow,' one of the other women volunteered pleasantly.

'Thank you very much,' Jane mumbled in furious embarrassment.

'You should come properly attired,' Lady Upnor continued to complain.

'I would have, if someone had told me what to wear,' Jane defended herself. Rather, if you'd had the bloody courtesy to tell me, she thought.

Jane's clothing finally sorted out, they climbed into Land-Rovers and drove up on the moor. As the vehicles climbed, they left the good weather behind and a soft mist began to fall. Eventually they could drive no further and so the party trudged across the moorland, the dogs leaping and barking excitedly around them. Jane soon discovered that the heather, which looked so soft and inviting to walk on, was very difficult to cross. Her Wellington boots kept slipping and, as she stumbled, she tended to drop behind the main party; she began to feel wet and miserable. She could sense Alistair's irritation as he had to stop frequently to wait for her.

They finally reached the butts, a long line of heather-covered fences shaped into little boxes. They found the butt which Rupert had allocated them and settled in on the damp earth, with Alistair's loader standing behind them.

'You shooting, M'Lady?' he asked.

'No, thanks,' she replied firmly.

'Of course she'll shoot, Fergus. Load her a gun. Look, Jane . . .' He proceeded to explain the gun's mechanism to her. 'There'll be a hell of a bang, so stand firm or it'll knock you over. Keep the stock tight against your shoulder and slide your left hand well up the gun, at the top to the fore-end. Then hand the gun back to Fergus here and he'll give you another. Look,' he said excitedly, 'look, here come the beaters. I used to do that as a lad.'

She peered through the mist and saw across the hillside a long line of boys and men walking towards them, their arms moving rhythmically as they beat the heather with their sticks. A flock of birds began to rise in front of them, and, in their panic to get away, swooped low towards the line of guns. The firing started.

The noise was deafening. The little birds, desperately trying to gain height away from this new danger, fell to the ground in droves. Jane crouched, horrified. The shooting ceased and out went the labradors, returning with the pathetic, dripping little carcasses in their mouths, tails wagging at their own cleverness. Alistair turned to her, his eyes blazing with excitement.

'Isn't it fun?'

The tears rolled down her cheeks. 'I think it's horrifying,' she cried.

'Christ, Jane, you can be such a bore at times. If you feel like that, why don't you bugger off then?' he shouted at her.

'I didn't want to come here in the first place!'

'I wish I had bloody well listened to you now!' They glared at each other with angry resentment. She turned her back on him and stalked off towards the Land-Rovers in the valley below. She tried to walk with dignity but her feet kept slipping and she lost count of the times she fell as she stumbled through the undergrowth. A young man was leaning against the nearest Land-Rover, and she noticed him hurriedly put out a cigarette as she approached.

'Would you be wanting tae get back tae the house, M'Lady?'

'Yes, please, if it's no bother.'

'Nothing's never nae bother, M'Lady.' Skilfully he turned the vehicle around in the soft mud. She offered him a cigarette.

'I shouldnae, really,' he said.

'Why not? You smoke, don't you?'

'Aye, but we're nae supposed to smoke in front of the gentry.'

'Well, I'm not gentry, so you're not breaking any rules if you smoke with me.' He gratefully accepted the cigarette, smiling at her words.

'D'ye nae like the shooting, then?'

'I hated it,' she said vehemently.

'Trouble is the wee birds make fine eating and someone's got tae shoot them if we're tae eat them.'

'Sure, but that's a massacre up there, and they call it sport!'

'Aye, shooting for the pot is fine. I have tae agree with you, it can go too far. A friend of mine works further south. He says the pheasants are the worst. They hand-rear them and then shoot them, and them poor birds learned to trust man. At least the grouse is wild.'

Jane shuddered. Sensing her mood he changed the subject, telling her the names of the various hills, talking about the wildlife which abounded, the badgers, the pine martens, the wild cats, the deer which, in winter when forage was low, would become so tame that he could feed them from his hand.

'Do you shoot them?'

'It's my job, M'Lady. It's necessary tae cull them or the poor beasties would get diseased and starve.'

'Do you like doing it?'

'It depends. If I've a stupid beast in me sights, then, aye, it deserves tae die for the sake of the rest, you see, before the bad blood gets passed on. But if I get a good, intelligent beast that I've stalked all day, and he's led me a real dance, then like as not I'll let him go. He'll breed again and maybe his intelligence and courage will enter his bairns.'

'I suppose it's really just another extension of the survival of the fittest.'

'Aye, M'Lady, something like that,' he said.

'But I don't understand how everyone enjoys it so. I mean, you do it for the good of the animals, really, but then Lord Upnor, why does he do it?'

'Ye know, M'Lady, he does nae shoot like he used tae. You see that, time and time again, the old men, they seem tae tire of it, would rather watch the animals than kill them. A day like today, well, it's traditional and his guests would expect it, but I've been on the hill with himself, and we've stalked a stag and at the end, he's got it in his sights, and he's just said bang and let the beastie live. Aye, you see it often. It's as if, as their own time approaches, they have nae got the same love for the killing. He's content with the fish.'

Jane liked this man who had such understanding of men as well as animals. She looked at him: he was tall and heavy, his muscles indicating enormous strength, but there was a sensitivity about him which seemed sadly lacking in the men of the house party. He promised to take her out one evening to see what they could find. 'The evening's best, they all pop out then. I suppose they feel safer. Perhaps they know that's when the guns are having a wee dram.' He laughed.

Back at the lodge, as she thanked him for bringing her home, the front door swung open and the rest of the female party appeared, carrying large picnic baskets.

'Given up then, sister-in-law? Get too much for you?' Clarissa taunted her. 'Couldn't take it?'

'I get cold easily.'

'Ha! Really? Expect us to believe that?'

'Believe what you bloody well like.' Jane turned away and climbed the steps to the house.

'Do you always have to sound like a fishwife?'

'It takes one to know one,' Jane countered.

'Mac, take us to the butts,' Clarissa imperiously ordered. Jane noticed with a quiet satisfaction that the man did not smile at Clarissa and her party as he had smiled at her.

She wandered down to the waterfall and watched what she now regarded as her fish. She had been married only seven weeks and already she and Alistair were having their first row. She wanted to leave this place where people only seemed to think and talk of killing. It was as if something had happened to change Alistair, who was behaving like a demon, she decided. She did not belong here and she did not want to belong. But she was married to Alistair, and that gave her every right to be here. She did not wish to be here, that was the difference. But what the hell was she to do? She could learn to set a table, seat people at it correctly, a million and one things, but she could never learn to enjoy the slaughter she had just seen.

She was reading on the big four-poster in their room when Alistair returned.

'Sulk over?' he snapped.

'I'm not sulking.'

'You could have fooled me.' He stomped about the room, scattering his damp clothes on the floor. 'You were a bloody disgrace up there on the moor. Made me look a bloody fool, stalking off like that, leaving me alone in the butt.'

'If I remember rightly, you told me to "bugger off",' she shouted angrily back at him.

'A real bloody fool,' he muttered as he stormed off to the bathroom. She lay on the bed tense with anger at the injustice.

'Why did you bloody well come then?' he asked, returning from his bath towelling his hair roughly in his rage.

'I won't again.'

'Good,' he snapped. 'At least I can have some fun if you're not there.'

'Fun! You call it fun, slaughtering poor little birds that don't stand a chance?'

'Jesus! I'm married to a St Francis of Assisi! Of course the birds stand a chance. We don't shoot them all – hundreds get away. In any case, how the hell do you think your food gets on the table? If you feel that strongly about it, then become a vegetarian. At least you wouldn't be a bloody hypocrite.'

'Don't you dare call me a hypocrite! That's the last thing I am. Your mother's reserved all the hypocrisy for herself. She's a bloody professor of hypocrisy!' Jane stormed.

'Leave my mother out of this.'

'A bit difficult to do as she's intent on making me look a fool at every turn.'

'You're fucking paranoid, I always said you were,' he shouted. 'You made yourself look a fool this morning, and me into the bargain. Bad-tempered little bitch, you were –'

'Alistair, stop shouting at me. I can't stand being shouted at. I'm sorry, I've said I'm sorry,' she screamed. 'I didn't know it was going to be like that, I've never seen anything killed in my life, it made me feel ill. If I'd known how awful it was going to be, I'd never have gone in the first place. But, please, for heaven's sake, stop saying what fun it is!'

Silently he started to get dressed. 'It's time you changed for dinner.'

'I don't want to go down to dinner.'

'You've got to.'

'I haven't got to do anything,' she snapped angrily.

'You're bloody well coming down to dinner. What the hell will people think if you stay sulking up here? They'll start to say I can't control my own wife.'

She picked at the bedcover. 'Did you enjoy the May ball?' As she spoke, she knew this was not the time to ask, but she could not seem to stop herself. He swung round, glancing quickly at her, but then averted his eyes, guiltily, Jane was certain. 'So, did you have a good time?' she persisted.

'Yes, as a matter of fact, I did,' he answered defiantly.

'Without me?'

'Yes, I'm quite capable of enjoying myself without you.'

'You probably enjoyed it more because I wasn't there.'

'I didn't say that.'

'You didn't have to.' They glared at each other across the white counterpane. Alistair began to brush his hair and then to splash after-shave on his cheeks, but in his agitation more landed on his shoulders than on his face. 'Why didn't you tell me?'

'I didn't think.'

'Why didn't you ask me to go?'

'I didn't think it was the sort of thing that you would be happy at.'

'Is that another way of saying — "out of place"?'

'If you like, yes.'

'Too posh for me?'

'Don't be silly.'

'I'm not being silly. I'm stating facts, aren't I? You didn't invite me because you were ashamed of me. Thought I'd be a duck out of water –'

'Christ, Jane, you've got one hell of a bloody chip on your shoulder!'

'Who did you take?' She had gone too far now, but she had to know all there was to know, no matter how much it hurt.

'I went with Clarissa and a whole gang. I didn't take anyone in particular.'

'I think you're a shit,' she hissed at him.

'God, woman, listen to you.' He looked at her with disgust. 'OK, I'll tell you the real reason. I didn't ask you because I knew you'd start bleating on about me drinking and having fun. There, that's the truth. You spoil things for me,' he added as a petulant afterthought.

Jane bent her head to hide the tears. His last remark was too near the bone. She had only herself to blame. She had engineered this row, just as her mother used to do. Alistair looked across the room at her, her dark hair falling loose across her breasts. Changing his tactics, he came over and put his arm about her.

'Jane, come on, love, I don't want to quarrel. You're right about everything. I should have warned you about the shoot. And it was unforgivable of me to go to the ball without telling you. It was the last, defiant gesture of a bachelor. I'm sorry, my darling. Forgive me. I didn't mean those horrible things I said.' He made her look at him. 'Come on, Jay, cheer up – let's be friends, Jane, please?' She put her arms up to him and he kissed her. 'That's better. Get changed, there's a good girl.'

Quickly she dressed and hand in hand they went down to dinner. The talk all through the long evening was of the 'bag': who had killed what and how many. The game book was produced and ceremoniously filled in with the details. Jane found she could hardly eat the food put in front of her.

That night, she again slipped off to bed before the others. In the middle of the night a drunken Alistair once more blundered into the room, into the bed. This time she recoiled in terror, desperately trying to escape his grasping hands. She rolled off the bed. He leaned across and grabbed her, pulling her back towards him. Her attempts to escape him seemed to amuse him for he laughed loudly as he tore the fabric of her nightie. Her nightdress in shreds, she covered her bare breasts with her hands.

'Alistair, please.' But her pleading only seemed to inflame his passion further, as violently he possessed her.

The two weeks dragged interminably for her. There was a wildness to them all here that was not present in England. Certainly everybody seemed to drink more, but Jane also wondered if some of the wildness was not induced by the excitement they found in the shooting. How else could she explain their pleasure in hurling billiard balls at each other, smashing the glass in the prints around the walls? Sometimes, in the night, one of them would climb the tower and hurl chamberpots from the battlements for the others to shoot at drunkenly. And what possessed them to 'mine' the carefully tended front lawn with thunder flashes which exploded with a terrifying crash when triggered by the front door being opened by an unsuspecting Banks? In the morning the lawn was completely wrecked, and the gardener was in despair, but it was still regarded as enormous 'fun' by everyone – except Jane. It was the violence of their humour that disturbed her most of all.

She was lonely. She spent most of her time reading, watched her fish for hours at a time and walked in the forest. Her mother-in-law continued to ignore her, which heightened her feeling of isolation. The talk seemed always to be of death: the dead animal's heads in the house haunted her. She wanted to be anywhere else. Each night the husband she loved, the gentle, considerate lover of her honeymoon, staggered late to bed and raped her.

She longed for her home, and for the Alistair she knew and loved, to return to her.

3

He did return, but not until they were safely back in their house at Respryn. He never mentioned his behaviour in Scotland, never apologized, as if he had no recollection of the incidents whatsoever. Jane reasoned that the courteous, kind person he normally was would certainly have said he was sorry. As in Cambridge, when he had crashed through the glass door, the only link was whisky. It seemed to act like a poison on him. Since he rarely drank spirits in England, there seemed no point in mentioning it. She would try to forget about it herself, but she knew that she never wanted to return to Scotland with him, never wanted to relive the nightmare of the past few weeks.

She settled happily into their house, Trinick. She took pride in the beautiful possessions which Alistair barely noticed. He was so used to being surrounded by lovely things, but they were a constant source of joy and wonder to Jane.

Upon their return, Alistair had arranged for her to interview several women for her staff. She was horrified at the prospect.

'But I don't want any staff,' she argued.

'Don't be silly, darling, of course you do. The house isn't that small. How could you possibly manage?'

'I'd go mad with not enough to do all day.'

'That's ridiculous, there would still be masses to do. I don't want you turning into a drudge, my sweet.'

'No, really, Alistair, I'd rather not. I want to do it myself.' She was afraid to have staff: she knew that she would not know how to handle them, or what to say to them.

'You're afraid to have staff,' he said accusingly.

'Don't be daft,' she lied. It was strange how often she told little lies to him these days, when in the past she had told only the truth, she thought.

'Well, at least have a char.'

'I might do that,' she acquiesced. She thought she could deal with a charwoman, it would be no different from asking one of the ward maids to do something. In fact, it would probably be far easier than dealing with the ward maids, a fiercely independent breed, united in their jealousy and hatred of the nurses. 'Yes, all right. I'll have a char.'

'Good. And a cook. Now we can't exist without a cook, can we?'

'Oh, Alistair, you are funny. Of course we can exist. I want to cook for you. That's most definitely my job. And, anyway, what about the expense?'

'The expense is no problem. When will you get it into your head that you don't have to worry about money any more? If that's all that's bothering you, we'll arrange a cook immediately.'

'No, no,' she said hastily. 'I want to do it myself.' She knew that she would be at a disadvantage with a cook, for the cook would know more than she, would sneer at her behind her back, at her ignorance of which sauce went with what. Not until she had taught herself some of the basics would she even consider such a prospect. But she did not explain any of this to Alistair.'

'But you can't cook.'

'I'm learning.'

'That could take ages. Think of my poor stomach, meanwhile.'

'I'll learn quickly, I promise.'

She kept her promise. She bought a pile of cook books which she studied as seriously as any student preparing for exams. She talked endlessly with the butcher and fishmonger, asking their advice. Complimented by her interest they were happy to advise her, selling her only the very best and recommending methods and times of cooking.

Inadvertently the butcher helped her to put her marriage drama into some sort of perspective. Returning one day, she unwrapped the dog's bones from the newspaper they were in, only to see her own and Alistair's faces smiling at her from the newsprint, like strangers. Why had she felt so ashamed at the time? She spread the crumpled paper on the kitchen table and studied the blurred image. Alistair had been right when he told her it was a one-day wonder and that they would be used to wrap fish and chips the next day. All that drama, the reporters popping out at them from the darkness, the feelings of panic, of shame, of embarrassment – to end up as a dog's bone wrapper! At last, this made it all seem as ridiculous as it should have seemed at the time.

Alistair had found a gardener who began rapidly to transform the garden. Jane took a great interest in everything he did and why, poring over seed catalogues and gardening books, but always referring back to the wisdom of Bert, who confided to his wife that he had never been happier in a job. He felt appreciated for once.

Alistair had given way to her on the question of servants but had insisted that, while she could do what she liked, he was going to have a valet. All married men in his position had valets, he stated. Mark joined their small household a few days later. Unlike most valets, he was willing to turn his hand to any job and help Jane with the odd repairs about the house: he cleaned the silver and even peeled the potatoes. He had been all over the world in his job and Jane would sit with a cup of coffee at the kitchen table, listening entranced to his gossip of life in high places. He was a mine of information of how things should be done and how people should be addressed – Jane used him as her personal etiquette expert. Unknown to her, their odd domestic arrangements were the talk of the neighbourhood.

Alistair had been right: she saw little of his mother. Lady Upnor came to Respryn only at weekends, preferring the social life of London during the week. They were rarely invited to the big house and then only when there was a large party where their absence would have been noted, and where it was possible for Lady Upnor to ignore Jane in the crowd. Yet while she was apparently ignored, Jane was aware of the older woman watching her all the time, waiting for her to make a fool of herself. It made Jane uncomfortable and even more nervous. She hated these evenings and attended them only for the sake of Alistair and his father.

Rupert had taken to popping in several times a week for coffee. He would sit at the kitchen table while Jane cooked, enjoying her company and talking about everything under the sun. Had she had a cook, she pointed out to Alistair gleefully, Rupert would not have felt nearly as free to come and relax with her. As the weeks went by, she began to love Rupert deeply for his kind, wise personality and his instinctive under-standing of her problems.

Honor was a regular visitor whenever she was staying at Respryn. She would often invite herself to dinner rather than eat at the big house. As she explained, the food and company were better. But Honor never stayed long enough for Jane, who would have been happy if she had stayed for months at a time. Instead she would alight at Respryn for a couple of days and then rush off to some distant spot.

Alistair enjoyed working for his father, learning much from him and Lockhart, the estate manager. He was away early each morning but he would return for breakfast and lunch, and with Rupert's visits as well,

Jane never felt lonely. As the weeks went by, the hard physical work that Alistair insisted on doing, for it was the only way to learn, he said, made his body more muscular and even more attractive to Jane. The long hours in the open ensured that he was always brown. She marvelled at the fact that the man she had thought perfect became daily more handsome in her eyes.

As her cooking improved, she gained confidence and they began to have friends to dinner. They had begun to form friendships with Lockhart, the local doctor and the vet, who were young and, like themselves, recently married. With these people she was relaxed; she could entertain them confidently, make them laugh, be herself. She was amazed one evening to discover that none of them had ever been invited socially to the big house.

'Never, Richard? But you're their doctor, too.'

'I know, but it's a throwback to the Victorian and Edwardian eras when doctors were classed with farriers and expected to use the tradesmen's entrance.'

'But, Richard, you don't use the tradesmen's entrance, do you?' she asked, shocked.

'Not likely. On principle. But my father did during all the years he treated them.'

'God, that's awful, isn't it, Alistair? After all, who's more important than your doctor and your vet?'

Alistair was as surprised as she. He had to apologize: he had never given it a thought, he explained. Later, among themselves, the others discussed how things would change when the old boy and his wife died and what a breath of fresh air Jane would be. But they never told her how they regarded her.

It was Alistair who suggested that her parents should come to stay. Her mother had answered the letter she had written the day before her marriage. It had been the only letter she had ever received from her parents and it was a strange mixture of forgiveness and admonishment. This was followed by a large parcel containing a lurid pink, heavily embroidered eiderdown which she loathed on sight and knew she would never use. Yet she wept over it, for it was far too expensive for them to afford and its very garishness seemed to highlight the great gulf that lay between them. That had been months ago and now she had guiltily to admit to herself that she rarely thought of them these days. The life she had led with them and this new life seemed a million miles apart. She confessed that she did not want them to be part of her new life. But Alistair insisted.

'You can't just cut yourself off. They are your parents, after all.'

'I know, but I've got you now. I don't need anyone else. We've nothing in common. Hell, they never write or anything.'

'I still think you should invite them. Perhaps they're waiting for you to approach them.'

'Father won't like it here. He'll probably be rude to you.'

'Then we'll be quits over my mother.' He laughed, and she had to invite them, despite her misgivings.

Alistair was busy, and since she had not yet passed her driving test she sent Mark to pick them up. Inadvertently she insulted her parents, who felt slighted and were a little sulky when they arrived.

Jane purposely kept the food simple, knowing her father's taste. Even so, he toyed with his roast beef and left all his vegetables.

'Didn't you like the veg, Dad?'

'They weren't cooked,' he grunted.

'But that's the proper way to cook them, with a little bite still in them,' she explained.

'It might be the "proper" way to you, it isn't to me. I don't like raw vegetables – gives you worms.'

Despite Jane's efforts, neither parent made any attempt at conversation during the meal and she remembered the silent meals of her youth. Already she had changed, already she regarded good conversation as important a part of the meal as the food.

She noted much about her parents that she had not seen before or of which she had been unaware. How loudly her father ate, how careless he was at putting the food in his mouth. He virtually shovelled it in so that it was unpleasant to watch him. She became fascinated by the way her mother grimly held her knife and fork between mouthfuls, the handles firmly clutched in her fists, standing sentinel over her plate as if she were afraid that if she laid them down, her food would disappear. Had she always eaten like that? With horror Jane listened to her mother's strangulated accent: presumably she thought that it was an improvement on her normal speech, that she sounded genteel, but it was merely dreadful. At the dining table and later in the drawing room, her mother sat poised and uncomfortable on the edge of her chair as if she were about to spring up and leave. Jane longed to push her back on the cushions, tell her to relax, wishing she could help her mother, who was so obviously ill at ease, but unable to think what to say. She asked if they would like to meet some of her friends while they were staying. Her mother hurriedly, too hurriedly, said no, they did not want to bother with other people: it was Jane and Alistair they had come to see.

The next morning Alistair took them both for a ride around the estate in the Land-Rover. He returned, looking hot and bothered, without her parents.

'What happened?' she asked.

'He refused to ride with me, insisted on getting out halfway round, after lecturing me that my father's ownership of the estate was an obscenity and that I was a parasite, and what would I be fit for when the great day came and all the land was nationalized? He's gone off now to talk to the "workers", as he put it. Wants to talk to them without any "bosses in tow".'

'That sounds like Dad. Where's Mum?'

'She went with him, looking all flustered.' He managed to laugh.

'Mum will have gone to try and stop him getting into any fights. I did say I didn't think there was much point in them coming. He was certain to hate all this. Like a lot of working-class socialists he's against anybody having anything he hasn't got – that is, until he gets it.' She laughed ruefully.

Eventually her parents returned and her father went immediately into the study and settled down silently with the newspaper.

'What happened, Mum?'

'Right bloody fool he made of himself. Started asking all manner of questions of these farmworkers we met – rude questions, I thought – like how much did they earn and how many hours they worked, and what about overtime, that sort of thing. Then he began to run the system here down, and those men gave him a right mouthful. They told him they didn't need his nasty Commie talk here, that they were very happy and if all he'd come for was to be rude about Lord Upnor and his son, then he had better get off their land or they'd throw him off!'

'Oh, dear. Poor Dad.'

'Poor Dad, my aunt Fanny. He's a bloody stubborn old fool and he just seems to get worse.'

'Mum, would you like to see the big house this afternoon? She's not there this weekend, so you won't run into the old ogress.' Her mother was thrilled at the idea but her father refused to accompany them, saying he did not want to see any more trappings of decadent wealth. They left him with his newspaper while she and her mother toured the house together. When they returned, it was to find her father standing in the hall, with their bags packed beside him, demanding to be taken home.

'But, Dad, this is silly,' Jane pleaded. 'You have a couple more days yet. And Alistair's father will be here tomorrow. He so wants to meet you.'

'I'm not being silly. I don't like it here, I don't like the system, I don't want to be part of it, even for a weekend. I feel I'm betraying my class by being here. And if you think I'm waiting around here to meet a bloody earl or whatever he is, you've another think coming.'

'Dad, that's ludicrous.'

'It's not ludicrous, Jane. You've gone over, but not me. We have nothing in common any longer with you, Jane, or your husband. I'd rather not be involved, I'd rather go.'

She arranged for Mark to drive them back. She felt she should be sad, but she was not. They had never been her friends, so why should anything have altered now? While she found her father stupidly bigoted, she had to admire the fact that he stuck so steadfastly to his principles. Her father was right, they did not have anything in common any more, only the accident of birth. This was her home now, her friends were here, her security was here. She took the eiderdown which she had put on her and Alistair's bed for the duration of her parents' visit, wrapped it carefully, packed it with mothballs and put it at the back of the large airing cupboard.

4

As the months sped by, Jane's confidence in herself and her ability to manage grew daily. Their circle of friends was still small, partly because they met few people. The people in the other large local houses did not invite them, except for the Duchess of Wessex, who had them to dinner several times and who, in turn, had visited them. Jane felt as much at ease with her as she did when Honor or the vet and his wife came to dinner.

'Did you use to be invited to all the other houses?' she asked her husband one evening. That morning Rupert had been telling her of the dinner dance they had been to at the neighbouring estate.

'Yes.'

'Then why not now? Because of me, I suppose?'

'I think it's more that they've heard that my mother doesn't approve and they're frightened to offend her and perhaps not get invited to the parties at Respryn.'

'But the Duchess has us over.'

'She doesn't have to give a monkey's what Mother thinks. It's all about the old pecking order, isn't it? The Duchess can do what she likes about us, because Mother dare not be offended or she won't get invited to the castle! Remember, duchesses are the heavy artillery in the English social scene.'

'Heavens, it's like a game of musical chairs. I hope I never get like that — not having people around because I'm frightened of what those higher in the pecking order might think.'

'No, darling, I don't think you'll get like that for one moment,' he laughingly assured her. 'I don't mind either, you know that.'

'But Linda and Bertie Talbot have been very kind, and she's as thick as thieves with your mother.' It was true, the Talbots had gone out of their way to be friendly, often having them to supper, and Jane had an open invitation to pop in any time she wanted, which she often did.

'I've wondered about them,' Alistair said thoughtfully. 'It's very strange. As you say, she's very close to Mother. Have you ever thought that perhaps Mother's using Linda to report back on what we're up to? Or maybe she believes in keeping a foot in each camp so we'll still have her over when I inherit.'

'Alistair, how can you think such a thing? They've been so kind to me. I think, having no children of their own, they like young people about. I was scared of them at first but now I'm really happy to go there. Perhaps because they're so eccentric your mother overlooks their being nice to me as just another quirk?'

'They certainly work hard at being eccentric,' Alistair answered enigmatically.

Eccentric they surely were. Jane delighted in it and admired the total confidence in themselves which enabled them to look and act as they wanted, and to hell with everyone else. They lived in a large Palladian house which, through sheer neglect, was falling apart about their ears, the Talbots being of that breed of house-owner which feels that owning a property is enough. In consequence the house was literally crumbling: large cracks had appeared in its façade, masonry lay where it had fallen from the balustrade. The steps were cracked and weed-choked, the drive a nightmare of unfilled potholes. The inside of the house was no better; their furniture looked shrivelled from neglect and lack of polish. The dogs dirtied the beautiful old carpets, the smell of boiled cabbage filled the air. Linda was very like her house, her once fine face now wrinkled and dried from years of neglect and undernourishment, her clothes a total hotch-potch of old tweeds and strange shapeless jumpers which she knitted in random stripes. A meal there could be a fine dinner eaten from lovely porcelain with crested silver, or baked beans on toast eaten sitting on the floor, with the dogs and cats fighting round about.

Both Talbots were more right-wing than anyone Jane had ever met, but she was able to enjoy their political views because they were too extreme to take seriously. Linda's conviction that Communists lurked everywhere, not only under the prime minister's bed but probably in it as well, only added to Jane's amusement. She liked them and she trusted them, found it easy to talk to Linda and had begun slowly to confide in her. She would often ask her advice about a menu or how to answer a letter or address an envelope to some titled person.

The Talbots' vegetable garden was as weed-choked as their drive. Now that, thanks to Mark's patient help, Jane had passed her driving test, she had fallen into the habit of dropping in with baskets of vegetables from the abundant flow her own gardener supplied. One morning she rang the bell as usual, but there was no reply. This was not uncommon, so she let herself in, as she had been told to do. She could hear Linda's strident voice on the telephone in a room off the hall, and she waited.

'I know, it's a desperate problem, she's out of her mind with worry,' Linda barked into the phone. There was a pause as the other person spoke. 'I have them over quite a bit, really, so that I can let her know what's going on. I mean, she tries hard enough, I'll give her that. She's always dropping in and asking advice. My dear, if I told you the things that gel doesn't know, you'd be amazed!' She laughed stridently. 'It's no good, though. It's not going to work. It's the vowels, you see, the vowels always let them down.' Another pause. 'Oh, very pretty, but it won't last, she'll run to fat. All tits and arse, as Bertie says.' Linda laughed again, loudly. Heavens, thought Jane, what a bitch Linda could be at times! Strange in such a kind woman. 'Yes, I know,' Linda's voice continued. 'Well, I've told her to pray for a divorce and hope it comes before a brat is born. Poor old Blanche, she doesn't deserve all this.'

Jane heard no more. She stood rooted to the spot. She wanted to run but her legs felt leaden and would not move. The blood was drumming in her ears and made her feel faint. Linda appeared in the doorway.

'Jane, what a lovely surprise! Let me get Bertie to see his favourite neighbour. How long have you been here?' she asked pleasantly.

'Long enough, you cow! You hypocritical cow!' Jane shouted. 'I trusted you,' she wailed, and with a heave she threw the bag of vegetables at the astonished Linda. Jane rushed out of the door and ran down the steps, stumbling in her haste on the moss-covered step. She drove at breakneck speed back to the haven of her house. She had no need to explain to Alistair, because, on his return home in the evening, he received a long phone call from his mother. When it was over, he came back into the drawing room.

'What happened?' he asked. When she told him he said, 'I see, I'm sorry. Perhaps it would have been better if you hadn't called her a cow and thrown the veg at her.'

'She is a cow.'

'I know, but you shouldn't have said it.'

'Why not?' Jane demanded angrily.

'It will only be used against you. You only prove to them their theories about you.'

'I don't care what they think about me. I'll say what I bloody well like.'

'I know, I know, Jay. But sometimes it's more dignified to walk away from a situation – silently.'

'Sod dignity. She hurt me, don't you understand?'

'I understand. I'm just trying to warn you, that's all. What's for dinner?' he asked, and the incident was never mentioned between them again.

But the damage to Jane was enormous. The confidence she had so painstakingly begun to build was shattered. She had lost her capacity to trust, and she had lost faith in her own ability to judge people. She met people now only with reluctance, and the happy little dinner parties ceased.

She had said she did not care what people thought, but that was not true: she cared very much. She had been so determined to succeed, to show them that she could learn, become what people wanted her to be. She bought the book on correct word usage that Alistair had mentioned once, as a joke, and studied it surreptitiously. She made lists of words to memorize. Some were easy – her 'handbag' became her 'bag', though she still winced when she bravely said 'loo' instead of 'toilet'. She now sat on her 'sofa' instead of her 'settee'. She had learned to say 'What?' to Alistair but maintained her 'pardon' for the char and the girl who helped with the ironing, for she still had a deep distrust of this rude word 'what'. But some words she could not remember: they sounded too awkward and clumsy on her tongue and refused to lodge in her brain so that she still had a 'mantelpiece' instead of a 'chimneypiece' and hers was a 'mirror' and not a 'looking glass'.

She approached vowels with wariness and fear. A, E and U seemed the kindest but even these, when combined with the dreaded O and I, lurked to trip her up. She learned cunning with her use of words and asked people if they wanted their tea black, for no matter how she tried she could not say 'milk' as she knew it should sound to 'them'. She invited people to her place instead of her house. In conversation she adopted a slight stutter in a pathetic attempt to disguise her panic as words full of the dreaded vowels loomed ahead in a sentence. Silliest of all, she could not say 'vowel' either.

Once a month they would go to London for a long weekend. She looked forward desperately to these trips. They would see Alistair's friends from Cambridge who now had jobs in the City, and Sandra would come to dinner. Sandra was now a staff nurse and engaged to an aspiring estate agent, Justin Clemance, who was quiet and a little pompous, not at all like the extrovert Sandra.

Only in London did the old Jane come out of her shell. Occasionally Alistair insisted they should give a dinner party at Trinick but she was never able to enjoy them. She felt sick with nerves for days beforehand. She was wary even with the few friends they had made. She would have only one friend here in the country, Alistair.

The following August she refused to go to Scotland with him. They had a blazing row, which frightened her with its intensity, and she nearly weakened in the face of Alistair's anger, but finally she was adamant. Alistair was furious and sulked for days but Jane was certain that by not going she was protecting their relationship, not harming it.

Their joy in each other when he returned was magical. She now knew she had been right not to go. On his return they made love with more depth and a new urgency. She was not surprised, a few weeks later, to find that she was pregnant. Alistair and his father were beside themselves with excitement. Even Alistair's mother relented sufficiently to buy some exquisite baby clothes, and Alistair reported that she was thrilled at the prospect of a grandchild, even if it was growing in the wrong body.

Jane had looked forward to being pregnant. She hated the reality. Not for her the joy of a placid pregnancy, or the compensation of floating through it with an ethereal beauty. She was sick. She felt clumsy. She became fat. She wanted her body back.

Alistair was a considerate expectant father. If Jane felt ugly, he was at pains to reassure her that to him she was beautiful. He put up with her fluctuating moods. The only disagreement between them was over the question of a nanny.

'But I don't want a nanny, I'm not letting some other woman look after my baby.'

'Jane, it's eccentric enough that you won't have a cook. We're having a nanny and that's that.'

'All right then, I'll get a cook and look after the baby myself.'

'No, my child has a nanny. You'll be tired when the baby is born. With a nanny here you'll have time to relax.'

The argument was still unresolved when Jane, on a beautiful June day, went into hospital and a boy was born. They called him James Rupert.

Jane held the unfamiliar bundle in her arms and scrutinized him for imperfections. But there were none; he was perfect. She wondered if he would love her and, as she wondered, became aware that, if he did, a day would come when he would love another woman more than her. In the acceptance and the mental preparation for it she had already shut a part of her heart away from him, though she did not realize it. Her feelings for him puzzled her, he must mean more than life itself to her – that was what being a mother was all about. But he did not. She still loved Alistair more than she loved her child.

Alistair described the party his father had given for the estate workers. The men had made a cradle for the baby and their wives had sewn a beautiful layette. Jane was touched beyond words when Alistair told her.

When she returned from the hospital with the baby, it was to find a sour-faced harridan in charge of the nursery and a cook in the kitchen.

'Alistair, she's horrible. She won't let me pick up James when I want, and I virtually have to make an appointment to go into the nursery.'

'It's your own fault. You should have agreed and then you could have chosen your own nanny, instead of my having to ask mother to find one.'

'Your mother! Oh no, they'll be in league together, she'll report back all the time. I can't live with her,' Jane wailed.

'All right then, make other arrangements. It's your department, not mine, but you'll have to sack her.'

Jane found a pleasant girl in the village who had trained as a nursery nurse and she plucked up courage to tell the terrifying nurse to go. It was the right decision. Both James and Jane liked Clare from the start and the baby thrived under her care.

Again August loomed, and Alistair asked her, 'Will you come to Drumloch this year, Jane?'

'I can't – the baby,' she excused herself.

'There's plenty of room for the baby and nanny and well you know it. Am I to take it you're refusing again?'

'I'd rather not go, Alistair.'

'Why not, for heaven's sake? I get bloody lonely up there without you – and horribly frustrated.'

'I'm sorry, I just can't come.'

'But why not? You needn't go on the shoots or anything, you know that – I agreed. Mother's easing up with you slowly, especially since James was born. You can't spend the rest of your life pleading that you don't fit in. You've got to sooner or later.'

He kept questioning her, demanding to know the real reason why she would not go. Eventually she broke her pledge to herself.

'It's the change in you, Alistair. I can't bear it. You become a different person when you're there.'

'So, occasionally I get drunk up there. Heavens, it's the only time I do.'

'It's not just that, I don't mind you getting drunk. It's the way you behave when you are. I can't cope with it.'

'I don't know what the hell you're talking about.'

'I know, Alistair. And that's half the problem.'

'Come on, Jane, what do you mean?'

'You rape me, Alistair. Each night last time at Drumloch you raped me.'

'Don't talk such rubbish, Jane. You're exaggerating. Rape, that's too strong a word.'

'It's not too strong a word. It's best I stay here.'

'Well, don't be surprised if I'm unfaithful to you up there one of these years,' he shouted at her.

'She's welcome to you like that,' she shouted back, as he stormed from the room. His head reappeared around the door.

'Sometimes, Jane, I want to hit you!' He slammed the door shut. Always Scotland, that was the only time they rowed. What was it about that house?

So this year, as before, he went without her. To distract herself, Jane did what she often did now when she was upset – she embarked on a bout of vigorous housework, and decided to spring-clean the house.

Alistair had been gone a week, and she was beginning to enjoy the sheer physical effort the house demanded of her. Her figure was rapidly returning to normal and she was full of energy again. She and her cleaning woman were busy in the drawing room late one morning, when the telephone rang.

'Jay, darling.' It was Alistair, but his voice sounded strange, thick and muffled.

'Darling, can you speak up? The line is dreadful. You sound as if you're at the bottom of the sea.' She laughed.

'Jane, it's Pa – he's dead. Please, come quickly.'

Jane stood stunned. 'Oh, my poor darling! Yes, of course, I'll come immediately.'

'Get Lockhart. Get him to arrange an aeroplane for you. You can fly from Plymouth to Inverness.'

'Yes, darling, of course. Are you all right?'

'Bloody.'

'I love you,' she said, but the phone had already gone dead.

Lockhart, stunned as she herself was, arranged the hire of a light aeroplane. Jane hurriedly packed their bags, while Clare, the nanny, prepared James for the journey. Within a couple of hours they were in the air. They had to refuel on the way and she waited impatiently, desperate to be with Alistair to find out what had happened, hardly able to believe what she had heard. There must be some ghastly mistake. Not Rupert, not that darling man.

They landed at Inverness. Tucker was waiting for her with the Rolls-Royce. He touched his cap.

'A sad day, Lady Upnor.'

Jane swung round, looking for her mother-in-law – but there was no one there but Clare and the baby. In that moment she knew that Rupert was dead, but in his dying her life had taken another enormous lurch forward. She was the countess now.

5

Jane settled the baby and Clare in the back of the Rolls and climbed in the front with Tucker.

'What happened, Tucker?' she asked as the car sped through the gathering dusk.

'We are not sure, M'Lady. After breakfast his lordship went for a walk. When he didn't come back, and the guns were waiting, we went in search of him. We found him down a gully by the Maid's Pool. You know, M'Lady, the stretch where the river really narrows through the rocks?' She nodded. 'Lying half in the water, he was, and soaked to the skin. He was still alive, but only just. We got him back to the house and called the doctor, but it was too late.'

'So he died of his injuries?'

'We don't know, M'Lady. They've taken him to Inverness for the doctors to find out, M'Lady.'

They drove on in silence. If only someone had been with him on his walk. If only he had called. If only . . . if, if, if . . . Had he lain in the water unable to move but conscious that he was dying? The thought was too painful to contemplate, as was the idea of such a kind man as Rupert dying alone.

'How's my husband?' Jane asked, trying to blot out the images in her mind.

'He's bearing up, M'Lady. It's been a terrible shock.'

They finally drew up in front of Drumloch Lodge. Jane did not wait for the door to be opened for her, but ran into the house. The large hall was deserted, and there was a strange stillness about the house as if it knew that its master was dead. Jane looked up and for one lunatic moment it was as if the animals' heads were smiling. She shook her head at the trick the light was playing and went quickly into the drawing room, where she found Alistair sitting with his mother and some house guests whom Jane vaguely remembered from her one visit here. As she entered, Alistair jumped up and rushed across the room to her, his face grey and drawn, his arms outstretched. As she held him, he clung to her with a desperation that made her wince with pain as his hands dug into the flesh of her upper arms.

'Jay, thank God, you've come. I needed you,' he said with quiet intensity.

'I know, my love, I know. I'm here now,' she comforted him.

'There really was no need for you to come, you know. Quite unnecessary,' her mother-in-law said sharply.

'Lady Upnor, I can't begin to tell you how sad I am. I had to come and be with you all,' Jane said gently, her eyes filling with the tears that until now she had controlled.

'Really? I wonder. Are you?' There was a cold cynicism in Lady Upnor's questioning.

'I loved him, Lady Upnor,' she answered simply. 'He was kind to me. I shall never forget him.'

Banks had quietly entered the room. 'Excuse me, M'Lady,' he said to Jane, 'but Nanny wants to know, should she take Lord James upstairs now?'

'Yes, please, Mr Banks.'

'You brought the baby?' Lady Upnor asked, her voice dangerously raised.

'Yes, of course.'

'What on earth for? There's enough to worry about without a baby.'

'But I couldn't leave him – I mean, his feeds.'

'Oh yes, of course.' A look of distaste spread over Lady Upnor's face. 'I would appreciate it if you could keep your bovine activities to the upper floor.'

Jane felt as if she had been attacked physically. She felt herself redden, but bit back her angry words. This was not the moment. The house guests shuffled out of the room awkwardly, both obviously shocked by the older woman's assault on Jane.

'Mother, for God's sake, can't you drop it? At a time like this, especially,' Alistair pleaded.

'What, Alistair? Drop what? To what are you referring?'

'I'm referring to your stupid attitude to Jane. Can't you let it drop, just for now? I wish you'd get it into your head, Mother, she's my wife, I love her, and you sicken me with this endless carping, especially now, with Pa . . .' He couldn't finish his sentence.

'I don't know what you mean. Of course, I realize that Jane is your wife, I'm hardly likely to forget, am I? All I asked was that she not feed the baby in public.'

'As if she's likely to.'

'One never knows with people of –' She stopped.

'Of my class? Was that what you were going to say?' Jane asked bitterly. 'We do know what modesty is, you know. I'm not exactly a peasant. Look, Lady Upnor, I came because I thought I could help. Please, I don't think any of us can cope with this sort of thing now.'

'Help? You? What could you possibly do to help me?' The older woman asked with a shrill laugh.

'She's a help to me, Mother, and I'd appreciate it if you didn't forget it. You're obviously overwrought, and there's no point in carrying on like this. Come on, Jane, let's go and see James. I've missed him.'

He put his arm about Jane and led her from the room.

'What on earth brought that on? I really had begun to hope that with James's birth things might get a little better,' Jane said sadly.

'Perhaps it's the jealousy of the old queen towards the new,' he answered wearily.

Jane took the baby from Nanny and carried him into their bedroom to feed him. She sat on the four-poster bed, cradling her son. Alistair paced up and down the room, stopping now and then to gaze at them, as James sucked contentedly at her breast. Satiated, the baby hiccoughed softly and went to sleep. Gently Jane laid him on the bedspread.

'James'll never know him now,' Alistair burst out. 'I wish he had. Pa still had so much to give us, so much to teach us.' As he spoke, the tears began to roll down his cheeks. Jane held up her arms to her husband and held him to her.

'Jay, I'm not going to cope. I'm not ready yet. It's too much for me, I don't know how to do it, not like he did.' His voice was muffled with tears.

'Darling, you will, you'll manage beautifully, I know you will. And I'll be with you, I'll help you.' She held him tightly as the sobs tore his body. Her heart ached for the pain he was suffering. Slowly he calmed down.

'I'm sorry, darling,' he spluttered. 'Blubbing like little James here.'

'No, it's better you should cry, darling. It'll make it easier for you in the long run.'

The crying subsided. Alistair wiped his eyes. 'He wanted me to go on that walk, he'd suggested it the night before, said he wanted to talk to me. And I bloody well overslept!'

'He'd have understood, Alistair. Anyone can oversleep.'

'Yes, but I feel so guilty. Oh, God, Jane, what have I done?'

'You've done nothing, darling. I expect the doctor's report will show he had a seizure or something. He wasn't young any more.'

'You don't understand, Jay.' He put his head in his hands. 'I overslept because I'd been awake all night making love to another woman.' He looked at her with anguished eyes.

Jane felt cold, ice cold. She let go of his hands. She stood up and walked like a mechanical doll to her case, and slowly and methodically searched for a sweater. Carefully she put the sweater on. She walked to the chest of drawers and poured a glass of water from the pitcher. She felt dizzy, the patterned rug seemed to leap from the floor towards her. She took a deep breath to quell the wave of nausea she felt. Her coldness persisted.

'For God's sake, stop fiddling about, say something,' Alistair begged. She turned to him, her eyes full of pain. He saw her expression and looked away. 'Don't look at me like that,' he shouted. 'I can't bear you looking at me like that.'

'I wish you hadn't told me,' was all she said. 'I'd rather not have known.'

'Jane, I'm sorry, so bloody sorry. I had to tell you. All day I felt so guilty. If I hadn't done it, Pa might still be alive.'

'And will telling me bring him back?'

'I had to confess.'

'So that you can feel better? Destroy me, so long as the guilt's removed?' She did not cry, she felt no tears. She wanted to be warm, feared she would never be warm again.

'I did warn you it might happen, if you persisted in not coming here,' Alistair said defiantly.

'Yes, you did, I remember.' She heard her voice, a long way away.

'So you're partly to blame too.'

'Yes, I probably am,' she said wearily.

'Is that all you've got to say?' he asked.

'I don't know what else there is to say, not now. I can't think of anything to say, I don't know what you want me to say.'

'I want you to understand and forgive me.'

Jane looked at him, silently, for a long time. She looked at his handsome face, the dear mouth, the mouth that kissed her and whispered sweet words to her. The mouth that had kissed another woman, given pleasure to another woman. Had it whispered sweet words to her too?

'I understand, you're different when you're here. I can understand that, but I can't forgive you yet. Don't even ask me to,' she said in a strange, controlled voice.

'She's nothing, Jane, she means nothing to me.'

'She meant something last night. And the night before?'

'She's gone. She's a friend of Clarissa's, she –'

'I don't want to know. I don't want ever to be told,' she suddenly screamed at him, making him jump back with surprise registering on his face. The baby jolted awake, his little fists windmilling in the air, and he began to cry.

'My darling, I'm sorry, did Mummy make you cry?' She scooped the baby into her arms, caressing the child, lulling him. All her attention was focused on the baby; Alistair stood helplessly by. He answered a gentle knock on the door, and she heard him talking.

'Jane, the doctor's back from Inverness. You coming? He's waiting for me.'

'No, Alistair, I want to sleep. I'll see you in the morning. I want to be alone.'

'Jane!' He stepped towards her.

'Don't touch me,' she hissed at him.

She gave the baby to the nanny to settle for the night and prepared for bed, moving like an automaton. She washed, brushed her teeth, got into bed and then, uncertain, got out and cleaned her teeth again. She lay in the dark and began to shiver. She could not stop. She wanted to think and she could not. She shivered, her teeth chattered, and all she could think of was Alistair's mouth on another woman's body.

She awoke at dawn exhausted. She lifted herself on one elbow. Across the room, slumped in a chair, Alistair slept, his head on his chest, his hair falling forward into his eyes as it so often did. Beside the chair was a half empty bottle of whisky. She watched him as he must have sat in the night and watched her. What thoughts, what fears had threatened him then?

Now, at last, she was able to think and with a clarity that surprised her. She loved him, nothing he ever did could alter that. She wanted him to hold her, to heal her pain with his kisses and his words of love. He had made one mistake. Was that enough to destroy all the happiness which they had and would have together in the future? She had always thought it would be, that if he touched another woman everything would be over, her love for him would die. But it had not. Her love was strong enough to weather this. She slipped from the bed, crossed the room and knelt beside him.

'Alistair,' she whispered, 'Alistair.' He stirred. 'Darling, I love you.' He was awake.

'Jane, my love, say that again.'

'I love you.'

'Thank God. Oh, my darling.' He lifted her and carried her to the bed. 'Jane, I love you. I've been a bloody fool. I'll love you always, Jane, I want you, only you.' He began to shower her with kisses, his fear heightening his passion and his need for her.

Later as they lay together, entwined about each other, tears finally came and, as his tears mingled with hers, he vowed that he would never hurt her again.

The next few days were a bustle, with guests arriving for the funeral and local people calling to pay their respects to the family. Jane was fully occupied, arranging food and drink and bedrooms for overnight guests.

The report from Inverness confirmed that Rupert had had a severe stroke which had rendered him unconscious immediately and that, had he survived, he would no doubt have been paralysed and speechless. They all felt secret relief at the doctors' report.

Lady Upnor was marvellous, Jane had to admit. She never broke down; she received sympathy from friends and neighbours with quiet dignity and her outburst of the first night was not repeated. Jane decided that her mother-in-law's attack must have been a distorted form of grief. With her own sadness for Rupert she found for once that she could forgive her. Finally Lady Upnor even went so far as to thank Jane for all she was doing.

Honor arrived. Her grief for her brother was terrible to see. It seemed she grieved more for her brother than Lady Upnor for her husband. Jane spent many hours with Honor, patiently listening as she went over and over stories of their childhood together. The two women walked miles over the estate and, without the guns banging in the distance, Jane could appreciate fully the beauty and the glory of the place.

'You know, Honor, if I was ever really rich, I'd buy a place up here and never let anything be killed on it, unless it was hurt or there wasn't enough food for them all. Wouldn't it be paradise?'

'What a lovely idea! I hate the killing, too. It's why I rarely come here. Let's hope you're rich one day and can do it.'

One morning they sat by Jane's salmon pool watching the fish, content in each other's company.

'You've changed, Jane, what's happened?'

'What do you mean, Honor?' Jane asked, startled.

'You've been hurt, Jane, it's in your eyes. There's a look that wasn't there before, a wariness. What happened?'

Slowly Jane began to tell Honor. She explained how she wanted to forgive Alistair and forget the whole incident, but that it would not go away, kept her awake at nights. When she looked at him she could not stop herself imagining his mouth on another woman's flesh.

'Poor Jane. Bloody fool Alistair. Why on earth did he tell you?'

'To remove his guilt, I think.'

'Men always think that, the fools . . . "If I tell, if I say I'm sorry, it will all be better again . . ." I sometimes despair of men: they are so infantile.'

'Yes, I think he thinks it's all over and forgotten, that he merely had a narrow escape.'

Honor nodded her head sadly. 'You don't have to tell me. They're all the same. The truth is the other women really are unimportant to them, mean nothing, and yet they never understand the pain they cause. Pain like that can alter a relationship for ever. Why they do it is beyond me, especially when they have a good marriage. I mean, there's nothing wrong in yours, is there?'

Jane looked at her hands. She knew it was not right that she had always to pretend an orgasm when they made love, but could Honor help, could she explain? No, she could not confide in her: it was wrong, disloyal to Alistair. Reluctantly she let the chance slip away.

'Honor, apart from his mother, and her awful friends, I thought everything was perfect.'

'What happens when he does it again?'

'No, Honor, I couldn't forgive a second time.'

'He'll be unfaithful again, you know. They always are, once they've taken the plunge. It's like a dog that's worried sheep and tasted blood. It becomes a compulsion with them.'

'Oh no, Honor, I don't think he will. He promised me. I think he thought he had lost me.'

'I sincerely hope you're right and I'm wrong then, Jane dear. You know,' she suddenly said, lightening the conversation, 'I sometimes wish I were a lesbian. I'm sure they're so much nicer to each other.'

'But what guarantee would you have, even then?' Jane asked, laughing at last.

'None, I suppose. God, life can be such a bitch at times, can't it?'

Linking arms, they strolled back to the house for tea.

Rupert was buried the following day in the Highlands he had loved so much. Led by a piper playing a lament, the mourners followed the coffin up a steep hill. The strong, kilted estate workers carrying the coffin strained under its weight and the steepness of the path. The cortege wound through the woods, past the river, and up – up to the top of the hill that looked down on Drumloch and, spread out as far as the eye could see, the old Laird's land. They laid him to rest, the plaintive skirl of the pipes echoing in the valley below and tearing at the pain of all those who heard.

The lawyers had come from London and, after the funeral, the will was read to the family. As expected, he had left all his estates and his house in London to Alistair. He had made provision for his wife to receive a sizeable income for the rest of her life and left a lump sum to Clarissa. There were small bequests to members of his staff who had served him for many years and then, right at the end of the will, was a bequest of a flat in Chelsea and £20,000 to a Miss Jean Robins.

Alistair spent long hours with the lawyers and when he finally came to bed, he looked ill with fatigue.

'It's bad, Jane,' he announced. 'The bloody death duties are enormous.'

'Tomorrow, darling, we'll worry about it then,' she said comfortingly. He smiled gratefully.

'Jane, my love, make love to me.'

Later as they were staring into the darkness Jane asked, 'Darling, who's Jean Robins?'

Alistair laughed. 'My mother wanted to know that, too. Miss Robins was Pa's mistress, and had been for the last twenty-odd years. She's a nice woman, I met her several times – she made lovely chocolate cake and was very funny.'

'What on earth did you tell your mother?'

'I lied. I said I didn't know who she was. I decided to let someone else tell her. I couldn't face it.'

'Weren't you shocked by your father when you found out?'

'Good God, no. Why? It didn't harm anyone, did it? And a fellow needs some fun,' he replied unthinkingly as he settled down in his pillows. But Jane could not get to sleep and lay worrying, Honor's words endlessly turning in her head – 'He'll do it again, they always do.'

When sleep finally came, her dreams were of savaged sheep and blood dripping from the fangs of large, grinning dogs.

6

Despite the loss of Rupert, the next couple of years were to prove two of the happiest of their married life. The financial problems facing Alistair were so enormous that they had to work as a team to solve them. And they worked well together.

They continued to live in the dower house at Trinick. Each morning, after they had breakfasted with James, Alistair would leave for the big house. Jane would stay and play with James for an hour. She would then drive to Respryn in her red Mini. At Respryn she had her own office. Her main job was to catalogue the contents of the house for the official valuation. She had happily started the job, ignorant of what was actually involved. It was a complicated and lengthy task. It was soon obvious that she was going to need help, so a secretary was employed; and in the university holidays, a student from Cambridge acted as her researcher. No inventory had ever been done before: there had been no need. But with death duties and the spectre of the Inland Revenue at their shoulders, it finally had to be tackled. Lady Upnor took great exception to her activities. To anyone who would listen she complained that Jane was checking up on what she owned. But Jane was learning to ignore her mother-in-law.

Together they worked and planned. Deciding on economies here, investment there, always planning for the long-term future – ensuring the continuation of Respryn for their son. Jane was in her element and happy that Alistair really needed her.

The talk was continually of the dreaded death duties. Properties were going to have to be sold, but which ones?

Two of the farms at Respryn were sold. Alistair had been told that by selling his father's collection of rare maps a very considerable sum would be raised, but he could not bring himself to sell these – his father had loved them so much. But he could not save the Book of Hours nor two paintings – a Constable and a particularly beautiful Stubbs – which were taken to the sale rooms, leaving unsightly patches on the walls where they had hung, no doubt, since the day they were painted.

Alistair insisted on going to the sale and Jane went with him. At the end of the sale of Rupert's paintings, Jane glared angrily at the man who had successfully bid for them both. A week later she and Alistair were intrigued when a large wooden crate was delivered. Inside were the paintings and a scrawled note: 'Hang these for me, darling. Love, Honor.' As they joyfully supervised their rehanging, it was like having old friends back again.

Still more money had to be raised. Jane secretly hoped that Alistair would decide to sell Drumloch. She would be content never to see it again. But Alistair, after endless meetings with accountants and lawyers, was advised to sell the London house. It was an unproductive but valuable piece of real estate, whereas Drumloch produced revenue. Alistair was happy with the decision: since his father was buried at Drumloch he had dreaded having to sell the Scottish estate. Lady Upnor was in hysterics. At least her anger at losing her London mansion sidetracked her from her suspicion of Jane's activities. Now it was her son she complained of, telling her friends that he was throwing her out of her town house. As his mother became more difficult, so Alistair's irritation with her grew. Jane would not have been human if she had not felt pleasure at the rift she saw growing daily wider between mother and son.

Lady Upnor continued to live in the large house. She was observing a year's mourning which, she had announced at the funeral, she would be spending at Respryn. The year had almost passed but still she showed no signs of moving, had kept all her staff and, despite her mourning, continued to entertain as she had done when her husband was alive. Alistair found himself paying her expenses, since his mother was adamant that the allowance her husband had left her was for her personal needs only, and not for wages and food.

'Look at these bills,' Alistair said angrily one morning in Jane's office, flinging a pile of statements on her desk. 'Just look at them! We can't afford this kind of expenditure.'

'You're going to have to tell your mother she must cut back.'

'She'll never cut back while she's here. We'll have to get her to move to Trinick.'

'Alistair, no!' Jane said, horrified. 'Please, don't even think of it. I love Trinick. She's welcome to stay in Respryn. I don't want to live here, the idea is too daunting. And think of the effect on your mother. We're happy as we are.'

'We have to move here, darling, you know we have to. It's expected of us. She knows the score better than you do, Jane. She knows she should have moved to Trinick months ago, that the widow always does. She's just being pigheaded —'

'Who's being pigheaded?' his mother asked, sweeping into the room. She smiled icily at her son. 'See to these, Jane.' She handed Jane a list.

'What do you want me to do with it, Lady Upnor?'

'Type it, of course, on that machine of yours.' Lady Upnor waved her hand vaguely at the typewriter and Jane's secretary who was cowering nervously behind it. 'It's my instructions for the staff for my house party at Drumloch.'

'Mother! You can't be thinking of a shooting party so soon.'

'Of course I am. Your father would have wanted it.'

'Firstly, Mother, I think we should give it a miss this year. After all, it's the first anniversary of Father's death. But also it's the expense.'

'I beg your pardon, Alistair,' Lady Upnor thundered at her son. The young secretary, fumbling for her notepad, quickly excused herself and scuttled from the room. 'How dare you speak to me like that in front of the staff?'

'I'm sorry, Mother. I forgot the girl was here. But I'm angry. This can't go on. Look.' He showed her the bills. 'The only solution I can think of is to shut up most of Respryn, to cut back on staff and, with some economies, I think you'd be more comfortable at Trinick.'

'I hate discussing money, Alistair, it's too vulgar.'

'I'm sorry you think so, Mother. But I'm afraid you're going to have to steel yourself to do so.' There was no humour in his voice.

'I could live in one wing.' She was bargaining now.

'Don't you listen to anything, Mother? We can't afford to keep a whole wing open. What's more, all the time you're here, Jane can't be mistress of her own house.'

'Fine mistress she is likely to make.' Jane looked coldly at her mother-in-law who continued as if she were not present. 'It will be the end of Respryn, if it's left in her hands.'

'Mother, don't start that. I'm not interested in your stupid vendetta. Be fair, I've leaned over backwards to help you. I can't afford it any longer. If you're off to Scotland next week, I suggest that, while you're away, we move your possessions over to Trinick for you.'

'I shall hate that poky little house.'

'And, while I'm on the subject of economies,' Alistair continued, ignoring her protest, 'we can't afford a large house party at Drumloch this year.'

'But I've invited everybody.'

'Well, you're just going to have to uninvite them. They're all friends, they'll understand.' His mother complained volubly and bitterly but Alistair was unyielding.

'Will you be coming to Drumloch with me, then?' She knew she was defeated.

'No, Mother, I've too much to do here.'

His mother swept out of the room as imperiously as she had entered. Jane relaxed in her seat. The woman was impossible, but still, Jane was beginning to feel sorry for her. The adjustments in the older woman's life were going to be enormous. But she was overjoyed at the news that Alistair would not be going to Scotland. She had been dreading it, knowing that this year, had he gone, she would have had to accompany him.

While his mother was away, Jane supervised the change of houses. For themselves, within the large house, they had a set of rooms which amounted to a house. In the west wing, which had a door to the courtyard, they had a large drawing room, a dining room and study. Upstairs was their own bedroom, dressing rooms and bathrooms and two guest rooms. On the next floor were James's nurseries and his nanny's room. The rest of the staff slept in the old servants' wing, just as they had always done. Alistair would occasionally sigh at the way they lived but Jane thought they were magnificently housed.

Laying off some of the house staff was painful for Alistair, who had known most of them all his life. Some were pensioned off in cottages on the estate; for others he found new jobs. There was endless talk of economy and discomfort. Jane's childhood was still too close for her to be anything but amused by this family's idea of hardship. Banks was kept on, with one footman. Lady Upnor's cook and kitchen maid decamped to Trinick. Jane had a new cook at Respryn, and a scullery maid. Alistair kept his valet, Mark, and insisted that because of her new position, Jane must have a lady's maid. With no hesitation she asked for May, and welcomed the girl like a long-lost friend. The chauffeur, Tucker, remained secure in his flat over the garage where the gleaming Rolls still stood; the baby had his nanny. The gardeners were cut from twelve to three and an army of cleaning women came in each day from the village. They still lived in one of the most beautiful houses in

England; they still had their house in Fulham and the estate in Scotland. Economy, she learned, was a relative word.

Suddenly the press re-emerged in Jane's life, taking an inordinate interest in her reactions to her new position. Once again the telephone became a threatening instrument which she avoided answering, in case it was an aggressive, nosy reporter. She was left with a fear of the machine which she was never able to conquer.

Despite the fact that she was now the countess, she did not feel that she was, just as she had never really felt she was Lady Redland. The use of her title continued to embarrass her: she always felt a fraud when using it. In London, where she could be anonymous, she took to calling herself Mrs Upnor, and felt much more comfortable with that. But Alistair found out and was furious. Angrily he told her to pull herself together and to stop being so neurotic; she was his wife and as such would be treated with the respect that his title deserved. This argument only made Jane more confused. How could a title, which after all was merely a word, confer respect? Only a person should be worthy of respect. 'Think of the advantages,' she was told, but she found it difficult to find any. Honor claimed that it ensured better cabins on liners, hotel rooms with the best views, and VIP treatment at airports, but since they never travelled, those advantages escaped her. There were distinct disadvantages, for Jane was convinced that prices went up when her title was mentioned. She soon realized that everyone reacted in some way to it when they were introduced to her. Some people became obsequious, others belligerent, and some tended to stand back as if fearing to be friendly, in case this should be misinterpreted. Sadly, these were the people whom Jane would most have liked to know. Even old friends' attitudes seemed to have changed: they were almost deferential, which only embarrassed Jane further. No one, it seemed, in this society, remained neutral to a title, except those who already possessed one, and Jane still felt ill at ease with them.

To Jane, her mother-in-law was still the countess. Jane was relieved that old Lady Upnor kept on various charitable positions which would otherwise have fallen to Jane, who did not feel ready to be the president or the chairman of anything yet, if ever.

Society, which had cut her dead, now courted her. The invitations poured in and the telephone rang continuously. Jane was amazed at the way these people chattered to her as if their silence and rejection of her had never happened. She was fêted, and she despised them for it. She was wise enough now to realize that should anything happen to Alistair, the procedure would go smartly into reverse. Had it been her choice, she would have had nothing to do with these people, but Alistair insisted that she entertain and be entertained by them. He was certain they were now aware of their error. 'You see, my darling,' he would say, 'they're acknowledging how wonderful you are. People aren't that bad, are they?' She wondered at his naivety, but did as he asked. She was amazed at how easy it was to be hypocritical, as she smiled at them, talked to them, ate with them, and still, inside, hated them. But about one thing she was adamant – Linda and Bertie Talbot entered Respryn over her dead body – and Alistair conceded.

Their trips to London were few – there was still too much work to do at Respryn – but occasionally Alistair had to go to see his lawyers, accountants and brokers, and Jane usually went with him. It gave her a chance to forget who she was.

Sandra was married and living in Cambridge. When Jane was in London she would try to get to town so that they could have lunch together and do some shopping.

Jane had visited her parents once since Rupert had died. But it had not been a success. It was not just the stares of the neighbours that bothered her, but the knowledge that her parents' way of life was so different now from her own. She wished she had money of her own to rehouse them. She did not like to ask Alistair, who had problems enough – if on a different scale. So she took to inviting them to London, where they would have tea, always in a Lyons Corner House, which was her mother's favourite. Then they would go to a show, usually a musical, and after a steak supper her parents would take the train back. She had given up trying to persuade them to stay the night. They seemed happy with these outings and it was a neat compromise as far as Jane was concerned.

Jane worried about Alistair. There were days when his new responsibilities seemed to weigh far too heavily upon him, and he seemed to age before her eyes. Then, just as she decided she must say something to him, he seemed to shake the problems away and the light-hearted, slightly wild Alistair of old would return. Usually, he would insist on a party, always at Fulham and always with the old friends from Cambridge. These parties seemed to be a safety valve for him. And if he got drunk on the wine, never whisky, she said nothing: it was as if he needed to.

They did not make love as often as they had. But Jane was not worried. She had read in a new women's magazine that sexual activity tailed off after the first couple of years and she guessed that she and Alistair were average in their lovemaking. In a way, she was relieved since, when she faked her orgasm, she always felt as if she were lying to Alistair. This way she did not have to lie so often.

As the problems at Respryn eased, Alistair finally took his seat in the House of Lords. Jane sat with Lady Upnor in the peeresses' gallery and watched the age-old ceremony unfold below her. The drama and solemnity of the occasion, in the dignified surroundings, brought home to Jane a fuller understanding of what her husband's position entailed.

London was beginning to swing, but Jane was happy for it to do so without her. She was happiest at Respryn. The city girl she had once been had completely disappeared. It was the country life she lived for. She began to take a great interest in the farm. With Lockhart's guidance she and Alistair began the long task of building a prize herd of cattle. They began to buy rare breeds, and imported a couple of Highland cattle from which to breed. Jane collected chickens and became a passionate admirer of goats. She lived in jeans and Wellington boots. She even went to the local point-to-points. So much for Lady Upnor's fears that Jane would miss the bright lights.

She had already discovered an interest in gardening while making the garden at Trinick, but now, with the large walled garden and the yards of greenhouses at her disposal, she was in her element. She planned and planted one garden, based on the scent of flowers, which even her mother-in-law admired.

Lady Upnor was less of a problem. Alistair had bought her a flat in London. At first she had complained that people of her status did not live in flats. This one was large, however, and, in Regent's Park: she soon discovered its advantages and returned to her previous life-style of weekdays in London and weekends in the country.

It was three years before Alistair could bring himself to go back to Drumloch, but the estate needed to make more money if he were to keep it. Jane and Alistair returned together. It was June and in the Highlands yellow gorse bloomed profusely, reflecting the bright sunshine that shone every day. The rhododendrons were a chaotic riot of colour. May blossom scented the air. There was none of the drizzle of August and there were no midges to drive them mad. Scotland was at its best and Alistair, relieved of the pressures of the south, was once again the carefree husband Jane remembered. In this peace, and her contentment, she began to love the place as Rupert must have done.

After long consultations with the factor and ghillies, it was decided to let the estate to the many rich Americans, Brazilians and Germans who were eager to rent stalking and fishing in Scotland. For the grouse-shooting in August and September it was decided that Jane and Alistair would host large parties which would be lavishly entertained in the old style.

That first August Jane discovered that the very rich were demanding and never ceased to complain. She found it almost impossible to pretend excitement over a large 'bag' which she was expected to admire. But she had to be there for only a month each year, and then she could return to Respryn. It was the price she had to pay so that Alistair could maintain his beloved Highland estate. Without her saying anything to him, Alistair had stopped drinking whisky while they were there.

James was a quiet little boy, thin and rather shy, but with his father's fair hair and brown eyes. By three he was already studious and would rather sit with a book than play with his soldiers. Of one thing there was no doubt, he adored his father, and would follow him everywhere about the estate, even copying the way Alistair walked. Jane was relieved that he felt so strongly for his father, for to her surprise, tinged with a certain amount of guilt, she found that though she loved the child, she did not have Alistair's patience with him. And she knew that, despite all the talk of the power of maternal love, she still loved Alistair more.

With memories of his own isolated childhood, Alistair agreed wholeheartedly with Jane's idea that they should set up a nursery school at Respryn for the child, and invite the very young children of the estate workers and village to join. Clare was in charge, and they were relieved to see that with his own age group James was not shy at all.

By the time he was five they decided to go one step further and enrolled him in the village school, the first Upnor child not to have a governess. Alistair's mother was up in arms and blamed Jane entirely for the decision.

Now that Alistair had taken his seat in the House, he was invited to join various boards of directors and he took over the charitable patron-ages of his father. A large part of his week had to be spent in London, but there were also the estates to oversee. Despite his initial fears, he was managing well. There was a new assurance and maturity to him.

For a couple of years Jane dutifully went to London as often as she could manage. It was hard for her: she found that she could not share his enthusiasm for his new life in London.

His business life she found dull. Many of the dinners he had to attend and give were boring affairs with people much older than themselves. Jane could now hold her own in country society talking of country matters but, having no interest in the world of business, she found herself once again reduced to monosyllabic conversation.

Alistair had also taken a fancy to the social life, which left Jane feeling that all the confidence she had managed to build was stripped away from her. She liked the tennis at Wimbledon, but Henley and Ascot were a different matter: there she had to talk to people, there she had to look elegant and self-possessed. She was aware that, compared with the other women in their set, she looked wrong. She could buy whatever she wanted – the problem was that to look 'right' entailed going into the sort of shops where Jane still felt intimidated by the assistants. She knew full well that she could now spend on a dress four times what these supercilious *vendeuses* earned in a week, but the knowledge did not help her. She was angry with herself but she was trapped, as always, in the mesh of insecurities which so often, she knew, were of her own making. In consequence, her outfits were often remarked upon unkindly. But if they sniped at her dress sense, no one could find anything unkind to say about her face, which with its haunting grey eyes was increasingly beautiful.

Alistair accepted every invitation that came his way. Tentatively she suggested that she would prefer to stay most of the time at Respryn, that she did not really like London and his friends. She was too relieved by his agreement to be hurt by it. This did not prevent her, though, from wishing that their old life could have continued as it used to be. And she spent her time longing for his return or a phone call from him.

Rupert had been dead for over five years when the most momentous changes began to take place. Respryn was losing money: something had to be done. It was Jane who first suggested that they should open the house to the public. It seemed wicked that all its beautiful contents should lie unseen, covered in dust sheets. Properly managed, the house should be able to pay for itself.

'Do you think you could organize it?' Alistair asked her one evening soon after she had suggested the idea.

'Me? You're joking!' She laughed.

'No, I'm not. I can't do it. I just don't have the time. I've too many commitments as it is.'

'I'm not sure I could.'

'Nonsense, of course you can. Look how well you run this place with me away so much. I sometimes feel I'm redundant at Respryn. It's always amused me how much you've proved my mother wrong.' He laughed. 'Think about it, Jay.'

Certainly, she had proved Lady Upnor wrong. Her training at St Cuthbert's, much as she had hated it, had taught her discipline and organization. She was surprised to find she enjoyed running the large, unwieldy household. She did not mind the cut-backs in staff and was quite capable of getting a bucket and mop and giving a hand when necessary.

But what Alistair said was not strictly true, for she had learned that most valuable of lessons, to delegate. Much of the running of the household was done by the true professionals, Banks, the cook, the head gardener and Lockhart. They were all far more capable than she of knowing what to do, what to serve, whom to place with whom, and what to plant and when to sell. Far from despising her, they appreciated her confidence in their abilities.

She decided to try to organize the opening of Respryn. She spent a busy few months touring other stately homes, sometimes as a guest of the owner, more often as a plain tourist – she found she learned more that way. The other owners were most helpful. Her head was dizzy from the advice they gave. Some advocated animals in the park; others told her to keep clear of them at all costs, that they would only ruin the trees. Some thought funfairs were the best money-spinners; others warned her that these only encouraged riff-raff. All were in agreement that the most important factors were good loos, and a restaurant serving nonstop tea. One duchess was adamant that half the trippers came just to say they had peed at her castle.

She naively hoped to open the following year, but she had not reckoned with the local planning authorities, who were obsessed with lavatories, fire regulations and crowd control.

It was not only the local authorities with whom she had to deal. Once their plans became known, representatives of protection and conservation societies appeared from nowhere leaping to the defence of Respryn. She wasted precious hours placating, reassuring and explaining to them. She was becoming expert at handling people.

She had the estate carpenter build her a mock-up of the house and she spent hours with it planning various routes for the guided tours.

She enjoyed compiling the guide book. Her work on the inventory had given her a good knowledge of the house's contents and of which things to illustrate in the book. She wrote a potted history of the house and family. She organized the printing. Alistair watched her activities with pride.

She turned the old servants' hall into the necessary cafeteria, with gingham tablecloths. She ordered robust china with the Upnor crest, arguing with Alistair that everyone liked eating off crested china. She arranged for a group of village women to make the jam and cakes they would sell. Since this would be the first money the women had ever earned in their own right, there was no shortage of volunteers.

She bought boats for the lake, had the swimming pool relined. Parts of the park were designated picnic zones and furnished with rustic tables and benches and giant wastepaper baskets. The old racquet court was converted into a gift shop. The mounting costs worried Jane but Alistair, bravely signing the cheques, pointed out that one never made money without spending it first.

The loos, though, were her pride and joy. Their white tiles gleaming, the brass taps burnished, the wooden seats shining, they were tucked away unobtrusively behind the stables.

She rejected the idea of wild animals in the park, or a funfair. Respryn would stand or fall on its beauty alone.

A year later than she had planned, they eventually opened. It was a success and the funniest thing of all was that Jane found she was one of the chief attractions. Everyone wanted to say they had met the 'working-class countess'.

Alistair's mother treated the whole operation with disdain, regarding it as nothing better than a vulgar circus for which she blamed Jane, and from which she distanced herself totally. Honor, on the other hand, was far more philosophical. Times had to change, she acknowledged. On her visits she became an enthusiastic and popular guide.

Outwardly the changes in Jane were many. She had a far more confident air: everyone was agreed on that. Her ability in organizing Respryn had given her a veneer of authority to which others responded. She did not even realize that she now said 'What?', 'loo' and even 'bog' and 'arse' as a matter of course. But inside her there was no change, she was still afraid, still self-conscious, still desperate for Alistair's love. What the years had given her was the ability to hide her inadequacies and to fool the world into believing that she was now a competent, self-assured woman.

She loved Alistair more with each passing year, but then she had always known that there could only ever be one man for her. It seemed unbelievable that they had been married for ten years, for the years had slipped by so quickly.

She was tired. It had been a busy day. She was glad of her bath and now, with her well-earned gin and tonic, she sat contentedly by the fire at Respryn waiting for Alistair to return from London. The phone rang.

'Darling?'

'Alistair, where are you?'

'London. Sorry, darling, but I've got tied up here in a business meeting and I can't get away.'

'Poor you. Never mind. We were going to have salmon – I'll get cook to put it back for tomorrow.' She started to chatter about her day, but he seemed distracted so, reluctantly, she rang off, disappointed. Recently Alistair had become so busy in London that he was often delayed.

The next day, Saturday, was a full day for Jane. She had acted as guide, sold souvenirs and helped out with the teas, and it was not until the last car drove away that she had time to realize that Alistair was not back and had not phoned. She tried the number of the Fulham house several times and listened bleakly as she heard the phone ring in the empty house. At ten he phoned.

'Darling, where are you? I was worried, I've been trying the Fulham number all evening.'

'Sorry, sweetheart, I got delayed. Look, it seems silly to come back now. I'll stay in town until next week.'

'Oh, Alistair, do you have to? I'm missing you.'

'I've got a board meeting on Monday anyway. It's daft to travel all the way down just for Sunday. I'll see you Monday evening.'

'Alistair, please come.'

'No, darling, I've just told you I'm bloody tired. It makes more sense this way.'

She heard a burst of laughter in the background.

'Alistair, where are you?'

'I'm at Clarissa's. Look, darling, I must fly,' and she heard the phone go dead.

She felt little tendrils of fear in her stomach. She thought he had not seen Clarissa for years, not since she married a merchant banker called Hector, who, like Clarissa, could hardly speak a civil word to Jane. Why go and see her now? He loathed her, he was always saying how much he disliked her. Had he, over the years, been seeing her, and thought it better not to tell Jane?

If he could deceive her over seeing Clarissa, what other things had he not told her? When he had first confessed his infidelity to her, she had watched him like a hawk, convinced that she would know if he were unfaithful again. There had been nothing, she was certain. But what did she expect? Was he to appear with a sign around his neck 'I am an adulterer', like some creature in the medieval stocks? How could she be so certain? How much about his life away from Respryn did she really know?

She cancelled dinner, she did not want to eat. She tried to watch TV but could not concentrate. She sat staring into the fire, a large gin and tonic in her hand, knowing instinctively that her greatest fear had materialized.

8

She spent a restless night, anger, mistrust and jealousy devouring her.

When morning broke Jane tried to rationalize her fears. Maybe she had overreacted. It was true, Alistair was very busy in London these days and he did get very tired. If he had bumped into Clarissa, what would be more natural than that she should ask him back for a drink, to see her new house perhaps?

All day Sunday she filled the hours with hard work, anything to stop herself thinking. That evening she sorted through all the cupboards and wardrobes in her dressing room. 'Busy, I must keep myself busy,' she kept telling herself.

On Monday evening she sat waiting nervously in the little study which, in the interests of economy, they used as a sitting room. She heard the dogs barking and knew that he had arrived. She felt certain that, when he entered the room, she would be able to read the truth in his face. But as he approached her he looked the same, the same sweet smile, the tender kiss. Perhaps she had imagined everything.

'My, you look pretty, M'Lady.' He grinned at her, poured himself a drink and freshened hers.

'Did you have a nice time?' she asked.

'Nice time? Oh, you mean at Clarissa's? Yes, fine. She doesn't send love, by the way!' He laughed at the thought.

'What's the house like?'

'Fine.'

'Is it big?'

'Average. Is dinner ready? I'm starving.'

'Nicely furnished?'

'Yes.' He studied his drink.

'Has she had designers in?'

'I wouldn't know. God, Jane, why all this sudden interest in Clarissa's house?' He poured himself another drink. 'When is dinner ready?' She sat opposite him and knew that he lied. He had not been to Clarissa's, his answers were too evasive. The thought lurched through her. She knew she was relying on instinct which could be a dangerous thing to do, but she could not stop herself.

'Who else was there?' she continued, relentlessly.

'At Clarissa's? No one, just Hector.'

'I thought I heard a lot of people laughing.'

'No. Just us. Ah, Banks! Dinner, at last.' He smiled at the butler. They settled themselves at the table in the little dining room. 'Tell me about your week,' he said.

'It's been a good one. We had over 600 on Saturday.'

'Splendid.'

'But I'm tired. I've been thinking, Lockhart could manage without me for a few days. How about you and me getting away for the weekend, together? How about next weekend?'

'Darling, I'm sorry. I accepted an invitation to go to Wallace Hawkins's and you know you never enjoy it there with all that horse talk.'

'Without me!'

'As I said, you hate the hunting and shooting fraternity. What's the point in your going?'

'I like the weekends with you, Alistair.'

'I know, my pet, but I really ought to cultivate Wallace a bit more. Just this once. We'll arrange something for another weekend, I promise.' He smiled at her.

After dinner they sat and watched television and she was almost grateful for the flickering screen which made conversation unnecessary. She wanted to probe further but at the same time she was afraid to.

'Will you be long?' she asked, deciding to go to bed.

'No, I'll just watch the end of this.'

She lay waiting for him. The light on the telephone console flickered on, indicating that the phone was being used. She longed for the courage to pick it up but was afraid of what she might hear. The call was a long one: it was a good half-hour before the little light went out and the receiver pinged. He came to bed.

'Not asleep?' he asked unnecessarily. 'God, I'm tired.' He yawned. He climbed in beside her but did not turn to take her in his arms as he always did when he had been away for a few days. Then she knew for certain. It had not been her imagination: the dream was over.

He was home for two more nights and, although he behaved to her in the same way, he never touched her or made love to her. Her body longed for him; she would lie beside him wanting to touch him but frightened of his rejection.

On Thursday he left, saying he would phone and that he would be back on Monday. She watched his car disappear down the drive and then, knowing what she must do, she called May.

'May, I want to go to London for some time. Do you think you could manage to look after James and me? It'll just be the two of us for a couple of months until James starts at his new prep school.'

'Of course, M'Lady, no problem at all.'

'I want to have a nice long holiday, alone with James, before he goes to boarding school. Perhaps you would pack his bag and some of his toys, and a couple of cases for me?'

She called Lockhart, told him she would be away for a while and instructed him to take charge for her. She got out her BMW, her thirtieth birthday present from Alistair last month. With May and James in the back she drove across the park which looked magnificent in the June sunshine. She did not once look back.

She knew that it would be safe to go to Fulham, it was unlikely he would take another woman there. May was thrilled with the little house and did not mind sharing a room with James.

'How long will we be here, M'Lady?'

'I don't know. May, would you do me a great favour? Please stop calling me "M'Lady", I hate it. Call me Jane.'

'M'Lady!' said May in a shocked voice. 'I don't think I could do that.'

'Please, May, I want you to. Everything's different now.'

'I'll try, but I think it will be difficult . . . Jane.'

There was no telephone call that evening. Not until late the following evening did it ring. She sat with her drink in her hand and watched it, willing it to stop. Over the weekend, the telephone sounded intermittently and each time she sat and looked at it, longing for the noise to cease in case she weakened and answered it.

It rang again when they were sitting at the kitchen table, while May and James ate their supper.

'Why don't you answer it?' May asked eventually.

'I don't want to,' Jane replied.

'Jane, I'm sorry to say this, it's not my place, but I've got to. M'Lady, you look terrible. You should eat. Just drinking is not good for you at all, and won't solve anything.'

'I can't eat, May, I just can't.'

'Oh, M'Lady, please, M'Lady, what's happening?' May began to cry.

'Don't cry, for God's sake, I can't stand it. I'll be all right, really I will. Just give me time to handle this in my own way. And I asked you to call me "Jane".' She heard the irritation in her voice and felt ashamed that she should snap at May.

On the Sunday he came. She was sitting in bed, too desolate to get up and face another day burdened with the knowledge which lay like a cancer within her. She heard May talking to him, heard her take James out for his walk, heard Alistair bounding up the stairs.

'Jane, for Christ's sake, what are you playing at? I've been worried. What the hell are you doing here? Why don't you answer the phone?'

'I've left you, Alistair.'

'You've what?' he said, astonished. 'Why, for God's sake?'

'You're being unfaithful to me again.'

'Don't be so bloody ridiculous, Jane – just because I go to Wallace's for the weekend without you.'

'Yes, but who did you take with you? Don't pretend, Alistair, there's no point. I know.'

'Who told you?' he asked urgently.

'No one.'

'Someone must have. That cow Clarissa!'

'No one had to tell me anything. I know, that's all.'

'How the hell could you possibly know?'

'Because I love you, Alistair. I didn't need anyone to tell me.'

He sat heavily on the bed. 'I am so sorry, so terribly sorry.'

'You said that last time.'

'But I mean it, it's nothing. She means nothing to me.'

'You said that last time, too. No doubt you would say it the next time.'

'But I love you, Jane.'

'I know, that's what makes it so bloody tragic.'

'Jane, come on, pack your bag. We'll all go home. I promise it will never happen again. We love each other, you've just said so, we can't throw that away. We'll work it out, I'm certain we can.'

'No, Alistair, you don't understand. I can't bear the thought of you touching someone else. I can't share you. It's all or nothing for me, it always has been, I told you that the day we got engaged. I warned you. How the hell do you think I felt lying next to you these last nights with you not touching me, not wanting me? I've thought a lot these last few days. I think I'll be better alone. The pain of being with you, like this, is too much to cope with.'

'Jane.' The anguish in his voice hurt her. She longed to hold him close to her. But she knew that if she touched him she would be lost and her pain would only intensify.

'I think you're being overdramatic,' he suddenly announced in a completely different tone of voice. 'It's only a little affair. I repeat, it means nothing to me.'

'It means everything to me.'

'Jane, be reasonable. How often do I go off the rails?'

'Once too often, I'm afraid, Alistair. Don't you remember we made vows to each other?'

'Oh, Jane, don't be so bloody working-class.'

'I am working-class, don't you remember? That's what all the fuss has been about all these years.'

'But everybody does it.'

'Everybody doesn't do it. I'd rather stick with my working-class morality, thank you, than be an aristocrat with the morals of an alley cat,' she spat at him. His hand flashed through the air and hit her hard across the face. She could feel her skin begin to swell, she felt her eyes smarting, but she did not flinch, did not touch her face. Instead, she looked at him, steadily.

'Jane, I'm sorry, I didn't mean to do that but I can't understand what's happening. If you love me, why leave me?'

'Because I want to continue to love you. If I stayed with you and this kept happening, then I might hate you.' He sat back on the bed, his head in his hands. 'But why, Alistair, tell me? I have to know. What did I do wrong?'

'Nothing, Jane, you've done nothing wrong. You've been marvellous, putting up with my mother and sister, all you've done at Respryn, your hard work at Drumloch, and loving me the way you have. It's I who am in the wrong. I admit it. I don't know why I do it.' He paused. 'I guess I get bored every so often and want some excitement, you know.'

'No, Alistair, I'm afraid I don't know.'

'Jane, all marriages end up like this. Surely you realize that? Hell, I wouldn't mind if you had the odd fling, provided you were discreet about it. It wouldn't alter our love for each other. My little adventures haven't, have they?'

'Oh, Alistair,' she said, a deep sadness in her voice. 'I've been such a stupid, blind fool. I thought it had just been that once in Scotland, but it hasn't, has it? There have been others, haven't there?' He did not answer.

He did not need to: the guilt on his face spoke for him. 'Then there really is no hope. No hope for us. I'd rather you went now.'

'But James, what about James? Have you thought of him?'

'Of course I've thought. You can have him each weekend – it's the only time you're at home anyway. I'll look after him in the week. In any case he goes to boarding school in September, poor little boy.'

'Poor little boy? It's a good job he's going if you're planning to be as stupid and selfish as this. What sort of life will that be for him? He needs us both.'

'We'll sort something out about the holidays. Share him, or take it in turns.'

'My God, you're a cold fish. I'd never dreamed it of you – parcelling out your son like that. I thought . . .' His voice was drilling into her skull. He was so clever, she knew that it was only a matter of time before he managed to make her feel guilty, as if it were all her fault. She had to stop him.

'Will you go now, please, Alistair? I'm very tired.'

'"I'm very tired." Christ, what are you made of? Break up my marriage, deprive our child of his home life and you sit there calm as can be and say you're bloody tired.' He stood over her, shouting.

She flinched from his anger. 'I didn't break up our marriage,' she said, fighting her tears. 'You did.'

'Oh, didn't you? Didn't you? The perfect Jane, the perfect bloody wife. Are you? Tell me, are you?'

'I tried to be.'

'Tried is the right word, and failed. Dear God, how you failed!'

'I don't understand. I loved you the only way I knew how.'

'Loved? Loved?' His voice rose to a screaming crescendo. 'You smothered me with your fucking love.'

'Don't say that,' she cried, putting her hands over her ears to shut out the hateful words.

'And do you think for one moment you fooled me with your moaning and writhing in bed, pretending to me, your husband? You and your famous honesty – the most important thing in our lives and you deceived me. You're no bloody use in bed. You're frigid, hear me? *Frigid!*'

'I'm not, I'm not,' she sobbed.

'And you're smug too. Bloody smug, thinking you're always right and criticizing my friends, my way of life and my family, ad nauseam. God, why did I ever marry you?'

She looked at him with horror. 'Christ, why were you ever born?' echoed in her memory from all those years ago.

'Why, then, tell me why you bothered, if you were going to give me all this pain?' she screamed.

'Because, fool that I am, I felt sorry for you.'

'Get out . . .'

'Yes, I'll go. I'll go where I can get some bloody warmth and understanding,' he shouted. The front door slammed and the sound made her wince with pain. She stared into space. She did not cry but sat silent as another part of her soul died within her.

She found the calm practicality of the lawyers helpful. They dissected her marriage and drew up the separation contract, in a clinical way, like legal pathologists. Alistair gave her the Fulham house, a sum was agreed for the support of James, and he insisted that May's wages were his responsibility. Then the lawyers began to negotiate her allowance.

'I don't want an allowance from you, Alistair, I'll get a job.'

'Doing what, for heaven's sake? What could you do?' Alistair sneered at her across the lawyer's desk.

'Perhaps if you'd pay for me to do a shorthand and typing course . . . I think I'd like that. Having organized the opening of a stately home to the public shows I have some ability,' she said with pride, fighting the tears she felt were not far away. How sad, she thought, that they did not seem able to speak to each other normally.

She enrolled at a secretarial school. It was strange to be back at school, sitting at a desk. The other girls were school-leavers and at first she felt shy of them as they talked nonstop of their boy friends and music groups of which she had never heard. She felt dowdy beside these exotic young women with their bright miniskirts and bleached beehive hair. But they were kind to her, took an interest in her. She decided that they were a much more caring generation than her own had been.

Life settled into an orderly routine which helped her. She attended school each morning and each afternoon, with May, she took James to a park, a museum or the zoo. Her evenings were devoted to studying the squiggles and swirls of shorthand. They lived simply. She found sleep difficult. And she felt completely dead inside.

Three months went by. Sandra called whenever she was in town. She had many worried conversations with May, without whom Jane would never have been able to manage. May cared for the house, looked after James when Jane was at school, cooked for them, and tried as best she could to help Jane through her depression. It was a difficult task which May had set herself, for Jane would sit for hours, a drink in her hand, listening to music, not wishing to talk.

'Jane, love, you've got to pull yourself together.'

'I'll be all right, May.'

'But you've been saying that for months now.'

'It takes time, I feel I'm mourning a death. It's the only way I can describe it. Please, May, be patient with me, give me time,' she pleaded.

Alistair phoned one day to suggest that he take James with him on a short trip to Italy, before the start of the school term. Jane agreed; it would be a holiday for the boy and it would give May a chance to go home and see her family. Since they had been in London the girl had not had a day off. Even so, May was worried about leaving her but Jane insisted; she felt that if she were completely alone for a time, perhaps she would be able to heal herself.

Alistair's car arrived. James had been watching for it from the window for the past hour.

'Come on, Mummy, Daddy's here.' The child rushed out to greet his father, who was standing on the doorstep. Behind him Jane could see the car and, sitting in it, a pretty blonde-haired girl. James rushed up to the girl and gave her a smacking kiss on the cheek; the girl greeted him with the ease of an old friend.

'Who's that?' Jane asked her husband, a dreadful coldness filling her.

'My girlfriend, Samantha.'

'You're not taking her to Italy?'

'Why shouldn't I?'

'But with our son? That villa, it's our place, our time.'

'Don't talk such romantic crap, Jane. That's all over now. I do need some comforts, you know. Of course she's coming. Really, Jane, it's none of your business whom I take with me,' he snapped. He looked at her closely. 'You look bloody awful, Jane, it's about time you pulled yourself together. You won't even get a job, let alone a lover, looking like that.' She slammed the door angrily in his face and turned to look nervously in the mirror. It was as if she looked at a stranger. A stranger with a puffy face from too much drink and too little food. Dull hair hung unkempt and limply about her face. The eyes that gazed back at her from this stranger's face were devoid of expression: they looked like the eyes of a dead person. She could not bear to look at this face – she picked up an ornament and smashed the mirror.

'I love you, you bastard!' she screamed, her voice echoing around the empty house, bouncing off the wall and beating into her brain. Sobbing, she poured herself a drink. With shaking hands she lifted the glass to her lips and downed the contents in one gulp, then quickly poured herself another one. With exaggerated care she placed her favourite recording of Sibelius's Fifth Symphony on the record player. From the cupboard under the stairs she dragged the large paisley cushion, now worn with age, and sat cross-legged on it in the middle of the floor, staring out of the window at the snippet of sky above the house opposite.

She remembered the very first time she had sat on this cushion, on this floor, in this room. Where had she gone? Where was he? What had happened to them? Where did dead love go? All that energy, created by their love, did it just dissipate into the air, did it wander about looking for other lovers? He hated her. She had heard it in his voice when he spoke to her. She had begun to cope with knowing that he no longer loved her, but how was she to live with the dreadful knowledge that he hated her? And now there was someone else, someone who knew how to love him and not smother him as he accused her of doing. Someone who screamed with real passion in his bed. He had gone for ever now; she had no place in his heart. Her love, her precious love, the only thing of any value she had to give him, was no longer needed. He was the only reason for living – and now he did not care if she lived or died.

She stretched her hands into the air and clutched at the space with desperation and folded her arms, cradling her unwanted love to her breast. She began to rock. Back and forth she rocked, and she began to make a strange whimpering, mewing noise. She watched her patch of sky as she rocked. She saw the night come and then the day, then night, then day again. The darkness and the daylight sped across her window as she rocked and mewed to herself.

Sandra found her three days later. Jane did not recognize her friend. She could not stop rocking, could not take her eyes from her little piece of sky.

Kind hands came and gingerly straightened her legs. She was not conscious of the pain in her cramped limbs. Gently they lifted her onto a stretcher and covered her with blankets.

She missed her sky, she could not rock but still she whimpered – her song for her dead love.

The days and nights filtered past her in uncounted progression. She felt she was a bird, a little green and yellow bird, and she watched patiently for hands to come and hold her, caress her gently, with tenderness. Hands that would love her.

Faces came and peered at her, talked about her as if she did not exist. She did not understand where they got the idea that she was unaware of them. It was funny because, of course, she knew them. She watched her friend Sandra, May, Mrs Evans; she learned to recognize the different doctors. She just did not want to speak to them, could not raise the energy, but, oh yes, she knew they were there. She waited for one face, but it never appeared. She longed for his face, then she would talk, she would make herself talk, she wanted to speak to him, explain everything, and once he understood then he would love her again. But she never saw his beloved face. They tried to frighten her into talking, for one man they sent had no face. Each day the faceless man looked at her and each day she screamed and screamed until they led him away. And then they stopped sending him and she felt happier.

She watched her sky, the sun shone brighter for her, the clouds scudded faster, the stars shone more clearly. She allowed the needles to be pushed into her. She liked the feeling that the drugs gave her: they allowed her to float above herself, as the bird that she had become.

She had been sleeping, drifting in and out of her own dream world, and when she awoke it was to see a new face looking at her with concern.

'Honor,' she cried, and she held her arms up. The woman took her and rocked her like a baby, crooning to her, and Jane began to cry. As the tears flowed from her eyes, as the pent-up emotions flooded out, she explained to this woman whom she loved the sadness that rotted her soul. Then and only then did her sanity begin slowly to return.

Her doctors were pleased with her: the change in her was miraculous, they declared. She had had a nervous breakdown, a severe emotional shock. Nothing to worry about, she would be fine now, she was well on the way to recovery, they told her. She knew that they were wrong; she knew that a part of her had died, that she could never be the same again. A new doctor came, a young man called Nigel, who talked to her, wanted to know about her. She found it easy to talk to him; to tell him of her need to be loved, the loneliness inside her, the emptiness she felt. In the talking came a measure of healing.

Honor came each day. They would walk in the grounds of the hospital and talk of everything – but never of Alistair. After that first outburst, Jane could not speak of him again, except to the nice, young doctor who, she felt, did not mind being told.

They sat in the sunshine in the garden and she felt peaceful and almost happy.

'I want to go home, Honor.'

'Yes, darling, you shall.'

'But today, Honor. Will you come with me? I want to be in my little house. I want to see James and hold him again.'

'Not today, darling, but soon,' Honor promised.

She talked often of James now, she could not imagine how she had forgotten him. They explained that she was not quite ready yet – a few more weeks and then she could return home. So she concentrated hard and willed herself better, incomplete as she was, so that she could see her son again.

Despite the racking pain of rejection which tore her apart inside, she had learned to smile calmly at them, to sit quietly, her hands folded in her lap. She knew this impressed the doctors, who would then keep telling her how well she was doing. There seemed no point in speaking of the pain within her: she doubted they would understand.

'We feel you are nearly ready to go, Jane,' the doctor told her. 'However, I don't think it's a good idea for you to go home yet. Lady Honor has suggested you go to Italy with her, but quite honestly I would prefer that you stayed in this country for, let's say, another three months. Then you could go to Italy for a good, long rest.'

'But I want to go home to James,' she complained. She noticed Honor and the doctor glance quickly at each other. 'What aren't you telling me? Is there something wrong with James? Tell me, please.' Her voice was raised with fear.

'James is fine, darling. He's with Alistair.' Again they glanced at each other and she saw the doctor nod his head almost imperceptibly. 'You see, darling,' Honor said gently, 'Alistair had to take the boy when you were so ill, and no one knew how long it would take for you to recover.'

Jane nodded, smiling. 'That was kind of him. But I want James back now.'

'The trouble is, Jane,' Honor continued, taking hold of her hand, 'when you were ill, well, Alistair applied to the courts and they gave James to him to care for.'

She sat in silence allowing Honor's words to sink in. 'You mean he had me declared unfit to care for him?'

'Yes.'

'Had me committed?' she asked calmly.

'Yes. He didn't know what else to do, Jane. Someone had to decide about James.'

She sat quietly, apparently examining this information. But within, she screamed in her anguish. She did not understand. 'Honor, he didn't have to go that far. I could only have James to myself while he was small. Alistair knew I understood that. I've always known that in the end he would be happier with Alistair, and he belongs at Respryn. A boy needs his father, doesn't he?' She knew she would begin to shake. She sat rigid, fighting the tremors which began to ripple through her body, fought with all her strength, for if they saw, they would never let her go.

'Jane, are you all right? Can I get you something?' the anxious doctor enquired, quickly opening the bag at his side.

'Don't worry, Nigel,' she said hurriedly. 'I don't need your drugs any more. I'll manage. I'll be all right in a moment. It's the shock, you see.' She turned her face to them and both Honor and the doctor averted their eyes from the pain in hers. 'I'm having to adjust to the fact that to all intents and purposes I've lost my son. I have, haven't I?' Honor was distressed at her words. 'But he need not have gone as far as to have me committed. I wouldn't have gone anywhere. I like it here.' The doctor and Honor looked intently at their hands. 'Why did he never come to see me, Honor? I waited every day for him to come. Had he come, I'm sure I'd have recovered faster.'

'But he did come, darling. Every day for weeks he came, but you screamed so much that in the end the doctors wouldn't let him see you. He's been beside himself with worry,' Honor explained.

'I didn't know that he had come. I couldn't see him.'

'No, of course not, darling, you weren't aware of anyone when you were so ill.'

She decided not to explain to them about the faceless man: it was too complicated and, as with everything else, she doubted if they would understand.

'Now, where are you to go? That's our immediate problem,' the doctor asked kindly. 'What about your parents?'

'God, no! They would be ashamed of me. Mental illness frightens people like them. It wouldn't go down well in the street.' She laughed a tiny laugh. 'In any case, I don't belong there any more, I wouldn't fit in. I do have one friend who might look after me before I go to Italy – Sandra, we nursed together.'

'That would be ideal. Especially since she's a trained nurse. Then she can keep an eye on you for us,' Nigel said, pleased with the arrangement. 'Do you want to see your husband?'

'No, thank you, not yet.' She could say it without thinking. She knew she had to have time before she could face him.

Everything was arranged for her. Sandra agreed immediately to take her friend and care for her until the doctors agreed that she was ready to fly to Italy for a long holiday with Honor.

A year after her collapse, outwardly well but precariously stitched together inside, Jane set out with Sandra, with whom she had shared her London adventure, to Cambridge, which had other memories for her.

Four

1969 – 70

I

Sandra drove Jane's car carefully. The traffic was heavy. Jane sat stiffly, flinching, as the large lorries hurtled towards them.

'It's all right, Jane. I know this road like the back of my hand.' She patted Jane's hand comfortingly.

'A year without traffic is a long time,' Jane explained. 'I'd forgotten how busy the roads can be.'

She made a conscious effort to relax, to let her hands lie flaccid on her lap. Breathe deeply, she told herself, as they had instructed her to do in the hospital, when, as now, anxiety crawled over her body insidiously, like invading slime. She felt transparent, as if her nerve endings were on the outside. Breathe deeply, she repeated to herself with more urgency. She had to control herself; it was important. She must not let anyone see how she was feeling, or she would be returned to the hospital she had just escaped from.

This must be how prisoners feel, newly released from jail, she thought, as she watched with strangely reawakened eyes the never ending flatness which stretched as far as the eye could see. Where the land met the sky, there appeared to be no division between earth and heaven. She remembered, fondly, the gentle hills of Respryn and the noble mountains of Drumloch, and she felt a wave of homesickness engulf her.

As if reading her thoughts, Sandra turned to her. 'You get used to the flatness. I didn't think I ever would, but I love it now. It has a beauty all of its own and, with no hills in the way, one is more aware of the fantastic skies.' Jane smiled at her friend. They had both changed. Jane was razor thin. Her cheekbones had deep hollows below them. Her clothes hung loosely on her. That was the first thing she must do: get something that fitted. How could one begin to feel normal in clothes like these? But Sandra had changed too. Her plumpness had gone — in its place an angular slimness, which did not suit her as well as her previous rounded curves — but the beautiful eyes and dimpled smile were still the same.

Sandra spoke of old friends from their hospital days. An inveterate letter-writer, she seemed to have news of everybody. They spoke of her family, her children, Lance and Michelle, of the new house they had just bought, and said nothing of Jane's illness or her marriage. Jane felt herself finally relaxing. The wave of anxiety had passed.

They left the main road and entered a village. Jane clapped her hands with pleasure as they sped past the village green where, in the shade of an oak, stood the quaint thatched pub; on the village pond ducks pottered busily; and the village shop had bottle-glass windows. It was a chocolate-box village, and brought a smile to Jane's face at last. The car snaked over a packhorse bridge, swung up a lane and they entered a modern housing estate. The houses stood in staggered formation, to give a measure of privacy to the occupants, but to Jane this element of privacy looked to be an illusion. Each house stood on an immaculate, unfenced lawn, giving the impression of wide open spaciousness, unless, like Jane, you were used to rolling parkland which made these lawns look like pocket handkerchiefs. Some attempt had been made to vary the minor details of each house. There were three types of front door and two types of door knocker, and some houses had porches while others did not. The houses were made individual only by the choice of curtains, or the make of car in the driveway. Since the houses had all been built at the same time, the gardens were at the same stage of development, and looking around it was as if only two trees, the weeping willow and the flowering cherry, were indigenous to these islands.

They came to a halt. 'There. What do you think?' Sandra asked.

'It's very nice,' answered Jane, unsure of what to say about a house that looked so uniformly ordinary.

'Of course, for you, after Respryn, it must seem like a hovel.'

'It's lovely, Sandra, really,' Jane said hurriedly. 'If I sounded a bit vague it was because I thought you still lived in Cambridge.'

Sandra's husband, Justin, was waiting for them in the sitting room. The first thing that struck Jane, as she looked about her, was how small the house was, and how bare it seemed, despite plenty of furniture. Everything gleamed in its newness, from the shiny Dralon-covered three-piece to the large wall unit which housed the stereo, TV and books. Apart from a Utrillo print and one vase, there were no ornaments and it was their absence that made the room seem naked. She felt as if she were standing in a showroom in a furniture store. The large picture windows were draped in net curtains so that it was impossible to see out. Dominating the room was a rough stone fireplace which rose from floor to ceiling; beneath a shiny copper hood was an electric fire, the artificial coals glowing too red.

'What do you think?' asked Justin, expansively waving his arm.

'It's a bit big, isn't it?' said Jane unthinkingly, fascinated by the monstrous fireplace.

'Yes, we're lucky. This style of house is the "Executive Elite", so we have a separate dining room, and four bedrooms. Our garden is the largest on the estate, always a good selling point, that,' he said proudly, misunderstanding Jane completely, much to her relief.

'Justin! You sound like an estate agent. I shouldn't think for one moment that Jane cares about the virtues of our house.'

'It's very interesting,' Jane said, quickly.

'Go on, I bet you'd be more interested in a drink. I know I would. I'll show Jane her room, Justin, while you organize the glasses.' Jane followed her friend up the open-plan staircase and into a back bedroom, whose walls were covered in a nursery wallpaper.

'Sandra, I didn't think. You haven't got room for me. The children . . .'

'Of course we've got room for you. The kids are bunking in together. They don't mind one bit.'

'But I thought that Justin said you had four bedrooms?'

'We have, but that's the agent in him talking. The fourth is so small you couldn't swing a cat in it. It's got my sewing machine in it – that's all there's room for.' Sandra laughed.

'Look, Sandra, I'll just stay the weekend. I'll be fine in Fulham.'

'You bloody well won't. We'll manage. I promised everybody I'd look after you. Hell, I virtually had to swear on the family Bible.' As she spoke, Sandra moved about the room, straightening the already straight curtains, smoothing down the smooth bedspread, checking the empty cupboards. 'The bathroom's across the landing. See you downstairs in the lounge.'

'Sitting room. Only hotels and airports have lounges,' Jane thought automatically, so well had she studied her book on accepted word usage. In the pretty, wallpapered bathroom, the tiles on the walls gleamed, the taps shone. Every corner of this house was a triumph of cleanliness and tidiness. Frilly net curtains hung unnecessarily at the small frosted window. She studied her face in the mirror of the medicine cabinet. Lounge, sitting room, drawing room, it did not matter a damn any more, and she could say what she wanted, But it was odd that she had flinched at that word 'lounge'.

Back in the sitting room, they waited for her. Small bowls of nuts and crisps now stood on the ceramic-tiled coffee table beside an ornately scrolled, silver-plated tray on which glinted carefully polished cut glass.

'What's your poison, Jane?'

'What?'

'To drink? Sherry?'

'Oh, gin and tonic, please, ice, no lemon.'

'Sorry, Jane, we're out of gin.'

'Don't fib, Justin. We don't run to spirits, Jane,' Sandra announced and her husband glared angrily at her. She stared back almost defiantly.

'Anything then, anything you're having,' Jane answered, flustered. 'Sherry will be lovely.'

As Justin poured the drinks, Jane saw that Sandra seemed incapable of relaxing. Even when she was sitting down her hands were endlessly fiddling, straightening the folds of her skirt, patting her hair, picking unseen threads from the arm of the chair.

Justin presented her with a small glass of sherry, which he carefully placed on an embossed leather coaster on the tiled table.

'Well,' they both said in unison, and then both laughed, awkwardly. 'After you, Justin.'

'I was going to say that my parents have invited us all to dinner the day after tomorrow. If you would like to come?'

'I'd like that very much, thanks.'

'I was going to suggest,' Sandra said in turn, 'that if we could get a baby-sitter, we should go out for a curry.'

'If you don't mind, I'd rather have an early night. But if you two want to go out, I'll baby-sit for you.'

'I don't think that's —' Justin stopped in midsentence.

'Thank you, Jane. We'll take you up on that, won't we, Justin?' Sandra said, looking pointedly at her husband.

'You needn't worry, Justin. I'm not dangerous. I didn't hurt anyone, only myself. The kids will be safe with me, I promise,' Jane said to a very red-faced Justin.

'Jane, I didn't mean . . .'

'Yes, you did, Justin.' Jane laughed good-naturedly at him and the embarrassing moment passed.

The children returned from their tea party and Sandra refused Jane's offer to help bath them. She was left alone with Justin. He stood with his back to the fire, legs straddled, the glass of sherry in his hand. He had a paunch now and the good looks of youth had given way to a smooth, self-satisfied face. Jane noticed the fingers around the stem of the glass were podgy and looked as if they'd be sweaty, too. He did not talk to her, rather he lectured in a hectoring tone. She listened but made no reply. Instinctively she felt he was not interested in anything she had to say. Jane thought that she did not like Justin very much any more.

At last, Sandra was ready and they left. Jane sat in the sitting room, the two children standing in front of her, solemnly inspecting her. She talked to them, but neither said a word, merely stared with round eyes in their angelic faces. Finally, she suggested that she read them a story.

'No!' five-year-old Lance said.

'No, thank you,' corrected Jane.

'Piss off,' the child replied.

'Pith off,' Michelle, his little sister, echoed.

'That's not a very nice thing to say to me, is it?' Jane asked, feeling more surprised than shocked.

'Don't want you here. Don't like you,' the boy announced.

'Don't like you . . .' his sister aped.

'I can't say I'm very impressed with either of you,' Jane said angrily. 'If you're going to be that rude, then you can both go to bed, now.'

'Shan't!'

'Shan't!'

'Yes, you damn well will, or I shall smack you.'

'You hit me, I'll tell my granny.'

'Tell her what you like. I'm sure she would agree with me that you deserve a good smack for such bad manners.'

'My mummy never hits us,' the boy stated proudly.

'Then perhaps she should.' Jane did not know how to handle this situation. She had never been very good with children, in fact, apart from James, she did not like them very much. Lance stuck his tongue out at her, and her hand itched to slap him. 'Go to bed,' she said as calmly as she could.

'Shan't!'

'Shan't!'

'Bed!' she yelled. Startled, the little girl ran screaming from the room, but the boy stood his ground, staring insolently at Jane. Suddenly he raised two fingers at her, stuck out his tongue again, and then dashed hurriedly from the room before she could reach him.

Jane poured herself another of Justin's far from good sherries and wished they had some gin. She leafed through the records but gave up on finding that they were mostly light music. She was surprised, Sandra had always loved classical music. She sat on the slippery, Dralon-covered armchair and remembered the wonderful softness of the velvets and cretonnes she had become used to.

That scene with the children had been extraordinary. They were awful, even someone who liked children would have to agree with her on that. They looked angelic and were monsters. She had presumed that Sandra's children, with her idyllic childhood behind her, would be perfect.

And why was Sandra so thin? There was a jumpiness about her which was alien to the carefree girl she had once been. There was something very wrong. Jane was certain she was not imagining it: her time in hospital had given her what she liked to think of as antennae which were able to pick up moods and atmospheres quickly and incisively. She had not yet worked out if this facility within herself had come as a result of her illness or whether, surrounded as she had been by people in a precarious mental state, she had developed it as a means of protection. There was an atmosphere of edginess bordering on aggression in this house which was a tangible thing to her.

She looked about her. This was a dreary room, it was totally lacking in character. She began to feel claustrophobic, especially with that vast fireplace looming over her. If one had pitons one could climb it.

She sat bolt upright in the chair. What had got into her? She should not be thinking this way. She was so used now to Alistair's standards that they were normal to her. Separated from them, she missed them, and realized she wanted to live no other way. Yet, when she had been a schoolgirl, this house would have been the height of her ambitions. Fifteen years later she sat here, sneering at it.

What right had she to sneer? It was bare, but from the odd remark that Sandra had dropped, it was obvious that they were short of money. She was turning into a possessions snob. It was not a pleasant thought.

Tired of all this self-criticism, she began to think of her future. After her holiday with Honor, what then? It had been one thing in the lawyer's office to state proudly that she wanted nothing from Alistair. Now, if she did get a job, she would certainly not earn as much as Justin. If they were hard up, how could she afford to pay the electricity bills, the rates, buy drinks? While she had had James, she could with a clear conscience accept an allowance for all those things, but now, what on earth was she to do? Maybe she had acted too rashly. She could not have known that she was going to be ill, and for so long, or that she would lose custody of James. The repercussions of that wretched illness were going to be with her for a long time. But one thing she had learned: never again would she be so involved with one person. In the future, in the unlikely event that she should meet someone she could care for, she would reserve a part of herself to fall back on if things went wrong. She would never allow herself to become so vulnerable again. She was certain that if she had not wallowed in her grief for Alistair, she would never have become ill. She had allowed her mental resistance to get too low and so she had succumbed. Just like catching flu, really, only more inconvenient.

It was strange that she should begin to think of all these things now. It was almost as if a curtain had lifted in her mind and she was faced with stark reality for the first time. It was a frightening prospect, but at the same time she realized with relief that she was facing it rationally and reasonably calmly, despite her fears.

She looked at the telephone on the table beside her and wished she felt free enough to phone Alistair, talk to him. Would she ever ask him for help? She did not know, she doubted it. Maybe one day she would have to swallow the stupid pride which had landed her in this muddle in the first place. Now all she wanted was to hear his voice, to tell him she was all right, that she missed him, that she was sorry, that she loved him. 'That she loved him' . . . it was always going to be like that. She might let herself think of being involved with someone else, but it was a futile exercise. She would never love anyone else: it was as simple as that, she thought. Hadn't she always said to Sandra, all those years ago, that there would only ever be one man for her? They were just romantic words then; now they were reality. Perhaps she should have shut her mind to his affairs. He would never have left her, she knew that; he would always have come back to her and their marriage. That pain would have been preferable to what she had just been through, preferable to this fear for the future. Would she ever have the courage to tell him all this? What if he gave her an ice-cold look? What if he spoke to her in that controlled way he now had, with barely concealed irritation? There were too many imponderables. By now, one whole year later, he was probably living happily with someone else. How was she to know – hadn't she refused to discuss him with anybody?'

She patted the telephone affectionately, drained her glass, switched off the light and went to bed in the room with aeroplane wallpaper, in the narrow child's bed, and lay a long time wondering what was to become of her.

2

Jane had overslept. She apologized to Sandra, whom she found, a can of Pledge in one hand, briskly polishing the kitchen cabinets.

'Tea or coffee?' asked Jane. 'I'll do it, just tell me where everything is.' Jane opened the cupboards Sandra indicated. 'Crikey, you've changed. They're so tidy!' She laughed. 'Remember your cupboards at the Nurses' Home? Always in a mess.'

'I wasn't that bad.'

'You were, you were dreadfully untidy, far worse than me,' Jane teased.

'I don't remember.'

Jane settled herself at the table and, digging in her dressing-gown pocket, took out her cigarette case and lit up. 'Got an ashtray?'

'I'd prefer it if you didn't smoke, Jane.'

'What?'

'It's a filthy habit.'

'I know, sorry.' Quickly she put the cigarette out. 'You given up, then?'

'Heavens, yes, ages ago. Justin doesn't like it.'

'I see. Does that mean I can't smoke here?'

'Good gracious, no. It's just I'd prefer you didn't in your bedroom and here in the kitchen.'

'Perhaps you've got a handy garden shed?' Jane grinned, but Sandra ignored the remark and continued with her polishing. 'Do you always polish the units? Isn't washing them enough?'

'I don't like to see finger marks,' she said, standing back and looking critically at the shining doors. Then she got a bucket, filled it with water, and proceeded to wash the floor.

'Don't you want your tea?'

'When I've finished this,' she replied.

'Why are you so unrelaxed?'

'Me? Unrelaxed? What a strange thing to say, Jane. I have work to do, I'm just getting on with it. We can't all afford servants to do it for us,' she said tartly.

'Sorry,' Jane said in a singsong voice and, clutching her mug of tea, tiptoed over the washed floor and into the sitting room. She lit a cigarette and took a few puffs but, conscious of the smoke curling into the air of the tidy room, she hurriedly put it out. Wandering back upstairs, she paused in the bathroom to run herself a bath. In her bedroom Sandra was making the bed.

'Heavens, Sandra! What the hell are you doing?' she exclaimed, shocked.

'Making your bed. What's it look like? I feel uncomfortable if I know there's an unmade bed in the house.' She busily straightened the counterpane.

'Sandra, love, I'd have done that. Honestly, you're making me feel embarrassed.'

'Sorry, I can't help that, I have to get finished. Is that the bath water running?'

'Yes.'

'I wish you'd asked, Jane. We only have so much hot water and I wanted to do a wash today.'

Jane felt herself blushing with confusion. 'Hell, I'm sorry, I didn't know. I'll stop it.'

'You might as well have it now, rather than waste it. We'll fix a time for you in future. It's the immersion heater, you see – for economy it's only on at certain times of day.' Satisfied with her bedmaking, she turned to the door. 'It's my morning for coffee, if you'd care to join us?' She smiled and left Jane alone.

Sandra was very confusing to be with, Jane thought, as she lay soaking in her bath. One minute she was so prickly, the next moment she was smiling that beautiful smile. The last person she had expected to become a houseproud woman was Sandra. She smiled as she remembered the arguments they had had when, for three months, they had shared a room in the Nurses' Home. Both were equally untidy, and the chaos they had created should have led to disaster, but somehow they had weathered it, and later used to laugh about it. Yet now Sandra denied that she had ever been untidy. She was hyperactive. Nobody changed that much without a reason. In her present sensitive state, Jane was finding Sandra and her house unnerving.

When she arrived in the sitting room, to her delight it was full of young women with their children. She stood in the doorway overcome by sudden shyness, watching them chattering happily with each other, as they drank coffee and ate cakes. The children divided into two groups, those who tumbled about together and those who clung to their mothers' skirts, sucking their thumbs, and solemnly watching the others as if wanting to join them but lacking the necessary courage – Jane knew exactly how they felt.

'Ah, Jane, here you are. Everybody, this is my best friend, Lady Upnor,' Sandra said in a proprietorial tone. The women stopped talking and, as one, turned and stared at Jane. 'Don't just stand there, Jane, come and have some coffee.'

One of the women made room for her on the sofa. Since some of the others were smoking, Jane took out her cigarette case and lighter and offered a cigarette to the plump, fluffy-haired girl who sat beside her. The girl was already balancing a baby, her coffee cup and cake plate with admirable dexterity, and still she managed to take a cigarette.

'Thanks.' She smiled. 'My name's Liz Turner-Green.' She looked longingly at the cigarette case. 'That's a beautiful thing. May I look at it?' Jane, not sure which to relieve her of, took her coffee cup in preference to the baby, and handed her the heavy gold case which carried her initials picked out in sapphires – a birthday present from Alistair. 'Gosh, it's heavy,' Liz exclaimed. 'Look, Dodo, isn't that the most beautiful thing you ever saw?'

'Is it real?' the woman called Dodo asked. She was red-haired, not in a soft, green-eyed way, but with sharp features and a spiteful expression.

'Of course it's real.' Liz laughed.

'I think it's vulgar,' Dodo said matter-of-factly. Jane felt acutely uncomfortable as the pale-blue eyes surveyed her coolly. She put out her hand to take the case back, but already it was being passed from one girl to another, making Jane wish she had left it upstairs.

'Does it offend your socialist principles then, Dodo?' asked another girl with rosy cheeks and large muscular legs which must have served her well on a hockey field. 'Lady Upnor, don't let Dodo upset you. She'd love to own it, really. She's just jealous.'

'Hilary, you needn't think for one moment that you can upset me. I only take note of people of intelligence,' Dodo said in a cool voice, but Jane saw that her eyes were blazing with anger. Jane braced herself for the ensuing row, but instead the large-legged girl merely laughed louder than ever, and Sandra took the heat out of the moment by offering more coffee.

'You staying here long, Lady Upnor?' Liz asked her.

'Jane, please call me Jane. Well, I was, but I didn't realize the house was so small. I don't think it's fair for me to stay too long.'

'Too small!' the young woman shrieked. 'Did you hear that, everyone – Jane here thinks this house is too small. Heavens, it's the biggest one of the whole estate.'

'I didn't mean it like that. Please. I mean with the children . . .' She blushed with confusion, and felt angry with herself. She had looked forward to meeting a group of women of her own age who lived normal lives. She wanted to talk to them, learn from them, and here she was inadvertently putting her foot in it at every turn.

Their astonishment at her remark subsided and conversation became general again. They discussed their electricity bills and there was a long debate about whether or not it was more economic to turn the immersion heaters off at night. They complained of how little their husbands helped them in the house. They all agreed that it was not immoral to economize on their housekeeping and to keep the excess for themselves to buy make-up and tights. Jane learned that the local shop had a sixpence discount on Nescafé – the middle-size jars, not the large. Hilary announced that she thought she might be on to a window cleaner, at last. This information caused great excitement. Jane listened intently and felt isolated. If she was to build a new life, she thought, how could she succeed if she felt she had nothing in common with women of her own age? She supposed she could learn, but, on the other hand, she was not sure if she wanted to: nothing they talked of interested her. Yet they seemed contented, and was not that what she herself longed for?

'Sandra's always talking about you,' Liz suddenly said, and Jane jumped, jolted out of her sense of isolation.

'We've known each other a long time.'

'She's wonderful, isn't she? I mean, she's so efficient, everything is always perfect. And her kids' socks are always immaculately white. Me? If I can find my lot one pair between them it's a miracle.' The girl laughed, and Jane warmed to her.

'You live here too?'

'Yes, opposite. We were first here. It was lonely to begin with, but now it's lovely with most of the houses sold – there's always someone to talk to.'

Jane wondered what they found to talk about, day after day. Sandra and she used to debate everything under the sun and yet there was her friend, across the room, deep in discussion on the best way to remove ring marks from furniture . . . Jane leashed in her thoughts and felt ashamed – she was getting arrogant, in the true Lady Upnor mould. She turned to talk to Liz. 'Tell me about your house,' she said.

'Oh, I'd much rather talk about yours,' Liz gushed. 'I visited it last year when we were on holiday. I shouldn't have been so rude, laughing like that when you said this one was small. I saw that I'd embarrassed you. Sorry. I mean, it really would be minute after Respryn, wouldn't it?'

Jane smiled gratefully at the plump young woman. 'It isn't really – you see, we only live in a small part. We can't afford to live in the whole house.' She realized she had used the present tense. How long would it take, she wondered, before she would be able to talk of having lived there?

'Do you mind the trippers crashing about?' Liz continued.

'No. Most people are very appreciative of what we do. It's good for the house, too, to be full of people and noise. And it helps with the expenses,' Jane replied, uncomfortably aware that the conversation had died down and that everyone was listening.

'Bet the heating bills are dreadful?' another voice enquired.

'Horrendous. But you learn to run a lot in winter to keep warm.' She managed a laugh but wished inwardly that they would return in their normal conversation. She found herself getting flustered as she was unable to answer some of their questions. The financial, day-to-day running had never been her concern.

'How many staff?' 'Do you have a butler?' 'Does a lady's maid wash your knickers?' 'Bet you've a Rolls-Royce?' 'A chauffeur?' 'What do you do all day?' The questions continued thick and fast. Jane wished her answers did not sound so apologetic. While some of the women had a genuine interest in Respryn, there were others from whom she sensed a distinct feeling of animosity. She had a strange feeling of *déjà vu*: she might just as well be back in Respryn, all those years ago, with Clarissa and her cohorts taunting her – except that now everything was reversed. Then she had been attacked for being working-class; now the ill-feeling was because she was a countess.

The door burst open and a harassed young woman, with a young child on each hip, stood anxiously in the doorway.

'Who owns that blue BMW out there?'

'I do,' Jane said, blushing inexplicably.

'Oh, Christ, I'm sorry – I've just reversed into it. My bloody foot slipped and I just shot backwards.'

'What's the damage?' asked Sandra anxiously.

'I've dented the bumper. I'm so sorry. I'll pay for it, of course. Christ, Chris will kill me,' the young woman wailed and both children, sensing her distress, began to cry loudly.

'That will cost a bomb, BMWs don't mend cheaply,' Dodo said unhelpfully.

'Oh, please, don't worry,' Jane said, relieved. 'If it's only a bumper, that's no problem – after all, what are bumpers for except to be bumped into?' She smiled brightly. No one smiled back.

'Shit! How grand can you get?' Dodo sneered.

'I don't understand,' Jane said worriedly, alarmed by the antagonism. 'What have I said?'

'Well, really, if you don't have to worry about a bent bumper, if you've got so much money it's of no importance, quite honestly I think it's disgustingly ostentatious of you.'

'What the hell do you mean? What the hell do you know about my finances?' Jane flared back, her vulnerability making her defensive.

'You've been boasting enough all morning.'

'Boasting? I have not, people asked me questions; I didn't bring up the subject of my home. Would you have preferred it if I'd ignored your friends' questions? In any case, it isn't – Sod it, I don't have to explain anything to you.' Jane felt herself begin to shake. Abruptly she stood up and walked across the room, conscious of the stares of the women upon her. As she got to the door, she turned and, forcing herself to smile, said in a dangerously sweet voice, 'But if it makes you feel happier, Dodo, I'll send your friend the bill.'

She swept from the room and into the kitchen. She started, vigorously, to do the washing-up. Suddenly her shoulders slumped and she clung to the edge of the sink. She took deep breaths, counting between each intake, just as they had taught her . . . but the control she needed eluded her. From deep within, anxiety wormed its insidious way to the surface, snaking along each nerve fibre, escaping from each follicle, bathing her in a fine film of sweat. She was conscious of the subdued voices of the women in the hall, and the unconcerned shouts of their children as the party broke up. Sandra must not find her like this, not even Sandra – they would shut her up again. Grabbing her handbag, she searched helplessly for her cigarettes. Turning the contents of the handbag out on the kitchen table, she hurriedly clicked open the case, put a cigarette in her mouth and, with trembling fingers, lit the lighter. The cigarette was soaked, her hands still damp from the washing-up. Cursing, she threw it away, quickly lighting another. Calm down, you stupid bitch, she told

herself with exasperation, inhaling deeply. The hospital had given her
pills. She wondered if for once she should take one. Until now she had
resisted them because she had an ex-nurse's fear of drugs, and also
because, if she were to regard herself as recovered, it had to be without
the crutch of tranquillizers.

Sandra came into the room, went straight to Jane and put her arm
about her.

'Jane, love, I'm so sorry about that.' Through the silk of her blouse,
Sandra felt Jane shaking. 'Love, don't get this upset. It's only Dodo, she's
a painful cow.' She looked intently at Jane, seeing fear in her grey eyes
which was out of all proportion to the incident. 'I don't know why we
put up with her. I suppose primarily because we feel sorry for her. Her
husband's a bastard – thinks he's God's gift to women and is always
having affairs with young students.' She spoke quickly in an attempt to
distract Jane.

'Is he a teacher?' Jane asked, not because she was interested, but
needing something to occupy her mind.

'He's a lecturer at the tech. He's got the most enormous chip on his
shoulder – feels second-rate compared with the university lecturers.'

'She reminded me of my sister-in-law, the dreadful Lady Clarissa.'

'God, how funny. I must tell the others. I mean, she's so left-wing she's
almost a Commie. But then that's the tech again: it's almost mandatory
there, it seems to me.' An uneasy silence settled over them, as Sandra
could not think of anything else to say. She looked anxiously at Jane as
she sat at the kitchen table, a blank look on her face.

Jane took another cigarette, forgetting Sandra's rule about smoking in
her kitchen. 'You see, Sandra, I begin to think I don't belong anywhere
any more. I don't know where I'll ever fit in,' she suddenly said, sadly.

'Oh, darling, of course you will. You and I get on just as before.'

'Yes, with you. But you don't understand. I can't go home to my
parents – there's nothing there for me now. I never really fitted into
Alistair's world. My hope was yours . . . but look what happened. So
where do I belong?' She looked anxiously at her friend, who had no
answer for her. 'Funny thing is, your friend Dodo's probably got more
money than me, anyway. I'm skint.'

'Jane!' Sandra exclaimed. 'You're not serious? Oh, God, you are.
Have you got a cigarette?'

'But you said –'

'I was being crabby. I hate these bloody coffee mornings – they bore
me to tears – and whenever it's my turn I'm bad-tempered. I don't

smoke officially: Justin would hit the roof. I'm a closet smoker.' She chuckled.

'Thank Christ for that,' said Jane as she opened the case which had started her downfall at the coffee party.

'Right, now tell me. What's all this nonsense? No money?'

Jane explained her problem and how she had no one to blame but herself. 'You're a bloody fool, Jane. You must go back to your lawyers,' Sandra advised.

'I can't do that. My pride won't let me.'

'Pride is a principle you can't afford, my girl.'

'I said I would manage and manage I will.'

'That's being pig-headed. It's as much his fault that you're not an SRN. He married you and prevented you from finishing your training. Had you done so, you wouldn't have had any job worries. Let's be practical then. What have you got? What can you do?'

'I'm very good at opening stately homes to the public.' At last Jane grinned.

'I don't think there's much call for that.' Sandra grinned back.

'I've done three months of a secretarial course – Alistair was paying for that. I don't mind asking him to pay for me to finish it. But how do I live until I get a job? Coming here has been a good lesson for me, Sandra. It's making me think of practical problems that I've never had to give a thought to – like how to pay electricity bills and the rates on the house. I haven't had to handle money since the day I married. I never see a bill. I have accounts everywhere. The most I ever carried with me was enough to pay a taxi. I used to joke about it and say I was like the Queen, never carrying money, but now –'

'House, you said, what house?' Sandra jumped eagerly on the word.

'Alistair gave me the house in Fulham, but I can't see how I can afford to live in it.'

'Jane, you're a clot. It's simple. You rent out the house, furnished – you'll get a small fortune for it. Then you rent something cheaper and live off the excess until you can get a job. Then you'll be laughing.'

'Do you really think it would be easy to rent? I hadn't thought of it.' At last Jane felt the vestiges of her panic recede. 'I thought I was going to have to sell it and I hated the idea.'

The back door burst open and Michelle rushed in, home from nursery school. Having kissed her mother, she turned and gave Jane a kiss, too.

'I thought you didn't like me?' Jane asked, surprised by the child's attention.

'I do,' the child answered indignantly. 'You're pretty,' she said as an aside, as she banged out of the room and rushed up the stairs.

'What was all that?' Sandra asked.

'Nothing, just a joke.'

'No, it wasn't. Lance was horrible to you last night, wasn't he?'

'Well . . . he's at a difficult age.'

'No, Jane, he's becoming a monster! I'm at my wits' end with him. What did he say?' Jane related what had happened and Sandra sighed. 'What upsets me is that he's beginning to affect Michelle and she's such a sweet child. It's his bloody grandfather – he spoils him rotten. He spends virtually every weekend there and comes back impossible.'

'Stop him going,' said Jane reasonably.

'Ha! Easier said than done. I can't. The old man would hit the roof, and Justin would be angry. His old man owns the agency Justin works for, you see. He's a real bastard, I hate him. He doesn't pay Justin nearly enough and always hanging over us is the threat that unless we toe the line he'll kick Justin out.'

'Sounds a really attractive character! But Justin, surely he'd rather be disinherited and be his own man?'

'I wish he would, but he's shit-scared all the time. The old bastard's a martinet. He's short, that's the problem.'

'Short! What on earth has that got to do with it?' Despite her friend's obvious distress, amusement sounded in Jane's voice.

'Don't you know the theory about short men? They have to bully to compensate for their lack of inches, to prove how masculine they are. Like Hitler and Mussolini. And I have to land up with one as a father-in-law.' As she talked, Sandra was picking away at the label on a sauce bottle.

'Sandra, stop fiddling. Do you realize, when you're not working, you're always fiddling with something?' To Jane's consternation Sandra began to cry.

'Oh, Jane, you don't know. I'm so bloody unhappy.' It was Jane's turn to put a comforting arm about her friend, but it was some time before Sandra's tears subsided.

'You're always listening to my problems. Now let me listen to yours for a change,' she said. Sandra blew her nose on a large piece of kitchen paper. 'Is this why you've turned into such a frenetic housewife?'

'I suppose it is. You see' – she helped herself to another of Jane's cigarettes – 'his father was so angry with Justin for marrying me in the first place. It's the only time he's crossed his old man, but then he didn't have much choice – I was pregnant.' She laughed, bitterly. 'I'm not good enough for his son, he thinks I'm a liability. I suppose that's why I have to have everything so perfect all the time, trying to prove what a good wife I am.' She began to pick at the sauce bottle label again and Jane waited patiently for her to continue, knowing there was more to come. 'And it's Justin, too. I mean, the kids come back from their grandparents like wild animals. They wreck the place and then if everything isn't all spick and span when he comes in, he hits the roof. He's so edgy these days, and so conscious, all the time, of what people will think and say. Sometimes I'm afraid he's going to end up just like his father. I seem to irritate him constantly. He's becoming a bully. He even hit me the other day.'

'Bloody hell!'

'It's this awful house: God, I hate it. We had a lovely house before, off Mill Road. It was smashing, but, no, Big Daddy decides the area isn't good enough for his son. That it's time we were incarcerated in this miserable executive box, on this bloody executive estate, with all the other boring young couples crawling painfully up the bloody ladder to success. And what happens? We're lumbered with an enormous mortgage we can't afford, for a house I never wanted in the first place.'

'But you seemed so happy just now?'

'Oh, don't get taken in by that. That's part of the "wife-of-successful-businessman" act that I'm very good at. Most of the women bore me to tears. They moan all the time – about their lives, their husbands, their bloody periods. And either they're getting too much sex or not enough. Sometimes, Jane, I feel that all my personality, what strength I had, has all been sucked out of me. But I love him. I just don't know what to do.' She began to sob. Jane took her hand, attempting to comfort her friend. 'Oh, hell, Jane. I'm sorry. I shouldn't be burdening you like this. I'm supposed to be cheering you up.'

'But you are helping me. You're putting my problems into perspective . . . and I thought I was alone . . . But you've got to put your foot down, Sandra, before it's too late. Get a job, that'll help with the mortgage and get you out to meet people,' she advised. 'You're going to crack up at this rate.'

'I know. It sounds awful, but when I used to visit you in hospital, I almost envied you your breakdown – you'd got right away from everything.'

'What's your mum say?' Jane asked.

'She doesn't know. She's so proud of me and my lovely home, I can't bear to disillusion her.'

Jane looked thoughtful. 'Come on, Sandra, we need cheering up. I'll go into town and get us some booze – we'll get pissed together.'

'Would you? Tonight's ideal. Justin's at some Rotary do. Get loads of fags, too!'

Jane drove into Cambridge. At least that had not changed, except that the students looked younger. She went first to the top floor of Heffers and browsed through the paintings. There were some good abstracts, but she decided on a conventional oil painting of the Fens, certain that Justin would prefer it. She went to Millers and bought recordings of the Brandenburg Concertos and Mahler's Third Symphony. She bought a bottle of gin and a couple of bottles of wine, then went to Adams and loaded up with exotic cheeses.

They put the children to bed early, saw Justin off to his dinner and, like conspirators, settled down to the serious business of getting drunk. For one blissful evening they were back together again – just as in the old days.

'There is just one thing, Sandra.'

'Wha's that?' Sandra slurred into her glass.

'Do me a favour, don't introduce me to people as Lady Upnor. I hate it, I get all embarrassed.'

Sandra sat bolt upright and looked earnestly at Jane, her eyes filling with tears. 'Oh, Jane. Don't ask me to do that. I love it, I'm so proud of you. I get such a kick saying it. Don't you realize – you're the excitement in my boring life.'

3

They drew up in front of Justin's parents' house, a pseudo-Georgian mansion, looking, with its columned portico, like a miniature Parthenon. They entered a large, imposing hall full of reproduction antiques, including a fake suit of armour.

Justin's mother, a thin, nervous woman, whose greying, mousy hair exactly matched the long dress she was wearing, showed them out to the swimming pool, where drinks were to be served. A shaggy green carpet stretched to the edge of the pool which was surrounded by gleaming plastic plants. Mrs Clemance could not settle, fluttered about them like a rather dull moth, serving drinks, plumping up cushions, emptying ashtrays. She seemed fond of Sandra, fussing over her almost protectively. Her genteel voice, a product of hours of elocution lessons, was hard to listen to, as each word issued forth half-strangled.

After an hour Mr Clemance finally joined them. Since Sandra always referred to him as 'the old man', Jane was unprepared for his apparently youthful appearance. With jet-black hair and dressed in fashionable, tight-fitting, flared trousers of green velvet, topped by a boldly striped shirt, he looked more like Justin's brother. But as he shook Jane's hand she saw that the hair was dyed, and the face was not, as she had thought, unlined – instead, the wrinkles were disguised by a heavy tan, which looked suspiciously even. The Clemances made an odd couple, so contrasted that Jane was reminded of a cock bird with his hen.

They began dinner, a meal of overcooked lamb and soggy vegetables, washed down by a 'Choice of the Month' wine from Mr Clemance's wine club, of which he was inordinately proud.

Mr Clemance dominated the conversation. He leaned back in a large, intricately carved chair, his stubby hands splayed out on the table in front of him. A miasma of smugness enveloped him. He did not speak to anyone in particular; rather he spoke as if the sound of his own voice was satisfaction enough.

Throughout the meal Sandra was silent. When not eating, she stared fixedly at the pattern on her plate. The only time she smiled was in response to her mother-in-law who fussed around them, communicating in a silent semaphore of arched eyebrow, questioning smiles and tentative gestures.

Justin seemed to enjoy his father's company. Sitting in a smaller chair, he leaned back, too, a carbon copy of his father, not in looks but in attitude.

Back at their house, Justin went to bed. The two friends settled for a nightcap.

'Your father-in-law is a male Lady Upnor. Perhaps they're related. What an ego! I don't think I've ever met anyone quite so pleased with himself before.' Jane laughed.

'I wish I could find him funny,' Sandra said. 'Do you see what I mean now? If it wasn't for Mrs Clemance, I'd begin to wonder if I existed.'

'Justin puzzled me, though. He was ignoring you too.'

'I know. So, am I to presume that he agrees with his father's opinion of me? That's the question that haunts me. And what makes me really sad is, I'm not a bad wife. But that old bastard won't rest until we're finished and he can marry him off to someone he thinks more suitable.'

'And I thought it was only me having problems about being accepted by gruesome in-laws. You'd think that now, in the so-called liberated sixties, things would have changed, wouldn't you?'

'Perhaps it's because we've done nothing. I mean, you read of working-class film and pop stars, even hairdressers, who're courted by everybody. Maybe if we'd done something with our lives we might have been more acceptable . . .'

'You have done something; you're an S R N. But those others, you can take my word for it, they're only taken up temporarily – like fashionable cabaret acts.'

They finished their drinks and made their way to bed. Jane lay in the dark, worrying about Sandra. All the fun and sparkle seemed to have gone out of her. She was in a vicious circle of being so terrified of Mr Clemance that she could not assert herself, and the more she cringed, the more he despised her. There was no doubt in Jane's mind: Sandra was on the verge of a breakdown. She would talk to Justin about it. One of the good things she had learned in the hospital was the value of talking things out; it solved so many problems before they took serious root in the mind. Self-awareness they called it, but Jane always felt that it was more like cleaning out a cupboard — taking the muddle out of one's mind.

The next morning while Sandra was doing the school run, Jane sat opposite Justin at the breakfast table.

'Justin, I'm worried about Sandra. I think she's on the verge of a nervous breakdown, unless we do something quickly,' she announced baldly.

'Really? I can't say I've noticed anything odd about her,' he said, sounding uninterested, peering over the top of his newspaper.

'Surely you have, Justin. She's so nervy. She never stops cleaning. Look how jumpy she is.'

'She takes pride in our home. I don't see anything wrong in that.'

'Of course not, not normally, but this cleaning of hers is obsessive, bordering on paranoid.'

'My, haven't you learned a lot in that hospital of yours?' he said, unpleasantly. 'Are you now trained in such matters?'

'Of course not, but I can't help noticing things. I think she needs to get right away. I think you should sit down with her and talk this through. It'll help both of you.'

'I don't think any of this is your business, Jane. I'd prefer it if you dropped the subject,' he said coldly.

'I can't. Hell, she's my oldest friend. I can't just sit back and see her cracking up because your father doesn't approve and is turning her into a nervous wreck. It has to be faced, discussed,' she said, a shade too excitedly.

'My father has nothing to do with this.' Justin methodically refolded his paper.

'But, Justin, your father has everything to do with it. Gracious, he's even turning her children against her.'

'That is arrant rubbish. How dare you. And who the hell are you to lecture me about my wife and my home? You haven't made such a great success yourself, have you? Just out of the loony bin, your marriage in tatters. What right have you to criticize me and mine?'

'It's because I've just got out of the "loony bin" that I'm in a position to say it. I can see signs in her that perhaps you're not aware of yourself. In the hospital —'

'I think, Jane, that you're a very arrogant woman. Just because you queen around with some stupid title doesn't give you the right to interfere like this.'

'I do not queen about. I am the last person who can be accused of that.'

'Oh no? You don't think I haven't noticed you sneering at our life style, because I have. And last night at my parents' you hardly opened your mouth and I know why, too — because you were uninterested and felt superior.'

'It's quite easy to feel superior to your father. Not your mother. I felt sorry for her — who wouldn't? But OK, yes, I didn't like your father: I thought he was pompous and rude, and horrible to my friend.' Horrified, she realized she was shouting. How much of that, she wondered, was to cover her discomfort at Justin's precise reading of her thoughts? The very thoughts she had been so ashamed of.

'Right, Jane,' he said, collecting his newspaper and coat, 'I thought it was a bad idea your coming here in the first place. I was certain that you would upset my wife. I would appreciate it if you weren't here when I return from work this evening. I really have no room for your interference and rudeness in my house.'

She should not have lost her temper, Jane thought, as she despondently packed her case. They had drummed that into her at the hospital. Calmness and logic, those were the keys, not flying off the handle and insulting a man's parents. She really had been trying to help. She had become so used to sitting in a circle, analysing others' problems, that she had quite forgotten that the outside, sane world did not behave that way.

'Oh, Christ!' Sandra exclaimed when Jane told her what had happened. 'But thank you for trying.'

'I did it all wrong. I was inexcusably rude about his father. And losing my temper, antagonizing him like that, isn't going to help you — and that's all I wanted to do. Oh, Sandra, I'm sorry.'

'I'm sorry you're going, but I'm proud you stuck up for me like that.' The two friends hugged each other.

'I suppose we'd better find somewhere for me to live.'

They phoned a couple of agencies and were given details of several flats. They telephoned one and made an appointment for Jane to view it later in the morning. Until it was time for her to go, they sat miserably smoking cigarettes and drinking cups of coffee.

'At least if you rent somewhere in Cambridge, you'll be near and I can pop in and see you to have a good old moan,' Sandra said bravely. But as Jane loaded her cases into the car, her friend began to cry.

The address she had been given was of a large house in Newnham. She drove up a shrub-infested drive and stopped outside a large house which looked in desperate need of a coat of paint. The garden was a riot of weeds, and the bell she rang was half hanging off the door. It was answered by a woman in her forties, her ample form covered in a multicoloured, flowing, none too clean kaftan. Her long hair was blonde, the roots showing black on her scalp; in her hand she wafted a long cigarette holder.

'Mrs Upnor? Welcome . . .' She waved Jane through the door, squeezing her bulk against the jamb so that Jane could manoeuvre past. 'Bloody hell, I just seem to get fatter and fatter.' She laughed loudly, as she showed Jane across the hall. Every inch of wall space was covered in paintings, the unpolished wood-block floor was strewn with random piles of books. They entered a bright kitchen which was a jumble of more paintings, books, plants, unwashed dishes and unironed clothes. 'Hope you don't mind clutter?' She grinned and pushed a fat, sleeping, white cat from the chair. 'Magnificat, move! Coffee?' She busied herself at the Aga, grinding beans, and moving, despite her obesity, with agile grace. Soon the kitchen was filled with the smell of freshly made coffee.

'They forgot to give me your name at the agency,' Jane said, savouring the delicious taste.

'Silly sods. Zoe Potterton, the old boiler, that's me.' She laughed loudly at her own joke. 'Have you lived in Cambridge before?' Jane was fascinated by her voice, which was low and husky: even when she was not smiling, laughter seemed to bubble through. It reminded Jane of Honor's voice with its hints of all manner of secret enjoyments.

'No, London mainly. But I have friends here, and when I found myself having to decide where to go, I thought of Cambridge.'

'Divorced?'

'Separated.'

'I hope you're not hoping to find a new husband here? Everyone's peculiar, you know. It's an odd place to live. Nothing's real here, it always seems to me. And the people take a bit of getting used to.'

'Marriage isn't a priority of mine at the moment,' Jane said lightly. 'I want to sort myself out, I've been ill, you see. I've just got to learn to pick up the pieces and build a new life.'

'You've chosen an odd place to try, then. Everyone seems to be off their rockers here. And most people are so self-centred, intent only on what they are doing, no real interest in anyone else. I always think that going to a dinner party in this city is like going to listen to half a dozen monologues.' She produced a large tin of cakes and offered them to Jane, who refused. As she bit hungrily into one, she suddenly said, 'I suppose you think I shouldn't be eating this, too fat already?'

'No, I wasn't.' Jane laughed at the question.

'Being fat is my own personal statement. This town is impossibly full of glorious, gorgeous, gilded youth. I can't compete, so I decided not to try and to be what I am, uncomplicatedly fat. No, I'd resolved not to say that any more. I'm not fat, really, I'm just under-tall. If you stretched me out a bit, I'd be lovely and thin, wouldn't I?' Again the full-blooded laugh rang out. 'Do you drink?' Jane nodded. 'Smoke?'

'Devotedly, I'm afraid.'

'Drugs?'

'Gracious, no.'

'Good. I like you, you'll fit in. I like people who drink and smoke. Drugs can be a bit wearying and trouble with the police and what have you. But I'd never have nondrinking, nonsmoking types as lodgers. They wouldn't fit in, and I'd be endlessly worrying myself about what vices they did have. Still, I expect you want to see the flat.' She led the way, talking nonstop so that Jane found herself watching carefully to see when she managed to take a breath. Jane could not understand how she could possibly have decided to like her since Jane had had little chance to say anything.

'See, you've got your own entrance,' Zoe said, unlocking the door and showing Jane into the flat. Built onto the back of the house, it had a large sitting room, with sliding glass doors opening onto the garden. A large, black, Swedish wood-burning stove stood on a central hearth; a spiral staircase led up on to a balcony which was arranged as a small study, and off it were two bedrooms. A beautiful kitchen, fitted in pine, and a bathroom completed the flat. 'You're welcome to use the garden, any time, and there's a lake at the bottom where we all swim and frolic in summer. What do you think?'

'It's perfect, Mrs Potterton. How much is the rent?'

'Call me Zoe, please. How much can you afford?'

'I'm not sure. I'm going to rent my house in London, I'm not sure what I'll get for it, but no doubt you want to rent straight away?'

Zoe thought for a moment. 'Tell you what we do. You rent your house in London and give me a third of what you get. How about that?'

'Are you sure?'

'Oh, I'm sure. The money doesn't matter. It's having congenial neighbours that's important. I've already said no to half a dozen the agency sent.'

'Heavens, what a compliment!'

'Do you want to move in now?'

'Well . . . I'm a bit short until I rent my own house.'

'Just owe it to me,' Zoe said airily.

Gratefully Jane accepted her offer, unloaded her cases, packed her things in the drawers, and then telephoned Sandra with her new number and address. After going to the shops to buy food and some drink, and fortified with a large gin and tonic, she telephoned Alistair.

It was a long time since they had last spoken – and then they had been screaming at each other in anger – but, when she heard his voice, all the old longing returned. Her mind raced with dreams and plans while her voice prosaically made arrangements to meet him at Fulham, to sort out what things he wanted to remove. She sat for a long time afterwards, her hand on the receiver, as if by touching the instrument she was, in some way, still in contact with him. He had sounded warm and kind and had offered to make the letting arrangements for her. It had been a big step for her to take, to speak to him, but now she wished they could have talked longer.

Jane was highly agitated as she approached the house in Fulham. It was the first time she had been there since her illness. She was almost afraid to enter in case she would catch it again, like a contagious disease, and never recover. She was afraid to see Alistair, too. It was one thing to talk on the telephone but an entirely different proposition to be face to face with him. But still, she argued with herself, speaking to him had been one hurdle, seeing him was only another. He was already there and opened the door as she put her key in the lock.

'You look well, Jane,' he said, kissing her quickly on the cheek.

'So do you,' she replied, unsure of what else to say.

'I think your Cambridge idea is a good one. Better to get right away.'

'Yes.'

'Are you sure you wouldn't prefer to sell the house altogether?'

'No. I'd rather rent it. I don't want to lose it, it's so much of the past . . . isn't it?'

'Quite.' He walked past her into the sitting room. She paused at the doorway, afraid to enter, afraid to look at the point on the carpet where her mind had left her that dreadful day. He stood in front of the Picasso. 'You can take this, if you like. You didn't believe me when I told you that you'd grow to love it, did you?'

'No.'

'So, do you want to take it?' he asked, unaware that she had not yet followed him into the room. He studied the painting. 'It needs reframing.

I'll get that done for you as well, shall I? And I think you should replace the china and glass: it's far too good for lodgers. I spoke to the agent and they'll see to all of that for you. Odd bits of silver should go. I don't want anything. You're welcome to the lot.' He was speaking quickly and, as he spoke, he roamed about the room collecting ornaments and pictures which he felt she should take with her. She watched the familiar figure, the beautiful hands which had caressed her, and she longed to shout, 'I want to come back to you. Take me back. I love you.' But fear would not let her speak; wordlessly she nodded at his suggestions and silently she packed the objects he gave her into the boxes he had thoughtfully provided. He did not look at her once; she wanted him to look at her – perhaps then he would see the naked longing in her eyes. 'Right, I think that's all. Didn't take long, did it? You'd better give me your phone number. I'll bring James over one of these weekends, shall I?'

'Yes, please,' she said huskily, the happy thought making her breathless.

'Right.' Satisfied, he looked about the room. 'That's it, isn't it?'

'Yes, I suppose so.'

'Funny, really, when you think of all the time we spent here, our life together. Now it's just a room, waiting for lodgers, isn't it?'

'No, it'll never be that to me,' she said, turning away, tears brimming in her eyes. He helped her carry the boxes out to her car, laid the paintings carefully on the back seat.

'Anything else?'

Hesitantly she explained her need for some money until the rent from the house started to arrive. Equally hesitantly she asked if he would pay her fees at a secretarial college. She wished he had simply offered and she had not had to ask.

'Of course. I think even with the rent coming in you'll have a struggle, you know. Better let me help you out on a regular basis.'

'That won't be necessary,' she said with dignity, as she accepted the wad of pound notes he gave her and climbed into her car.

As she cleared the London traffic, she felt overwhelmingly sad. What had she expected – that on seeing her he would run into her arms and beg her forgiveness, plead with her to return? Yes, she supposed that was exactly what she had hoped for, but things like that only happened in fairy tales. This was life, real life, where it seemed there were to be no happy endings.

4

She settled into her new life in Zoe's flat. She had wondered if it would be difficult for her to meet people, but as an endless procession of people visited Zoe, so she would be summoned by Zoe yelling out of a window for her to come and be introduced. Her life became a succession of new faces and celebrations, since Zoe needed only the weakest of excuses to open yet another bottle of wine.

They would sit for hours around the large pine kitchen table, Bach or Mozart filling the room from the giant-reeled tape recorder. They were a motley crew – university lecturers, worried by their work or disillusioned by it; homesick students; lovesick nurses; menopausal women whose children had left home and who could no longer find ways of filling their days; men whose wives had just left them; homosexuals set on another destructive affair – all of them in some way wounded by life.

People would arrive at any time, day or night. Coffee would be put on or wine opened. Zoe would settle her expansive bottom on her special cushion, in the biggest chair. With her giant breakfast cup or the equally large rummer in front of her, she looked just like one of Goldilocks's bears. She could coax, wheedle and persuade them to tell her everything – and they did, at length. Zoe always seemed to have time. In fact there was not even a clock in the kitchen to remind anyone of time passing by.

In this company Jane felt at ease. She listened to their tales, and just as Sandra's problems had helped her put her own life into perspective, these new friends consolidated that perception. Her sudden bouts of anxiety passed, the pills were flushed down the lavatory. Jane felt calm. Luckily, she was aware that it might be a false calm, for she could not say she lived in a normal world. She was surrounded by the walking wounded of life; apart from trips to the corner shop she never went out; and she had the security of Zoe's strength to protect her like a huge, warm blanket. But it was giving Jane respite, a plateau on which her mind could heal and renew itself.

The reason for Zoe's size soon became apparent. She was a cook of passionate genius. She never minded how many she cooked for; her only proviso was that she was never to be left alone in the kitchen.

'I can't stand being alone. I start thinking, and too much thought is a dangerous exercise,' she laughingly explained to Jane one day, as she avidly and expertly chopped the ingredients for another gargantuan casserole. The rest of the house seemed to hold no interest for her. Jane only ever saw her in the kitchen. She supposed that Zoe must have a bedroom somewhere, and that there were other rooms, but Jane never saw them, and could only presume that they were slowly falling into decline from neglect, as the front of the house was doing.

From far away in the large house, Jane would hear Benjamin tapping away on his typewriter. He was a successful novelist. He worked hard and was rarely seen in daylight hours. Telephone messages would be taken for him; anyone who wanted to see him would have to wait patiently until his tall, lolloping figure wandered into the kitchen, his big nose over his wild, bushy beard sniffing the air like a huge shaggy dog's at the tempting smells coming from Zoe's Aga. They adored each other, and Jane loved to watch them as they greeted each other every evening as if they had been separated for weeks, not just for one working day.

'Benjamin works so hard,' Jane commented one afternoon: the tapping of the typewriter had been a constant background noise all day.

'Yes, it sounds as if it's going well. I dread it when a book's finished: he gets very depressed that all the characters he's created have gone away. Then he stays depressed until he starts another one.'

'It must be wonderful to be that successful.'

'It is. On the other hand, because he's successful, the intellectual snobs here sneer at him. He was a Fellow, you see, once, then he committed the unforgivable crime of writing a bestseller. Now some of his old colleagues ignore him. He says it doesn't matter, but I know it hurts him.' Zoe looked angry at the thought.

'They're probably jealous of all the money he earns.'

'Yes, that's probably it.' Zoe laughed, her expression lightening.

Jane spent more and more time with Zoe as the weeks went by. Zoe cooked and Jane would help clear up, do the washing and ironing; and she took on the weeding of Zoe's precious herb beds and vegetable garden. If the front garden was a jungle, the back was a model of order, with row upon row of vegetables flourishing. The arrangement worked well, for Zoe had all the tasks she hated to do done for her, and Jane was never alone.

Jane had always enjoyed writing letters, and now she had the time. Honor was high on her list, Alistair and May, too, and Nigel, her doctor, and her parents. It was as if by writing long chatty letters to them she was proving how much better she was. Each week she wrote to James, hating the thought of him now at boarding school, and though it was often difficult to know what to write, she was certain he must look forward to the post. Each week he replied, short stilted little notes, thanking her for hers, rarely any news.

Sometimes three or four letters would be posted before Alistair would reply, always news of the estate, nothing personal. His phone calls were infrequent, and she began to feel more isolated from him.

Honor never wrote but instead phoned often in reply, enquiring how she was and never failing to ask if there was anything she wanted. Each time the invitation to go to Italy was repeated and each time Jane declined. For the moment, Jane felt safer with Zoe and Benjamin; her days were full of chores and people. At Honor's Jane knew that she would have too much time with nothing to do but to think, and she was not ready for thinking, yet.

The letters done, Jane began to write for the pleasure of it. She tried to put into words what had happened to her and to her surprise found that the exercise helped her further. As the days sped past, Jane kept putting off her plan to enrol at the secretarial college, there just didn't seem any need somehow.

Sandra called whenever she was in Cambridge. On each visit, Jane was aware that she was witnessing the gradual disintegration of her friend. Each time she looked gaunter, each time she was thinner. She chain-smoked now, and her hand as she reached for her cup had an almost imperceptible tremor. One day she was more agitated than usual. Not only had Mr Clemance announced that he was taking the children on a month-long cruise, but he had suggested that on his return they move into the big house with him. Justin seemed to think all this a good idea: it would solve his money worries. But Sandra was in despair.

'That friend of yours is going to have a breakdown any day now,' Zoe declared after Sandra's latest visit.

'I know. I don't know what to do. I tried talking to her husband but he threw me out. She's frightened to do anything in case Justin sues for divorce and gets the children.'

'That's unlikely.'

'His father's very rich. He'd finance Justin to fight her through every court in the land for those brats. She loves him, you see, though I don't understand why. I think he's a creep.'

'Does her mother know?'

'No, she's too ashamed to tell her.'

'Phone her up, you tell her.'

'I can't do that . . . it's none of my business.'

'I've never heard anything so wet in my life, Jane. I thought you were her friend. I'll phone, what's the number?'

Zoe went straight to the phone and in graphic detail told Mrs Evans what was happening to her daughter. The next day, a shocked Mrs Evans arrived and, within an hour, had assessed the situation, had packed Sandra's and the children's cases and was speeding back to Battersea with the three of them. That evening the telephone lines to Cambridge bristled as Mrs Evans vented her spleen on Justin and his father. She was adamant: Sandra and the children were to stay with her until Justin decided what he wanted – his father or his wife. Zoe and Jane waited impatiently for the outcome.

Six weeks later a radiant Sandra appeared. She seemed beside herself with happiness. She and Justin had been on holiday together while Mrs Evans looked after the children. She was coming back, but on her own terms. Now the children were only to see their grandparents once a month. According to Sandra, the time spent with her mother had worked wonders on the children, especially Lance. The house outside Cambridge was up for sale and they were searching in the city for something cheaper. Once she had left him, Justin had realized how much he loved her, and had plucked up the courage to demand a raise from his father. With the mortgage pressures off him, and more money in his pocket, Sandra was certain that the bullying, hectoring Justin would disappear – everything had been getting him down too. Sandra herself was applying for a part-time job at the hospital. Jane watched this speedy revolution with envy and wished that she had been able to solve her own problems as neatly as Sandra had done, but then, as Zoe pointed out, Jane did not have the formidable Mrs Evans behind her.

The weekend she had longed for arrived, and on a crisp autumn day, Alistair was due with James. She was nervous as she awaited their arrival, and unsure if this stemmed from the prospect of seeing Alistair or excitement at seeing her son again. When she saw Alistair getting out of his car, the old longing flared up in her body. The little boy who climbed out of the car in his smart school uniform looked like a stranger to her.

The boy stood in the driveway, his cap clenched in his hand, staring intently at the ground and aimlessly kicking a pebble with his shoe, as his father kissed Jane on the cheek. James turned his head away, abruptly, as she tried to kiss him.

'Kiss your mother, James,' Alistair demanded. Anxiously Jane saw the small hands clench his cap more firmly, his jaw set in a determined line as he went on kicking the pebbles. 'James!'

'It doesn't matter, Alistair. He'll kiss me when he wants to, won't you, James?'

The boy did not answer. His eyes darted everywhere, looking at everything but Jane. She was distressed that his lovely blonde hair had been cut with short back and sides, accentuating the slimness of his young boy's neck. She saw the fine blonde down on the nape of his neck and she longed to nuzzle him there, suddenly remembering the warm, earthy smell of little boys. She asked him about school. He replied shortly, called her 'sir', and kept a mental as well as a physical distance from her. Over a year was a long time in the life of a child of nine. She would have to learn to be patient with him; but, even as she thought this, she realized that she did not mind his distance; shockingly, it did not seem to matter.

They spent a stiff afternoon in the botanical gardens. Jane and Alistair walked ahead of James who lagged a good ten yards behind, as if proclaiming to the passers-by that he was not with them, or rather, she thought, with her. Alistair, irritated, would call him, they would pause and wait for him, but as soon as they set off, the boy would lag behind again. They had tea in the Copper Kettle, then wandered back to Newnham. She gave Alistair a drink. James sat on the edge of the sofa, giving the impression that he was ready for instant flight. She turned the television on for him, but he did not watch; instead his eyes never left his father, waiting for the first sign that they were about to leave. When it was time for them to go, it was Alistair to whom she hated to say goodbye.

After this initial visit, they came twice a month during the school holidays. James's air of detachment persisted. Alistair was distressed by the boy's behaviour. He cajoled, nagged, reasoned with and yelled at James, but to no effect. Jane suggested that, perhaps, if she were alone with him for a few days, it would be easier for them to reforge a relationship. Alistair refused her request: he was regretful but he quite openly admitted to her that he was afraid she was not fully recovered yet. She could have argued with him, she supposed, but she did not want any bad feeling between them, so she dropped the idea. In a way, she was relieved at Alistair's refusal. She felt she had suggested it because she should, not because she wanted to. In reality, what would she have talked to the boy about? What could she give the boy when he so obviously did not want any part of her?

On each visit, her main hope was that Alistair would say something of how he felt about her, about them. But he never did. Instead, she felt he treated her with a distant but tender concern.

'Will you ever go back to him?' Zoe asked her one night as they sat alone, drinking chilled white wine and eating dolmades.

'I shouldn't think so. He's never shown that he wants me back.'

'I wouldn't say that – he looks at you at times as if he could eat you.'

'I've never noticed. He never makes any advances and he's never said he misses me.'

'Has he found anyone else?'

'I should think there's an army of them.' Jane laughed.

'Perhaps he's waiting for you to make the first move. He strikes me as a somewhat inhibited individual where emotions are involved.'

'He's not particularly inhibited where leaping into beds is concerned,' she said ironically. 'I couldn't make the first move, though. What if he rejected me? I just don't know how I could cope with that.'

'You'll never know unless you try. You can't hide behind your breakdown for ever, miss.'

There were times, Jane thought, when Zoe's bluntness was hard to take. But she was right. Jane knew she used her illness as a barrier to life, something behind which to cower. She never went anywhere, clung always to the security of Zoe and her kitchen. She was going to have to do something about it – well, some time, she would.

'There's something else, Jane.' Zoe interrupted her thoughts. 'You'll probably hit me for saying it, but you don't seem to be involved with that little boy of yours. You seem –'

Jane stood up abruptly. 'You're right, Zoe. I would like to hit you. If you'll excuse me, I'm off to bed,' she said coolly, picking up her cardigan and leaving Zoe to the rest of the wine.

She lay on her bed, frowning at the ceiling. She felt threatened by Zoe's assessment. But she was not ready to talk about it to anyone. Alone, she often worried about her attitude to James but, even so, she felt she did not worry enough. When she was with James, it was as if she were watching someone else with the boy. She was certain that the boy regarded her as a boring duty, a visit that had to be got through, politely, before he could get back to the life she now knew nothing about. It should make her sad; it was odd that it did not. Part of the trouble was that, try as she might, she could not remember what it was like to be a mother. She just could not seem to remember what their relationship had been like before her illness. When she thought of the past it was always of her life with Alistair, almost as if the child were an adjunct to that life, not a true part of it.

She fumbled on the bedside table for her packet of cigarettes, lit one and watched the smoke curl up to the ceiling. Perhaps her attitude was a defence mechanism. Having lost Alistair, was her mind refusing to cope with the possibility of losing her son? Or was it that they were reaping the whirlwind of her childhood? How could you love as a parent if you had not been loved as a child? Maybe Alistair was right: maybe, as a result, she could not love, only possess. Agitatedly she puffed at the cigarette. That could not be true. She knew she loved Alistair, whatever he chose to say. And knowing how she felt about Alistair, there was Zoe, always nagging her to find a boyfriend, telling her she would get crabby without sex. Jane laughed softly. If only Zoe knew – sex, and the lack of it, did not bother Jane one jot. It was the lack of love that made her sad.

She stubbed out her cigarette, and searched for the light switch. Beside the lamp, Alistair's face smiled at her from a photograph. She gently traced the outline of his lips. She had placed it there so that it was the first and last thing she saw in her day. Alistair, not James.

'Oh, dear, I am weird,' she said to the darkness.

5

Autumn slid into the marrow-freezing cold of a Cambridge winter. The winds whistled in from the North Sea, crossing the Fens but apparently losing none of their bitterness and ferocity on the way. They even acquired the ability to go around corners, so that wherever one huddled in the city, the wind would find one out. This would, Jane thought, have been a logical time to go to Honor's, but Zoe had invited her for Christmas, which coincided with Benjamin's birthday and the big party they always held. In the New Year she would go to Italy for a month, and when she returned she would start her secretarial course again.

The food for the party would have fed an army. Hearty, robust stuff to line the gut and mop up the wine, in total contrast to the delicate canapés and wafer-thin sandwiches she had ordered for parties at Respryn.

Armed with a big brush, Zoe marched across the kitchen. 'Care to help get the party room ready?'

Jane willingly followed her across the hall and into two intercommunicating, darkened rooms. Zoe wrestled with the shutters and, as the thin winter light filtered into the room, Jane burst out laughing. Before her was a room totally bare of furniture, except for large cushions scattered about the floor, a stereo unit with massive speakers, and everywhere dirty ashtrays, upturned bottles and empty glasses.

'Oh, dear, I should have cleared it up after the last party. I always forget. Still, it hardly matters now, does it? We'll just empty the ashtrays and wash the glasses, it'll be in just as much of a mess again in the morning.'

'Zoe, I love your logical mind!'

Jane was excited at the prospect of the evening. It was such a long time since she had been to a party. She dressed with care in a new black suit she had bought from Wallis especially for the occasion. She studied herself in the mirror. She had never worn so short a miniskirt before: the style had never seemed right at Respryn. She liked the way it seemed to make her legs look longer, and the fact that the chunky patent-leather shoes accentuated their slimness. She buckled a chain belt around her waist and decided to wear her hair loose. The black suit with her dark hair made her look interesting and intellectual, she decided, laughing at this new image. Now that, thanks to Zoe's cooking, she had filled out a little, the new clothes suited her.

Zoe looked magnificent in a turquoise kaftan, shimmering with gold thread which competed with her freshly bleached hair. As Zoe glittered about the room putting the finishing touches to the food, Jane was aware that she was nervous. It was an extraordinary discovery: she had thought that nothing could frighten Zoe. But here she was, fretting and worrying in the same way that Jane had done at Respryn.

Jane circulated dutifully about the room, but could find no one to talk to – plenty to listen to but none to talk with. She wondered what it was about male academics that made them smell, a strange musty sort of odour, akin to unwashed socks or a damp day on the London tube.

She finally gave up circulating and stood quietly watching the crowd form and reform like live cells under a microscope. She smiled at the sight of Zoe, deep in conversation, her arms whirling like a turquoise windmill as she argued animatedly with another middle-aged woman.

'Hullo, who are you?' A dark-haired young man with a distinct cockney accent was standing beside her.

'I'm Jane Upnor, Zoe's lodger, in the flat.'

'One of her lame ducks, are you?'

'Yes.' She laughed. 'I suppose that's a fair description of me.'

They stood side by side, surveying the crowd. She glanced at him out of the corner of her eye. He looked interesting, different, she thought. She searched for something to say to prevent him moving off.

'What do you do?' He spoke for her.

'Nothing, just trying to survive at the moment.'

'Hope you haven't told the other geezers here that you do nothing. It wouldn't go down at all well.'

'I've learned that already. It's the glazed look that comes over them and the speed with which they shuffle off.'

'That's 'cause you're no use to them, you see, if you do nothing. Everyone is on the lookout for contacts, people who'll give 'em a leg up, see?'

'You mean no one wants to know me for myself?' Jane said in mock horror.

'Christ, no. What an antiquated idea! Only use you'd be to this lot is to listen to 'em.'

'I've done a lot of that tonight, actually.'

'"Actually", have you?' he said, mocking her voice, but this only amused her. 'What you've got to do, my girl, is to emote. *E-bleeding-mote*, as our American mates would say.'

'Sounds messy, like having an emetic.'

'I like that. You're funny. Yes, emetic, much the same really, give out, spew your personality out. 'S good, that.' He laughed, showing a fine set of white teeth, so white they made his full lips look redder than they really were. There was a film of moisture on his lips which, to her astonishment, Jane found she would like to touch.

He stood in front of her now, as if shielding her from the other guests. She was pressed back against the wall. Used to peering up at tall men she found, for a change, that she was looking at his face with ease: he could only be a few inches taller than she. Dark, piercing brown eyes looked at her with an amused glint. His hair was long and black and one hank kept falling across his forehead which he would impatiently flick back with his hand – just like Alistair did. He leaned forward, and the black shirt he wore, unbuttoned, revealed a hairy and muscular chest. She felt totally encompassed by his short but powerful body. There was an animal quality about him which, with mounting surprise, she realized was exciting her. 'So, what do you do?' she asked, the huskiness in her voice betraying what her body was feeling.

'Tom Hutchins. Painter by profession.'

'A painter? Of houses?'

'Good God, no. Pictures.'

'You mean, you're an artist.'

'No, I mean I'm a painter. I can't call myself an artist. Picasso, he's an artist, or Bosch, or Turner. Me, I'm learning, I'm still a painter.'

'So one day you'll be an artist.'

'Oh yes.' He smiled a strange sardonic smile, removing, momentarily, the deep furrows on either side of his mouth which gave a look of bitterness to his face. She listened fascinated as he talked with intensity of painting, of pictures he loved, of how important his work was to him; a day without putting brush to canvas made him feel incomplete, he said.

'Would you like to see my work?'

She hesitated only for a moment. 'Yes.'

'Come on, then.'

'But . . .'

'You either do or you don't.'

There was such a crush that they would certainly not be missed. It would not matter, she thought, if she popped out for an hour.

They heaved their way out of the crowded house. He walked so rapidly that she almost had to run to keep up with his hurried strides. They finally turned into the warren of streets behind Mill Road and stopped in front of a small terraced house. By the street lamp she could see that the windows were covered in dust and that the curtains were old blankets. The door was painted a bright emerald green and in the very centre a large, painted, purple eye looked at them. He pushed the door open. A plump, rather dirty-looking young woman was in the hallway. Her long, dark hair reached her waistline; she wore flowing, brightly coloured clothes which swirled about her, and around the hem of her dress were little bells which tinkled as she moved.

'This is Beth, she's our group mum.'

'How do you do, Beth?' Jane said politely.

'Peace,' the young girl said, raising her hand. Smiling a dreamy, unseeing smile, she glided into the front room, tinkling as she went. The smell of joss sticks pervaded the air. Tom led her up the steep, uncarpeted staircase. The walls of the small room into which he showed her were covered from floor to ceiling in paintings. Canvases were stacked one on top of each other against the walls, and the smell of turps was overpowering. There was a small table covered in paints and a mattress on the floor, but nowhere to sit, as far as Jane could see.

'That's where you sit,' he said, indicating the far from clean mattress. Jane lowered herself onto it and he handed her wine in a cracked cup. Gingerly she sipped it: the sharp, acrid taste made her throat constrict and she coughed.

'Used to better, I suppose?' he asked, holding up the bottle.

'It went down the wrong way,' she lied.

He took a painting from the stack against the wall.

'What do you think?' The large canvas, painted in primary colours, was full of enormous, laughing people. The group was at the seaside, fat bottoms straining the brightly striped deckchairs, plump children eating ice creams covered in sand. It was like the postcards which her aunt used to send from the seaside, with one difference. There was one monstrous figure in the painting, with an ugly, distorted face – and it was not laughing.

'They're so funny. But why the devil, who's that?' she asked. He ignored the question. 'Tom, they're so true. It reminds me of my childhood.'

'Your childhood.' He snorted.

'Oh yes, caravan trips to the seaside with my aunt. She had a big bottom like that. I was always scared that the canvas would rip whenever she sat on a deckchair. Is it for sale? I'd love to buy it.'

'No.'

'Which ones are?'

'None of them.'

'Don't you sell your work?'

'I'll have to one day, just to make room for more. I don't want to. I don't want to become some fat pig's investment. I've warned 'em, mind you, that some of 'em are going to have to go. They didn't like it much, I can tell you, bleeding well sulked for days.' He continued to talk as if the people in his picture were real. He produced more and more of the funny paintings, each with its devil leering in the corner. He seemed too serious and intense a person to paint such happy paintings.

'Good, aren't they.' It was a statement rather than a question. She watched fascinated as he produced a tobacco pouch and began to make a roll-up cigarette. She had forgotten about them; she had not seen it done since she had watched her father. From another pouch he took a strange-looking lump, which looked like a nutmeg, and with a sharp knife began to shave some of it into the tobacco. Carefully he rolled it up.

'What's that?' she asked curiously.

'Oh, come off it, you're not telling me you don't know hash when you see it?' She looked shocked and he laughed at her expression. 'It's good for you, gets rid of all those bleeding inhibitions,' he said, lighting it and inhaling deeply. Then he handed it to her.

'No, thank you,' she said primly.

'Oh, come on, don't be unfriendly. Try it.' Cautiously she sucked at the cigarette, inhaling the strange-tasting smoke. Nothing happened, so she inhaled some more.

'Here, don't hog it.' He snatched the joint back. 'Why do you live here in Cambridge?'

'I've friends here, and I like the atmosphere. I like all the young people about the place.'

'You're not that young though, are you?'

'Put so bluntly, no.'

'How old are you?' he asked, and passed her the joint.

'Thirty-two in May.'

'Over the top, aren't you?'

'How charming you are, Mr Hutchins. How old are you, then?'

'Twenty-nine.'

'There isn't that much difference between us, then.' She laughed.

'Oh yes, there is, lady. I'm still young, you see, and you're middle-aged. It's all in one's attitude, you were probably born middle-aged.' He began to giggle inanely. 'You getting high, my poor old middle-aged bird?'

'I don't think so.'

'It'll work next time.' He lay contentedly on the pillow looking at the ceiling, apparently oblivious to her presence. She began to wonder if she should leave, when suddenly he sat up again. 'I should like to see your tits,' he announced. Instinctively she crossed her arms across her chest, which only made him giggle again. 'God, Jane, you're so funny, so bleeding funny. Like an old maid.'

'You surprised me. I'm not used to people speaking to me like that.'

'Jane, you can't be true. You must know you've got great boobs. What's more natural than that I should want to have a dekko at them? Come on.'

'No, I think I'd better go.' His only response was to laugh even more loudly. He began to roll another cigarette.

He handed it to her. 'It's lonely being high on your own. Come on, love, try again.'

She knew she should get out, knew that it was madness to be here smoking joints with this strange, wild young man, but she did not want to go. There was a fascination about him and the whole situation that kept her. Again she took a deep breath of the pungent smoke, felt it burning as it swirled down her throat, decided that she did not like the taste one little bit and that this was a pointless activity when . . . she felt suddenly as if her blood was made of honey. She felt her brain expand: suddenly she was totally free, she had no problems. She laughed and the characters in the paintings laughed back at her.

'Good girl,' whispered Tom. 'Now let's see those lovely tits.' She enjoyed being undressed by him, enjoyed the wonderful feeling as his large, sensuous mouth closed over her nipple. How slowly he did everything! She felt she was floating, certain that she was the little green and yellow bird again, but this time the little bird was safely held in loving hands, oh, such loving hands . . .

'Tweet, tweet.' She laughed uncontrollably. 'Tweet, tweet.'

'To-wit-to-woo,' Tom replied. It was all so funny, so deliciously, sensuously funny. Why on earth had she ever thought she could never be happy again, never enjoy what this wonderful man was doing to her? She heard a strange moaning, which grew louder and louder, and she realized that it was herself; she heard herself moaning and sighing until with a body-shattering explosion, and for the first time in her life, she reached a shuddering climax.

6

'Aha, and where did you get to last night?' Zoe teased Jane when she finally arrived back at the house.

'Well I . . . I . . .' Jane did not know what to reply and, to her annoyance, felt herself blushing. She wondered if there would ever come a time when she would no longer blush – it seemed so undignified in a grown woman.

'There's no need to answer, Jane – you look marvellous.'

'I feel marvellous. I feel so relaxed, so . . .' She hugged herself.

'Splendid. May I ask who the lucky fellow is?'

'He's a painter, Tom Hutchins.'

Immediately, the benevolent smile disappeared from Zoe's face. 'Oh, Jane. Not Tom, he's not right for you. You could find somebody much better than that creep.'

Jane felt a surge of anger. 'What do you mean? What makes you say that?' she demanded. Zoe ignored her questions and continued, energetically, to whisk the cake she was making. 'I like him.' Still there was no response from Zoe. 'I said, I like him, he's fun. I had a lovely evening. I'm not going to fall in love, Zoe. Neither of us wants any great involvement, just to enjoy each other. That's what's so marvellous about it.'

'You've changed your tune in a hurry, haven't you?' The two women glared angrily at each other across the kitchen table. 'I'll remind you, you said it was all or nothing for you –'

'I didn't know I was going to meet anyone like Tom, then, did I? I've changed.'

'You haven't changed. Not enough for a sexual fling with a bastard like Tom. That isn't you. You'll be disgusted with yourself if you go on with this. Hell, Jane, I'm so angry.'

'I can see that.' Jane laughed bitterly. 'So what is it about Tom that makes you so angry?'

'I could write a book on what I've got against that young man.' She shook her balloon whisk at Jane before returning to the cake with renewed fury. 'You bloody fool, don't you see, I'm angry with you because I love you, and you're in danger and you don't have the sense to judge and to see. You've led such a sheltered life that you don't know danger when it's staring you in the face.'

'I don't think being ditched by my husband and having a nervous breakdown is leading a sheltered life.'

'Of course it bloody well is. If you had lived a bit more you wouldn't have crumbled so dramatically, would you?'

'You're not answering the question. Leave that flaming cake alone and tell me,' Jane shouted.

'He's dishonest. He steals things, usually from his friends – that sort of charming dishonesty.'

'That's slander.'

'No, it's not, it's true. Ask anyone.' An oppressive silence hung over the kitchen. Jane was too shocked to speak and Zoe still too angry to do anything but beat the poor innocent cake. 'He takes drugs, too,' she added, finally.

'Everyone takes drugs these days.'

'Everyone doesn't, my girl.'

'It's only pot and that doesn't hurt you. I'm sure he's not taking anything else, and pot's not serious.'

'That remark shows just how little you know, then, young woman. One thing leads to another. I've seen it time and again.'

'For goodness' sake, Zoe, stop mothering me. Let me lead my own life.'

'Normally I would, I'm only interfering because of that creep. I bet you smoked pot last night?'

'Yes, but only a little, and I won't do it again, I promise.' She saw Zoe's massive bulk relax. 'Please, Zoe, let's be friends. I'm so excited, I wanted to tell you about it. You see, I had an orgasm last night for the first time in my entire life. Isn't that amazing?' The wonder of the experience still lingered in her voice.

'Oh, child, if you were high on pot . . . that was an illusion. Don't you see? There's no difference between that and if he had fucked you while you were pissed out of your mind.'

'You don't understand, Zoe. It was real. I know, I've tried before – making love drunk – but it never happened . . . and then last night . . . And he didn't "fuck" me – he made love to me.'

'Tom! He's incapable of anything but fucking. All he does is copulate.'

'Shut up, Zoe!' Jane screamed putting her hands over her ears. 'Don't use such horrible language to me. Don't spoil my happiness.'

'I'm not, I'm trying to preserve what little happiness you've managed to make for yourself. I warn you, Jane, he will use you, just as he uses everyone.'

'Maybe I'm using him too,' Jane replied defiantly. Zoe sat down heavily on her chair. She looked defeated and weary.

'Zoe, please don't make me fight you. I need you.'

Zoe sat silent for a moment, deep in thought. 'You're right, Jane, it's your life.' She smiled at Jane. 'I'll say no more. But I warn you, when he's hurt you and you come in here crying, I shall say "I told you so" – I promise you that.'

On the few occasions that Jane saw Zoe in the following weeks, she kept her promise. Tom was not mentioned by the two women again.

Jane's happiness was total. She felt like a sixteen-year-old again. They seemed able to extract enjoyment from the silliest things. They would go to the park and swing on the swings, shriek as they slid down the slide, and when the park-keeper appeared to tell them angrily to clear off, they would run away, giggling, like the naughty children they felt they were. They played 'knock door ginger' and Jane could not remember when she had had such fun or laughed so much. They ate fish and chips from the paper, washed down with cheap red wine. And they made love – long sensuous hours of exploring each other's bodies. She did not try very hard to keep her promise not to smoke more hash. The liberated feeling it gave her was too seductive. She spent little time in her flat; most nights she slept in Tom's room in the dusty, dirty little house in the back streets of Cambridge.

Tom shared the small house with Beth and four other men. The lack of privacy made Jane feel uneasy: casually she suggested after a few weeks that she get a new flat where they could move in together.

Tom thought for a moment. 'All right,' he finally said. 'But there is one thing. If I move in with you, don't you get all "married" with me, will you? No set meal times, no "Where have you been?", no washing my socks.'

'I promise, darling.' She laughed with relief. She knew she would have promised him anything.

'And don't call me "darling", it's bourgeois. I can't stand it.'

'All right – Tom.' She smiled, too happy to feel hurt.

She returned to the house in Newnham to pack her possessions. Zoe appeared in the doorway.

'What are you doing?'

'I was just about to pop over and see you, Zoe. I think I should look for another flat.'

'Jane, why? Don't do that. We enjoy having you here so much.'

'It's difficult. You see, Tom and I have decided to move in together and I know how you feel – you wouldn't want him in your flat.'

Zoe stood silent for a moment. 'No, you're wrong. It's your home and you have every right to have whoever you want with you. I've not mentioned again how I feel, have I? I've kept my promise: I shall continue to keep it.'

'Really? You wouldn't mind?' She flung her arms round Zoe. 'That would be so marvellous. I don't want to go. And really, Zoe, I think he's changed. You might even begin to like him again,' she said hopefully.

'Yes, Jane, maybe I will, for you.'

She rushed back to Tom with the news, and cheerfully helped him pack his few possessions into the back of her car. Almost triumphantly, she drove him to her flat.

Tom took one of the bedrooms for a studio and moved in his paints and pictures, which was all he seemed to own. That first evening they hung his paintings throughout the flat, light-heartedly arguing about where best to put each one. She enjoyed the novelty of having a man to cook for, and with their first meal there they drank a bottle of good wine.

'That's one proviso I make,' she said, laughing at him over the rim of her glass of wine. 'No more vinegar plonk. My liver can't stand much more.'

'So long as you don't expect me to pay for it, who am I to complain?'

She watched eagerly as he got out his tin of tobacco and began the ritual of rolling the reefer for them. She shut her mind to the thought of Zoe across the patio in her kitchen, and the promise she was about to break again. All she could think of was the effect the drug had on her, longing already for the physical release it gave.

They settled into a routine. She would get up in the morning, leaving him asleep, and would clean the flat as quietly as possible, so as not to wake him. Then she would go to the shops and buy their food, feeling like a million other housewives for the first time in her life. But there the similarity ended, for when she came home, he was either locked in his studio, which he would never let her enter, or he was out. She never knew where he went and did not dare to ask because he was increasingly irritable. Each evening she would cook their supper, hoping that he would come back in time to eat it. More often than not he did not. So, although he lived with her, she saw less of him than she had in that first rapturous month. And a different sort of loneliness began to seep into her life.

Most evenings she sat alone in the flat. She had stopped writing her letters to her friends – she was afraid she might reveal too much of herself in them. Instead she began again to write, playing with words. Nearly all of her efforts ended up in the wastepaper basket. But Jane found she enjoyed seeing her thoughts emerge in black and white.

Late one night when he returned home, Jane was already in bed but got up to tell him his supper was in the oven.

'I told you,' he shouted, 'no bloody hot dinners. I don't want to be looked after. Don't you understand plain English, you stupid bloody cow?'

'Don't speak to me like that, Tom, I can't bear it.'

'You'd better get used to it. You're living with me now, not some bloody lord.' He leaned menacingly over her and, frightened by his anger, she went back to bed as he slammed into his studio.

So she gave up cooking for him, and since she could not be bothered to cook for herself, she began to lose weight at an alarming rate. She lost interest in her looks. She would have been welcome in Zoe's kitchen at any time, but she avoided going there. She was far too proud to confess her increasing unhappiness. In a strange way she felt that Tom was testing her, setting the parameters of their relationship. Surely, she thought, things would improve once he was convinced that she would make no demands.

Now, it was only in bed at night that she thought she was happy – when the ritual smoking took place, and her body relaxed, her pent-up and complicated emotions evaporated. In the mornings she tried not to face reality. But her fear of being alone again made her cling to Tom.

He had been picking on her all morning. Whatever she did was wrong. He objected to the record she put on and tore it from the turntable, scratching its surface. Perversely, he grumbled that she did not feed him, then threw the fried egg she had cooked across the kitchen, complaining that she could not even cook an egg. He criticized her choice of books, her clothes, her hair. She stood listening to the familiar tirade and wondered why she did not cry. Instead, she wanted to scream at him. Longed to tell him what a cruel, thoughtless bastard he was, twisted, abnormal, a deviant – the angry words tumbled about in her brain. But, she remained silent. Silently she wiped the egg from the wall, and picked up the shards of broken plate.

'What the bloody hell is this?' He was standing in the doorway, holding a pair of jeans in front of him. 'Why have you been going through my things?'

'There was a tear in them – I mended them.'

'Leave my clothes alone!' he stormed.

'I was only trying to help.'

'Then don't. I like them torn.'

'Tom, that's ridiculous, you can't wear them torn.'

'I can, and I do. I don't want you doing things for me, all right? I don't want a domestic scene, I don't want to have to say "thank you" to you for anything,' he shouted.

Neatly she washed the egg out of the cloth. Rinsed out the plastic bowl. Wiped the draining board. Then she collected her coat and bag and, while Tom was in midsentence, slipped out of the flat.

She walked along the Backs, not seeing the beauty of the colleges, the skeletal fingers of the winter trees. She sank down on the bank, oblivious of the damp grass, and intently watched the river slide by. Something had happened, she decided – she had not cried, had not even wanted to. Was she becoming impervious to his intolerable moods?

Distractedly she tugged at the grass. Why did she stay with him? She did not even like him any more; he did not make her laugh as he used to do. She did not seem to care whether he stayed or not. She knew she did not hate him: hate was a violent, passionate emotion but she felt empty.

How could she have ended up with someone like him after Alistair? Perhaps because they were complete opposites – the only similarity was the way their hair fell down over their foreheads. Was she punishing herself? she wondered. But for what? For failing, perhaps. Failing in that previous, precious relationship. Wouldn't Nigel and the other psychiatrists have a field day with that theory? she thought, smiling to herself.

A swan approached the bank, looking for titbits, and stared solemnly at her. She remembered that other river, that other swan, and her whole being ached for the past, the lost happiness.

But what was she to do? She dreaded the thought of being alone again: she knew she could not face it. And there was the sex. She smiled. Zoe had been right: that was all it was – copulation, not lovemaking. But she enjoyed it still, would go so far as to say she was hooked on it. Without doubt Tom was good in bed. How could she adjust to living without the physical excitement he gave her? Perhaps he was the only man in the world who ever would. Again she tugged at the grass: a small pile now lay beneath her hand. She would get rid of him soon, she promised herself. But not yet. It was as if her body were demanding the orgasms it had been cheated of in the past.

Purpose in her life – that was what she needed. She stood up, aware at last of the damp patch on her trousers. She shivered, pulled her coat secure about her and walked purposefully into town.

She found the office of a secretarial college she had seen advertised. She enrolled herself as a full-time student and, to the principal's surprise, asked if she could start there and then. When she returned to the flat that evening, Tom was out.

As before, Jane enjoyed the course. Once again, the shorthand needed such concentration that she was able to shut out the part of her mind where her worries and discontent lurked. Tom, too, seemed much happier with this arrangement and nagged her less, even became quite pleasant again.

'Nothing personal,' he explained. 'It made me feel uncomfortable with you being around all the time, I felt I had to talk to you.' He even surprised her by giving her £50 one day. 'I like to pay my way,' he muttered, giving her one of his rare, sardonic grins.

'But you needn't,' she exclaimed. Even as he insisted that she took the money, she wondered where he had got it from. At regular intervals after that he would appear with odd sums of money for her.

During the day, while Jane was at college, he filled the flat with his friends. She did not like them: she thought they despised her, and they made her feel uncomfortable. She did not confide her feelings to Tom for she was too afraid to hear him accuse her of paranoia: it was not a word that she could contemplate with ease. If she did not like his friends, he had no time for hers, either. She had foolishly invited Sandra and Justin to dinner one night. The evening was a disaster, as she should have predicted. How on earth had she expected Justin and Tom to get on?

It was as if she led two lives. In the daytime she had college and visited her friends on her own; at night she became another woman, moaning, writhing. It was as if they only met on the mattress these days. She knew it could not go on; she knew that this self-deception was likely to damage her, but still the fear of loneliness persisted. And always the thought of their sexual passion kept her in a trap of her own making.

She had not seen Alistair for nearly three months. Blizzards, a flu epidemic, everything seemed to have conspired to prevent him coming with James. Not until late February was it possible for him to come. She was relieved when Tom announced he would be out during Alistair's visit.

When Alistair arrived on his own, she was surprised.

'Where's James?'

'He's got a filthy cold, I thought it better to leave him at home.'

'You shouldn't have bothered to come, then,' she said, but was pleased that he had.

'I like to see you,' he said simply. 'In any case I had to deliver the Picasso: it's been reframed,' he said, putting the parcel on the floor. 'You hardly need it, though, do you?' He nodded at the paintings on the wall. 'Who did them?'

'A friend of mine. Thanks for the Picasso. I love that picture. It's a sort of bond with the past, if you know what I mean.' She smiled shyly.

'I ought to give it to you outright.'

'Good gracious, no. You've been generous enough to me. No, just allowing me to borrow it is enough.'

He took her to Panos's restaurant for a long lunch and afterwards they walked along the backs, their breath curling in white tendrils in the cold air. They paused and watched the birds on the water.

'Do you remember our swans on the Thames?'

'Yes, and Mr Rat, do you remember Mr Rat and how he looked at us with those intelligent black eyes? And that breakfast – I still think of that as the best breakfast I ever had,' he replied. For the first time she found that they were able to talk about the past, reminisce about places and people.

'Do you have to get back to London early?'

'Not particularly.'

'Shall we go to Fitzbillies and get some crumpets and chocolate cake? Remember how we used to spoil ourselves when you were an undergrad?'

He took her hand as if it were the most natural thing to do. They collected their cakes and walked back to her flat; she could almost pretend that nothing had ever changed between them. She made the tea, and they toasted the crumpets on the fire. She sat on the floor as Alistair relaxed in the big armchair, his long legs stretched out in front of him. They sat in the half-light watching the flames.

'Jane, come back,' he said suddenly.

'Alistair . . .'

'I need you, Jane, I love you.' She could not believe the words she was hearing. She had dreamed of this scene, known exactly what she would say, and now she sat in stunned silence.

'Look, Jay, I've been a fool, a bloody fool. I miss you and I need you – that hasn't altered. There's never a day goes by that I don't regret what I said to you, what I did. I can't pretend there haven't been other women since you left, but it's you I want.'

'Alistair, I —' she started to say.

'Anyone home?' With sinking heart she heard the front door slam and the sound of Tom's voice before he burst into the room. Alistair stood up, rigidly. He looked from Jane to Tom and back again. 'Darling, crumpets, how lovely,' she was astonished to hear Tom say.

'I see, Jane. I really must apologize. It was very presumptuous of me,' Alistair said with a hard look on his face. 'I'm obviously not up on the developments in your life. I'll be in touch.' Before Jane could speak he had left the room, slamming the door shut.

'Did I butt in?' asked Tom.

'What?'

'Did I interrupt a pretty little reunion scene just then?'

'No, of course not. He was just leaving,' she lied. She had no intention of giving him the satisfaction of knowing what he had done.

'What's that?' He indicated the parcel.

'It was meant to be a surprise,' she answered, but with little enthusiasm in her voice. Tom tore the wrappings off the painting.

'Bleeding hell, I don't believe it!' Reverently he touched the painting with his fingertips. 'I can't believe I'm touching this, that it's here. You never told me about this.' He sat cross-legged on the floor gazing at the painting. 'I wouldn't want to live on this planet without Picasso on it, too.'

'You're going to have to one day, he's an old man after all,' she said in an automatic voice, wondering what the hell she was doing discussing Picasso's death when her own heart was breaking.

'No, when he dies, I go too. I wouldn't see the point of living when he's no longer around. I don't want to talk any more. I just want to be left alone to look at this.'

She was only too relieved that he did not want to talk, for she wanted to think. She lay on her bed in the dark. Life played such cruel tricks. She had been so close to having the man she loved back again, and now he was gone and, from the look on his face, no doubt for ever. How unfair it was: he had had God knows how many affairs, and she had had only this inadequate relationship. He had obviously, over these months, imagined her alone and waiting for him. She had waited for him but she had been lonely. Tom had none of her love: he did not want any and would run away from such involvement. The only thing he would ever love was an old man far away in a château below a French mountain; second-best for him would be to sit and gaze at the old man's paintings. How could she explain that she lived with Tom out of loneliness? How could she ever explain that the only way she could make love to Tom was to smoke his dope so that the drug took her out of herself and she became another person?

She buried her head in her pillow and cried softly.

Much later Tom came to the room. He began the ritual of rolling his cigarette; she watched him uninterestedly.

'Tom, don't bother for me, I'm not in the mood.'

'You what?' He looked hard at her. 'Been crying?'

'No.'

'Yes, you have. You don't mean you've been crying over that wet drip of a husband, for heaven's sake?' He laughed unpleasantly.

'I have not been crying, and he is not a wet drip,' she said angrily.

'I hate twits like him, never had to graft and scrounge to survive. Smug self-satisfied bastard.'

'Tom, please . . .'

'I'm so sorry, do I offend M'Lady?'

'Tom, I don't want to row.'

'Neither do I. You're not worth rowing with. You're a nothing and a nobody. What have you ever done in your life except lie on your back, open your legs and let a man screw you? That's how you've got where you are – you're a bleeding parasite! Christ, you bore me.' He slammed out of the flat. She could only feel relief that tonight he had gone, for now she could lie in the dark and think of Alistair. She could dream of a different future, and plan the letter she must write to him explaining everything.

The next day she posted her letter. Each day she waited in vain for a reply or for the phone to ring. She was puzzled. If he had really wanted her back, would he let Tom stand in his way? Had he perhaps been seduced by the happy day, the firelight, the memories of his youth here? Had it all been one of those illusions that seemed to pepper her life at the moment?

There was no word from Tom. She was relieved that he had gone, that she had not had to make the decision. Occasionally she felt sexually frustrated but soon learned that if she did something active, something as mundane as scrubbing the kitchen floor, the feeling went away. And why had she mooned around thinking she was alone? She had a good friend in Zoe – how could anyone be alone with a Zoe in her life?

Two weeks later, Tom returned.

She took him back, she never knew why.

They slept together but in the mornings, although her body might feel relaxed, her mind was in increasing turmoil. With her emphatic views on love, she was cheating on herself, and the knowledge was becoming increasingly difficult to live with. She had lost patience with him weeks ago; now she was losing patience with herself.

The winter finally faded and Easter came. A stilted letter arrived from James but still no word from Alistair. Sandra had invited her to lunch at her new house across the city in Chesterton. A German friend who was staying with her had spent hours painting eggs in beautiful intricate patterns for a treasure hunt. Before, Jane would have hoped to interest Tom in the eggs, now she did not even bother to tell him she was going.

'No Tom?' said Sandra.

'No, he's doing one of his walkabouts. I don't know where he is.'

'I can honestly say that I don't think we'll miss him,' Sandra said with a grin. 'Rotten for you, though.'

'Oh, I don't mind.'

'Yes, you do. It's Sandra here, Jane, your old mate. You don't have to pretend to me.'

'Okay, so I mind. I mind not having a relationship I mind about. If you can work out such a convoluted sentence.' She laughed wryly.

'Jane, for heaven's sake kick him out. Can't you see what he's doing to you? You're as thin as a rake and you've a dreadful, haunted look about you. You can't cope with this sort of setup. You need to be loved, Jane, and he's on such an ego trip that he can only love himself.'

'I know you're right, Sandra. It's easy to say. But falling in love doesn't happen that easily. Maybe it'll never happen to me again. Remember, I always said it would be once for me.' She sighed. 'I suppose I've got into a sort of rut. If I throw him out, what then? Try again? Have the same thing happen again?'

'I should never have let you go. You weren't ready, I knew that. I should have stopped you, sorted something out with Justin . . . You were ripe for landing in a messy relationship like this.'

'No, Sandra. I've got to learn. It would have happened whenever I set up on my own. I know I would still have gone through something like this.'

'Not if you'd met someone decent, someone who really cared about you. That's the trouble with Zoe's, she only ever seems to have misfits or crackpots there – never anybody normal.'

Jane had to laugh. This was the old Sandra. 'Well, I certainly fit that description!'

'I didn't mean you, you clot. Do you keep him?' she suddenly asked.

'No, he gives me money from time to time for his keep. He's intermittently quite generous.'

'Where does he get it from?'

'I don't know, I presume he must sell the odd painting,' she said hurriedly, wishing that Sandra had not, as usual, gone straight to the crux of the matter and asked the very question that worried Jane.

'I doubt it. Zoe says he never sells any of his paintings. Zoe says she reckons he's dealing in drugs.'

'Oh, Zoe's got a thing about drugs. I'm certain he's not on anything. I'd know if he was.'

'Would you? I don't think I would. Wherever he gets it from, I doubt if it's honestly.'

'Sandra! I know he's a bit odd, artists usually are, aren't they? But I don't think he's a criminal. He can be fun sometimes, Sandra, honestly, and it's someone to look after,' she finished lamely.

'Pity he doesn't appreciate you more. Trouble is, all the time you're with him, how are you going to meet anyone else?'

The children clattered into the room, and the question remained unanswered. Jane enjoyed the lunch, which stretched into tea and then supper. It was past eleven before she left. She refused a lift. She wanted to walk back and enjoy the smell of spring in the air. It would not be long till summer now: in the sunshine everything would look better. It was probably this long, endless Cambridge winter which was making her see everything so bleakly. As she let herself into the flat, she was pleased to see that the lights were on: she hated coming back alone to a darkened house.

The sitting room was full. Apart from Beth, the faces were all new to her. Jane felt conspicuous and overdressed in her pretty Laura Ashley dress. The men were in jeans and T-shirts, with dirty sneakers on their feet, and most of the women were in long, flowing Indian dresses, with dirty, bare feet protruding beneath the hems. The smell was overpowering: mixed with the heavy, musty smell of marijuana was the acrid smell of unwashed bodies. The room was a shambles. There were bodies everywhere, and upturned wine glasses on the carpet. She swooped on a cigarette end as it burned the edge of the coffee table.

'Tom,' she said, trying to keep the irritation out of her voice, 'are you going to introduce me, then?'

'My apologies.' Tom jumped up. 'Everybody, I'm so sorry, I forgot my manners. Let me introduce your hostess, Countess of Somewhere, Lady of Nowhere. Now everyone up and curtsy to your betters.' The group stumbled to its feet and, laughing and falling about, curtsied to her in a grotesque parody.

'Tom, please,' she pleaded.

'No, M'Lady, we all know our place. We must touch the proverbial forelock to you now, mustn't we?'

'Or foreskin!' someone shouted, 'We must touch our foreskins to her ladyship!' Unzipping his trousers he took out his penis and waved it in the air, tugging at his foreskin. The other men began to remove their trousers. With mounting horror Jane watched the ugly scene, her face twisted in disgust as the men began to dance about her, writhing obscenely. Repulsion filled her as the women's cackling rang in her ears.

'Tom, stop them!' she screamed.

'I think it's great.'

'I want them out, now.'

'No, I'll say when they're to go. They're my friends. If you don't like it, then piss off, you boring cow,' he spat at her. 'Get out, Jane!' he shouted. Frightened by the violence she saw in his eyes, she ran up the stairs and, pulling a chest of drawers across the doorway, barricaded herself into her room. Sleep was impossible, not just because of the noise they made but because of her feelings of self-disgust. She had become a nobody in her own home. He was mad. If she were not careful, he would make her mad again. Suddenly she saw the dreadful risk she was running. She had been so busy bothering herself with her introverted self-analysis that she had not seen the real danger she was in. She had had enough. He had to go.

At daybreak she went downstairs. Bodies lay everywhere in jumbled heaps. Ornaments were smashed on the floor; the carpet was covered in wine stains and would have to be cleaned if not renewed. With dismay

she saw that the curtains had been pulled down, the curtain rod
wrenched from the wall. Cold anger gripped her, and she kicked Tom,
who stirred lazily.

'Tom,' she said clearly, 'I am going out. I shall be back early this
afternoon. When I return I expect to find you and your friends out of
here and this mess cleared up.'

'Sod off,' he grunted in reply.

She walked for miles about the city, then had lunch in a pub and drank
two large brandies.

The flat was quiet as she entered it. She opened the sitting-room door:
the room looked devastated but at least it was empty. With manic energy
she began to clear the chaos; she scrubbed the carpet, washed the walls,
tenderly picked up the pieces of broken porcelain. She threw the
windows wide open and the foetid smell began to disappear.

When order was restored she went up to her bedroom. Nausea filled
her as she saw Tom and Beth sprawled naked across the bed. She shook
Tom.

'Wake up, you bastard!' she screamed. Tom turned over and stretched
contentedly. 'Get up and get that woman out!' she continued to shout.
Beth woke and smiled dreamily at Jane.

'Do you have to shout so loud?' Tom asked in a reasonable tone of
voice.

'Yes, I do, I'm angry.'

'I don't like anger. I don't like aggressive vibrations,' announced Beth,
sliding off the bed and walking, naked and unconcerned, across the
room.

'You get that ugly, dirty cow out of my house!' Jane yelled.

'She isn't that dirty,' Tom said, laughing. 'Or you'd have caught
something yourself by now.'

'What the hell do you mean?'

'I mean what I'm saying. I've been screwing Beth every day since I met
you. She's better than you are. Laugh is, you were too bloody dumb to
realize it.' Jane stood speechless with anger. 'I've been thinking,' he
continued in his reasonable voice. 'I've decided to move her in here with
us – a nice cosy *ménage à trois*. It'll cut down on my travelling and you
might manage to learn a thing or two about screwing from her.' He
smiled at Jane.

The smile was the last straw. Jane leaped across the room and hit Tom
hard across the cheek. Very calmly and precisely he hit her back.

'Look, Jane, I'm not angry yet, but I'm likely to be. I do as I want, you understand. No one orders me around. Get that into your stupid, thick skull and I'll stay, otherwise I'm off.'

'Get out, you bum, you sickening filthy bum!'

'Language, M'Lady. You can't insult me – there's no point in trying. And don't look all hurt and offended. I've only given you what you wanted, kept you from going barmy, fucked you. You've been taking from me just as I've been taking from you.'

'I want you *out*. I mean it, I never want to see you – ever again. Get out!' Her voice rose, as she used every filthy word she could think of. But as she shouted, she knew that her anger was more at herself than at him.

'OK, don't yell. Keep your hair on. We'll go.'

Jane did not wait to hear more but raced to the bathroom and locked the door. She stripped, jumped under the shower and began methodically to scrub every inch of her body with her nailbrush, oblivious to the pain.

'Dirty bastard. Dirty bastard,' she repeated to herself over and over again, like a mantra.

When she emerged, the flat was empty. All his paintings had gone, his studio was bare. The silence hung oppressively about her. She slumped on the sofa, wanting to curl away in some dark corner – ashamed. She sat there as if frozen. Then slowly and gradually she felt the web of anxiety begin to build within her. She began to rock, back and forth, rhythmically.

'Not bloody likely. He's not worth that,' she said aloud, grabbing the phone and asking for International. She waited impatiently for the connection to be made.

'Honor, please, can I come?'

'Darling, immediately, I insist,' she heard the loved voice say. Five minutes later her plane ticket was reserved: Jane was amazed at how simple it had all been.

Through that night, she packed. It was only then that she realized what Tom had meant when he had said 'taken from you'. He had been clever, he had not stolen anything big that would be noticed straight away, so she had not registered that the odd piece of silver was missing. It was the same with her jewellery: he must have noted what she wore, and then taken only small pieces that he had seen she rarely used. How he must have laughed at the joke of paying her with money raised from the sale of her own possessions. She cursed her stupidity, but at least her anger with him and with herself doused any hysteria.

'Zoe?' she said, entering the kitchen the next morning and seeing the familiar figure at the kitchen table. 'Zoe, I'm sorry . . .' She stood with her shoulders slumped. 'You can say it, Zoe, – "I told you so."' She managed a weak smile.

'I've nothing to say,' Zoe replied. 'But you look as if you could do with a good breakfast.'

'Zoe, the flat is in a dreadful mess. I've cleaned up as best I could. Can I leave you a blank cheque to replace the carpet and get the place redecorated?'

'Are you going away?'

'Yes, to my friend, Honor, in Italy. I know I ought to stay and sort out the flat but I feel I've just got to get right away, now.'

'Don't worry, I'll see to it. Are you coming back to us?'

'If you'll have me. I was happy in the flat until . . .'

'Of course we want you back. How long will you be gone?'

'Three weeks, a month at the most.'

Zoe insisted on driving Jane to the station; it was the first time that Jane had ever seen her outside her house. She hardly noticed the journey. Not until she was on the plane and looked down to see the coastline of England receding did her mind jolt into focus. Things were not as bad as they seemed. So, she was still vulnerable. Perhaps she was not as stable as she had fondly thought. But, on the other hand, in the months with Tom, she had never let go, had not had any crises of anxiety; her mind had weathered Tom.

Finally she decided what she was going to do. She knew that she could not return, not until she was so strong that no one could hurt her or use her – so strong that she would never again involve herself in a second-class relationship in the hope of solving her problems and, in so doing, make them worse. She had to take care, for some time to come, but she knew it: that was the beauty of it.

Five

1969 − 76

I

Everything was the same and yet everything was different. She stood on the terrace of Honor's villa, knowing, as she looked at the timeless view, that she was a different woman from the young girl who had stood here on her honeymoon – not so long ago in time but a long time in living.

She felt, on her arrival, almost like an invalid, and from the concerned way in which Honor looked at her she had to presume that she looked like one, too. She allowed herself to be looked after, sitting on the terrace wrapped in a blanket by Guido, Honor's manservant. Guido was horrified that she wished to swim – April was far too early in the year, she might catch cold, it could only harm her, Guido fretted. She ate well because Guido seemed to take it as a personal insult if each dish was not finished. She drank too much Frascati, but consoled herself that it did less damage than the gin, of which she had begun to drink far too much in Cambridge.

As the spring sun gathered strength her skin became golden. The mouthwatering Italian food brought the gentle curves back to her body. Zoe would have been proud of her. Her long hair began to shine once more and the grey eyes regained their sparkle, appearing even larger in her tanned face. Jane was becoming a beautiful woman again.

The peace of the place was everything she needed. She was not yet ready to talk or to explain and Honor, sensing this, did not pry. As her physical state improved, so did her mental wellbeing, until she was able to begin to sort through the turmoil of her mind. Like a filing clerk, she extracted each problem, each puzzle. Whether it was to do with Alistair, James, Tom, herself, or a combination of all of them, she would examine and study it, then file it back into her mind. Each time she went through this process, she began to create new order within herself.

Over a month had passed in this way. One evening the two women sat after dinner in a companionable silence, when suddenly, without preamble, Jane began to talk. She began at the very beginning. She told of her childhood, right through to the shame of the last four months. She told of her fears. Of her worry about her son. Of her craving to be loved. She opened compartments of her mind which, until now, she had kept closed. She felt no embarrassment as she spoke of love — her needs, her failures — for Honor knew so much about love and being loved. It was as if she were talking of another woman in another time. Honor sat, moving only to pour more wine into a glass or to light another cigarette, and she listened with an intensity that made talking easier. When the monologue finally ceased, she kissed Jane tenderly, 'It will be better now, I promise.' She led the now exhausted Jane to her bed, and tucked her in as if she were a small child.

Jane slept a long, deep sleep. When she awoke, she found that Honor had been right — she did feel better — and she found that her hope for happiness, which had for so long deserted her, had returned.

They never sat and discussed all the things that Jane had told Honor. But as the days slipped by, an odd word here or a sentence there would remind one or other of them of that long conversation and then, minutely, they would discuss some issue of Jane's life.

'You are wise,' proclaimed Jane one morning after Honor had for the umpteenth time put into perspective the jigsaw puzzle of her mind.

'God, darling, don't even think it. Me, wise? It's too funny to contemplate. I've just lived longer, that's all. It's always so much easier to see other people's problems. You never recognize your own. If I were wise, I should hardly have made the balls-up of my life that I have, would I, darling?' She chuckled in her deep-throated manner.

'Do you wish you'd had children?'

'Good God, no! I'd have been the world's worst mother.'

'I think you would have made a super mother.'

'No, you're wrong. I could never have stayed still long enough, and I can't stand babies. I might have enjoyed my children when they were adults, as I enjoy you and Alistair, but think of all the damage I could have done in the intervening years.' She laughed at the very idea.

'I don't think I'm a good mother.'

'What if you're not? James has a good father, hasn't he? We may not agree with what he's done to you, but he seems to be a caring father, much to my surprise. Why should you automatically be expected to be a good mother? That's the problem with having babies. You don't really know until you've had one if you're going to be any good at it, do you? So dreadfully random of nature, don't you think?'

Jane smiled. 'It must be lovely being you – so confident about everything.'

'Rubbish, no one's that confident about anything. If they are, they've usually led dreadfully boring lives. The trouble with you, Jane dear, is that you think too much. It's a dangerous occupation.'

'Zoe says that, too.'

'She's right. You spend hours worrying about love and being loved. All the time that you're thinking about it, you're never going to find it, are you? You must try to forget about it. It's more likely to happen then.'

'But, Honor, you've misunderstood. I don't want anyone else's love but Alistair's.'

'Piffle! You can't spend the rest of your life clinging to the past.'

'I'm not clinging to the past. It's in my present that I still love him. I know I couldn't love anyone else and I can't have a relationship without love. Look what happened with me and Tom.'

'Bah, Tom was an unpleasant interlude, a little bitty mistake. We've all made them,' she said with a shrug. 'You'll see, he'll be of no importance in a few weeks' time.'

Once again Jane returned to the problem of James.

'Jane, darling, all the time he's at Respryn there's nothing you can do. It's that old bitch, I'm sure of it, poisoning his little mind against you.'

'She wouldn't go that far, surely?'

'That old cow is capable of anything.' Honor was launched on her favourite subject – Blanche Upnor. Honor seemed to have an inexhaustible supply of stories about her and every wrong that the woman had ever done.

'What irritated me most about her was that she was always ready to criticize me. Always watching for me to make a cock-up, but she never once told me what to do or how to do it,' Jane complained.

'But darling, she wanted you to fail, to prove her right. She's so stupid, so bigoted. If Alistair lets her back into the house, he's madder than I thought he was.'

'Is he thinking of it?'

'He hasn't so far, but men are funny about their mothers, aren't they? I've often wondered if it's guilt – giving them all that pain to come into the world. And mothers of sons always seem to win in the end, haven't you noticed?'

Jane loved it best when Honor reminisced about her youth and how Respryn had been in the old days; her life as a debutante in London, the crazy things she and her friends had done. It was like listening to someone who had lived in another century rather than someone who was describing a way of life recent in years but irretrievably destroyed by the war.

The advantage of being here with Honor was that it bore no relationship to her other life. The opulent luxury, the release from the worries of day-to-day living, the upside-down life style – where they might sit the night away talking and then sleep all morning – all helped Jane to divorce herself from her past and to see herself as a different person.

Occasionally, half-heartedly, Jane would say she really should go back to England. She felt guilty about Zoe and the empty flat. But Honor would hear none of it and was adamant that Jane should stay for as long as she liked, for ever, if she wanted. Jane needed little persuading.

'Jane, darling, next month masses of friends will be coming. Will you mind?'

'Why should I mind? Who's coming? How exciting!'

'The whole of the world.' Honor laughed. 'The season begins now. You see, as it gets hotter the cities empty and the villas are all opened up until by midsummer there's no one left in the cities except the tourists and the poor souls who have to work for a living. We shall be very busy. Will you like that?'

'Yes, I think I will.' Jane was genuinely surprised at her reaction. 'In any case you must be bored stiff with just me.'

'What a silly thing to say! I've loved having you here all to myself. I've enjoyed watching you get better and feeling that I might have helped. Normally I should have been off on my travels, round and round like a goldfish in a bowl. Instead, I feel relaxed and at ease, wondering why on earth I spend all that time rushing about when I have this lovely home. No, it's been such fun having you here, watching you – what is that divine new expression? – "get your head on"!' She laughed. 'Oh, I do wish I was young enough to be a hippy, such fun!'

That week they shopped. Honor approached shopping like a general planning a campaign. Magazines were consulted for the latest trends, phone calls were made to friends in the fashion industry in London and Paris. Lists were drawn up. Wardrobes were inspected and ruthlessly culled of garments of the wrong length, line, colour or fabric. Shoes of the wrong height went the same way and only hats that could be retrimmed were reprieved. It was a long process, for so many of the clothes that had to be discarded reminded Honor of a happy day, or some lover until now forgotten, and she would sit on her heels in the chaotic muddle and tell Jane of this and that in her life. Eventually, enough space had been cleared and ideas gleaned for the serious shopping to begin.

They did not so much enter a shop as descend upon it, for at the sight of Honor owners and managers would drop everything, as if she were the only customer. In each shop she was welcomed like a long-lost friend, chairs were arranged for her, drinks appeared, and hours passed in the choice of fabrics and the exchange of gossip. If a shade were not quite right, new bolts would be ordered from Rome. Nothing was too much trouble to make M'Lady Honor happy. Jane seemed to live in a sea of silks, crêpes and chiffons. Once the fabrics had been chosen, each seamstress had to be visited. Honor had a different woman for each garment for, as she explained, you could not expect one who could make a jacket to be an expert on trousers, skirts and blouses as well. So Maria made their shirts for them, Pepe the trousers, Franca the day dresses, Lela the evening dresses and, of course, only Sofia could be trusted with the chiffons. Shoemakers measured their feet, patterns for handbags were selected and the glovemaker brought out his best skins.

The biggest surprise of all was how swiftly the clothes appeared. They were cut and fitted one day, given a second fitting the next, and finished the following, each one beautifully sewn, each a perfect fit.

'They're lovely,' exclaimed Jane.

'Yes. I'm satisfied.'

'But, Honor, I can't afford all these. One or two, yes, but not this avalanche.'

'Don't be ridiculous, darling, I'm paying.'

'Honor, I can't possibly accept.'

'Why not? Don't be so stuffy. Of course you can accept, it's giving me pleasure, and in any case I can't have my niece appearing in front of my friends dressed exclusively by Marks & Spencer. What would they say?'

'But the expense!'

'Don't be vulgar, darling, what would Blanche say – talking money?' She laughed loudly at her joke. 'I can afford it, I like to do it. Please don't spoil my fun.'

Jane relented. It was not difficult, for the clothes were more beautiful than any she had ever worn and, as each box was delivered, she would unpack excitedly and try on the contents, gazing with satisfaction at the image that the mirror reflected. She wore colours that she would never have dared choose herself: rich, jewel-like colours which, in this bright sunlight, enhanced her dark looks to perfection.

Honor prowled around her protégée, scrutinizing the fall of the skirt, smoothing a wrinkle which only her eyes, seeking perfection, saw.

Jane was an apt pupil, taking Honor's advice without question. Each day she became sleeker, better groomed and more confident.

'You're spoiling me rotten.'

'Fun, isn't it?' Honor smiled gleefully at her. 'I do so enjoy being rich. What's the point of money, if you don't spend it? I think it's wicked just to stick it in a bank, amassing away. But the bloody stuff just keeps coming, so I have to spend as much as I can, spread it around a bit. See what a good socialist I am.' The husky laugh rang out happily.

'But where does it keep coming from?'

'Did I never tell you?' Jane shook her head. 'I told you about my Bob, didn't I? The one who's now a cabinet minister? Divine man.' She sighed. 'Well, when my parents wouldn't allow me to marry him I was so angry – dear God, how angry I was – I wanted revenge. I bided my time, looked around and eventually found the ideal candidate in an American called Wilbur Calem. Imagine, a self-made American, my father nearly had apoplexy. He was thirty years older than me, and even his name sent shivers down their spines – there's something ridiculous about Wilbur; sounds like a hamster, doesn't it? Worst of all, he was in "trade" – dirty word in my family. He'd been everything in his life: lumberjack, waiter, crook, probably, you name it, Wilbur had done it. Then somehow he got into making sausages. It was too perfect: imagine the only daughter of the Earl of Upnor married to a man who made sausages. You can imagine the shock and horror at Respryn. So, I eloped with him.

'When I met him I'd realized that he was rich. I mean, there would have been no point in eloping with someone penniless just to get my own back, because father would be sure to cut me off without a penny, and the satisfaction in a cold garret would have been less than in a suite at Claridge's. But it wasn't until we were married that I realized how rich. The dear man was absolutely loaded with money. By then the sausages had enabled him to go into real estate, oil, everything under the sun. It was lovely, the way he spent money on me, like living in an avalanche of gorgeous presents. But then it all went wrong. I'd intended to marry him to teach them a lesson. Then I was going to ditch him and they were going to welcome me back with open arms – really dreadful bitch I must have been. But I fell in love with him, crazily, totally besotted. I couldn't help myself: he was the kindest, most considerate man I have ever met. Of course I had to tell him what I'd done and he roared with laughter and said he'd known all along and he hadn't minded because he loved me and was convinced I would grow to love him, given time. He'd even guessed why I had married him, and the dear soul just thought it was dreadfully funny. God, how I adored him – that's why I still use his name after all my other marriages.'

Honor paused a long time. Jane sat on the edge of her seat, eager to hear more.

Honor sighed. 'He died. The silly man died after only five wonderful years. Just got up one morning, turned to me, told me he loved me, and then simply keeled over, stone-cold dead. I wanted to die, too: there seemed no point in living without him.' Tears formed in her eyes at the memory but she quickly brushed them away. 'He had no family, you see, no one but me, and so I inherited everything. There's so much income that I couldn't possibly spend it all each year – silly isn't it, all that money just for me? I don't have anything to do with administering it, of course: lawyers and accountants beaver away looking after it and they just send me cheques which I busily try to spend.' She laughed.

'Then what happened?'

'Disaster, that's what happened, unmitigated disasters – three, to be precise. First an alcoholic racing driver, failed, of course. But luckily his liver hated him as much as I did, in the end. Then I married Marcus Telling, poor man, such a dreadful actor. The trouble was he didn't think to tell me he was queer.'

'And then?'

'Wayne Higgins – I do seem to have a thing about odd names, don't I? I met him soon after he'd come out of jail. But he just couldn't stop being a crook, you see, even when he had all my money to spend. He seemed to need the excitement. We were in America – off he trots and robs a filling station, bopping this poor man on the head. That was the end.' Honor got up to pour more drinks.

'But what happened to him?'

'Oh, he got life. And I got a divorce.'

'Honor, you're so funny. Do you think you'll ever marry again?'

'Good God, no! I suppose, in a way, I'm like you: I'll always love my darling Wilbur. But, unlike you, I enjoy my little adventures. And the way I live now, I'm in control. They go when I tell them, no nonsense, no alimony.'

'I'm so sorry about Wilbur,' Jane said gently.

'Bloody inconsiderate of him, if you ask me,' replied Honor, but she was not laughing.

As Honor had promised, it did seem as if, suddenly, the whole world had arrived in this tranquil spot. The quiet roads began to fill with the roar of expensive motor cars, Maseratis and Ferraris in droves. New boutiques appeared like a rash in the small town at the foot of the hill. Smart hairdressers from Rome opened their summer salons. The beaches filled with the beautiful bodies of young men and women, staking out their positions for the duration of the season, greeting each other excitedly after the winter. At night their hillside, which until now had been dark, glistened with lights like giant glow-worms as villa after villa was opened up. Jane hadn't even been aware that the villas were there.

Now the phone rang constantly, people dropped in, and a quiet evening at home on the terrace was only a memory, for each evening they went out to dinners or parties. She would watch Honor's friends, admiring their elegance, their perfect grooming, their confidence, wanting to be like them. They were kind and charming to her, and she blossomed but could not help being amused at the way they all called her the *contessa inglese*.

Dutifully she flirted with the men, for it seemed to be *de rigueur*. But, as she flirted, she felt nothing. It was just a social game to be played; it was expected of her and she did not wish to offend.

She regretted that she only had O-level French while this glittering group would switch from English to French, German and Italian, almost without taking breath, and she determined that this winter she would learn a language.

Usually she left long before Honor, and always alone. Honor seemed to have an insatiable appetite for socializing. Jane found she did not have the same stamina. In any case Jane loved the mornings. She would sit on the terrace and watch the mist roll up the hillside from the town, until everything was bathed in the glorious sunshine; and she liked to swim at this time of day, before her breakfast, while it was still cool enough to be exhilarating.

She never saw Honor in the mornings, and only occasionally at lunchtime. Honor would appear in the afternoon, showing no signs of fatigue and eager to start the social whirl again.

One morning, Jane found the lunch table on the terrace set for four. Two handsome young Italians suddenly appeared and bowed graciously over her hand.

'Umberto,' announced one.

'Federico,' said the other.

She could only smile for she had no Italian and they appeared devoid of English. So they sat smiling inanely at each other until Honor arrived.

'Darlings, you've met.' She swished to her seat. 'What do you think of my find, Jane? Aren't they divine? So handsome and virile. Umberto is superb.'

'But . . .' Jane glanced embarrassed at the young men.

'Don't worry, darling, they can't understand a word we say.'

'Are they staying here?'

'For the time being. I met them at Constanza's last night after you'd scuttled off, and I just couldn't let them escape. They're just too marvellous, like book ends.' She laughed and the young men grinned happily. Honor talked rapidly to them in Italian, at which they bowed again to Jane and she laughed too; then everyone was laughing but no one except Honor knew at what.

'But two of them, Honor?'

'I know, terrible, isn't it? But such fun. When one flags you've always got the other one,' and she burst out laughing again.

'But Honor . . .' The sound of shock was apparent in Jane's voice.

'Now, darling, don't be so stuffy. You're a big girl. I told you ages ago I liked living here because it was easier to be naughty, didn't I?'

Jane looked around the happy, smiling group. There was a strange innocence about them all and Jane felt ashamed of her initial reaction. It was none of her business; Honor was a grown woman, free to do as she wanted, and she was hurting no one.

Now, when they went shopping, there were four of them clattering about the streets, exploding into the shops, sipping Campari and soda under the huge umbrellas of the pavement cafés, watching the world go by. Each morning the young men joined Jane for her swim and began to teach her Italian. She supposed that when people saw them all together, they presumed that one of the boys was Jane's lover: as she did not want to be involved with anyone, the arrangement was really quite convenient.

2

'What a busy little scribbler you are, Jane.'

'Honor! You're up early, it's not even lunchtime,' Jane teased.

'Couldn't sleep. Who are you writing to, anyone I know? Can I put a message in?'

'That one's to James. Shall I add your love? Now I'm writing to my friend, Sandra, and I was just thinking – it's strange: if you asked me, I'd say I prefer men to women, but all my best friends are women and they're all very similar, too. You, Sandra and Zoe are all warm, practical and logical. I was wondering if one chooses one's friends because they have the qualities lacking in oneself.'

'I'd hardly say you lack those qualities, my sweet.'

Jane lay back on the lounger. 'I've been trying to describe my life here to Sandra, but it's impossible. This life is like a dream: it's all so exotic and glamorous and I think I'm beginning to forget what ordinary life is like.'

'Would you like to lead an ordinary life?'

'Like Sandra? I envy her security, but I don't know if I want to live like that, or even if I could.'

'You couldn't. Once you get taken out of your environment, there's no going back. Alistair spoiled you for any other sort of life. You can go up in style, but you can't go backwards.'

'Hell, Honor. Don't depress me. I'm going to have to learn to settle for less.'

'Nonsense, not if you play your cards right.'

'You mean if Alistair wants me back.'

'Certainly not. The world is full of miserable people giving marriages a second try. It never works. I mean here – you could find someone if you wanted to.'

'Oh, Honor, you never give up, do you?' Jane smiled fondly at the older woman.

'Have you any emeralds?' Honor abruptly changed the subject.

'No, I'm clean out of emeralds,' Jane replied with a giggle.

'I've noticed you never wear jewellery. You didn't leave it all behind, did you?' Honor asked anxiously.

'Of course I did, except for my engagement ring, a cigarette case and some small pieces. And the choker you gave me.'

'That was silly, Jane. You should always hang on to your jewels and furs. You never know when you'll get replacements and buying them for yourself is never the same as being given them by a lover.'

'Honor, you're so funny. I could hardly have walked off with the Upnor collection, could I? Alistair never had enough money to buy me expensive stuff anyway. Why do I need emeralds?'

'Tonight we go to a ball at the Palazzo Villizano, and everyone will be there, in best bib and tucker. I thought you should wear the green silk that Lela made for you. You'd better borrow my emeralds, they'll be a perfect match. I don't need them – I'm wearing my sapphires tonight.'

'Whatever you say, Honor. You're the boss.'

'It'll be enormous fun. There'll be masses of divine men for you and by the end of this evening I expect to find you in love. Otherwise, I shall have lent you my emeralds for nothing.' Honor laughed at her.

That evening Guido drove them up into the mountains. The boys had been sent into town earlier by Honor. Umberto and Federico seemed to accept their occasional dismissals with good humour.

Across a steep valley, Jane saw the castle. It stood, floodlit, on top of a steep hill, a small town clustering around the lower slopes like the folds of a skirt. It was so improbably beautiful, with its turrets, its hundreds of glinting windows, that it was like an illustration in a book of fairy tales. The car stopped in the town square at the bottom of a steep hill, and they joined the long line of people walking up to the castle. Several horse-drawn carriages clattered past, taking the elderly and those who could not manage the climb. On either side of the road, the townspeople stood, applauding dresses that pleased them, and shouting encouragement to the party-goers. As Honor and Jane appeared, there were cries of '*bellissima!*'

Through massive, heavy, wooden gates they entered an immense stone courtyard lit by flickering tapers. Here they joined the queue of people climbing a long flight of worn stone steps to the entrance which led into a large medieval hall. Jane stood awestruck at the sight. The hall was already crowded and the women in their bright silks and satins whirled in a never ending kaleidoscope of colour. From the ceiling brilliantly coloured pennants hung, swaying in the heat from the throng below. An orchestra was playing and, at every turn, servants in scarlet silk knee breeches with white slashed doublets were serving drinks. Jane felt she was stepping into a Renaissance painting.

She had never seen so many exquisitely dressed women. But in her classically draped emerald-green silk dress, Jane, though she was unaware of the impression she made, could hold her own with any woman in the room. Her dark hair gleamed and her golden skin looked flawless. Honor's emeralds shone at her neck and wrist but were no match for the excited sparkle in her wide grey eyes.

Honor swooped like an exotic bird from one group of friends to another. People had travelled from all over the world to this ball, and Jane found herself searching hopelessly for a face she knew.

'Honor!' They both swung round at the voice. A dark-haired man approached them, his hands spread wide in expansive greeting to Honor, who fell immediately into his arms, shrieking with pleasure. Perhaps this man was the reason why Umberto and Federico had been left behind, thought Jane, and she looked at him with renewed interest. She guessed that he was in his forties but could not be certain. She had learned that it was difficult to assess the age of the rich, for it seemed that, lacking financial worries, their faces did not wrinkle in the same way as those of ordinary people, and their permanent tans made the middle-aged look years younger than they really were. At least this man made no attempt to hide the silver speckling his dark hair. He was far from handsome, with a large aquiline nose which gave his face an arrogant look that disappeared the moment he smiled. His shoulders were wide and muscular, his hips trim, and his physique so well proportioned that Jane was at first unaware of his lack of height. Yes, thought Jane, he would be admirably suited for Honor: though younger, he was nearer to her in age than the two boys. He had that indefinable aura which, she was now aware, invisibly cloaked only the very wealthy.

'Roberto, darling!' Honor cried. 'Where have you been? Why were you so long in coming this year? We have missed you dreadfully.'

'Problems, Honor. Always problems.' For the first time he smiled and looked enquiringly at Jane.

'Jane, allow me to introduce your host, Il Principe Roberto Michele de' Verantil di Villizano.' The names rolled expertly off her tongue. 'Roberto, this is my niece, Lady Upnor.'

Jane's confusion at the long list showed on her face. 'Roberto is sufficient,' he said, in an attractive, deep voice with only the merest hint of an accent, as he bowed elegantly over her hand.

'Roberto.' To her annoyance Jane realized that her voice emerged as almost a whisper. The dark eyes watched her intently, making her uncomfortable, and she lowered her eyes from his stare.

'Charming, charming. It is my greatest pleasure at last to meet the beautiful *contessa inglese*. Everybody speaks of your beauty, Contessa.' He smiled warmly at her. 'But, I forget myself, have you two ladies dined? No? Allow me.' He guided them to a table set in a bower of flowers away from the main throng. Several of the exotic servants appeared immediately at his side and he issued instructions. Their dinner arrived, a bewildering assortment of beautifully prepared dishes, and wine in huge crystal goblets. She did not need to talk for, throughout the meal, Honor kept up a stream of chatter, animatedly telling their host of all the parties and the people he had missed. As they talked of people she did not know, Jane allowed her attention to wander around the vast room, enjoying the parade of elegantly dressed people, the display of jewellery which must be worth a king's ransom. Once or twice she glanced at the Prince, and each time her glance seemed to coincide with a look from his fine, dark eyes, smiling at her. Hurriedly she looked at her hands in confusion, and could not understand why. It was as if, at one glance from this man, all the gloss and sophistication she fondly thought she had acquired in the past weeks deserted her completely.

'Darlings, there's Josh Phelps, I haven't seen him all summer, do be angels and excuse me a moment.' Before Jane had a chance to stand and join her, Honor swept away. She was at a loss for what to say to the prince.

'Please don't bother with me,' she finally said. 'You have so many guests to attend to.'

'They seem quite happy.' He gestured to the throng. 'Would you care to dance, then you won't have to try to think of what to say to me?' He was laughing at her, but she stood up with relief. 'Which do you prefer, Contessa? Dancing to this orchestra, or I have one of those 'groups' the young seem so fond of. You are so young, perhaps you would prefer the latter?'

'I really don't mind. I like old-fashioned dancing.'

'Old-fashioned – how charming!' He laughed.

'I'm old enough and young enough to enjoy both.'

'How fortunate you are. Me? I don't pass this test, I prefer the old style. I like to hold a woman when I dance with her. And some of the gyrations I see I prefer in the bedroom and not in public. I suppose it means I grow old.' He sighed, laughingly, as he took her arm and led her into a quickstep. He did not talk as they danced and Jane could concentrate on the music and the pure pleasure of dancing with someone so adept and easy to follow. The music changed to a cha-cha. His hips moved only slightly, but provocatively. Jane liked to dance but she had never before danced with a man who could make her feel as sensuous as this. She was disappointed when the music stopped and the musicians, taking a break, put their instruments away. He led her back to their seat, where there was no sign of Honor. She expected him to excuse himself but instead he sat down beside her, ordered more wine, and offered her a cigarette.

'You're a good dancer,' he said as he leaned forward to light her cigarette.

'Not as good as you.'

'Not yet, but you will be. You have the feel for it. It's rare in an Englishwoman.'

'Aren't generalizations dangerous?'

'I'm not generalizing, it's a fact. They're too self-conscious, always aware of people looking at them, wondering what effect they're creating. You can't dance like that. Only the music, the rhythm and your partner should matter, you see, just like making love – the sound, the rhythm, your partner.' He smiled mischievously at her.

'Really?' She hoped she sounded more confident than she felt.

'Ah, yes. You'll be good at that too – one day.'

'One day? And what makes you think that I'm not good now?' Her rising anger made her speak boldly.

'I know these things.' He laughed at her. 'I make you angry, I like that. I like the sparkle in your eyes that your anger gives.'

'I'm not angry. Why should I be? You can think what you like. You're unlikely to find out one way or the other.'

'Yes, Contessa.'

'I'm not angry,' she almost shouted.

'Yes, Contessa.' He continued to smile his infuriating smile. He was insufferably rude, she thought. The dignified thing would be to move away – but she did not.

'I wish you would stop calling me Contessa, too. My name is Jane.'

'Then I accept the honour you give me and I'll call you – Jane.' It was ridiculous, how could the sound of her name make her feel as if she had been caressed?

'Are you enjoying Italy?' he asked, switching back to the role of considerate host, so that she could almost believe she had imagined the suggestive conversation.

'It's wonderful.' With relief she began to tell him what she loved about Italy.

'Is this your first visit to my country?'

'No. I was here several years ago. I regret that I didn't return sooner.'

'I too.'

'I'm sorry?'

'I regret that you didn't return sooner also. It would have been a joy to me to know you better.' Once again the tone of his voice had changed. She felt herself blushing and cursed inwardly as the familiar warmth suffused her face. She lowered her head, hoping that he had not seen, but he put his hand under her chin and made her look up at him.

'Charming,' he whispered. She did not want to look at him. He was not just flirting with her, he was seducing her with his beautiful voice and the suggestion in his eyes. It frightened and, at the same time, excited her. But it was not what she wanted. She did not want to be involved with anyone – except Alistair. She closed her eyes to shut out his expression.

'Are you tired?' he asked, concerned.

'A little hot.'

'Would you like to walk outside? It's very warm in here.' He led her through the crowds, not stopping to speak to anyone despite the dozens striving to catch his attention. They walked out onto a wide terrace where the heady scent of jasmine filled the warm evening air. They leaned on the wall and together they looked down at the village twinkling far below.

'It was a clever place to build a castle,' she said.

'Yes, no one has ever managed to conquer it. If my ancestors didn't like someone they could just drop them over the wall.' He laughed. The music seemed a long way away now. She was conscious of his closeness, would have liked him to touch her, yet perversely dreaded his doing so.

'You are a sad lady,' he stated.

'I'm not sad. I'm having a lovely time.'

'Ah, the famous British stiff upper lip. You cannot deceive me: it is in your eyes, such sadness.' He touched her hand. 'I would love to be the man to remove that sadness.' She turned her face away from him. 'I'm sorry. I startle you. Look at me, please. My dear Contessa, I can tell you one thing: we shall be important to each other, I promise.'

'Please,' she said, suddenly shivering, 'I want to go in now. I should try to find Honor.'

'Of course, forgive me.'

Back in the castle they could not find Honor in the crowded halls.

'Honor will not want to go yet, I'm sure,' he said, taking her arm. 'Perhaps you would like to see my gallery? I promise, I will behave like the perfect gentleman.' He smiled good-naturedly at her. 'Come, we shall be respectable art lovers together, instead of the other sort.'

At the top of a long flight of shallow stone steps was his gallery, which housed a fine collection of paintings. At each picture they stopped to admire, and Roberto told her its provenance, about its artist, the mediums used.

'You know so much about the paintings. Are you an expert?'

'Good heavens, no, but you cannot live all your life with these beautiful paintings and not know them, not explore every inch of them as one would a woman one loved.' That voice again, Jane thought, flustered. 'Come and meet my family,' he said, leading her into a side gallery. 'Ancestors, may I introduce to you all Lady Upnor, the charming English countess?' Laughingly he waved at the ranks of portraits on the walls. Jane sank low in an elegant curtsy to the paintings. Roberto, enjoying her gesture, with equal elegance gave her his hand as he helped her rise. 'You see, Jane, what dreadful rascals some of them look, but others I think I would have liked to know.'

'There's a definite family likeness, I think it must be the nose,' she said, scrutinizing his face.

'Yes, the famous Villizano nose, as bad as the Habsburg lip, isn't it?'

'Oh no, I think it's a very regal nose,' she protested.

'Regal?' He postured, turning his profile to her. 'Yes, I like that concept of my nose,' and he laughed. She decided then that she liked him: he could laugh at himself. So many men and most of the Italians she had met took themselves far too seriously.

'What a lovely portrait!' Jane exclaimed as they halted in front of the last picture. 'The artist has caught your expression and your fine eyes exactly.'

'Have I fine eyes?'

'Beautiful eyes.'

'If they are so, I think, it is only because I look at beauty and it reflects in my dull eyes.' He turned to her and smiled. His extravagant compliments made her feel awkward, like a gauche young girl again. A little too quickly, to cover her confusion, she said, 'Why is there this big gap here?'

'That is for the portrait of my wife.' At his words she felt a momentary and ridiculous sense of disappointment.

'Has she not had her portrait painted yet?'

'No, not yet. She can't, you see, I haven't found her yet.'

'Oh, I see,' she said and was shocked at the sudden happiness his words gave her. They were interrupted by the swishing of silk as Honor fluttered towards them.

'Darlings, I hate to interrupt, but I've got this dreadful headache. Would you mind terribly, Jane, if I left you? I can send Guido straight back to wait for you.'

'That's not necessary, Honor. I'll come with you,' Jane said, concerned.

'No, darling, I wouldn't hear of it. And Roberto here would never forgive me for dragging you away.'

'No, I insist. If you're not well, I'll come with you.'

'Dear Honor, of course Jane must travel with you. I am only sad to lose two such lovely women from my party, but . . .' he said, shrugging his shoulders.

He insisted on escorting them to the courtyard and waited while their car was summoned. As Jane settled herself in the back, Roberto spoke softly with Honor. He came around to her side of the car.

'Jane, I hope we meet again very soon.' He bowed and kissed her hand.

'That would be lovely,' she heard herself say. Guido skilfully edged the car out of the courtyard. Jane would have liked to look back to see if he were still there, but she knew it would look unsophisticated.

'Sorry, Jane, darling, to drag you away like that.'

'I was ready to go, Honor. I really am tired,' she lied. 'Are you all right? I've never seen you ill before.'

'Heavens, I'm not ill. Just a stupid, silly headache. Too much booze recently, I should think. An early night and I'll be as right as rain.' She grabbed Jane's hand. 'I think our prince is rather taken with you. He asked me if he could call on you, as if I were a chaperone – too divinely quaint.'

'He's very nice.'

'"Nice" isn't exactly the word I would choose to describe Roberto.' Honor laughed. 'He's an impossible fish to land, that one.'

'Oh, Honor, I don't want to "land him". It was a lovely evening and he was the perfect host, nothing more. In fact, I thought it was you he was interested in.'

'Me?' Honor hooted with laughter, wincing with pain as she did so.

'Oh, this stupid head. Darling, I'm far too old for Roberto. In fact, I'm even surprised at his interest in you. Don't get me wrong, I only meant that he's normally trailing some empty-headed creature of twenty around with him.'

'To be honest, he frightens me.'

'Darling, I know what you mean. It's that world-weary air of dissipation about him. Dreadfully exciting, though, isn't it?' She chuckled quietly.

3

The haze that shimmered above the sea began to lift as if an invisible hand were gently unpeeling the mist to reveal the little town. It was Jane's favourite time of the day, and she watched entranced, as she did each morning after her early swim. Guido appeared across the terrace, the phone in his hand.

'Il Principe di Villizano,' he announced, indicating the phone.

'I don't think we should wake Lady Honor this early, Guido, not even for the Prince.'

'No, Contessa, he wishes to talk with you.'

Nervously she took the telephone. 'Hullo?'

'Jane, good morning. I just knew that if I called this early I would find you awake. It's a beautiful morning, isn't it?'

'Fantastic. Thank you for the lovely party, Roberto.'

'It was my pleasure. Honor is better, I hope?'

'I don't think we shall know that until this afternoon,' Jane said, laughing.

'So, your aunt will sleep all day? You'll be alone?'

'Well, yes,' she said uncertainly.

'Perhaps, then, you would take luncheon with me? It would give me great pleasure.'

Jane did not hesitate. 'Thank you, Roberto, I should like that.'

'I shall call for you at eleven.'

Replacing the receiver, she looked at the telephone and wondered why on earth she had accepted with such alacrity. It was hardly the sophisticated thing to do, and it was not as if she were really interested in him. He was not her type, and he was too old. Gracious, he was not even handsome. Still, there was no harm in lunch – dinner might have been a different proposition. She jumped up and, grabbing her large beach bag, hurried to her room – Honor would never forgive her if she went out with the Prince, of all people, not looking her best.

Everything went wrong. Her hair refused to do what she wanted and she had to wash it again. The same with her nails: twice she had to start from scratch and repaint them. Choosing something to wear took for ever. Honor's generosity meant she now had so many clothes that it was always difficult to choose, but today she was even more indecisive. She tried on half a dozen outfits, pirouetting in front of the mirror, before deciding on an aquamarine silk pyjama suit, which she dressed up with the junk jewellery that Honor adored and had taught her how to wear with style. She never failed to be surprised by the difference wrought by her new clothes and accessories. None of her friends in England would have recognized this sleek, bronzed woman.

Having scribbled a note to Honor, she was waiting on the steps when, on the dot of eleven, Roberto's black Maserati drove up in a cloud of dust. This morning he was dressed in the casual clothes that Italian men wear so well. He settled her in the car as if she were a precious package, and within a minute they were roaring off down the drive.

'I do like punctuality, thank you,' he said, and smiled at her. She had not noticed last night what a generous mouth he had, nor that his teeth were so white and even. She hoped they were his own, it would be awful to be kissed by someone with false teeth. What a silly thing to think – she was not going to kiss him, anyway, so what did it matter? She smiled back at him, not knowing what to say. She hated being punctual; all her life she had wanted to be one of those scatter-brained women who are late for everything, and with whom no one ever seems to be cross. Her inner clock always made certain that she arrived on time, and frequently early. But this was the first time anyone had ever complimented her on this.

He drove at a fast and furious pace, sounding his horn loudly and making other cars scuttle out of the path of this gleaming, black monster. She closed her eyes with terror as the car seemed to skim the very edge of the coast road: the drop to the sea looked far too steep for survival if anything went wrong.

'Are you afraid?'

'The road is very narrow.' She managed to control her voice.

'Don't you find speed sexually exciting? I do.'

'No.' She laughed nervously. 'That's the last thing I find it. All I feel is sheer terror.'

'Then I shall slow down,' he announced, and reduced his speed to 70 miles an hour, still far too fast for comfort on these winding roads. Jane gritted her teeth and, for the next hour, closed her eyes every time they hurtled round a bend. Her sigh of relief when the car finally screeched to a halt turned to a cry of pleasure as she opened her eyes to see the small white hotel nestling in a cove, the blue sea lapping a pale sandy beach, pine woods protecting it on the landward side.

'Roberto, what a heavenly hideaway!' she exclaimed.

'Worth the journey, wasn't it?' He grinned at her, and then gently took her hand and brushed his lips against it. She felt a surge of excitement as he touched her, which was not at all what she wanted. He let go of her hand. 'I have told no one of this little place, none of my friends. That way it stays like this. It's very simple food but excellent.'

The innkeeper appeared, bowing low to Roberto, speaking excitedly, far too quickly for Jane to catch a word. Roberto's reply was equally unintelligible to her, but the man nodded his head in vigorous agreement before turning to scuttle away up the road down which they had just come.

'What on earth did you say to the poor man to make him run away like that?' she asked.

'I have asked him to go and put up his "Full" sign. I don't want anyone else here to spoil our peace.'

'Roberto, you're joking. And he agreed?' she said, astonished.

'Of course.' He shrugged his shoulders. 'At a price, naturally.'

'Roberto, you're extraordinary!'

'No, not extraordinary. What is more natural than that I should want to be alone with you, here?' She laughed, delighted at his extravagant compliment but disconcerted by the pounding of her disobedient heart.

'Did you bring a swimming costume?' he asked suddenly.

'Yes, I've learned never to go anywhere in Italy without this,' and from the car she pulled the large beach bag that went everywhere with her these days.

'Come.' He took her hand and led her into the hotel. The shadows of the interior and the coolness of the tiled floor were a welcome contrast to the heat outside. Still holding her hand, he led her up the plain pine stairs and opened a door to a bedroom. The immaculately clean room was dominated by a wide pine bed with startlingly white sheets. Jane looked nervously at the bed.

'You change here, Jane, I will await you on the beach,' Roberto said, quietly closing the door behind him and leaving her in the room. Jane sighed audibly: for one dreadful moment she had thought that the whole day was about to be spoiled by a clumsy attempt at seduction. Even as she changed she realized that this had been a stupid thought – that would not be Roberto's style.

On the beach she found Roberto supervising the *padrone*, who was folding up the sunbeds and replacing them with large beach blankets. An umbrella shaded a wine cooler in which a bottle was already chilling.

'So much better for one's tan, don't you agree?' he said, indicating the blankets. 'And so much more intimate,' he added, smiling mischievously. Instead of replying, and to cover her confusion, she plunged into the sea and swam through the crystal-clear water to a large rock. From its top she could see the tiny fish darting in and out of the rocks. She watched, amused, Roberto on the beach still issuing instructions to their host, who rushed about anxiously fulfilling them. Then, with firm strokes, Roberto swam out to the rock and climbed up beside her.

'Wonderful, isn't it?' he said. 'The water is always so clean here, because of that line of rocks, I presume. Did you enjoy your swim?' She nodded, and sat, knees drawn up, arms folded about them, her body safely cocooned from eyes that constantly looked at her. Gently he brushed the sea water from her upper lip, his finger softly outlining her mouth. She shivered at his touch, quickly stood up, dived into the sea, and swam back to the beach. She flopped onto the rug, put on her dark glasses and lay down, facing the sea. Behind the dark lenses she watched him secretly as he dived time and again from the rock, his muscular body arcing gracefully. She was amused at the knowledge that this display was for her. He joined her, sinking down on the rug beside her. Gently he removed her sunglasses.

'Don't hide those wonderful eyes. I think you're a witch. Only a witch would have such grey eyes with black hair. A man could die just looking at those eyes.' Jane was sure there must be a sophisticated response to such compliments, but she could only laugh, shaking her wet hair which splashed him with water. Blushing at her clumsiness, she lay on her back, and pretended to soak up the sun. Even with her eyes closed she knew he was looking at her, felt certain that now he was studying the swell of her breasts. She half opened her eyes. She was right: Roberto was leaning on one elbow, gazing down at her. She sat up and, groping for her towel, hurriedly wrapped it round her shoulders.

'May I not look? Just look? You're so English. Why be ashamed of such beauty?'

'You make me feel uncomfortable and you make me blush just like an adolescent.'

'I know, I find it adorable. I love that delicate blush. It shows you're still pure.'

'I can hardly be that,' she replied wryly.

'It's possible, rare but certainly possible, to lose one's virginity and still remain a virgin in the mind,' he said seriously. Jane smiled vaguely: she did not understand his riddles.

'Come, lie back. I will not touch you, I promise.' She lay back; though he was not touching her, it felt as if he was. He lay so close to her that she could feel his breath on her skin, feel the warmth of his body, conscious always of his dark-brown eyes upon her.

'You're laughing at me,' she protested.

'Am I?'

'Yes. It makes me feel awkward.'

'I apologize. I don't wish to disconcert you – never. Instead of my gazing at you with adoration – not laughing at you, as you claim – we shall talk. OK?' He grinned at her and for a moment she felt safe.

'You speak wonderful English. You've hardly any accent at all.'

'You shame me that I have any accent. I get lazy these days.'

'Where did you learn?'

'I was at school in your country and I was at Oxford.'

'That explains it, then. Did you enjoy it?'

'Yes and no. England is such a civilized country to live in, such delights to be found there – the tea, the armchairs, crumpets, Ascot, the shopping, the Russian-roulette weather, Guinness. But on the other hand, I hate the weather, the rude shop assistants, warm beer, dog hairs on the armchairs – endless lists. Worst of all is that the English are never comfortable with foreigners. I found it difficult to make close friends. I had friends but I was always conscious that I didn't really belong, that behind my back I was "that greasy wop". My breeding and my background meant nothing to the arrogant English.'

'How did you stand it?'

'At first I felt enormous anger, but then it amused me. Such incredible arrogance has to be admired, such total conviction that God is English, C of E and a Tory.' He laughed loudly.

'You know I'm married?' she asked suddenly.

'Yes, I was told. Your husband must be a madman to allow you to be alone, here.'

'I don't think my husband gives a damn where I am.' She gave a sad, bitter little laugh.

'Then he's not simply mad, but certifiably so.' A shadow flickered across her face and, sensitive to her mood, he changed the subject. 'How long will you stay?'

'I don't know. Honor keeps persuading me to stay longer. It's easy to give in, it's so lovely here, it makes my problems seem a million miles away. I'll probably stay to the end of the summer, then return to Cambridge and look for a job.'

'A job? What for?' He sounded surprised.

'To earn money, of course.' She knew her answer would surprise him even more. Suddenly she wanted to challenge his assumptions about her.

'But it's your husband's duty to look after you.'

'He would. I don't want him to. I don't want his help or his money.'

'You're a woman of spirit, too. You must hate him a lot not to be willing to accept his money.'

'Oh, I don't hate him, I love him,' she said simply. 'No, I want to be independent. I want to do something for myself, I don't want just to be the wife of someone. You see them all the time, everywhere, in the shops, at the hairdresser's, women full of self-importance, which they've done nothing to earn. They spend the rest of their lives feeling important, being noisy about it, because of their husband's position or wealth. I don't want to be like that, I want to be myself. And if I achieve anything, it will be because of what I've done – not because I happened to have slept with someone. Even if it's only a typing job. Otherwise, it's a form of whoredom, really, isn't it?'

'You've set yourself a difficult goal. Young as you are, it's a little late to start again, isn't it? I think it might be easy to think this way, now. But what about when you're older? How will you feel then?'

'I shall have a career behind me and a pension.' She could not help laughing at his pained expression. 'And you, what will you do when the summer is over?' she asked.

'I have to go to Rome for a while. And then to Paris in the autumn: it's always more amusing there. In winter, I go to my estate in the north for the shooting of the wild boar. You pull a face? It's a great sport, but not for women. I don't like these women who shoot, pretending to be men, it's unfeminine. I might go skiing, see old friends, and if the winter gets too depressing I'll go to the sun. It's a busy life.' He laughed at himself.

'So you're what they call a jet-setter, then?'

'Good God, no. Nothing as glamorous, or vulgar.' He looked appalled at the idea.

'Do you work?'

'Yes, very much so. I have estates to administer, and I have other business interests. Even my socializing is a form of work: I know a lot of people, they tell me things. I hear of a deal here, another there. I weigh them up, investigate, contact other people about them, and because I met so-and-so at Gstaad, for example, I can fix something up. It all depends on whom you know, really, the way I do business.'

'Doesn't it always?' she asked with a touch of bitterness. 'What matters is who you were at school with, Oxbridge, who your cousin married and who you're related to. I hate that system,' she said with vehemence.

'I'm sure you do, my love, many do. But you'll never alter it. Occasionally people think they have broken in, been accepted, but if their credentials are not quite right they never are, and when the chips are down, no one will go to their rescue. It's always been that way, no doubt it will continue so. But don't let's quarrel. This conversation is much too serious for such a beautiful day.' He filled her glass.

They sipped their wine. She did not know if it was because of the heat, the wine or the proximity of his body, but she felt dizzy. He was telling her about the wine, but she did not hear the words. As she listened to his voice, she felt a physical need which had been dormant in her for some time. She felt that if he touched her again she would be lost . . . but he kept his promise and did not do so. Only his voice caressed her, as he spoke of impersonal things.

Their host arrived to tell them that lunch was ready.

'Do you wish to change?' Roberto asked.

'No, if you and the *padrone* don't mind me like this,' she replied as she slipped a short towelling robe over her bikini.

'I'm sure he's as happy with the way you look as I am.'

It was cool in the deserted dining room. They selected a table by the window. The food was delicious, as he had promised. All the time the *padrone* hovered near their table, his keen eyes watching for any signal from Roberto. Roberto ordered several bottles of wine, insisting that she sample each. She noticed that, though he drank with pleasure, he never finished a glass.

'This one is lovely,' she said, sipping the golden, chilled wine. 'Where is this one from?'

'I want to touch your breasts.' His hand snaked across the table and took hold of hers before she had time to remove it. 'I want to see them, I want to take them in my mouth, I want to feel your softness. Dear God, I ache with wanting you.'

Jane sat transfixed with astonishment, his words, echoing Tom's so closely, sent shivers through her body and made her shake. Still he held her hand. 'I want to bruise you, I want to make you moan with desire for me.' She looked at him, her eyes wide with horror, and she saw naked desire in his eyes, saw that his mouth was slightly parted, imagined that mouth on her. She felt a shiver of excitement flood through her, and snatched her hand away.

'Roberto, please. The man!' Beside them the *padrone* still stood, smiling and nodding his head. Jane hastily wrapped her robe tighter about her.

'Ignore him. He speaks no English.'

'He doesn't have to. Just one look at you, and he must know what you're saying,' she said spiritedly.

'Darling Jane. Forgive me, I couldn't stay silent any longer. Last night, the moment I saw you, I wanted you. I wanted to take you away from the ball. On the beach just now I wanted to tear your costume from you and mount you and possess you . . .'

'I'm not a bloody horse.' She tried to laugh but the laugh died and emerged as a half-strangled sigh.

'I don't joke, Jane. I want to give you the pleasure that I know you have never known. Let me be the one to teach you.'

'For Christ's sake, Roberto, send that man away, I can't bear him grinning at me like that.'

He spoke quickly to the man who virtually ran from the room. Roberto turned back to Jane, and took her hand again. 'Now, my darling, now, let me make love to you for the rest of the day and all night.'

'Roberto!' Her eyes pleaded with him.

'You're not going to let me, are you?'

'No, Roberto, I can't.'

'Why not? Who is here to see? There's that wonderful bed upstairs waiting for us. Can you not imagine what beauty of feeling awaits us, in that room, on that bed?'

'Please stop, I'm sorry you feel this way. But I don't think I've done anything to make you think that I would or could.'

'You may think that but your body feels differently. All morning I've sensed your need for me. I know you've been fighting this feeling all the time. Jane, imagine my weight on you, the power of me within you.' He spoke quietly, urgently.

'Roberto, it wouldn't be right. I don't want to, you're wrong, I don't want ever to make love to another man.'

She wished he would stop. With every word he spoke she could feel herself weakening.

'No, my sweet one, you must not talk like that. Of course you must make love to me. Your beautiful body was made for it. You have nothing to fear, my darling. This fellow is very discreet.'

'Is he?' Jane sat upright, anger flashing in her eyes. 'You know that for a fact, do you? Come here often, then, do you? It must cost you a small fortune hiring the place so often to be on your own with your latest pick-up.'

'Contessa, don't be angry with me. As a matter of fact, I don't make a habit of coming here. I thought it would appeal to you,' he said gently. 'I did not plan this. I beg your forgiveness, Contessa. I apologize, blame the wine, the sun, your intolerable beauty.'

Jane ran from the room and blindly up the stairs. Her legs were shaking. What the hell was wrong with her? Her body was completely aroused. She looked at the bed: he had been right, she did want to make love to him. She wanted to see his body naked looming above her, to smell him, to . . . 'No!' she shouted out loud. 'No!' That was lust. She did not love him; she loved only Alistair. If she went to bed with him, she would despise herself. She could live without sex. She was not going to repeat the mistakes of the last six months in Cambridge with anyone.

He was waiting for her in the hallway. He helped her into the car, and she thanked the *padrone* in her faltering Italian. As they drove back, quite slowly, he talked casually and did not attempt to touch her, and it was as if the incident had never happened.

Back at the villa, Honor was on the terrace with Umberto and Federico. The two boys eyed Roberto with unconcealed resentment. He merely glanced at them once and then ignored them.

'And what have you two darlings been up to?' Honor asked archly, raising her eyebrows.

'Nothing, my dear Honor. I took your lovely niece for a swim, a delicious lunch, perhaps a little too much wine, and I return her safely to you.'

'*Quel dommage.*' Honor looked unconvinced. 'I was anticipating news of a delightful little affair. How sad!'

Roberto accepted tea – Honor's was the only house where proper tea was served, he said – but declined her invitation to dinner. Jane, becoming used to the complexities of her new feelings, found that she wished he had accepted. Afte tea, she walked with him to his car.

'It would have been nice if you could have stayed to dinner,' she said shyly.

'Not for me, my entrancing Jane. It would have been unbearable. To sit in a room with you, for hours, to look at you, and to want to touch you without being allowed to – that's too much for me. I can only permit myself to see you for a few short hours.' He bent forward and kissed her full on her mouth and the shock of his lips on hers made her quiver. He stood back and looked at her with a strange, knowing smile, and almost imperceptibly nodded.

'All in good time, my little one. All in good time.' He waved his hand and was gone.

4

That evening, pleading tiredness, Jane did not go to a party with Honor and the boys. She wanted to be on her own. She had forgotten that for months she had been terrified of being on her own; now at last she had chosen it.

She had intended to write some letters. Instead she sat on the terrace, attempting to analyse her fluctuating emotions and attitudes. One moment she wanted never to see Roberto again, the next she was miserable at the thought of not seeing him. Later, when he phoned to invite her to lunch the following day, she accepted, feeling elated and excited at the prospect.

This time they drove into the mountains. He laughed at her expression, as she surveyed the crowded restaurant into which he led her.

'You see, my darling Jane, you will be safe from me here.'

'Roberto, I don't think one is ever safe with you anywhere,' she countered.

'Perhaps you've been thinking; perhaps you don't really want to be safe?'

'Oh yes, I do. But I'm sure you're a gentleman, and I enjoy your company, so I thought it was worth taking the risk,' she parried.

The head waiter made much of them. With a flourish which entailed much flexing of his elbows, he removed Jane's chair and seated her. He flicked open a large damask napkin with a sharp movement of his wrist, making the linen crack like the sail of a boat. With hands darting like quicksilver he rearranged the flowers, altered the position of the ashtray, and straightened the already perfectly aligned silver. He clicked his fingers at his acolytes and with a bow presented Jane with the menu. Jane was aware that she had just witnessed a virtuoso performance.

Roberto surveyed the other diners. There was much waving and bowing. Jane noticed that some he rewarded with more enthusiastic waves than others. For some he bowed from the waist, to others he inclined his head. Having done so, he then proceeded to ignore them all.

'Please, if you want to go and speak to your friends . . .' Jane smiled, indicating the room with a wave of her hand.

'No, my darling, I am with you. They're of no importance,' he replied with an ingenuous arrogance that made Jane smile even more.

'You seem to know everyone here. It's extraordinary, I think I've met more people since I've been staying with Honor than I ever did while I was with Alistair. We lived in the country, you see. We didn't mix much socially.'

'This husband of yours is a strange man. He allows you to be here on your own, but when you're at home he does not introduce you to society. He should want all the world to know and admire you.'

'But I didn't want to be part of society. It had rejected me and I was frightened by it. It was a very difficult situation for Alistair, too,' she said lamely. She wanted Roberto to understand, but here in this restaurant it all sounded so unlikely, even to her.

'And why did this society reject you?'

'As you would say, my credentials were wrong.' She smiled wryly.

'Poor little one. Your husband failed you. He married you, so he should have made society accept you.'

'It's more difficult in England.'

'No, it's worse here – the society, the caste system. Having married you, he should have made a stand. He knew before he married you how it would be; he knew the system better than you. He sounds a very stupid man; what was he trying to do, change the order of things?'

'Oh no, I don't think he ever thought about it. He said he married me because he felt sorry for me after his family had been horrible to me.'

'Then I was right, he is very stupid. He only made matters worse for you, didn't he?'

'I suppose so but, honestly, I don't think he knew it was going to be as difficult as it turned out to be. He meant well, and he loved me.'

Roberto frowned. 'I find this conversation makes me angry. I don't want to talk about your husband, Jane.' His voice was suddenly cold.

'Then you shouldn't have brought the subject up, should you?' she replied, heatedly.

'I don't like to think of you in the arms of another man.'

'But that's silly, Roberto. I'm not a twenty-year-old virgin.'

'I wish you were, and had known only me,' he said wistfully.

'This food is delicious.'

'Dear Jane, always so English when the conversation goes the way she does not wish it to go.'

Their coffee was served and they lingered over a brandy. 'Why does your aunt live with those dreadful gigolos?' he asked abruptly.

'They're not dreadful and I'm sure they're not gigolos.' She felt indignant on Honor's behalf.

'Of course they are. It's such a sad waste.'

'What's a gigolo, then?'

'Jane, you know full well.'

'I want to know what you think a gigolo is,' she persisted.

'A gigolo is a young man who makes love to an older woman for money.'

'How do you know she pays them? I'm sure she doesn't.'

'Well, perhaps not in money, but she feeds them, takes them about with her, probably buys them clothes and jewellery.'

'And had I gone to bed with you yesterday, what would have been the difference between them and me? Would you have despised me, too, thought me dreadful?' She stared angrily at him, exasperated with his pompous hypocrisy.

'Of course not, that's entirely different.'

'What's different? You're older than I am, you buy me meals, no doubt if I had an affair with you you would buy me presents, too, and clothes. I've no money, I can't repay your hospitality.'

'Darling, I adore you when you're angry. Those eyes of yours are even more beautiful then. That wonderful grey takes on an entirely new depth, a depth with great fire . . . wonderful.'

'You don't take me seriously,' she said, growing more irritated.

'Of course not, I think you might be winning the argument.' He smiled, took her hand, raised it to his mouth and she felt his breath on it. It was a sensuous act, more so than if he had kissed her hand.

'What you should have said was, "Why does your aunt have such young lovers?" Then I would not have taken umbrage, but gigolo – it's not a pretty word, is it?' She took her hand from his grasp but she smiled at him.

'True. So why does she?'

'I think she's fed up with husbands. She says they're too expensive a hobby.' Roberto laughed loudly. 'This way she's in control, they go when she wants, no alimony. If you're a very rich woman, I suppose it's a good system. Don't think I disapprove, because I don't. They're very kind to her, and they're really very sweet. They make her happy, so I'm grateful to them because I love her.'

'I was wrong to criticize. I apologize. You're right, if she's happy, then . . . She must be very lonely sometimes.'

'Honor, lonely? I've never thought of that. She's always surrounded by so many people that it doesn't seem possible.'

'That's a sure sign of loneliness. She drives some of my friends mad, you know. There are many who would love to please her,' he said with such a soulful expression that Jane had to smile.

Their lunch finished, he drove her home. Again he had tea with them, and again refused an invitation to dinner. For a week the routine was varied only by the restaurants to which he took her for lunch. Each day he flirted gently with her, but he made no further attempt to force himself upon her.

She did not go out in the evenings any more. He always phoned in the evening, and always at a different time. Until his phone call, she was restless and would wander about the villa aimlessly.

One evening, Honor was having a rare quiet night at home.

'For heaven's sake, Jane, do settle. Read or something.'

'I'm sorry, Honor. I can't settle. I'm like this every evening until Roberto phones. I'm always afraid that this evening is the one that he won't. But I'm still restless even once he has phoned, I don't know why.'

'Jane, you're impossible. Of course you're restless. You go out with a sensuous man like Roberto, he brings you home by early evening and then leaves. I'm not surprised you're like this. Why, you should be in bed with him by now, not wandering around here driving me mad. I presume he has tried to seduce you?'

'Yes,' Jane said, half embarrassed and half proud that he had.

'And you turned him down?'

'Of course.'

'Why "of course"? I should think he's everything a young woman wants. He's not handsome in a conventional sense but he's bloody attractive in an off-beat way, such fun to be with, and very kind. Mind you, I doubt if he's ever been treated like this before. He must be intrigued by you – women are queueing up to get into his bed. It's very clever of you, darling.'

'I'm not trying to be clever. I could never sleep with him, Honor, I don't love him.'

'Piffle, of course you could.'

'It would be all wrong. How could I sleep with him, pretending it was Alistair?'

Honor shrieked with laughter. 'Jane, darling, if you slept with Roberto, I can guarantee there's not the slightest chance you'd want to pretend that it was Alistair – or anyone else. The very idea,' she snorted, obviously well pleased with the joke. 'But Jane, seriously, you can't spend the rest of your life with no interest in men. Be sensible.'

'I admit I'm very attracted to him: it would be difficult not to be. And if I'm honest I'll admit I love his attention. But if I slept with him it would just be for sex and I never want to do that again.'

'Jane, you're so divinely old-fashioned.' Honor chuckled, but then added seriously, 'You're not still hoping to go back to Alistair?'

'Well . . .'

'Jane,' Honor exclaimed, 'I don't understand you. After the dreadful way he treated you.'

'Sometimes I think I was too rash. If I'd kept my eyes and mouth shut, I'd be happy now.'

'Bullshit! I've never heard anything so stupid in my life. You'd be perfectly miserable by now. I love him dearly but he'll never change: he's too much like my brother – he always had to have a little woman on the side, too. You'd become a martyr – the shires are full of them. You see them at point-to-points, too hippy, too loud, too fond of the sherry, with set mouths, sad eyes, and besotted with their dogs.' Jane had seen so many women who fitted Honor's description that she could not laugh. 'You're too young to live in the past,' Honor went on. 'Remember, Jane, you're living your memories now: make sure they're not dull, sterile ones for the sake of the old woman you'll be one day.' Jane shivered at Honor's chilling remark. 'Roberto would be an ideal start for you. He's charming, rich, sophisticated, experienced in bed and he would make you happy.' Honor efficiently enumerated Roberto's virtues.

'But I don't want to marry again.'

'Darling, I'm not talking about marriage. Oh, dear, you're so innocent. I'm talking about a delightful affair, a light summer soufflé of a relationship. You take everything so seriously, too seriously.'

'That's true.' Jane smiled.

'You must forget about marriage where Roberto is concerned. Firstly, you'd be a divorced woman, which would kill his stuffy old mother and he'd have a guilt complex for the rest of his life. And, you know, despite appearances, Roberto and people like him stick to the strict order of things. When he's fifty, he'll marry a suitable young girl from a suitable family, who, no doubt, has already been picked out for him. She will produce his babies and he will continue to have mistresses, several of them.'

Jane shivered, as if with cold. 'Several, really?' She tried to sound nonchalant, but she felt sick inside, and that night she found it difficult to get to sleep.

It seemed that finally he was bored with her. Now that she knew he had many mistresses, this was not surprising. For five days he did not telephone, despite her making all manner of bargains with God. On the sixth day, when the phone rang she ignored it. When Guido handed her the phone, she knew she sounded overeager as she accepted his invitation to dinner the following night.

'Honor, he's invited me to dinner, not to lunch.' A flushed and happy Jane exploded into the room.

'Thank goodness for that. For Christ's sake, sleep with the delicious man this time, then perhaps we can all have some peace.' Honor laughed at her.

The following night she asked Honor's advice about what to wear at least half a dozen times before settling on a plain, full-skirted, black taffeta dress which made a delightful swish as she moved. Honor insisted on lending her a diamond necklace and earrings. It was a very sophisticated-looking woman who rushed out of the door like an excited schoolgirl as she heard his car arriving promptly at eight.

The road seemed familiar to her this time. 'Where are we going to dine?'

'At my home. I'm tired of crowded restaurants and noise. We shall dine peacefully *à deux*.' Jane found herself both relieved and apprehensive at the words.

Tonight there were no lights in the castle as they drew up. As he led her through a side door, along stone-flagged corridors and up and down innumerable stone staircases, her high-heeled shoes clattered and echoed in the silence. He ushered her into a room which, but for the view, could have been one in any large English house. Comfortable chintz-covered chairs and sofas, a log fire and, to complete the picture, two large dogs which merely raised their heads as they entered, then returned to their contented slumber in front of the fire.

'Gracious, it's so English. Even an open fire, in Italy, in summer!'

'It can get very chilly in the evenings in these mountains. I'm glad you think it's so English. I went to great trouble to create the illusion.'

'Except for the view, it could be England,' she said, crossing to the large full-length window which framed a view of mountains tinged with the rose colour of the setting sun.

'Crikey!' She jumped back in fright: beneath her was a sheer drop to the valley far below. Roberto caught her as she stepped back, twisting on her heels in her haste. As he touched her she leaned her body slightly towards him, but he steadied her and then, to her disappointment, let go, crossing the room to pour the drinks.

'I'm sorry, I should have warned you. It's quite safe, though, the glass is very thick. It looks dangerous, that's all.'

'I forgot for a moment that the glass was there, it made me jump,' she said in confusion, caused, she knew, more by his touch than by her fright. He settled her in a chair beside the fire with her drink and, selecting a record, put it on the turntable. As the beginning of Sibelius's Fifth Symphony filled the room, Jane jerked nervously and spilled half her drink.

'Jane, darling, what is the matter? You're a bundle of nerves tonight – and you're as white as a ghost. Darling, what has frightened you?'

'It's the music, Roberto, please, anything but that . . . I can't stand it.'

'But it's so beautiful to listen to, especially when the sun is setting on the mountains.'

'Please, Roberto, please change it.' The urgency in her voice made him cross to the record player at once. Instead, he put on some Mahler.

'Does Mahler frighten you, too?' He smiled gently as she began, frantically, to dab at her dress. 'Would you like me to get a robe for you? The servants can see to your dress.'

'No, it's nothing. Look, it's all mopped up – so clumsy of me. The Mahler is lovely,' she said quickly.

'What was it?'

'Oh, I was being silly. It reminded me of something that happened a long time ago and that I prefer not to remember, that's all. I'm fine now.' She smiled brightly at him.

'Was it reminding you of some sad love affair?' he persisted.

'No, nothing like that.'

'Pain in a woman's life is always caused by a man, even at second hand.'

'I suppose that's right.'

'Will you tell me about it?'

'I can't, Roberto, I'm sorry.'

'I want to know everything about you, even the bad things.'

'But I can't think about it, let alone talk about it.'

'I would like to kill anyone who has ever hurt you,' he said vehemently, and kissed her gently on the forehead. 'You will tell me one day, you promise?'

'I'll try. But not yet, Roberto, please,' and the almost begging tone of her voice made him change the subject.

A servant appeared and stood silently to one side. He said nothing to Roberto, who continued to talk and sip his drink. Ten minutes must have passed while the mute servant stood there, before Roberto stood up and told her that dinner was ready. The servant moved silently and opened a door concealed in the bookcase to reveal a dining room, also furnished entirely in English style. Two more servants stood there, dressed in black livery with gold trimmings and immaculate white gloves. While they ate, the men stood at attention behind their chairs. As courses were finished, they moved in unison to remove the dishes and replace them with new ones; in tandem they poured the wine. Jane watched but she could see no signals pass between them.

'I thought you said we were dining *à deux*?' she said pointedly.

'We are.' He sounded surprised.

'How can it be *à deux* with so many in the room?'

'They're servants: they don't count.'

'That's a dreadful attitude, Roberto. I hope they don't understand English.'

'Of course they don't. But if they did, it wouldn't alter the fact. They know their place and I know mine.'

'I could never adjust at Respryn to having servants. It always embarrassed me, being waited on – I always seemed to be apologizing.' She laughed at the memory.

'How strange. You must have confused them terribly.'

'Did I?'

'There's no shame in being a servant, you know, provided you're a good one. Your embarrassment could have insulted them.'

He turned and spoke quietly to the men, who silently left the room. 'Better?' he enquired, smiling at her. 'I don't want you to feel uncomfortable, do I?'

'I hope they don't feel insulted.'

'On the contrary, they will assume that I have dismissed them because I want to be alone with you. But obviously you were not brought up with servants. Tell me about your life.'

She told him her story, everything but the illness. She was ashamed of that.

'Of course, now I remember you. I remember your face – I saw it in the newspapers. I thought then what a beautiful face it was, but you look very different.'

'Thanks to Honor. I was pretty dowdy before. She's done what she calls "glossing me up".' Jane laughed good-naturedly.

'She has done a wonderful job, but she had the best material to work on. You have no vanity: that's rare in a beautiful woman.'

'But I don't think I'm beautiful; in fact, for years I thought I was ugly. My mother was always at pains to tell me so.'

'How very strange of her. Your parents, do you see them often?'

'No. My father thinks I'm a traitor to my class, poor old thing. And my mother, well, I just don't seem to have anything in common with her. We're both uncomfortable with each other. I write and let them know how I am, and send presents, but I haven't seen them for ages.'

'It wasn't just your husband who put that sadness in your eyes.'

'I wasn't sad,' she said. 'Not really. Just angry, and determined that things would get better. But there are advantages to an unhappy childhood: nothing ever hurts you as much again, after being rejected as a child.'

'Doesn't it?' he said, unconvinced.

'Well, it's different, shall we say? And you have a better chance of surviving what gets thrown at you.'

'And what has been thrown at you?'

'Rejection. My parents first, then society, my husband . . .'

'How did he reject you?'

'He had an affair.'

'So, you left this husband, whom you claim to love, because he had an affair?'

'Well, several, it turned out. But one or several, it's all the same.'

'Poor man. To lose you . . . He should have been more discreet.'

'It wouldn't have made it any better and I would have found out anyway. There were people who would have made certain I did.'

'Don't you think you were too hard on him? We men are weak creatures, you know.' He smiled, spreading his hands expansively as if in apology for all men.

'No, I don't. I expected fidelity. I was faithful to him. If I were to be unfaithful it would be because I no longer loved. It has to be the same with a man.'

'Does it? You sound so sure.' All the time he spoke he smiled gently, but Jane had the feeling that he was laughing at her, that her views were amusing him. She found it disconcerting.

'I *am* sure,' she said emphatically.

'I have always found it difficult to be certain of anything in this life.' He sipped his wine and gazed at her over the rim of his glass for what seemed a long time. 'And me, when you have your affair with me, what if I am unfaithful?'

'It would be the same.'

'I see. And what about now, what if I told you I had a mistress?'

'I know you have. Several in fact.'

'How interesting. Who told you?'

'A little bird. But we are not having an affair, so it's none of my business what you do, is it?'

'True. But how do you feel at the thought that, when I take you home tonight, I shall kiss you chastely, go to the arms of another woman, and spend the night making love to her, when it should be you?'

'Should it?'

'Of course, as you well know.'

'But it won't be, so again it is none of my business where you sleep tonight,' she answered lightly, but inside her was a tumult of distaste and distress at the very idea of him with another woman.

He smiled enigmatically. 'Shall we take our *digestif* in the sitting room?'

No servants appeared. She curled up on the comfortable sofa. He put on more music and sat down opposite her.

'You don't flirt with me any more,' she said almost petulantly.

'I never stop,' he replied, laughing.

'I haven't noticed.' She pouted.

'What was I doing just now?'

'I don't think talking about your mistresses amounts to flirting with me.'

'Doesn't it?' He smiled. 'Are you getting just a little jealous, Contessa?'

'Of course not, I don't mind what you do. We're good friends – that's all.'

'And do good friends normally flirt?'

'Some do.'

'Jane, Jane, you're so contrary. What you mean is that I have stopped trying to seduce you. I haven't stopped flirting with you. But I thought we had a pact?'

'Oh.'

'You tell me not to seduce you, so I don't. Then you don't like it when I stop.' She smiled shyly at him. 'Do you want me to start seducing you again? I will with pleasure.' She saw the merriment in his eyes.

'I really did mean flirting,' she parried.

'You did not answer my question.'

'I don't know what to say,' she replied, becoming flustered.

'Then you're a little more uncertain than before, which is good. It's a pity you're not yet totally convinced that I'm right for you. Never mind, you will be.'

'You're always so certain.'

'It's easy. It's in your eyes when you look at me so shyly, so slyly. It's in the way you move your body when you're close to me. You want me. You're deciding – even at this moment you argue with yourself. You waste time with your games, your little teases, but no matter. We have time, and it adds to my pleasure in savouring the prospect of you.'

'You make me sound like a dish of food.' She laughed, but he looked seriously at her from across the room and said, 'When you have decided, you will let me know immediately, won't you?'

'Yes,' she said breathlessly, willing him to come to her and touch her, knowing that if he did, she would not resist, not tonight.

'Good. And now it's late, and as we both know, I have business to attend to. I think we had better go,' he said, to her acute disappointment and annoyance.

5

'Jane, you've let me down. What on earth are you doing here?' Honor asked, as she swept into the room with Umberto and Federico.

'What's the time?' Jane asked blearily.

'It's gone four. What happened?' Honor asked, and then told the two young men to go to bed.

'Nothing happened,' Jane said when they had gone. 'Nothing at all. We talked about his mistresses – that was the high spot of the evening. I think he's bored with me. He didn't ask me to go to bed with him, anyhow.'

'Darling Jane. He's not bored with you, he's playing games with you. I bet he knew exactly how you were feeling tonight and decided to pay you back for all the indecisions of the past weeks. In any case, men like Roberto don't ask you to go to bed with them – the very idea! – they lead you to it with a word here, a glance, an innuendo. Nothing as vulgar as asking.' Honor snorted with laughter at the thought. 'You're so divinely unsophisticated, Jane, it must be driving Roberto mad with desire.'

'I couldn't sleep so I came in here to listen to music and at least I've made my decision. I'm not going to have an affair with him. He's conceited and I think there's something decadent about him. Imagine having a whole army of mistresses – it's revolting.' But Honor's only reply was to laugh even louder. 'I don't think it's funny. Anyhow, I've decided that I don't want to be a member of his private sex army.'

'Perhaps, if he had you, he wouldn't want the others.'

'I doubt it. You yourself said the other day that men never change, they just begin to lie better. I'm not taking the risk.'

'Well, it's your decision. I still think it's a pity. He would have been such a good education for you. So, can we go to bed now, if that's decided? I've a splitting headache.'

'Honor, don't you think you should go and see a doctor? You often have these headaches now,' Jane asked anxiously.

'No. It's too many late nights at my advanced age, and I drink too much. I ought to wear my specs for reading, too, but I can't bear to. I look so ugly in them!' She chuckled.

In bed, Jane tossed and turned. It was hard to contemplate not seeing him again, but it was stupid to continue like this: it was not fair to either of them. When he next phoned, she would thank him politely for the good times they had had and explain that since she could not be what he wanted, it was better that they stop seeing each other.

But she did not get the chance, for he did not phone.

'Don't mope, Jane,' Honor said briskly. 'You've only yourself to blame, and it's boring me, this long miserable face about the villa. I like happy people. Pull yourself together and come to the Pattersons' with me tonight?'

But the evening did not distract her. She was even more despondent when they returned to the villa to find a note from Guido saying that the Prince had telephoned four times.

'Four times?' shrieked Honor excitedly. 'Now we know he's been playing games. When he finally phones – how long has it been, a week? – instead of your being in, which he's now used to, you're out all evening and Guido is far too discreet to tell him where. Oh, what fun, four phone calls! I think he must be feeling that he's overplayed his hand just a teeny-weeny bit.'

'You make it all sound so complicated. There must be a reasonable explanation.'

'Affairs are complicated things. I've had years of practice and I know what's going on in our divine prince's head.' She clapped her hands with glee. 'What's the time? One o'clock? Right, I guarantee he will call by two. If you've any sense, you won't answer it – really give him something to worry about.'

'How can you be so certain?'

'Oh, I am. I'll switch the phone through to your room – that's how certain I am.'

At two minutes past two, Jane wearily put her light out. At five past she quickly switched it on again. She sat mesmerized watching the phone as it rang. She let it ring half a dozen times before she picked it up.

'Hullo?' She tried to sound sleepy.

'Jane? Is that you? Jane, I am in Rome. I was called away.' He paused. 'Jane, are you there?'

'Yes, Roberto, I'm here.' Her ploy to sound sleepy was not working: she could hear the eagerness in her voice.

'Where have you been? I was calling all evening.'

'Out,' she said casually.

There was a pause before he asked, 'Darling, how are you?'

'Oh, I'm fine. I've been busy.'

'Did you miss me?'

'Yes.'

'Good. Perhaps you weaken, a little?'

'Maybe.'

'Nothing more definite?'

'No.'

'Look, Jane, I may be delayed in Rome a few days yet. Should you need me, Honor has my number. I would love to talk to you but, darling, I'm busy, I must go now. Ciao.' The phone went dead. To hell with him, she thought angrily, what could be keeping him busy at two in the morning but another woman? He had probably crept from her bed to call Jane. Damn him, he could go and boil his head as far as she was concerned. It was ridiculous that grown men and women should be playing games like this.

Honor, though satisfied to have been proved right, was not happy about the outcome of the call, especially when Jane began to suggest that she should return to England to start looking for a job.

'Darling, you can stay with me for ever. I love having you here.'

'You're sweet, but I can't live off you like this for ever, can I?'

'I don't see why not. If it doesn't bother me, why should it bother you? Too silly.'

Jane finally promised to stay for another month. Honor went out to lunch and then with Guido to the shops. Jane was left alone in the villa. When the phone rang, her instinct was to ignore it, but the caller was persistent and finally Jane went to answer it.

'Honor?' The voice made Jane start. 'Honor, is that you?' it asked. The sound of the familiar, warm voice excited Jane.

'No, Alistair, it's Jane.'

'Oh.' There was silence as she waited for him to continue.

'How's James?' she eventually asked.

'He's fine. He's really happy at his prep school.' Perhaps it was her imagination, or did his voice sound colder?

'And how are you?' she asked almost shyly.

'Rattling around, much the same as usual.' There was a pause. 'Jane, I'm glad I got you. I want to talk to you, it's important.'

'Yes?' she said breathlessly, happy that, at last, he wanted to talk to her.

'You are O K now, aren't you? I mean, fully recovered?'

'Oh yes, Alistair. I'm right as rain now.' The words bubbled out of her: she was sure his questions could mean only one thing.

'Anyone else?'

'No, no one,' she answered, perhaps a shade too quickly.

'I see,' he said shortly. She had expected him to sound more pleased.

'So?' She laughed.

'I think it's time we got a divorce.'

Momentarily, she took the receiver away from her ear and stared at it with a puzzled expression. She could not have heard him correctly.

'It really would make everything simpler and a lot tidier if we got divorced,' she heard him continue.

Jane felt as if she were boxed into total silence. This was not how the conversation should go. And what had happened to the clock – why wasn't the clock ticking? What the hell had gone wrong? He should be asking her to catch the next flight out.

'Look, you needn't bother yourself with a thing. I'll get the lawyers onto it straight away. Of course, it goes without saying that you can divorce me for adultery – it's customary,' his voice went on relentlessly.

'You'll what?' Her voice suddenly exploded into life. 'Oh, thank you, Alistair,' she said with heavy irony. 'How really kind of you. What an honour, letting me sue you.'

'Jane? What's got into you?'

'What's got into me? I'm angry at your bloody nerve.'

'I don't know what you're going on about. It's always the gentleman who is sued: that's how things are done. But don't forget I could, in law, sue you with that weirdo in Cambridge.'

'You might have the legal right, Alistair, but what about the moral right? I never wanted any of this to happen. If you hadn't played around, we wouldn't be in this position now. Do you remember, or have you conveniently forgotten?'

'It takes two to break a marriage, or have you forgotten that?' he countered.

'Bastard!' she snapped.

'Look, Jane, I don't want to argue with you.'

'Don't you? I don't hear from you for months and then you blithely phone up and ask for a divorce. What do you expect?'

'At least we can try to be civilized about it.'

'Civilized? You?' she sneered, while her mind was screaming, I don't want a divorce. I love you. Instead she yelled, 'Oh, do what you bloody well like!'

'I will!' he shouted back, and the phone was abruptly disconnected.

The clock was working. That was strange – she had been certain it had stopped, but now its relentless ticking was deafening. She picked it up and stuffed it under a cushion to prevent herself hurling it out of the window. The bastard had hurt her again. He knew how she felt: she had poured it all out in that letter which he had not seen fit to answer. And this, at last, was his reply. She kicked the sofa. What about her pride, her wonderful pride which was in shreds now? How could she ever face him? The sod, the rotten sod! She sat with her head in her hands. If only she had not answered the bloody phone, then none of this would have happened . . . She felt the prick of tears, and shook her head. She was not going to cry: she had cried enough over him. 'I'll show the rotten bastard,' she muttered to herself as, feverishly, she rifled Honor's desk, searching for her address book. Half an hour later, tears were running down her cheeks but they were tears of frustration at her inability to make the operator understand what she wanted. She heard Guido's car and rushed to meet him.

'Guido, thank God you're here. Please get me this number, quick.'

Guido calmly obtained the number and smilingly handed the phone back to her.

'Roberto?'

'Contessa?'

'I miss you. I'm so miserable.'

'I'm sorry you're so sad.'

'Roberto, may I come to Rome?'

'Of course.'

'Tonight?'

'You've decided?'

'Yes.'

'Then come, my love, come quickly.'

It was Guido who found out the times of trains for her, and it was Guido who lent her the money for the fare to Rome. A single ticket would do, she told him, and he smiled knowingly. She raced up the stairs two at a time and frenetically began to pack her bags, hurling an assortment of clothes into them, instinctively picking her best clothes. She swept the contents of her dressing table into her make-up valise. Never, since she had been at Honor's, had she ever showered, changed and made up in such record time. Guido drove her to the station and promised a hundred times that he would phone the Prince the minute he got back to tell him her time of arrival.

The train was travelling too fast for her and yet not fast enough – such was the turmoil inside her. She wanted to see Roberto before she changed her mind again. She wanted this train to speed up and to race her away from the past. And yet it thundered towards him too swiftly. This time she knew that she could not resist: the time for playing games was over. But after so many doubts, what sort of happiness could she expect with him? What number mistress was she to become? How could she learn to bury the principles of a lifetime and accept the inevitable infidelities? How could she learn to hide a love for another man which had burned in her for so many years? She was going for all the wrong reasons – what if he detected this and left her in anger? What the hell was she to do with her life? Mercifully, the emotions of the last few hours, the endless questioning of her mind, forced sleep upon her and she awoke with a start when, at nine, the train pulled into the station.

Anxiously she searched the faces on the platform as she stood alone, isolated in the seething crowd of Italians noisily and emotionally greeting each other. Perhaps he had changed his mind, perhaps he would not come . . .

'Jane.' He was beside her, his arm protectively about her. He was smothering her face with hungry kisses and suddenly she was part of the milling Italian throng.

'I missed you, Roberto, darling,' she said honestly.

'That is the first time you have called me "darling" or anything but Roberto,' he said happily, as he took her arm and held her tightly, as if fearful that she might slip away from him. Gently he ushered her through the hordes of pushing, shouting people. Having stowed her cases in the boot, he got into the car beside her and took her hand.

'Do you want me to book you a room in a hotel, Jane?'

'No.'

'You're certain. No more games?'

'No, darling, no more games. I want to sleep with you tonight, if you want me.'

'Want you? Oh, sweet Jane.' He laughed at her. 'Yes, I want you, I want you.'

With skill he threaded the car through the crowded streets, in the fast city traffic. She had never been to Rome but this night she saw only him. In the train she had feared that she had come only because of Alistair's rejection of her – she had been certain of it. But now, beside him, able to touch him, to smell him, it seemed equally certain that she had come because Alistair's news had jolted her into a decision that she needed to make, that it was natural for her to make. She lifted her hand and stroked his cheek.

'What happened?' he asked, taking his attention off the road for a second as he looked at her searchingly.

'What do you mean?'

'What made you decide to come?'

'I missed you too much. I realized what I wanted and how stupid I had been.'

'Nothing more? Nothing happened to make you change your mind?'

'No, nothing,' she lied.

6

Everything in Roberto's life seemed to move on oiled wheels. The wrought-iron gates of his Roman house opened silently as they approached. The front door was opened, like the gates, by unseen hands. In the huge, white marble hall stood a row of silent servants in dramatic black and gold livery. When they moved, it was with silence and smoothness across the marble floor. The sound of Jane's heels seemed unnaturally loud.

To her surprise, Jane was immediately dispatched to her room with instructions to change quickly for dinner. She was in such a hurry that she had no time to take in the splendour of her room, did not see the Manet hanging on the wall or the fine Venetian looking-glass. Not till later did she notice the exquisitely inlaid French bureau, the Persian rugs scattered on the highly polished floor. She cursed herself for having packed so fast – everything was badly creased, and only the black taffeta she had worn the other night was wearable. She felt even more dishevelled when she skidded back to the hall to find Roberto immaculate in his dinner jacket.

'Are we going out to dinner?'

'Yes. You'll like the place we are going, it's a beautiful old monastery which Mussolini turned into a restaurant.'

'There's no need: a sandwich will do me.'

'What you're really saying is that you're surprised I did not rush you into bed immediately?' He smiled teasingly at her.

'Well . . .' She felt a traitorous blush flit over her face.

'No, my darling, that's not my way. These things have to be done properly, with grace and with – anticipation.'

The restaurant was everything he had promised. Old as time, and yet with all the comfort of the twentieth century. The view across the Tiber to the floodlit Castel Sant' Angelo could not have been more romantic. He had ordered their meal while she was on the train and seemed genuinely delighted at her pleasure in his choice. As the meal progressed he talked easily and entertainingly, leaning across the table to her, speaking with intensity on many subjects but not once about themselves. Occasionally he would stroke her arm, touch her hair; and always there was his warm, seductive smile. But she began to feel edgy. She supposed she had expected a repeat of the frenetic seduction scene at the beach hotel – but there was nothing.

As the time passed and he continued to talk animatedly to her as if she were a good friend, she began to wonder if she had imagined everything. And yet he had asked her if she wanted to stay in a hotel. Surely that could mean only one thing? Maybe she was not beautiful enough for him this evening in her crumpled dress. Maybe he had met someone else and this dinner was to let her down lightly. Maybe she had delayed too long and he had tired of the idea of her. She had been determined never to have an affair with him; now, contrarily, she felt acute disappointment at the thought that nothing would happen. He did not hurry his food, as one might have expected an eager lover to do, but lingered over each mouthful. Even when the meal was finished, he did not ask for a bill, but ordered cognac and slowly, oh so slowly, he drank it. It was past two before they left the restaurant and made their way back to the house.

Even at that time in the morning the ritual of the swinging gates was repeated. This time, Jane spied a very old man, bent almost double as he bowed low to them. In the hall the servants waited, taking their coats, opening doors for them. She found these silent figures everywhere disconcerting.

'When on earth do they go to bed?' she asked in a whisper.

'Why, when I do, of course.'

'But that poor old man outside, he should be retired, or at least in bed hours ago.'

'If I did not use Giovanni he would die: if I suggested he had an early night he would think that I did not like the way he worked. I am his life, my darling, don't you understand?'

'No, I don't – it's feudal.'

'Yes, it is. So feudal that it makes my responsibilities, my expenses, enormous. But why do we always end up discussing servants?' He looked pained.

'It's a subject that fascinates me.'

'Reserve some of the fascination for me, will you?' He smiled as he crossed the room and poured them each a brandy. She did not want a drink: her nervous anticipation had reached a peak where she felt she would scream at him if he did not touch her soon, kiss her, anything . . .

'Oh no!' she wailed.

'What is the matter, my darling?'

'My handbag, I left it in the restaurant.'

'It will be perfectly safe, don't upset yourself. I'll send one of the men first thing in the morning to collect it for you.' She gulped nervously at her drink. 'Darling, what is the matter? It will be returned.' He smiled at her, amused by her agitation. She was in despair: inside the bag was the last of the marijuana she had had from Tom. If she had not fooled Alistair with her faked ecstasy, she was hardly likely to fool someone like Roberto. Why couldn't she just be honest with him?

Having put on the same Mahler record he had played at dinner the other evening, Roberto came and sat opposite her, not beside her as she would have liked. He sat in his chair, his glass in his hand and stared at her with that deep, dark, penetrating stare which, although it frightened her, excited her too. She sat transfixed as she felt his gaze wander over her body, resting for a moment on her breasts, then moving on down her body. She wished he would speak, for she could think of nothing to say.

'Darling Jane, you're so tense, what is the matter?'

'It's the way you stare at me, I don't like it.'

'I'm sorry. I am enjoying so much looking at you. I've waited: it would be wrong to rush things now. I told you, I enjoy anticipation. Take your shoes off, lie back and relax, darling.' His beautiful voice did not soothe her as she lay back on the couch, feeling as stiff as a board.

'It's no good.' She swung her feet to the floor and looked at him with desperation in her eyes. 'Roberto, I . . .' She stopped, blushing, and hating as always that telltale colouring of her face. He looked at her enquiringly. 'Roberto, have you by any chance . . . have you got any dope?' she said in a rush, in a tight, little voice, her blush deepening.

'Did I hear correctly, Contessa? Dope?'

'Yes.' The redness deepened.

'What for?'

'It's nice, of course.'

'I'm aware it's nice. No, it was something in your voice, the way you asked, it was strange.' He crossed the room and sat, at last, beside her. He took her hand, but she could not look at him. 'Yes, I've some grass, but I would like to know first why you want it so desperately.'

'I just like it.'

'That's not the only reason.'

'It helps me.'

'Helps you what?' Stubbornly she sat silent. Putting his hand under her chin, Roberto forced her to look at him. 'Helps you what?'

'I don't want to tell you. Can't you just give it to me?'

'No, darling, I want to know. I don't like this air of desperation about you. Tell me. I insist.'

'Well, if you must know. It helps me make love.'

'But darling, we need nothing, especially tonight.'

'You don't understand. I can't make love unless I'm high.'

'Jane, darling?' he said, concerned as he saw tears begin to gather in her eyes. 'My darling, don't upset yourself.'

'It's true,' she sniffed. 'I just can't, not without dope in some shape or form. And I don't want to deceive you by pretending.'

'Dearest, you could not deceive me. Don't you realize I already understand every mood you have? How could you deceive me in our bed?'

'It's the only other way. I don't want to spoil your pleasure so I would have to pretend. You see, I like the beginning and the end, it's the important bit in the middle that leaves me cold.' She smiled a lopsided smile.

'Darling, it's all important, every moment. I will show you what it is like to be really made love to: you won't need anything with me.' As he spoke he began gently to kiss her face, her neck, nibbled her ear. She lay back against the cushions as his hands moved over her. He bent and through the silk of her stockings she felt his soft mouth as he began to kiss her feet, her ankles. She felt his hands search for the softness of the inside of her thigh, involuntarily she arched her back. 'Come, my love,' he said and, sweeping her into his arms as if she were a child, carried her from the room and up the stairs.

They entered a different bedroom. In the centre of the room stood a large, gilded four-poster bed; enormous candles lit the room but their light did not penetrate to the corners. He laid her, gently, on the bed. Looking up, she saw that the canopy of the bed was a huge mirror and she lay watching fascinated as with grace and expertise he began to undress her. With an exquisite slowness he peeled her stockings from her. With care he removed her dress. He paused, admiring her in her black silk lingerie, all the time telling her how beautiful she was to him. He uncovered her full breasts: she would have loved him to touch them, caress them, but instead he feasted his eyes on them. The slowness of his movements, the deliberation, his sensual expression, the low, sexual tone of his voice, heightened all her emotions. She felt no shame, only total abandonment to him. Never taking his eyes from her he began to undress himself, pausing frequently to gaze at her with naked longing in his eyes, talking gently to her. Naked he knelt beside her; languidly she raised her hand to caress his fine muscular body. Still he knelt, quietly talking to her, telling her of his joy in her, of the pleasures of the night ahead, of what he was going to do to her, and what she would do for him. At the sound of his relentless voice, the husky sexuality of it, her desire for him became a desperate need. She began to rock her head from side to side, her body began to writhe rhythmically. 'Please, darling. Please,' she heard herself plead. His answer was to touch her gently. The relentless whispering continued, gently his lips brushed her breast, first his fingers sought her, then his mouth and her body shook uncontrollably as he brought her to a climax. She sank back on the pillows. He knelt above her and laughed.

'Don't!' she yelled, hiding her head in the pillows.

'Such a sensuous little English girl. Does she still need her dope to enjoy me?' He continued to laugh with delight.

'Roberto, don't look at me. I feel so ashamed!'

'Ashamed? What on earth for?'

'You hardly touched me and look what happened. How is that possible?'

'Many things are possible, my darling, many things.' He bore down upon her and kissed her with a hard passion, his lips bruising her mouth in their intensity. As his hands, his lips, his tongue ranged over her body, searching out the secrets of her flesh, she was begging him to enter her and take her. She screamed with her longing, and then he was driving himself into her.

She was to learn so much that night. Not only that such lovemaking existed, but also that she could come again and again, as if her body was an instrument he could control at will. She found that as she climaxed so she wanted more of him, that overnight she had become insatiable in her need of this man and his body. She learned so many variations, each appearing more enjoyable than the one before. He taught her that there was no shame in love, if both enjoyed what they did to each other, then there was no sin, no disgust, only pleasure. She learned to let him do whatever he wanted to her for what he wanted she wanted, and she experienced total possession. She had not known that her body could feel like this, and had never known what wantonness was within her. And for the first time she met the unselfishness of a man who desired only her pleasure and delayed his own until she felt sure she was almost dead from the passion of the night.

She awoke to his voice and his gentle kiss. He stood beside the rumpled bed, freshly bathed and shaved, in an elegant silk robe. Beside him was a tray of coffee and croissants.

'Breakfast, my love?'

'I don't need food.' She smiled at him, contented as a cat, as she lazily stretched against the fine lawn pillows trimmed with lace.

He laughed. 'So, do you think I cured you?'

'Oh, Roberto, you were . . . I had no idea what love could be like.'

'I told you you were pure. You see, I knew that body had never known real love. Had never been truly awoken. We make good love together. Now you will never want to leave me, will you?'

'Never. I couldn't anyway, it would never be like that with anyone else, never, never. You may live to regret last night – I shall always be creeping into your bed now.' She laughed with delight at how bold she felt.

They drank their coffee and suddenly she found she was ravenous. They ate the plateful of croissants and then rang for more. She bathed, a long, luxurious bath, the water full of sweet-smelling oils, and he sat beside the bath and talked and talked; and he insisted on washing her, and drying her, and powdering her. He brushed her hair, he dressed her in a negligee of cream silk, handmade lace cascading around its neck and hem.

'There, my first present to you.'

'It's so lovely, Roberto, when did you buy it?'

'Yesterday.'

They returned to the bedroom. The bed had been made with fresh sheets.

'Oh, my God, look! Someone's made the bed. Crikey, those sheets, what will people think? How embarrassing!'

'Not at all. My laundress will be very happy for me. There is no shame in lovemaking in this country, my darling, only joy. You must get used to that.'

They lingered all day in the room, making love, talking, laughing.

'Don't you have work to do?' she asked guiltily.

'No.' He smiled.

'But I thought you had been called away on important business.'

'No.' He burst out laughing. 'That was a little lie. I thought if I went away suddenly, it might help you make your mind up faster.'

'Roberto, that's deceitful!'

'Of course, but then about the only sensible platitude in your language is that "all is fair in love and war".'

They bathed and dressed; Jane found her clothes neatly pressed and hanging in his dressing room. Roberto took her out to dinner. He took her to Frascati to drink the wine, and then they returned to the giant, mirror-canopied bed which seemed to be becoming the centre of her world.

For five days the routine was the same. She was satiated with love and she had never looked more beautiful or felt more relaxed and content.

On the sixth day he asked her to live with him. And on the sixth day they had their first row.

7

'So, will you come and live with me?'

Jane looked up, startled, from her coffee cup, at Roberto lying languidly at the foot of the bed, casually lighting his cigarette. His tone of voice seemed to her the same as if he had asked her where she would care to dine.

'The way you ask me makes me think that my reply is about as important to you as if you had asked me if I prefer tea or coffee,' she replied sharply. It was Roberto's turn to look in surprise at Jane, reclining against the pillows, her long, dark hair spread over their silky smoothness, apparently enjoying her morning coffee, her skin glowing with that special sheen of a woman well loved.

'I beg your pardon?'

'You heard!' she snapped.

'I heard, I mean I don't understand the sharpness in your tone.'

'It's a very big question you are asking me, one that could alter my life, and you lie there as if you were totally unconcerned what my answer might be. Or are you so conceited that you have taken my saying yes as a foregone conclusion?'

'Jane, what has got into you? You're very grumpy this morning.' He was laughing as he leaned across the bed to take her hand. Angrily she brushed his hand away. 'Darling, please.' He looked perplexed. 'Of course it is a big question, for both of us. And it is one that I do not ask lightly.'

'Then why sound so offhand? It's my life we're talking about.'

'My life, too.'

'It's a bigger step for me than for you. I can say goodbye to my reputation.'

'My love, I am aware of that, but you will have my protection. My friends will understand. What is more natural than that two people in love should want to be together all the time?'

'What about your family?'

'They would think it perfectly normal that I should take . . . that I should live with the woman I love.'

'Mistress. You wanted to say "mistress".'

'Yes, my mistress. It is an old-fashioned word, but yes, that is what you would be. I see no shame in it for you.'

'What we lack is a word for you, really, isn't it? Pity I'm not filthy rich – then you could be my gigolo, and we'd be quits.'

'Darling, don't sound so bitter. I would offer you more if I could.'

'Offer me what? Marriage? Hardly.' She laughed but it was a short and hard sound.

'Don't you think that if I could marry you, I would?'

'I can get a divorce,' Jane said quickly.

Roberto was silent.

Jane did not know what devil was working in her. Part of her was ecstatic that he had asked her and the other part of her was a tumult of anger that he should dare. She knew full well that had he asked her to marry him, she would have refused. She knew she could not face again the social problems such a marriage would cause. So why was she making such a fuss, why was she needling him like this? 'It's not just that I would be a divorced woman in a Catholic country, is it?' Still Roberto did not reply. 'Is it?' she persisted.

'No.'

'What is it then?' He did not answer. 'It's because I'm a peasant, isn't it, not good enough for your snooty family, is that it? I wish you would speak to me,' she said, her voice sharp with anger.

'Jane, that is a silly thing to say. You of all people should know that it is not possible. Good God, girl, there are families in my society who will not entertain people in their houses who are not in the Almanach de Gotha. Can you imagine what those people would do to you? It wouldn't stop with us: they wouldn't accept our children either. Could you live with that? Compared to my society, your English one is liberated.'

'And of course you are in the Almanach de Gotha,' she sneered.

'Jane, don't be perverse. Please try and understand my position. If I could change things for you, I would, but I can't. I have my family to consider, too, my mother – it would kill her.'

'Isn't her son's happiness important to her?'

'She belongs to a different generation. Duty is of more importance to her than happiness.'

'Christ, it's archaic! It makes me so angry. What is so wrong with me? I'm not a bad person, a thief, a bitch. I just want to love you, and to do that I have to accept that I'm second-class. Well, I'm not and I won't accept it.'

'Darling, everything you say is true. But we cannot change things. This society would destroy us.'

'It's such dreadful hypocrisy – they will accept me if you're screwing me, but not if you marry me.'

'Jane, Jane, this language does not become you.' They sat on the bed, glaring angrily at each other. 'I'm sorry to hurt you, Jane. I thought you understood, after your experiences. I would never have asked you if I had thought to hurt you so. I cannot marry you, I am sorry, there is no argument to pursue. But as my mistress you will be accepted in the circles I move in. I can offer you my protection, which is immense, and my love for you, which goes without saying.'

'And what about me when you get married?'

'I have no thoughts of marriage.'

'No, but in the future when they wheel out that little schoolgirl for you. What about me then?'

'What schoolgirl, what are you talking about?'

'That kid that your family has already decided you will marry, when you're fifty.'

'Darling, where do you get these ideas from? There is no one chosen for me, I promise you.' He almost laughed at her notions.

'It's not funny. You could desert me.'

'Of course. And you could desert me, it goes both ways. Look, darling, I'm not offering you an affair that will be over by Christmas. I'm offering you a life with me as my companion until the day we no longer make each other happy. And when that day comes, I promise to look after you until you meet someone else, or all your life if necessary. I cannot be fairer than that, can I?'

'Marvellous. A pension plan. Is it index-linked?'

'Jane, you are making me angry.'

'You've already made me angry!' An oppressive silence descended on them. 'Mistresses? What about all your mistresses?'

'I wouldn't have any.'

'Oh no?' she said, the disbelief evident in her voice.

'No, I would not do that to you. I am an honourable man. If I say I will not, you will believe that I won't,' he shouted at her.

'It's going to cost you dear, moving that lot out of your various houses, pensioning them off.'

'Jane, you must believe me, I have slept with hundreds of women. I have always had women available to me, but I have never lived with one of them. Not as I'm inviting you. If you don't want to come and live with me, share my life, then just say so, but don't create all this unpleasantness about us. Jane, I love you.'

'It's easy to say.'

'At least I say it. You haven't once told me you love me,' he shouted back. 'Do you love me?' She sat silently. 'Jane, I asked you a question. Do you love me? Answer me! I demand to know.' He was shouting again.

'No, I don't love you, so there,' she said in a singsong voice like a petulant child.

'I don't believe you. We could never have what we do without love.'

'You use the word so easily – probably a lot of practice with it. But for me, it's a bloody big word in my vocabulary.'

'I am amazed it is even included in your somewhat limited vocabulary.'

'I haven't had your advantages in life, so you needn't start sneering at me.' She wanted to cry. She had awoken so happy and now she felt wretched. But like someone on a helter-skelter, she felt she could not stop, now they had started.

'I apologize, that was low and unforgivable of me. Please, Jane, forgive me? Please?' He put out his hand and lifted hers to his mouth and kissed it. She looked at him, tears overflowing her eyes. 'Oh, my darling, this is so wicked of us, we have such happiness and we begin to destroy it.' He kissed her full on the mouth and she responded to his touch. 'Do you really not love me?'

'Roberto, we have just made friends, don't start again.'

'But if you don't, why can't you lie? Why do you have to hurt me?'

'We have gone too deep for lies.'

'I can't believe you don't love me, I just can't. If it's true, what do I have to do to make you love me? I will, you know, I will make you love me.'

'You can't make someone love you. It happens or it doesn't.'

'We have everything. What is stopping you acknowledging it? I want to know,' he persisted.

'I would rather not say.'

'I insist. Jane, tell me, now.'

'I love my husband. I told you right at the beginning, nothing is going to change that. I always knew I could only ever love one man. What I have for you is nearly that, but not quite.'

'You talk rubbish, utter rubbish.' He looked as if he wanted to shake her with exasperation.

'I didn't want to tell you: you made me.'

'You are cruel, Jane. You have your little fantasy and you inflict it on me. And you risk destroying what we have with your stupid lie.'

'It's not a lie. I love him,' she shouted defiantly. Roberto swung round and hit her hard across the face, then he twisted her long hair around his hand and shook her.

'You little bitch! How dare you talk of loving him in front of me when I give you so much and he has given you so little. The bastard couldn't even make you happy in bed.'

'That wasn't his fault, it was mine,' she shrieked back at him. 'And don't you hit me, don't you ever dare hit me again!'

'Listen, you stupid little fool. You're in love with a memory, don't you understand? A memory, that's all it is, memory of your first love – we all have that sort of memories but we don't mistake them for love.' He was screaming and she was crying now, and still he continued. 'You cling to it from fear. You're afraid of life! That's why you took so long to come to me. But don't for one minute think that what you feel is love, it isn't. It's me you love, me, you understand.' He threw her back across the bed.

He paced agitatedly about the room as she lay on the bed sobbing. His anger was a fierce force in the room. Why had he asked her? she thought. Everything was spoiled now, it would never be the same again. She felt the bed give as he came and sat beside her.

'Jane, I'm sorry. I should not have hit you. I lost my temper because I am so afraid of losing you. You think I'm a playboy, that I'm toying with you, that I'm not serious about you. If only you could understand, my darling, how much I need you, how desperate I have been for a love like this. And now I've probably lost you.'

Blindly, through her tears, she held up her arms to him. 'Roberto, I don't want to fight. Of course I want to live with you, I certainly can't live without you now. I was being oversensitive. You're right, marriage would be impossible: I know I couldn't go through the sort of rejection Alistair's mother and friends inflicted on me, ever again. I know you're trying to protect me, I really do. Forgive me.'

They made tender love and when they later lay on the bed, watching their reflections in the mirror, Roberto turned to her.

'I will make you love me,' he whispered. 'That's a promise.'

'Yes, darling.' She smiled.

'We shall live as if we were married but, with us, when there's no love left, we shall separate with respect, dignity, no recriminations and friendship.'

'Maybe we shall never separate?'

'True. In that case, my love, I shall marry you when I'm seventy and to hell with all of them.' He laughed.

They lingered on in Rome. The city was empty of people he knew, all his friends had gone to the mountains or the sea to get away from the heat of the city and so Rome was left to them and the tourists. They joined the throngs of sightseers and he showed her the city he loved. He knew of little, out-of-the-way churches which the tourists never found. And tiny squares with bubbling fountains where the tourists never wished. He showered gifts upon her and took her to small restaurants where they would sit for hours, talking. She began to think that life with him would be a joy. Only that loveless child of years ago who still dwelled within her stubbornly prevented her acknowledging that she loved him. But those who saw them together – holding hands, devouring each other with their eyes, unashamed of their blatant, physical need for each other – knew that she did.

Finally and reluctantly they returned to the coast. A party had been arranged at the castle, and it would have been unthinkable to cancel it. Late one afternoon they drove up to Honor's villa.

'So here you are! What on earth was there in Rome to keep you two in that dreadful heat?' she teased them fondly. Jane clung to Roberto's arm.

'We fell in love, Honor,' he said simply, and grinned as sheepishly as any callow youth.

'Darlings, how marvellous.' Honor clapped her hands excitedly. 'It's a champagne occasion, isn't it?' She called to Guido to bring champagne. 'Now, tell me all.'

'I've come back to pack, that's if you don't mind, Honor. I'm moving in with Roberto.'

'Why on earth should I mind? At last you've taken my advice.'

'I want her to move immediately before she has a chance to change her mind,' Roberto explained.

'Is she likely to?'

'If you knew the job I had persuading her.'

'She's always had a streak of obstinacy,' Honor said with a husky laugh.

'So I learned. And pride.'

'Oh, dreadful pride, I thought it would be the ruination of her,' Honor merrily retorted.

'Would you two mind not talking about me as if I wasn't in the room?' Jane grinned. 'Any mail for me, Honor?'

'On my bureau.'

While the two friends chatted, Jane collected her mail. Apart from a letter from the bank there were three letters for her. Recognizing James's childish writing she tore that one open first, and shrieked with joy as she read it. 'Oh, Roberto, Honor, it's from James, he wants to come and visit. I haven't seen him for months. He's always so shy and awkward with me, I never dreamed he'd actually ask to come and see me. All I ever get are his funny, stilted little letters. Roberto, can he come?'

'Of course, my darling, but he is the only male from your past I'll welcome.' The significance of his remark was not lost on Honor, who glanced sharply from one to the other.

'Oh, how sad!' said Jane, reading her second letter.

'What's sad?' Honor asked inquisitively.

'It's from May, do you remember her, Honor? My lovely maid from Respryn who came to London with me? She got married but it's broken up. She's back at Respryn and she's unhappy there – she says it's not the same without me and is there any chance of a job with me? I wish I could help her.'

'Write back and ask her if she minds working all round the world.'

'Roberto?'

'Darling, you'll need a personal maid, what better than to have an English one? Mind you, she'll have to be good.'

'Oh, she's the best. But Roberto, I can't afford her.'

'I'm not asking you to, I'll pay her, you silly girl.'

'Roberto!' She jumped across the room and flung her arms about him. 'She's so special to me, Roberto, thank you so much. Gracious, how much happier can I get?'

Honor and Roberto smiled indulgently as she ripped open her last letter. As she read it, the smile disappeared from her face to be replaced by a heavy frown.

'I don't believe it,' she said, horrified, sitting down heavily, her face white. 'The bastard!'

'Jane, what is it?' Honor rushed to her side.

'It's from my lawyer. Alistair is suing me for divorce and he's named Roberto as co-respondent. But the date –' She scanned the letter for the date. 'This is impossible, it's dated a couple of days after I left for Rome.

How did he know, how did he find out? He lied, he said I could sue him. I told him there was no one in my life: how could he have known? How could he do this to me?'

'You told him when?' Roberto asked sharply.

'The day I left for Rome,' Jane said, unthinkingly.

'So you spoke to your husband that day?'

'Yes, Roberto.'

'I see,' Roberto said, his face closing with anger.

'No, Roberto, you don't see. It wasn't like that. I promise you it made no difference.'

'What are you two talking about? So many people are here, he probably found out from someone who had seen you two together.'

'It's unimportant how he found out. That does not concern me. I talk of lies and deceptions, Honor, that's what concerns me.' He looked coldly at Jane.

'Roberto?' Jane looked at him with anguish.

'If you are coming, Jane, I suggest you pack quickly. I have much to do at home,' he said suddenly, and Jane with relief excused herself and went to pack some more clothes, leaving Honor apologizing for her nephew. When Jane returned, she crossed the room to Roberto and kissed him on the cheek.

'I'm sorry, darling, to cause you these problems.'

'I do not mind being named as co-respondent. No, Jane, that's not the problem we have to resolve,' he said ominously.

They left Honor still admonishing them not to let anything spoil their happiness and warning Jane to contact her lawyer immediately. She was still calling to them as the car began to spin down the drive. It was a silent drive back to the castle. Roberto was hunched over the steering wheel, a cold and angry expression on his face. As usual he drove far too fast but Jane was too afraid of his anger to say anything. She should have told him about Alistair's call before. It was so easy to be wise now, but at the time, silence had seemed the best policy.

Roberto must have warned the servants that she was coming, for a set of rooms had been prepared for her. Of all the bedrooms she had occupied in her life, this was by far the most beautiful. She sat at her dressing table gazing through the large windows to the valley and watched the sun setting behind the mountains. It was a breathtaking view. She wandered about the room admiring the pictures, amounting to a fortune, which hung on the walls. How strange her life was! Sitting in this beautiful room she could hardly remember the tiny bedroom of her childhood. To have come from that life to all of this was like some fairy story. In England the memories of her previous life had never left her: always she had remembered her past, it had been a strong part of her present. But here in this foreign land, in this castle, with Roberto by her side, it was no longer part of her. The past was the dream world, not the present, and when she looked back at the girl she had been, she saw someone else.

8

'Do you like your rooms?'

Jane swung around from her dressing table, startled by his voice, to see Roberto standing in a doorway which was so cleverly concealed in the massive wall tapestry that she had not noticed it. The maid who had been tidying her clothes bobbed to Roberto and silently left the room.

'I didn't hear you come in, you made me jump.' She laughed nervously. After the silent drive, she had not seen him until now, a full four hours later. His absence had made her nervous, for he usually came, drink in hand, and talked to her while she had her evening bath. It had become a ritual with them, until tonight, when she had waited in vain for him. 'I missed you,' she said simply.

'I had much to attend to.' His words reassured her: perhaps it was not anger, after all, which had kept him away from her.

'So do you like your rooms?'

'Darling, they are superb. I spent ages just gazing at that wonderful view and watching the sun set. They're perfect, I've never lived in such style.' Again the nervous laugh. 'I mean, my dressing room and bathroom, they're so luxurious, and this room, just look at it, it's big enough to have a ball in . . .' She heard herself prattling on. 'Is that really a Gauguin over there?'

'Yes, of course.'

'It's lovely,' she said lamely, her nervousness making conversation difficult. He crossed to her dressing table and opened her small jewel box.

'Who gave you these?'

'Honor gave me the pearls, the rest were presents from my husband.'

'I would prefer it if you did not refer to that man as your husband. He does not deserve the title.' He scattered the jewellery on the dressing-table top. 'Apart from Honor's gift, I would prefer it if you did not wear any of this, do you understand?' He gestured, dismissively, at her small collection of jewellery. She nodded, though she did not understand. 'I will buy you whatever jewellery you need. I don't want you to wear another man's gifts in my sight.' The coldness in his voice was mirrored in his expression. 'And while I'm on the subject, I do not want you to have any contact with this man, except through your lawyer. Should he telephone, or write, I wish to be informed. I have left instructions with my staff and I expect you to obey my wishes also. It is an order, Jane.'

'But —'

'There are no buts. You accept these conditions, or you pack and return to your aunt.'

'Darling, please don't be so angry with me. I know I was wrong, that I should have told you about Alistair phoning. I was going to, really. I would have, honestly, I just forgot . . . you see how unimportant it was to me, I forgot.' Even as she spoke, she had a chilling feeling that he knew she lied.

'Sadly, dear Jane, we shall never know if you would have told me. At least one thing we do know for sure, you lied to me at the station. I shall take time to forget that lie.' She could not meet his eyes but instead intently studied her hands. She had apologized but she refused to beg. The silence between them was oppressive.

'Is your maid adequate for you until your own arrives from England?' She was relieved not only by the change of subject but also by the change in his tone.

'She's fine, thank you. Mind you, we had a bit of a job understanding each other — we managed finally with mime and drawings.' Her laugh sounded more natural this time.

'You must learn my language.'

'Yes, I must. I know a few words already but I would like to speak it properly.'

'I shall find you a tutor.'

'Books or Linguaphone will do fine. I don't think I would like a tutor, someone actually hearing my ghastly mistakes.'

'Jane, you're a funny creature. So sophisticated in some ways and still a child in others.' Lovingly he caressed her hair. It was going to be all right, she told herself. He crossed the room into the dressing room, threw open the large mahogany wardrobes, lined with white silk, and began to study her clothes, which looked so few in the cavernous interior. 'We shall have such fun filling these cupboards,' he announced. His cold mood seemed to have disappeared completely. Taking her by the hand, he led her to the small sitting room where they had sat the first night she had dined here. It was becoming apparent to her that their quarters were in one wing of the castle, a house within a house, like Respryn except that everything was larger and grander. Over dinner they began to talk of the party to be held the following day.

'What should I do about the party?'

'Do? Darling, what do you mean?'

'I'd like to help, and I'm good at organizing things – food, flowers, that sort of thing.'

'Good heavens, that won't be necessary. The staff know exactly what has to be done. You needn't worry about such matters.'

'But the household, I must be able to help manage the household?'

'I wouldn't hear of such a thing. My darling – worrying about such mundane matters. My staff run all my homes expertly, they would be horrified if you wanted to help.' He looked equally shocked at the notion.

'But what on earth shall I do all day?'

'Be beautiful, for me.'

'You say the loveliest things, Roberto, but I can't spend my life titivating – I'd go bonkers again.'

'Again?' he enquired sharply. Jane felt herself blushing, and began to study her hands. 'You know, darling Jane, it's a good job you have hands to stare at so intently each time you are confused.' She looked up to see him smiling fondly at her. 'So what is this? Something else you haven't told me?'

'Only because I feel ashamed – no other reason.'

'Why be ashamed? I presume you were ill? What is there in illness to be ashamed of?'

'I suppose it's a hangover from my childhood – mental illness must never be discussed, must be hushed up, a slur on the family, that sort of thing.'

'Poor Jane, was it dreadful?'

'Yes, it was . . .' Almost with relief she began to tell him of the horror that had engulfed her, swept her away with it as if on a rip tide.

'And yet you still say you love this man?'

Again the long studying of her hands. 'Yes.'

'Such strange creatures, women,' was all he said.

'Anyhow' – she shook her head, as if shaking the conversation away – 'what am I to do all day?'

'As I have said, you'll devote yourself to beauty.'

'All day? It can't take all day!'

'That is all my mother ever did, that and a little charity work.'

'I don't think mistresses would be welcome as charity workers in Italy,' she said lightly. 'I shall have to find a hobby. Painting, I liked painting at school: that would be fun.'

'And your Italian. You will be so busy at this rate you won't have time for me,' he teased.

After dinner, they lingered over their cognacs, and took a last walk on the terrace. When Roberto suggested it was time for bed, she agreed eagerly. In her room he kissed her cheek, and then passed through the concealed door in the tapestry. Quickly she prepared for bed. She sat in the vast four-poster and waited. She read for a while, but he did not come. Her body began to ache for him. As she remembered their nights in Rome, she became restless. The book did not interest her; she kept rereading the same page. She fell asleep, propped up against the pillows, the book open in her hand, the light making an oasis of the bed in the large darkened room.

She awoke with a start. Daylight was streaming into the room and he stood by her bed, an old woman beside him with a breakfast tray.

'Good morning, Jane. Your breakfast is here.'

'But I hate breakfast in bed.'

'You liked it in Rome.'

'That was different, you were with me.'

'I have work to do, I have been up since six and now it is nine. Rome was a holiday for me.'

'Then I shall get up at six, too.'

'For heaven's sake, you will not! A lady should breakfast in her room.'

'I don't want to. I hate eating in bed.'

'Then you must get used to it, it's not seemly that you should breakfast with me.'

'You are being stuffy, Roberto,' she cajoled him.

'No. I am teaching you how you will behave in my household,' he replied carefully and yet Jane heard a sternness in his voice which worried her.

'You did not sleep with me, last night,' she complained.

'No. Now we lead a new life. You have your suite of rooms, I mine. When I want you, I will come to you. Last night I did not want you,' he said coldly and Jane felt her smile freeze on her face. 'So,' he continued as if he did not notice her expression, 'so, the party is tonight. As I told you there is nothing for you to worry yourself with. I shall be unable to see you until tonight, I have business to attend to. I apologize, but it is unavoidable.' Now his tone of voice was pleasant again and he kissed her gently and left.

As she drank her tea, she was perplexed. He seemed to switch from mood to mood in the space of a sentence: one minute gentle with her, the next with that dreadful coldness in his voice which confused and frightened her.

Jane spent the day wandering aimlessly about the castle. The staff scurried busily about, each knowing exactly what they were to do. Even her offer to help with the flowers was curtly refused by an abrupt and efficient young woman. She was aware that wherever she walked, busy as they were, the servants stole sly glances at her and once or twice she was certain she heard a muffled giggle. Irritated by their staring and by her own uselessness, she strolled out of the castle and down the hill to the village. From behind windows and half-open doors she was again aware of the sly glances, the whispering, certain now that she heard giggling as she walked past. She must curb her irritation and the feeling of anger that was welling up in her. This was not England in the early seventies, this was Italy, and an Italy which time seemed to have passed by. She could not expect understanding from these people: to them she was a kept woman. If she were to win any respect from them, then she would have to behave with circumspection and dignity, not anger.

The heat was intolerable and she had not thought to wear a hat. As the midday sun beat down on her she felt dizzy and exhausted. Listlessly she reclimbed the steep slope to the castle and with some difficulty found her way to her room. She supposed it was lunchtime but where a meal would be served she did not know, and had not the energy to find out. Instead she lay on her bed trying to cool herself and realized that, if she were to survive here, she would have to find something to do with herself. Otherwise this inactivity would drive her mad. She would have to campaign to be allowed to do something about the running of the house, or else she feared she would always feel like a guest in it. She had never been able to understand women who took hours to have a bath: she could not imagine what took them so long.

Her walk and her worries had tired her and she slept fitfully, to be woken by the smiling maid waiting to help her to dress for the party.

As the party progressed, she forgot her daytime fears. Roberto was as charming and attentive as he had been on that first night when they had met. He never left her side, held her hand, caressed her hair, her cheek, proudly introduced her to his friends. At about one in the morning he insisted she was tired and must go to bed; she longed to stay but he was adamant and escorted her to her room and kissed her cheek as he said goodnight. She lay in the dark listening to the distant music, longing to be part of it, perplexed that he had made her leave when she was obviously enjoying herself. She strained her ears, hoping to hear his footsteps returning to her. The dawn was breaking, music still filtering into her room when she finally fell into an exhausted and restless sleep.

The days began to fall into a lonely pattern. She found it surprisingly easy to take hours over her bath. She wrote endless letters – to James, to Zoe and Sandra, to Honor. She devoured books but without enjoyment, and she would stare for hours out of her window at the view without really seeing it. She felt the dreadful lurching sensation of misery returning.

They went to parties and to dinners, or would dine at home, and wherever they were he was charming and affectionate to her. Each night she was certain that his mood had passed and each night she waited in vain, peering through the darkness at the little door in the tapestry, praying for it to open, cursing it for always being closed. One night she tried to open the door but found that there was no handle, it was a secret door with a secret mechanism. She ran her fingers over the tapestry, trying to find the hidden lock. In a frenzy of frustration she beat on the door, hoping he would hear her, not knowing if he was on the other side, or even where it led, or even where his rooms were. Her sobs rang around the empty room and she cried herself to sleep, huddled by the little door. He found her there in the morning and gently picked her up and carried her to her bed, but said nothing about it, merely talking of the weather and his plans for the day.

Inside she was screaming with the pain of his rejection but she was beginning to feel a terrible rage, too. She had thrown herself on his protection, the protection he had promised her. She began to withdraw into herself and, as one week passed into another, began to fear that she was in danger of another mental breakdown. All the signs were there. She had to force herself to eat, force herself to concentrate, force herself to smile, to talk to people, wanting only to be alone, to hide away. She was certain that she was dying inside. And then he would smile at her across the room, that secret smile of lovers, and hope would surge within her that the nightmare was over. She began to hate her hope, wished it would evaporate, and finally let despair take over completely, for perhaps desperation would force her to decide what to do.

One evening, two weeks after she had moved in with him, after a quiet and pleasant dinner with him, he had, as usual, left her, and she sat in front of her dressing table absent-mindedly brushing her hair. She began to remember how peaceful it had been in the hospital – one whole year of peace and quiet, no worries, no responsibilities – everyone had been so kind to her then. Why couldn't she now shut out of her mind anything that upset her, as she had previously made Alistair's face disappear? If she was honest, it had been quite a happy time, really . . . The hairbrush clattered onto the dressing table. With horror she stared at her reflection. Christ! She was beginning to think of the oblivion of her breakdown with affection. She must leave, she must get right away from him. It was dangerous for her here. She did not understand this game he played. Whatever his motives, it was a cruel game. She had had enough, more than any soul should be expected to endure. With rising panic she began to suspect that he was attempting to destroy her. This was no innocent play, this was retribution. Fighting the hysteria welling within her, she wrenched one of her cases from the wardrobe and began to throw her clothes into it. She would go to Honor, first thing in the morning . . . thank God for Honor. Sobbing, she cleared the bottles from her dressing table.

'And what is my little one doing?' The bottle of perfume clattered from her hands onto the floor; the stopper rolled under the table and the liquid began to make a rivulet across the marble floor, the large room filling with its scent. 'I shall have to buy you another one,' he said, smiling gently at her.

'Roberto,' she sobbed. 'I don't want to leave you.'

'Then don't, my darling.' He swept her into his arms and carried her to the bed, where she clung to him with all the desperation of her near madness. He began to make love to her and time and again he brought her to a screaming climax. The relief of her body and mind reduced her to a frenzy of tears.

They lay exhausted in each other's arms. 'Why, Roberto?'

'I wanted to make you hate me.'

'Oh, Roberto! I could never hate you. You frightened and saddened me, but to hate you . . . never!'

'But I thought if you hated me you would leave.'

'But why? Do you want me to go?' Icicles of fear tingled through her.

'God help me, no.'

'Then why did you do this to me, to us?'

'Each morning I would stand by this bed determined to tell you to go, to get out of my life. And you would open your beautiful eyes and smile at me and I was lost . . . And then, each night I would pace the floor fighting with myself not to come to you, to take and possess you, and each night I resolved again to tell you to go and then each morning . . . the same helpless ritual. I told you weeks ago you were a witch.' He smiled and, lifting a strand of her hair, kissed it. Jane sat up and looked intently at him.

'Roberto, darling. Please, I don't understand why, when we mean so much to each other, you put me through these two terrible weeks.'

'You lied to me about your reasons for coming to me in Rome.'

'What if I had been honest with you that night? What would have happened? Would you still have wanted me? What else could I have done?'

'But I thought you had come to me. And then to find out that you were running away from your so-called husband . . .' His mouth twisted with bitterness. 'To have to know that I was being used as a means to forget your own unhappiness.'

'But darling, that night I didn't really know what I was thinking. How could I be totally honest with you when I wasn't sure if I was being honest with myself? Like you, at first, I thought that was the reason I had come, but then I began to think differently, I began to realize that in fact he had jolted me into a decision I had wanted to make all along.'

'How can I ever be certain?'

'You have my word.'

'Will you ever know what you did when you lied? But I don't seem to be capable of deciding to stop loving you.' He laughed at her. 'It has been a great shock to me. From the very start I couldn't believe it, I, Roberto Villizano – rake, sophisticate, womanizer, in love! I didn't even recognize it at first. How could I, it had never happened to me before? I thought you were just another conquest, but each time I saw you, I wanted you so desperately that other women ceased to exist. You have made me so vulnerable: that's what fills me with fear, that is why I wanted you to go. I feel as if I am in uncharted seas in my relationship with you.' He sat staring moodily into space, 'And you had the coolness to tell me that you loved him. I wanted to die when you said that, but I wanted to kill him first.'

'But, Roberto, listen to me.' She took his hand in hers. 'Listen, I begin to think it's a different kind of love.'

'You just say these things to make me feel better.'

'No, darling, I don't. I'm being honest with you as best I can. Heavens, Alistair and I were children when we married, mere kids, we grew up together, went through a lot together. I can't just stop loving him, but I begin to see that it isn't the love of a lover. You can't just throw away the past.'

'If only I could be certain. If only . . .' He looked longingly at her. She bent towards him, her bare breasts brushing against his skin. Aroused, he took her in his arms and kissed her with a forceful intensity. As he drove himself into her his great need filled her with such happiness but this time, as she reached her climax and cried with joy as he always made her do, she also cried, 'I love you!'

He wept. This strong, confident man sobbed in her arms and at last, as she held him and consoled him, she believed that she loved him.

'Roberto, I've been such a bloody fool. We nearly lost so much,' she said.

9

Her long lonely days were a thing of the past for she and Roberto were now almost inseparable. If he had business on his vast estate she would go with him, sitting patiently for hours while he talked with his tenants in a patois she could not understand. Just to be near him was happiness enough. She was welcomed by these simple people with a dignified deference. If this woman made their prince happy then she was welcome. Nobody stared at her, or sniggered, when he was with her. Now he lunched with her, took English tea with her. Only breakfast he ate alone. The morning ritual remained unchanged. Each day she was woken by him, the old maid beside him with her breakfast tray, grinning her toothless smile.

Roberto had changed her. She was always conscious of her body now. She cared how she looked, for him. No matter what she was doing, she was aware of herself, aware of her femininity. The more he made love to her, the more she craved from him. She was always ready for him at any time of the day or night.

Sunday was the only day she disliked. She hated the tolling bell that never seemed to cease, the sound dolefully soaring up the valley from the village below. It was not a joyous noise, not like the church bells at home. Its mournful note matched her mood on Sundays, for Roberto would visit his mother that day, and though nothing had ever been said, she knew better than to ask if she could go too. The old princess, well into her eighties, lived across the valley in yet another castle owned by this astonishing family. 'How many castles does one family need?' she had asked him, laughing, one day.

'Too many,' he replied. 'They ruin me, these dreadful stone mistresses.'

If she was lucky, Honor might visit, but that was rare, for Honor disliked travelling so far into the hills, away from her villa and friends. Roberto would not hear of her going to Honor's without him. So

Sundays were a hateful day, but the memory of his treatment of her when she first arrived was too fresh in her mind for her to object strongly. She waited, from ten in the morning until ten at night when he returned, trying to hide her growing resentment. Once or twice he brought some cousins back with him, but always male cousins: her correct assumption was that she was deemed too wicked to meet his female ones. Sometimes she raged inwardly at the injustice but otherwise she was happy and, she reminded herself, it was only one day out of the seven.

When alone she would spend hours exploring the castle, realizing that she had seen only a small part of it. There was none of the cheerful clutter of possessions she was used to at Respryn or Drumloch, where different styles and periods of furniture stood happily side by side, where unimportant and inexpensive objects could be found scattered among the priceless pieces. Here each piece of furniture, each ornament, each sculpture was placed so that its beauty could be seen to perfection. At Respryn, she had felt free to rearrange things, but here there was no question of it, for everything had its place: it would have seemed a sacrilege, she felt, to move anything. Roberto's two houses, despite their differences of style, period and size, were similar. There was a silence about them both which was almost tangible. The servants here moved in the same silent way, like noiseless acolytes, so that sometimes she would jump, thinking that they were ghosts as they flitted past her. Both houses were places of dark shadows, which varied from the deepest black through all the shades of grey and green, so that sometimes she felt she lived in a magic castle under water. It was the shutters and blinds that created this illusion: their gentle movement as they swayed in the breeze, or the sun sneaking through the latticework, made rippling patterns of the shadows. In every room the sun was fought as a fierce enemy of the treasures inside. Both houses echoed. As she explored, her footsteps would make a deafening clatter on the stone or marble. Feeling guilty at breaking the silence of centuries, she would tiptoe or often, to the staff's amusement, could be seen, shoes in hand, as silent as they, wandering through the rooms and galleries. Respryn was like a doll's house compared with this magnificent, castellated, arrogant building.

He had been right: her help was not needed and would probably have been resented by the servants, who went smoothly about their allotted tasks.

She found Roberto's attitude to his staff strange. He never seemed to speak to them, and yet they always knew exactly what he wanted. It would not have been unfair to say that he virtually ignored them, as though they were pieces of furniture. But instead of the smouldering resentment that she expected, she began to notice, with astonishment, that they looked at him with undisguised adoration.

A letter arrived from Alistair.

'Do you want to read it first?' She waved it at him. 'It's probably about James's visit. Nothing more ominous.' She grinned, confident now in their love for each other.

'Read it to me,' he replied with a smile. Within seconds of opening it, she was in tears.

'He won't let James come and stay with us,' she said in disbelief. 'Listen: 'I have spoken to my lawyers, who agree with me that the household in which you are now living is not a suitable one for a child of James's tender years to visit",' she read.

'What?' Roberto stood up, an expression of anger spreading across his face.

'There's more. "Until you get rid of the gigolo with whom you choose to live, I'm afraid, Jane, you can't see James. Sorry about this, but I have to think about the boy, and my lawyers assure me I'm within my rights . . ." Roberto!' She looked at him with an expression of horror, only to see that he was beginning to laugh. 'What's so bloody funny? How dare you laugh when I'm so unhappy?' she stormed at him.

'My darling, forgive me, it's the idea of me as a gigolo – I find it so amusing. But you're right, I should not laugh. This Alistair of yours is a very arrogant young man.' Pulling himself together, he crossed the room and put his arms about her. 'He is wicked, this man, I shall never forgive him the repeated pain he causes you. Come, my little one. We shall consult lawyers, too.'

'It won't do any good. They will probably all say the same thing.'

'It's a dreadful price you are being asked to pay. I would understand if you felt you had to leave me for your son – that I could forgive.'

'I couldn't leave you, Roberto.' Her voice was firm now. 'It would make little difference, he'd find some other excuse to stop me, or rather his bloody old mother would. This is her work, I can smell her in this.'

'He must be a very weak man then, if he allows his mother to rule him so.'

'He's not weak, it's just his mother's so bloody strong. Even the devil would run and hide from that terrifying old hag.' She managed a bitter little laugh, thinking, as she did so, that there did not seem much to choose between Alistair's mother and Roberto's.

'Then he's trying to get you back.'

'Alistair, wanting me back? No, there's no risk of that,' she snorted derisively.

But that day she did not go with Roberto; instead she went to her room, pleading tiredness. It was cruel and unfair, she thought. Was she supposed to believe that Alistair lived like a monk at Respryn, never had girlfriends to stay? Unlikely, unless he had changed out of all recognition. But to have her declared an unfit mother on moral grounds, that was despicable. She knew there was not a court in the land that would allow her to have her son now. Only a year ago he had asked her to return to him, yet now he could do this to her. He wasn't a vindictive sort of person, nor was he a prude; it had to be that old bitch, still warring away in the background against Jane. Still terrified that if her grandson saw too much of his mother, she might contaminate him with what Blanche saw as the obscenity of her background. It might be wicked to hate but, by God, she could not help herself. She thought of the consequence of leaving Roberto, but what for? She knew the answer – a life of loneliness, devoid of love, and, if she were lucky, the chance to see her son once a month. She could not live like that, not again. Perhaps later, when Roberto was more secure in his relationship with her, trusted her again, perhaps then he would let her go alone to spend a few days with her son. It was the only thing she could hope for.

She was depressed for several days and only cheered up with the arrival of May. Roberto shrugged resignedly when she insisted they meet her off the plane rather than send a car. He watched with disbelief as the two women excitedly hugged each other in greeting, tears streaming down both their faces.

'But May's not just a servant, Roberto, she's my friend,' Jane explained to him later, but the concept was beyond his comprehension.

Happy as she was here, she was hungry for news of Respryn. Who had had babies, who had died, who was feuding with whom?

'And you got married, May?'

'Yes, daft thing to do. I'd always said I'd never marry and I should have stuck to the idea. Daft I was. Drove me mad, he did, nasty smelly thing, and he snored too.'

'Who was he?'

'A new footman, Felix. Oh, he's good-looking enough, and he was pleasant, but his socks smelled something dreadful . . .'

'Hardly grounds for divorce, May.' Jane laughed.

'No, it was wrong of me to marry him in the first place. I don't know what got into me, I suppose I was lonely. Respryn isn't the same without you, and of course I'd had to go back to being a parlour maid. I didn't like that, I can tell you – the other cows laughing at me behind my back 'cause I'd come down in the world. In the middle of me being fed up, Felix popped the question and I said yes, and after I'd said it, he seemed so pleased I didn't like to say, "Sorry, I've changed my mind."'

'Oh, May!'

'His Lordship was real kind to us, he really was, gave us a lovely cottage, up by the home farm. I enjoyed doing it up, getting it nice, then I got bored and Felix wouldn't let me go back to work . . . and he drank . . . and . . .' She looked at Jane as if making up her mind about something. 'It was the sex,' she stated. Jane sat silently, waiting for her to continue. 'Well, I couldn't be doing with it, it was disgusting, he was like a bloody animal . . .'

'May, I am sorry.'

'Nothing to be sorry about. It's my own fault – always listen to your inner voice, my mum says, and I didn't. Anyhow, it's one of them new quick divorces for us, two years apart and it'll be over.'

'I meant I was sorry you didn't enjoy the sex,' Jane said gently.

May shrugged dismissively. 'Landed right on your feet here, haven't you, him a prince and this lovely castle. No day trippers here, I'll be bound!'

'No, May, more's the pity. There should be.'

'I never did understand you and the trippers – you actually seemed to enjoy them. Untidy lot, leaving their litter about. These houses should be for the families and nobody else.'

'May, you sound just like old Lady Upnor,' Jane protested.

'When you getting married then? When your divorce comes through?'

'I'm not getting married, May.'

'Why ever not?'

'It would be too difficult and complicated, me with my background and being a divorced woman. One's bad enough, but the two together –' She flicked her fingers, as if cooling them, in an unselfconscious Italian gesture.

'Who says?'

'We both do, May.'

'Does he love you?'

'Oh yes, he does.' Jane smiled.

'Then I don't see the problem. Lord Upnor didn't let society stand in his way with you, so who's this prince think he is to treat you like this?' May said angrily.

'May, don't be cross with him. It's my choice, too, I couldn't go through all that social thing again, I couldn't. We're happy as we are, very happy.'

'Well, I don't like it and that's flat. You someone's mistress: it doesn't seem right.'

'It's the seventies now, May. Times have changed.'

'Not that much, they haven't. Where's your security, I'd like to know? And if times have changed so much as you say, then why can't he do the proper thing and marry you?'

Her logic was unassailable. Jane gave up the argument. 'May, let's leave it alone, eh? I love him, he loves me; I'd rather be with him like this than live without him, don't you see?'

'He seems very nice and a real gentleman, for a foreigner. And he has got lovely eyes, and that voice . . . it makes me go all wobbly.' May giggled. They never discussed the situation again.

Jane's Italian lessons had started in earnest. Each day a young woman appeared and for two hours they toiled away together. Jane had not found languages easy at school, but now, wanting to please Roberto, she learned quickly.

Roberto was away for the day and Jane had taken the opportunity to do some extra work in the comfortable study he had given her to use. Her pen ran out, and she opened the desk drawers to search for another. A large box full of reels of films caught her eye. Home movies! How lovely. She pressed the button that swung the bookcase open to reveal a screen, another button and the projector appeared from the wall. Expertly she wound the reel of film on to the machine: she had watched Roberto do it often for he refused to go to the local cinema, which was a dingy, smelly fleapit, and had new films sent from Rome. Jane settled down in the large, leather chair as the film flickered into focus.

A young girl appeared on the screen, lying on a large bed. Unselfconsciously she began to undress. Jane's eyes opened as wide as saucers: it was a blue movie. She had never seen one in her life and she sat forward in the chair with excited curiosity. A man loomed out of the shadows and began to caress the girl, his face turned to the camera. It was Roberto. Transfixed Jane watched as his hands slid over the girl's breasts . . . with a horrified gasp, and with nausea rising within her, she leaped for the projector and with shaking fingers switched the machine off. She could not believe what she had just seen. It was disgusting and there was something else about it – that bed, it was somehow familiar. Dear God in heaven, she exclaimed, it was the bed in the house in Rome. The bed they had made love in, the bed with the mirrored canopy . . .

It was evening before Roberto returned. All afternoon Jane had been in a turmoil of indecision about whether to mention the film or to ignore it, pretend it had not happened. As their dinner wore on she found it increasingly difficult to forget what she had seen. They took their cognac through to the adjacent sitting room.

'You're very quiet, Jane. Is anything the matter?'

'Nothing.'

'It doesn't seem like nothing to me. Tell me, what is the problem?'

She looked at him, as he smiled his gentle smile, remembering the sight of his hands creeping sensuously over the naked girl's body.

'I found some films,' she stated baldly.

'I see.'

'Well, I don't!'

'Perhaps you shouldn't pry in people's drawers.'

'I wasn't prying. I was looking for a pen. And you said I could use that room as if it were my own.'

'Yes, I did, that's true. I was stupid – I should have moved the box.'

'You certainly should have moved the box. It was disgusting . . .' Roberto said nothing. 'I mean, how could you? It's sick, degrading.'

'Why did you watch it, then?'

'I only watched the beginning. When I realized you were in it I switched it off immediately.'

'Ah! I see. It's not the fact that it's a pornographic movie, it's the fact that I'm in it that disturbs you so?'

She ignored the implication of his argument. 'And the others, are they dirty pictures too?'

'Yes.'

'You're perverted!' she shouted at him.

'They were made before I met you, I can't see what concern they are of yours.'

'Can't you? I think it's very much my concern that you are decadent.'

'Yes, you are right, I was decadent, but no more, don't you understand, my darling? It's the old romantic story, the dissolute hero reformed by the love of a good woman,' he said calmly.

'You're bloody well laughing at me! How dare you? How can you be so cool about it when I'm feeling sick inside with disgust and anger?' she shouted.

'Jane, calm down, let me try and explain to you, please. I don't apologize for those films being made. I'm sorry you found them and that your curiosity got the better of you –'

'You don't apologize?' she snapped with disbelief.

'Shut up a minute and listen to me,' he commanded. Jane subsided in her chair, still smouldering with anger. 'Yes, I was a different man then. I had been spoiled in life, so much money makes conquests easy, you know. By the time I was twenty I was well tutored in love. By my midthirties, I was bored and jaded. Nothing excited me anymore. These films, they were a little conceit and, eventually, they were an aid to me. It excited me to know what the camera was recording, it made it easier for me to copulate with those young women. That's what it was ... a physical copulation, nothing to do with the mind.' He poured himself another drink. Jane, despite her anger, sat listening intently to every word. He continued. 'There is much in my life that I hope you will not discover. I have done many dark things, mainly from despair, but, oh yes, I was decadent. And then the miracle happened and I met you. I could not believe what was happening to me: to make love to you was a joyous experience, you reawoke my body, you gave me a physical and mental satisfaction I had not known since I was a young man. You gave me back dignified love ... If only you could understand. That was another man, it's not the person I am now.'

'I suppose I can understand, a little,' she said doubtfully. 'But it was such a shock. And seeing you with another woman, I wanted to kill her.'

'My poor love.'

'I didn't trust that bed when I saw it.'

'It is very vulgar,' he said sheepishly. 'Am I forgiven?'

'If you destroy the films.'

'Immediately.' He hurried from the room and was gone for some time. When he returned he smiled apologetically at her. 'They are all burned.'

'All of them?' He nodded. 'Roberto, I've been thinking. That bed, where was the camera?'

'Above the mirror.'

'And ...'

'Yes, my darling, I'm sorry, you too – but only once.'

Jane put her head in her hands, 'Roberto, how could you?'

'I can only say I'm sorry.'

'Get rid of that bloody bed, promise me?'

'Yes, I promise.'

She had been afraid that the thought of the films would destroy her need for him, but when they went to bed, to her relief, she found she was as eager for him as before. But first, much to his amusement, she insisted on clambering on a chair to inspect the canopy of this bed for hidden cameras. Later, as they lay in each other's arms, she turned to him.

'Roberto? Have you ever slept with another woman in this bed?'

He kissed her gently. 'No, my sweet. Only you.' Satisfied with his answer, she drifted into sleep.

The summer ended. They were in Rome for three weeks. Roberto kept his promise and the bed with the mirrored canopy was gone. But still Jane could not feel relaxed, not until they had moved to another room. Even then she began to doubt if she would ever be happy in this house: it had an air of foreboding about it, which she had not noticed before but which haunted her now. In a strange way, she felt the house did not like her and wanted her to go, and she began to feel homesick for the castle.

She could not have been happier when Roberto announced that they were going to Paris. May was beside herself with excitement. Until her trip to Italy, the furthest she had travelled had been from Respryn to London, and now the whole world was beginning to open up for her.

Roberto had a large, elegant flat in Passy, staffed by French servants. All Jane's hard work at learning Italian was of no use to her here, and she knew that her attempts to communicate with the staff in her bad schoolgirl French only made them laugh.

'They're sneering at me behind my back,' she complained to Roberto.

'Darling, you're too sensitive. What does it matter? They're only employees. In any case the French sneer at anyone who doesn't speak their language perfectly.'

'How can you talk about your employees like that? Your arrogance is incredible sometimes,' Jane said with a brief laugh. 'But maybe you're right about the French. That housekeeper's certainly a stuck-up old bitch.'

'Then she shall go.'

'Roberto, I didn't mean . . . Heavens, I don't want to be responsible for someone losing their job,' she said lamely.

'Then she should do it better.'

The next morning Jane realized with guilty relief that the housekeeper was not to be seen, and she felt it was not her imagination that the staff were treating her with much more respect. May hated the place. She had liked Italy, had enjoyed the Italian food, had made friends with the servants, had even picked up enough Italian to talk with them. But in France she had nothing but complaints. She moaned about the plumbing, the water, the house, the smell of garlic. She hated the food – convinced that the sauces were only to cover up the taste of bad meat – and existed on a diet of poached eggs which entailed a daily row with the arrogant young chef, who resented her presence in his kitchen. To add insult to injury, May refused to allow him to cook her eggs.

'He'll only put some filthy sauce all over them,' she complained to Jane. Because of Jane's bad French it was left to Roberto to create calm in the kitchen, a role he did not relish.

'That is the first and the last time I have been in one of my kitchens. It is no good, Jane, you will have to learn French. I am not going to spend my time sorting out the domestic arguments created by your maid.'

'But I haven't learned Italian yet,' she wailed.

A compromise was reached by employing a new housekeeper who spoke English, was courtesy itself and who made friends with May. It was just as well for, as the days sped past, Jane doubted if she would have had time to learn another language. Her days were full.

With great seriousness Roberto supervised the restocking of Jane's wardrobe. She was fascinated that a man should take as much interest and care in how she looked as Honor had done.

'It takes a man to dress a woman,' he informed her. 'Left to their own devices they look a mess.'

'Thank you very much.' She grinned. 'I'll tell Honor that.'

'Ah, Honor is unique in women – she has real style.'

'I really don't need any more clothes, Roberto. Honor bought me so many.'

'But winter comes. You need a different wardrobe. And in any case you need better clothes. I shall be judged by how you look.'

His boyish arrogance amused her and she allowed herself to be led from one great couture house to another. He would sit critically eyeing the clothes paraded before them, choosing first one garment, then another, never allowing her any say no matter how much she protested.

'But, Roberto, I love that dress so much.' Wistfully Jane eyed a dreamy concoction of frilled broderie anglaise.

'It is not your style, darling. That is for an ingénue. You would look wrong in it, totally.' The *vendeuse* nodded her agreement.

The *vendeuse* in each house terrified Jane. It was not that they were unkind or rude, only that they were so perfectly groomed that no matter how good she thought she looked when she arrived, the moment she saw these impeccable women in their neat black dresses, with their smooth make-up and pristine hair, she felt a mess. Their skirts never seemed to wrinkle, their make-up never needed touching up, their shoes were never dusty.

'Why can't I look like them?' she would complain to Roberto.

'You will. It is just a matter of time. Your deportment needs attention. Watch how they move, how they sit. Always they are conscious of their bodies. Note how unobtrusively they arrange their clothes as they sit. They wear the clothes, not vice versa: they do not allow themselves to be intimidated by what they wear. Watch the mannequins, they are saying, "Look at me, I am beautiful", but they say it with their bodies, their subtle movement.'

'I can't strut around like them, don't be daft! Everyone would laugh at me. I don't want to look like that.'

'Of course not, but you must learn to be proud of your beauty. Then you will walk correctly, then the clothes will look right on you.'

'But I don't think I'm beautiful.'

'Don't be silly, Jane, and stop fishing for compliments.'

But it was true. She was not confident in her own looks. She wanted to be blonde and have curls, to be tall and willowy, not dark and small. She could not see that in Roberto's eyes her petiteness was one of her great charms. Her total lack of conceit was another.

Her efforts always to look her best were an exhausting regime to maintain. May was kept hard at work pressing and sponging, dressing her hair, manicuring her nails. Visits from beauticians and masseuses took up much of her time. It was unthinkable to Roberto that she should go to a salon – the salon came to her. If they were invited to an important dinner or reception, he would enjoy watching as her *maquillage* was applied – she could no longer think of it as mere make-up, because the preparation of her face now was a very skilled and long process, almost an art form. Roberto would sit looking at her with loving pride, offering suggestions. Sometimes, she told him, she felt like a giant Barbie doll he had bought to play with. He found the idea amusing and would enrage her by calling her Barbie at the most inopportune times.

She had thought, after the practical life she had led, that she would hate it all; in fact she found she loved it. She loved the beautiful clothes and what they did for her, she loved the attention and the fuss. She loved the pride Roberto had in her, and she worked hard to please him. She even learned to walk differently for him, when a dreadful, bossy woman was employed to improve her posture. She had changed, she knew it: she was no longer the frightened girl who shopped in Marks and Spencer because the assistants in the dress shops terrified her. She was growing in confidence, which lay thick upon her, not from the knowledge that she looked wonderful but from the certainty of this man's love.

They returned to Italy for the shooting, staying at another of Roberto's houses. In this shooting lodge deep in the forest she immediately felt at home. The scenery reminded her of Drumloch, but the house was far more beautiful and comfortable than Drumloch had ever been. Since Roberto did not want her to go shooting with him, she could pretend it was not happening and would while away the days reading, walking and making herself beautiful for his return. The house party was large and she began fully to appreciate that Roberto's households ran themselves. Despite thirty house guests, and sometimes as many as fifty for dinner, none of the problems were hers. The major-domo arranged everything: where people were to sleep, where they were to sit at dinner, what they were to eat. She had all the time in the world to look after herself, and each evening, as the company assembled, she found it easier and easier to move among them as the gracious hostess Roberto expected her to be.

They skied. They went to the West Indies. They joined an American on his yacht. They sailed the Java sea. She fell in love with Bali. Everywhere there were new people, new experiences, and the amusing realization that she need never be without a tan.

His friends were charming to her. With them she felt welcome and never tongue-tied or gauche. Here the criteria were that, as a man, you should be rich, successful and amusing, and, as a woman, beautiful, intelligent and amusing. She did not know why but she had presumed that these people would be empty and frivolous, and that she would be bored. Nothing was further from the truth. The women shamed her with how well read they were. Their knowledge of art and music was frequently encyclopaedic. In England she had been used to a society that regarded an intelligent woman as unfeminine and a threat, whereas here she was regarded as a jewel. Beside them she felt ignorant. As she had learned how to dress and how to present herself, now she began with a ferocious intensity to learn.

She had expected the press would be everywhere, but their peace was never disturbed. But they did not go to nightclubs or first nights, they dined in one another's homes or on each other's boats. She learned that publicity could be avoided if one were rich enough and chose to be invisible to the press.

Most of Roberto's friends, like him, owned land and dabbled in business; it was as if they moved around the world in a large club. They were a sophisticated group and Jane's role in his life was accepted without question. There were many other women who were mistresses, too, but Jane soon learned that she was luckier than they, for Roberto loved her, and she was a rarity in that she was permanent in his life, whereas most of the others came and went. It was not unusual to be friends with a man's mistress one week, the next to be chatting to his wife. And when it was the turn of the wives, she was always the only mistress present and knew that therefore she had a special place in his life.

The world was suddenly a very small and different place. These people caught planes as other people caught buses; to fly across a continent for a party was not uncommon; excellence in everything was the unspoken norm. She noticed that, in her new world, colours of clothes had a greater subtlety, silkworms seemed to make softer silk, sheep grew finer wool, brocades and velvets were more lush. Doors seemed thicker and they shut with a satisfying clunk, as did the doors on her cars now. Windows shone more cleanly, the glass was thicker. Gold was heavier and glowed more richly. Dirt did not exist and ugliness was removed. Poverty was something glimpsed distantly from a limousine window or read about in the newspapers.

When she thought of Alistair these days, she found that her life with him seemed as far removed from the present as her childhood had been from her life with him. This elegant woman could happily hold her own wherever she was.

A whole year had passed and they were back in Italy. There had been nothing further from Alistair about their divorce and she had almost forgotten about it, thought it was of no importance to her. It was Roberto, his face black with rage, who heard first of Alistair's plans.

'He is suing me in the Italian courts for enticing you away from him, and thus denying him his conjugal rights. Such a charming gentleman, your beloved husband!' He stormed about the room, waving his lawyer's letter angrily in his hand.

'I don't believe it. But you didn't entice me away, I didn't know you.'

'Exactly.'

'What are you going to do?'

'Kill him, probably.'

Instead, many phone calls and an aeroplane flight later, Jane found herself in Alistair's lawyer's office. The room seemed full. Her own lawyer and aide were present, and Alistair with his, but it was Roberto and his anger that seemed to fill the room. It saddened her to see Alistair in these circumstances – still the fine, boyish face, the elegance, the way he had of flicking his hair from his eyes. He had not altered: he was still beautiful to her eyes. But how had it all come to this? What had happened that they could not be friends?

'I had presumed, Prince Villizano, that you would have brought your advisers with you from Rome,' Alistair's lawyer, Mr Strong, said.

'That won't be necessary,' Roberto replied shortly.

Alistair stepped forward, his hand outstretched. 'We've never met,' he said. Roberto looked at the hand offered him and slowly turned his back. Alistair coughed. 'You look wonderful, Jane.' He sounded surprised.

'Thank you, so do you.'

Roberto swung round and glared angrily at Jane, who hurriedly took her seat. Without preamble, the two sets of lawyers began to argue terms. As she listened, Jane felt humiliated. They talked as if she were some sort of package, up for barter to the highest bidder.

'Am I to gather that this meeting is for us to come to a financial arrangement so that it will not be necesssary for this distasteful matter to be brought to the Italian courts?' Roberto enquired so calmly that Jane felt a flicker of irritation that he was not upset for her.

'Exactly, Prince Villizano,' said Mr Strong, with obvious relief that he was speaking to a man of the world who understood these matters.

'And that you are bringing this action in the Italian courts because of the liberal divorce laws you now have in this country, since 1971, I believe?'

'Quite.'

'If the law says I have to pay for the privilege of Lady Upnor's love, so be it.'

Alistair and his lawyer sat back appearing relaxed and satisfied, content in the knowledge that only the amount remained to be decided.

'However,' continued Roberto, 'it does seem somewhat unfair to me, since it was Lord Upnor who was the first to commit adultery, thus precipitating Lady Upnor into a serious nervous breakdown which culminated in this gentleman here having her committed as a lunatic to an asylum. Am I correct?'

'Well, a private mental hospital, a very luxurious hospital, may I add?' Alistair's lawyer interrupted hastily.

'He then acquired custody of their child since he had her declared an unfit person to care for him?'

'Er, well, yes,' Alistair's lawyers agreed, somewhat uncomfortably.

'I'm not surprised you don't want all this brought out in the English courts. We have all heard of British justice: I can imagine what the famous British justice would think of this claim. But we have justice in my country, too. I doubt if the courts there would consider my having to pay for a cast-off, lunatic, childless wife as being exactly fair justice, would you?'

'Well, couched like that, no. But you have to admit that because of you, Lord Upnor has been deprived of the love and comfort of his wife.'

'But they weren't living together.'

'They might have been reconciled had it not been for you, Prince Villizano.'

'But he doesn't seem to have made much effort to effect a reconciliation.'

'We do not know what attempts he has made,' Mr Strong argued.

'He does and I do.'

'Prince Villizano, I do not understand what you are getting at.' Mr Strong was agitated now.

'Then I shall explain. Lady Upnor and I have discussed this at great length. We have decided that she has paid enough already in pain, humiliation and anguish. We are quite happy for the whole sad story to come out in court in whatever country you choose. Then the judges can decide if I am to pay or not.'

Pandemonium broke out. Roberto stood up. 'No doubt you will wish to discuss this matter. Come, my darling.' He offered his hand to Jane. 'We are at Claridge's, gentlemen – once you have decided.'

Alistair jumped to his feet. 'Jane?' He looked at her and she felt there was almost a look of pleading in his face, which puzzled her.

'Goodbye, Alistair,' she said with dignity, and hand in hand with Roberto she left the room. Outside, she turned to him. 'You fox, we never discussed anything! How I kept quiet I shall never know.'

'They annoyed me, talking about you as if you were a commodity, something in the marketplace. It was distasteful. They won't press the claim, we shall hear no more. Now, my darling, where would you like to have lunch?'

He was right, they heard no more. The months slipped by and the whole sordid incident passed from her mind. Their life settled into its exotic routine. She was in the West Indies when she was informed that her divorce was going ahead and several months later, in Singapore, she heard that a decree nisi had been granted. Three months later she was in New York when the news reached her that it had been made absolute. She looked at the paper in her hand and she felt an overwhelming sense of loss and failure. She had embarked on that marriage with such shining hope and confidence, all her youth had been invested in that union. Now this paper said it was no more. It really was the end of that era in her life. Strangely, although so much time had gone by, and despite her happiness with Roberto, as she looked at the paper, she suddenly felt an emptiness within her.

11

Another year with Roberto slipped by with clockwork smoothness. She had lived with him for three years. And for three years she had not seen her son.

At first she had written every week but as the time went by it became more difficult for her to write to a child who was rapidly becoming a stranger, one whom she no longer knew. Soon she was writing once a month, then only intermittently and at birthdays and Christmas.

In an ornately carved sandalwood box, tied with blue satin ribbon like the letters from a lover, she hoarded the few letters the child had written her, dog-eared now from endless rereading.

She had photographs of him, too, which she would study by the hour, sometimes with a large magnifying glass, poring over them, searching his features for a sign of herself. The shape of his eyes, she felt, was like hers, otherwise he was a replica of how Alistair must have looked at thirteen. She knew so little about him, what his interests were, who his friends were, for his letters were dutiful and unemotional. She wished now that she had been more positive when he had come to visit her in Cambridge, had made more effort to get to know the child. For now she wanted to know him and it seemed it was too late.

To all intents and purposes she was Roberto's wife. Each year the rules of their relationship relaxed a little more, so that now she had met most of his family, women as well as men. The moves to meet his family had started tentatively with the arrival at the castle of a cousin and his new wife. His report back to the family on Jane must have been favourable for it was followed by an invitation from his father, Roberto's uncle, and from this visit others grew.

Jane was amazed by this family and the scale of their living. She had often heard, in England, snide remarks made about European aristocracy, as if their claims were spurious, and they were regarded as poverty-stricken, living in crumbling ruins, taking jobs as guides to rich

Americans to make ends meet. Certainly not in the class of their secure and smug English counterparts. Nothing was further from the truth with the Villizano family. Each branch of the family had its own castle, a palazzo in Rome, and at least one shooting lodge.

The wives were always Italian, always of noble birth – not one corpuscle of unacceptable blood flowed in their veins. They were appalled by the English aristocracy's habit of, as they put it, 'marrying out', a dangerous foible which would only dilute the precious blood. Jane had tried to explain that it did not weaken, but strengthened. And in this century the American heiresses, whom many families had sought, had saved a number of country estates. 'Tut, tut,' the Italian women exclaimed, flicking their elegantly manicured hands through the air, the light shining on rings at least 200 years old, and again they explained to Jane the necessity of pure blood lines. They did not speak of social unsuitability, of liability – such mundane thoughts did not enter their heads. No, they talked as racehorse owners talk. Looking at them, Jane saw that these women had been bred and refined to a fine-boned elegance, just like the horses whose blood was regarded with equal importance. So Jane was never offended, it was a theory they discussed: she never felt here that the conversation was directed at her.

Closest to them in distance as well as age were Emilio and his wife Francesca. Both were cousins of Roberto, from different sides of the family. Emilio was the same age as Roberto and his wife a year younger than Jane, a sophisticated couple whom Jane particularly liked and felt as if she had known for years.

She sometimes began to hope that Roberto would relent and marry her. From being adamant that she would never marry him, it was now the thing she wanted most in the world – that, and to see her son. Only Roberto's mother, she was certain, stood in their way. Perhaps when she died? But as the old lady entered her nineties, hale and hearty, Jane learned how young men must feel waiting for dead men's shoes. She had never discussed the subject with Roberto – but she had a sense of permanance with him, an inability to imagine life without him.

May had at long last come out of what Jane referred to as her 'bangers and mash' period and had become a true cosmopolitan. She loved her work, took great pride in Jane's appearance, had even forgiven Roberto for not marrying her. Wherever they went, there was May, an iron in one hand and the heated rollers in the other, no mean feat on safari in Africa.

At thirty-five, Jane showed she was one of those lucky women who improve with age, as if her inner contentment and confidence had worked outwards to her skin, her hair, her figure. As the beauty of youth faded, another, more striking beauty took its place.

They were back from their annual travels to spend the summer in the castle in Italy. It was the usual mix of summer people including, as always, Honor, whose friendship Jane valued increasingly. Roberto, trusting her more, had relaxed, and on Sundays as his car turned one way to visit his mother, hers would turn the other and she would visit Honor.

Honor never failed to astound Jane. She had known her now for over fifteen years and in all that time she had barely changed in looks, outlook or manner. Jane had no idea how old she was: Honor was not the kind of woman who discussed her age. Jane was sure this was not out of conceit but because, to Honor, age was irrelevant and she would have been surprised by anyone finding it necessary to ask such a question. Jane presumed she must be in her late fifties, could be sixty even, but she still had the looks and vitality of a thirty-year-old.

It was a hot Sunday in August, and the two women were relaxing by the pool after a light lunch, gently gossiping, Jane's foot stirring the water of the pool. They would have a siesta soon, then friends would arrive for cocktails and dinner, before Jane went home to Roberto. That was her unchanging routine every Sunday.

'What on earth's the matter with Guido? He never runs,' Honor commented as they watched the now decidedly portly Guido puffing towards them along the terrace, the long extension cable of the telephone trailing behind him like a writhing snake.

'He looks dreadful. Something's happened, Honor,' Jane said, alarmed, her first thoughts of Roberto, who, despite her protestations, still drove like a maniac.

Too breathless for speech, Guido handed Jane the phone.

'Hullo? Jane Upnor speaking,' she said cautiously.

'Jane, love. Sorry to disturb you. It's James. Little blighter fell out of a tree . . .' she heard Alistair say.

'Is he all right?' she asked, knowing as she spoke what a futile question it was. Alistair would hardly be calling her if it was not serious.

'No, he's not too good, Jane. He's been calling for you . . . and the quacks think . . .'

'Where is he?'

'St Cuthbert's.'

'I'll be there this evening.' She quickly replaced the receiver and, for the first time ever, dialled the number of Roberto's mother. As the phone rang she turned to Honor, with terror on her face. 'It's James, he fell out of a tree, he's in hospital!'

'Don't panic, Jane. If he's got the Upnor head, he'll be OK.' She smiled supportively. 'I'll get some things packed for you.'

Roberto came to the phone, his voice full of concern, knowing that for her to call him there, something very wrong had happened. She explained.

'Get Guido to drive you to the airport, I'll get the pilot organized. Be brave, little one, I'll see you there.'

'Will you come with me, darling? I'm so afraid.'

'I have that meeting with those German financiers tomorrow and the Americans on Tuesday. I can hardly —'

'Please, Roberto.'

'Darling, I can't get hold of Herr Schramm at such short notice, but I can cancel the Americans. Send the plane back and I'll fly to London tomorrow afternoon. OK?'

'Bless you, Roberto.'

In the car, Honor held her hand as Guido raced like a demon down the mountain roads. Roberto was waiting for her by his new aeroplane, which was ready to taxi off.

'My passport, I haven't got my passport . . .'

Smiling, he handed her the familiar blue book. 'I called May,' he explained. He took her into his arms and kissed her forehead. 'Now, my love, stop worrying so. Boys are always falling out of trees and landing on their heads.'

'But he could be paralysed, or dying of a brain haemorrhage . . .'

'Then the sooner you get there and find out, the better, my sweet.' He helped her into the plane. She looked down at the two people she loved so dearly, and as the plane took off and circled the dusty little airport she waved and waved until their figures were two tiny dots she could scarcely see.

It was early evening, and raining, as the taxi drew up in front of the familiar doors of St Cuthbert's, but the worried woman who got out seemed unaware of where she was, appeared to have forgotten the years she had spent here herself as a nurse. She entered the private wing and was shown immediately to the third floor. It needed every ounce of her reserves to push open the door of the room the nurse indicated. It was three years since she had seen her son, and now it might be too late.

She burst into an anguished cry of relief as she saw the young boy with a sticking plaster on his forehead and a wide grin on his face, shovelling large spoonfuls of ice cream into his mouth.

'Thank God!' she said, unaware that in that exclamation lay all the maternal love she had feared she was incapable of. Alistair stepped quickly across the room and took her arm.

'Sorry, Jane. Right scare I must have given you. But he suddenly sat up as bright as a button. It was too late to call you back.'

'Hullo, Ma.' James smiled shyly at her.

'James.' Jane rushed across the room, forgetting in her relief that the boy did not like to be kissed, and flung her arms about him and hugged him to her, smothering his face with kisses. It was some time before she realized that the child was cuddling her back with equal intensity. 'Crikey, you frightened me. What happened?'

'I was climbing a tree, and a branch broke. I landed on my head. Did I see stars! Everything went black . . .' James laughed, evidently enjoying the drama he had created.

'Is he all right?'

'The doctors say yes, he's been X-rayed, no concussion. They want to keep him in overnight, that's all. Sorry, big drama over nothing.'

'Don't be sorry. I'm just so relieved he's going to be fine.' She smiled fondly at them both. She had often wondered how she would feel on seeing Alistair again. This was the first time she had seen him and their son since the divorce. Would she be bitter, would she be cold with him, would she tell him how much anger and pain he had caused? None of these – she could never remain angry with him. Whenever she saw him, that smile, the unruly hank of hair flopping forward on his forehead, and his guilty, boyish expression enabled her to forgive him anything. She knew that it would always be like this.

At eight they were asked to leave. Outside it was still pouring with rain.

'Haven't you got a coat?'

'No. It doesn't often rain in Italy in August, remember?'

'Put this round you then.' He took his jacket off and slipped it around her shoulders. 'I'll get a taxi.' She stood in the doorway, aware suddenly of the familiar smell of his coat round her. Strange how one never forgot smells, and how quickly and sharply they brought back memories. Alistair's smiling face appeared at the taxi door. 'Have you eaten? Fancy a bite?' he asked.

'I should get to a phone and call Roberto.'

'Phone from the restaurant,' Alistair suggested.

It was a pleasant little French restaurant in Kensington. The proprietors were none too happy at her request to call Italy, since there was no pay phone. Persuaded by a ten pound note from Alistair, they agreed. Roberto had not yet returned from his mother's. She left a message.

'That must be about the most expensive two-minute phone call to Italy ever,' she said, laughing, as they settled at their table.

'Anything, for M'Lady.' He bowed.

She was surprised how easy it was to talk to him. This is how it should be between two people who once loved each other, she thought contentedly, as she sipped the wine he had ordered.

'You know, Jane, I've been a real bastard over James. When that poor little bugger was calling for you, I realized the dreadful thing I'd done to him and to you. I'd no right to stop you seeing him.'

'It was cruel, Alistair. But I must admit, there was a time when I didn't seem to mind. I don't know why. But in the last couple of years I've ached to see him.'

'I'll make up for it now, I promise. Would you like to have him come to stay with you when he's over the bang on his head? Before he goes back to school?'

'Alistair, would you? I'd love that.' Her eyes shone with excitement. 'With Roberto there too?'

'Yes, of course. I hear he's a nice enough bloke for a wop.'

'Alistair, you fool! James will love Italy. We're there until the end of September. Perhaps you would let him come skiing with us after Christmas?' she asked hopefully.

'We could see how it fits in with his school terms.'

'How wonderful, how bloody wonderful!'

'It's quite a life you lead now, isn't it?'

'It's different.' She grinned at him.

'When are you going back?'

'I had planned to stay until James was better so that I could see as much of him as possible – while you allowed it.' She smiled slyly at him. 'But if the doctors are satisfied with him and if you promise that he can come in the next few days . . . well, tomorrow, I guess.'

'Can I book him on a flight to that local airport that's opened up?'

'Don't bother. I'll get the plane sent to pick him up. He'd probably love that.'

'Christ, Jane, how grand!'

'Sorry, does sound a bit flash, doesn't it? It's Roberto's latest toy – he's in love with it, I think. It makes sense, though. You see, we spend so much time travelling and he's always having to rush back from somewhere or other. But what about you? What are you up to these days?'

'Oh, I flit about, bit like a bee really, little bit of nectar here, then on to the next flower. I keep busy, nothing serious. Just hasn't turned up.' He shrugged.

'You'll probably meet someone when you least expect it. That's what happened to me.' She smiled fondly at him and patted his hand. 'How's your mother?'

'Still bossing.' He groaned. 'Still hating you,' he added with a grin.

'After all this time. Extraordinary. And Clarissa?'

'She's got two kids now. Poor little sods, she ignores them completely. Mind you, she ignores poor old Hector too.' He laughed. 'She's very bitter, of course.'

'Bitter, why?'

'Didn't you hear? Hector lost a packet in some mad investment scheme, nearly wiped him out. Clarissa's standing by him, though if I were Hector, I'd wish she'd piss off.'

'Poor Clarissa.'

'Do you mean, poor as in "what a shame" or poor as in "got no money"?'

'I meant I was sorry for her. I should think Clarissa would find it more difficult than most to adjust to less money.'

'You're something else, Jane! Why should you feel sorry for her when she's been such a bitch to you?'

'That was all a long time ago. It's very easy to be forgiving when one is happy, isn't it?' She smiled.

'I shouldn't feel too sorry. She's not that poor. It's all relative. To most people she's still rich: it's only Clarissa who thinks she's on the breadline.'

'Poor Hector, then.'

'That's much more to the point. Of course I have a great time telling Clarissa of your various adventures. You see, I keep tabs on what you're doing.'

'What on earth for?'

'I like to see her go green.' He roared with laugther.

'I meant, why the interest in what I'm up to?'

'I do care about you, you know.' He smiled his devastating smile at her and she warmed to him, but then she remembered the trouble his interest had caused, and she frowned. 'Honest,' he said, taking her hand and squeezing it. 'Let's have another bottle of this Sancerre, shall we?'

They lingered over the wine.

'Where are you booked in?'

'Gracious, what's the time? Damn, it's gone eleven. I didn't bother. I went straight to the hospital. I'd best get a taxi to Claridgés and hope they're not full.'

'Why not stay at the house in Fulham?'

'It must be all damp and musty.'

'No, I often stay there, since you don't rent it out any more. I didn't think you'd mind. In fact, that's where James and I were staying – it was the tree in the garden.'

'I don't want to put you out.'

'Hell, you wouldn't be putting me out. It's your house, anyway. It's damn cheeky of me to squat in it, I suppose. No, I'll go to my club, no problem, and I can assure you the house is as dry as a bone.'

'It would be nicer than a hotel . . .'

'Of course it is. I'll come and settle you in, make sure there are no mice. Do you remember how scared of mice you used to be?' he reminded her as he paid the bill and hailed a taxi. They drove to the familiar street. It seemed strange to be standing once more beside Alistair as he put the key in the lock. The house even had the same smell about it, she thought as she walked into the hall.

She went straight to the study to telephone Roberto. He laughed at the excitement in her voice as she told him that James was to come and stay. 'I'll get a commercial flight back. I want to stop off in Paris.'

'Why?'

'It's a surprise. You must wait until tomorrow night to find out,' she teased him. 'I love you.'

'Hurry home, my little one.'

In the drawing room Alistair was uncorking a bottle of champagne. 'Remember the first time we had champagne together?' He grinned.

'Am I ever likely to forget?'

'That was a special night, and so is this one,' he said, pouring the wine into the flutes.

'Why?'

'Because we're friends again. Because we can begin to forget all the bad things we've done to each other.' He lifted his glass to her in a silent toast.

She looked at him sharply. She could not recollect anything that she had ever done to him, but he was in such a good mood and the evening had been so perfect that she let the remark pass. She wandered about the room, admiring the new pieces that Alistair had added, exclaiming with pleasure as she recognized an ornament, a painting. Their old sofa was still here, and the ornately carved Indian table.

'Remember how proud of that sofa we were?' He noticed her looking at it.

'Yes. And how your mother hated it.'

'The day it came, wasn't that when I took you to your first Italian meal?'

'You know, I think it was.' She looked about the room. 'It's still the same, isn't it?'

'Nothing ever really changes.'

She had been happily exploring the room until she reached the spot on the carpet where, on that dreadful day, she had sat and had slowly and deliberately, she now believed, let her mind drift away from her. She shivered. She felt his arm about her shoulders. He turned her towards him.

'Don't think about it, Jane.' He took a strand of her hair and twisted it between his finger and thumb, playing with it as, long ago, he had loved to do. 'Forget the sadness,' he whispered.

'You're right. It's fatal to remember the past. I learned that.'

'But how do you forget, how do you erase all the magic and beauty that's there in the past too?' he asked her huskily. 'Jane! Jane!' he said urgently. 'I've been such a bloody fool. I love you, I need you. Come back to me, I beg you.'

'Alistair . . .' she began to say in astonishment, but before she could finish the sentence his lips were on hers and she was held securely in his arms, his hands feverishly running over her body. 'Alistair . . . it's all too late . . .' but her body and her memories betrayed her. She was too tired and too vulnerable to protest further, and she leaned against him. It seemed to her the most natural thing to do. As she felt she belonged in this room, was relaxed in it, so she belonged in his arms. He took her hand and quickly led her up the stairs. She followed like someone in a dream. In their old bedroom, he held her, gazing at her face, and kissed her again.

'You're so beautiful,' he sighed as he gently laid her on the bed and crossed the room to pull the curtains. 'Jay . . .' He knelt down on the bed beside her. 'At last . . .'

From far away in time the physical excitement that his touch had always given her was reawoken. As his hands once more explored her body so she was lost. She had no past, no future, only this exhilarating moment.

His passion intensified and she felt that timeless power that all women feel as a man loses all consciousness except for her, her body and the pleasure she can give.

Wiser now in the ways of his body and her own, as she had not been in the past, she responded expertly. Their bodies entwined, broke loose, re-entwined. Their passion mounted in unison. He rode into her with an intensity that neither had experienced together before. Deeper and deeper he plunged into her. Her body arched to receive him, inviting him, exciting him, sucking him into that minideath of shared oblivion. Her voice screamed, 'I love you!' and together they climaxed. She held his sweat-soaked body to her as he lay slumped with exhaustion upon her. At last, at long last, she had given him what he had always wanted from her. This time she had not failed him.

He rolled away, lit two cigarettes, and handed her one. His arm about her, they lay in silence, the smoke from their cigarettes entwining above them just as their bodies had done. To Jane, it was as if the years in between had never happened.

'Jane, darling,' he said at last. 'My God, that was wonderful. You were sensational.'

'I didn't have to pretend this time.'

'No, that was obvious. Heavens, it was shattering, wasn't it? Marvellous!' Pleased with his words she snuggled closer against him, feeling secure as she lay beside the beautiful body she had never forgotten. 'Crikey, Jane, I've had plenty of sex in my life but I tell you one thing, you've learned one hell of a lot since the last time,' he said sleepily.

At his words, the blood in Jane's veins seemed to turn to ice. She shivered, and did not know what to say. But there was no need for words: with disbelief she heard Alistair's breathing settle into the regular rhythm of someone deeply asleep.

She lay in the dark, frozen with despair. Nauseated with reality. A yawning void opened where her heart should have been.

Relentlessly her mind came back to life, and she wished it had not, as myriad emotions assailed her. She had to be the stupidest woman that walked this earth. She had fooled herself. She always seemed to do that. He didn't love her, he hadn't said any words of love to her, only congratulated her on her sexual ability. Nothing had changed. No doubt at this very moment he was being unfaithful to some other woman, with her. She dreamed of love and to him she was only another conquest.

How could she be so stupid? Why did she always have to wrap everything up in romance?

And here she was blaming Alistair, but really wasn't she the same? So for a split second then she had dreamed of a future with him but wasn't that because of the pleasure they had enjoyed with each other? She had allowed her vagina to rule her head and her heart, so who was she to criticize him? She was Roberto's and she had betrayed him. There was nothing to choose between the two of them.

Roberto! All the love he gave her, all the passion. Roberto never had 'sex'. Roberto made love. And he made love with an unselfish generosity which perhaps she had begun to take for granted. How could she possibly muddle the two like this time and again? She had had a narrow escape – she should have been content with the deep affection, love, call it what you will, that she and Alistair had for each other. With Roberto she was loved as other women could only dream of being loved.

She slipped from Alistair's arms and hurriedly dressed. For the rest of the night she sat in the drawing room watching the slowness of the clock, wishing she was safely back in Italy. She thought to wake Alistair to explain that she had been a fool and had made a dreadful mistake, but decided against it. She did not want Alistair to think she put too much emphasis on what had happened. It was best just to slip from the house – no note, no explanation. That way, with luck, he would think she, in turn, regarded him as just an amorous adventure.

At five she silently let herself out of the house and by seven was on the plane to Paris.

Her appointment there took longer than she had anticipated and she missed her flight for Italy. She caught the later one, and it was late evening before her car swung into the courtyard of the castle.

The castle had a strange, deserted air about it. She had expected to find the German industrialists there. It was odd that Roberto had not invited them to stay – he usually did. Their private sitting room and his study were both empty. She raced up the stairs but he was not in her bedroom. She ran along the corridor and swung open the door of his room. 'Roberto! Such exciting news!'

'What news, Jane?'

'*Roberto!*' Her mouth formed the word but no sound came out. Across the room, in the large bed, lay Roberto; beside him was a young fair-haired man. She lifted her hand and swept it before her eyes as if to remove the image she saw. She wanted to move, to run away, but her legs felt as if they were filled with lead. With enormous effort, she turned and

walked slowly from the room, stumbling as she did so. She fumbled her
way along the corridor, groping against the walls for support, bumping
into furniture as she went, bruising herself yet not noticing the knocks.
She moved like a zombie into the safety of her own room. She leaned
against the bed, fighting for breath. A strange noise was issuing from her
throat: she was trying to say 'Roberto', but instead she sounded like an
animal in pain.

The door in the tapestry opened, silently. 'Tell me, Jane. What is this
exciting news you have for me?' He smiled coldly at her.

'I don't understand,' she managed to say.

'What don't you understand, my dear Jane?'

'Roberto, what is happening?'

'Aren't you in a better position to tell me that?'

'I don't understand!'

'So you keep saying,' he replied in an ice-cold voice.

'How could you do this to me?' she cried.

'Do what?'

'You know bloody well what! That bastard in your bed.'

'That young man. Very good-looking, don't you think?' Jane could
feel her mouth hanging open with astonishment. 'Don't look so startled,
Jane. Didn't you know I liked young men, too? How remiss of me not to
tell you. How impolite.' He laughed. He was actually laughing. Jane
clasped her hand over her mouth as a great engulfing wave of nausea hit
her. She raced for the bathroom and, shoulders heaving, she hung over
the lavatory bowl. Loud retching noises filled the room, but she had not
eaten, she could not be sick, could not relieve this nausea within her. She
slumped on the floor, sweat running down her face, dry, racking sobs
shaking her body.

'Calm down, Jane, for goodness sake. You sound like an animal.'
Roberto stood in the doorway.

'Calm down! After what I've just seen. How could you, Roberto?
How could you be so cruel? And when we have so much . . .'

'What have we got, Jane? Lies and deception? I'm not the only person
in this room capable of cruelty.' From his pocket he took a piece of
paper, a telex message. He thrust it at her. 'Read that,' he ordered. It said
little and it said everything; as she read it she thought she was going to
faint.

'26, BATHURST ROAD, FULHAM. 11.30 P.M. – 5 A.M.' The words of
the telex seemed to dance before her. Blood was drumming in her head.
She shook herself: she was angry now, very angry.

'You had me watched! You had me followed! How dare you? What right had you to do that?'

'The right of every man who doubts the integrity of his woman, as I doubted you.'

'So,' she snapped. 'Five a.m. So what? Yes, I went to Fulham, I didn't want to stay in a hotel. It is my house, after all. What's wrong in my going there? What your telex doesn't tell you was that Alistair was with me, I freely admit it. He came with me because I was afraid to be on my own. And I left at the crack of dawn to fly back to you. To you!' she shouted. 'It doesn't mean anything.'

'The subsequent telephone call did. You were seen in the bedroom, silhouetted artistically against the window, before you pulled the curtains. You in the arms of that unspeakable bastard!'

She sank against the side of the bath, despair filling her. 'Nothing happened,' she lied desperately.

'I don't believe you, Contessa.'

'Is this to be my punishment then? That creep in your bed?'

'It amused me. After all, you had been amusing yourself, so why should I not have a little fun, too?' He smiled at her, but it was the smile of a death mask, the muscles rigid, no warmth in the eyes.

'You cruel bastard!' she spat at him. 'Not even a woman to punish me with, but a boy to humiliate me. You rotten sod!'

Swiftly he crossed the room and hit her hard, her head banging against the marble wall. 'Don't you ever call me names.' He hit her again. His heavy, muscular body loomed above her.

She scrambled to her feet. 'Don't you hit me! What right do you think you have? You don't own me. I'm not your bloody wife.' She spat the words, angrily, at him.

'Just as well you're not my wife, in the circumstances,' he shouted back.

Their anger filled the room, each one fuelling the fury of the other. Suddenly he slumped against the wall, staring at Jane, an expression of disbelief on his face. 'Oh, Jane, how could you?' She averted her eyes with shame. 'You took my love and you squandered it,' he said in a quiet voice which was more menacing than if he had continued to shout at her.

'No, Roberto. You're wrong. I was coming back. I was so excited. Roberto, listen to me. Please.' She grabbed his arm as he turned as if to leave the room. 'I'm sorry, Roberto. I know "sorry" sounds inadequate for what I've done. Believe me, I don't know how it happened, or what got into me. I was drunk. You must believe I was drunk, I didn't know what I was doing. It just happened, forgive me, for God's sake.' He did not look at her as she tugged desperately at his clothes. 'Darling, I know I did wrong. But, truly, I think it will help us. I'm sure I've buried the ghost of the past once and for all. I've been fooling myself. I pretended to myself that Alistair didn't matter but he's always been there like a ghost between us. Now, he really has gone. I know for certain, totally and utterly, that it's you I love. And I realize now how much you love me.'

'I fear you may have reached these conclusions too late, Jane. I despise you. You have no dignity. That you could let that man even touch you is beyond belief.'

'But it meant nothing – nothing at all. I thought for a minute . . . but it's gone, it's over . . .'

'You whore!' he shouted, his words echoing off the marble walls. 'You stinking, filthy whore!'

'I love you,' she pleaded.

'Love! You love? You cannot begin to comprehend what love is. You took my love, you used me, declared your love for me and all the time creeping about in your sordid mind were thoughts of him. When I fucked you, did you pretend it was him? Did you want it to be him?' He was screaming at her, his face almost black with rage.

'No, I didn't. It wasn't like that. It was all so complicated. It just happened, I don't know how or why. And, Christ, I wish it hadn't, don't you see?'

'All I see is a hypocritical whore who pontificated about fidelity, how faithful she was, and she was lying. You are deceitful. I shouldn't even call you a whore – at least a whore is honest. You're lower than that.' He looked at her with such loathing in his eyes that Jane had to look away. 'You cheap bitch! Get back to the gutter where you belong. Get out of my house and out of my life. Now!'

'But Roberto, I went to the doctor in Paris. Roberto, I'm pregnant.'

He looked at her coldly as he opened the door. 'Then, Madame Contessa, I suggest you have an abortion.'

12

'Oh dear!' said Honor, sitting Jane down and pouring her a very stiff drink. 'You're going to have a splendid black eye, too. What on earth have you and Roberto been up to?'

Through her tears, Jane told Honor the whole story. 'Honor, I'm so unhappy. What am I to do?' She looked up and saw a stony-faced Honor staring at her. 'Honor, don't be cross with me, not you as well.'

'I'm more than cross. I'm furious. You stupid, silly little bitch! What on earth got into you? I thought you were so happy with Roberto. Good gracious, just recently I had begun to think he might even end up marrying you.'

'Me too. But he won't now.'

'Of course he won't and can you blame him?'

'What about him? In bed with a man! He's not so innocent, either,' Jane defended herself indignantly.

'I would bet everything I own that it was just an act. He wasn't doing anything with that fellow, had no intention of doing so. It was meant to humiliate you.'

'He succeeded. The shock! I'd no idea he was queer, no idea at all.'

'He isn't. Even when he was really wild, in the days before he met you, I heard all sorts of tales of orgies and drugs and so on, but never men. Not our Roberto.' Honor gave a short laugh. 'You have hurt him dreadfully, young woman. And with Alistair of all men! I thought that was dead and buried ages ago. If you had doubts, why on earth didn't you come and talk to me about it? I would have put you straight. God, you've been so stupid!'

'Please, Honor. Don't keep telling me I'm stupid. Don't you think I know?'

'But what on earth made you do it?'

'I don't know. I really don't know. It just seemed ... shit! I was emotional about seeing James again, and so relieved he was all right, there was nothing to worry about. Alistair took me out to dinner, we drank too much, it was fun, and then, back at the little house which had been our home . . . I can't explain it, Honor, but it just seemed so natural.'

'It's a pretty lame excuse. We've all had nice evenings out with too much to drink but they don't end in going to bed with the one person who can ruin one's life. I just don't understand you – I thought you were so sensible.'

'I don't understand myself. He just kept saying, "Do you remember . . . ?", and it just all sort of happened.' She shrugged her shoulders despairingly.

'Ah! "Do you remember . . . ?" Dreadfully dangerous words they are! Yes, I begin to see. What a mess.'

'You see, Honor, I'm so confused, but I think I love them both. To be honest, I didn't just jump into bed with Alistair without a thought. I wanted to. And yet I know I love Roberto. His hating me is the worst thing to bear. I'll never forget that look of hate I saw in his eyes.'

'Poor Jane. It's quite common to love two men – but one has to make a choice and live with it. You're not the first woman to wish we lived in a polyandrous society. At least you have a solution – forget Roberto and go and live with Alistair,' Honor suggested, practically.

'But he doesn't love me. I'm just a sexual conquest to him. And in any case I'm pregnant with Roberto's child.'

'Good God, girl, how careless of you! Do you have any more shocks for me, or is that it?'

'Nothing more. In any case it couldn't get worse, could it?' She smiled weakly.

'Maybe, with the baby on the way, Roberto's crazy enough about you to forgive you, eventually,' Honor said, but Jane heard the lack of conviction in her voice and it made her start to cry again. 'For Christ's sake, Jane, do pull yourself together. All this crying is just going to give you wrinkles. It's not getting us anywhere. We must be practical and think what you're to do. You know you're very welcome to stay here, both you and May, there's plenty of room. It would be such fun to have a baby about the place. Guido would be beside himself with happiness. Yes, do stay . . .' Honor held her hand out to Jane.

'Honor, it's sweet of you. I can't. It's too near him, too near all the happiness we shared. No, I had best get right away. I'll go back to Cambridge. I've friends there.'

'As you wish, darling,' Honor said lightly. 'But what about money? Will you let me help with that?'

'Hell, Honor, you're too good. No, I managed before, I'll manage this time.'

'But with a baby on the way, darling? You won't have two halfpennies to rub together. Let me help you, I'd like to.'

'I got myself into this mess, I'll get myself out of it. I can always finish my secretarial course.' She managed to laugh. 'That bloody course. I seem to have been doing it for years, and whenever I do, something catastrophic happens.'

'It's going to be a fearful adjustment for you to make after your life with Roberto. It really will be riches to rags, won't it?'

But it was not the loss of riches that was worrying Jane. It was the thought of a life with no love in it that frightened her.

Early the following morning cases came from the castle containing all Jane's possessions. She sat on the floor sifting through them, repacking all the clothes Roberto had given her, and his presents of jewellery.

'God, girl, you're not sending that all back, are you?'

'Yes, and a note to tell him to dispose of my clothes in his other houses.'

'Is that all it says? Isn't that a bit cold?'

'I did all the begging I'm going to do last night. He's made his mind up. There's nothing else to say.'

'You're too proud, Jane. It's been your downfall once before. And you're making a dreadful mistake – at least keep some of the jewellery. It will keep you for years. Heavens, Roberto can afford it, and it's his baby after all.'

'I can't, Honor. You know I can't.'

'Such a pity! Goodness knows when you'll get another wardrobe like this. He's got such good taste for a man.'

'They're not exactly the sort of clothes that would look right trundling a baby round the supermarket, are they?' Jane managed a weak laugh. Even so, she thought that Honor would cry as the trunks full of her lovely wardrobe were loaded back on the vans to be returned to the castle.

It was a wrench saying goodbye to Honor. But by late afternoon she and May were on the plane to England and by late evening they were sitting in Zoe's kitchen with Zoe and Sandra. Jane had telephoned them both from Heathrow. It was like coming home. She had forgotten what a haven Zoe's kitchen was.

'You must stay here, Jane. I never re-rented the flat when you wrote to say you wouldn't be back. Too lazy, I suppose. Your stuff's still there. It's plenty big enough for you and May.'

'Could I really? Just for a while. Zoe, you're an angel. There's another problem, you see. I'm pregnant.'

'Oh no!' Sandra exclaimed.

'That complicates things,' Zoe stated.

'Does he know?' Sandra asked.

'Yes. He suggested I had an abortion,' Jane replied, fighting back the tears.

'The bastard!' said Sandra.

'Men!' exploded Zoe.

'No, I don't blame him. I treated him atrociously.' To the astonished ears of her two friends she confessed, fearful as she did so of their condemnation, but feeling a compulsion to tell it in all its sordid detail.

'What a sorry tale, Jane. You've been such a clot. But you must think of the future now, and the baby. And, speaking of babies, the most sensible thing is that you get some sleep,' Zoe bossed.

Zoe, May and Sandra sat for hours drinking wine and discussing Jane's situation, once she was in bed.

'That bloody Alistair! He's always popping into her life and wanting her back and then pissing off again. I could kill him,' Zoe said angrily. 'If he'd just kept out of her life she would probably have got over him years ago.'

'I think he meant it, this time,' May said. 'After she left Respryn he had a procession of girls but none of them lasted long. You could see he knew he'd made a mistake.'

'I think he was serious, too. After Jane telephoned today, I phoned St Cuthbert's. I know the sister on that ward, she trained with us. James was never in danger, he was just in for routine observation. He was never delirious nor was he calling for her.'

'My, my. I take it all back then. But how could she go back to him if she's pregnant with Roberto's baby?' Zoe asked logically.

'She can't, can she?' Sandra looked depressed.

'She might have an abortion, as Roberto suggested.'

'Jane? Never. I can't see her doing that.' They solemnly sipped their wine. 'What's Roberto like, May?' Sandra asked.

'He's lovely. He's not handsome or anything – he always reminded me of a monkey, he's got one of those funny, ugly, attractive sort of faces. And so kind, I think he's the kindest man I ever met. And he adored her.'

'Then maybe he'll forgive her, take her back?' Zoe said hopefully.

'No, Mrs Potterton, I doubt that. If he'd loved her a little bit less he might have done, but she was on such a pedestal to him. And he's a Latin, of course, they don't easily forget, do they?'

In the morning, a much calmer Jane began to sort out the muddle of her life. The first priority was money. She telephoned Alistair, who did not sound in the least surprised to hear from her so soon and was eager to see her.

'No, Alistair. I don't want to see you, not for some time. The other night was a stupid mistake. I'm phoning to say that I want to sell the house in Fulham and perhaps get something smaller here, in Cambridge. I hoped you would make the arrangements for me – you know how useless I am.'

'You've left him, then?'

'You could say that, yes.'

'I'm glad. That wasn't the life for you.'

'About the house . . .' Jane continued, ignoring Alistair's remark. She had no intention of arguing with him about Roberto, not now, especially.

She was not alone in making decisions. Zoe and May had made them too. Over lunch they told Jane the conclusions they had reached. Zoe wanted no rent for the flat, and when the baby came May would move into the main house to sleep. May would help Zoe in the house so that Jane need not worry about her wages.

'I can't let you do that.'

'Why not? I like May, provided I can get her to call me Zoe, I couldn't stand that "Mrs Potterton" bit day and night.' Zoe smiled at May. 'No, it makes sense, I need help, you know better than most what a pigsty this place is. And you needn't bother spending your money on a house. It's simple.'

'Yes, it's beautifully simple. But don't you see, Zoe, it's too generous of you. I've got to learn to stand on my own two feet.'

'Why? It's a silly saying that. You needn't worry about money anyway: Benjamin's making so much, now his books are being made into films, money is the least of our worries. Those Hollywood nymphets, that's what my nightmares are about.' Zoe laughed her loud, good-natured laugh.

'Until the baby's born, then. But once he's here, I have to think again.'

'I have every confidence you'll bounce back some way or other, Jane. You seem to be destined to be one of those people who drive around in Rolls-Royces or Minis but nothing in between. You'll soon get out of this year's Mini,' Zoe said.

'I like your faith in me. For the moment I can't see a way out. No, it's modest living from now on for yours truly.'

It was comforting being back in these familiar surroundings, with Zoe just across the patio whenever she needed her, with May coming in and out; and there were the large, rowdy meals in Zoe's kitchen with a new batch of lame ducks. She missed Roberto desperately, far more than she let the others know. She would sit for hours looking at the phone, trying to muster the courage to telephone him, but she never succeeded.

Jane was baby-sitting for Sandra. When Sandra and Justin returned and Justin had gone to bed, the two women sat up talking, just as they used to do.

'Jane, I never told you before but, you know, Alistair set you up. James was never at risk.'

'I know, Sandra, "set up" just about sums it up.'

'You know? Oh. But that was the wrong phrase to use. I really think he wanted you back.'

'Sandra, I was just another body to him. It was probably his way of getting back at Roberto.'

'Alistair? He never struck me as a vindictive type. You sure?'

'Positive.'

They sat for a while in silence. 'Jane, can I ask you something?' Jane looked quizzically at her friend. 'It'll probably sound daft, but . . . I've only slept with Justin . . . what's it like with a different man? I mean is *it* different?'

Jane laughed. 'Wondering if you're missing out, Sandra? Yes, it was different . . . but then it wasn't . . . maybe I was different – I just don't know.' Sandra looked puzzled at Jane's riddle of an answer. 'Oh, God, I miss him!' she suddenly burst out. 'I ache for him. I want him so badly. No one will ever be able to make love to me like that again.'

'Jane, I'm so sorry, I thought you'd got over him, you never say anything. But you'll find someone else, I'm certain.'

'No, Sandra, you don't know what it was like. He made my body come alive and he kept it that way. When he took me it wasn't just my body he took, it was a part of my soul, too. Each time he made love to me, I thought I would die from the sheer ecstasy of it.'

'It doesn't sound at all what Justin and I get up to,' Sandra said with irony. 'I mean, it's all very nice and enjoyable but I can't imagine our little gropings could ever reach those exalted heights.' She laughed, making Jane smile at last. 'You know, you and I were born at the wrong time. We missed out on the sixties. All that fun and freedom, the pill. Hell, I'd got varicose veins by the time it was being prescribed, and how can you be promiscuous lugging a Dutch cap around in your handbag? There we were beavering away looking after husbands, house, brats, all the things we had been told it was our duty to do, and everybody else was having such fun! Now it's all too late – 35-year-old hippies just look sad.'

'I wonder if it is such fun. I wonder if they really enjoy all that casual freedom. I think we felt safer.'

'God, Jane, you're a right one to talk – at least you've lived in sin.'

'"Living in sin" sounds so wicked, as if you're having an orgy every night. But Roberto and I weren't like that. We lived a very staid life, really, a very married life: all that was missing was that little bit of paper.'

'But think of all the opportunities that are open to young women these days, don't you envy them that? I do.'

'Not really. I haven't changed much, Sandra. I still would love to have a man to look after, to be waiting for the sound of his key in the lock every evening. Someone to grow old with.'

'I'll swop for your past any day,' Sandra said wistfully.

'I think you'd want to swop back pretty fast. I'd have given anything for the sort of security you have with Justin. You might think it dull, but I envy you it.'

'Then don't ever get involved in an argument with the Cambridge women's libbers. They'll tear you apart with fury.'

What she had said was true, she thought, as she drove herself home. Her desires were simple and seemed destined to be unfulfilled. She did not want freedom, sexual or otherwise. She did not want a career. She wanted a husband and the emotional security such a relationship would give her. But, feeling as she did about Roberto and Alistair, how could she ever hope to find another man?

Honor came on one of her whirlwind visits. As Jane had expected, her three friends took an immediate liking to each other. Honor even persuaded Zoe to leave her kitchen and took them all out to lunch at

Panos's. It was a noisy lunch. Jane thought that May would die from laughing as Honor, Zoe and Sandra capped each other's funny stories, one after the other, like machine-gun fire. They then trooped through the city, like a gaggle of giggling schoolgirls, marching into one department store after another, where Honor insisted on buying not only a complete layette, but all the furniture for the nursery, too. Before she left at the same breakneck speed, Honor took Jane on one side.

'Have you written to Roberto?'

'No, Honor, I can't.'

'I think you should. He's desperately unhappy. He's virtually a recluse, darling. No one sees him, poor old thing.'

'No parties or anything like that?'

'Nothing. The castle appears closed up, but I know he's there, lurking in the shadows, like a sad ghost. Too morbid, darling.' She shuddered.

But she did not write. What was there to say? She had told him she was sorry, had begged his forgiveness, said that she loved him, and he had not wanted to know. What else was there to write to say?

A month after Honor's visit, she was in Zoe's kitchen when a breathless May rushed in.

'He's here,' she blurted out, interrupting Zoe in midsentence.

'Who's here?' Jane and Zoe asked in unison.

'The Prince!'

She looked a mess, she thought, as with pounding heart she raced across the patio. All this time and all she could think of was how she looked! She was convinced she had not heard May correctly. But there he stood, in the middle of her sitting room, looking out of place in his elegant clothes in the ordinary surroundings of her flat. He looked tired, desperately so, and she felt anguish for him and wanted to rush across the room and hold him to her.

'Hullo,' she said shyly, instead. She was conscious of his eyes looking at her swollen belly and she instinctively put her hands in front of her. 'It's getting big. Not very glamorous, I'm afraid.' She tried to laugh, but her nerves would not let her. Instead a strangled, stupid giggle emerged.

'Honor told me about the baby,' he said without preamble.

'She was here last month. Where did you see her?'

'Paris.'

'You went to Paris as usual, then?'

'Yes.'

'How's the apartment?'

'Why didn't you let me know about the baby?'

'I did. I told you that . . .' She could not finish the sentence.

'I didn't believe you. I thought it was a trick. Why didn't you get rid of it?'

'It isn't the baby's fault. It didn't ask to be conceived. And . . .' She stopped.

'And?'

'It's part of you.' Her eyes filled with tears and she hurriedly turned away.

'Jane, I think we should get married.'

Her head jerked up. She could not believe what she was hearing, she knew that her mouth hung open inanely in astonishment. She could not speak from excitement.

'It would be better for the baby, if he were legitimate. It would not be fair to deprive him of his heritage because of our errors. As you say, he did not ask to be conceived.'

'It might be a girl,' was all she could think to say.

'If we marry, he is secure,' Roberto continued as if she had not interrupted. 'I wouldn't try to take him from you, not like Alistair, I'm not cruel like that. No, but I would expect to share him with you. I would like to see him each summer, and I would like to have him for the skiing and, when he is older, for the boar-shooting. I would like that all decisions to do with his education are mine. I would prefer him to be educated in Italy, I should like him to be an Italian, not an Englishman. I would wish to pay for his upkeep and his servants and, of course, for you.'

'It would be fairer to him,' she said softly, amazed that she could sound so reasonable as she stood, her hopes smashed in little pieces about her. 'I wouldn't want you to pay anything for me, I don't deserve anything, but I can see you would want to support your child. It wouldn't be a question of servants – there's only May.'

'This is not suitable accommodation for you,' he said, looking about the sitting room. 'You must look for a house and I will buy it for you. Perhaps an estate in the country, it would be healthier for the boy, and he should learn to ride . . .'

'I like it here, Roberto. I don't want to move. My friends are very kind to me, we don't need a big place.'

'I don't wish to be difficult. Stay here by all means for a while, until he is older. Should you change your mind meanwhile, then let me know.'

It was all so coldly businesslike. She looked at him with longing.

Nervously she stretched out her hand and gently touched his. 'I love you.'

'I love you too, Jane.'

'Then why?'

'I cannot forgive what you did to me. I could never trust you again.'

'Will you stay with me here, now?' Her voice implored him.

'No. I've rooms at the Garden House, I shall see you each day.'

He kept his word in the days before their wedding. He took her to dinner each day, and there were moments of such ordinary intimacy between them that she would allow herself to hope. But then she would say something, or touch him, and he would look at her coldly and all hope for reconciliation was dashed. The very closeness of him was a perpetual agony to her as she remembered the joy his lovemaking had given her. At night she would plan not to see him, but each morning she relented — just in case.

He had planned their marriage with great care. He had chosen a day when a world-famous film star was to marry in London, and his ploy worked: not one reporter appeared at their wedding. Sandra and Benjamin were their witnesses and Zoe and May their only guests. They stood in the biting December wind on the steps of the Shire Hall while May insisted on taking their photograph with her Instamatic camera. Jane thought wryly how different it was from the last time, as she smiled into the lens. Zoe cooked a magnificent dinner, and Benjamin served champagne, but it was a restrained party.

Then it was time for Roberto to leave. They crossed to the flat for a moment alone together.

'You really are going then?' she asked.

'Yes, I fly home tomorrow.'

'We could make it work, Roberto,' she said, urgency giving her the courage to say what she thought — what had she to lose?

'I would make your life hell, Jane, never trusting you, never letting you out of my sight. You would be a prisoner.'

'I'd learn to cope.'

'No, in time you would hate me. This way is better. The baby has his father's name, his inheritance is secure and you'll be free to lead your own life.'

'But I want to be with you, on any terms.'

'Then you don't know yourself at all, my dear Jane. You have too much spirit for the restrictions that I would put upon you. I don't wish to argue any more, Jane. I have decided.'

'Very well.' She tossed her head with a gesture of defiance. 'You will regret it, though.'

'We shall see,' he said as he made for the door.

In the months that followed she would often wonder if she should have pleaded with him more, if she should have begged, implored. Could she have handled him better? But it was all too late, she told herself frequently. She had only herself to blame this time.

She wrote to James to tell him about the baby, fearful of his reaction. But now she concentrated all her energies on the baby growing within her. She fought any sign of depression, fearful that her moods might infect the child. She wrote long rambling letters to Roberto, which she never posted, knowing that he would not have answered them. But the letter-writing was a form of contact with him that was necessary to her.

In March, on a crisp, golden day, when the crocuses ran riot on the Backs, a lusty, black-haired boy was born, just as Roberto had predicted.

Sandra had arranged to inform Roberto of the arrival of his son, and the following day a large basket of flowers arrived at the nursing home, followed by a telegram which said simply, 'Welcome, Giovanni Roberto Michele Umberto.' Jane laughed: such a long list of names for such a little soul.

She had him christened in the Roman Catholic church. It seemed the right thing to do. She had written to Roberto to tell him which day it was to be. But he did not come.

She was left with his son, his name, and an unquenchable fire in her body for him.

13

Jane had wondered what she was to do with herself once the baby was born. She had not realized that, to this child, she was to give willingly her total time and attention. She would begin her secretarial course at the technical college next term, she said. Next term became the term after. And finally next year seemed early enough to start. Roberto's allowance was generous, so that, having no need to look for a job, she concentrated happily on the child. She knew that even had she lacked money, she would have moved heaven and earth not to have to work, so that she could spend her time with him.

She was the first to admit that she enjoyed this baby in a way that she had not enjoyed her first-born. Perhaps it was because she was older and had more patience and was more aware of how transient babyhood was; or because, she thought, when she had had Alistair to love as well, her affections had been more divided. Or maybe, having been deprived of so much of James' life, she now overcompensated with this little one. Whatever the reason, it made her single-minded and surprisingly content in her life with her son.

She had forced herself not to think about Roberto. At first she had spent hours longing for him, remembering the past, planning a future: then, one day, she realized with a jolt that once again she was allowing the past to rule and threaten her present. She had to stop this, take a grip on herself. It was finished with Roberto: her son needed her full attention, not the depressed, discontented woman she risked becoming if she allowed herself to dream. It had been difficult. The intensity of Roberto's passion had followed her, it seemed. But slowly she succeeded until, a year later, she could live a whole day without thinking of him. But at night it was different – then she would lie in bed and her mind, relaxing its guard, allowed her body to announce its hungry need for him.

She had expected that she would have difficulty adjusting to a more

undane existence, that she would long for the excitement of life with
oberto, the travelling, the clothes, the parties, the endless parade of
:ople. But she did not miss this life at all. Now she began to realize that
e life which she had thought so full had, in fact, been empty. It was
e perpetual motion more than anything else that had generated the
ea of excitement. Roberto and his friends, she realized, lived a life with
. much rigid routine as the office worker catching the 8.35 each
orning. It was the exotic locations that had confused her.

With a sense of relief she found she could delay washing her hair until
e next day – it did not matter. She enjoyed putting on old jeans and
eakers and staying in them all day. It was wonderful that a broken nail
as no longer a major tragedy. It was odd, though, she would think: she
as certain that, when she was living the exotic life, she had enjoyed it.
Maybe she was far more adaptable than she had thought.

One thing upset her. She never heard from Roberto's friends. She sent
hristmas cards but received none in return. She had felt that they had
ked her for herself but clearly she had been mistaken. Only Roberto's
usins, Emilio and Francesca, kept in touch, though she would have
xpected them automatically to side with Roberto. Francesca wrote
egularly with news and sent photos of her son, born two weeks after
iovanni; and they even invited her to stay.

But none of these conclusions was reached overnight. And now she
new herself well enough to wonder whether she could have reacted and
dapted so well without Giovanni's welcome demands on her.

She did not lack friends, however. Living with Zoe, it was impossible
 be lonely, and it was a rare day that she did not see Sandra. But she
ade no attempt to find a lover. She did not look at men as posssible
vers. It was as if Roberto had destroyed that potential in other men for
er. And what if he still had her watched? It was not worth the risk.

Alistair telephoned frequently. He would ask her out to dinner, and
everal times he invited her to join him at a house party. She always
efused; she was afraid to accept. Alistair, she feared, was the one man
vho could still excite her physically. She could not face the old romantic
eed for him, either. She knew that such reactions would make her
lespise herself. She wanted to long only for Roberto.

James came. Of his own initiative he phoned one day to ask if he could
ome for half term. Jane was torn between terror at the prospect of
pending days alone with the boy, and longing to see him again. He was
ifteen now: a solemn and serious young man arrived on her doorstep
vith none of his father's charm and lightness. His first visit was strained

but it was as if the child wanted to build a relationship with her, for he persisted and called regularly.

Her greatest joy was to see her two sons together. Despite the great age difference, James was entranced by his small brother and would play with him for hours. She learned that he was not as humourless and serious as she had thought: he had a delightful, off-beat sense of humour. He was still not demonstrative but the dreadful distance she had felt in the past had gone. It should have been worse since Lady Upnor now lived at Respryn with her son. Jane wondered if, perhaps, the old lady had overplayed her hand, had gone too far in her condemnation of Jane, and had turned the boy towards her. She did not know for certain, she never asked and, since the boy did not talk of his life at home, the subject was never raised between them.

One year passed without her having to relinquish Giovanni to his father, but in the second year, Roberto insisted and May and the toddler travelled to Italy for the summer, leaving Jane alone. She missed both the child and May, and one evening, sitting alone in the flat, feeling too depressed to join the others, she was surprised when Alistair appeared at her door, unannounced, resplendent in his dinner jacket.

'I'm up for a college dinner,' he explained. 'I've got a couple of hours to spare. Thought it was silly that we see so little of each other these days. We should see each other more.'

'Should we?' she asked, pouring them drinks, already uncomfortably aware that she was pleased to see him.

'Yes. Jane, I've known you longer than most of my friends. Makes me shudder to think just how long. It's terrifying the way the years are slithering by, isn't it?'

'I'm not sure what you mean.'

Alistair took a gulp of his drink, stared intently at the glass, and then said quickly, 'I've been a real bastard to you in the past, haven't I?'

Jane smiled. Alistair seemed nervous. She wondered why and what he was leading up to.

'Jane, there's something I've wanted to say for ages. It was bloody of me to try and sue Roberto like that, wasn't it?'

'It was a long time ago.'

'Well, it was, wasn't it?' He leaned towards her, frowning, as he waited for her answer.

'Yes, Alistair, if it makes you feel better, it was bloody of you.' She laughed at him.

He seemed to relax a little and sat back in the armchair. 'I was angry ou know, and jealous. That's why I did it. That day in Cambridge when asked you to come back to me, I had taken months to pluck up the ourage to ask you, and when I did eventually ask, that bastard Tom alked in. I could have killed him!'

'But Tom was nothing to me, I explained all that in my letter to you.'

'What letter?' He looked up sharply from his glass.

'I wrote to you that same night, telling you that I loved you and trying o explain about Tom and me.'

'Jane, I never got any letter! Where did you send it?' he asked acredulously.

'To Respryn, of course.'

'But I went to London. I went on a monumental binge. I can't emember much of what happened but I do know there was no letter.'

'It must have got lost in the post, then. How strange! I wonder what vould have happened to our lives if you had got it?'

'Letters don't get lost in the post, Jane. It's the sort of thing one says to ne's bank manager.' Anger flickered across his face. 'I know what appened to it.'

'Your mother?'

'I'd stake my life on it. Interfering old bitch. God, what else has she lone to ruin my life?'

'She is a bitch. But she interferes only because she loves you, Alistair.'

'Jane, sometimes you can be too reasonable. You ought to hate her for vhat she has done.'

'I used to, but I can't now. I just don't have it in me to hate anyone. In ny case, I believe in fate: we weren't meant to get back together, so your nother was just an instrument of fate. You've got to admire her tenacity, hough, she never gives up on me, does she?' Jane gave a rueful smile.

'But we could have been so happy,' he said seriously.

'On the other hand, we might have been as miserable as sin together. nd I wouldn't have Giovanni. Perhaps, inadvertently, I have your nother to thank for him.' She smiled to herself at the thought of the trange tricks life played.

'And now?' His voice insistently interrupted her thoughts.

Jane looked at her hands. She remembered that night, in Fulham, emembered so clearly her moment of joy; but she also remembered his vords, 'You've learned a lot since the last time'. Those words she could never forget. She shuddered almost imperceptibly.

'So?' she heard him say, softly.

Jane looked at him. Apart from the grey in his hair he looked the same, still handsome, still charming. It would be so easy, she thought. One word and there was the chance that he could be hers again. But could Alistair ever be anyone's totally? How long before the affairs started again? How long before the rot of rejection would eat into her soul?

'We're friends now, aren't we? Let's keep it that way. I value our friendship,' she said, her calm voice belying the control she was exerting.

He seemed about to say something else, but stood up suddenly, his drink unfinished. 'Well, the Master and Fellows await me, I'd better be going. But I meant it, Jane – let's have the odd dinner together. You can't spend the rest of your life mooning about in this little flat, worrying about babies.'

'That would be nice, dinner occasionally,' she said, letting him out of the door.

After he'd gone she sat for a long time in the twilight. It was as she had feared. It had taken all her willpower not to slip into his arms, feel his lips on hers, want to feel his naked body and his hardness within her. What was it about her? Other women were content with one man in their lives but not she – always the same, always wanting the two and now unable to have either. She smiled at herself. It wasn't strictly true that she just thought of babies; she had not told him, but she had a job now.

It had happened completely by accident. She had always enjoyed writing letters, long newsy ones. As she scribbled away in Zoe's kitchen one day it was that practical woman who suggested she should try writing for money. She had sent off an article to the local paper on a subject close to her heart, the difficulties of marrying out of one's class. To her excited astonishment they printed it and sent her a cheque. It was a one-off, she decided, and was surprised when they asked for a series of articles. In the evenings and while Giovanni rested in the afternoons, she had sat at her desk tapping away at her new portable typewriter. She was thankful that at least her haphazard attendance at secretarial course had taught her to type. She found the articles surprisingly easy to write and she loved the thrill of rushing round to the newspaper office to meet the copy deadline. She was amazed one day to get a phone call from a national women's magazine, commissioning some articles. Staggered by how much they were prepared to pay, she took particular care over them, and sent them off nervously. Three weeks later the assistant editor rang to ask if she would be interested in writing an advice column. The prospect unnerved Jane, but Zoe brushed aside her objections and insisted she accept.

It was a success. She enjoyed the work, which she could do at home as happy if she could help people, and was appalled by the sadness and fear in so many women's lives. She discovered it was not just women like herself who had married into difficulties: there were those working-class women who had married a working-class sweetheart only to find that, as the man's career advanced, the pressures on them were enormous – how to do things correctly became an ever present nightmare. It seemed silly to think that not knowing how to lay a table when the boss was coming to dinner might lead to divorce, but Jane got letter after letter that said just that.

What saddened her most was that nothing had changed. She might be happy in liberal, easy-going Cambridge but out there the social jungle was in good heart. Society was still as spiteful and those on top were still as busy kicking at the fingers of those just below them on the ladder of success.

Being able to say she was a professional journalist made life in Cambridge a lot easier for her. She no longer had to suffer the blank, bored stares that saying she did nothing had elicited.

Her life seemed to have settled into a pleasant, comfortable routine, one which, if she was lucky, would go on for ever.

It was late as she sat at her desk writing her column. The flat was lonely without Giovanni, but she had peace to work. The phone rang shrilly. Irritated, she looked at her watch as she crossed the room to answer it.

'Jane, darling. It's Alistair. I don't know quite how to tell you this. It's bad news, it's Honor. I'm afraid she's dead.'

Jane leaned against the wall as she felt her legs buckling under her. She felt enveloped in ice.

'Honor? What on earth are you talking about?'

'It's a shock, I know, Jay, but I'm afraid it's true.'

'This is crazy. I was going to phone her tomorrow, ask her if I could go and stay with her for a couple of weeks,' she said, as if the fact of her intended phone call proved the falseness of his news. 'She can't be dead, I won't believe it.'

'Guido just phoned –'

'A car crash, that was it, wasn't it? Maybe she's just hurt.'

'Jane, love, I'm sorry. It wasn't a crash. Guido found her in bed a couple of hours ago.'

'Of course he'd find her in bed, it's late, isn't it?' she snapped, her rising hysteria reaching her voice.

'Jane, love, you standing up? If so then sit down, take some deep breaths. I know it's hard but you've got to take a grip on yoursel Obediently she did as he said. The deep breathing made her rega control but did not remove the ice-cold blackness that surrounded he 'Her light was on, apparently she hadn't been too well recently. He we to see if there was anything she needed, and he found her, dead.'

'Alistair!' She began to sob. 'I wish you were here.'

'I wish I was, too, Jay. It's a devastating blow. I know how fond of h you were. I thought I should tell you immediately, I didn't want yo reading about it in the newspapers.'

'But what did she die of? She always seemed so fit.'

'I don't know, love. I expect there'll be a post mortem.'

'God, how ghastly! Poor Honor.'

'I thought you'd want to be at the funeral. It's next Wednesday Respryn. You must stay the night, it's too long a drive. James will wa to have you here, he's upset. He was very fond of her.'

'Of course, Alistair. Thank you for letting me know.' She was calme now but it was the calm of disbelief. She replaced the receiver and sa there well into the night, her mind refusing to accept that a worl without Honor was possible.

14

The following Wednesday as she drove through the lodge gates of Respryn and crossed the familiar park she felt a mixture of emotions. Above all she felt an overwhelming sadness that bright, shining Honor was no more, that a glittering piece of magic had gone from the world. She felt a loneliness tinged with fear that Honor would never be there to turn to again. She felt guilt that she had not been to see her sooner – if only she had been there, Honor need not have died alone. She stopped the car and looked round at the beautiful parkland and took comfort that some things never changed. She felt strangely happy to be back here again on the land that for so long had been her home. As she sat and watched the deer, she laughed at herself, for lurking under all these varying emotions was an old familiar feeling of apprehension at the prospect of seeing Alistair's mother again. It wasn't just the parkland that never changed.

Alistair and James were waiting for her and Banks gave her a kindly, warm welcome. She was shown to her room. It was the same room she had occupied the very first time she had come here. She sat on the bed and, looking around the room, saw that nothing had changed here either, except herself. She wondered if the gauche, badly dressed young girl who had sat here, too afraid even to leave the room on her own, would recognize herself in this groomed, sophisticated woman? She had been too long with Roberto and he had been too good a teacher for the veneer that he had given her to disappear. She might not wear couturier clothes any more, but with her acquired sense of style it was easy for her to make her cheaper clothes appear far more expensive than they were. She knew instinctively now the best way to dress her long hair. Her make-up was discreet and perfectly enhanced the large, grey eyes, still unlined, the high cheekbones. Her figure had a svelteness that made it hard to believe she was the mother of two children, one of whom was almost an adult.

Yet, Jane knew that the changes were outward; inside, the differences between the girl she had been and the woman she had become were minimal. She was still longing for love, still not really belonging anywhere, and always, it seemed, in awe of Alistair's mother. But there was one difference: her feelings for Lady Upnor could amuse her now.

Lady Upnor had hardly changed. A few more lines on her face, perhaps, but the same upright carriage which belied her years. Clarissa would not age as well as her mother. There was too much hardness and bitterness in her face, and already she had the set lines of a sour middle age.

Jane was greeted by both in the same manner: an almost royal inclination of the head, a limp handshake. Sufficient courtesy for her not to be offended, but not enough to make her feel welcome. At least the years seemed to have taught Clarissa to disguise her contempt.

August. It seemed to be a significant month in her life. In that month she had met Alistair, Rupert had died, she had finally given herself to Roberto, had betrayed him in that month and had left him too. And now Honor . . . she wondered if Honor's death had interfered with the shooting party at Drumloch. She hoped it had; perhaps it had had to be cancelled. How annoyed Blanche Upnor must have been!

The funeral was beautiful in its simplicity. Estate workers carried the coffin from the house through the knot garden, the rose garden, as if Honor were saying goodbye to them, through the little garden gate and into the tiny church so close to the house that it appeared part of it. The church was packed. As the men lowered the coffin onto the bier in front of the altar, Jane began to weep, it looked so small. Honor had been tall in life, and it was strange that death should make her seem tiny. They buried her in the family vault alongside her ancestors, beneath the oaks, looking down on the home of her childhood.

The congregation made its way silently back to the house. Drinks were served and people stood in embarrassed little clusters whispering to each other. 'You all right?' Alistair asked her, handing her another drink. 'I got you a gin and tonic. I know you loathe sherry.' He smiled at her.

'I hate to think of her alone out there.'

'She's not alone. Calem, her first husband, is with her.'

'How come?'

'She had his ashes in an urn. She's carted them around the world with her for years. She told me yonks ago, "When I snuff it, put Calem in my coffin with me. He was so divine in bed, I'd like to share my coffin with him." So I did. They're both tucked up together.'

'Dear Honor, how lovely! Outrageous to the end.' Jane laughed with delight at the thought of Honor reunited with her Wilbur Calem. As her laugh rang out, several groups turned and stared at her with disbelief and she saw Lady Upnor's mouth twist with distaste. 'Alistair, tell me a funny story, quick, make me laugh again. Honor would have hated us like this, all sad and miserable.'

'You're right. Let me see.' He embarked on a long shaggy-dog story, and when he got to the punch line, Jane laughed loudly, joined this time by Alistair. A deathly silence fell upon the room, and there were more disapproving looks. Alistair clapped his hands. 'Everyone, listen, don't be shocked. Jane had just pointed out to me that Honor would have wanted us to have a happy time. You remember, all of you, how she loved a good party. Well, I suggest that we cheer up in respect and honour of her memory.'

There were murmurs of assent, the whispering ceased and conversations were in normal voices. A laugh rang out, then another, and the volume of noise increased until soon the level was that of a good cocktail party in full swing, one in which Honor would have been very much at home. Instead of the customary two sherries for the ladies and whiskies for the men, Banks and the footmen were dispatched for more liquor and the party went on into the early evening. It was such a success that, as he left, one young scion of a noble house thanked Lady Upnor for 'an absolutely super party' . . .

Finally only Jane, the family and their lawyer, Mr Strong, were left. Jane noticed the lawyer begin to remove a sheaf of papers from his briefcase. She moved silently towards the door; if the will was about to be read, she would slip away.

'Excuse me, Princess, I would be grateful if you would stay.' Jane turned in the doorway.

'I really don't see any reason for this woman to stay, Mr Strong. This is family business,' Lady Upnor said imperiously.

'With Your Ladyship's permission, I would prefer it if she stayed,' Mr Strong said smoothly as he settled his papers on the desk in front of him, ignoring the glare that Lady Upnor gave him. Jane, looking around for somewhere to sit, chose as always a window seat.

The lawyer began to read the will. It was long, for Honor had had many friends and everyone seemed to be remembered. As each bequest was read out, there was a message from Honor for the recipient, whether they were present or not, all read in Strong's passionless, legal voice. It was a touching will and a funny one too – she had left a large sum of money to Guido with the instructions that he buy himself some land, but Honor suggested he stick to olive-growing since, with his liver, vines might be too big a temptation. Jane heard Alistair's name mentioned: Honor had left him the land she owned here, saying that she wanted it to revert to the Respryn estate. For the first time Jane realized that Honor must have bought much of the land which had had to be sold when Rupert died.

The lawyer took a sip of his drink and looked anxiously around the room. Clarissa and her mother sat on the edge of their chairs, probably unaware of how eager they both looked as they strained to catch every word. The nub of the will, announcing the disposal of Honor's considerable fortune, had been reached.

Mr Strong cleared his throat and went on. 'My paintings, my furniture, my motor cars, my jewellery, my flats in New York and London, my villa in Italy, I leave outright to my dear niece and true friend, Jane Upnor née Reed.'

The gasps in the room were audible. 'Really!' Jane heard Lady Upnor exclaim, but, undeterred, the lawyer, having taken another sip of his drink, continued. '"The rest of my estate, my portfolio of stocks and shares, my various businesses and business interests, and any monies I have at the time of my death, I leave to my great-nephew Viscount Redland, possession of which he is to enjoy only upon the death of his mother Jane. Total control of my estate and its income is to be hers to enjoy outright with, as Jane would say, 'no strings attached' until her death.

'"Now I expect at this very moment there's a lot of muttering going on, so let me explain. I have done this, Jane, because I learned to love you and you became a good friend to me. I admire your integrity, and I know James's money will be safe with you.

'"I have done this, Clarissa, because you have always been a mean-minded, spiteful little bitch and you were cruel to Jane when she needed friends and understanding. But in any case I never liked you and, Jane apart, would never have bothered to leave you anything.

'"As for you, Alistair, I could never forgive the way you treated Jane, the dreadful cruelty of taking away her child at a time when she needed love. No doubt you were influenced by your dreadful mother, but that is no excuse. I tried to forgive you but I couldn't. I could never understand Jane's faithfulness to you and the love she bore you for so long. Since I spent long hours trying to persuade her to ditch you, it would be hypocritical of me to leave you anything other than what belongs to Respryn and the future. So I chose to benefit your son.

"'I would prefer, though I doubt if it is likely in the circumstances, that you do not vent your spite in your collective disappointment upon Jane. It is not her fault I have chosen to act in this way.'"

The lawyer paused a long time and took another long sip of his drink. Finally, as if screwing up all his courage, he continued, "'My only regret is that I won't be with you all just to see the expression that is, undoubtedly, on Blanche's face right now.'"

Everyone turned to look at Lady Upnor, whose face was mottled grey and maroon and twisted with anger. The lawyer laid the papers down, took off his spectacles and polished them carefully. He looked like a man who knows that all the furies of hell are about to break upon him. The silence hung oppressively. Jane waited for the onslaught to begin.

'I don't believe it!' Lady Upnor finally said, her voice strangely thick with emotion.

'The bitch, the filthy degenerate old bitch!' Clarissa screeched.

'Does that mean I'm rich?' James asked.

'Not for a very long time, it seems, James, unless you're lucky,' his grandmother interjected, glaring at Jane venomously.

'Can you two shut up a minute and let me say something?' Alistair demanded but Clarissa ignored him and continued unabated, though in a quieter voice, which, after her initial hysterics, was more frightening.

'You're a cunning bitch, aren't you, Jane? Wheedling your way into the lonely old bat's life, always looking as if butter wouldn't melt in your mouth, and bloody scheming all the time.' To Jane's astonishment she saw that Clarissa was crying; somehow she had never thought her capable of tears. Hector, her husband, put his arm about her shoulder to comfort her but angrily she shrugged him away. 'It's not fair, we needed that money so badly,' she wailed. 'She's not even family.' Angrily wiping the tears from her eyes, she jumped to her feet. 'We'll fight it, that's what we'll do. We'll get the will overturned.'

'Lady Clarissa, I do not advise that,' the lawyer interrupted. 'You would spend a lot of money and get nowhere. A will made by a person sound in mind is almost impossible to upset and only then by a close relative. Your relationship with Lady Honor would not be regarded as close enough.'

'But she wasn't of sound mind. She was mad, always had been, everyone knew that. You knew her, Mr Strong.'

'Eccentric, yes, Lady Clarissa, but mad in medical and legal terms — no.'

'I think it is appalling, Mr Strong, that my children should be deprived of their rightful inheritance in this way. That's the will of a spiteful, vindictive woman,' Lady Upnor said angrily, the mottling on her face even more marked. 'It doesn't sound like a proper will to me. I'm sure no court would accept it.'

'I know what you mean, Lady Upnor. It is a most unusual will, but then Lady Honor was a most unusual person.' The lawyer tried a placatory smile but, getting no response, he continued. 'However, it has been duly witnessed and I can assure you Lady Honor was of sound mind when she made it. I remember her exact words to me. "I want a will that everyone can understand, no legal jargon," she said. It is a proper will, albeit not couched in legal terms. Of course you may take other opinions, Lady Upnor, but you will find they agree with me.'

'When was that will made?' Lady Upnor angrily enquired.

'It is dated December 1970. Nearly three years ago by my reckoning. She came to my office when she was here on a Christmas visit.'

'You were in Italy then,' Lady Upnor said accusingly, stabbing the air with a long bony finger.

'Yes, I was,' Jane said quietly.

'There you are, then, Mr Strong, undue influence from certain quarters, no doubt.' Lady Upnor continued to emphasize her words by pointing her finger menacingly at Jane.

'I was no longer living with Lady Honor, I had left. I take exception to your accusations, Lady Upnor. And I would appreciate it if you would stop wagging your finger at me in that aggressive manner,' Jane said in such an even tone that only Alistair was aware of the hint of humour in her voice.

'How dare you? You impudent hussy!' Lady Upnor spluttered, but Jane noted with satisfaction that she folded her hands on her lap.

'Shacked up with your gigolo, were you?' Clarissa snapped.

'Clarissa, what is the point in insulting me like this? Don't you ever give up?' Jane felt exasperated.

'What do you expect? That I just sit back and let you steal our money?'

'I'm not stealing anything. I repeat, I knew nothing about Honor's intentions. I knew she didn't like you and I admit that I agreed with her assessment of you. What the hell did you expect after all the years of sniping I had to put up with? But I'd no idea she'd go this far.'

'You see, Mr Strong, she admits it. She worked on the old cow, it's obvious,' Clarissa shrieked.

'If I can get a word in edgeways in the midst of all this backbiting, I for one would like to say I'm very pleased for Jane. You keep going on about rightful inheritance, Mother. This money has nothing to do with us. It was Wilbur Calem's originally: Honor was free to leave it to a cats' home if she wanted.'

'She's done that,' Clarissa said childishly.

'I would prefer it if you didn't mention that loathsome Calem's name.' Lady Upnor said haughtily.

'You might have found him loathsome, Mother, but your loathing appears to stop short of his money.' Alistair grinned triumphantly.

His mother shook her head angrily but ignored his jibe. 'I think Clarissa is right. I think Jane wormed her way into my sister-in-law's affection, Mr Strong. Something she had no right to do.'

'That's not fair, Lady Upnor. I loved Honor, she was a good friend to me. I always presumed that Alistair would get everything.'

'Liar!' shouted Clarissa. 'Your whole life has been one long scheme. Look how you conned Alistair into marrying you. He denies it, but I bet you told him you were pregnant. He'd never have married a common little tart like you for any other reason.'

'Aunt Clarissa!' James had leaped to his feet. 'How dare you speak to my mother like that?' He crossed the room to stand protectively beside Jane, who smiled gratefully up at him.

'You don't know her, James. Christ, I always had my doubts about Honor, I wouldn't be surprised if the two of them were a couple of lesbians and we didn't know.'

'Clarissa! You've gone too far,' Alistair shouted at his sister.

'A little family loyalty from you wouldn't go amiss, Alistair. Hoping to screw your way back in to some money, little brother?'

'Clarissa, so help me, I'll hit you.' Alistair lunged forward as if to strike her but Jane grabbed at him.

'Alistair, please don't bother. It doesn't matter. Honestly.'

'I'd no idea this family could be so bloody,' young James said with disbelief.

'You haven't heard the half of it, James. Why do you think your father wouldn't let her have you? Ever thought of that? I'll tell you, because he knew her for what she is, and he didn't want any of her nasty working-class mentality rubbing off on you.'

'Grandmother, this is terrible. Please stop, Aunt Clarissa.' The youth looked, wide-eyed with horror, from one relation to another. Jane took hold of her son's hand and squeezed it, hoping to convey that she was no longer upset by this family and its attitude to her. She looked at the angry faces, Lady Upnor's still dangerously mottled – absent-mindedly, Jane wondered if she had had her blood pressure checked recently. Clarissa's carefully larded make-up was beginning to melt with the perspiration her anger was creating – she'd be furious when she saw her face in the mirror. She watched and listened and realized that they were no different from any family haggling over an unfortunate will: money really brought out the best and worst in people. Money. How much? she wondered. It must be a considerable amount. Look at the way Honor had lived; look at the hysterics she was witnessing. Inwardly she smiled. What fun, what power! No, that wasn't a pleasant thought – Honor had never used it as a weapon and she wouldn't, either. Imagine, though, after all these years, here she sat, no longer the least bit in awe or hurt, and rich, too. A smile broke on her face – what a sense of humour Honor had! She became aware that Lady Upnor was talking to James. She shelved her thoughts for the moment, and concentrated on what the old bitch was saying.

'I'm sorry, James, but you're a man now, it's better that you know the truth. This family has never been the same since that woman, your mother, came into it.'

'I'll tell you the truth, James.' Alistair spoke up. 'My mother thinks I got custody of you because I loathed your mother and she thinks she persuaded me. It wasn't that. I thought, wrongly, as it turned out, that if I got you she would come back to me, but she didn't. You were all I had left from our marriage, and when she didn't want me, I knew that if you got to know her too well you would love her more than me. That's the truth. And I suggest that, if you two can't shut up and behave with a modicum of civility, you both leave the room,' he added forcefully to his mother and sister.

'I'll leave the room, willingly. Oh yes, I'll leave the room but I'll see that bitch in court. Come on, Hector, Mother.' The two women swept from the room with a sheepish Hector tagging along behind.

'Another Scotch, Strong? You look as though you've earned it,' Alistair said, the tension visibly draining out of him.

'Thank you, Lord Upnor, another drink would go down well. I do so hate these occasions when people are disappointed. The trouble is, they get so carried away that I think they forget I'm here,' he said, almost sadly.

'Mr Strong, what does this will mean?' Jane asked.

'It means, Princess, that you are an extremely wealthy woman. Not only do you have complete control over Lady Honor's assets, but you will enjoy her very large income from them for life. You are also free to dispose of those properties left to you outright. She did mention that she thought you might like to keep the Italian villa: she felt it was a special place to you.'

'Yes, that's true. But I would like to help Alistair in some way. James's school fees are so high and in a few years there'll be the cost of university. His expenses will be heavy. I'd like to pay them if there's enough.'

'Very proper in the circumstances, might I say? It's your privilege entirely whom you assist.'

'After death duties, there would be enough, then?'

'My dear Princess, I don't think you have any idea of the vastness of Lady Honor's estate, even after death duties are taken into consideration.'

'Dear old Calem.' Jane smiled.

'Jane, I don't want you helping me out. James, yes, but not me, I don't deserve it.'

'Yes, you do, they were magic years.' She held out her hand to Alistair. Mr Strong packed his papers away.

'I almost forgot. There's one thing here for you, Princess, a letter. The instructions are on the envelope.'

Jane took the thick white envelope with Honor's distinctive, bold handwriting on the front: 'Jane, read this when on your own, your feet up and a large G & T in your hand.' She slipped it into her handbag.

The lawyer left and Alistair poured his son and Jane another drink.

'Here you are, James. I think today is a day we won't count your drinks.' He laughed affectionately at his son.

'Can I get this straight, Pa? Ma has control of Aunt Honor's money but it's all mine one day?'

'That's right. I don't think you have any cause to worry. I can't imagine your mother ever letting you run short.'

'So we're rich?'

'You could say that – filthy rich would be more accurate.'

'Wow!' exclaimed his son.

'Do you have any idea how much, Alistair?' Jane asked.

'None whatsoever. I do know that the Calem empire is enormous and very diversified. She explained it to me once but I wasn't really listening –

it all seemed to be companies within companies. I don't think darling old Honor really understood, she just spent it.'

'What about death duties?' Jane asked, remembering Alistair's problems at Respryn.

'It won't be like when my father died. She had an army of accountants and lawyers looking after her affairs, and she was no longer resident in this country. Don't look so worried, Jane. You'll inherit her advisers along with the money. I should just listen to them.'

'Granny and Aunt Clarissa were bloody,' the young boy announced suddenly, looking anxiously at his mother. 'Poor Ma.'

'James, don't worry yourself, it's been going on for so long now that I'd have felt there was something terribly wrong if they had been nice to me,' Jane said with a shrug.

'I have listened to them sometimes in the past. Ma, I'm sorry . . .' The boy's face twisted as he fought to control tears that were not far beneath the surface.

'Darling, I understand.' She put her arm around her son and looked closely at him. 'Darling, listen to me. It's not important. We're friends. We love each other, that's all that matters.'

Mother and son stood holding each other. Alistair crossed the room and in turn put his arms around them both. The three of them stood silently holding each other, taking comfort from each other.

She could not stay the night now. Alistair accepted that the atmosphere would be intolerable for her. In the small hours she finally arrived home. She was tired from the long drive, but still she poured herself the drink Honor insisted on, and sat down, her feet up, as instructed, and opened the letter.

Darling, darling Jane,

Isn't this too divinely ghoulish? Just like in the films!

Did Blanche's face go all slack with shock and horror? Such fun, I do wish I could have been there. I did toy with the idea of making one of those video tapes from the grave, like they have in America, but I decided that was a wee bit too vulgar!

I expect you were called all manner of names, scheming bitch etc. But you know and I know and that's all that matters. With no children, it is sad and chilling to know that one is dying with no one to leave favourite knickknacks to. But I loved you, so you were the logical choice.

Yes, I knew I was dying. Remember those silly headaches?

They'd started just before you came to stay. I saw the doctors and they gave me a year to live. Be buggered, I thought, I'll fight this, and I did. Nothing for three years and then, whoosh, the bastard peeped up again. It was when you left Roberto. I so wanted you to stay, I was so low then and afraid. I should have told you, begged you to stay, I suppose, but you were so afraid of seeing Roberto, remember? Anyhow, with my luck the tumour went dormant again. I was a bit weak and wobbly but by cutting down on the late nights and the booze I could manage reasonably. Then this year it came back with a vengeance, there was no mistaking its intentions this time. It's here to stay and the pain is sometimes intolerable. It's obvious which of us will win the battle this time.

They can't operate, you see. The only thing they could offer me was radiation treatment and chemotherapy, but with a very slim chance of recovery. They were quite honest with me, I'd lose my hair (imagine, after all the money I've spent on the bloody stuff, having it all fall out!), I'd slip slowly into being a paralysed, incontinent vegetable. Well, I can't let it happen, Jane, I just can't.

I found an obliging doc who's given me some pills that will just carry me off, no fuss, and everyone will think my heart gave out.

I shall take them one day when the pain is like a circular saw in my head. I'll lie down with a nice gin and tonic and beat the bastard at its own game.

Forgive me, darling, but there's no other way. I wanted you to know, but don't tell a living soul. You see, I want to be buried at Respryn with the rooks and wood pigeons cawing and cooing away above me, and the scent from the rose garden wafting up to the cemetery. I don't know what the law is about suicides in consecrated ground, and all that guff – or is that just Roman Catholics? Anyhow, I'd rather not take the risk of some busybody finding out and insisting on digging me up. Too macabre for words, darling!

Remember when we were at Drumloch, when poor old Rupert died, you said if you had a place like that you'd never kill anything. Buy one, darling, you can afford it, and it's a nice idea. Do get in touch with Roberto, I beg you.

                                                            Honor

Jane sat clutching the letter for a long time, her large gin and tonic forgotten. Her mind led her back unbidden over all those years to the many times when her wise friend had comforted, counselled and loved her. Gradually the awful void Honor's death had left in her heart began to fill up with the memories, both happy and sad, that their friendship had left. Honor had been too full of the joy of living to endure a living death. She had taken the only way.

Curiously at peace with herself now, alone, Jane said goodbye to her beautiful, glittering friend.

15

A piece of paper had so changed her circumstances that there was no way she could ever lead a normal life again. Overnight she had become a very wealthy woman and from now on, her accountants advised her, a tax exile. Long hours were spent with lawyers and the ever present accountants, rationalizing her fortune and her future.

Her days seemed full of decisions and the nights full of wondering if she had made the right ones. Decisions about Honor's investments were easy to make – she just left everything as it was, and would rely on the same team of experts that Honor had depended upon. Deciding to sell the New York flat was easy, too. She did not want to live that far away, so everything was sold. She dithered about the flat in London. It might be useful, and James could use it when in London, and Alistair too, if he wanted. But then she saw it. Elegant and enormous, the flat was for parties and soirées; she would merely rattle about in it on her own. She put it on the market immediately.

A few weeks into her wealth, the realization that it was not all going to disappear overnight finally fixed itself in her mind. She travelled to her home town, and within a couple of hours had found a house on a leafy avenue, with gardens at the front and back, bay windows, a fitted kitchen and a tiled bathroom. Not until the contracts had been ex-changed did she return.

It was strange entering her childhood home. It was even smaller than she remembered and shabbier, too.

'This is a surprise. We thought you'd given us up,' her mother welcomed her. Jane chose to ignore the gibe. What was the point in arguing that they hadn't gone out of their way to keep in touch with her? Instead she jangled the keys of the new house and put them on the table.

'That's for you two.'

Her father picked the keys up, suspiciously. 'What are they?'

'They're keys to a house on Sunny Avenue. I remember Mum always dreamed of a house there. And it's close to the football ground for you, Dad.'

'What's this, then, conscience money?' her mother asked, her customary bitter expression distorting her face.

'No Mum, it isn't. I would have done this years ago, but I was never in the position to. Now I can. I want to see you both more comfortably settled.'

'This money hasn't come from that greasy wop you've been living with, has it? 'Cause I'll tell you now, if it has, you can tell him where he can stuff his bleeding keys.'

'No, Mum, it hasn't come from him. I was left some money by Alistair's aunt. It's my money.'

'Why did she leave it to you? What about Alistair? And James?' she asked sharply.

'She left it to me and James.'

'Oh, that poor dear boy Alistair, what he's suffered because of you. You were a stupid cow to ever leave him, a nice gentleman like that.'

'Who left who is academic. He broke the marriage up, not me.'

'Not without reason, I'm sure. You always were impossible to live with, and that's a fact. And then to choose a greasy wop!'

'Mum, I'm beginning to get irritated by you. He's not a greasy wop, and I'd prefer it if you didn't talk about him like that. Now, do you want this bloody house or don't you?'

She had planned this surprise so meticulously; she had presumed her mother would be beside herself with happiness, but it wasn't going at all as she had anticipated.

'Thank you, Jane, it's very generous of you. We'll enjoy living there.' To Jane's astonishment, it was her father, accepting graciously.

'I thought you always said you'd never accept charity,' her mother snapped at him.

'I don't regard a gift like this from our only child as charity. Can we go and see it?'

On seeing the back garden, he immediately and enthusiastically began to plan what he was going to plant. Her mother stalked about the house, inspecting it, sniffing audibly as she opened cupboards and tried the windows.

'It's filthy!'

'Empty houses always look dirtier than they are. They were very nice people, I'm sure you'll find it's just the bareness makes it look dirty.'

'It's a nice kitchen,' her mother said grudgingly. 'But the heating — it'll cost a small fortune. Your father's retired now, we're not rolling in money, you know.'

'I've thought of that. I'll make you an allowance for things like rates and heating.'

'It's a long way from the shops.'

'Mum, stop carping. If you look in the garage, you'll see a Mini. Why don't you just give in and accept it as a nice house, and one you'll be happy in? I sometimes think you prefer being miserable.' Jane was rapidly becoming disenchanted with the whole exercise. She wandered into the garden and joined her father.

'What d'you think, Dad?'

'It's a little palace, Jane. It's very good of you. We weren't exactly the best parents, me especially. And then you do this. You're a good girl, Jane.'

Unused to kind words from him, she was puzzled by the change in him and did not know what to say. So she leaned forward and kissed him on the cheek. It felt odd to be doing so, the flesh unfamiliar, the flesh of a stranger. Her father began to cry.

'Oh, Dad, please don't cry, it's supposed to be a happy day. That's if Mum will allow it to be.' She was embarrassed, she hated to see him cry, but was not sure what to do or say to him. She did not know him well enough to be able to comfort him.

'Sorry, I'm getting to be a sentimental fool in my old age. And ashamed, too. It should have been me buying this house for your mum, but somehow, I never seemed to make it.'

'You've got it now. Does it matter who bought it? Perhaps she wouldn't have moaned so much if it had been you.'

She managed a weak laugh. Perhaps that was the reason for the change in her father: old age, as he said, making him look differently at things, at her.

'Yes, she would. But she'll come round. Your mum's only really happy when she can have a good moan, bless her. It's more a ritual, really.' He smiled at her. 'Heavens, even God can't get it right for her! It's either too hot or too cold, too wet or too dry.'

'Maybe she should have been a farmer.' The sad moment had passed. She had always presumed that they hated each other, but now her father had just shown that he was fond of his wife. As love could turn into hate, was it possible that hate could turn to love?

She stayed a week in the old house with them. Her Vuitton luggage looked incongruous in the bedroom of her childhood. She washed at the kitchen sink, she trotted out to the outside lavatory. Stoically she ate her mother's cooking. Having had her token moan, her mother settled happily into planning for the new house. Each day they set out shopping for furniture, carpets and curtains, a washing machine, a gleaming new cooker. What had started as a duty became a pleasure and Jane was as excited as her mother when they found exactly the right wallpaper for the sitting room. It was an odd experience, being in her home town again. Had it always been so drab? Had the people always looked so downtrodden and dejected? It fascinated her to think that as she walked along the High Street, she was probably brushing shoulders with women she had been at school with. She scanned the faces of those who she thought were her own age. It was days before she realized that she was searching for the wrong faces. She had been looking at women with young faces, like hers; now she realized that had she stayed here, she would have been one of those with faces marked with premature middle age. It was a sobering experience. Once or twice her mother stopped someone and said, 'Jane, you remember so and so here,' and Jane would lie and say, 'Yes,' and a stilted conversation would begin; then the old acquaintance would start to look embarrassed and, since there seemed nothing to say, they would move on.

She was glad to get back to Cambridge and to May and Giovanni returning from Italy. A momentous amount had happened since they left. Tanned by the sun, Giovanni looked far more Italian: he could even say one or two words in the language. She purposely did not ask May about Roberto, and May, presuming she did not want to know, said nothing. Giovanni was too young to say more than a few garbled phrases about 'Papa'.

That Christmas Jane went wild. She was so happy to be able to give. She showered all her friends with presents. When invited out, she took only the best wine, a pot of caviar, fruit out of season, exotic plants. Just like Honor, she found it 'such fun'. If rich people were unhappy, it was because they had not learned the sheer exhilarating joy of giving, she decided.

And then the unpleasantness started. Snide remarks were made about her wealth, and sly comments on the cost of her clothes. Her jewellery was inspected a mite too closely. She began to feel intensely guilty that she had so much. Some blatantly asked for help and she was only too happy to give it, but she was puzzled when she saw them later: often these same people would cross the street to avoid her. Others came to her with schemes that needed investment, all of them impossible, but she was not prepared for the abuse she received when she refused to invest. Only Zoe and Sandra never changed, but then Zoe was wealthy, too, and understood, and Sandra had been a friend too long to be anything but happy for her and was, in any case, incapable of malice.

The last straw came when Jane found herself in the ladies' in Eaden Lilley, stuffing the dress she had just bought in Vogue – the exclusive shop she loved – into a Marks and Spencer bag, just in case she met someone she knew on the way back home; anything to prevent the catty remarks that would be made about her choice of shop. 'This is crazy,' she thought. 'I can't live the rest of my life being ashamed, and doing potty things like this.' Sadly, the conclusion she reached was that she could not stay in Cambridge. Being rich had its penalties and other people's envy was the hardest. Since her lawyers had advised her that after a year she would have to become a tax exile, she decided to go now. To Italy. If she bumped into Roberto it was too bad, but at least in financial terms she could face him as an equal. And if she found she could not live so close to him, then she would sell Honor's villa and find somewhere else in the world to make her home.

She gave May the option of staying with Zoe, but May insisted on going with her and Giovanni.

'You need me more, now you're rich. At least I might stop you doing anything daft.'

To her surprise, Guido was still at the villa. He looked sheepish as he opened the door for them.

'But what about the smallholding that Lady Honor gave you the money to buy?' Jane asked him.

'Principessa, I couldn't leave this beautiful villa, it has been my home for too long,' he burst out desperately. 'Principessa, you will allow me to stay here with you, please?' His pleading decided her that there could be no sale of Honor's villa. If Roberto were to be awkward, she would just have to learn to live with the problem. In any case, Honor had been right: this was a special place to her. Already she felt relaxed and happier.

She meant to telephone Roberto as soon as she arrived but she delayed, admitting to herself that she was frightened, fearful of the effect the sound of his voice would have on her hard-won equilibrium. The summer slipped by in a haze of happy days with Giovanni by the pool. The villa was a quieter place without Honor's friends racketing in and out and with the phones rarely ringing.

Autumn came and still she had not phoned. But now, Christmas was only a few weeks away, and in fairness to their son, she must speak to him – they should, for the child's sake, celebrate it together. She telephoned the castle. The Prince, his major-domo told her, was still in Rome, too ill to come this year.

'Too ill? What's wrong with him? Is he in hospital?'

'No, Principessa, he is in his house in Rome.' A strange moaning noise issued from the telephone. 'Principessa! He is dying!'

Never had she packed so fast and never had Guido driven so rapidly. He drove direct to Rome, she did not have patience to wait for a train. She needed to be moving. When they arrived at the *palazzo*, Jane leaped from the car before it had even halted. The same old man opened the gate for her, his body still bent, but now with the added burden of grief. On seeing her, he looked as if he would cry, speaking in Italian too garbled and fast for her to understand. She raced up the sweeping marble staircase. The house oppressed her immediately. She opened the door of Roberto's suite of rooms and found her way barred by two nurses.

'No visitors allowed,' they said stiffly, in unison. The male nurse grabbed her arm and pushed her back through the doorway.

'Get out of my way. I am the Principessa Villizano, I demand to see my husband.' It was the first time she had ever called herself that and she must have said it with authority, for the nurses stood respectfully aside to let her pass. She crossed the anteroom and gently opened the door into his bedroom. Tiptoeing towards the ornately canopied bed, she stopped, transfixed with horror at what she saw. A frail old man slept there, his thinness accentuated by the large, opulent bed. His body was not fine and muscular like Roberto's but wasted, the skin stretched taut across the bones. Roberto was always tanned but this man's skin was putty-coloured, with a sickly, yellow tinge. Roberto was dark-haired, not grey like this man. There must have been a hideous mistake, someone was playing cruel tricks on her. Then the figure on the bed opened his eyes, the fine, dark-brown eyes focused on her, and she put her hand to her mouth to stifle the gasp. Only the eyes were those of the Roberto she knew.

'Ah, my Contessa.' He took her hand and with difficulty lifted it to his mouth. 'You came.' The words were a sigh on his lips.

'Roberto, my darling, what has happened to you? What is wrong with you? How long have you been like this?' The urgent questions tumbled out of her.

'Forgive me, my dear, I know, I look terrible, not the Roberto you remember. It is difficult to realize that it is me, isn't it?' He tried to smile.

'Why on earth didn't you send for me?'

'How could I? What right had I?'

'You should have sent for the woman you knew loved you.'

'Do you still love me, Contessa?'

'I never stopped loving you, my darling.'

'You never took another lover?'

'No, my darling.'

'Then it is an even greater tragedy.' He sighed.

'But what on earth is wrong with you?'

'I have a form of leukaemia. It has been mercifully quick. I feel no pain, but I am very tired.'

'America! We must go to America, immediately. They are so much more advanced there,' she said in desperation.

'No, my sweet. It's no use. It is my time to die.'

'You mustn't talk like that. I won't hear it! You will live, I will make you live.'

'As I made you love me? Remember how you said it was impossible?' He laughed, but the effort was too much for him. He closed his eyes and she held him to her, terrified that the shock of seeing her had weakened him and that he would die now, just as she had found him again.

'We've been such fools, Roberto, such bloody stupid proud fools,' she said as he opened his eyes and smiled. She took his hand and covered it with frantic kisses.

'It's so easy to be proud and foolish when you think you have years of life ahead of you. But you're here now. You'll stay? You will stay with me to the end?'

'Darling, of course I'm staying. For all the years we have left, I'll be with you. You're not getting rid of me this time.' She tried to joke. He sighed contentedly and she sat and held his hand and watched him as he slid back into a deep sleep.

While he slept she summoned his doctors. They assured her that there was nothing further to be done. There was no point in taking him to America; they themselves had arranged for the world's experts, including the Americans, to see the Prince. They felt that her coming was the best thing for him, for he had spoken often of her.

'But this house. I hate this place. It's so gloomy. Could we not take him to the castle? He loves that best of all: I'm sure he'd get better there.'

'I very much doubt if he would survive the journey, Principessa.'

'We could fly him.'

'Not even a short flight.'

'How long then?' The dreaded question hung in the air between her and the sober-suited doctors.

'A month, Principessa, at the most.'

She turned away from them. It was impossible, a month. She could not, and she would not, believe it.

There was already the gloom of death about the house. The servants shuffled silently about, their faces long and mournful. The windows were shuttered, and the large rambling palazzo was a place of shadows and despair.

Before Roberto awoke, she had ordered the shutters to be opened. Roberto had loved the sun, had followed it all his life; if he were to die, it was intolerable that he should die in this half-gloom. Even the weak December sun which filtered through was better for him than that. She ordered boxes of flowers to be delivered immediately. And she told the servants that, on pain of dismissal, they were to smile and be cheerful in front of the Prince – they could keep their mournful looks to themselves. Once he was awake, she had all the medical paraphernalia removed to the anteroom; his bedside table was cleared of medicines and bottles, and flowers took their place. She had the large stereo set up in his room, so that throughout the day and at night when he could not sleep he could have beautiful music filling his room. The first record she placed on the turntable was the Mahler he had played her years ago.

'Already, it is better.' He smiled at her. 'It becomes a home and not a charnel house.'

In her room she found nothing altered. The wardrobes were still full of her clothes, the dressing table contained her make-up and perfumes. Each day she would change her clothes several times, even though they were now very out of date. She would groom herself with the special care that he had once demanded. He remembered each outfit, where they had bought it, where they had had lunch that day, whom they had met, and where they had gone that evening.

Each night she would prepare herself for bed with elaborate care as if going to a lover and each night she would lie beside him and hold him, talk to him when he could not sleep, snatching sleep herself whenever he drifted off, but waking the minute he stirred. Only his eyes could express the longing that he still felt for her.

His spirits improved as she fought for him, like a tigress. The dreaded month passed and he was still with her. The doctors had been wrong.

Christmas came and, against the doctors' advice, she sent for Giovanni and May. The doctors feared that the child would weaken and tire him. Instead, the presence of his son and the child's happiness strengthened him. They decorated the tree; Roberto was carried downstairs and sat in his favourite chair, issuing instructions on where the coloured lights should be, teasing her, bantering with her, and smiling now, always smiling.

This house had become her world, his room the centre of that world. She never went out, was never far from his side. She began to plan; they would talk of Giovanni and what they both wanted for him. In the New Year they started him in kindergarten, and in the evenings, the child would sit on his father's bed and together they would look at his books and what he had done that day. She began to plan for them, where they would go this summer, whom they would see. He would smile at her and agree and she would try not to see the sad resignation in his eyes.

Now it was spring. There were days when the sun was warm enough for them to wheel Roberto into the garden, and he would sit, his face turned to the sun he loved so much. But there were days he could not be moved. Her indomitable spirit and her devotion impressed everyone. She would not speak of death, she would not accept it. As spring turned into summer she began to believe that she had won. A month, they had said, and that had been seven months ago.

He was sleeping peacefully. She sat beside the bed, holding his hand, gazing with love at the face which, even with this terrible illness, still had a nobility to it. He awoke and his dark eyes smiled at her.

'Promise not to live in the past, little one,' he whispered. 'Don't waste any more of your life. We've wasted too much already. You promise? You must live. You promise, my Contessa?' he asked with a strange urgency. They were the last words he was to speak to her. He fell asleep but this time did not wake up. He slipped silently and imperceptibly away from her into a deep coma. He lay suspended in that sleep before death for three long days. Days when Jane could not accept what was happening, a time when she never slept but talked to him, softly, willing him back to her. She knew he heard, for sometimes he smiled. Jane was certain that, since he could hear her pleading, he would fight, he would return to her. But, on the fourth day, he died in her arms. She held him a long time after he was dead, loath to let him go, loath to give his body to the waiting nurses. Eventually, ignoring her cries of anger, they forced her to give him to them.

It was a sad return to the castle. As the train bearing Roberto home drove into the station, it appeared that the whole village of Villizano was waiting. First they went to the church for a solemn requiem mass. Then the coffin was placed in the gleaming, black and silver hearse, pulled by six fine, black horses, black plumes dancing on their heads, their feet muffled as they pulled the precious load up to the castle, along the road lined with silent, weeping people. Roberto was laid to rest in the white marble mausoleum of his ancestors. Through it all, Jane, with Giovanni at her side, felt as if she too were dead: she seemed to feel nothing. She wondered why she did not cry, loving him as she did. All around her people wept, but Jane stood stoically, her face a rigid mask.

His family closed ranks around her, shielding her from the curious. For the first time she felt part of his Italian family. Francesca took Giovanni and drove off with him to play with her son. Supported by Emilio, Jane steeled herself to enter the castle. In the large, formal salon, the windows, the mirrors, the paintings were all draped in the same fine, black material which billowed in the gentle breeze like the sails of ships in mourning. Only large arum lilies, their sickly-sweet smell filling the air, decorated the room. Groups of people stood in whispering, huddled groups, dressed from head to toe in black. There was no question of this gathering becoming the light-hearted party that Honor's wake had been. Here the ceremony was so awesome that it shrivelled the soul.

Emilio led her by the arm to the centre of the room. In a large chair sat an old woman, wizened with age and the only person seated.

'You must meet my aunt, Jane, Princess Renata Villizano, Roberto's mother.' Nervously Jane approached the black-clad figure whose face was entirely covered in a heavy veil. Emilio spoke quickly to his aunt. With a surprisingly agile flick of her wrist she swept the veil back. Beautiful dark eyes shone brilliantly in a face wrinkled and yellowed by age. They were so like the eyes of her son that Jane suppressed the cry that welled up within her. The eyes studied her closely.

'This is a sad day, daughter,' the old woman said in a strong voice and in impeccable English.

'Sadder than I have words for, Principessa,' Jane replied softly.

'I am more fortunate than you, I shall see him sooner,' the old woman announced with no embarrassment, and Jane envied her such faith. 'But we have his son, and for him I thank you, Jane.' Jane bowed her head. 'I gather my son had told you of his wish that Giovanni be brought up as an Italian?'

'Yes, Principessa, please do not fear. I shall fulfil Roberto's wishes.'

The old woman fell back against the cushions of the chair. Her eyes suddenly dulled as if a light in them had been extinguished. 'Thank God,' she sighed in a quiet, tired voice. She waved wearily to a manservant who came and with ease lifted the old woman into his arms and carried her away. She had achieved what she had come to do.

Somehow, Jane saw the other guests away and was finally left with Emilio, James, who had flown out to be with her, and yet another army of lawyers. There was no need to worry that Giovanni's estates would not be well managed: it was clear that they would go on just as before. But she decided to shut up the houses until he was old enough to take charge of them. She loved this castle but, without Roberto here, it was too painful for her to remain.

Now, with everyone gone and the lawyers dispatched, James suggested they explore the castle, which he had never seen before.

'Darling, I don't think I could. It's too painful for me yet. I'll wait here for you. Maybe Emilio would be kind enough to show you?' The two men left her, and she opened the door to what had been their private sitting room. She wanted to be alone. Perhaps here, where they had spent so many happy hours, the tears that were inside her like a painful tumour would be set free. She had known him seven years, but she had only lived with him for three years and seven months. Encapsulated in that short time were all the memories she had of him. She heard a scratching noise. When she opened the door, a golden retriever entered. It crossed the room and sat gazing at Roberto's chair, and whined. She knelt down and stroked the dog.

'Hullo, old boy, who are you? Did you love him too?' She comforted the whining dog, but still she could not cry.

'Ma! Ma! Come quick,' James called. Nervously she ran to him. He was standing on the steps to the picture gallery. 'You never told us about this. It's sensational,' he said, walking quickly ahead of her to the wing where the portraits hung. 'Look!'

Jane cried out with disbelief. Beside Roberto's portrait was a full-length one of herself. She was dressed in the emerald-green silk dress she had worn when she had first met him, Honor's emeralds about her throat. It was an astonishing likeness.

'You never told me you'd had such a beautiful picture done?'

'I couldn't tell you, I didn't know.'

'But . . . ?'

'Roberto arranged it,' Emilio explained. 'He called in several artists. The place was full of giant photographs of you, Jane. Honor lent him the jewels and I gather the dress was already here. He must have had a dozen paintings done before he was satisfied with this one.'

'It was what I was wearing the night we first met.' Jane's voice faltered.

'He loved you very much, Jane.'

'I know, Emilio, as I loved him. We were fools, I most of all. But Emilio, why didn't you tell me he was so ill? Why didn't you send for me sooner?' It was a question that had haunted her ever since she had seen Roberto. Why had no one, not even May, told her?

'He forbade us, Jane. All of us. He said he didn't want you to come back out of pity . . .'

'Oh God,' she sighed, turning away from her portrait, not daring to glance at the one of Roberto hanging by its side. 'I must get out of here,' she said hurriedly.

As they were getting into the car, the major-domo gave her a heavy wooden box which the Prince had instructed him to give to her after his death. The dog still twined itself around her legs.

'Was this the Prince's dog?'

'Yes, Principessa. He has not seen the Prince for a year and he pined dreadfully. And today, it is quite extraordinary, but today, I know he knew he had come home and he has been inconsolable.'

'What's he called?'

'Harry, Principessa.'

'Harry! What a weird name for a dog,' James exclaimed.

'I think it's a fine name. Prince Hal. Shall we take Roberto's dog with us?'

They loaded the box and the dog into the car.

'Jane, do you think it would be better if Francesca and I kept Giovanni for a few days more?'

'Would you, Emilio? It would be kind of you. I don't think I could be a good mother at the moment.' Emilio kissed her hand. Jane eased the car out of the courtyard and down the mountain to the villa.

Late that night, alone in her room, the dog already settled for the night on her bed, she gingerly opened the box. Inside lay all the jewellery he had given her. And beneath, wrapped in tissue paper, was a cine film, with a note attached. She had hoped that there would be a letter, like the one Honor had written her; instead there were only a few words: 'Forgive me, Contessa, I lied, I could never destroy your beauty!'

'Roberto!' Her longing and agony for him sounded in the cry. The dog raised its head and nuzzled her. She sank her head into his soft fur and she began to cry.

Six

1977

ane seemed to live in a world full of the swirling fogs of grief. Daily she
grieved for Honor and Roberto. At first she could not go out, nor did she
want to see anybody. She knew that this was wrong, that she should be
attempting to build a new life. But as she began to fight back from her
despair, it was as if she were suffocating in a giant sponge of cloying loss
that would not let go of her.

James stayed in the villa with her for a few weeks after the funeral, but
when he announced he must return to England she felt only relief that
he was to be left alone. Giovanni returned from his cousins'. She looked
forward to the child's return, certain that with him to consider she would
soon recover. Instead, she found his demands irritating, and the child
increased her irritation by making her feel guilty that she should feel this
way. When Giovanni, fractious with boredom, demanded to return to
the happy home of his cousins, she quickly, too quickly, she knew, made
the necessary arrangements.

'You can't go on like this, Jane. It's ridiculous,' May admonished her
as the car, taking her young son away, disappeared round the curve of
the drive.

'May, don't nag me. He's better off at Emilio's. There are kids to play
with, there's more for him to do.'

'He needs his mother now that his father's gone, poor little
mite.'

'I know what I'm doing. I need this time alone.'

'Self-indulgent, that's what it is.'

'May! You can be so hard. I have to grieve, and in my way.'

'It's Giovanni I worry about. When he was here you hardly noticed
him. Poor kid, he must wonder what's going on, when you virtually
smothered him with love before.'

'Christ, May, I've just lost my husband! Don't you see it'll take me
time?'

'It's not as if he was a proper husband. You hadn't lived with him for years.' May stood, arms akimbo, looking sternly at Jane.

'Don't you ever say that to me again, May!' Jane swung round angrily to face her friend. 'I never stopped loving him, as you bloody well know. He was my husband here . . .' Dramatically she thumped her breast.

'I shouldn't have said that, Jane, I'm sorry. Of course you never stopped loving him, but life must go on. I don't want you getting ill like you did over his lordship.'

'I won't do that, I promise. I just need time. I know I'll never be the same again, but eventually I might find a different way of living.'

She knew May was telling her the truth in her usual down-to-earth manner. She knew she was doing wrong. She just did not seem to have the will or energy to do anything about it.

Christmas came and Giovanni returned. They bought a tree and decorated it. They shopped for presents and Jane carefully wrapped them. Guido dressed up as Father Christmas. They had turkey, wore funny hats from the crackers and Guido and May played blind man's buff and hide-and-seek with the child, while Jane sat curled up in a chair a gin and tonic in her hand, and watched them, unsmiling.

Giovanni went back to his cousins. Jane was left wandering aimlessly about the beautiful white villa, fully aware that the ghost of Honor would be appalled by her.

'You'll end up losing him just like you lost James if you're not careful. You're a fool, Jane. You need that boy. Don't push him away like this,' May pleaded.

'I know what I'm doing. Give me a year.'

'What then? I bet you'll be whining, "Give me another year"! You're drinking too much, too.' May frowned at the glass in Jane's hand. 'Oh, and by the way, Guido and I have decided to get married.'

'You've what?' Jane's glass clattered onto the marble table. 'That's wonderful news. I had no idea.'

'Of course you hadn't, you've been so wrapped up in yourself you wouldn't have noticed if we'd developed bubonic plague.'

'May, I'm sorry. Am I that dreadful?'

'Yes. Not enough to do, that's your trouble. If you'd been left with kids to support instead of all this money, you'd have had to pull yourself together.'

As always, May was right. Having money should have made deciding what to do easier, instead it made it harder.

he wedding of May and Guido in February seemed the only happy
ccasion for a long time. It was also the event that finally forced Jane into
tion. She decided to take a holiday and leave the couple alone for a few
onths.

But where to go? With no set plans she motored slowly up through
urope, stopping where the mood took her, sometimes for a day,
ometimes for a week, visiting the cathedrals, castles and museums
ithout the summer crowds about her. She seemed to have been
happy for so long that it was several weeks before she realized that she
as enjoying herself.

Finding herself on the coast of France, on a whim, she took the ferry
r England. As the boat churned across the channel she sat in the bar
id wondered where to go next. It was then she decided to go to
cotland and find the house that Honor had urged her to buy. It was an
bligation, and one that must be fulfilled.

She took the motor rail to Edinburgh, visited estate agents and then
rove, zigzagging across the country, searching for perfection. She saw
any estates; they were all beautiful but none of them seemed just right.
he exasperated estate agents began to despair of her. She tried to
xplain that she would know the minute she saw it, that an inner voice
ould tell her she had found it, and they, behind her back, decided she
as demented.

She went further and further north in her search. As she drove over
rumochter Pass, despite the bright sunshine, there was still a scattering
f snow on the tops of the mountains which made them look like giant
almatian puppies huddled in sleep. A strange elation filled her and she
as certain she was near the end of her search.

Jane had not realized that buying a house could be like falling in love,
ut she learned. As she drove around the corner of a sadly neglected
rive, the house loomed in front of her in the bright Highland light, and
te fell in love. It could have been riddled with dry rot and deathwatch
eetle, but she did not care – she had to have it.

The house was white, tall and proud; two large towers with fine
epperpot roofs stood at either end, like sentinels. The windows were
rge, the door wide and welcoming. The house stood protected against
te winds by old beech trees and the views to the moorland were
reathtaking. It looked as if it had been transported by magic from some
alley in the Dordogne: it was far more like a small French château than
er idea of a Scottish castle. As she drove towards it, she knew the search
as over.

She waited impatiently for the lawyers to complete the sale. While they worked, she stayed in the local hotel. There was an elation in her now, long missing, a new excitement. In a strange way she felt she had come home. If this was to be a new start, she must slough off the past. She decided to revert to her maiden name, and determined that no one here should know her as anything else.

She ferried herself about searching for furniture and pictures, arranging for builders and workmen to be ready to start the day the house was hers. She had the furniture from Honor's London flat, which had been in store, sent up. She wrote excited letters home to May in Italy, to tell her of her find, and was unaware that the letters relieved May of a lot of worry. Jane, she felt, was going to be all right.

At last she had possession. And the work began. Eager for it to be finished she donned dungarees, wrapped her hair in a scarf and made herself the decorators' mate, much to the workmen's surprise. It was not at all how they expected rich Sassenachs to behave, but they respected her for it. And each night she went to bed exhausted and happy. She found a gamekeeper willing to work her land with the strange instructions that nothing should be killed, unless it was necessary, or for his pot. He would laugh about her to his mates, but the more he thought about it, the more he liked the idea. She found a couple willing to move in and look after her while she was there, who would care for the house when she had to return to Italy. She loved their soft Highland accent, and recognized in Margaret, with her kind face and deceptively gentle manner, the same steely personality as May, which would put up with no nonsense and would tell her what was what in no uncertain terms. Only the accent was different.

Her birthday came. Alone, she faced the fact that she was forty. The years had slipped by with an unfair rapidity, she thought, and laughed at herself, knowing full well that this was what everyone reaching that ominous milestone must think. She looked at herself critically in the mirror. She looked good, she told her reflection. A few lines now, but as she turned her face from one side to the other, she decided they added rather than detracted from her face. She had no grey hair yet, and her figure looked as firm as ever. The gloss that Roberto had given her still remained. Even in jeans and headscarf there was an elegance to her.

Scotland healed her. As she walked across her gun-free land, she could enjoy the peace and tranquillity of the place, the lack of urgency that pervaded it. The vastness of the scenery helped her to put a sense of perspective into her life. She would stand on the top of a hill and admire a

ew unchanged for a million years and it made her, Jane Reed, seem
ry unimportant.

One day a large trunk arrived. Hearing of her new home, Alistair had
rwarded the things she had left at Respryn when she had left in such a
urry. It was an odd feeling to open this casket from the past. It held little
ings she had collected over the years – photographs, letters. She spent a
ppily morbid afternoon rereading Alistair's love letters to her, their
tempts at poetry. She found the book she had bought with the list of
ords that it was O K to use, and she laughed at the memory of the poor,
secure creature she must once have been. With due ceremony she put it
the fire and let the flames destroy her old self once and for all.

Her accountants pestered her daily to return to Italy before the Inland
evenue ruined her. Reluctantly she began to pack. She did not want to
ave this new home, which had assumed so great an importance in her
e in such a short time. Was it because it was the only house that had
ally been hers? All her life she had lived in other people's houses, never
e that she had created. And because she had never lived here with a
an, it was devoid of painful memories. She hated to leave but she
anted to see Giovanni, needed to see him. She had been right and May
rong, she had needed time away from him to resolve their future
gether.

She knew now without a doubt what she had to do. She realized that
e had distanced herself from him almost as if in some strange way she
d been preparing herself for the decisions she was finally to make. As,
the end, it had been better for James, with his heritage, to stay with his
ther, so she resolved it was best for Giovanni to spend a large part of
e year with his Italian family. She could not teach him to be Italian, she
uld not help him learn how to be a great landowner. If he stayed with
er, in a few years he would go to prep school: she could not let him go
rough that, not years of being despised by the English for his noble
alian blood. She would ask Emilio and Francesca to keep him with
eir ever increasing family, to grow up as an Italian. She would have
im for the holidays and would visit him much more than she had visited
mes. There would be people who would say she did not love her child,
ad cast him aside, but they would be wrong. This was the right decision
r Roberto's son.

s she sat in the dining car of the train taking her to England, she was
addenly aware of a woman behind her reading a story to her children.
low strange, she thought, she knew the words, knew what was coming

next. With a start she remembered – it was the book about Jane Squir‹
which her father had given her so long ago and which she still cherish‹
for he had inscribed it 'with love'. It pleased her to think that the bo‹
was still read and loved.

She took the long car ferry from Southampton to Le Havre. W‹
Roberto she had never really enjoyed hurtling from one country and o‹
culture to another. She enjoyed the hours on the ferry which gave ‹
time to adjust from Britain to the continent. She sat in the bar, by ‹
window, watching the grey waters of the Channel slip by.

'May I have the pleasure of buying you a drink?' a heavily accent‹
voice asked her. She looked up to see a young man smiling at h‹
Dark-haired and dark-eyed, his face had the intelligent intensity peculi‹
to Frenchmen. His clothes were expensively well cut, his body lithe ‹
slim. She paused imperceptibly before accepting, with an equally wa‹
smile. His English was bad, and she was surprised to find how mu‹
French she managed to dredge up from her memory. As drink follow‹
drink, her French became more fluent. He told her he was from Paris, ‹
name was Jacques, he was thirty-two and worked in banking. He ask‹
her where she was travelling to and when she said Italy, he smil‹
broadly.

'How wonderful! I am going to Rome.'

'Are you driving?'

'No.' He patted his pocket. 'Train.'

'Do you drive?'

'But of course.'

'If you wouldn't mind sharing the driving, I can give you a lift ‹
Florence, if you like.'

'That would be marvellous.'

'Are you in a hurry?'

'No, no, I have all the time in the world.'

The boat docked at Le Havre and together they made their way to t‹
boat deck. She was amused by the startled expression on his face as s‹
unlocked the door of the Rolls-Royce.

'I had no idea,' he said, almost as if in apology.

'It's very easy to drive.'

Since speed was unimportant, they decided to avoid the motorwa‹
and to meander down through France on the secondary roads, doir‹
some sightseeing, stopping when the fancy took them.

'Do you know the Relais Château hotels?' she asked him. 'They'‹
wonderful.'

'Of course,' he replied, but for the first time she heard uncertainty in his voice.

'I would like to stay in them. I shall insist on paying.'

'But, Madame, I could not hear of such a thing.'

'In return for your helping with the driving, of course.'

'Ah, well, in return for the driving, *d'accord*.'

It was pleasant driving through the beautiful French countryside with a companion. He was knowledgeable about his country's history and architecture. He was funny, too, and made her laugh. Using the joke that he was her chauffeur, she was able to pay for their meals and hotels with no embarrassment to either of them.

On the third night, as she settled down to sleep, he crept stealthily into her room and climbed wordlessly into her bed. For a second she thought she must ask him to leave, but as his arms went around her and she felt the comforting sensation of his bare flesh against hers, she wondered whom it could hurt now. No one. It would be nice to know a man again, to feel him in her, and so she turned to him and the pleasure of his soft mouth on her body.

He was not going to Rome. There was no job in banking, and with disarming honesty he told her he had not even the money for a train ticket. She liked his honesty, enjoyed his company. She was happy with his lovemaking, which was skilled and expert, and unselfish. It did not drive her to the heights of ecstasy that she had experienced with Roberto, but she knew that physical perfection like theirs happened only once in a lifetime, if that. So in some strange way she felt she was not being unfaithful to Roberto's memory. She decided to take him back to the villa with her.

On their arrival, May could hardly wait to get Jane alone. She was beside herself with anger.

'He's young enough to be your son!'

'Hardly,' Jane insisted. 'He's over thirty.'

'Is that what he told you? Twenty-five, more like.' She sniffed audibly.

'May, don't sniff like that, you remind me of my mother.' Jane laughed but May did not join in.

'What happened to all that famous grief, then? Barely a year since the Prince died. It's disgusting, Jane, that's what it is.'

'I thought you were the one who told me to pull myself together,' Jane replied smartly.

'So I did, but not this way. You're making a fool of yourself.'

'May, it's my life and I would appreciate your not speaking to me like that. I do employ you, after all, or have you forgotten?' Jane flashed angrily.

'No, I haven't forgotten and you'd better give me the sack now if you expect me to do anything for him, 'cause I won't serve someone like that.'

'May, dear God, what are we doing? I don't want to fall out with you.'

'I've always spoken my mind, you can't expect me to stop now,' May replied, tears glinting in her proud eyes.

'I know it must be a shock to you, but May, he makes me forget, he gives me a sort of happiness. I still grieve for Roberto, I will for the rest of my life. This is something different, Roberto would understand.'

'He wouldn't, he'd have had a fit. You with a gigolo!'

'If it was good enough for Honor then it's good enough for me.'

'You don't think that woman was happy, do you, the way she carried on?'

'No, not really happy. I shall be surprised if that ever comes again, but this is a good second-best. He's a nice enough young man.'

'You've got into a panic, haven't you, just 'cause you're forty?'

'May, don't talk so daft. Being forty has nothing to do with it.'

'Well, the only solution I can see if he stays is that you get someone else to look after him, 'cause I'm not and that's flat.'

'May!' Jane exclaimed.

'You can "May!" me all you like. I'm not waiting on the likes of him.'

'You are being stuffy, May. Who can it possibly hurt?'

'*You*, you fool!' and May slammed out of the room.

Exasperated, Jane phoned the agency for a new servant. When the woman arrived, May calmed down, but she kept her promise and would do nothing for Jacques. But for once May was wrong, it did not seem to hurt Jane. The lovemaking was pleasant enough but it was his company she enjoyed most. It was good to have someone with whom to go shopping and sightseeing, someone to talk to as she ate her dinner, instead of those interminable, lonely meals.

The summer slipped by. She did not know what made her change her mind. Perhaps the blue-rinsed American matron they had seen last week, with a young man fawning over her. Or was it the way she had noticed Jacques look at young girls in bikinis? Or was it, finally, her honesty which had made her see the way she was going, realize that perhaps May had been half right about Jane's reaction to that fortieth birthday? Whatever the reason, she decided suddenly that he had to go.

As she watched Jacques pack his bags, she felt no remorse, no pleasure. If she felt anything at all, it was a mild irritation that he was taking so long.

'I don't understand, Jane. Why do I have to go?' He kicked the door of the wardrobe shut as he removed the last of his clothes. She heard the question but she did not reply for she did not know the answer.

'What has made you change so suddenly?' he asked as he bundled his clothes into the last open case. That was very unlike him, she thought; he was usually such a tidy person, almost obsessively neat with his clothes.

'You shouldn't pack your things like that, they'll get all creased,' she commented helpfully.

'What do I care about that?' He turned to face her, holding out his hands. 'Jane, please, for God's sake, tell me, what have I done wrong?' She heard the note of pleading in his voice and she shut her ears to the tone, not wishing to hear it, not wanting to start feeling sorry for him. She regretted now that she had not left him to his packing. She did not even feel guilty for her lack of feeling. She just wanted to get the whole scene over and to be on her own.

She could understand his bewilderment, it had been a very sudden decision on her part. Her lack of explanation must be perplexing for him, but, in truth, she felt as confused as he. His normally handsome face was now set in sad lines. He usually looked so happy. She hated to see him look like this, and for what? Was it worth it? Would she miss him? How would she manage being alone again?

His heavy gold bracelet caught on the webbing of his case, and he swore softly. She hated that bracelet, and the gold medallion he always wore around his neck. She hated them, not because he had been given them by her American predecessor, but because, like badges of office, they proclaimed what he was and so what she had become. She shuddered. Vigorously she shook her head to dispel the indecisions worming into her brain. He had to go.

She smiled at him, fondly, she hoped.

'You've done nothing wrong, Jacques. It's me, I want to be by myself, that's all.' She searched in her handbag and took out an envelope stuffed with dollar bills. 'Here, take this.' She handed him the money. He made no attempt to refuse.

At last he had loaded the car. She had forgotten about the car. She had given it to him on his birthday and maybe, in view of it, she had been too generous with the money in the envelope. Did it matter? It was too late now, she could hardly ask him to give her some of it back.

'You're a strange woman, Jane,' he said as he climbed into his car. 'Look, here's an address where you can find me when you change your mind.' He gave her a card and attempted a smile.

'I won't change my mind, Jacques. I'll just remember what a wonderful summer we had.'

She did not know what had made her say that. It had been pleasant enough, but not wonderful, not like some of the summers she had known. In contrast this had been a sad substitute.

She gave a small wave as he drove off, its brevity calculated. He might have misinterpreted a more energetic goodbye, especially after her remark about the summer.

She stood and listened until she could no longer hear his car and then walked back into the empty villa. In the white marble hallway, she paused – it felt odd. The house was not used to silence either. It stood in its white, luxuriant splendour as if listening for the noises to return. She lingered for a moment, accustoming herself to this unusual quiet, allowing it to wrap around her. She crossed into the long, white drawing room, poured herself a large gin and tonic and went out on the terrace. The sun was beginning to set in the hurried way it always does in the Mediterranean, the sky ablaze with improbable colour. Only in Britain did the sun seem to set gently and with dignity. She felt an overwhelming longing to be home again, to be sitting in the soft, balmy cool of a Scottish evening, not here in this searing, baked heat. What on earth was she doing here, anyway? She should never have allowed herself to be persuaded to live abroad, always to be a stranger. She had already found her place to live, the place where she was most at peace with herself. She was homesick. Not just for the house but for the contentment she had begun to feel there. She had listened to accountants and lawyers, people concerned only with her balance sheets, and she had let them persuade her to leave the security of her home and to come to this foreign land in order to save, in taxes, money that she did not need.

She sipped her drink and watched as the lights came on in the bay far below her. Across the terrace Harry, Roberto's dog, padded towards her. He sat at her feet and regarded her with an expression of devotion. Idly she patted his head. How lovely to be a dog, she thought, everyone accepted that a dog just wanted to be loved. God, she was getting so full of self-pity these days . . .

She had to find something to do, May was right, she was too rich, too idle. She did not know what that something would turn out to be, but she was sure that some day she would know.

Seven

1977–85

I

For nearly three years she had lived in Scotland. Her business affairs meant that she had to make trips to London and New York, but she made them as short as possible and then quickly returned to her haven in the northern Highlands, so quickly that she would sometimes liken herself to a furry animal scuttling back to its lair.

She had not returned to Italy but allowed friends to use her villa whenever they wanted, for she was happier and felt safer where she was. The villa had too many memories that still haunted her. But she had not been short of company. Giovanni came four or five times a year, often with his cousins. Various combinations of Sandra's large family visited, all married now, with children of their own. And Sandra herself, sometimes with her family, often on her own. In summer there was an endless tide of James's university friends and when the other lodges opened, the young from them visited in droves, so that it seemed her son was embroiled in one endless party. And there was the memorable and drunken week when Zoe had finally abandoned her kitchen and caught the shuttle, complaining bitterly at the size of the seats. Her parents came once, but moaned constantly about the weather and the isolation, and cut short their visit to return to their suburban comfort.

But something had happened to Jane. While she would look forward, eagerly, to these visitors, within a couple of days she resented their presence, with the exception of her sons, found the duties of being a hostess irksome and longed to be alone again. She never once saw anyone off on the plane or train with regret.

She saw little of Alistair. When she was in London, she rarely saw him, for he had given up most of the directorships and committees that had kept them apart when they were married, and preferred these days to spend most of his time at Respryn. He had invited her to Drumloch several times but she had refused. The Highlands had become an oasis of calm and peace for her, and she knew the guns at Drumloch would distress her more than ever. He was always too busy to come and stay with her and in a way she was relieved, for she did not want to find that she would want him, like the others, gone in a couple of days. But still, it seemed a shame that they had drifted apart, especially now when she was certain that she could see him and not want him, for since Jacques she had not felt the need to bother with another man.

She would have been hard pressed to explain how she filled her days, but she did. She spent hours walking her dogs, now six in number, and just watching the light on the hills, enjoying the colours, the changing seasons and the birds and animals.

But the longer she stayed, the more she realized that living in Scotland was full of paradoxes. She learned that she could love and hate this strange, wild country at the same time. Always, Scotland had two faces, like a beautiful and deceitful woman. A lush and lovely day with the air gin-clear could turn within the hour to a nightmare of mist or blizzard. A stretch of green that invited her to walk on it would become a slimy, stinking bog. The placid sea, with the rocks sitting in the sparkling water as if scattered by God in a playful mood, could, the next day, turn into a writhing maelstrom and, whipping up a shrieking wind to cover their screams, dash a boatload of strong men onto the jagged rocks.

This duplicity seemed reflected in the people: honest as the day is long and yet capable of cunning trickery; kind and thoughtful or mean and cruel in their thoughtlessness; funny to the point of hysteria or dour to a soul-numbing dullness; proud with the pride of centuries and tribal laws and loyalties, or craven with a shame of their heritage. Men who could one day risk their lives to save a man and yet the next damn him to isolation with their malicious, meaningless gossip.

Jane learned that even as the sun beat down on them, the long preparations for their cruel winter began. Winter here was an old enemy to be faced and beaten by careful planning. And so, while the holiday-makers enjoyed the quaint, idyllic scene, the Highlander cut his peats and stacked and dried them in neat piles beside each door. The fish and meat were hung and smoked, the eggs were pickled, the potatoes stored, the wood cut. The cracks in the house were mended, the shutters secured. Winter here stormed in, a heartless enemy.

She sensed a wariness towards her in the locals which only time would allay. She realized that because she was English she would never be fully accepted but she wanted to live here and was willing to settle for second-best. She could understand the hatred for her race engendered by years of oppression and abuse. She could see that in each generation it was blue-printed in their very cells, so that even if they knew no history, even if they could not read, the hate was second nature. So she would hear such comments as 'He's nae so bad for an Englishman!' and know that this was the nearest to a compliment their heritage would allow.

She distrusted the 'gentry'. Such an antiquated term to describe them; one long dead in England, but used daily here. Listening to the tone of the Highlanders' voices as they said it, she was aware it was not a term of respect. The 'gentry' were divided into two groups, those who stayed the year long, most of whom strutted around like feudal kings, and those who came for the shooting and scuttled back to the delights of the south as winter came. Of the two, it was the latter the locals most disliked. The absentee landlords were an emotive and a political issue. But when they came up for the fishing and shooting they seemed blithely unaware of the resentment they caused with their big, fast cars on the narrow roads, destroying the peace for the weeks they were here. It was a shock to Jane when she became aware that Rupert, greatly respected though he was, had been one of these. And Alistair – he was still one of the absentee landlords, she thought wryly. Most of all, she saw, the Highlander's loathing was reserved for the young of the house parties who descended on the local bars and, with their loud, braying voices and their arrogant manners, fertilized annually the hatred for the English lurking in the Highlander's soul. But the Highlander needed them and the money they brought and, canny to the last, would touch his forelock, oblige, perform and, in the safety of his croft, would laugh at and hate them.

On her arrival, there had been a flurry of invitations for Jane; her coming had sent a wave of titillating curiosity through the local 'gentry'. But once they had met her and, like dogs sniffing out each other's pedigrees, had found she was not one of them, the invitations ceased. She did not mind. She had not come here to try, after all this time, to be accepted. And, in any case, as she saw endless replicas of Lady Upnor, she was relieved to be left alone. Nothing was ever going to change. But she had changed, for it no longer mattered to her: she could watch them and not want to be part of their society. It puzzled her now why she had ever wanted it.

Since throughout her adult life she had not felt she belonged any-where, there was a comfort in knowing that here in the north of Scotland the rejection was historical, not personal.

2

Jane sat at the dinner table of the Impingtons, the only local couple she visited regularly. She liked Liz Impington who, being American, sailed unbothered through the sea of class divisions, inviting to her table anyone she liked and who amused her. But tonight, surrounded as she was by owners of great estates, Jane should have known better . . .

'But what about the ordinary people?' Her question hung in the air of one of those pools of silence that occur at a dinner party, waiting for the ill-timed remark to drop noisily into its waters.

'There's more at stake here than people,' thundered the red-faced and heavily chinned man opposite her.

'What can be more important than people?'

'Our heritage, Mrs Reed. Our heritage, our land. We're only custodians of all of this, you know.' His chubby, lily-white hands swept vaguely through the air. 'We don't own it, we care for it for future generations.' Noisily he took a sip of his wine and sat back, pleased with his sentiments. Jane looked around the assembled company at the well-fed, well-wined faces as they, sanctimoniously and in unison, nodded agreement – like a row of well-controlled puppets, Jane thought. 'The land is sacred,' the noisy, hectoring voice persisted. 'The beasts, the fowl, the flora must be protected. Allow this development to take place here and what have you got? Before you know it, Mrs Reed, another part of our heritage ruined for all times.'

'I agree with you that our heritage should be guarded wherever possible, but people's needs must still come first. I mean, the level of unemployment here is dreadful.'

'You don't for one moment think this development will create jobs locally, Mrs Reed? They will utilize the local work force to do the labouring, and when that's done, they'll be laid off, as poor as ever, but discontented that the big wage packets are over, and with another part of their heritage lost for ever.'

'Then, this time, extract guarantees for permanent employment for the community,' Jane answered reasonably.

'You are singularly naive, Mrs Reed, if you think that there is a remote possibility that such guarantees would be forthcoming. And, if they were, employ them as what? Navvying is all they're fit for –'

'Really, Lord Ludlow, I hardly think that's a fair statement to make. I've been struck by just how intelligent people are here. I reckon they could be retrained to do anything.'

'As an incomer, Mrs Reed, I don't really think you're qualified to have an opinion and I don't think any of this is your business. Like so many, you arrive, think you know it all in six months, and, probably, in another six months you'll be gone.'

'And how can you be so sure?'

'Seen it all before. I've seen your type before.'

'And what's my type, Lord Ludlow?' Jane asked, her eyes glinting dangerously.

'Too much money, too little sense. You're not born to the land, you don't understand it and the passions it rouses. I hear you don't even allow any shooting on your land.' The man snorted derisively.

'Oh yes, Percy, and how long have your family owned your estate? Fifteen years or thereabouts, isn't it? Just after you got your life peerage, wasn't it? Where were you before, Birmingham, was it, or Manchester? I doubt passions about land run very high there.' Jane looked up to see a pair of clear, intelligent, blue eyes smiling mischievously at her. As Jane smiled gratefully, one of them winked at her. 'I think Mrs Reed is right, people are more important than a stretch of scrubland running down to a beach that no one ever goes to anyway.'

'But the birds,' Percy Ludlow persisted.

'Bah the birds. They're not daft, you know. They'll soon find somewhere else to go.'

'You're a philistine, Fran, and we all know about your politics,' he said darkly, appealing to the others, and a rumbling murmur went round the table.

'I'm not a philistine, Percy, I'm a realist. And my politics are irrelevant when we're discussing something as fundamental as the future of a whole community. Jobs, Percy, that's what this area needs, jobs, not more birds. Jobs for men to go to, earn a decent wage packet, regain their dignity. There's thousands of acres left for the birds.' The blue-eyed woman thundered as loudly as Lord Ludlow.

'Dignity,' boomed his lordship. 'What dignity? They're all layabouts anyway, you won't get them interested in work. All they're interested in is their government hand-out, paid for by you and me . . .' The row swirled on, and Jane sighed inwardly: it was as if she were back on that first night at Respryn.

'Fran, Percy, you're getting overexcited down that end, and ruining my dinner party. I'm sure you're both right.' Mrs Impington smiled with a patient expression which showed she was used to Fran and Percy's battles. She rose to her feet. 'Ladies, shall we . . . ?' Gracefully she gathered the ladies about her, like a careful hen with her chicks, leaving the men to the port. The old order, thought Jane; just as things were getting interesting, off they had to troop to powder noses, drink filthy coffee and talk about servants and education.

In the drawing room the blue-eyed woman made straight for Jane.

'Fran Nettlebed. I was longing to meet you before dinner. You're the glamorous mystery woman who bought the Murchon estate a couple of years back, aren't you?'

'I'm not so sure about glamorous.' Jane laughed. 'But yes, I'm Jane Reed.' They shook hands. The blue eyes sparkled in a face that glowed with health and was as square as her body which, enveloped in a royal-blue kaftan, looked twice the size it probably was. She reminded Jane of Zoe.

'It's odd we haven't met before.'

'I don't go out much. I enjoy the solitude. But I like Liz Impington, she's interesting. So I usually come here when they're up.'

'Implying you don't think much of the others?' The bright-blue eyes twinkled at her.

'Let's just say we don't have an awesome amount in common,' Jane said. 'I was so enjoying that argument in there.'

'I'd promised myself I wouldn't get involved tonight. Now I'll have to apologize to Liz. But that bloody man gets right in my craw, he really does. He's so pompous – silly old fart.'

'Wasn't he the man who made a fortune out of property and gave the socialists a pile of money?' Jane said, laughing at Fran's colourful language.

'That's him.'

'He doesn't sound very much like a socialist.'

'He isn't any more.' Fran laughed loudly. 'Human leopards are quite capable of changing their spots.' She slung the end of a long feather boa over her shoulder, the feathers floating agitatedly through the air as she did so. Unconcerned, she spat out those feathers which had found her mouth. 'Load of crap this lot spout, I can tell you.'

'Do they all think like that?'

'Mostly. And none of them has a right to an opinion anyway, they're never here — come up for the shooting, casting the fly, and then sod off back to London when the weather gets tough. No time for them at all.'

'You live here all year, then?' Jane asked.

'Yes, in fact I prefer the winters when this lot go. Mind you, I don't count Liz in that number.'

'Why have anything to do with the others, then?'

'I have to be seen to be one of them, you see. You have to in local politics — keep up, I mean.'

'Why?'

'They own everything. Even from London they bloody control what's going on. So you've got to keep in to know what's what, what plans are afoot, who to contact, who to try and coerce.' Fran threw back her head and guffawed, just the way Zoe did.

'This planned development — where is it, and what is it? I'm afraid I just dived in without knowing anything about it.'

'You interested? Great!' The stubby hands clapped together with glee. 'Come to lunch tomorrow, I'll take you over. About twelve do you? Then you can tell me all about yourself, I'm dying to know. No one seems to know a thing about you.' She gave Jane her card.

'There's nothing interesting about me,' Jane assured her.

'Ha! Don't give me that. I can sniff out interesting people at a hundred yards.'

Noisily, the men rejoined the party and, as in a game of musical chairs, everyone changed places. Jane walked towards Liz and Percy Ludlow, whose fat paunch made his sporran stick out at an angle as if he were blessed with a permanent erection. Seeing her coming, he pointedly turned his back. Ah, well, thought Jane, what does it really matter? Instead she talked to a young New Zealand playwright whom Liz had picked up as a hitchhiker. One dram later, Jane found herself yawning. She thanked Liz Impington and left the party.

3

Next day, at noon, Jane drove up Fran's driveway. She had not known what to expect – not a croft, certainly, but neither did she expect the beautiful Georgian house she found. A pack of dogs tumbled down the steps in friendly greeting. Fran came out to welcome her and in cords and sweater she looked not only thinner but far more comfortable than she had the night before.

Jane had imagined that Fran would live in chaos and was unprepared for the muted, beige-and-white, ordered elegance into which she was shown.

'It is lovely, isn't it?' Fran said, noticing Jane's admiring gaze. 'But difficult to keep with the brats about. I ban them from here. You have to have one safe haven, don't you?'

'How old are they?'

'Fourteen and twelve, vaguely civilized at last, thank God. Gin?'

'Is your husband here?'

'No. He's got itchy feet; he's a geologist, spends more time abroad than at home, unfortunately.' She handed Jane her drink and pushed an enormous ashtray towards her.

'He doesn't want to settle and farm, then? I mean, is that your land out there?'

'Yes, but we rent it out. Jack doesn't like the countryside, you see. He distrusts it. He'd much rather live in the middle of some filthy city, but, since he's away so much, it seemed only fair that I should choose where we live. Good old London boy, my Jack: the country is for looking at, nothing more. You farming?'

'No.'

'What do you do, then?'

'Not much, really. I walk the dogs and think about what I ought to do,' Jane said lamely. 'What about you?'

'Meddle in politics – I'm on the local council, small stuff. I'd like a real job now the kids are older but I don't know what I want to do, and fitting in with Jack's schedule makes any nine-to-five job impossible.'

'How did you get involved?'

'Accident, really, and conscience. Jack earns a fortune and I've got some money of my own, so I have the time. I think you have to put back into the community if you're one of the fortunates, don't you?'

'I'm ashamed to say I've never given it much thought. Too self-centred, I suppose,' Jane said apologetically.

'Perhaps you've never regarded yourself as one of the fortunates?' There was no note of sarcasm in Fran's voice but Jane looked sharply at her and was rewarded with Fran's expansive smile. 'So, Jane. Put me out of my misery. Explain all the mystery. Who are you? What are you doing here?'

'Got a few hours?' Jane smiled. She found it easy to talk to Fran.

'All day.'

She had lived so long as Jane Reed now that as she told her tale, it felt almost as if she were talking about someone else.

'I thought I knew you. Your face, it was plastered all over the papers for years, wasn't it? Of course, and the Prince. What a gas! And no one here has twigged?'

'Well, no, I just say I'm called Reed, you see. And it was all so long ago.'

'I suppose you want to keep it deadly secret. Hell, I'd love to tell some of the old crows around here. The last story I heard about you was that you had won the football pools.'

'How typical!' Jane said lightly.

'So tell me, in this extraordinary life of yours, what affected you the most?'

'Bathrooms,' Jane said without hesitation. 'I have never got over the luxury of having a bathroom and running hot water.' She laughed at the surprise on Fran's face. 'Did you think I was going to say something a lot more socially significant?'

'Well, yes, I thought you'd rattle on about becoming obsessed with class or something, not bathrooms,' she protested.

'But I did become obsessed with class. I still am.'

'And how do you regard yourself now, as a princess?'

'Good God, no. Working-class, of course.'

'You certainly don't look it in clothes like that.' Fran eyed the understated Yves St Laurent suit, the Hermès bag and shoes.

Jane laughed, smoothing her skirt. 'That's the influence of my second husband. He made me into a clothes snob, I'm afraid. But seriously, if I had said I thought of myself as an aristocrat when I was married to Alistair, I bet you'd have thought, "Who the hell does she think she is?" If you're a working-class child, that's what you stay, especially when the chips are down. Haven't you noticed, when people are angry, they always revert to the accents of their origins? You can't have a decent row in an assumed accent.'

Fran laughed in agreement. 'You're like my husband – he's working-class and makes no secret of it – but what about those who manage to cover their tracks?'

'They never do, they're only fooling themselves. The upper classes will always sniff them out. It's a closed shop with its own rules, codes and network absorbed with their mother's milk. They might let me in to the club but only as an honorary member and only for as long as it suits them.'

'True. Right old expert on the subject, aren't you? Are you rich?'

'Yes.'

'Hasn't that made a difference?'

'I don't really know. I don't think anyone here knows how rich I am.'

'It would make one hell of a difference, I can assure you. You should see them with the sheik who bought that estate last year.'

'Bet they're foul about him behind his back.'

'True.'

'So it wouldn't make any difference, would it? No, thanks. I don't give a fig any more.'

'Good for you. How about some lunch?'

Fran led her into a farmhouse-style kitchen. The red Aga, the long pine table, the Portmeirion pottery, the herbs hanging drying from the ceiling, all reminded her of Zoe's kitchen. She felt at home. Fran was one of those rare people, warm and giving, whom she felt she had known for years. Jane was not in the least put out when Fran suddenly asked, 'Do you think you'll get married again?'

'I shouldn't think so. I was lucky twice, I can't expect such luck a third time.'

'You don't sound as if you've had much luck – one divorce, then being widowed.'

'I meant I can't complain about my marriages. You make mistakes, and the tragedy is you only realize when you're older and it's all too late. But still I'm lucky. I've got two marvellous sons, and I'm very fond of Alistair.'

'Most people seem to hate their exes' guts, not talk of being fond of them.'

'Well, that's their loss,' Jane said.

Fran was an excellent cook and the wine was superb, and it was a contented and well-insulated Jane who set off with Fran to look at the land that was causing all the problems.

Strathleith was a small estate of 15,000 acres. Unusual for this area, it was mainly flat, and swept from the foothills of the mountains to the sea. The land was rough, not agricultural, and there were no trees. It was rather dull except for the beach, which was a beautiful sweep of golden sands. The two women stood on a headland, the wind from the sea whipping at their clothes.

'The beach is lovely but I've seen more beautiful places up here. Surely no one could object to this being used?' Jane said helpfully.

'Everywhere you go up here is beautiful. It's our blessing and our curse. No matter what you want to do, the environmentalists do have a case, it's all so sodding lovely.' Fran angrily tugged at a piece of couch grass.

'I'd have to look on the map, but I'm certain my land must join onto this.'

'It does,' said Fran. 'I checked last night.'

'And what exactly is it you want to do here?'

'There's a small group of us on the council would give our eye teeth for this land. We want to start an industrial complex here, small work units. We don't want big business here. Have you heard of the smelter they built over on the east? Marvellous, it was, until it went bust and all the men were laid off. We can't afford all our eggs in one basket – we must diversify.'

'That makes sense.'

'Fantastic! You understand,' Fran shouted excitedly, beaming from ear to ear as if Jane had understood the secret of the universe. 'You've no idea how many don't understand that concept. They drive me bonkers.'

'But surely everyone wants to bring employment into the area?'

'Those fat cats sit on their estates pontificating away about the benefits of bringing employment to Scotland, but only if the industry stays in Glasgow and Motherwell – it mustn't come and upset their grouse and their stalking. A hint of that and they're on the ecology bandwagon straight away.'

'And what about the government? Can't the government buy it?'

'Christ, Jane, haven't you been listening? Those bastards *are* the government. If not in power, my love, they know or are related to those who are. Went to school with them, served in the army with them, shoot with them, fornicate with them.'

'Times are changing.'

'Balderdash! What were you saying back at the house? The system never changes and the people up here are the victims of it just as you were, but in their case we're talking of survival, not just the odd insult at a dinner party.' Fran's face was red with anger.

'But I've seen in the paper . . . large grants from the government . . .'

'Fish farms and craft shops, Jane. I tell you, if I see a planning application for another craft shop I'll run naked through the streets of Inverness, and that'll frighten them.' She laughed loudly, the wind scooping up the laugh, accentuating its hollowness.

'What do you think will happen?'

'I expect old Rimbish will buy it, it marches with his land.'

'It's all so depressing.'

'That it is, my girl. It's perfect for what we want. The main road is only three miles away, no distance for up here. The bay is deep enough for ships. Hell, the railway cuts across it, that is, if the line isn't axed . . .'

'Poor Fran.'

'Poor Fran, my arse. Poor Highlanders.' She kicked angrily at the sand. 'I don't know why I get so worked up, no one gives a damn.' The blue eyes looked angrily out across the water. 'My particular bandwagon.' She suddenly grinned again. 'Come on, Jane, fancy some tea?'

That evening, at home, Jane sat in her small library, surrounded by her dogs, and thought for a long time. She wanted the woman to like her. She feared that Fran despised her for the rich, spoilt, self-centred person she must seem. She had wasted too much of her life worrying and caring what people thought, seeing injustice at every turn. She knew she had lied when she said she did not care what people said any more. Obviously, if she were honest, one of the reasons she had hidden away up here was to escape, not to have to face reality, to avoid being hurt. She had been wrong. She had allowed herself to become obsessed with slights and insults instead of getting on with living.

She spent the next morning with paper, pencil and a calculator, making telephone calls. She made copious notes. She surprised her accountants, whom she had meekly obeyed until now, signing whatever was put in front of her, by asking for a complete set of her business accounts and a total breakdown of all her assets. she had a long telephone conversation with James. And she returned to Strathleith and walked the land.

She waited anxiously for the parcels of accounts, balance sheets and bank statements to arrive. Once they had, the large drawing-room carpet disappeared under a sea of paper. Never seriously involved in business, Jane worked late into the night and all the next day trying to untangle the web of how much she was worth.

'Donald, it's Jane.' She finally phoned her chief accountant. 'There's an estate up here I want to buy.'

'Another one, Jane? Of course, if you want, just give me the name of the agents.'

'I don't want to live on this one, Donald. I want to do something with it.'

'Like what?'

'I want to build an industrial estate on it.'

'There's a lot of money to be made that way these days, Jane. A good investment.'

'No, Donald, you don't understand. I don't want it, I want to give it away.'

There was a long silence on the phone. 'Give it away?' Jane smiled at the pain in her accountant's voice.

'Yes. I've worked it all out. I'll set up a trust and the people who work it will own it. It will need houses and schools, even an airport eventually . . .'

'Jane! Jane! What on earth are you talking about?'

'I'm talking about putting back into the community, Donald.'

'But, Jane, you're talking about millions if not billions.'

'I know, isn't it exciting? I realize it can't all happen at once, but I intend to raise money from everywhere – industry, banks, government.'

'And what sort of industry have you in mind, Jane?'

'Computers to start with, a Highland Silicon Valley, the air's so clean up here –'

'But you don't know anything about computers, Jane.'

'Of course I don't, as I know nothing about creating industrial estates. I shall employ those who do,' she heard herself snap in reply to his patronizing tone of voice. 'I shall buy the land out of income, Donald, and when it gets going I want to use my money, none of James's. I've worked it out – I can well afford it.'

'What about James in all this? I mean, even if you use what's yours, he has every right to expect it to be his one day.'

'He's excited. He's coming up next week to see it and he's got masses of ideas, too.'

'And does this land you want have planning permission?'

'No.'

'Then I must ask you to be cautious. Without planning permission the land will be almost worthless.'

'I'll get planning permission.'

'Jane, it isn't that easy. It might prove impossible to get the necessary permits.'

'Oh no, Donald, it won't. I know exactly what I'm going to do.'

4

Two months later the *Scotsman* had barely hit the breakfast tables before the phone began to ring. It was not surprising – 'Italian Princess saves Strathleith Estate.' Two cats out of the bag, she thought.

Lord Ludlow was one of the first to congratulate her. Jane explained nothing; she did not want to and, in any case, Ludlow did not give her time to, so fulsome was his praise of her. The phone never stopped ringing: the local nobility were welcoming her with open arms – for the time being.

As the phone rang for the umpteenth time, Jane heard the noise she had been expecting all morning, the roar of Fran's Ferrari as it screeched to a halt outside. Fran burst angrily into the room.

'You bitch! What the hell are you playing at?'

'Fran, I –'

'You're just like the rest of them and I, bloody fool, thought you were something different,' Fran shouted, tears welling in the beautiful blue eyes.

'Fran. Shut up! Sit down and listen for once,' Jane ordered. Fran sank sulkily into a chair, still blazing with anger.

'Want a job?' Jane asked.

'Job? What job?'

'Chairman of the trust I'm setting up.'

'Chairman? Trust? What the hell . . . ?' The intelligent eyes watched Jane sharply.

'Strathleith. I'm forming a trust. I'm giving it to the people who'll work it.'

'Sodding hell!'

'Very expressive, Fran.' Jane laughed at the open-mouthed astonishment on her friend's face. 'You see, your industrial estate will be built. But I want to go one further, I want a whole town built. It's to be done well, the best architects. I want it beautifully landscaped so that no one can say, "Look at that God-awful hole."'

'Jane, I don't know what to say . . .' There were tears again in Fran's eyes.

'We'll need training facilities. We shall insist that as many locals as possible are used, not just as labourers to build the place but trained to do skilled work. It'll take time but that must be the end result. This is to help this community, not to make money for people down south. The women, too. And the children – I must go round all the schools and see what computer courses are being taught.' The words bubbled out of Jane in a breathless torrent.

'Computers?'

'We won't just stop at computer-related industries. There's so much unused talent here. We can have our own weaving factories, textiles. Laura Ashley did it, why not us? Bottled water – hell, it's wonderful stuff here, why buy Perrier? I've so many ideas. Fran, it's so exciting! I've been dying to tell you but I was frightened something would go wrong and I didn't want to disappoint you.'

'Exciting! Jane, it's mind-blowing. But hang on a minute, how?'

'I'll kick it off. Hopefully it'll all be self-sufficient in ten years or so.'

'But it will cost –'

'Millions. I know.'

'But, Jane, where's the money coming from?'

'I'll start, and others will help us – industrialists, big businesses, banks and then the government will have to chip in. This is the big one, Fran. Everyone will want to help . . .'

'And you mean you can even contemplate this sort of money? Christ, are you that rich? Like Hughes, like Getty?'

'Not personally, but I have access to almost as much.'

'Bloody hell,' Fran said, open-mouthed with astonishment. 'But Jane, what about the planning permission? They'll still stop it.'

'No, they can't. We won't be applying for planning permission for individuals, we'll be applying for a whole community, a whole new way of life. With the general election eighteen months away, who the hell will dare to refuse us with the unemployment at the level it is here?'

'They will. They'll shut it up somehow. You don't know those bastards like I do. It'll be done in such a way that no one will ever get to hear of your plans.'

'But people will know. I'm that weird thing in our society, a personality. For years I've hidden from the press; now, if necessary, I'll court ἀem, newspapers, radio and TV. No, I don't think we'll have any ⌐roblems with our applications.'

Fran looked unconvinced. 'They'll throw everything at you – con-⌐rvation of endangered species, destruction of the environment. They'll ⌐op you,' she declared knowledgeably.

'Look at all those horrible conifer plantations, they've destroyed more ⌐f the Highlands than any light industry has ever done. And who planted ἀem? Why, the people you think will stop us.'

'That's different, nice little tax breaks in forestry. They'll find some ⌐are bug, last on the planet.'

'Then I shall employ experts to check every inch of land to make sure ἀat we aren't about to destroy anything.'

'You'll make enemies, Jane.'

'I'll make friends, too.'

'But who will really join us?'

Jane reeled off a list of internationally known names.

'Wow! You know all those people?'

'Yes. Roberto knew everyone and he was in business with lots of them. 've talked to them, they're interested. There's loads of reasons why they ⌐hould be – old obligations to Roberto, tax breaks, honours, you'll see.'

'Why, Jane? Why are you doing all this?'

'So many reasons, Fran. Something you said that first day we had ⌐unch together, it made me sit up and take stock. I'd been feeling sorry ⌐or myself for too long, wallowing in self-pity, thinking too much. I love ⌐ here, I want to give in return. And, to be honest, I want something to ⌐o. I guess I've always wanted something. I never found out until now ⌐hat it was.'

'Hell, I started all this. So let me just say two things, love. First, I think ⌐ou should keep some financial involvement in this project, say 25 per ⌐ent.'

'But I don't want any financial benefit from it.'

'Maybe not, but people won't trust you if you don't. If they see that ⌐ou've invested in it for yourself, put your money where your mouth is, ⌐hen they're much more likely to regard it favourably, and help. Other-⌐vise it all sounds a little too good to be true.'

'Do you think so? Yes, I see what you mean. All right, I'll keep a ⌐ortion for myself. At least it'll please my accountant.'

'The other thing is, I don't want the job as chairman.'

'Oh, Fran, I can't do it without you.'

'You don't have to. I'd love a job, but as your assistant or something.

You have to be the chairman. You're the one who's worked it all out, you're the one with the clout.'

'OK, assistant chairman or chairperson, or whatever you like.' She danced a little step of glee. 'Oh, Fran, darling, isn't it all so wonderfully exciting?'

'Jane, I didn't know you had it in you.'

'Neither did I, Fran, neither did I!'

590   Discussion of Policy

You have to do it. I think if you
you're the best company to...

5

...an advised that they should work secretly in the planning stages. She ...ared that, if news of Jane's intentions got out, objections would snow ...own thick and fast, and the less warning the opposition had, the better. ...an's husband was the only local whom they told. He wished them well ... he left for his job in the East again, but he sounded as if he doubted ...ere could ever be a happy outcome.

...Together they travelled the length and breadth of the country and to ...urope, to America, anywhere they could study the concept of a new ...own. They visited factories by the dozen, workshop units by the ...ndred. And after each trip the files containing their plans and ideas ...ew larger.

...Within the first month an American company, in which Roberto had ...vested heavily, showed interest in the possibility of setting up a ...uropean factory. At a party in London, Jane met the head of a large ...osmetics firm, who began to think seriously of setting up in her town. ...esigners who had until now seen Jane as just a good customer began to ...gard her, excitedly, in a new light, when she asked them to investigate ...e weaving of fine silks in the Highlands, thus saving them the need to ...alk the suppliers of Europe. Taking a necklace whose clasp had broken ...to the jeweller's in London that Roberto had always patronized, Jane ...oved quickly on hearing the owner say he was toying with the idea of ...oing into clockmaking. A furniture manufacturer, a toymaker, the ...leas flowed thick and fast: getting tenants was not going to be a ...roblem, and they had not even started to investigate how many small, ...ubsidized units would be needed by people who could not afford to ...art big. Everyone was sworn to secrecy at this stage.

...She was listened to sympathetically by businessmen who had been ...art of Roberto's vast network of contacts. As they had respected the ...an, so they respected his memory, and to his widow they pledged the ...vel of donations she would need.

With this backup, they decided the time was ripe to begin to hav
unofficial, exploratory talks with the local planning officer. Since th
council had wanted the land in the first place, Jane was not surprised b
the enthusiasm and advice they received from him; and, knowing th
problems they were likely to face, he was equally keen that, for the tim
being, their talks should be confidential.

The botanists, zoologists, ornithologists and all the other experts Jar
had marshalled searched and scoured the land. It took weeks, but finall
their reports arrived. Nothing of any rarity or of an endangered specie
had been found on the estate.

James, newly graduated from university, was excited by his mother
plans. He tried, unsuccessfully, to persuade her to use some of th
Wilbur Calem millions that would one day be his, and then, the greate
surprise of all, he gave up his new job in a City bank to join her and Frar
It was like a shot in the arm to Jane that he should have such faith in th
outcome and that he wanted to live and work with her.

'It's incredible,' Fran said as they relaxed over dinner in London afte
a long afternoon spent in the deep leather armchairs and gentlemen'
club atmosphere of the senior partner of Ormerod Brothers, th
merchant bankers. 'Money really does make money, doesn't it?'

'True, and so unfair.'

'Not this time, my old mate, not this time. There are moment
though, Jane, when I think it's all too easy, that something's got to g
wrong.'

'You're a dreadful pessimist, Fran.'

'No, Jane, I'm not. You're just an incorrigible optimist!'

Over six months later their outline planning application was rejected o
its first presentation. Jane and James waited with frustrated anger fo
Fran to arrive.

'The sods!' exclaimed Fran as she bounced angrily into the room. '
shouldn't have resigned from the flaming council. At least we'd hav
known something was going wrong.'

'You would have had to declare an interest, Fran, so it probabl
wouldn't have made any difference,' James pointed out.

'But we would have had some warning that things weren't goin
completely our way.'

'The Neanderthals must have known right from the outset. So muc
for all the promises of confidentiality.'

'Neanderthals?' asked Fran.

'James's word for the opposition.'

'But it was inevitable. After all, our application had to be published ~eks ago,' Fran said as reasonably as she could manage.

'But not time enough, Fran, to set up all these new environmental ~oups. No, they've known right from the beginning, I reckon.'

'What groups?' Fran demanded. James began to read a long list of ~cieties dedicated to the protection of every aspect of flora and fauna, ~m the birds to the buttercups, from the sea to the slugs. 'I've never ~ard of half of them.'

'Exactly, Fran, that's what James means: they've been set up in the ~st twelve months – probably the same people belong to all of them.'

'It was pretty naive of us, really, if you think about it, Jane. Once we ~gan putting feelers out in the City, then the word must have been out in ~e bloody clubs, gossip shops more like.'

'But they promised, all of them, even Ormerods.'

'Yes, Ma, but to them, promising to you was one thing; their loyalty ~s to be with their own sort, so they could welsh on you with a clear ~nscience. It's the old-boy network.'

'I can't see your father doing something like that.'

'But he's not really one of them, Ma, is he? Never has been.'

'That's true.' She laughed. 'Or you wouldn't be here, would you?'

The old Jane would have been cast down with dejection but this new ~ne resolved to fight back. And she needed every ounce of that resolve, ~r the tentacles of vested interest seemed to be everywhere. There were ~ays when she felt she was in a web of intrigue and plotting so dense that ~ere was no way out. Time and again the people she tried to contact, to ~lk to, to persuade them to see things her way, were out to her calls and ~ever returned them. Many letters to important people mysteriously ~ent astray.

Since so many avenues seemed suddenly closed to her, she approached ~e one group who welcomed her with open arms – the press. She ~ourted them, but it was hard: she had hidden from them for so many ~ears. Everything about her past was dragged into the light. For each ~omplimentary article there was always an equally derogatory one. ~nce again her steps were dogged by eager young reporters with ~otepads, while photographers ran backwards in front of her. She had to ~teel herself to see her face on television. She had to adjust to losing her ~nonymity.

The first letter came as a shock. Her hands shook violently as she saw ~he word DEATH crudely made from newspaper headlines. But this one

was mild compared with those which followed: from them she learned
new vocabulary of invective. When the abusive phone calls started, s
retreated behind a screen of secretaries who sifted and sorted throu
the mail, answered the phone for her, and protected her from hate.

When her car was pushed off the road and into the river she emerg
unhurt but soaked, her rage delaying the inevitable shock, as s
screamed angrily at the retreating black car which sped back up the gle

The police, though they assured her it was probably a chance ca
of reckless driving, thought it would do no harm if she had a bod
guard with her at all times. She was not fooled by their bland-fac
reassurance.

Now, not only could she not open her mail, pick up her phone, answ
her own front door, but she had lost the freedom to drive wherever s
wanted and, worst of all, to wander alone on her beloved moor.

It was not surprising that there were days when she wondered if sh
should not give up. But then the spirit which had saved Respryn fro
financial chaos, given her the courage to raise Giovanni, and the streng
to will Roberto to live for those precious extra months, re-emerged a
she and Fran carried stoically on.

When the second planning application was thrown out, Jane decid
she had to see someone at the top. Since so many doors were now clos
to her, she used her new allies, the press, to announce her intention to p
her case to the minister for industrial planning. In the face of so ma
questions in the tabloids about why he did not see her, he had to rele

As Jane was shown into his office, her heart sank. In front of her stoo
a replica of so many of her adversaries – the neat pinstriped suit, almos
uniform; the Guards' tie; the smiling mouth beneath the unsmiling eye
His cheeks, pouched like a well-fed hamster's, were an ominously hig
colour – the bright red of years of best claret and hours spent stalking
the hills. His colour said it all: she did not need to look at the photograp
in the crested silver frame to know what his wife would look like, and sh
did not need to ask if the painting on the wall was of his own ancestr
pile. He was charming, almost unctuously so. How grateful they we
for her generous intentions but he was powerless to help, he smooth
informed her. 'A local matter,' he said, one eyebrow arched expressivel

'But I can't see it as just a local matter, like something of n
importance. I've promises from manufacturers that, for a start, w
ensure 2000 jobs. That's just the beginning. And you know that numbe
of jobs in the Highlands is like 10,000 jobs anywhere else.'

'Princess . . .' he started.

'Reed, Jane Reed.'

'Miss Reed, of course, how remiss, I had quite forgotten you prefer . . .
at have you thought perhaps, if you wish to give so generously, that the
ational Trust for Scotland or the RSPB would be only too pleased . . .'

'I didn't buy it for them. I want to create jobs in a community that
sperately needs them, permanent jobs that last all year, not just when
e tourists come, with the long winter lay-off when they've gone. I want
build decent houses, with room for people to move in, not rabbit
atches. I want to give people hope.'

'Most commendable, Miss Reed, but I'm afraid my hands are tied.'

'And you won't untie them?'

'It's not that easy, my dear. As I've explained, this is not a government
sue.'

'Then it bloody well ought to be and if you were half a minister you
ould get off your arse and make it one.' Angrily she picked up her
andbag and gloves. 'And, minister, I'm not your "dear" anything. I
ould be obliged if you would remember that in the future dealings we
all be having with each other.'

She had the satisfaction of seeing him speechless, gulping like a
randed fish, though she realized she could now expect no help from
im. Still, she knew no help would have been forthcoming anyway.

The solution, like most solutions, came in the middle of the night. And
ke the best solutions it was so blindingly simple that she wondered why
n earth she had not thought of it before.

She would play the game their way, with their ploys and using their
ules.

Anonymously, she joined all the societies for environmental concern
at had suddenly proliferated like mushrooms. She compiled a list of
e principal officers and telexed the list to the New York offices of the
Vilbur Calem conglomerate. The powerful computers sifted, searched
nd analysed and less than twenty-four hours later the answer lay in her
ands.

Jane telephoned Alistair and two nights later she sat opposite him in
he Caprice.

'Like old times, Jane.'

'I don't remember ever coming here with you. Roberto, yes, but
s?'

'I meant being together. We should see more of each other, Jane.'

'It's my fault, but I'm so busy, there's so much to do. And you're rarely
n London these days.'

'I'm getting like my father, I suppose. I'm happiest at Respryn, I ca[n']
be bothered with the rat race of London.'

'But you used to love the London scene so much.'

'That was just a youthful phase,' he said, looking sheepish. 'Perha[ps]
I've grown up.'

'Oh, Alistair, don't do that, it would be awful if you grew up. Jame[s is]
grown-up enough for the two of us.' She laughed.

'But a fifty-year-old Peter Pan is somewhat undignified, don't y[ou]
think?'

'No, and in any case I can't believe that you're fifty – it only seems li[ke]
yesterday, doesn't it?'

'Yesterday and a million years ago. Jay . . .' He put his hand across t[he]
table and covered hers. The movement was so unexpected that for a lo[ng]
moment Jane left her hand where it was. At his touch her mind rac[ed]
back to that last time they had made love. The nerves of her body tens[ed]
as she remembered the feel of his lean, strong body. She looked at t[he]
generous line of his mouth . . .

'Penny for them?' He was smiling easily at her.

'I wanted to talk to you about my trust,' she said quickly, fearful th[at]
her eyes must reflect the intimacy of her thoughts.

He removed his hand from hers. 'Don't you think that perhaps y[ou]
have taken on a bit more than you can chew, Jay?'

'It's funny to hear you call me Jay. No one else does,' she said, findi[ng]
it increasingly difficult to concentrate on the reason they were here.

'Our word. That's nice.'

She looked across at him, now, in his middle years, even mo[re]
attractive than in his youth, something she would not have thoug[ht]
possible. The blonde hair was now totally white, the same silver whi[te]
that his father's had been. The lines on his face added to its distinctio[n]
and his body was as slim and spare as when she had married him. A[nd]
strange, too, being with him and remembering the past, how quickly h[er]
pulse seemed to race . . .

She shook her head, trying to erase the thoughts that were plagui[ng]
her. This was ridiculous – Honor would have told her to go out and fi[nd]
some nice, uncomplicated young man. 'Alistair, do you approve of wh[at]
I'm doing?' she said, suddenly unsure of herself.

'The idea, yes, of course. It's a wonderful concept and typical of you[;]
you always had a guilt thing about wealth and privilege, didn't you?'

'With my background, what would you expect?'

'Remember how you used to sit on the floor of the Rolls when we we[re]

hrough towns because you were embarrassed to let anyone see you in
t?'

'It wasn't just that. I always thought how disappointed people would
e, expecting to see a film star or a pop star and instead getting us.' She
aughed at the memory.

'The idea's all right,' he said, suddenly serious. 'But I worry what it
night be doing to you. James told me about those pleasant fellows in the
ar and how you now have a personal ape to mind you.'

'Oh, that's nothing, people will soon forget, once I've really got it
going. But you do approve?' she asked anxiously, realizing that she
eeded his approval more than anyone else's.

'I approve. Of course Mother doesn't. She's convinced you're fritter-
ng James's inheritance away.'

'I'm not, Alistair, I'd never do that.' She leaned across the table,
studying his face for any hint of suspicion.

'I know, darling. She's old and she can't grasp it. I've tried explaining
and James has, too, but at eighty-five it's all too much for her.'

'I shouldn't think her age has anything to do with it. She would have to
bject on principle, if I was involved.' The mention of Lady Upnor
rought her back to the purpose of their meeting. 'Anyhow. Would you
o me a favour?'

'I'll try.'

'Do you know Lord Ludlow and George Fraser-Brown?'

'I know George. I was at Cambridge with his son, John – you know,
he minister for industrial planning.'

'We met,' she snorted derisively. 'What about Ludlow?'

'I don't know him socially, only in the Lords. Can't say I like him
much. I mean, if you get your life peerage from one party I think it's
pretty cheap to cross the floor the minute you're safely ensconced.
Bombastic old toad I've always thought him. What's your interest in
hem?'

'Those two are stopping my plans.'

'You sure?'

'Oh yes. There are others but they're the main ones. If I can make them
rumble, the rest will soon follow.'

'I can't see either of them giving way, especially to a woman. God, they
oth live in the Middle Ages where women are concerned. You do realize
hat George is old Rimbish's brother-in-law, and his estate is bang next
oor to your little venture – you could hardly expect him to agree.'

'But, Alistair, he's got thousands of acres and he's so rarely there.'

'I take your point. Of course Ludlow would object on principle, just to ingratiate himself with the real nobs he aspires to be like. So what's your plan?'

'I've discovered that an American bank, a subsidiary of the banking section of the Calem conglomerate, has large loans out to Ludlow and Fraser-Brown. Put simply, either they get off my back or I arrange to have the loans called in.'

'Ha! I like it! How much?'

'Ludlow nearly 5 million, Fraser-Brown just two.'

'Shit! It would finish Ludlow. I know for certain he's in a bit of a mess at the moment, had one or two catastrophes. He'd never get anyone else to back a loan of that size. But Fraser-Brown's a different matter, lot of money there, you know. It would just be a temporary setback for him, he'd raise it again, no problem. My, my. Little Jane, you have changed. Quite the ruthless career woman, aren't you?'

'I don't like doing it – I think it stinks – but then what they're doing to me stinks, too. Do you know, Alistair, that land had been on the market for five years before I came along? No one wanted it then, hardly anyone knew of its existence. I know it's a rotten thing I'm planning, but they chose the rules, not me. I'm only playing the sort of hand they're expert at.'

'So where do I fit in?'

'I hoped you'd know something about them, have some idea what I could do.'

'We're going to have to find something else on the Fraser-Brown lot. Obviously it would be most helpful if we could find something on Fraser-Brown junior, wouldn't it?' He smiled at Jane, his eyes sparkling.

'Most definitely. I think I'm going to enjoy all this.'

'If we could get something on the pompous minister, it would be marvellous. You see, it's all getting to be so big that we'll need the government in on this eventually.'

'I'll do it.' He laughed. 'I know how to handle John Fraser-Brown. Not very pleasant but then he was a pompous fart at Magdalene, and Ludlow's the sort of lord that gets us all a bad name. Don't worry, we'll sort them out, together.' He looked at her, momentarily serious. 'It's amazing, Jane, but you seem to get more beautiful the older you get.'

'It's all an illusion, Alistair. It's wonderful what money can do.' She tried to sound casual. Alistair was not given to compliments.

'I want to make love to you, Jane.'

To Jane it was as if the sound in the restaurant was suddenly shut off,

She felt she was in a child's game of statues, as if the other diners and waiters were frozen in that moment. She looked at Alistair, saw the naked longing in his eyes, felt the fatal longing of her body for him. And then remembered, 'You've learned a lot since the last time . . .', his voice echoing back and forth in her brain. The noises of the restaurant returned, the waiters and diners were moving. She turned her face away.

'Don't spoil the evening, Alistair,' she heard herself say, almost primly.

'Sorry, Jane. But I had to say it.'

The spell was broken. They finished their coffee, and Alistair handed her into a taxi, kissing her lightly on the brow. From the taxi she watched his familiar, long-legged walk as he disappeared down the street, and she wished that things, that she, could be different.

A week later the phone rang in her Scottish home. 'Jane? Alistair here. Mission accomplished, collapse of stout parties. Have you ever seen a puce-faced peer turn green before your eyes? I have. Not a pretty sight. Anyhow, the word's out to all their little minions. I should reapply forthwith if I were you.'

'What did you turn up on John Fraser-Brown?'

'Oh, that was rather naughty of me,' he said with a chuckle. 'I just conveniently remembered that one day at Cambridge, he hadn't sported his oak, and I walked in. It seemed odd that he should have his trousers down round his ankles and the beefy fencing blue with him likewise. I just reminded him, that's all, and out of friendship thought I'd better mention that I'd probably told you at some point along the way.'

'Alistair, fantastic!'

'It is, isn't it? He can't afford any scandal, especially not of that nature, if he's to fulfil his ambition and become prime minister.'

'Alistair, you're wonderful. I love you, I really do,' she said with glee. There was an awkward pause. What on earth had possessed her to say that? she thought.

'I'm glad to hear it, Jay. Perhaps you could whisper it in my shell-like ear one day soon, instead of down this infernal machine,' he quipped with practised, social ease. She relaxed: that was the kind of bantering flirtation in which her bank manager indulged.

This time everything progressed with the smoothness of the best-oiled machinery. Jane's trust application was passed and, over a year since the day she had bought the estate, Jane watched Fran turn the first sod of

earth. The minister for industrial planning made a smiling and well
received speech of gratitude as he declared the Wilbur Calem Trust a
reality.

Jane, in turn, smiled charmingly at him. To give him and his father
their due, they had lost graciously, unlike Ludlow, who continued to
bore anyone who would listen about the ruthlessness of Jane Reed. But
in the way of the world, no one listened to him any more: as always
money and success triumphed.

6

Everything began to move with satisfying speed. It would have moved faster but for Jane, who rejected one set of plans after another from an ever increasing army of architects. She knew what she wanted: they were just not producing it. She had explained, she thought, quite clearly. She wanted buildings that would blend as far as possible into the environment in which they stood, and that would offer functional yet pleasant working conditions. In her endless travels, time and again she found factories where the offices, the planners and the designers worked in large-windowed, carpeted luxury, while the work force toiled in noisy, windowless, featureless blocks. It seemed illogical to Jane that those with the more interesting jobs enjoyed the most comfort, while those with the dull, repetitive tasks had the least.

She had hoped for a Scottish firm, but her search finally ended in a pretty, wooded valley in Devon at a small textile factory. The architects were two young men whose largest contract this factory had been. As they listened to her plans, their dark, intense eyes glittered and their floppy bow ties seemed to quiver with excitement. Their views mirrored hers, her enthusiasm matched theirs.

Around her now she had an army of advisers. Her solicitors and accountants had been joined by financial experts, marketing and publicity men. All were up in arms at her rejection of yet another set of plans and at her choice of new architects. She had been foolish, they would have liked to say; instead they contented themselves with telling her she needed a large, experienced firm, not two young lads fresh out of college, and the publicity and marketing people, who were Scottish, deplored her choice of Englishmen. But Jane was learning fast and getting tougher with the learning – she knew what she wanted and no one was going to stop her, certainly not local nationalist feeling.

'I'm the one who's been doing the searching, and I know just how difficult it's been to find a firm who understand what we want. I couldn't care less what nationality they are. If they were Eskimos I'd still have asked them.' Such views, now expressed firmly and with confidence silenced her advisers. They might moan behind her back, but it suited Jane to use her power and their burgeoning fear of her to achieve her own ends.

The plans for the factories and work units that they already knew they would require began to arrive. Jane was thrilled; the two young men had planned exactly what, until now, had been her dream.

Their plans for the housing, therefore, came as a disappointing shock.

Jane stood in the small, cluttered, but brightly lit office of Colin and Renton and silently studied the exquisitely drawn plans for the housing development. She frowned. Colin nervously straightened his red polka dot tie; Renton's hands restlessly played with the large cowboy buckle on his belt. The silence seemed endless; they were not used to Jane frowning.

'This isn't what Fran and I asked for,' she said quietly.

'There are 200 units, Jane, the number you stipulated,' Renton's high-pitched voice explained.

'In boring, uniform rows! It looks like a plan more suited to the Industrial Revolution.'

'It's the most cost-effective use of land.'

'We're not exactly short of land, Renton.'

'I realize, Jane, but with the factories costing so much, we thought we should economize somewhere.'

'Who asked you to?'

'Well, no one . . .'

'These are rabbit hutches. You can't expect people to live in conditions like that.'

'They conform to the minimum square footage for living space laid down in the building regulations.'

'Then the building regulations are inhuman. Sod regulations. This whole concept is built on defying rules and regulations. I want large houses, landscaped for privacy, big gardens – we're dealing with country people, they're going to want gardens they can plant vegetables in, not just sit in.'

'How about a large allotment plot, Jane, each house to have its own if they want? Then the gardens needn't be so big,' Fran suggested helpfully.

'Oh yes, Fran, I like the allotment idea. That's good – we'll do that. It doesn't alter the fact that I want them to have good-sized gardens.' She continued her careful study. 'But they're all the same – why are they all the same?'

'Well, cost-effectively –'

'Renton, Colin, I don't think you can have listened to a word that Fran and I said to you.' Her irritation made her voice hard. 'Maybe we need a different firm for the housing.'

'You tell us what you want, we'll do it,' Colin said hurriedly.

'But we did tell you what we wanted, excellent housing. How can you design such beautiful factories and then do this?' Angrily she stabbed at the offending plan.

'We're rather good at factories.' Renton laughed nervously, only to be silenced by Jane's angry glare.

'For your benefit I'll outline it just once more. We want houses of different sizes – not all people have 2.2 children. I don't want our children sleeping four to a room. We need small units for the unmarried only. Family houses must have at least two rooms downstairs.'

'But we've done them with two rooms just as you said; both Colin and I would much rather have had a large open-plan room, but you were so insistent on two rooms.'

'You couldn't swing a cat in either of those rooms. We want a large family room, and a smaller, quieter room, for being alone, a study . . .'

'Study? Jane, you're kidding! These houses are for artisans.'

'And don't workers also need peace and quiet? Doing homework in a crowded family room is an impossibility.'

'There are the bedrooms.'

'Bedrooms are always colder. Children like to be near what's going on, not isolated in their bedrooms.'

'As you like, Jane, but it'll be few families who'll use them that way.'

'You don't know that,' Jane snapped sharply. 'And why are the walls so thin?'

'That's how houses are built these days, Jane.'

'Then I don't like it. We must have solid, soundproof houses.'

'But the cost?'

'That's my worry, not yours.'

'Honestly, Jane, I think you would just be throwing money away. This is normal building-reg housing.'

'Have either of you ever lived in a house where you can hear your neighbours rowing, gobbing, farting, copulating?' she asked angrily.

'Well, no, but –'

'I have. It's hell. It creates family tension and arguments, let alone

ruining your sex life.' She was almost shouting at the two startled young
men. From Fran a large snort of laughter exploded.

'She's right, boys. Hell, we can't be responsible for ruining the
Highlanders' libido, can we?'

Suddenly they were all laughing and Jane calmed down, her point
made and taken. She surprised herself these days by just how forceful
and arrogant she could be to ensure the realization of her dream.

A month later she was in possession of the housing plans, and at last
they met with her approval. The building began in earnest.

For three years Jane worked, planned and schemed. She found reserves of energy she did not know she possessed; her attention to detail, her insistence on perfection became legendary. As her town grew, as more factories opened and new families moved in, she had thought that she would not need to work so hard, but nothing was further from the truth. As her fame spread, so the demands on her time were increased and she spent weeks and months away, travelling the world, lecturing, advising, consulting – her diary full for months to come.

She was proud of her success but as the years sped by, seeds of discontent began to grow within her. To achieve what she had, her personal life had been sacrificed. She saw far too little of Giovanni, who was becoming more Italian than English, instead of the mixture she had hoped he would be. She had not had a holiday in years. She rarely saw her old friends now. She still wrote to Sandra and Zoe, but their replies only emphasized the growing gulf between her life style and theirs in Cambridge. Though she met people by the thousand, she was never in one place long enough to establish any friendships. She was forty-seven, beautiful, elegant and assured, but she had become resigned, not without regret, to the idea that she would end her days alone.

When she saw Alistair it was only ever for a quick meal, before jetting off somewhere. She made sure they were never alone together. She was still afraid of the effect he had on her. It would have been so easy to phone him, arrange a meeting, get into bed with him. But Jane was determined not to repeat her mistakes. Other men left her cold; she kept them firmly at arm's length. Despite her wealth and success, her fear of rejection was a powerful force. Jane was unaware that her frenetic work schedule was in fact a defence mechanism – it did not allow her time to think of her own life.

Into her organized, tabulated world, the news that her father was ill

came as a shock. In her new life there was no time for illness. But for hi
she made time.

She flew down to England and took the car to the neat house whic
was now her mother's pride and joy. His decline had been rapid and sh
was not prepared for the emaciated figure she found, huddled in front o
a large fire that did not seem to warm him, the *Daily Mirror* folded on hi
lap. His radio had been replaced by a large television set which flickere
in the corner, the sound off.

'What's this then, Dad? Malingering, are we?' She tried to joke t
cover the pain she felt at his appearance.

'Something I ate, I reckon, don't know what all the fuss is about,' h
said lightly, but looked at her with frightened grey eyes, flecked no
with the yellow of age, which seemed to plead at her for an explanation
'I can't seem to keep anything down. It's like a bloody hangover tha
won't go away.'

'Should put more water in it.' She laughed nervously and averted he
eyes from his agonizing gaze. 'Who's your doctor?'

'Useless bugger!' her mother exclaimed. 'Fresh out of medical school
he doesn't know his arse from his elbow, if you ask me. He isn't eve
English,' she added darkly.

'I'll arrange for you to see a specialist in London, Dad.'

'See, I said she would –'

'No, you bloody well won't!' Her father managed to raise himself i
his chair, indignation giving him strength. 'I've never approved o
private medicine, jumping the queue, you can't expect me to change m
ways now.'

'Oh, come on, Dad. It would put Mum's mind at rest –'

'No. National Health's good enough for me.'

'But Dad . . .'

'I know you mean well, girl, but I've got my principles.'

'Fat lot of good they ever done you.' He chose to ignore the flash of he
old bitterness in his wife's voice.

'I understand, Dad. Forget it.' And she squeezed the thin, blue-veine
hand. It looked transparent and frail.

He picked at the rug that covered his knees and, without looking a
her, said in a barely audible voice, 'I'm very proud of you and wha
you're doing in Scotland. Seems there must be some of me in yo
after all.' She heard an unfamiliar, almost embarrassed pride in hi
voice.

'It looks like it, Dad.'

'Bloody waste of money, if you ask me. I bet Lady Upnor thinks the same way, wasting James's money like that.'

'I'm not wasting James's money, Mum.' She tried to sound patient instead of irritated. 'I used my own money and we raised the rest. In any case, Lady Upnor's dead, so her views don't come into it any more.'

'Dead? Why didn't you tell me? When? What she die of?' Her mother leaned forward with her customary interest in the news of death, illness and catastrophe.

'You'd never met so I didn't think to tell you. She died in her sleep, at Respryn, last year. She was in her eighties, after all.'

'She'd had a good innings, then.' There was a hint of disappointment in the woman's voice as she trotted out the platitude. Jane's mother preferred gory deaths. 'Did you go to the funeral?'

'No. I didn't see the point.'

'See the point! You have to go to funerals, Jane, even if you don't want to. That wasn't nice of you at all.'

'She'd hated me for so long and I never liked the woman. It would have been hypocritical to go. Alistair understood.'

'Quite right, Jane. I'm glad to see you've got principles. Now, if you two would stop your clacking, I want to check my pools.' The clawlike hand manipulated the remote-control button and the television set burst into noisy life.

Jane followed her mother into the kitchen where the older woman, filling the kettle, suddenly slumped against the draining board looking weary and beaten.

'You shouldn't have given up so easily, Jane. You should have insisted on another doctor.'

'You know what he's like, Mum. I'll phone his doctor and check what's going on, see if there's any more we can do. But in the end it's up to him, we can't make him see a specialist. It's his life, after all.'

'His death, more like.'

'Oh, Mum, don't say that.'

'It's the truth. And it's not just him. What about me, doesn't anyone ever think of me? I've a right to insist on him seeing another doctor.'

'I'm sorry, Mum.'

'You seem to have spent your life saying "sorry" to me. About time it stopped.'

'What, saying sorry?'

'No, doing things that make it necessary for you to say it.' She lit the gas, angrily, it seemed to Jane, who sighed inwardly at the prospect

that things were likely to degenerate into a row, even at a time like
this.

'I'll lay the tray,' she said hurriedly.

'What am I to do, Jane, how the hell am I to manage?' the older
woman suddenly burst out. She stood awkwardly, knotting and un-
knotting the teatowel in her hands, appearing embarrassed by her own
sudden outburst. Jane looked up, taken by surprise at the change in her
mother's voice. 'I don't understand anything any more. All those years
when I wished the old bugger would fall under a bus, the quarrels, the
rows, why, I've never stopped nagging him, I still do. And yet, I'm filled
with such dread at him leaving me, the emptiness there'll be . . .' She
began to cry noisily, using the teatowel as a handkerchief.

'It's because you do love him, Mum.'

'Don't talk so bloody daft.' She sniffed derisively and with shaking
fingers attempted to light a cigarette. Jane steadied the match for her.
'You always were sloppy, Jane.'

'There's nothing sloppy in acknowledging you love somebody.'

'I've never been one for words.'

'I know, Mum. He loves you too, I'm sure of it.'

'Well, he's never said so, and he's a funny way of showing it.' She sat
down heavily on the kitchen chair.

'You stayed together, didn't you, despite everything? And you're not
the easiest person to tell, you know. I love you, but I've never been able to
say it.'

Her mother sniffed again loudly. 'We don't see much of you – if you
love us so much you'd think you could find the time to see more of us.'

'We don't get on, Mum, we never have, it's safer if I don't see you, but
that doesn't stop me loving and caring for you.'

Her mother twisted in the chair as if she were uncomfortable with the
way the conversation was going. She appeared relieved when the kettle
began to whistle, and she got up to make the tea. 'He's going to get
worse, Jane.'

'When he does I'll pay for a nurse to help you.'

'He won't have that.'

'Then lie to him, tell him it's on the NHS.'

'Yes, I might do that,' she said, picking up the tray.

Later that afternoon Jane visited her father's doctor. He confirmed her
fears, the prognosis was bad. All the tests that could be done had been
done, all the treatment available had been tried. Her father's tumour was
inoperable. Another opinion, the doctor felt, would only confirm what

they already knew and would exhaust her father further. To her mother's anger, she accepted the decision.

Jane would have stayed longer but an urgent call from Scotland arrived and her father insisted she left to attend to it. She planned to be away for only a short time.

The nurse was not needed. A week later, her father died, neatly and quietly, watching a football match on the giant television set she had bought him.

Jane stood by the open grave, her body shuddering with sobs. Back at the house, she helped serve the ritual ham-salad tea, with South African sherry. The tears kept streaming down her face.

'I don't see why you're so upset. He was never much of a father to you,' her mother said, when the few guests had gone, and they sat sipping tea that neither of them really wanted.

'We had the odd moment of closeness,' Jane said, a strange mixture of defence and pride in her voice.

'Few and far between, if you ask me. I don't think he ever liked you, if you want to know the truth.'

'I'm not asking you and I don't want to know. That's cruel, Mum.'

'It's the truth, but then you never liked the truth, Jane, all that airy-fairy romantic guff in your head. For goodness' sake, pull yourself together,' she snapped as Jane began to cry again.

'If you must know, I'm crying because it's all too late, he'll never love me now,' she cried out.

'There you go, sloppy talk again.'

'Christ, Mum, don't you ever give up?' Jane shouted angrily at her mother who sat rigidly in the chair opposite.

'There's no need to shout at me like that. You are getting bad-tempered, Jane.' Huffily she sipped her tea. 'I was surprised Alistair didn't come.'

'He offered, I said no.'

'And what right had you to do that?'

'It was the same as me with Alistair's mother: Dad never approved, so it wouldn't have been right for him to be there. Alistair understood.'

'Your father liked Alistair, it was what he was he didn't like.'

'Oh, I see, he liked Alistair but not me?' She sounded bitter.

'Alistair's a fine man. You were a fool ever to leave him. Look at you now, all this money, rushing about the world, showing off. It's all right now, but what about the future? Look at you — you'll be fifty before you know where you are. Still on your own, a fine, lonely old age you're

going to have.' Jane admired the way her mother could sniff her critica
snort and sip her tea at the same time.

'Age isn't that important. Fifty isn't old these days, and the attitud
that every woman needs a man is gone – that's old hat,' she said wit
spirit.

'Old hat it might be, but it's still the truth, people need people. An
mark my words, seventy will come galloping along in no time.'

'Thanks for cheering me up, Mum.'

'I think I might move in with your aunt.' Her mother abruptly change
the subject. 'She's on her own now and it's silly, the two of us rattling
around in two houses. She's always good for a laugh, too – not that I ca
see much to laugh about at the moment.'

'That's a good idea. I would have been happy for you to come to live
with me.'

'No, you wouldn't. As you said the other day, we've never got on. In
any case I don't like Scotland and I couldn't live in your grand way.'

'I don't live in a grand way. My life style is quite simple, really.'

'Bah, don't give me that! Do you see much of Alistair these days?'
Again she changed the subject as if suddenly tiring of one and needing to
distract herself with another topic.

'Not as much. But I'm seeing him next week. It's his birthday – he's
having a big party at Respryn. I promised I'd go.'

'That's nice. I must remember to send him a card.'

At last her mother stopped talking and Jane was relieved when she
announced that she thought she would have an early night. It had been
an emotional day for Jane and she was finding it a strain to deal with the
sudden shifts in her mother's moods. As always she did not really know
what to talk to her about.

As she lay in the dark, thinking of the day, she puzzled over her
mother's attitude. Less than two weeks ago she had been dreading this
day, and had been in tears at the prospect, and yet today she had shown
no emotion and had even been irritated by Jane's grief. So Jane was both
surprised and relieved when through the wall she heard the unfamiliar
sound of her mother weeping. She did care, after all. Jane lay listening,
wishing she could go and comfort her mother but knowing she would
not appreciate the intrusion on her grief. It was sad, thought Jane, that
one could know someone all one's life and still not be close enough to
help them.

8

It was a strange feeling for Jane to be motoring through the park at Respryn and to know that there was no Lady Upnor waiting at the end to sneer at and torment her. She had felt guiltily elated when the old woman died but now, as she approached the house, she felt a sense of emptiness. How strange. Just like her parents – hating in life and grieving in death.

She swung the car into the courtyard. She must be the first guest to arrive: there were no other cars parked.

Banks was no longer there to greet her. He had retired to a cottage on the estate several years ago, and she hoped she would have time to visit him. The door was opened by an impeccably dressed young butler with a superior air and more than a hint of a sneer on his face. His manner was correct but Jane felt he was too perfect – more like a stage butler than the warm and welcoming Banks.

She was shown to her habitual room and given Alistair's apologies for his absence: a drama with his prize bull had called him away to the farm.

She was glad to have time to rest: she seemed to have been travelling for weeks. She bathed, and selected a dress of kaleidoscopically coloured silk she had bought at Saks in New York. She stood in front of the cheval glass and studied her image. She smiled at the thought that this mirror had seen Jane in all her different phases, from the gauche, badly dressed young nurse through her dowdy period to the present day and the sleek, perfectly groomed woman she was. Jane could now look at herself and acknowledge that she was beautiful. Lucky, too, for age had been kind to her and her face with its fine bones was still lovely, the eyes were still clear, the long hair still shone luxuriantly.

At the summons of the first gong she made her way to the drawing room and found Alistair alone, waiting for her.

'Happy birthday!'

'Jay, you look ravishing. What a dress – Honor would have approved.'

She spun round, demonstrating the fullness of the brightly coloured silk. 'Yes, it's very Honorish, isn't it, more suited to Italy – but I felt like cheering myself up.'

'Of course, your father – how did it go?'

She shrugged. 'All right, I suppose, as funerals go, but difficult. You know. Mother and I still not communicating, Mother still carping. Nothing's changed – I guess it never will. Here . . .' She handed him the carefully wrapped parcel she had brought. Like the little boy she so often thought he was, he unwrapped it eagerly.

'Hey, look at this, it's sensational,' he said, placing the large glass bowl gently on a table. 'Look at the workmanship!' He studied the engravings of Respryn, Drumloch and Trinick which she had commissioned.

'Look at the bottom.' She was smiling, pleased with the success of her idea.

He peered into the bowl. 'Why, it's the little house in Fulham.'

'All the houses you've lived in, you see.'

'All the houses we've lived in, you mean. It's the most thoughtful present I've ever had.' He kissed her cheek, his hand lingering a second longer on her arm. 'G & T?'

'Where's everybody?' she asked, as she took the drink.

'Everybody who?'

'The party guests.'

'Oh, I cancelled it,' he replied airily. 'Couldn't be bothered.'

'What am I doing here, then?'

'I can always be bothered with you.' He grinned the still boyish grin. 'I'll be honest – there never was going to be a party. I pretended.'

'What on earth for?'

'You're always so busy and surrounded with acres of people these days, I thought it was about time we had dinner on our own, without half a dozen of your minions around. I sometimes feel you do it on purpose – the people I mean – as if you're avoiding me.'

'Alistair, don't be silly.' She laughed.

'Am I? Anyhow, I hope you don't mind.'

'How could I? It's a very sweet compliment. So it's just the two of us, no other house guests?'

'Totally *à deux*, as the Frogs would say.' The silly, weak joke made him seem almost shy with her.

The butler appeared and announced unctuously that their dinner was served. Ceremoniously taking her arm, Alistair led her into the small family dining room.

Jane looked around the familiar room where they had eaten so many times together in the past. The blessing of Respryn was its continuity. It gave her, as it always had, a sense of security.

'So how's James? Still beavering away for you up north?' Alistair asked when the butler finally withdrew.

'He's wonderful!' Jane's eyes gleamed with pride. 'He works so hard, I really don't know how I would cope without him. He does more and more off his own bat now. He's so smart: he's more aware of what's going on than I am. I think I'm becoming redundant.'

'Good, then maybe the rest of us will see more of you.' He grinned.

'Actually, I've some exciting news. He asked me to tell you . . . he's getting engaged.'

'Really? To whom? Do I know her?'

'I doubt it. As soon as he arrived, the local matrons trotted out their daughters but it didn't work. He's fallen in love with my gamekeeper's daughter – she's one of my secretaries.'

'Ha!' Alistair roared with laughter. 'I like it. Full circle. A chip off the old block, after all, and I thought he was too serious ever to be like me.'

'Perhaps it's as well that your mother didn't live to see it. I'd have got the blame for influencing him.' She laughed too.

'Let's hope he doesn't make a mess of it, as I did.'

'Oh, come on, Alistair. We were both at fault. It took me a long time to realize it but I must have been a pain, with my insecurities and those massive chips I carried around on my shoulders. Katriona's different, though: she's far stronger and knows exactly who she is – God help anyone who tries to put her down.'

'Nice name. Is she pretty?'

'She's stunning – black-haired and grey-eyed, you know, with that lovely pale complexion some Scots have.'

'It's not just the Scots who look like that.' He lifted his glass to her and, stupidly, she thought, after all these years, she was blushing. 'When do I get to meet her?'

'I have to fly to New York again this week. He's planning to announce it when we get back. Perhaps you could come up that weekend?'

'I'd love to.'

'I was thinking of offering them the villa for their honeymoon, but I wondered if that was too schmaltzy.'

'I don't think it's schmaltzy at all. As I remember, we had a rather spectacular time there. Let's hope they do too. I often think –'

The oily butler reappeared, and Alistair stopped in midsentence. With exaggerated ceremony, the butler served them the next course, bowing as he withdrew.

'He's creepy.'

'Who, Uriah?'

'That can't possibly be his name. Uriah!' she protested.

'Uriah Heep – it's my secret name for him. I think he's called Justin de Beaune or something. I usually avoid calling him anything.'

'He's not like a butler at all. Banks would have a fit.'

'I don't think he is, I'm sure his references were fake, but you know me, I meant to check and never got around to it – you used to do all that sort of thing. I reckon he's an out-of-work actor playing the part.'

'That's what I thought the minute I set eyes on him. It's funny how we think the same things after all this time.'

'Are you lonely?' he suddenly asked.

'I don't get the time.' She did not know why she lied: remnants of her stupid pride, she presumed. 'And you?'

'Very. I doubt if there's a day when I don't kick myself for losing you.'

'Alistair, don't fall into that trap,' she said quickly. 'For years I rued the day I walked out. But I learned there's no point in ruining the present because of past mistakes. Honestly, love.'

'Don't look so alarmed.' He was laughing. 'Candlelight always has this effect on me,' he said, grinning, lightening the mood. Jane looked across the table at him: the light shining on the white hair played tricks with her eyes so that it looked as blond as it was when she had first met him. With his boyish charm it was always difficult to know when he was serious and when he was joking, she thought.

'What would happen, Jane, if I crept into your room tonight?'

Jane just caught the glass that she knocked sideways. 'I'd scream for Uriah Heep.' She giggled, desperately covering her confusion.

'It was a serious question, Jane.'

She stopped laughing. 'I don't know, Alistair, I don't even know if I'd have the courage to say come in.'

He smiled. 'I know how you feel. I wonder if I would have the courage even to knock.' He laughed again. 'Ah, well, if we're such cowards I guess we'll never know.' He shrugged his shoulders and poured more wine. As if the previous conversation had not taken place, he asked politely about the town's new airport. The moment had passed. Jane felt a strange mixture of relief and regret.

He took her arm to lead her into the small drawing room, and sat opposite her. It was a pleasant evening and passed quickly as they talked of old days and friends, of incidents that one remembered and the other had forgotten and some memories still fresh to both of them. They discussed James's wedding and what they should give him. Then Alistair escorted her to her room.

'Night, Jane,' he said, kissing her gently on the mouth. 'Thanks for a super birthday – best for a long time.'

She watched him as he disappeared along the red corridor that led to what had once been their suite of rooms.

Jane was restless as she lay in the dark, waiting for sleep. She wished she had not come: she knew the effect he could have on her. It was unfair of him to tease her. Look at her now, tossing and turning, half longing to hear his knock on the door and half terrified that she would. She wished that when he had kissed her, she had responded; she should have flung her arms about him, kissed him back. So, if she really wanted to sleep with him, why hadn't she? Even as she thought the question, she knew the answer – her fear of rejection, the hurt pride of that young woman she had once been. She knew that his mild flirting was part of a game, his suggestion that he visit her, simply an exaggerated form of politeness. She could hardly think him shy – after all, he'd shown no shyness in the past with his numerous sexual adventures – so why should he suddenly be timid now, especially with her? It was just a diversion to him.

But all the same, if he did come, she wondered what she would do. She could acknowledge she was beautiful still: people were always telling her that. Her hands ran up and down her body. She was slim, and still had a good figure, but it was not the body or the skin of the young woman he had known. Even if he really did want her, his desire was probably for the woman she had once been and not the one she was now. Eventually sleep rescued her, and when she awoke in the morning, he had not come.

They had breakfast together. Neither referred to the conversation of the night before. Alistair came with her to visit Banks in his cottage by the home farm. She inspected his horses, and felt almost relieved when it was time to go.

'Keep in touch, Jay.' He smiled at her through the window of the car and, kissing his fingers, gently placed them on her lips. 'See you next week.' He waved gaily as her car slid out of the courtyard.

Her appointments kept her in London for three days before she was able to travel north to pack and to collect her papers and her thoughts for the trip to New York. Hating flying, she dreaded these trips, but it was necessary for her to attend regular meetings at the Calem conglomerate.

And there was increasing interest in her trust in America and more of her time these days was spent lecturing and explaining the concept.

Among the pile of mail that awaited her, she was surprised to find one in Alistair's familiar handwriting, with 'Very personal' underlined twice. It was years since she had had a letter from him – he always phoned. She opened it. It was short but to the point.

Jane,
I always make a mess of things with you. I had laid my plans so carefully. I was going to seduce you, somehow wheedle my way back into your life. I haven't got the technique, that's my problem – need lessons, I suppose. I admit it's never been a problem before! But I'm so afraid of hearing you reject me.

Please come back to me, please love me again, please marry me again. There, no flowery language, just plain English, but said with as much if not more feeling than if it was all wrapped up in pretty phrases.

I keep telling you what a bloody fool I've been over the years. Last time I managed to get you into my bed I knew, even as I spoke, that I had blown it. I lay there pretending to be asleep, sensing you awake, hurt and thinking what to do. I just didn't know what to say to make it right. And I think that sometimes when I'm trying to tell you you just think I'm flirting with you. Odd, I've never been a letter writer but it seems easier to write than to say it to you. Maybe I should have taken up letter-writing sooner . . .

I've done so much to hurt you in the past, I know, but now please let me love you. I need you, Jane.

                                                          A.

Jane sat stunned. She reread the letter three times. How extraordinary: all that time he was afraid of rejection, too. Her hand went out to pick up the telephone –

'There you are, Ma. I heard you were back. I hope you don't mind but I've arranged for us to go a day early. We're flying out tonight.'

'Perhaps that would be better,' she said in a faraway voice.

'What do you mean, better? I thought you'd be annoyed.'

She smiled. 'Have I time for a bath at least?'

'If you're quick.'

She bathed hurriedly; her cases were already packed. Her mind was in turmoil, but she would have time to think on the plane. Her hand shook as she slipped the letter into her handbag.

Epilogue

The jet skimmed eastward across the Atlantic. Jane was returning home to Scotland.

'Jane,' Fran's voice whispered. She opened her eyes. 'Fancy a drink before we eat?'

'Lovely.' Jane stretched her body.

'Nice sleep?'

'I was thinking.'

'Long think. Anything interesting?' Fran asked, alert, her hand darting towards the ever present pen and pad.

'No, Fran, you can relax. I was just thinking about myself and my life.'

'How boring,' Fran teased.

'Totally self-indulgent. Bloody hell, I'm tired, Fran. Dynamic, go-getting Jane Reed is tired.'

'I'm not surprised. The number of meetings you managed to squeeze into four days was ridiculous. Why, you even exhausted the Americans. You need a holiday, my old mate. Why don't you go to that lovely villa of yours? You never use it.'

'Do you know, Fran, since Honor died, I guess I've only been there half a dozen times. It would be nice, a holiday – any chance of your coming?'

'Jane, love, I'm the last person you need. We practically live together as it is. What you need is a feller with you, my girl. Why not ask Alistair, I bet he'd jump at it?'

Jane leaned back on the cushions. There Fran went again. She's psychic, thought Jane; how the hell could Fran know that Jane had been thinking about Alistair since they left Scotland? Maybe she had talked about him without realizing it, maybe she had let something drop.

The villa. Honor's magic world. It would be nice to be there and relax for a couple of weeks, to forget all the business problems, the worry, shed the responsibilities. Could she do that at the villa? Wouldn't the memories she'd been so intent on running away from haunt her?

Across the aisle, James sat quietly working through a mountain of paperwork. He worked so hard, was so conscientious, she knew he would be only too happy to take more of the load off her. If she were honest with herself, she had to admit that he was quite capable of running everything himself. She was a figurehead, really: she could and should do less.

He sensed her looking at him and smiled. How like his father he looked, she thought — the same blonde hair, the fine-boned face. He was too serious, though, and lacked his father's sense of fun. That was their fault: he had had a lonely childhood which could not have been made easier by his grandmother's continual interference. Jane could still remember the illogical sense of freedom she had felt the day Alistair had phoned to say his mother was dead, freedom from that malevolent spirit.

Giovanni had been lucky not to have a Lady Upnor in his young life. Her two sons were so different; it amazed her that they should be such good friends. She thought fondly of her Italian son, so handsome with his flashing brown eyes, improbably white teeth and Roberto's wonderfully sensuous smile. He did not seem to have a serious thought in his head. Already at twelve he showed signs of turning into an out-and-out playboy, interested only in fast cars. Before long, no doubt, it would be girls. Maybe one day he would settle down, just as his father had done.

Absent-mindedly she picked at the food the stewardess had given her. Perhaps Italy would be a good idea. But she would have to take somebody with her, someone to shield her from the past.

Could it work? She took the letter from her handbag and read it for the umpteenth time. She smiled as she remembered the years when she would have gone flying to him. What stopped her now? The romantic girl who still lurked within her, dreaming of the perfect love? No, that wasn't true. About one thing, Jane had been right all her life. She had said she would love Alistair and through everything she had. No, it was fear and pride. Stupid wasteful emotions. What if he were unfaithful to her? Hadn't she for years now admitted her mistake, admitted that infidelity need not mean the end of love? Yes, it would hurt but not as it had before. He did seem to have changed. And with the sexuality that Roberto had unlocked in her, she too had changed. Could she make love to Alistair again, though? She knew now that sexual attraction was still an important ingredient in her feelings towards him. Platonic love lay many years away for her yet. But she felt strangely shy at the thought of is seeing her naked again. In an odd way it would be easier to go to bed with that Brazilian diplomat she had met last night than with Alistair.

'Oh, Lor'.' She sighed. It would be lovely to be back at Respryn, with someone else to fill her thoughts, someone to care for her and to love her. She sighed again. It would be wonderful to wake up in the night and sense him beside her. She moved restlessly in her seat. God, that last time had been wonderful: she remembered the way she had screamed as he brought her to her climax. What was so wrong in having learned to use her body, how to excite his? Stupid Calvinistic shame which the sophisticated Jane Reed could never quite shake off. She smiled at herself, and at the memory of that night.

'What's that strange smile for, Mother?' she heard James ask.

'I was just thinking how nice it would be to sleep with a man again,' she replied, startled out of her reverie.

'Mother!' James laughed in surprise.

'Did I shock you? Maybe I'm not as old as you think. The old hormones are still scudding about.' She laughed.

'There's always Father.'

'Darling James, you never give up, do you?'

'Neither does Father. He still loves you, Mother.'

'I love him, too.'

'Then what's stopping you? I think you're both bloody mad, rattling around in your huge, great houses. You'd save a fortune in housekeeping.'

'My darling son, where did you inherit such an accountant's mind from? I don't think housekeeping economies are quite the best basis upon which to rebuild relationships.'

'You know what I mean, Ma. And I still think you're both daft.' He returned to his papers.

Maybe Alistair would like to come to Italy with her . . . after all, if the memories were what frightened her, what was more logical than to invite one of the memories to come with her? Perhaps in Italy she could come to a decision – just the two of them alone – and maybe the villa would work its old magic.

It was obvious what she wanted. Then why didn't she grasp it? What held her back? Fear, stupid fears that had plagued her all her life.

Roberto had understood. That first argument, he had told her the truth about herself. That she was afraid of life, of loving. Roberto would have thought she was wasting her life now. He would have accepted her

business success with pride; but he would never have comprehended h
denying herself physical pleasure.

Thinking, thinking, that's all she seemed good for. And where did
get her?

The seatbelt light came on. She slipped the letter back into her bag. S
checked her make-up. The plane banked and swept in a circle over t
town below. This was the only moment in the flight that Jane loved. S
could see the whole town beneath her, ablaze with light.

The plane swirled down and landed on the newly built runway. At t
terminal building, cars waited. The door of the plane swung open an
she stepped out. Dame Jane Reed was home in Strathleith.

She stood beside the plane. Across the tarmac a crowd was rushin
towards her. She could see the architects, her accountant, at the fro
one of her secretaries clutching a sheaf of messages for her. Beyond the
the hospital committee waited. Beyond them who else?

Jane opened her handbag. From inside she took a pad and pen. T
pen poised indecisively for a moment. She wrote hurriedly. 'Darling,' sh
said, turning to her son. 'Could you telex this to your father? I haven
time. I promised to go to a meeting of the new hospital committee befo
I go home.'

James glanced at the paper. 'You haven't put your name on it.
doesn't make sense.'

'He'll understand.' She smiled.

James glanced again at his mother's familiar handwriting an
shrugged his shoulders. He turned into the administrative building an
soon the telex chattered.

'Why not? But get rid of Uriah Heep!'

Alice Adams
Superior Women £2.95

They met at Radcliffe in 1943. Their friendship survived four
turbulent decades – World War II, the civil rights struggle, the drug
scene, the sexual revolution, Vietnam. Their destinies seemed
assured. But the fickle finger of fate cannot distinguish even superior
women . . .

Annabel Carothers
Kilcaraig £2.95

A turbulent saga of three generations set against the grandeur of the
Scottish isles . . . The Lamonts of Kilcaraig belonged to the Isle of
Mull as surely as the proud birds of prey belonged to the mountains
of Glen More. Through six decades their chronicle unfolds –
Catriona, the grandmother whose dark secret shadowed the family's
future; Grania, the daughter who finds love only after she has chosen
a husband; Niall and Rorie, twin grandsons of contrasting destinies,
and Catriona the granddaughter, as beautiful as her namesake . . .

Pamela Belle
The Moon in the Water £2.95

Thomazine was born heiress to the lands and fortune of the Heron
dynasty, and she was born under a dark and troublesome star.
Orphaned at ten years old, growing to womanhood among cousins,
she met the headstrong Francis and they both dreamed of the mystic
unicorn. The sweep of the times was against them. Francis was
banished and imprisoned, Thomazine forced into loveless wedlock,
and the onrush of beating drums and naked steel heralded England's
Civil War.

'Masterly ... vivid tapestry of a family saga, richly crowded with
flesh-and-blood people' ROSEMARY SUTCLIFFE

The Chains of Fate £2.95

The blood-red tide of civil war ran deep over the land, and
Thomazine became the wife of a man she would learn to hate,
believing her Francis to be dead. When she learned the truth – that
Francis lived – Thomazine rode north on a mission hung with the
chains of fate. Those chains weighed down her journey as she
moved through land occupied by enemy soldiers, found the man she
loved at the price of deserting her own child, and lost Francis again
to the cause of Montrose ... Time and again Thomazine and Francis
would be torn apart, yet one day, the chains of love must prove
stronger ...

Alathea £2.95

The brilliant new novel from the bestselling author of *The Moon in
the Water* and *The Chains of Fate*.

Surviving family tragedy, the threatening attentions of her jealous
half-brother, the devastation of both the Plague and the Great Fire,
and forsaking marriage for her career, the beautiful, headstrong,
gifted Alathea grows up into fame and fortune, and is the mistress of
a notorious rake.

But the destiny of this fiercely independent artist is as yet unfulfilled,
and in time the wheel will come full circle for Alathea, child of
dreams and truths and Unicorns ...

Caroline Bridgwood
The Dew of Heaven £2.95

As the dark clouds of World War 2 cast their shadow over a country
fighting for survival, Britanny Stein and her American banker
husband Jake face the uncertain future secure in their deep love for
each other. But for their beautiful daughter Nancy, as stubborn,
impetuous and lustful as her mother ever was, the turmoil of the
rapidly changing times is a golden opportunity to make her mark on
the world . . .

Sweeping from the rural tranquillity of Somerset to the hustle and
bustle of London, *The Dew of Heaven* follows the fluctuating
fortunes of the Steins of Graylings and their neighbours the Steeles
of Heathcote through two decades of love, ambition and struggle –
and the guilt of an illicit passion that will forever shape the destinie
of those caught up in it.

This Wicked Generation £2.95

For more than a hundred years there had been Colbys at Graylings,
the beautiful Georgian country estate in the heart of Somerset. But
now, as a result of her father's cold, implacable treachery and a
neighbouring landowner's ruthless, unpitying ambition, Britanny
Colby was about to lose her inheritance . . .

From the quiet of the English countryside in the years leading to the
cataclysm of the Great War to the frantic and glittering high society
life of London and New York in the Roaring Twenties, the loves and
the chequered fortunes of the passionate and wilful Brittany Colby,
the cold and calculating landowner Adrian Steele, and the rich and
powerful American bankers Jake and David Stein are recreated with
the clash of character and the sweep of narrative that marks the
emergence of a major new storyteller.

Hilary Bailey
All the Days of My Life £3.50

Mary Waterhouse grew up fatally pretty. Evacuated from the London slums during the war, pregnant at fifteen, a murderer's widow at sixteen, Mary was swept into the glamorous and dangerous world of London's low life when she fell for debonair hoodlum Johnnie Bridges ... The chronicles of one of the most outrageous and irresistible heroines of modern times, *All the Days of My Life* is a rollicking and rumbustious romp through fifty years of post-war Britain.

Magda Sweetland
Eightsome Reel £2.95

The death of Rhona Rosowicz brings her remaining family to the decaying Edinburgh mansion where she and her daughter Esme had lived a solitary life. Surrounded by people she hardly knows, Esme's behaviour excites attracts and infuriates her relations as their lives intertwine in the mode of a dance. Esme's growing friendship with her aunt's husband leads to forbidden fruits, and through him she discovers the existence of her Polish father whom she thought long-dead. To escape the scandal, Esme goes to see her father in Canada. There she meets a handsome RCAF officer and the mistakes of her forefathers begin to repeat themselves.

All Pan books are available at your local bookshop or newsagent, or can be ordered direct from the publisher. Indicate the number of copies required and fill in the form below.

Send to: **CS Department, Pan Books Ltd., P.O. Box 40, Basingstoke, Hants.   RG21 2YT.**

or phone: 0256 469551 (Ansaphone), quoting title, author and Credit Card number.

Please enclose a remittance* to the value of the cover price plus: 60p for the first book plus 30p per copy for each additional book ordered to a maximum charge of £2.40 to cover postage and packing.

*Payment may be made in sterling by UK personal cheque, postal order, sterling draft or international money order, made payable to Pan Books Ltd.

Alternatively by Barclaycard/Access:

Card No. | | | | | | | | | | | | | | | | | | |

Signature:

Applicable only in the UK and Republic of Ireland.

While every effort is made to keep prices low, it is sometimes necessary to increase prices at short notice. Pan Books reserve the right to show on covers and charge new retail prices which may differ from those advertised in the text or elsewhere.

NAME AND ADDRESS IN BLOCK LETTERS PLEASE:

....

Name ————————————————————————————

Address ————————————————————————————

————————————————————————————

————————————————————————————

————————————————————————————

3/87